WARSAW

OSPREY
PUBLISHING

DEDICATION

To Gary and Stephanie Taylor

PRIT BUTTAR & LOTTIE TAYLOR

WARSAW

A CITY AT WAR 1939–45

OSPREY PUBLISHING
Bloomsbury Publishing Plc
Kemp House, Chawley Park, Cumnor Hill, Oxford OX2 9PH, UK
Bloomsbury Publishing Ireland Limited,
29 Earlsfort Terrace, Dublin 2, D02 AY28, Ireland
1385 Broadway, 5th Floor, New York, NY 10018, USA
E-mail: info@ospreypublishing.com
www.ospreypublishing.com

OSPREY is a trademark of Osprey Publishing Ltd

First published in Great Britain in 2026

A catalogue record for this book is available from the British Library.

ISBN: HB 9781472873514; eBook 9781472873408; ePDF 9781472873422; XML 9781472873446; Audio 9781472873439

26 27 28 29 30 10 9 8 7 6 5 4 3 2 1

Plate section image credits are given in full in the List of Illustrations (pp. 7–9).
Maps by Prit Buttar
Index by Mark Swift

Typeset by Lumina Datamatics Ltd
Printed and bound in Great Britain by Clays Ltd, Elcograf S.p.A.

Editor's note
For ease of comparison, please refer to the following conversion table:
1 mile = 1.6km
1 yd = 0.9m
1 ft = 0.3m
1 in. = 2.54cm/25.4mm
1 lb = 0.45kg

MIX
Paper | Supporting responsible forestry
FSC® C018072
FSC www.fsc.org

Osprey Publishing supports the Woodland Trust, the UK's leading woodland conservation charity.

To find out more about our authors and books visit www.ospreypublishing.com. Here you will find extracts, author interviews, details of forthcoming events and the option to sign up for our newsletter.

For product safety related questions contact productsafety@bloomsbury.com

CONTENTS

LIST OF ILLUSTRATIONS

By mid-1942, the *Umschlagplatz* ('Exchange Place') became the holding area for Jewish deportees bound for Treblinka and a site of horrors in its own right. Unknown numbers were executed, beaten, and raped in and around the railyard whilst awaiting transport. On some days, as many as 12,000 Jews could be deported from here. (Universal History Archive/Getty Images)

The camp at Pruszków was established during the first week of the Warsaw Uprising to process refugees before transporting them elsewhere; by September, it was rumoured that all Varsovians were being sent on to concentration camps. The railway halls became critically overcrowded and were a hotbed for disease, leading to spiralling mortality rates. (HUM Images/Universal Images Group via Getty Images)

The later weeks of the Ghetto Uprising are remembered as the 'battle of the bunkers', with guerrilla skirmishes and frantic escapes as the Germans choked the remaining life out of the ghetto. The image of this boy raising his hands, photographed for Stroop's self-congratulatory report, became a recurring motif in the paintings of Samuel Bak, a survivor of the Vilnius Ghetto. (Keystone/Hulton Archive/Getty Images)

Initially, Stroop was ordered to preserve workshop premises as far as possible, but the Jews' resistance frustrated progress enough to warrant the indiscriminate razing of property. By 25 April, fires were widely sanctioned, and troops received this order: 'if any resistance is encountered or if dugouts cannot be reached, the buildings are to be burnt down.' (© Hulton-Deutsch Collection/CORBIS/Corbis via Getty Images)

In Warsaw, men and women from across the social spectrum found themselves swept into resistance groups such as the *ZWZ* or the *AK*. Thousands of Varsovian teenagers, too young to have fought in 1939 but filled with youthful energy and a sense of immortality, joined the Uprising, as did a number of Jewish fighters who had survived the Ghetto Uprising. (Hulton Archive/Getty Images)

On 27 September 1944, Polish rebels in Mokotów tried to escape their encircled position via the sewer system, only to emerge straight into German hands. Jerzy 'Zbroja' Umiński, pictured, was captured and taken to a POW camp; around 120 others were shot on Dworkowa Street. (Mondadori via Getty Images)

The Red Army moved into Warsaw on 17 January to find that about 85 per cent of the city had been utterly destroyed. Between 2,000 and 3,000 so-called 'Robinson Crusoes' survived by hiding in these ruins; one of them was Władysław Szpilman. (Roger Viollet via Getty Images)

LIST OF MAPS

DRAMATIS PERSONAE

POLAND

Anders, Władysław – Commander of Polish II Corps formed in Soviet Union (known as the 'Anders Army')
Auerbach, Rokhl – Jewish writer, ally of Emmanual Ringelblum, member of *Oneg Shabbat* project
Bartoszewski, Władysław – Auschwitz survivor, *AK* fighter, post-war politician, prolific activist and historian
Beck, Józef – Minister of Foreign Affairs in 1932–39
Berg, Mary – Jewish diarist, survivor of the Warsaw Ghetto
Berling, Zygmunt – Commander of pro-Communist First Polish Army
Białoszewski, Miron – Uprising diarist, survivor, poet
Bytnar, Jan – Grey Ranks scoutmaster, member of the *Wawer* group
Chruściel, Antoni 'Monter' – *AK* chief of staff, commander of armed forces during the Warsaw Uprising
Czerniaków, Adam – Chairman of the Warsaw Ghetto *Judenrat*
Czuma, Walerian – Commander of the defence of Warsaw in 1939
Dąbrowska, Maria – Novelist, diarist
Dmowski, Roman – National Democrat politician
Donat, Aleksander (Michał Berg) – Holocaust survivor, journalist
Ehrlich, Josef 'Kapota' – Jewish collaborator
Gancwajch, Abraham (Chaim) – Head of 'The Thirteen'
Iranek-Osmecki, Kazimierz – Head of intelligence for the *AK* in 1944
Jankowski, Jan – Delegate for government-in-exile
Kamiński, Aleksander – Scoutmaster, commander of *Wawer* group, editor of *Biuletyn Informacyjny*
Komorowski, Tadeusz 'Bór' – Commander-in-chief of *AK* during the Warsaw Uprising

Korboński, Stefan – Commander of Directorate of Civil Resistance, government delegate
Korczak, Janusz (Henryk Goldszmit) – Doctor, philanthropist, victim of the *Grossaktion*
Kossack-Szcucka, Zofia – Novelist, philanthropist, co-founder of *Żegota*
Kott, Kazimierz – Leader of *PLAN*, famous escapee of Pawiak
Kozielewski, Jan 'Karski' – Underground activist, courier, diplomat
Kozielewski, Marian – Pre-war policeman, first commander of the Warsaw Blue Police
Krawczyńska, Jadwiga – Writer, underground journalist
Krzyżanowski, Aleksander – Commander of *Burza* in Vilnius
Kulski, Julian – Deputy to Stefan Starzyński, mayor of Warsaw after the former's arrest
Kulski, Julian Eugeniusz – Son of the above and *AK* fighter, 15 years old at the outbreak of the 1944 Uprising
Kusociński, Janusz – Olympic gold-medallist runner, member of the underground
Kutrzeba, Tadeusz – General of Poznań Army in 1939 at the Battle of Bzura, deputy commander of Warsaw Army before capitulation
Lejkin, Jakub – Notorious deputy of Warsaw Jewish Ghetto Police
Lipiński, Wacław – Chief of Polish propaganda during the 1939 invasion
Lipski, Józef – Polish ambassador in Berlin 1934–39
Micuta, Wacław 'Wacek' – Grey Ranks instructor, officer to Scout Battalion *Zośka* during the 1944 Uprising
Mościcki, Ignacy – President of the Second Polish Republic 1926–39
Nałkowska, Zofia – Writer, activist, diarist
Niedziałkowski, Mieczysław – Pre-war member of the *Sejm*, underground civilian commissioner during occupation
Nowak-Jeziorański, Jan – Member of *Akcja N*, underground courier
Okulicki, Leopold – Chief of staff of the *AK* during the 1944 Uprising, successor to Komorowski as overall commander
Paderewski, Ignacy – First elected prime minister of Second Polish Republic
Pełczyński, Tadeusz – Chief of staff of the *AK* during the 1944 Uprising
Piłsudski, Józef – Polish statesman, commander-in-chief, considered founder of the Second Polish Republic
Raczkiewicz, Władysław – President of the government-in-exile 1939–47
Rataj, Maciej – Pre-war president, member of the *Sejm*
Ringelblum, Emmanuel – Jewish historian, activist, diarist, leader of the *Oneg Shabbat* project
Rómmel, Juliusz – General of Łódź Army at the time of the 1939 invasion,

general of Warsaw Army before capitulation
Rosinski, Jan – Member of the *AK* in Warsaw
Rowecki, Stefan – Commander of *ZWZ* and *AK* 1939–43
Rydz-Śmigły, Edward – Commander-in-chief of Polish forces at the time of the 1939 invasion
Rzepecki, Jan – Commander of *AK* Bureau for Propaganda and Information
Sikorski, Władysław – Prime minister, commander-in-chief in exile, 1939–43
Sosnkowski, Kazimierz – Successor to Sikorski as commander-in-chief 1943–44
Starzyński, Stefan – Mayor of Warsaw 1934–39
Szeryński, Józef – Detested commissioner of Warsaw Jewish Ghetto Police, known collaborator
Szpilman, Władysław – Musician, diarist
Tokarzewski-Karaszewicz, Michał – Leader of *SZP*, founder of *ZWZ*
Zygielbojm, Szmul – Political activist, member of the National Council for the government-in-exile

Germany

Auerswald, Heinz – *Kommissar* for the Warsaw Ghetto
Bach-Zelewski, Erich von dem – Senior SS officer, commander of suppression of Warsaw Uprising
Beutel, Lothar – Commander *Einsatzgruppe IV*
Bürkl, Franz – Security police NCO
Dirlewanger, Oskar – SS brigade commander
Eberl, Irmfried – Commandant of Treblinka
Eichmann, Adolf – Senior SS officer involved in the Holocaust
Fischer, Ludwig – Governor, Warsaw District
Forster, Albert – *Gauleiter* Danzig-Westpreussen
Frank, Hans – Governor, *Generalgouvernement*
Globočnik, Odilo – Senior SS officer involved in the Holocaust
Gottberg, Curt von – SS commander on the Eastern Front
Hahn, Ludwig – Security police chief, Warsaw
Heydrich, Reinhard – Senior SS officer, head of *RSHA*
Höfle, Hermann – Deputy to Globočnik
Keitel, Wilhelm – Head of *OKW*
Krüger, Friedrich-Wilhelm – *HSSPF* in *Generalgouvernement*
Meisinger, Josef Albert – Commander *Einsatzgruppe IV*
Model, Walter – Commander Army Group Centre from mid-1944

Otto, Helmut – *Reichskommissar* in Warsaw
Reinefarth, Heinz – Senior SS officer involved in suppression of Warsaw Uprising
Ribbentrop, Joachim von – German foreign minister
Sammern-Frankenegg, Ferdinand von – *SSPF* Warsaw District
Schön, Waldemar – *Kommissar* for the Warsaw Ghetto
Schulenburg, Friedrich Werner Graf von – Pre-war German ambassador in Berlin
Schultz, Herbert – SS police officer
Stahel, Rainer – Senior Luftwaffe officer, original fortress commandant in Warsaw
Stangl, Franz – Commandant of Treblinka
Stroop, Jürgen – SS officer in command of suppression of Ghetto Uprising
Vormann, Nikolaus von – Commander Ninth Army from mid-1944

SOVIET UNION

Cherniakhovsky, Ivan Danilovich – Commander 3rd Belarusian Front
Kaminski, Bronislav Vladislavovich – Commander of *RONA* forces
Mayski, Ivan Mikhailovich – Soviet ambassador to the United Kingdom, 1932–43
Molotov, Vyacheslav Mikhailovich – Soviet foreign minister
Rokossovsky, Konstantin Konstantinovich – Commander 1st Belarusian Front in 1944

OTHERS

Gubbins, Colin (Britain) – Head of SOE

INTRODUCTION

'And when difficult times come … in years of injustice and defeat, the roar of the Vistula's waves will sing to your descendants of hope, strength, and victory'

Artur Oppman, '*Syrena*', 1925

Hundreds of years ago, the poet Artur Oppman tells us, in a small fishing settlement on the west bank of the Vistula, two fishermen were enraptured by the heavenly strains of a mermaid's song. The fish could wait, they decided, and they set about capturing the mermaid as a gift for a local prince. The magical creature escaped her bonds – but she vowed to hide in the waves of the river and to watch over the people of the city and the generations that came after them.

There are many myths surrounding the mermaid on Warsaw's coat of arms. If we were to indulge ourselves in reading between the lines of Oppman's version, we might say it tells us something about how Varsovian people have seen themselves through history: canny, opportunistic – or resourceful – and prone to seduction by mysticism. In any case, the mermaid has become an integral part of Warsaw's aesthetic culture and public imagination, woven into the urban landscape through innumerable statues, reliefs, and murals from which she looks over the city and its people as promised.

Oppman's fairy tale points to another truth: that the history of a city is more than its foundation, its architecture, and its skyline. Warsaw – the city that was razed to the ground not once, not twice, but three times in 400 years – is one of the best testaments to this. The so-called 'Phoenix City' stands as a monument less to a sense of historical continuity than to its tireless resurgence and its ability to weather the most brutal of storms; not for nothing is the city's motto *Semper invicta*, 'ever invincible'. This means that to understand the history of Warsaw, we have to go deeper than the aesthetic and material record – much of which has been deliberately destroyed. We have to look at the people, their experiences, the stories they told about themselves: what they chose to rebuild, what they left unearthed, which questions remain unanswered – and which unasked.

On the one hand, Warsaw can be viewed as a microcosm of the convoluted, tumultuous, and troubled history of Polish people as a whole. In 966, the first Duchy of Polonia was established to unite the 'people of the field' who set themselves apart from neighbouring Bohemian, Czech, and Rus Slav tribes by their distinct language. This also marked the inculcation of the *Polanie* people into Christendom, and there followed centuries of dynastic ebbs and flows, frontier shifts, and regional adjustments that left their mark in kaleidoscopic ethnic and cultural variation. Jewish, German, and Bohemian immigrants were generally welcomed to contribute their services beyond the native agrarian economy, and ethnic definitions of statehood were almost completely absent during the Middle Ages. By the 15th century, the fishing settlement of *Warszawa* – then part of the Duchy of Masovia – had grown into a bustling hub, the steady flow of migrants into the city fuelling its expansion beyond its original core (later known as Old Town) and turning it into a home for diverse crafts and trades. The potential for conflict between 'native' *Polanie* and newly arrived migrants was amplified in the streets of Warsaw, where economic and administrative disparities between the city's precincts inevitably bred resentment towards specific population groups – especially the Jews of New Town.

There was nothing particularly unique in the Polish kingdom's ethnic diversity during this period, especially in Eastern Europe. What did set the Polish dynasties apart from their feudal European neighbours was a unique lack of vassalage which kept the *szlachta* – or gentry class – independent, and the power of centralised authority in check. The result was a 'compromise between regionalist tendencies and an underlying sense of kinship and political unity'; identifying oneself with the Polish kingdom relied less on rigid bureaucratic hierarchies and more on political and, increasingly, religious affiliation.[1] Another important difference was that, from the 14th century onwards, Polish monarchs were denied automatic hereditary succession and were instead elected to serve by the *szlachta* – and later, by the parliamentary *Sejm*. This concept of government by consent was still a long way from constitutional democracy, but crucially, it deprived Polish rulers of the unalienable 'divine right' to rule enjoyed by monarchs elsewhere on the continent. By the 16th century, the *szlachta* actually held a legal right to resist the authority of the king and instigate a revolution – or *rokosz* – if they felt their liberties were under threat.

Why does this background matter in the context of a world war that broke out centuries later? The answer is that distinctive patterns of Polish identity, attitudes towards authority, and mechanisms of resistance – all severely tested between 1939 and 1945 – were beginning to emerge long before questions of political nationhood and independence came to the fore. When we tease out stories from occupied Poland, we pull on the threads of social, cultural, and political forces centuries in the making.

Firstly, we see Warsaw as the centre of Poland's political life and place on the world stage – with all the highs and lows this entailed. In the 1520s, the city was formally reincorporated under the Polish Crown and established as the seat of the *Sejm*; by the end of the century, its position between Polish Kraków and Lithuanian Vilnius made it the ideal capital for the Polish–Lithuanian Commonwealth. The city's growth accelerated in line with its political status – and also made it a significant target for foreign invaders. As much as 90 per cent of Warsaw's population was wiped out in the Swedish Deluge of 1656, marking the start of a tragic pattern of destruction that would become horribly familiar.[2] The opening years of the 18th century brought another portentous glimpse of Poland's future as it was transformed into a battleground – this time, between the Swedes and the Russians – at the expense of Polish people. It was only in the second half of the century that the city's development picked up pace once more – just in time for another political setback.

In 1772, the three powerful neighbours of the Commonwealth – Russia to the east, Austria to the south, and Prussia to the west – agreed to redraw the map of the region, each taking control of large swathes of territory. Their troops moved into the Commonwealth and rapidly overcame local resistance. King Stanisław August Poniatowski, the ruler of Poland, appealed in vain to other European powers for aid and support, and with varying degrees of reluctance Poland accepted the imposed redrawing of its borders. The brazen land grab came as a shock to much of European public opinion, but Catherine the Great and Frederick the Great were able to seize on the criticisms of French philosophers to justify the invasion and portrayed the partition as a mission to civilise an 'obscurantist backwater' plagued by disputes of succession. That these conflicts were in large part stoked by foreign intervention was beside the point; as Voltaire declared, the First Partition came both as a result of and as an attempt to overcome 'Polish disorder'.[3] Attempts to continue to function as an independent state resulted in war with Russia in 1792 after Poland entered into a treaty with Prussia. To the dismay of the Poles, their new allies quickly abandoned them in exchange for further territorial gains, resulting in the Second Partition of Poland in 1793. More than half of the remaining territory of the Polish–Lithuanian Commonwealth was annexed by its rapacious neighbours. Allies had proven unreliable, enemies merciless.

Warsaw emerged from the Napoleonic Wars as the capital of Congress Poland – which comprised the territories formally ceded to Russia at the 1815 Congress of Vienna. Alongside Łódź and the Dąbrowa Basin it became one of the centres of rapid industrialisation that was so long overdue and began to reshape Poland's agricultural economy. Workers flocked to the city in search of work in the new manufacturing industries, including textiles, metallurgy, and glassware, and this flow only increased with the Russian abolition of serfdom in the 1860s. By 1897, it had grown to be the third largest city in the Russian Empire behind Moscow and St Petersburg, numbering 626,000 inhabitants. Although the majority were Catholic Poles, the city was also home to large numbers of Belarusians, Ukrainians, and Jews; the population of the latter had grown significantly as Jews migrated from other parts of the Russian Empire in an attempt to escape antisemitic policies and pogroms.

Secondly, we can also trace the character of Varsovian attitudes to authority – and resistance – through the centuries that precede our main story. The seeds of Warsaw's revolutionary spirit were sown as far back as 1525, when rampant abuse of power and wealth on the part of city authorities inspired a popular revolt. Over three hundred years later, under partition, the Poles rallied around the figure of Tadeusz Kościuszko, a military commander who had led his troops with distinction against the Russians and had served in Washington's army in the American War of Independence. The consequence was an uprising across Poland in 1794, which yielded notable success; a combined attempt from Prussian and Russian troops to capture Warsaw was thwarted by a widespread civilian insurgency in the city and inspired further uprisings across the country. Also in Warsaw, Kościuszko was petitioned to issue a call to arms in Yiddish and assembled the 'Beardlings', the first all-Jewish military unit since the previous millennium.

Not for the first time, the population proved willing to put aside their ethnic and cultural differences in the interest of confronting a foreign occupier. Nor was this the last time that they would pay a heavy price for doing so: it is estimated that over 20,000 Poles – a mixture of civilians and soldiers – were killed as the Russians sacked Warsaw and quelled the uprising.[4] After the last remnants of the insurgents were mopped up, the remnants of the Polish–Lithuanian Commonwealth disappeared in the Third Partition of Poland. Henceforth, Warsaw's experience of foreign occupation and its resistance towards authority diverged from other Polish territories. Whilst relationships with Russian imperial rule were universally fractious, Polish suspicions, antagonisms, and reactions were generally magnified in Warsaw.

Thirdly, Warsaw served as the cultural heart of the discourses and debates shaping Polish identity – both despite and because of the city's repeated occupations by various powers and the continuous redefinition of Polish territories. At the start of the 19th century, it seemed to many in Poland that their homeland was on the verge of becoming an independent nation once more.

The arrival of the armies of Napoleon Bonaparte was greeted with great enthusiasm, and when the French created the Grand Duchy of Warsaw in 1807, the Poles placed their faith in Napoleon to restore Poland. The new statelet turned out to be very much under the sway of Napoleon, who was content to encourage Polish national aspirations while banking the region's recruits and resources. Nevertheless, Polish support for Napoleon went deeper than uniting against a common enemy. For Napoleon, Poland was just another stepping stone on the path to eastern expansion, but to the Poles, marching alongside the *Grande Armée* was their chance to claim a place in the glorious annals of military history and to be more than an occupied territory. In 1808, 125 men of the Polish *Chevaux-Légers* charged 16 Spanish cannon at the Battle of Somosierra, to commander Jan Kozietulski's cries of '*Vive L'Empereur*' (or perhaps more likely, '*naprzód psiekrwie, Cesarz patrzy*' – 'forward, you sons of dogs, the Emperor is watching').[5] In any case, it is telling that of the guard that accompanied the banished emperor to Elba, half were Polish troops from the Chevaux-Légers; also that Prince Józef Antoni Poniatowski, Kościuszko's supporter and nephew of the last king of Poland, was one of the most enthusiastic supporters of Napoleon. It was all too easy for Poles to see their defeat at the hands of the partitioning powers mirrored in the exile of Bonaparte – their tragic underdog hero.

Efforts to eliminate Polish and Lithuanian nationalism arose across the partitioned territories, but most intensely in the Russian-occupied regions. Being largely Catholic, the occupied populations caught here showed little inclination to accept their status as part of the Orthodox-first Russian Empire, and despite heavy-handed Russian regulations that banned many books and attempted to control schools and universities, the cultures of Poland and Lithuania not only survived but consciously crystallised under partition. Starting in the 1770s, the Polish cultural scene revitalised in opposition to the imperial powers with a burgeoning native enlightenment movement that became more reflective and didactic. Later, this gave way to a more self-conscious, nostalgic movement that lamented the invasion of foreign oppressors and hearkened back to the noble Sarmatism of pre-partition Poland. The works of Adam Mickiewicz, Józef Ignacy Kraszewski, Juliusz Słowacki, and, of course, Frédéric Chopin were celebrations of Polish history, and an affirmation of a cultural vitality that would not be wiped out. The occupied peoples took Rousseau's words to heart: 'You may not be able to prevent them from swallowing you up; see to it at least that they will not be able to digest you.'[6]

Polish identity had a unique flavour precisely because it transcended lines on the map. As the historian Brian Porter argues, nascent Polish nationalism demanded active affiliation, not passive acceptance; patriotic intellectuals were able to 'reconceptualis[e] the nation as a spirit or an ideal' beyond (and indeed, to escape) the grim geopolitical realities of partition.[7] Crucially, this concept of 'Polishness' was not ethnically exclusive, or at least, not as explicit as it would become over the following century. To be 'Polish' was to long for the restoration of territories and to hope for independence. For the Lithuanians, Belarusians, Germans, and Jews who had lived side by side for centuries, it was inclusive, not divisive – united as they were in their struggle against the tyranny and oppression of the partitioning powers. As the prominent patriotic historian Joachim Lelewel encouraged his readers, it was important not to 'differentiate the sons of Poland, whether they speak the Ruthenian, Polish, or Lithuanian language.'[8]

After another unsuccessful rebellion against Russian rule in Warsaw in November 1830, debates over Polish identity became more heated. The term *naród* (nation) began to be associated more frequently with the concept of *lud* (the people), raising inevitable questions about exactly who could call themselves Polish. Some, like activist Jan Janowski, started to leverage concepts of birth and ethnicity to exclude the international elites they blamed for subjugating the country.[9] But the failure of the November Uprising revealed to those in the patriotic intellectual sphere the challenge of generating active support amongst 'the people' – most of whom had been apathetic to the rebellion. One result of this was a strong messianic movement that placed Poles at the centre of not just their own destiny, but the universal struggle against evil:

> … for the Polish nation did not die. Its body lay in the grave and its soul had gone from the earth, that is, from public life, into purgatory, that is, into the domestic life of [those nations] suffering from slavery … And on the third day the soul will return to the body and the nation will rise again and free all the peoples of Europe from slavery.[10]

Adam Mickiewicz described Poland as the 'Christ of Nations', using the imagery of reincarnation to sustain visions of future renewal in a lexicon both familiar and awe-inspiring to Catholic Poles. What is interesting is that even this framing of nationalism did not come at the expense of religious toleration. Judeophobia continued to exist (as it had for centuries), but it was sidelined in the interests of fulfilling Poland's historical destiny. When the next major Polish revolt erupted in 1863, Catholic, Protestant, and Jewish communities marched shoulder to shoulder in Warsaw and mourned each other's losses in the fight for freedom.

Examining life in Warsaw during the partition era not only foreshadows but also goes someway to explain the Varsovian response to German occupation in the 20th century. When Georg Brandes, a visiting scholar from Denmark, arrived in Warsaw in 1885, he couldn't help but notice the sinister effects of partition on the city:

> The city is of great extent, but with its decayed grandeur and the horrible memories it calls up at every turn, it makes a mournful impression. In the last century, next to Paris, it was the most brilliant city in Europe; now it is a Russian provincial town. It then had the character of prodigal splendour; now it is a forlorn, neglected place, which declines more and more every day … Warsaw is the capital of a country whose existence the government does not recognise, and is a city whose pride the government wishes to humble in every way.[11]

Sometimes an outsider is the most honest observer – especially one such as Brandes, who arrived in Warsaw from Vienna, the 'city of freedom from restraint', the jewel in the crown of the Austro-Hungarian Empire. His account gives an insight into how Warsaw was perceived by foreigners, both as a shell of its former self and as an alien amongst other Polish cities. By this time, Russian authorities had closed Polish schools, pushed for Russian to be spoken in Catholic churches, and made it illegal for Polish to be spoken in public. In many ways, Warsaw had become a 'city of contradictions'.[12] The pressure of Russification policies after 1863 seriously stymied education and cultural expression; censorship was far harsher for Warsaw than it was in its cultural rival, Kraków, in Austrian Galicia. Russian authorities feared that Poland could become a gateway for Western European propaganda that would invigorate workers' movements and upset existing hierarchies across the empire.[13] Brandes' Kafkaesque exchange with customs authorities at the Russian Frontier reveals that the resulting incoherence and absurdity of Russian oppression was just as much of a nuisance to visiting foreigners as it was to the native population, leading him to conclude that 'from this point we were outside the real precincts of European civilization':

> It was in vain that I called their attention to the fact that they might safely leave me the Danish books and newspapers, since no harm could be done with them in Poland, where no one understands Danish. 'In the censor's office they understand all languages,' was the answer. – 'Grant that that is true, although I have my doubts; but the government censor, who is Russian, I cannot corrupt, and the other people do not understand Danish, do they?' – 'That is true from your point of view,' was the answer, and, acting from their point of view, they kept the books.[14]

Yet despite all this, the fact that by 1901 Warsaw outstripped St Petersburg in production of daily newspapers speaks to a vivacity of cultural activity that connected residents – or at least, the literate – in a shared intellectual space. Warsaw theatre, subsidised by St Petersburg, became a popular outlet for creative expression and the airing of grievances, especially as it was one of the only spaces free from linguistic censorship. Brandes found the Warsaw people to be humble and hospitable towards foreigners, and passionate and energetic with regard to their heritage and traditions. In an assessment that could be applied as aptly half a century later, he stated:

> … the gaiety with which they whirl is not the common joy of life; it reminds us rather of that which the prisoners of the [French] Revolution displayed in their ignorance as to what the next day would bring forth. This levity is not common levity, but a lightness often found in those who daily defy suffering and death.[15]

And indeed, the Russian authorities' fear (and, no doubt, anticipation) of further rebellion was so high that the most inconsequential of actions could lead to devastating reprisals. However nebulous popular Polish nationalism might have been at this point, it is difficult to understate the psychological fallout of Russian oppression. Brandes went on to describe an incident with a family he visited during his stay in Warsaw:

> The son of the family, a boy of sixteen, the only son of a widow, one evening in the theatre had thrown a wreath … A few days later, in obedience to an order from the Minister of Education, the principal of the school called him up, and told him that he must not only leave the school, but that all future admission to any other school whatever was forbidden him; it was the punishment for having been guilty of a *Polish demonstration*. The boy went home and put a bullet through his head.[16]

The city's sense of dislocation was heightened by the fact that Poles, Jews, and Russians occupied parallel worlds separated by religion, language, dress, and culture. There existed a stratum of more affluent Jews who opted to speak Polish as opposed to Yiddish and adopted elements of European dress alongside their Polish neighbours, but these suggestions of assimilation were inconsistent and often caused consternation amongst Catholic Poles and traditional Jews alike. The writer Aleksander Kraushar encapsulated a sense of identity crisis that would have been common to many assimilationist Jews:

> What kind of future awaits my poor child? He was born a Pole, the Muscovites demand that he be a Muscovite, [notorious antisemitic journalist] Jeleński forbids him to be a Pole, he doesn't want to be a German, and he's incapable of being a Jew.[17]

With dissent increasingly dangerous and few channels to vent their frustrations, Polish residents of Warsaw still held tight to their cultural roots. Every incident of confrontation fuelled the simmering resentment against foreign rule whilst raising the temperature of patriotic feeling. The controversy around the Mickiewicz monument was a case in point. In 1897, nearly a quarter of a million rubles was raised via public newspapers and journals after the governor-general of the city approved the erection of a monument to the national poet. The following year, sculptors worked feverishly to complete the project in time for the centenary of the poet's birth on 24 December, when an heir of his literary tradition, Henryk Sienkiewicz, was to play a leading role in the unveiling ceremony. At the last minute, the Russians had misgivings over Sienkiewicz's potential influence and Minister of the Interior Ivan Goremykin forbade the writer from speaking in public. Other speakers pulled out in protest, and in the end the statue's unveiling was accompanied only by music and a few religious ceremonies. Once again, the Russians' inconsistent and clumsy displays of power managed to dispel any potential reconciliation with the native population. The memory of this kind of repression would linger for decades in Warsaw's collective consciousness and compound the sense of distrust towards foreign powers.

The patterns of the history of pre-20th-century Poland are frequently overlooked when historians focus on more recent events. What is most striking about the writings of Kraushar and Brandes quoted above is that their descriptions of life under Russian imperial rule could have been just as apt in describing conditions under German occupation between 1939 and 1945 – and, of course, the 44 years of Soviet rule that came after. Indeed, the experience of invasion, occupation, subjugation, and efforts at cultural annihilation unleashed during the Second World War were not without precedent; nor were the patterns of social and political rebellion or cultural resistance on the part of the Poles. To be clear, the scale of suffering and destruction during the Nazi occupation was unparalleled, but many of the corollary themes would have felt distressingly familiar to Poles whose parents and grandparents had endured the partition era: Poland became a battlefield for warring neighbours, and Warsaw the epicentre; everyday life was dictated by foreign invaders; the population was at once bound together by common hardship and fractured by mutual suspicion; allies failed to intervene in Poland's interests; and assertions of Polish identity and independence fell on deaf ears on the global stage.

By 1945, over 80 per cent of Warsaw had been reduced to rubble. At that point in time, the city was little more than an index of the tragedy inflicted upon it, 'a Nazi script that demanded [its] complete disappearance'. It is no coincidence that 96 per cent of landmarks deemed historically significant before the war were either fully or partially erased in the Germans' systematic annihilation of the city's identity.[18] If piecing together the story of a ruined city wasn't hard enough, years of Soviet censorship added another layer of obfuscation to the historical record and hindered attempts to restore the city's collective memory. History is never truly objective, but, as the historian David Crowley puts it, Warsaw's ruination provided a blank canvas for 'acts of ventriloquism by architects, politicians, film-makers, artists and writers over a period of more than six decades.'[19]

Today, some of the most powerful memorials to the city's past aren't immediately obvious. To the average visitor, the monument to Adam Mickiewicz on Krakowskie Przedmieście appears at first glance unremarkable – a memorial to a cultural icon in a capital city. But digging deeper, we realise it is a monument to something much more profound: the expression, survival, and revitalisation of Polishness in spite of repeated attempts at its annihilation. Half a century after its controversial unveiling ceremony, the Mickiewicz monument became a prime target in the Nazis' campaign against Polish culture; like thousands of other such statues across the occupied territories, it was dismantled and cut into pieces to be melted down and transformed into materiel for the Nazi war machine. The majority of the statue was therefore lost, but incredibly, the head survived – so whilst the body of the modern iteration differs slightly from the original, Mickiewicz's head was recast as a perfect replica. The statue we see today serves as a perfect metaphor for Warsaw itself: much of the city, like Mickiewicz's body, was irretrievably lost, and has been rebuilt or reimagined in new ways; some parts – like the statue's pedestal – are original, but indelibly marked by the scars of war. But the most important things, the windows to the soul of the city, can still be found – if you know where to look.

We hope to show that Warsaw should not be defined by these circumstances, especially since the city, like any other, was always defined by its people more than its landmarks. This is a story not only of Varsovian natives but of refugees, of occupiers, and of others who found themselves tied up in the city's fate. In some ways it is a microcosm of the Polish war experience; in others, of any civilian population at war. But most of all, it is a story of a unique city with a distinct character that was made to suffer incomparable devastation. It is testament to the strength of the spirit of Poland as a whole and Warsaw in particular that recurring cycles of violence, occupation, and repression failed to extinguish the flame of Polish identity. Oppman's mermaid would have been proud to see the city she sheltered rise up time and again, *semper invicta*.

CHAPTER 1

THE REBIRTH OF A NATION

... And happy he that perished in the strife
If for the others he'd prepared the stage
Of fame and honored life.
En masse, *Young Friends!*
Though steep and icy be our path
Though force and frailty guard the door:
When force is used, with force respond and wrath;
While young, upon our frailty wage a war ...

Adam Mickiewicz, 'Ode to Youth', 1820[1]

THE NOWHERE STATE

On 15 May 1935, a procession departed the Belvedere Palace in Warsaw to commence its three-mile journey to St John's Cathedral. The cortege passed slowly through Warsaw along streets lined with police officers, soldiers, and clergy – at its heart, a horse-drawn carriage bore a flag-draped coffin, flanked by guards in dress uniform. At the cathedral, the coffin containing Marshal Józef Piłsudski, the man who had towered over Poland since its rebirth from the ashes of the First World War, was transferred to an artillery carriage, which was then taken to the main railway station in the city. Here, it was carefully loaded aboard an open railcar and commenced a slow journey across Poland to Kraków. It was estimated that during the 14 hours the train crawled across the country, half a million Poles stood bare-headed at the railway tracks and stations to pay their respects;

the entire nation seemed to recognise that something of great significance had taken place.[2] Warsaw resident Irena Protassewicz noted the extraordinary effect the marshal's death produced on city life: 'It was said that when Marshal Pilsudski died, not a single burglary took place in Warsaw; the criminal world too felt the solemnity of the moment.'[3]

At a time when storm clouds were gathering across Europe and the threats to Poland seemed to be encroaching from all sides, it was a singularly bad moment for the country to lose such a powerful figurehead. In so many aspects, Piłsudski – like Warsaw – had come to embody all of the contradictions of Poland, and without his presence the future suddenly seemed very uncertain.

How did Warsaw get here? How did the city that started the century under the fist of foreign occupation find itself lamenting the hero of Poland's newfound independence just three decades later? And, before the end of the decade, how did it enter yet another era of occupation – one unmatched in its brutality?

The answers reveal just how cataclysmic and consequential the opening decades of the 20th century were in Poland. By the time Hitler invaded in September 1939, the Polish had survived a world war, thrown off an enemy occupier, repelled an unprecedented ideological threat, witnessed a *coup d'état*, and reinserted themselves – or at least, attempted to do so – onto the world's diplomatic stage. The drama of these years is the story of the ethnic and political tensions within Poland as well as the difficulties it faced in its dealings with the rest of the world. These issues, and how the Poles attempted to address them, shaped the social, political, and cultural fabric that was torn apart by the Nazi invasion and came into sharp focus in Warsaw; they also give an insight into the Poles' sense of identity, internal social conflicts, and their instinct for resistance. Perhaps most of all, the journey from partition to independence to occupation puts into stark relief the nation's historical tragedy – one that might be overlooked were we only to start our narrative in 1939.

Alfred Jarry's 1896 play, *Ubu Roi*, opened with a comment that was as prescient as it was surreal: 'As to the action which is about to begin, it takes place in Poland – that is to say, nowhere.'[4] Not only was a unified Poland missing from the map at the turn of the century, its statelessness meant it was little more than an afterthought in mainstream political discourse. To outsiders, it was literally and conceptually 'nowhere'. As for Warsaw, the city was little more than any other provincial centre – a pin in the map of the sprawling Russian Empire. The trends of rapid urbanisation and industrialisation that were surging around Europe arrived slightly later in Warsaw, which only added to the suddenness of the city's population explosion; during the 50 years prior to the First World War, its population quadrupled from approximately 200,000 to 900,000 residents.[5]

Warsaw had always been a trading hub, but the growth of manufacturing during this period contributed to the city earning a 'great reputation' for high-quality goods in Russia and beyond, especially in the textile, button making, and knitting industries, but also metallurgy, artisanal crafts, and, later, arms.[6] As the 1911 *Encyclopaedia Britannica* noted, this was in spite of considerable political and economic disadvantages: 'The barrier of custom-houses all round Poland, and the Russian rule, which militates against the progress of Polish science, technology and art, are so many obstacles to the development of its natural resources.'[7] Inevitably, and despite Russian interference, Varsovian society and culture diversified too. Amongst the myriad ethnic groups that now called the city their home, the most populous were Poles, Jews – accounting for around one third of the city's population – and Russians. Of these three groups, the last were the least numerous but the most powerful; both Poles and Jews were excluded from public office and local government, living at arm's length from the Russian authorities who viewed both groups with suspicion.

This is not to say they lacked political ambition. Internally, Poland's statelessness gave rise to an ideological vacuum around the concept of national identity, with extensive censorship under partition – especially in Russian-controlled Warsaw – making it difficult for Poles to study their own history and even harder to reach a consensus on what 'Polishness' represented. This was more than an academic problem. The definition of national identity was considered integral to the shaping of an independent Polish state, and to answering the question of which groups amongst the current population were to be included or excluded. This ideological vacuum naturally attracted a broad spectrum of competing discourses, but the most influential – and most consequential to the nation's future – were emblemised in two political rivals: Józef Klemens Piłsudski and Roman Dmowski.

NATIONALISM DIVIDED

Piłsudski was born in 1867 in a manor house close to the village of Zułów (now the Lithuanian Zalavas), about 35 miles northeast of Vilnius. His mother Maria was a strong influence, giving him a lifelong love of Polish history and literature; she also insisted that her children show respect for all people with no regard to social rank, and domestic servants in the manor were instructed to ignore the children if they did not show proper politeness and respect. The Piłsudskis came to prefer the writings of Słowacki, who wrote in 1848 that the liberation of Poland required not just the expulsion of foreign occupiers, but also the end of aristocratic privilege.[8]

By 1885, the young Piłsudski was active in underground politics, and, convinced that independence had to be accompanied by great social change, increasingly interested in the growing socialist movements in the Russian Empire. Inevitably, this led to clashes with the authorities, and he would be imprisoned or exiled more than once. He became a supporter of the new *Polska Partia Socjalistyczna* ('Polish Socialist Party' or *PPS*), which called for universal suffrage, a ban on legal discrimination between religious or ethnic groups, a minimum wage, equal employment rights for women, and an independent Polish state. This state would have as its boundaries the historic frontiers of the Polish–Lithuanian Commonwealth, and would inevitably incorporate large populations who were ethnically not Polish – Lithuanians, Belarusians, Ukrainians, Germans, and Jews. Piłsudski recognised the importance of gaining the support of the Jewish community for the Polish independence movement and categorically rejected the antisemitic views of those who favoured the creation of an ethnically pure Poland. In 1898, he wrote in the journal *Robotnik*, the underground newspaper of the *PPS*: 'Any trace of antisemitism among our comrades will be persistently fought against, and under no conditions will we allow its manifestation in the life of our movement.'[9]

These principles of toleration were not, however, universal. Roman Dmowski, the son of a Warsaw stonemason, was another rising star in Polish political circles; in later years, he was the co-founder of the-right-wing *Narodowa Dekoracja* ('National Democracy') or *Endecja* movement. He took a very different approach to that of Piłsudski and the *PPS* in terms of both what independence should look like and how it should be achieved. The confrontation between the two men – one born from a working Varsovian family, the other the Polish–Lithuanian gentry – came to symbolise the unbridgeable divide in the Polish nationalist movement. While Piłsudski rankled under Russian oppression, Dmowski's formative years exposed him to the reality that questions of national sovereignty came secondary to those of subsistence for the average working-class or peasant Pole. In 1893 he co-founded the right-wing National League, which later grew into the *Endecja*, a body that would constitute the major opposition to the *PPS* and Piłsudski's insurrectionist tactics.

Dmowski eschewed all ideas of armed resistance and adopted a social-Darwinist stance on ethnic assimilation. He envisioned a Catholic Poland that would fulfil a 'healthy egoism' by rejecting non-Polish minorities that threatened its integrity and unity. He himself was openly antisemitic, often describing Jewish schemes to take control of the world, and doubted whether the 'Polonisation' of minorities would be possible for the Jews – not least because unlike Lithuanians, they weren't Catholics. He feared that the creation of a Jewish homeland in the

Middle East would be the start of Jewish attempts to establish worldwide hegemony, but at the same time saw mass emigration of Jews from Poland as essential. Like the struggle for independence, however, he saw this being achieved by social and economic pressure rather than direct violence.

Hostility towards Jewish groups had of course existed for centuries, and attacks on Jews were widespread throughout Central and Eastern Europe in the 19th century. The expression *pogrom* – derived from a Russian term for violent destruction – was first applied to such attacks in about 1881. After he came to power in 1894, Tsar Nicholas II made no secret of his personal hostility towards Jews in private. Like other rulers throughout history, he recognised the benefit of identifying a group within society as 'the enemy within' and although his government condemned antisemitic attacks, Nicholas saw such incidents as a useful diversion of the anger of ordinary people away from the government. It is unsurprising that so many Jews within the Russian Empire became supporters of anti-monarchist groups like the fledgling Bolshevik movement.

In Poland too, there was a long history of hostility towards Jews, but it was not ubiquitous. Whilst the Catholic church was often a source of cultural resistance to attempts to Russify the population (and to impose Orthodox Christianity), it also had a long history of suspicion and hostility towards Jews. Nevertheless, the Russian authorities failed to acknowledge the fluidity of allegiances amongst the occupied peoples, and efforts to create division along religious lines didn't always go to plan. After an *agent provocateur* paid by the Russians initiated the Białystok pogrom of 1906, for instance, survivors described how many local Poles had opted to shelter Jews rather than participate in the violence.[10] The right-leaning Polish nationalist movement would become notorious for its antisemitism, but this was by no means a foregone conclusion in the 19th century. The claim by the historian Ezra Mendelsohn that 'the triumph of unbridled Polish nationalism was bound to be accompanied by antisemitism, given the legacy of Polish–Jewish relations and the supreme Polish nationalist doctrine of "Poland for the Poles"' overlooks the complexity of nationalist discourses of the time, not least because many Jews were fierce supporters of Polish independence and wanted to be part of the future independent Poland.[11] The martyrdom of Michał Landy, a Jew killed in Warsaw during a pro-independence march for raising up a fallen Christian cross, was just one symbol of this.

Another nuance in the Polish–Jewish dynamic was the plurality within Jewish society itself, which varied widely in culture, politics, social status, and beliefs. The Jewish community in Warsaw exemplified the broad spectrum of Jewish experiences of urbanisation, ranging from strictly Yiddish-speaking Orthodox groups who isolated themselves from non-Jewish society, to the growing proportion of generally wealthier assimilationist or acculturated groups who adopted European dress, did business and integrated with non-Jews. Degrees of assimilation and acceptance fluctuated over the following decades, but with movements spanning from the socialist Bund labour union to the anti-assimilationist *Folkspartei* ('People's Party') to various competing Zionist factions, the Jews consistently matched their Polish neighbours in engagement across the political spectrum.

When war broke out between Japan and Russia in 1904, Piłsudski travelled to Japan in the hope of securing aid, only to be frustrated by an intervention on the part of his rival, Dmowski, who advised the Japanese that a Polish uprising would have little support from the working classes. But when Piłsudski returned to Europe in 1905, a wave of strikes was sweeping through the Russian Empire, and he and his followers quickly set about inciting Polish participation. The results were impressive, with over 90 per cent of Polish workers walking out. Over the following days, scuffles with police escalated, culminating in a major uprising in Łódź in June; to Piłsudski's dismay, the *PPS*-supported insurgents found themselves fighting not only Russian military and police forces, but also armed members of the *Endecja* faction loyal to Dmowski, who opposed the strikes and protests and favoured cooperation with Russia. After three days of fighting, the uprising was crushed, and between 200 and 800 people were killed with many more wounded. Eventually, order was restored in the Russian Empire. Tsar Nicholas grudgingly agreed what became known as the October Manifesto, guaranteeing freedom of speech, assembly, and religion, and the creation of an elected Duma. Many in the *PPS* regarded this as a positive development, but Piłsudski was highly sceptical, and his doubts proved to be justified: within a few years, most of the freedoms granted in the October Manifesto were clawed back.

WAR UNDER PARTITION

The outbreak of the First World War in August 1914 breathed new life into dreams of establishing an independent Polish state. With help from the Austro-Hungarian Empire, Piłsudski had established a body known as the Polish Riflemen, which subsequently became the Polish Legions of the Austro-Hungarian forces. The Polish Legions ultimately grew to number about 30,000 men, but far larger numbers of Poles were simply conscripted into the armies of the three empires that had seized Polish territory in the 18th century, and on many occasions Polish soldiers found themselves fighting each other. When Piłsudski's legionnaires faced Poles in the Russian Army in the first winter of the First World War, the two sides joined in the singing of traditional Polish Christmas songs, singing verses in turn across no-man's land.[12] A bookseller from Kraków later wrote that of his 12 nephews, eight served in the ranks of the *k.u.k.* (abbreviated from *Kaiserlich und Königliche*, 'Imperial and Royal') Austro-Hungarian Army, two in the Russian Army, one in the German Army, and one in the US Army.[13]

The original war plan for the Russian Army had called for swift advances into East Prussia in the north and Galicia in the south. After early failures, the commander-in-chief of the Russian Army, Grand Duke Nikolai Mikhailovich, issued a proclamation calling upon Poland to fight to 'be reunited under the sceptre of the Russian tsar … reborn, free in her faith, language and self-government'.[14] This ignored the reality that Russia had played a leading role in the dismemberment of Poland, and that repression of Polish culture had been more severe in Congress Poland than the regions under Prussian (later German) and Austrian control. Nor did the manifesto offer true independence, merely a degree of home rule as part of the Russian Empire. Dmowski and his supporters greeted the proclamation with enthusiasm whilst Piłsudski dismissed it as worthless. Russia had shown no commitment to the October Manifesto, and there was nothing to suggest that matters would be any different this time.

Indeed, Dmowski had chosen a very different path to pursue independence, and in late 1914 formed the *Komitet Narodowski Polski* ('Polish National Committee' or *KNP*) to further Polish nationalism through cooperation with Russia. Piłsudski, in contrast, remained committed to a multi-ethnic Poland, and readily recruited Jews into his Legions whose experiences with Russian military abuses made them natural allies against occupation forces. A young lieutenant in the 1st Brigade of the Legions wrote a proclamation that was widely distributed across Polish territories in which he underlines the divergence between Piłsudski's uncompromising demands for independence and Dmowski's attempts to secure autonomy within the aegis of the Russian Empire:

> We must rise up against Russia and the Russian executioners – our greatest enemy and oppressor who has committed hundreds of massacres and pogroms upon a defenceless Jewish population – but not like slaves licking the feet of their master …
>
> Today, we march under the banner of the Polish Legions in a common fight for the freedom of Poland – a Poland that for 800 years has taken us under its roof, a Poland that does not know violence and pogroms …

> Remember that Poland shall belong to those who fight for her. He who loves freedom and desires to be the citizen of a free country, who does not want to live in tsarist captivity, who does not want to rot and live a dull life under the Muscovite yoke, who want to live and thrive in the light of freedom – come with us.[15]

The leaflet was less than entirely honest: Poland was no stranger to violence against Jews.

Dmowski's attempts to extract concrete concessions from the Russians were to no avail. When Warsaw fell to the Germans in August 1915, he sensed that the war was turning and left Petrograd in search of western allies. Meanwhile, Piłsudski dispatched Ingacy Boerner, an officer in the Polish Legions, to Warsaw to make preparations for a new national government, sharing an astute prediction of how the conflict would unfold:

> Already, it is entirely clear that Russia will be defeated, but the Central Powers will be defeated as well. In Russia, sooner or later, a revolution will break out, followed by a revolution … in Austria and finally in Germany. At the moment Polish lands are liberated from the Russian yoke, the purpose of the Legions will come to an end, as the struggle to expel Russia will have been accomplished. We shall then build up our strength for the second phase … when we have to deal with Austria and Germany.[16]

However unconvincing the October Manifesto was to Piłsudski, the debate around it sent worrying signals to the British and French governments who feared the possibility of Poles defecting to the Central Powers. Both nations were wary of supporting anti-Russian nationalists so long as Russia remained an ally; but nor was the possibility of Russia absorbing German and Austrian Polish territories welcome at a time when the European balance of power lay in tatters. The war had put into sharp relief the issue of Polish nationhood that had been largely ignored in the west for decades, but it 'remained secondary to the defeat of Germany and victory on the Western Front.'[17] As Edvard Beneš, prime minister of Czechoslovakia either side of the Second World War, declared with understandable cynicism, the Great Powers 'treat [small nations] as they find it convenient at the moment.'[18]

The First World War inflicted great hardships on the Polish people. The country became the battleground of the Germans, Russians, and Austro-Hungarians, with all three carrying out scorched earth policies at different times. Any sense of affiliation to the Russian Empire was decisively severed as the imperial troops plundered their way back east, looting property and deporting at least 743,000 Poles on accusations of conspiracy.[19] There were numerous occasions when, prior to the arrival of the armies of the Central Powers, Russian soldiers carried out pogroms against Jewish populations; when German and Austro-Hungarian troops recaptured Przemyśl, the city's Jews were the most enthusiastic in welcoming their arrival. The destitute population of Poland received little support from the incoming Germans, not least because the British blockade was stretching German resources thin. Nor were the British willing to undermine the blockade by attempting to send aid to the Poles that might fall into the wrong hands. Not for the first time, and certainly not for the last, the civilian population could do nothing except pray for survival.

Meanwhile, as Dmowski was seeking support in Paris, London, and Rome, his nationalist vision shifted once more. Territorial autonomy was no longer enough; the Polish people deserved nothing short of full national sovereignty. To this end, Dmowski set up a new *KNP* in Lausanne with the intention of establishing an official Polish army and presiding over the restitution of Polish lands in future peace negotiations. Another *KNP* member helped raise western awareness of the Polish question; in 1915, pianist, composer, and future prime minister Ignacy Jan Paderewski began lobbying for popular relief and support for the nationalist cause, establishing the Polish Relief Fund in London and the White Cross Society in the United States. Paderewski found the ear of one of President Woodrow Wilson's closest advisors, Colonel Edward House, and by 1917, the Allied Powers had recognised the *KNP* as the official representative body of Poland. It is unlikely this support can be traced solely back to sympathy for Polish nationalism, or even for the plight of the civilian population. In President Wilson's eyes, Poland was nothing more than a victim of 19th-century European *Realpolitik*, in the same way that the war represented the 'bankruptcy of modern European politics' and failure of 'Old Diplomacy'.[20] In any case, the president laid out his vision of a more moral political future in his famous 'Peace without Victory' speech of January 1917, and, crucially, voiced the assurance Dmowski was seeking: 'statesmen everywhere are agreed that there should be a united, independent, and autonomous Poland.'[21]

But what were the attitudes of the Polish people towards independence at this point in time? Poland was once again being ravaged by foreign combatants, so civilians were understandably frustrated that their promises of independence remained unfulfilled even after the departure of the Russians. 'Political parties reveal so much impotence and dilemma,' the writer Maria Dąbrowska noted in her diary, 'who knows whether they are not actually a manifestation of the disintegration and bankruptcy of certain values.'[22] Dąbrowska embodied the energetic political engagement that was characteristic of Warsaw's intelligentsia during this period. An active supporter of the *Liga Kobiet Polskich Pogotowia Wojennego* ('League of Polish Women of the War Emergency Service'), she was married to socialist Piłsudski ally Marian Dąbrowski, but remained, like many others, sceptical of political parties whose 'desire to dominate' only seemed to be stalling the independence movement. 'We said before the war: "Down with parties. Unity, independence for all is the first goal,"' she recounted in late 1915, voicing her growing sense of disillusionment and 'great heartbreak' that was making her consider withdrawing from activism altogether.[23] The Jewish community, meanwhile, could only hope that future independence would break the patterns of oppression they had come to expect under occupation. As Yiddish writer and journalist Ber Kutsher wrote:

> One event after another arrives, overlapping, as if in a film, as if in a kaleidoscope, impossible to see with the naked eye, impossible to comprehend … Regents, state council, ministers, legionnaires, soldiers … And if there are soldiers – they will lash Jewish backs … And pull Jewish beards … You know it. You get it. It's nothing new. History repeats itself. Just yesterday, under the tsarist boots, today under the German fist.[24]

In 1916, the material costs of the war became increasingly important. German forces lost huge numbers of men, first at Verdun and then during the Battle of the Somme; in the east, the *k.u.k.* Army was equally badly degraded in the Brusilov Offensive. In all, the Central Powers lost over 3.5 million men. The only obvious source of relatively untapped human materiel was Poland and there were calls for widespread conscription. From Warsaw, General Hans Hartwig von Beseler, the German governor-general, warned that any such initiative would be difficult to implement unless it was preceded by a clear decision on the future of Poland. Eventually, trying to offer the Poles sufficient reasons to agree to their plans, the Central Powers issued what became known as the 'Two Emperors' Manifesto'. This recognised Poland as an independent state, comprising what had been Congress Poland, though its precise frontiers would be decided at the end of the war. Significantly, neither Germany nor Austria-Hungary were willing to hand over any Polish territory that they had occupied at the start of the war.

Whilst recognition of an independent Poland was widely welcomed by nationalists, it was abundantly clear that the Central Powers had offered the very minimum they could to secure Polish troops for their war. The *Centralny Komitet Narodowy w Warszawie* ('Central National Committee of Warsaw' or *CKN*) rejected Beseler's call for mass recruitment of Polish troops to serve with the armies of the Central Powers, insisting that any Polish forces should be independent and under Piłsudski's control; he had already resigned from the Polish Legions over similar demands. Beseler replied, with some justification, that Piłsudski had no military training and was therefore unsuitable to lead a field army. Negotiations dragged on through the winter of 1916–17; then, the events of March 1917 changed the world forever.

THE OLD WORLD COLLAPSES

Unrest had been building in Petrograd, the capital of Imperial Russia, for some time. The city was highly dependent on the railway network for its food supply and the strains of war had brought the Russian railways to the brink of collapse; food shortages triggered a new wave of strikes and protests and on 8 March (23 February in the old Russian calendar), thousands took to the streets. As had happened in previous protests in Russia, the marchers found themselves confronted by soldiers in the days that followed. In some cases, the troops and accompanying police opened fire on civilians, but when Cossacks blocked a bridge over the Neva and a large crowd of women protesters attempted to cross, the Cossacks simply moved aside. Other soldiers joined the protesters, firing on troops still loyal to the government. Within days, both the government and the Romanov dynasty had been swept away.

Russia was now under the control of a new Provisional Government. One of its first steps was to recognise the right of Poles to determine their own future.[25] For Piłsudski, this effectively brought an end to any need for Polish troops to serve alongside German and Austro-Hungarian soldiers against Russia. To the dismay of many Polish nationalists, Charles I, the new Austro-Hungarian emperor, ordered the transfer of the Polish forces under the control of the *k.u.k.* Army to German control a few days after the declaration by the Russian Provisional Government. Piłsudski was offered command of a future Polish Army, but when he responded by making new demands, Beseler ran out of patience and had him arrested.

If the Germans hoped that this step would curb Polish nationalist sentiment, they were badly mistaken. There were large demonstrations in Warsaw and growing disaffection within the ranks of the Polish Legions, and the new *Tymczasowa Rada Stanu* ('Provisional State Council' or *TRS*), resigned in protest against Piłsudski's arrest in August 1917. The Germans reacted by creating a three-man Regency Council led by Prince Zdzisław Lubomirski, but most Poles regarded this body as being primarily concerned with serving German rather than Polish interests, and the four largest political parties in Warsaw declared that its actions were illegitimate while Piłsudski remained in prison. Even from the isolation of his (fairly comfortable) prison in Magdeburg, Piłsudski continued to dominate politics in Poland.

There was one more major development in 1917 that would have huge ramifications on Poland's future: the United States officially entered the war against Germany in April. It is hard to overstate the importance of this; to many Americans, President Wilson included, the conflicts across Europe were nothing more than the death throes of an obsolete old world order. The United States had shown minimal interest in stepping into a war that did not directly affect it or its borders, and had little understanding of the dense geopolitical and ethnic dynamics at play in Europe. Entering the war at this stage meant taking the honourable high ground over the old world powers in order to build a new system, not to defend specific interests or to reinstate the status quo. In acknowledging his country's reluctance to go to war, Wilson invoked a moral crusade that could only be led by the United States:

> We shall fight for the things which we have always carried nearest our hearts, for democracy, for the right of those who submit to authority to have a voice in their own Governments, for the rights and liberties of small nations, for a universal dominion of right by such a concert of free peoples as shall bring peace and safety to all nations and make the world itself at last free.[26]

On 8 January 1918, President Wilson presented his Fourteen Points to the US Congress and in so doing laid out his blueprint for the post-war world. The penultimate point was significant:

> An independent Polish state should be erected which should include the territories inhabited by indisputably Polish populations, which should be assured a free and secure access to the sea, and whose political and economic independence and territorial integrity should be guaranteed by international covenant.[27]

There was certainly cause for celebration, but further scrutiny of Wilson's statement gave nationalists pause: the word 'should' was applied to Poland while 'must' was used for Belgium.[28] Colonel House's explanation that the word 'must' had only been applied to conditions that were not up for discussion was hardly reassuring.[29] Then there was the question of how an 'erected' Poland would differ from a 'restored' or 'reunified' state; did an assured passage to the sea mean the inclusion of Gdańsk or only access to it? For the nationalists, Wilson's statement was a semantic can of worms. The restitution of the Polish state was still far from a foregone conclusion. If Poland was to win her place in a renewed world order, some of the old world powers had to fall first.

One of the three empires that had dismembered Poland was already effectively eliminated; the others, as Piłsudski had foreseen, soon followed. The Habsburg government had struggled for years against a rising tide of nationalism in the Austro-Hungarian Empire and in October 1918, a last-minute offer of increased autonomy for all regions was not enough to prevent the disintegration of the empire. Several regions broke away and declared independence, forcing the emperor to abdicate. Germany was also engulfed in unrest, leaving Kaiser Wilhelm II no option but to step down, and both nations agreed an armistice with the victorious Western Powers.

Imperfect Independence

On 8 November 1918, Piłsudski was released from Magdeburg. News of his release quickly reached Warsaw and crowds began to gather at the railway station in anticipation of his return. On 10 November, Piłsudski arrived, and was met by Prince Lubomirski and Adam Koc, the head of the clandestine *Polska Organizacja Wojskowa* ('Polish Military Organisation' or *POW*). The earlier crowds at the railway station had drifted away over the preceding day, but as Lubomirski and Piłsudski drove to the prince's residence, people gathered once more and cheered jubilantly. Regardless of the views of Dmowski and others in Paris, there was little doubt about who was seen by Poles as their leader. On 11 November, the day that Piłsudski was named commander-in-chief of the Polish forces and entrusted to form a new national government, Poland marked her independence day and brought 123 years of foreign rule to close.

Drawing a line under the war would prove complex. When Piłsudski arrived in Warsaw, there were around 30,000 German troops who had yet to evacuate the city, and though putting police headquarters and armouries back under Polish control was a priority, he was wary of violence flaring up between retreating Germans and the Poles reclaiming their city. Addressing a committee of German soldiers, Piłsudski guaranteed their safe evacuation so long as they surrendered captured property, lay down their arms, and avoided provoking the Poles. At the same time, the *POW* issued an order that Germans were not to be attacked and that they were to be left to return to their country in peace. The result was a remarkably orderly transfer of power across the city, with only a few casualties recorded. At the behest of the astute Piłsudski, the *POW* had monitored (and played upon) war-weariness in the German ranks and knew that the demoralised troops were unlikely to put up much resistance. Moreover, Piłsudski's triumphant entry into Warsaw made its citizens more jubilant than vengeful. As Maria, Lubomirski's wife, recorded:

> We're free! We get to govern ourselves! This really happened and in such an unexpected fashion at that … The Germans are dumbfounded, they're sporadically resisting, but they allow themselves to be disarmed not only by military men, but also by common civilian whippersnappers … Strange things in our capital! ... The present day is historic, unforgettable, filled with happiness and triumphant! [30]

At this moment, it didn't matter to Varsovians that the boundaries of the new Poland were still unfixed; that its future was in the hands of international powers; or that Polish nationalists were still pulling in different directions. For people who had lived their whole lives under foreign rule, the week of 11 November was coloured by a sense of real change and a hope that Poland had finally retaken control over her destiny. The writer Maria Dąbrowska couldn't help but note that even the weather was 'absolutely beautiful' on their day of independence:

> Throughout the day, military assets and civilian authorities are being taken from the Germans. All day long, the streets are crowded. The trams are running as usual. There are cars with our soldiers everywhere … In the midst of all this, Poland is rising. And nobody sees how beautiful it is. Nobody notices in this commotion.[31]

All that remained was for Piłsudski to inform the Allied Powers in no uncertain terms that the hour for Poland's reunification had arrived. On 16 November, he sent a telegram to the leaders of Germany, USA, Britain, and other Allies:

> As the commander-in-chief of the Polish Army, I hereby notify belligerent and neutral governments and nations of the existence of an independent Polish State encompassing all lands of united Poland … The Polish State arises from the will of the entire nation and shall be based on democratic principles … I have the firm hope that the powerful democracies of the West will lend their aid and fraternal support to the reconstituted and independent Polish Republic.[32]

This declaration of independence raised as many questions as it answered. In France, Dmowski and the *KNP* were recognised by the Western Allies as the official representatives of the Polish people, but there were other competing bodies in Galicia, Poznań, Lwów, and Lublin. Moreover, few in the west had any understanding of the ethnic mixture of the Polish population; international recognition of the new state only came in February 1919 after the first *Sejm* elections, but western suspicions about potential pro-Bolshevik leanings remained.

Meanwhile, the ethnic powder-keg had ignited into open violence. When Ukrainians attempted to seize territories in the eastern part of Galicia, it didn't take long for Polish recriminations against the insurgents to degenerate into opportunistic pogroms against the Jewish population. In Kielce, in a forerunner of the terminology later adopted by the Germans, there were attacks against *żydzi-bolszewicy* ('Jewish Bolsheviks') and smaller-scale attacks elsewhere. As one Polish Jew commented, 'the birth of Poland was accompanied by rivers of Jewish blood'.[33] The violence was widely reported around the world, and Piłsudski faced the first practical test of his declarations that antisemitism had no place in Polish life. His promises to investigate the violence against Jews came to no avail and when challenged on why his orders that the army protect Jews were unknown to the general public, Piłsudski replied that he wasn't an autocrat and couldn't issue proclamations of a political character.

It was a disappointing and weak response. Piłsudski had shown no hesitation in issuing political decrees in the past, and it seems that the outbreaks of anti-Jewish violence – many of which rumbled on for several months more – took him by surprise. Considering Dmowski's openly antisemitic attitude, he may have feared that any firm action to punish those responsible for the attacks would play into his rival's hands – and so, he treated the violence as a passing phenomenon and hoped it would quickly die down.

There were other difficulties too. Polish people had completely different experiences of authority depending on whether they'd lived under tsarist, Prussian, or Habsburg rule, so establishing any form of consensus – let alone trust – in centralised power was almost impossible. In the words of the historian Adam Zamoyski, 'during the period of partition, [suspicion of central authority] had morphed into more or less active and patriotically motivated civil disobedience and subversion aimed at the occupying authorities.'[34] The Poles had accepted their oppositional status for so long that the concept of being able to voice their national interests via democratic mechanisms, whilst ideal in principle, proved utterly alien to them in practice. Nevertheless, Piłsudski was able gradually to gain support from the Western Powers, not least by portraying Dmowski as being out of touch with the situation within Poland. Reports from western diplomats in Warsaw were increasingly favourable towards Piłsudski, who had responded to Dmowski's personal antipathy by describing his rival as 'reactionary, antisemitic and unacceptable to the people at large'. By contrast, Piłsudski was seen as an engaging, often humorous person who appeared to be acting on behalf of all the people of Poland.[35] Or, as one British diplomat put it, bearing 'None of the usual amenities of civilised intercourse, but all the apparatus of sombre genius.'[36]

A NEW WORLD ORDER?

The Allies' mission to shape post-war Europe hinged on many challenges: navigating the collapse of the great imperial powers; restoring territory and ensuring self-determination for minor nation states; and, perhaps most importantly, constructing a balance of power that would work in their favour. The question of Poland sat at the intersection of all these issues, but the Allies were not united in how to proceed. With the threat of Bolshevik Russia casting a long shadow over Eastern Europe, Poland was in a pivotal position to either staunch or quicken the flow of radical Communism westwards. All the Western Powers thought of Poland in the context of using the new state to further their own agendas; there was little consideration of the wishes of the people who called it their homeland.

That said, the Allies could not look away from their responsibilities to the Polish civilian population who had borne the brunt of the war. Future president Herbert Hoover experienced first-hand the extent of Polish suffering:

> Here were about 28,000,000 people who had for four years been ravished by four separate invasions during this one war, where battles and retreating armies had destroyed and destroyed again … In parts there had been seven invasions and seven destructive retreats. Many hundreds of thousands had died of starvation. The homes of millions had been destroyed and the people in those areas were living in hovels. Their agricultural implements had been depleted, their animals had been taken by armies, their crops had been only partly harvested. Industry in the cities was dead from lack of raw materials. The people were unemployed and millions were destitute. They had been flooded with roubles and kronen, all of which were now valueless. The railroads were barely functioning. The cities were almost without food; typhus and other diseases raged over whole provinces.[37]

To leave destitution and poverty unchecked was to leave the door open to further social disorder and political radicalism and undermine their fundamental vision for peace in Europe. As Wilson himself put it, 'Bolshevism is steadily advancing westward; it is poisoning Germany. It cannot be stopped by force, but it can be stopped by food.'[38] In February 1919, the United States Congress established the American Relief Administration (ARA) under Hoover's directorship to aid post-war recovery in the Eastern European states. Of the ARA's $100 million budget, around $200,000 was dedicated per month to the relief of Polish children whose plight Hoover had found profoundly moving:

> We saw very few children playing in the streets of Warsaw. Why were they not playing? The answer was simple and sufficient: The children of Warsaw were not strong enough to play in the streets. They could not run; many could not walk; some could not even stand up. Their weak little bodies were bones clothed with skin, but not muscles. They simply could not play.[39]

By August, tons of food supplies were being shipped to Poland and the ARA had coordinated kitchens to feed 500,000 children per day. The relief mission would go on to provide much needed clothing, shoes, and typhus treatment, as well as technical support in rebuilding infrastructure and railways. For hundreds of thousands of Polish residents who had survived the war only to find themselves in a ruined nation, Hoover had provided salvation. Biologist Vernon Kellogg summarised this perfectly: while 'the name of another great American (Woodrow Wilson) spelled freedom for them; the name Herbert Hoover spelled life to them.' Within a year, Hoover had a street named in his honour in Warsaw; later, he would be made an honorary citizen of the city and give his name to the square in which a Monument of Gratitude was erected to commemorate the ARA's efforts. When Hoover arrived in Warsaw, unannounced, thousands of children turned out to show their gratitude:

> … one thing they decided to do, which was the best thing for the happiness of their guest they could possibly have done. They decided to show him that the children of Warsaw could now walk!
>
> So seventy thousand boys and girls were summoned hastily from the schools. They came with the very tin cups and pannikins from which they had just had their special meal of the day, served at noon in all the schools and special children's canteens, thanks to the charity of America … But they were astonished to see as they gave him their gift, that this great strong man did just what you or I or any other human sort of human being could not have helped doing under like circumstances. They saw him cry.[40]

Hoover believed that the future of Europe depended on its children and that ensuring the health and security of the next generation was a matter of existential importance. Yet 27 years later, he would once again be providing aid to Warsaw's children. By that time, the monument erected in his honour would stand headless thanks to a German grenade, and the 'shattering experience' of walking through the city's streets in the wake of the Second World War would haunt his dreams for years afterwards.[41] Despite Hoover's best efforts, this was not the last time Warsaw would know devastation.

In 1919, under the terms of the Treaty of Versailles, Germany was forced to give up parts of East Prussia, Upper Silesia, Eastern Pomerania, and Posen (Poznań to the Poles), with further territories to be decided through public plebiscites. Paderewski – now prime minister and foreign minister – made clear that these boundaries '[differed] somewhat from the preliminary peace terms' owing to German objections, but on the whole, he presented it as a success for the reunification of ethnic Poles. Germany would retain territory that was home to nearly 100,000 Germans, while Poland's gains would bring 60,000 Poles into the new state.[42]

One point of contention was the fact that Poland was also compelled to sign the 'Little Treaty of Versailles' that bound the government to ensure 'total and complete protection of life and freedom of all people regardless of their birth, nationality, language, race or religion.'[43] This was the first of the Minority Treaties imposed on newly independent states as a condition of membership into the League of Nations. To the Poles, it was perceived as a slight to their history of tolerance and, more broadly, another example of the condescension and hypocrisy of the Western Powers.[44] On the whole, Paderewski was careful to paint the treaties in a positive light and to encourage the Polish people to look forward, not backward, to 'forget all past sorrows and experienced sufferings'. Criticism and pessimism towards the peace agreement was, he said, just symptomatic of the 'long years' of bondage Poland had suffered. But in hindsight, his final words on the Treaty of Versailles, full of joy as they were, turned out to be ironically prescient: 'Wake up, arise … there is no day more beautiful, more glorious, more eventful; no date more lucky, and more fruitful than the day of 28 June 1919.'[45]

Paderewski's appointment as prime minister was the result of detailed negotiations with Piłsudski, who saw him as the best compromise figure to lead Poland; in particular, his contacts with the Western Powers were essential for securing supplies for the new Polish Army. In any case, Piłsudski remained both head of state and commander of the armed forces. The agreement between

Piłsudski and Paderewski shocked Dmowski, not least because the *KNP* now increased the size of its representation in Paris. He had little choice but to accept reality.

New Threats, Old Existentialist Crises

In the meantime, Poland found itself at war with Bolshevik Russia. The cession of the Baltic States, Congress Poland, and Ukraine to the Central Powers in the Treaty of Brest-Litovsk in 1918 was, from the point of view of the Soviet leadership, no more than an expedient move to buy time. With its grip on power apparently secured, the Bolshevik regime turned its attention to recovering its lost territories and several armies invaded the Baltic region. Eastern Lithuania, centred on the ancient Lithuanian capital of Vilnius, had perhaps the most tangled history and ethnicity of the region. For Piłsudski, this was where he had been born and was inextricably part of Poland. In what was known in the inter-war years as the 'federalist programme' (or *Międzymorze*, literally 'between seas' or *Intermarium*, in reference to the Baltic and Adriatic Seas) he hoped for the restoration of the old Polish–Lithuanian Commonwealth, with Poland as the dominant partner. The Lithuanians were anxious to establish their own independence from all outside influences, be they Russian, German, or Polish. In the confused fighting that followed, the Vilnius region changed hands several times before finally being seized by the Poles. Lithuanian protests to the Western Powers were to no avail, but the dispute would poison any attempts to forge closer links between the two countries as the Second World War approached.

In the summer of 1920, the advance of the Soviet armies – led in the north by Mikhail Nikolayevich Tukhachevsky and in the south by Semyon Mikhailovich Budyennyi – was deeply threatening to Poland, and the Western Powers expected Warsaw to fall within days. Winston Churchill, then British Secretary of State for War, lamented, 'nothing can now save Poland … the Russian part of her will be re-absorbed in the Russian system.'[46] But the Soviet advance turned out to be poorly coordinated. Budyennyi failed to turn northwest towards Warsaw, allowing the Polish forces gathered in and around the capital a brief window of opportunity to strike into the southern flank of Tukhachevsky's advance. The result was the Battle of Warsaw in the second week of August 1920. The Polish forces were close to their supply bases, whereas the Soviet armies were running out of supplies. Personally taking command of the 20,000-strong *Grupa Uderzeniowa* ('Strike Group'), Piłsudski planned to strike north in a complex operation that was widely criticised by western observers as overly ambitious, especially given Piłsudski's personal lack of military training. But when the counteroffensive began, it was immediately successful. The Polish Fifth Army, commanded by General Władysław Sikorski, drove back the Soviet units that were threatening to encircle Warsaw from the northwest, and a few days later Piłsudski's group struck north to the east of the Vistula. The Poles advanced into almost open space, covering about 42 miles in a day and a half.

Tukhachevsky rapidly realised the catastrophe that was unfolding and ordered the armies that had swept west to pull back, but lines of communication were badly disrupted by the Polish advance and few units received his orders. By 21 August, coordinated fighting by the Soviet units had almost completely ceased, with each formation operating with little or no knowledge of the whereabouts of friendly and hostile forces. With 15,000 dead and 65,000 men taken prisoner, Tukhachevsky's armies disintegrated. The Poles had lost about 4,500 men, with a further 10,000 missing.

The jubilation around the 'Miracle of the Vistula' – as some called the battle – marked a zenith in Polish nationalist sentiment. Both Lenin and the Western Powers had underestimated Poland's ability to resist invasion and the solidarity of the Polish public. Many survivors of the Battle of Warsaw attributed the victory to the Blessed Virgin Mary and even claimed to have seen her on the battlefield, which only reinforced the narrative of the Poles as God's people, once again fighting to save themselves – and the world – from annihilation at the hands of the ungodly. Meanwhile, the Catholic Church was instrumental in whipping up patriotic fervour and encouraging Poles to repel the foreign evil of Communism, while the government and other agencies spread propaganda underlining the existential threats to the newly independent nation.

Propaganda aside, Poland's allies in the west attributed enormous significance to the outcome of the battle for closing Bolshevism out of Europe. No doubt relieved to have been proven wrong in his previous predictions, Churchill celebrated that Poland 'is not to perish but to live', and that thanks to her, 'Europe, her liberties and her glory, are not to succumb to Kaiserism or to Communism.'[47] English diplomat Lord Edgar Vincent d'Abernon would go on to describe the battle as 'the eighteenth decisive battle of the world', and decry the fact that there was 'none of which the significance is less appreciated.'[48] Indeed, it is unlikely that even the Varsovians understood the full historical significance of their triumph. But for a people whose independence was freshly won, and whose memories of occupation were so raw, it would have been a moment of immense ideological potency.

Unfortunately, the victory was soured by events away from the battlefield. Even as Piłsudski's troops began their counteroffensive, Kazimierz Sosnkowski, the

Polish Minister of War, issued an order for all Jewish soldiers in the Polish Army to be interned in a camp near Jabłonna, a short distance to the north of Warsaw. The order was issued without any discussion with the rest of the government and was almost immediately condemned by Ignacy Daszyński, the deputy prime minister. Sosnkowski was unrepentant, claiming increasing cases of harmful Jewish activity. Despite further protests from Jewish parliamentarians and others, Sosnkowski refused to rescind the order; when challenged in parliament to name a single Jewish soldier who was guilty of treason, he failed to do so. Once again, Piłsudski failed to stand by his earlier words regarding equality for all ethnic groups. He told journalists that the behaviour of the Jewish population was varied – in some areas, they had fought bravely against the Soviet invaders, but in others, 'sometimes even on a mass scale, treason could be found on the Jewish side.'[49] Although there is no clear evidence of Piłsudski's involvement in the order to create the internment camp, it is highly unlikely that Sosnkowski would have acted without Piłsudski's knowledge and agreement. The outcome was a souring of relations with parts of the Jewish community; the Jabłonna camp was closed down a few weeks later without any charges being brought against any of its occupants.

COUP D'ÉTAT

Internal political life in the early 1920s continued to be characterised by conflict, division, and stalemate. Increasingly frustrated by the political wrangles in Warsaw, Piłsudski announced his retirement in 1923 'after making so violent a speech against his political opponents that he was challenged to a duel', or, as he would later explain:[50]

> After I had led the war for giving Poland independence, I wanted to leave Poland to her own devices ... The Polish *Sejm*, which I call a prostitute, purposely framed the Constitution so that the greatest shame which savage ignorant brains could devise would be placed on the nations' most popular men ... The only way of escape was by resignation ... even though I could have crushed the whole outfit under my thumb like a vile worm.[51]

Not everyone was happy to see the back of Piłsudski. Many nationalists – both on the right and left – remained convinced that the 'strong man' who had brought them this far still had work to do. They saw Poland struggling not just internally, but also on the international stage, where the nation looked increasingly vulnerable. The Locarno Treaties of 1925 were a set of seven separate agreements intended to settle remaining border issues across Europe, but although Germany agreed to arbitration in the event of territorial disputes with Poland, the eastern borders of Germany were not defined in the treaties; nor was any arbitration binding. The Western Powers saw the treaties as ushering in a 'spirit of hope' to post-war Europe, but to many Poles, they represented the exact opposite. France committed itself to mutual assistance of both Poland and Czechoslovakia in the event of either nation coming under attack contrary to the terms of the Locarno Treaties, but the details remained vague. The following year, the German–Soviet Berlin Treaty of non-aggression added further gloom in Polish circles.

The ineffective *Sejm* had significantly undermined public faith in Poland's new democratic experiment and left nationalists longing for a strong government to restore order and accelerate post-war recovery; the fresh memory of Piłsudski made them feel the 'great moral force' was tantalisingly close, even if he had sidelined himself for the time being.[52] One can only wonder where they would have looked for rescue had he not existed – or whether, without his legacy, the draw of a strongman would have been quite so compelling. In any case, the crisis and the events of 1926 marked a turning point in the direction of Polish political life and foreign policy that continued until the outbreak of the Second World War.

In 1926, amidst economic turmoil, right-leaning parliamentary factions appointed Wincenty Witos as prime minister in an attempt to restore national order. Piłsudski was no supporter of Witos, whom he saw as emblematic of the *Sejm*'s moral degradation, and on the same day made his feelings clear in an interview with the *Kurier Poranny* ('Morning Courier') newspaper: 'I stand up to fight, just like before, against the main evil of the state: the rule of unruly parties and factions over Poland, forgetting about imponderables, and remembering only about pennies and benefits.'[53]

The Witos regime seized the newspaper edition, but Piłsudski's supporters were already in motion. The next day, General Lucjan Żeligowski resigned from his role as Minister of Military Affairs and mobilised the Warsaw garrison to Rembertów, where he put the troops under Piłsudski's command. Other officers loyal to Piłsudski were already advancing on the capital, and on 12 May, the marshal invited President Stanisław Wojciechowski to a face-to-face meeting on the Poniatowski Bridge in the hopes the latter would agree to a peaceful transfer of power. It was not to be: Wojciechowski's declaration that he was responsible for the army enraged Piłsudski and caused him to storm off in frustration. Hours later, troops loyal to Piłsudski swept across the Kierbedzia Bridge into Castle Square and pushed the government forces to the south of the city. The government evacuated and announced a state of emergency, but their forces were already outnumbered two to one by Piłsudski's loyal followers. The next day, the Central

Committee of the *PPS* instigated a general strike in support of the marshal, which, thanks to the participation of the *Związek Zawodowy Kolejarzy* ('Railway Workers' Trade Union'), had the effect of cutting government communications and lines of reinforcement. By 14 May, Piłsudski's forces numbered 8,000 troops, four times the number defending the government. Wojciechowski and Witos finally accepted the irrevocable momentum of the coup and resigned to prevent the violence spreading, leaving the death toll at 379 and injuries numbering almost a thousand. According to Piłsudski, the confrontation was conducted, on the whole, in a 'most chivalrous and courteous' manner: 'Machine-gunners were obliged to drive off curious throngs to right or left. Sometimes a whole battle was stopped to let women and children cross the street.'[54]

It does appear that both sides took care not to target non-combatants; as the historian Andrzej Garlicki points out, civilians were literally caught in the crossfire 'because they did not know how to behave' in the urban conflict.[55] Varsovians watched the confrontations in the street, from open windows, and balconies, oblivious to the danger of stray bullets; little did they know that this kind of random violence and the daily brush with death would come to characterise life in their city a couple of decades later. As for their political outlook, Dąbrowska voiced the enthusiasm of those celebrating the coup as Warsaw's moment of revolution, 'like a chapter from Greek history':

> Two moral nations clashed in Poland. One nation of creativity and self-improvement, reaching the essence of issues, and the other nation – a nation of lies and convention … The conditions were created for a new life. But what will we, the public, do with it. Piłsudski cannot do everything for us. It is too difficult to write about it all. Huge issues and tasks loom.

Perhaps more telling was the footnote Dąbrowska added to this passage in 1943: 'God, what a mistake this [optimism] turned out to be.'[56]

This was the first occasion that Polish forces had fired on each other since independence, and after the initial novelty of watching the fighting, the citizens of Warsaw began to contemplate what might lie ahead. Piłsudski was all too aware of how the coup would look to his opponents; it was yet more proof of his 'overweening conceit' as much as it was of his 'astounding popularity and influence with the army and with the people.'[57] Yet when the *Sejm* elected him as president at the end of May, he refused the position, not because of any scruples over his *coup d'état* but because he resented the constitutional limits of presidential power. He accepted the position of Minister of Military Affairs and declared that he did not intend to turn his coup into a Fascist revolution, but it was clear who held the real power in Poland: when the new prime minister, Kazimierz Bartel (and prime ministers after him) formed a new government, it was Piłsudski whose approval he sought first, not the president.

SANACJA

Piłsudski wasted no time in rolling out his *Sanacja* ('Sanitation') project for government reform. The movement attracted support from right- and left-wing politicians and military officers who sought to eradicate corruption and resecure the Polish economy but stopped short of coalescing into a formal political party. Instead, *Sanacja* occupied a nebulous middle-ground between autocracy and democracy. Piłsudski cemented his hold on political power by becoming permanent commander-in-chief of the Polish military, and his followers used every technicality (and occasionally extra-legal means) to exclude opposition parties or facilitate their division. But in pigeon-holing him as just another 'dictator', foreign reporters failed to understand the nuance of the marshal's interests. Piłsudski had little interest in interfering in the daily society of Polish people, and freedoms of speech, press, and political association were not legally restricted. Jerzy Szapiro, editor of the socialist newspaper ***Robotnik***, was a vocal critic of Piłsudski's regime but wrote that the marshal was 'no Mussolini' and had 'no scheme for organising Poland according to his wishes'; he was simply acting according to his 'personal' antipathy towards the *Sejm* and its members.[58] But Piłsudski's plans to reform Poland's political system were badly disrupted in April 1929 when he suffered a mini-stroke, depriving him of the use of his right arm for several days.

Disputes with the *Sejm* continued and Piłsudski sent 90 armed officers into the *Sejm* chamber in an attempt to intimidate its members – a measure that in any other state might have been an indicator of totalitarianism, but many Poles welcomed it as an example of the strong patriarchal influence needed to manage their immature democratic system. From 1929 onwards, however, *Sanacja*'s political tactics became even more openly repressive, with political opponents frequently intimidated or arrested. Such acts left an indelible black mark on Piłsudski's reputation. It was becoming apparent that the same man who had tried time and again to impose order on the Polish system could also be its greatest flaw, as Szapiro identified in 1929:

> Poland's problem is not so much a problem of Government, as a crisis with regard to the source of power. As things are now, Piłsudski is the only source of power in

> Poland. The parliament has been temporarily destroyed as the institution which creates power and gives power. What happens if the source of power, now vested in Piłsudski, dies out?[59]

But Piłsudski remained a popular figure among the Polish public and particularly national minority groups, who by then accounted for around 31 per cent of the population. This was in no small part thanks to Piłsudski's concept of 'state-assimilation', which, unlike the National Democrats' 'ethnic-assimilation' approach, placed loyalty to the nation at the heart of Polish identity over ethnicity. As a result – and despite his far from perfect record on standing up to antisemitism – Piłsudski enjoyed considerable support from the Jewish population (which numbered over 3 million at this time) who were relieved to see the National Democrats' overt antisemitic leanings falling out of favour. Most of the country's 740,000 *Volksdeutsche* ('ethnic Germans') welcomed the coup, rightly seeing Piłsudski as less threatening to them than the National Democrats. Nevertheless, it remained difficult to bind the post-partition populations and integrate their myriad cultural, economic, and religious interests. In some cases, this was due to long-standing inequalities that prevailed in the Polish system; for example, people from minorities in poorer, less developed areas of the country found it difficult to advance in the civil service or army. In other cases, existing rifts were manipulated – often intentionally – by foreign developments. In the early 1930s, the *Orhanizatsiia Ukrainskykh Natsionalistiv* ('Ukrainian Nationalist Organisation' or *OUN*) launched a series of terrorist attacks that sought to undermine Piłsudski's programme of assimilation, receiving funding and support from Germany. In the autumn of 1930, Piłsudski ordered a repression of Ukrainian nationalist groups, and thousands were detained, including 84 parliamentarians.

If western powers were sceptical of Piłsudski's autocratic tendencies, they were equally – if not more – cynical towards his approach to foreign policy. From 1932 onwards, with staunch Piłsudski supporter and former coup commander Józef Beck at the helm of the Ministry of Foreign Affairs, Polish policy took a decidedly self-interested stance to which many in the west were quick to assign sinister motives. The 1932 Polish–Soviet Non-Aggression Pact and a similar agreement with Germany in 1934 were interpreted as deliberate attempts to undermine the defence alliances between League of Nations members. In 1942, historian Hugh Seton-Watson even went so far as to imply that Polish policy opened the door to Nazi expansion in the east:

> The basis of Polish policy, then, was not love of Germany but a combination of territorial greed, fear of revolution on the part of the landowners and colonels,

> mistrust of the strength and will to resistance of the Western Powers, and the supreme confidence of Colonel Beck in his own Machiavellian genius. This policy played an important part in the preparation of German plans for Eastern Europe.[60]

This exemplifies a common misunderstanding amongst western critics with regards to the *Sanacja* regime's ideological outlook. In their eyes, the Polish government had moulded itself into a military dictatorship, and, like most regimes of this type, was beholden to the interests of conservative landowners and the military. Beck's policy outlook was 'Machiavellian' in so much as it prioritised national interests at the expense of western preferences, but this was not down to aggressive militarism. On the contrary, Beck was seeking to create a new 'equilibrium' between Poland's two most dangerous neighbours, Germany and the USSR: 'History teaches us that the greatest catastrophe to affect our nation resulted from the activity of those two states. And secondly, in the desperate situation in which we then found ourselves, no state in the world could be found to hasten with help to us ... Warsaw's policy can never depend either on Moscow or Berlin.'[61]

The Poles still smarted from the memory of partition and the failure of the Western Powers to help until the country had been devastated by war. The tragedy lies in the fact that Polish Machiavellianism was doomed to failure, and that Warsaw would in fact be dependent on the whims of Berlin, Moscow, and the Western Allies for most of the century.

Moreover, Piłsudski and Beck were keen to redress the inadequacies of the Locarno Treaties, which they felt had sidelined Poland for the sake of security in the west. Both realised the precariousness of balancing relationships with both Germany and the Soviet Union but believed the collapse of one or the other of these threats was imminent. Until then, they were increasingly unwilling to entrust security to a League of Nations on whose list of priorities Poland seemed to feature extremely low.

STORM CLOUDS GATHERING

The first decade after the end of the Great War in 1918 saw clashes with Germany, particularly in Silesia, but little to threaten Poland. But in 1930, German politicians began to question the border between the two countries. In particular, the 'Polish Corridor' – the neck of land that stretched north to the Baltic coast near Danzig, which had returned to its historical status as a 'free city' – separated the German province of East Prussia from the rest of Germany. To the dismay of many in Poland, many US politicians seemed to be sympathetic to restoring this region to German control, and despite President Herbert Hoover offering supportive statements, Piłsudski couldn't hide his anger when Sir John Simon, the British foreign minister, asked if there was any room for compromise on Poland's part. Almost as soon as Hitler came to power in 1933, the status of both the corridor and Danzig was raised once more. Emboldened by Hitler's statements, the senate in Danzig – the city had a majority German population – informed the Poles that a detachment of Polish police that had been stationed in the harbour since 1923 was no longer welcome. Piłsudski immediately dispatched a Polish warship, which disembarked 120 soldiers. On this occasion, Hitler backed down.

Piłsudski knew that despite past Polish military successes against Soviet forces in the east, Poland desperately needed allies. In 1933, he held preliminary talks with the French; according to some sources, these discussions included consideration of a pre-emptive war against Germany.[62] Whatever was or wasn't discussed, the Germans became aware of Polish preparations for potential hostilities, not least because Piłsudski deliberately didn't hide them – he used the preparations as a means of increasing pressure on Hitler to hold discussions to secure Germany's adherence to the status of Danzig and the Polish Corridor. In May 1933, Hitler agreed to meet Alfred Wysocki, Piłsudski's personal envoy in Berlin. Perhaps to the surprise of the Poles, the new Führer of Germany agreed to their demands and issued a statement that Germany would abide by the existing treaties.

Any sense of relief at this was short-lived. Before the end of 1933, Germany had left the League of Nations and its Disarmament Conference, raising once more the question of the reliability of Hitler's assurances about treaty obligations. When Piłsudski sent an envoy to France to seek a clear French commitment to come to the aid of Poland in the event of war, the best that he could secure was a promise of military aid, but no commitment to use its army against Germany. It was against this background that a non-aggression agreement between Poland and Germany was negotiated in November 1933 and ratified early in 1934, but Piłsudski told an aide that he doubted the agreement would last even four years, and questioned German commitment to the status quo about Danzig. It is telling that the German foreign ministry objected to the declaration being referred to as a pact in case it implied the Polish–German border was no longer up for debate.

The credibility of the League of Nations had always been questionable, and Piłsudski and Beck saw their actions as merely ensuring that Poland's future remained in Polish hands. But the ethnic tensions within Poland continued to cause difficulties. Germany submitted complaints to the League on behalf of 'oppressed' *Volksdeutsche* in Poland, something the Poles suspected as a means of undermining Polish governance. There is no question that complaints on behalf of many minorities (especially Ukrainians) might have been justified, but interestingly, no complaints were made on behalf of Jews during Piłsudski's rule. For the Poles, the issue was not so much the idea of protecting minorities as the 'depletion of sovereignty' caused by the Minorities Treaties and the fact that they divided 'the League of Nations into two groups, one of which has far-reaching international commitments … while the other is free from minority obligations.'[63] As early as 1922, Polish delegates were advocating for a 'generalisation' of minority policy for all League members to remove this double standard, but to no avail.[64] During the 1932 Disarmament Conference, with arguments over *Gleichberechtigung* ('equal treatment') for German armaments, the Poles seized their chance to push their agenda of generalisation on the subject of minority obligations forward once more. But when, in 1933, Hitler withdrew Germany from the conference and the League itself, the treaties were undermined even further; ethnic Poles residing on German soil were no longer guaranteed the same legal protection as *Volksdeutsche* in Poland. With Hitler's persecution of Jewish minorities beginning to ramp up and Germany openly re-arming, and the Soviet Union being considered for accession to the League, Poland made a final appeal for the Minorities Treaties to be revised. Diplomat Count Bernard Raczyński complained that despite being free from obligations towards minorities, the Soviet Union could exploit the Minorities Treaties to the detriment of Poland.[65]

On 13 September, 1934, Beck announced the suspension of the Minorities Treaties in Poland until more universal minority protections were established. The Western Powers responded with predictable outrage, arguing that Poland's dissent undermined the authority of the League, while simultaneously using it as a pretext to dismiss further discussion of generalisation. But it is likely Beck and Piłsudski had long given up on the League and sensed that its influence was on the wane. The issue of minority protection had never really been a domestic one; Beck had been careful to stress that the suspension of the treaties was in no way an act of hostility against minorities, and his declaration did not draw any major internal protest.

The Legacy of a Giant

After the war, many historians were quick to lay the blame for Poland's occupation at the door of Beck and Piłsudski's foreign policy. For the historians Seton-Watson and A. J. P. Taylor, the Declaration of Non-Aggression, withdrawal from the Minorities Treaties, and the German–Polish Minorities Treaty of 1937 were all early signs that Poland was drifting away from the League's orbit, alienating vital French support, and actively enabling Hitler's expansionist policy. But, once again, this is to misunderstand the consistent pragmatism of Polish strategy. The Poles had learned through bitter experience that Western Allied support wasn't guaranteed. It was natural that a newly independent nation in historically unstable Eastern Europe might fear its existential concerns would not be a priority for western powers – especially ones who hadn't experienced partition and occupation in recent history. Secondly, Beck and Piłsudski's pursuit of equilibrium between Germany and the USSR was a natural successor to the *Intermarium* programme that had tried and failed to re-secure alliances between the Polish–Lithuanian Commonwealth territories; these were not policies drawn by ideological ends so much as they were means of securing Poland's presence in the fractious post-war world. After 1935, Beck continued in this vein with his 'Third Europe' conception, a new *Intermarium* alliance that would unite Poland with Italy, Yugoslavia, Hungary, and Romania. The Third Europe idea never came to fruition, and Beck remained aware that Poland wouldn't be able to repel an attack from either the USSR or Germany on her own. But complete ideological alignment with either was always out of the question, and to argue otherwise is to underestimate the fierce independence of Polish outlook and her refusal to become a vassal state to a bigger power. As the old Polish saying went, *Nic o nas bez nas* ('Nothing [is to be decided] about us without us') – and this applied as much to Germany and the USSR as it did to the League of Nations.[66]

Internally, the last years of Piłsudski's power were marked by an increase in authoritarianism. The creation of the *Obóz Narodowo-Radykalny* ('National-Radical Camp' or *ONR*), a Polish quasi-Fascist group, in 1934 was unwelcome for many reasons, including its open and virulent antisemitism. Interior Minister Bronisław Pieracki was shot and killed in June 1934 just before he was about to announce that the *ONR* had been banned, and Piłsudski immediately ordered a wave of arrests. There was widespread praise and support for this across the world, but the government now created an internment camp at Bereza Kartuska, where members of both the *ONR* and the Ukrainian *OUN* were held. The lack of any judicial process or opportunity to challenge the detention of hundreds of opponents caused widespread alarm. To add to the growing sense of gloom in Warsaw, there was another assassination. French Foreign Minister Louis Barthou was visiting the Balkan region in the autumn of 1934, trying to create a widespread alliance that would act as a counterweight to Germany, and a Bulgarian nationalist shot and killed King Alexander I. In the exchange of fire that followed, Barthou was also killed; ballistic reports showed that the bullet that killed him was probably fired by a French close protection officer, but this remained secret until 1974. Barthou's death ended any lingering hope of a widespread alliance, and Piłsudski was deeply depressed by the news. His own health was now failing, and in April 1935 he was diagnosed as having cancer of the liver. A month later, his death was announced to a shocked Poland.

For all his – very evident – faults, Piłsudski's death cut to the heart of Polish public life. On 13 May, the *Kurjer Warszawski* lamented the end of an era:

> The news that hung over Warsaw yesterday at 9 o'clock in the evening in the flutter of death's wings is so grave and momentous that everyone understands its supreme importance without words … A man in whose hands for the last nine years the rule of the country has rested substantially and indivisibly … This is so much so that this period must be considered an epoch in our history, and the man who embodied it, gives this epoch its name.[67]

In the days following his death, 'an unbroken stream' of Varsovians and well-wishers converged on Warsaw's Old Town where Piłsudski lay in St John's Cathedral, huddling together under umbrellas as they edged through the rain along Miodowa Street and Podwale, from Kapitaluna Street and beyond.[68] The cabinet announced a period of six months of national mourning in honour of the man President Mościcki described as 'the greatest [man] in the whole vast sweep of our history', and the *Warsaw Weekly* reported flags lowered to half-mast in Germany and Italy as condolences came in from abroad. But in addressing the enormity of Piłsudski's legacy, his spirit of dominance, and his nationalist vision, Mościcki was also alluding to the vacuum left in the marshal's wake:

> To the nation, he has left a heritage of duty toward the honour and power of the State … we must take up and carry on. And our grief and pain, may it but deepen in us, in the whole nation, the understanding of our responsibility before his spirit and before the generation yet to be.[69]

Ever since the restoration of Polish independence, Piłsudski had been almost indistinguishable from Poland as a whole. The degree to which he shaped – and was shaped by – Poland is difficult to overstress. Through force of personality and determination, he towered over his contemporaries, often showing little or no tolerance for the views of others. Perhaps the biggest flaw in his time in office was his repeated failure to protect Jews as fully as he might have done, which both alienated potential Jewish support for his nationalist movement and lent more support to his right-leaning, antisemitic rivals. Still, there was widespread mourning of his death amongst Jewish communities, both in Poland and abroad. In words, if not always in actions, he had been a defender of the rights of all parts of the Polish population, and many feared future developments in his absence. But his death meant much more than an increased threat to Polish Jews. The system of government that he had largely created was a unique blend of democracy and authoritarianism, and functioned only because of his presence. Without him at the helm, this system could not continue; nor was there any tradition of democratic rule to which Poland could resort. With the constant threat of the Soviet Union to the east and a growing menace in Germany to the west, it was a singularly bad time for Poland to be left in such an uncertain state.

Moreover, the Second Republic was almost two decades old and was now a very different place compared to when Piłsudski had first stepped into the political limelight. A whole new generation of Poles had emerged which would later be dubbed the 'Columbus generation', a term taken from Roman Bratny's 1957 novel, *Kolumbowie. Rocznik 20*, and described youngsters born in the 1920s who were 'discovering' their nation in its new form and giving voice to its independent identity when war broke out in 1939. This was the first generation in 123 years not to know the yoke of partition, but it would not be spared the trauma of occupation for long. Coming of age during a new existential conflict with disturbing echoes of the past, this generation's struggle would embody Poland's tragic historical pattern: freedoms heroically won, then ruthlessly extinguished.

CHAPTER 2

LEBENSRAUM

The german won't spit in our face,
Nor germanise our children …

We won't have Poland's name defamed,
We won't step alive into a coffin.
In Poland's name, in her honor
We lift our foreheads proudly …

Maria Konopnicka, 'The Oath', 1908

THE LEGACY OF VERSAILLES

There are few occasions in history when dictators have informed the world in advance of their aggressive intentions. Published in Germany in 1925, Hitler's *Mein Kampf* laid out his hopes of establishing a German land empire in Eastern Europe that would rival the territorial size of the British and French empires and the United States. At the time, few took the declarations of the leader of a small political party too seriously, but Hitler made no secret of the fact that he considered restoration of the 1914 frontiers as inadequate; the territories controlled by Germany at that time, he argued, had been too small to support its population, and it was essential to secure larger holdings to protect the German population from future threats of naval blockade. Ultimately, the building of this empire would come mainly at the expense of the Soviet Union, with most of Poland absorbed into Germany – or re-incorporated, as he preferred to frame it.

The towns and villages immediately to the east of the Oder River had been home to large Polish communities for centuries, often with their own schools, churches, and other institutions. After the partitions of Poland, the numbers of Poles living under Prussian control increased considerably. The southern part of East Prussia, most of Pomerania, the city of Poznań, and many of the newly gained areas of Silesia had long supported intermingled German and Polish populations. But the Prussian – and later, German – authorities largely left the Poles alone. There may have been discrimination in terms of employment, and antisemitic sentiment was never far away, but there was nothing that resembled the heavy-handed policies of Russia in the 19th century to eliminate Polish culture, language, or religious practice. By the 20th century, however, most Germans regarded the lands that had been gained from Poland as unquestionably German. This was despite many of them retaining Polish majorities, and the fact that Poland's independence prompted considerable numbers of Germans to return to their diminished homeland. Meanwhile the lost territories – the entire region around Poznań, parts of Silesia, the 'Polish Corridor', and the city of Danzig – were seen by many Germans as parts of their nation that had been unjustly excised.

But territorial acquisition was merely the start of Hitler's ambition. He rejected the French and British conceptions of empire on the grounds that by leaving large non-European populations in their colonies, these two nations failed to exploit their empires fully. In the case of France, he went further:

> If France develops along the lines it has taken in our day, and should that development continue for the next three hundred years, all traces of French blood will finally be submerged in the formation of a Euro-African Mulatto State. This would represent a formidable and compact colonial territory stretching from the Rhine to the Congo, inhabited by an inferior race which had developed through a slow and steady process of bastardisation.[1]

Instead, Hitler saw his future empire developing in a manner similar to the European conquest of North America. On more than one occasion, he reminded his followers of the fate of native North Americans, arguing that they had been replaced by a superior culture and were now largely forgotten. It should be remembered that such views were not unusual at the time; the era of belief in social Darwinism – applying concepts of natural selection to ethnic groups and nations – was coming to an end, but plenty of politicians were couching similar ideas in different terms. Speaking in parliament in a debate about Jewish settlement in Palestine, Winston Churchill said:

> I do not admit that the dog in the manger has the final right to the manger; though he may have lain there for a very long time, I do not admit that right. I do not admit for instance that a great wrong has been done to the Red Indians of America or the black people of Australia. I do not admit that a wrong has been done to those people by the fact that a stronger race, a higher-grade race or at any rate a more worldly-wise race, to put it that way, has come in and taken their place. I do not admit it. I do not think the Red Indians had any right to say, 'The American continent belongs to us and we are not going to have any of these European settlers coming in here.' They had not the right, nor had they the power.[2]

In the same way, Hitler argued, German settlers would spread through conquered lands in Eastern Europe, replacing the existing population. There was no intention of establishing permanent client regimes in the lands he planned to conquer – any such administrations would exist only for the shortest possible period.

For Hitler, there was no question that the Slavs and Jews – who collectively made up almost all the population of Poland – were racially inferior to Germans, and therefore had no right to prevent superior races from seizing their land. At best, they might be useful as labourers, but his dream of a huge empire peopled by German settlers would necessitate a drastic culling of their numbers; after all, exploitation of the new territories for the benefit of Germany would only be possible if the non-German population was greatly reduced. In particular, the urban populations of Poland and the western Soviet Union would serve no purpose in the new German territories, and, from the outset, were earmarked for elimination.

Before he could turn his attention to Poland, however, Hitler faced several challenges. The first was the greatly reduced size of the German military as a consequence of the Versailles Treaty though, even before Hitler came to power, the German government had made plans for expansion. An extensively militarised police force together with the large numbers of highly trained NCOs in the army effectively created cadres around whom forces could later be expanded. Late in 1931, funding was approved for the creation of industrial infrastructure that would allow Germany to maintain an army of 21 divisions with substantial numbers of aircraft, artillery, and tanks.[3]

Almost immediately after he came to power in 1933, Hitler channelled both his and the German public's widespread resentment towards the Treaty of

Versailles and its signatories into action. He started by pulling Germany out of the League of Nations and the World Disarmament Conference; reparations payments had effectively been suspended during the Great Depression and by 1935, almost all restrictions imposed upon Germany had been broken. Rapidly gaining confidence, Hitler announced widespread conscription, and officially unveiled the Luftwaffe – which had been created in secret in 1933.

APPEASEMENT AND EQUILIBRIUM

For their part, the Allied Powers proved surprisingly malleable in their attitudes towards Germany after 1919. Long before Hitler came to power, there was an acknowledgement that, to ensure peace, German grievances towards the Treaty ought to be addressed. One reason was that Germany remained a key economic player in post-war Europe, relied upon by France for steel and coal and Britain as an export market. Moreover, at a time when Britain was struggling to hold together its fraying global empire, the idea of committing resources to further conflict in Europe was out of the question; hence why in matters such as Germany's claims to Danzig and parts of the Polish Corridor, the Allies were often sympathetic to complaints made at Poland's expense. As had happened before (and would happen again), the Poles saw the Western Powers prioritising their own interests over the security of Eastern Europe.

If Germany's foreign policy was an exercise in assertion, Poland's outlook was one of reaction. Unlike Hitler, Beck never sought actively to undermine the League of Nations' concept of collective security upon which Poland was so dependent in the post-war years. But Germany's withdrawal from the League and Hitler's brazen re-armament showed the League of Nations to be utterly toothless with regard to one of Poland's biggest threats, and this context is crucial to understanding Poland's position in the run up to war in 1939. Zamoyski has observed, 'it is hard to suggest a foreign policy that might have saved Poland' in the 1930s; her leaders knew that they could not count on the Allies for unconditional protection and were aware of Poland's insignificance on the diplomatic stage.[4] In the words of the historian Donald Buzinkai, 'if Britain and France were still attempting to work with Germany outside the purview of the League, then why should Poland not do likewise?'[5] Even so, Piłsudski and Beck's policy of 'equilibrium' between Germany and the USSR was only ever intended to be a temporary solution. Its effectiveness was predicated on the presumption that only one of Poland's neighbours would turn out to be a threat; Beck never dreamed that both would turn on Poland at the same time, let alone that they would form an alliance. In fact, to Beck, it was the Communist threat from the east and its internationalist intentions that appeared more pernicious, especially when the League of Nations extended membership to the USSR:

> We Poles have no confidence in Russia, or in her political aims. On the strength of our experience, we see there two imperialisms: the old Tsarist one and that of Communism. In practice, as far as our affairs are concerned, it comes to the same thing ... We do not believe that Russia would engage herself ... on our side.[6]

The policy of equilibrium did not die with Piłsudski in 1935. Beck continued to walk a fine line between the dictatorships looming on Poland's borders in a way that was at best ruthlessly self-interested and at worst dangerously short-sighted. We can imagine he carried with him Piłsudski's deep suspicion that the Western Powers saw Poland as a pawn, a lapdog to the whims of their closest allies in France; Beck certainly earned a reputation for being brusque, arrogant, and downright rude when challenged in person.[7] After withdrawing from the Minorities Treaties, he was only too happy to prove Poland perfectly capable of negotiating minority issues in Danzig independently of the League – something Hitler was no doubt aware of when he commented: 'The main fact is that the two Governments ... possess the firm will and determination to improve their relations. It was a real work of peace, of more value than all the chattering in the League of Nations.'[8]

Whether Beck suffered from an excess of pride, sense of honour, arrogance, or complacency, the fact that Poland had distanced itself from the League of Nations made it an easy target for Hitler to exploit and isolate further. When, in 1938, Hitler spoke about the 1934 declaration of non-aggression, he was careful to flatter Poland's independent political spirit and pay homage to the inimitable late marshal. Even if Piłsudski (and his autocratic tendencies) did garner Hitler's genuine respect, in hindsight, and knowing what we know of the Führer, it is hard not to hear the calculated cynicism in his words:

> The most difficult problem with which I was confronted was that of our relations with Poland ... that Poles and Germans would regard each other as hereditary enemies. I wanted to prevent this. I know well enough that I would not have been successful if Poland had had a democratic constitution. For these democracies which indulge in phrases about peace are the most blood-thirsty agitators. In Poland there ruled not a democracy, but a man; and with him I succeeded ... in coming to an agreement which ... entirely removed the danger of conflict.[9]

Given his explicit intentions to create a land empire across Eastern Europe and to recover the 'lost territories' that had been given to Poland at the end of the First World War, any wish to remove 'the danger of conflict' must be seen as merely postponing confrontation until a more favourable moment.

In the meantime, by acting as a cooperative partner in bilateral talks, Germany was quietly drawing Poland further away from the League of Nations. This was exemplified when, in 1935, Hitler announced what most of Europe had already anticipated: Germany was re-arming. Britain, France, and Italy drew up a resolution to condemn the development, but stopped short of suggesting any direct retaliatory measures; Beck, meanwhile, took the opportunity to denigrate the League's proposals to expand its political activity, citing its previous failures and excessive bureaucracy as proof that its authority as a security body was on the wane. He also pointed out that Poland had already secured agreements of non-aggression from both Germany and the USSR, and even went as far as implying the Polish people feared League interference would 'undermine that state of peace which had been established by a sincere and loyal political effort.'[10] This high-handed attitude irritated the Western Powers, but especially Poland's closest alleged partners; when a Franco-Soviet proposal for an Eastern European security pact fell through, the USSR was quick to blame Poland, insisting that its aversion to collective agreements could have 'nothing in common with peaceful intentions.'[11]

Hitler had other pressing territorial priorities closer to home. Alarm was mounting both within Germany and elsewhere at his steady and ruthless acquisition of territories with German populations. Many Austrians had hankered for union with Germany for decades, and the *Anschluss* – the formal annexation of Austria – was greeted with huge enthusiasm across Austria, but with dismay in Warsaw. 'God save Austria!' ran the *Kurjer Warszawski* headline, dismissing Hitler's claims of peaceful occupation as the 'traditional fairy tale in German politics at the moment of armed entry into the territory of another country'.[12] Next came the Sudetenland, where about 3 million ethnic Germans had been left outside of Germany after the creation of Czechoslovakia in 1918. At Hitler's behest, the *Sudetendeutsche Partei* ('Sudeten German Party' or *SdP*) presented demands carefully calibrated to be unacceptable in Prague, ensuring the failure of negotiations and forcing the Czechoslovak government to order partial mobilisation.

The Munich Agreement

Aware that sooner or later, German attention would turn to ethnic German minorities within Poland, the Warsaw government watched developments closely – but, oddly, without a great deal of concern. The Polish ambassador in

Paris informed the French foreign minister that Poland would not take any military action even if France attempted to provide Czechoslovakia with military support, while, at the same time, Beck publicly stated that Poland would join Britain and France if they went to war with Germany. When the Czechoslovak government ordered full mobilisation, the Soviet Union offered military support provided Poland and Romania permitted Red Army units to cross to Czechoslovakia through their territory; both nations refused. After a flurry of diplomatic messages, a further meeting between Hitler, Chamberlain, Mussolini, and French prime minister Éduard Daladier was arranged for the end of September. The outcome was the infamous Munich Agreement: Germany gained control of the Sudetenland, and an international commission would be convened to consider other disputed areas. Characteristically, the Western Powers made this agreement without anything approaching full discussions with the Prague government; instead, Beneš was informed that if his nation chose to fight, it could expect no help from the west. Despite the strength of his forces, he knew that he was greatly outgunned by the Germans and had little choice but to accept.[13]

At first glance, the Poles' apparent reticence towards the crisis over the Sudetenland seems surprising. Like Czechoslovakia, Poland had regions with substantial ethnic German populations and it was surely inevitable that if he succeeded in the Sudetenland, Hitler would turn his attention to Poland – even if he had assured Chamberlain that he had no further territorial ambitions in the east. But the relationship between Czechoslovakia and Poland was a difficult one. In 1920, taking advantage of Polish commitments in its war against Bolshevik Russia, Czechoslovakia had seized the oil-rich area known as Cieszyn Silesia or Trans-Olza, and after a seven-day conflict, retained roughly two thirds of the disputed area. When he learned how the British, French, and Germans had decided the fate of the Sudetenland without any reference to the Czechoslovak government or the Polish minorities involved, Beck felt slighted. At his instigation, the Warsaw government issued Prague its own ultimatum, demanding the immediate Czechoslovak withdrawal from Trans-Olza.

Under immense pressure from all sides, Beneš concluded that Czech resistance against Germany remained viable only if Poland remained neutral rather than becoming a second front; thus the Polish ultimatum pushed him to accept the terms of the Munich Agreement. In many respects, it was a cynical and short-sighted move by the Polish government, allowing Hitler to widen the blame for the dismemberment of Czechoslovakia. When Slovakia declared independence in March 1939, the Germans quickly seized what remained of Czechoslovakia, creating the *Protektorat Böhmen und Mären* ('Protectorate of Bohemia and Moravia'). The new Slovakia was little more than a client state under German control, and the consequence of the fall of Czechoslovakia was that the frontier Poland shared with Germany was now far longer. Much of the region facing Slovakia and the Protectorate was mountainous, and the Polish Army would have to divert significant numbers of troops to cover against an attack from this region, weakening defences elsewhere.

TENSIONS IN THE FREE CITY

Immediately after the dismemberment of Czechoslovakia, Berlin's focus moved to Poland and Danzig, on the Baltic coast. When the USA entered the First World War, President Woodrow Wilson stipulated that an independent Polish state 'should be assured a free and secure access to the sea'.[14] Dmowski had insisted during the Versailles Conference that Danzig – Gdańsk to the Poles – was unarguably Polish as it had been part of pre-partition Poland, but the US government faced a dilemma as it had also stated that self-determination should form the basis of territorial adjustments. At this time, about 90 per cent of the urban population of Danzig was German, and given that it would be impossible (and potentially explosive) to place a city with such a large German majority under Polish control, a compromise was agreed. Danzig would become a free city, with Poland being granted substantial special rights. Polish access to the coast was achieved by granting territory to the west and north of Danzig to Poland, creating the Polish Corridor. The British in particular were opposed to giving Poland control over the city itself, while the French and American governments were equally opposed to allowing it to remain in German control. But the agreement – particularly as the population of the rural area handed to Poland had a large Polish majority – was seen as the best solution.

Relations between Poland and Danzig's predominantly ethnic German administration were fraught from the start. When German dockers went on strike in 1920 and refused to unload vital munitions needed for the fighting against Bolshevik Russia, the Polish government took steps to ensure uninterrupted access to Baltic shipping by ordering the construction of a new seaport to the north of Danzig in the Polish Corridor; the ensuing diversion of trade from Danzig to the small town of Gdynia only increased the tension. Although the Polish population of Danzig increased in the years after the First World War – rising from about 10 per cent in 1918 to perhaps 20 per cent or more in the late 1930s – the German majority remained in firm control and there was widespread discrimination against the Poles. The local branch of the Nazi Party dominated the city's politics from the early 1930s and began organising noisy demonstrations demanding reunification with Germany. Ernst Ziehm, the president of the Senate of Danzig, attempted to impose a ban on further marches. Even Hitler grew alarmed at the increasingly strident demands of Albert Forster, the Nazi Party *Gauleiter* (regional Nazi Party chief) in Danzig, and ordered him to desist; but new elections in the city in May 1933 resulted in a stunning victory for Forster, with the Nazi Party securing over 50 per cent of the vote. Ziehm was replaced by Hermann Rauschning, who favoured a diplomatic path in discussions with the Polish government; whether by chance or design, the impositions of Forster and Arthur Greiser, the Senate vice-president, provided Rauschning with leverage. Nevertheless, the Polish–German non-aggression declaration of 1934 seemed to offer further hope that direct conflict could be avoided.

Setting aside – for the time being – his goals of immediate reunification with Germany, Forster instead focused on steadily tightening the party's grip on Danzig. Discrimination against Poles intensified, including interference in religious affairs. Meanwhile, animosity was growing between Forster and Rauschning; the Senate president's frustration and exasperation with the *Gauleiter* led to him threatening to resign on several occasions. In addition to anti-Polish activities, Forster and his comrades broke up meetings organised by other political parties and attacked their supporters in the streets. Persecution of the city's Jewish population was gathering pace. In the summer of 1934, Forster wrote:

> For a National Socialist, there is no such thing as a decent Jew. This race is and remains our mortal enemy. All the hardship and misery that we have experienced and are still experiencing has been instigated by these people … We must eliminate the Jew wherever possible. Any magnanimity towards the Jew is misguided.[15]

Rauschning finally resigned in November 1934. He was an ardent supporter of German territorial ambitions with regard to Poland but opposed to the violence with which the Nazis built and held onto their power base, and in the months that followed his resignation he openly supported politicians who contested Nazi authority. This led to him fleeing to Poland in 1936. Greiser replaced him as Senate president, and as the Nazi Party in Danzig escalated its repression with minimal resistance, relations with the Polish minority became ever more fractious.

After the absorption of the Sudetenland, Hitler abandoned the generally conciliatory and diplomatic tone that he had taken with Warsaw. In October 1938 the German foreign minister, Joachim von Ribbentrop, demanded the reunification of Danzig with Germany. The Poles rejected this demand as unacceptable to the Polish people, but Forster was already stepping up demonstrations in the city and the German press began a vociferous campaign. At the same time, Ribbentrop ordered Hans-Adolf von Moltke, the German ambassador in Warsaw, not to engage in negotiations; Germany was deliberately making demands that would not be acceptable to Poland in order to trigger war, with Danzig and the Polish Corridor serving as the *casus belli*. For their part, the Poles felt that although 'great progress' had been made in improving German–Polish relations, the growing atmosphere of 'general political chaos' in Europe made the question of Danzig more critical than ever.[16] To Beck, the idea that the newly independent Polish state would concede to Hitler's demands and be subsumed as a German vassal state was inconceivable, even if it risked a hopeless war. To quote the historian Gerhard Weinberg, 'Choosing between surrender and desperate fight – the experience of the years 1772–1919 dictated a fight against all odds.'[17]

Wary of Forster's tendency to overreach, both Ribbentrop and Reich propaganda minister Joseph Goebbels instructed the *Gauleiter* of Danzig not to take unilateral steps; any further escalation was to be orchestrated carefully. The smallest matters risked inflaming antagonism on one side or the other, and even if Forster was minded to follow the orders he had been given, others took matters into their own hands. In February 1939, a dinner-dance was organised in a café in Danzig frequented by students, and a sign appeared in the café window: 'Dogs and Poles are not allowed entry! Poor dogs!'[18] There was great anger in the Polish press, particularly when the Germans tried to claim that the notice had been put up by a Polish student as a deliberate provocation.

'EASY GAINS'

If the situation in Danzig wasn't worrying enough, Hitler was already closing in on another 'free city'. To the north of East Prussia, the city of Memel (now the Lithuanian city of Klaipėda) had demographic issues similar to those of Danzig: within the city, the German population formed the majority, but the surrounding countryside was dominated by non-German people, in this case, Lithuanians. Prior to the First World War, the city was the most northern part of East Prussia, but after the war the newly independent Lithuania sought to take control of both the city and the strip of coastline extending from East Prussia to the south to Memel. However, the League of Nations declared that Memel would be a free city. A small French military presence was intended to serve as a guarantee of this, but in 1923 the Lithuanian government instigated a revolt and sent troops into the territory. Despite its protests, the League of Nations was forced to accept the *fait accompli*. But following the fall of Czechoslovakia, Hitler demanded the return of the city to German control. In parallel with the demands sent to Warsaw about Danzig, Berlin insisted on the surrender of the city and its hinterland to Germany, and in late March 1939 the Lithuanian government reluctantly agreed, having no means of opposing military action by Germany.

The consternation in Warsaw at this latest development was considerable: with Hitler having seized Memel, a move against Danzig seemed inevitable. Finally, it seemed to the Poles, the Western Powers sat up and took notice. At the end of March, Chamberlain stated in parliament that Britain would support Poland, strengthened a week later by a military alliance. Hitler was initially furious, but Ribbentrop advised him that, as had been the case over Austria and Czechoslovakia, the British would avoid getting involved in any conflict between Germany and Poland. Moreover, this development allowed the Germans to claim that Poland, in its preference for 'a promise of hope from a third Power to a direct guarantee of peace by the German Government', was already violating the 1934 non-aggression agreement. It is interesting that in their chastisement of the Poles, the Germans made frequent allusions to the 'late Marshal Piłsudski, praising his vision and his willingness to break with the political methods of the past', as if trying to make out that it was Poland that was now acting dishonourably – a major insult to any Polish patriot.[19] In any case, the British guarantee did not necessarily represent a reversal in Beck's approach to foreign policy. Having watched Hitler make 'easy gains' by exploiting the Western Powers' policy of appeasement, Beck probably hoped that Germany would stop short of further action towards Poland if it risked direct conflict with Britain and France.[20]

In the meantime, Hitler had to reorganise his programme of European conquest. Since Polish neutrality could no longer be relied upon in the east if the Germans attacked westward, the Wehrmacht began to draw up plans for annexation instead. As early as April 1939, secret orders were passed to high-level commands to prepare for war, and although the Germans had directed the world's attention on Danzig, the orders made clear the greater agenda: the mission of the Wehrmacht would be the complete destruction of the Polish Army.[21] A month later, Hitler addressed the military high command. General Rudolf Schmundt, who was present, wrote a *précis* of the speech in a document that would later be used in the Nuremberg Tribunals. According to this record, Hitler made clear that he wished to attack Poland 'at the first suitable opportunity', adding that 'Danzig is not the object at stake. For us, it is about expanding *Lebensraum* in the east and securing food supplies'. Schmundt added:

> [Hitler] must reserve the right to give the final order to strike. There must not be a simultaneous confrontation with the west (France and England). There is no doubt that a surprise attack can lead to a quick solution. The aim remains to deal the enemy a devastating blow at the outset. Right or wrong or treaties have no role here.[22]

The subsequent weeks erupted in frantic diplomatic manoeuvring; in reality, Berlin was busy sabotaging any potential resolutions to the dispute. Despite Ribbentrop's assurances, the British and French made clear at the end of June that they would not stand aside if the Germans attempted to change the status quo in Danzig, and this strengthened the resolve of the Polish government still further; a week later, Moltke reported to Berlin from Warsaw: 'There can hardly be any doubt that, given the heated atmosphere that prevails across the entire country today, a clear violation of Polish rights in Danzig would not be tolerated.'[23]

MANUFACTURING THREATS TO THE REICH

Even if the British and French didn't intervene, Hitler had a serious domestic problem to contend with: German public opinion was against a major war. If his ambitions to conquer and dismember Poland were to be realised, the mood within Germany would have to change; and so, the Nazi propaganda machine ramped up. German newspapers were full of exaggerated stories of violent acts by Poles against these German minority communities in Danzig and other places in western Poland. There were a few incidents along the frontier where small groups of soldiers or border guards – often no more than one or two individuals – strayed across the border; in the past, such episodes would have been dealt with administratively and without fuss, but now each was treated as a significant, headline-worthy violation. Steps were taken by the Germans to increase their strength within Danzig: the police force was militarised and placed under the control of the SS, and several freighters carrying armaments from German ports in the Baltic to East Prussia inexplicably developed 'engine trouble' as they were passing Danzig, forcing them into harbour to seek help. The Poles protested in vain, and when they responded by moving military units closer to Danzig, the German press seized on this as proof of Polish aggression.

German agents also worked to incite Polish violence against ethnic Germans to bolster the narrative of victimhood. In the last days of August, there was an explosion in the railway station in Tarnów, in southern Poland. Part of the building was destroyed and 24 people were killed. Almost immediately, police arrested Antoni Guzy, an unemployed former locksmith who had a German mother and Polish father. When he was interrogated, he revealed that after joining the *Gewerkschaft Deutscher Arbeiter* ('German Workers' Trade Union'), he was sent to Germany where he received a modest amount of training in covert operations. In response to a coded message broadcast by a German radio station in Breslau (now the Polish Wrocław), he went to Kraków and collected two large suitcases. He was then told to take the suitcases to Tarnów, where he was to put them in a left luggage locker, before returning to Kraków.

It seems likely that Guzy had no idea of the contents of the suitcases. He made no attempt to leave the station, waiting patiently for a train back to Kraków, and was present when the explosion occurred, suggesting his controllers intended for him to be killed in the explosion.[24] Although Tarnów was a transit point for trains carrying the rapidly mobilising personnel of the Polish Army, the intention seems to have been to incite revenge attacks against ethnic Germans, but no such attacks took place. There were many other staged incidents. All along the German frontier, Reinhard Heydrich, who at that time was head of the Gestapo and the *Sicherheitspolizei* ('Security Police'), had ordered the removal of elements of the population that were deemed to be politically unreliable. As part of a plan variously codenamed *Konserve* and *Himmler*, isolated farms and other buildings in this belt were then identified and arson attacks were carried out, which were then blamed on 'Polish elements'.[25] The growing voraciousness of the German press and persecution of the Poles did not go unnoticed in Warsaw. In August, the Polish embassy in Berlin reported to the Ministry of Foreign Affairs that the Poles were evidently the Nazis' next major target:

> This [press] campaign bears a remarkable resemblance to that waged last year against Czechoslovakia, except that the present propaganda is being carried on with far greater intensity than on that occasion ... to-day the German Government's conduct is not veiled by even the flimsiest of pretexts, and this clearly indicates that the German authorities do not count on any negotiations in the future ...
>
> What we are now witnessing is the authorities' wholesale closing down of Polish associations ... mass expropriations of Polish farmers and the everyday deportation of large numbers of persons of Polish race from the frontier regions.[26]

With the threat of war growing ever greater, Beck made a concessionary offer. In mid-August, he informed the Berlin government that Poland was willing to give up control of the customs offices in Danzig; Hitler rejected this angrily as being far too little. A week later, *Gauleiter* Forster – now elevated to Senate president in Danzig – tabled a motion for the city to rejoin Germany. This was in violation of the League of Nations charter that had established the free city, and the British and French intervened to prevent an escalation. Warsaw was pressured to avoid further military measures and to appoint a mediator; for the moment, it seemed to Hitler that as had been the case in 1938, the Western Powers would not intervene.

EQUILIBRIUM SHATTERED

Even if Ribbentrop was right and Britain and France chose to look away at the last moment, there was a further issue in the stance of the Soviet Union. Throughout 1939, Soviet delegates had been holding talks with Britain and France – but only at a perfunctory level with Poland – about collective measures they could take to contain German expansionism. When he became aware of these discussions, Hitler made secret contact with Soviet diplomats, offering a bilateral arrangement that would be more favourable to the Soviet Union than any agreement with Britain and France.

The early stages of negotiations faced difficulties. The Soviet Commissar for Foreign Affairs, Maksim Maksimovich Litvinov, had repeatedly warned Stalin that Nazi Germany was the greatest threat to the Soviet Union. The best policy, he advised, was to try to contain German ambitions by building a series of links with the Western Powers, even if these fell short of formal military alliances. But there was another reason for German dissatisfaction with Litvinov: his Jewish ancestry. After receiving repeated hints from Berlin that Litvinov was an insurmountable barrier to an agreement that would be greatly in the interests of the Soviet Union, Stalin dismissed Litvinov in May 1939.[27] Given Stalin's purges of so many parts of the Soviet government and military, it was surely no surprise when large numbers of *Narodnyy Komissariat Vnutrennikh Del* ('People's Commissariat for Internal Affairs' or *NKVD*) officers descended on the Commissariat of Foreign Affairs and arrested many of Litvinov's aides; most were subjected to severe interrogations in attempts to secure incriminating evidence against their former boss.

Litvinov's replacement was Vyacheslav Mikhailovich Molotov. Like many Soviet figures he had chosen to discard his birthname – Scriabin – in favour of a revolutionary pseudonym: in his case, a derivation from the Russian word *molot* ('hammer'). His reputation for working long hours earned him the nickname 'Stone Arse' and he was also known to be excessively pedantic – a trait he willingly demonstrated when he told those around him that Lenin had originally referred to him as 'Iron Arse', and that this was his preferred nickname. But Lenin had also condemned him for writing documents that were 'the most shameful bureaucratism, and the most stupid'.[28] Despite his punishing work schedule, he owed his rise more to his unswerving loyalty to Stalin than to any personal aptitude. Stalin appointed him as Litvinov's replacement with orders that he was to 'clean out the synagogue' – a reference to Litvinov's Jewish origins – and Molotov agreed readily that there were too many Jews in the ranks of the Soviet leadership and ambassadors. The fact that his own wife was Jewish was far less important than rigid adherence to Stalin's wishes.

At first, discussions with Ribbentrop focused on matters of trade and technology transfer, and Moscow continued negotiations with France and Britain. The sticking point with the Western Powers was how events might unfold in the event of war. Stalin wanted guarantees that the Red Army would be able to enter Polish territory in order to fight the Germans, but Beck had already stated the position of his government – given the past history between Russia and Poland, there was widespread fear that if Soviet troops entered Polish territory, it would be impossible to compel their departure.[29] At the same time, the Poles hoped that they could stave off a potential invasion so long as the Soviets remained engaged and that talks with the Western Powers continued. But by the third week of August, the unthinkable had happened: German representatives had effectively completed a trade agreement and Stalin suspended talks with Britain and France.

That Poland had failed to recognise a German–Soviet rapprochement as a possibility was tragically ironic. On the one hand, Beck had stayed true to the late marshal's policy of equilibrium in keeping both German and Soviet threats at arm's length and standing firm when necessary; everything in his diplomatic approach hinged on the idea that Poland would never again be occupied or partitioned by foreign powers. On the other, he – like many others in the foreign ministry – made the mistake of assuming that as ideological enemies, Nazi Germany and the Soviet Union were irrevocably incompatible in diplomatic outlook. Hitler's distaste for Communism was no secret and, in the form of the 1936 Anti-Comintern Pact, had provided the basis for an alliance with Japan against the Soviet Union. Conversely, from Stalin's point of view, there was little to separate Germany from other 'bourgeois' capitalist enemies aside from the fact it happened to subscribe to 'bourgeois militarism'.[30] Wacław Grzybowski, the Polish ambassador to Moscow, judged that Stalin would refuse to be drawn into a war between the imperialist Western Powers, preferring to wait on the sidelines until an advantageous moment presented itself. When pressed in June 1939 to account for rumours of German–Soviet talks at

Poland's expense, Grzybowski doubled down, insisting that an agreement remained impossible because '(1) Russia could not allow a German victory; (2) Russia could not consent to have a common border with Germany.' In his opinion, the suggestion that a rapprochement was within reach could be little more than a 'bluff' because Germany would hardly risk losing Japan in return for gaining the USSR as an ally.[31]

As early as October 1938, there had been signs that German–Soviet relations were shifting, but the Poles refused to take them seriously. By May 1939, a close confidant of Marshal Hermann Göring was quoted as saying that Hitler and Ribbentrop were planning to divide Poland between Germany and the Soviet Union in a fourth partition, and although Berlin ambassador Józef Lipski received numerous reports along these lines, he dismissed them as non-credible conspiracies that were designed 'clearly to intimidate us'.[32] Even in August, when the news of Ribbentrop's meeting with Molotov trickled out of Moscow, the immediate response from Warsaw was muted. The press presented the development less as a direct threat to Polish security than as further proof of Hitler's ideological bankruptcy:

> For what is a non-aggression pact with the Soviets, entered into by a state proclaiming that it is ideologically fighting the Comintern? ... Today no one defends Nazism as a supposedly programmatic direction any longer … The programme and principles are collapsing like a house of cards! It turns out that everything is just ways and means in the struggle for German supremacy over the world. There is no ideology![33]

But in truth, ideology had never been a sticking point in Hitler's foreign policy. He had always been fiercely pragmatic in testing and exploiting diplomatic opportunities in a way that Poland – and her western allies – still hadn't grasped. Far from being a sign of weakness, this was in fact his greatest strength, because the European powers were so blinded by the localised interests of National Socialism that they failed to appreciate Hitler's larger plans for geopolitical conquest.

In his immediate assessment of the German–Soviet rapprochement, Beck felt that nothing had really changed: the Soviets were still unlikely to engage in European conflict, and it was hard to see a robust Nazi–Communist alliance working in practice. He believed that both sides were probably enjoying the opportunity to exert psychological pressure on Poland and that the only necessary response was to 'substantiate the firm position of England, France, and Poland' for European security.[34] When the Molotov–Ribbentrop Pact was officially signed on

23 August, the Poles were forced to consider a more sinister question: did the pact contain secret clauses to bind the interests of the Germans and Soviets together, and if so, what were the implications for the eastern states? In the week that followed, rumours abounded that the Pact included a clause concerning the partition of Poland. It seems that the British, United States, and French had credible reports confirming this, but chose not to share their intelligence with the Warsaw government, perhaps fearing that it would break the Poles' resolve and cause the country to capitulate to the Germans without a fight.[35]

Even at the end of the month, as conflict seemed all but inevitable, Beck showed astonishing confidence in declaring that Poland's situation was 'not so bad', alluding to secret preparatory mobilisation and praising France's 'enormous military effort ... a two-million-strong army on the Maginot Line.'[36] Yet there was no question that the Warsaw government was mentally preparing for war. With the signing of the Polish–British Defence Pact on 25 August, Poland was reassured that Britain (and France) were ready to come to its aid. As news of this broke, Hitler made a final diplomatic effort to dissuade the Western Powers from intervening, hoping to exploit the policy of appeasement one more time by demanding the restoration of Danzig and the Polish Corridor. However, when the British learned that talks were conditional on the presence of a Polish representative with full signing powers, they suspected Poland was being set up to follow in Czechoslovakia's footsteps to full capitulation.

OPERATION *HIMMLER*

The full significance of the Molotov–Ribbentrop Pact, as it soon became known, was beginning to surface. On 29 August, the *New York Times* reported the words of Samuel Harper, an eminent American Slavicist and historian, who told the newspaper that the non-aggression pact probably did include secret protocols that would divide Eastern Europe into spheres of influence between Germany and the Soviet Union.[37] Whether this was based upon Harper's suspicions or from other sources, it was entirely accurate. The existence of the protocol would only be proven after the end of the war, and the Soviet Union would continue denying the facts for decades. Under this protocol, Finland, Estonia, and Latvia were assigned to the Soviet sphere of influence. Poland was to be divided between Germany and the Soviet Union, with Lithuania falling into the German sphere of influence. This latter provision was altered after Poland's capitulation since the Wehrmacht ended up seizing Polish areas originally slated for Soviet annexation, and Germany compromised by giving the Soviets a free hand over Lithuania.

Finally, Germany agreed to refrain from action over Soviet claims to territory on its frontier with Romania. It was another example of the extreme cynicism of the Nazi regime. Germany's readiness to sacrifice the territorial integrity of Finland and Romania – both friendly powers – revealed a striking level of contempt and strategic opportunism.

The world watched with bated breath as German troops assembled along the frontier with Poland. In the remote southeastern corner of German Silesia, the town of Gleiwitz (now Gliwice in modern Poland) was about to gain particular attention; home to a significant radio transmitter tower, it would soon be the site of another staged provocation under Operation *Himmler*. On 22 August, as negotiations continued in Moscow and the Wehrmacht was completing its preparations for war, Hitler told his senior generals: 'I will provide a propagandistic *casus belli*, no matter whether it is plausible or not. The victor will not be asked afterwards whether he told the truth.'[38]

As part of Operation *Himmler*, Heydrich had set up a training camp to the north of Berlin where about 300 soldiers of the SS were issued with Polish uniforms and weapons. They were then deployed in a series of attacks on German customs posts and other locations, firing wildly into the air, singing patriotic Polish songs, and leaving behind the corpses of six men – inmates of concentration camps – dressed in Polish uniforms. The most ambitious such mission took place at Gleiwitz under the command of Sturmbannführer Alfred Naujocks. Late on 31 August, he and a small group of men dressed in civilian clothing drove to the transmitter tower and seized control. One of the men then used a small radio set attached to the tower and used for emergency weather warnings to transmit a proclamation. The original intention was to commence with an announcement that the radio station was in Polish hands, and then to call for Poles in Silesia to rise up and conduct sabotage attacks prior to the arrival of the Polish Army, which would invade Germany in support; for unknown reasons, only the opening statement was transmitted, and even this was heard only in the local area.[39] Franciszek Honiok, an ethnic Pole who was associated with anti-German groups, had been arrested the previous day by the Gestapo and was now brought to the Gleiwitz transmitter, drugged and unconscious; he was shot and killed, and his corpse left in the building while Naujocks and his team fled. The *Abwehr* (German Military Intelligence) agent responsible for sourcing Polish uniforms, weapons, and other props for the incident was one Oskar Schindler, who would achieve fame for his later acts to obstruct Nazi policies.[40]

The attack was proclaimed by the Germans as a further example of intolerable Polish action. The world's press, however, was rightly sceptical. On the same day, in a last attempt to try to avoid war, Lipski presented himself to Ribbentrop and declared Poland open to negotiation, but was dismissed as soon as it became clear he did not have signing rights. With the Germans blaming Poland for the talks breaking down, there was now no denying that war was imminent. What could not be anticipated was the ferocity of the attack on Poland that would eclipse all previous experiences of suffering in the nation's troubled history.

Whilst Poland had underestimated the significance of the Molotov–Ribbentrop Pact, Hitler, for his part, had convinced himself that Britain and France would be reluctant to commit to another European war over his eastern expansion. On 22 August, Hitler gathered Wehrmacht commanders in his Obersalzburg home and delivered a speech outlining his plans for the (now inevitable) invasion of Poland. He assessed that even if they wished to resist the Germans, Britain and France's armament situation rendered an attack from the Maginot Line highly unlikely; their only other option would be to impose a blockade, which Hitler felt confident he could endure thanks to Germany's autarky and Eastern European resource bases.[41] He followed this up with a second speech that made clear the campaign objective would 'not consist in reaching certain lines, but in the physical destruction of the enemy':

> Our strength consists in our speed and in our brutality. Genghis Khan led millions of women and children to slaughter – with premeditation and a happy heart. History sees in him solely the founder of a state. It's a matter of indifference to me what a weak western European civilization will say about me.
>
> ... Accordingly, I have placed my Deaths-Head formations in readiness – for the present only in the East – with orders to them to send to death mercilessly and without compassion, men, women, and children of Polish derivation and language. Only thus shall we gain the *Lebensraum* ['living space'] which we need.[42]

Of the many territories and states that fell victim to Hitler, few inspired as much murderous hatred as Poland. Where other populations were to be co-opted, subdued, or put to work, Hitler's mission in Poland was one of extermination, in which all kinds of hellish brutality and mindless violence were to be justified. In the Führer's eyes, the annihilation of Polish culture and society would one day be little more than a footnote in the history of the Thousand Year Reich.

CHAPTER 3

FALL WEISS

O Polish mother! …

Your son is called to battle devoid of glory –
To martyrdom that brings no resurrection.

The only gravestone that will mark his plight
Will be the gallows' somber wooden frame;
A woman's stifled tears his only fame:
That, and Poles talking long into the night.

Adam Mickiewicz, 'To Polish Mother', 1830
Translated by Bill Johnston[1]

A NEW WAR

After ten years of iterations, Hitler's operational plan for the invasion of Poland was finalised by mid-June 1939. Codenamed *Fall Weiss* ('Case White'), it called for a direct attack from Poland's west across the German border; an attack from the north via East Prussia; and a final attack from the south across the Slovakian border. At the same time, the *Volksdeutsch* population inside Poland would be called upon to support the Nazi advance in their ultimate military objective to encircle Warsaw and cut off the Polish Army on the west bank of the Vistula. The operation was to commence at 0445 on 1 September; two minutes before this, the old battleship *Schleswig-Holstein*, which had been at anchor in the Bay of Danzig, moved slowly into position facing the small Polish garrison in Westerplatte, a small peninsula near the old channel of the Vistula River. As German troops crossed the border along a 995-mile front line – with just 200 miles separating the main assault from the Polish capital – *Schleswig-Holstein* opened fire with her four 11-inch guns and several smaller 20mm guns. The bombardment lasted less than ten minutes and delivered over five tons of explosives, but the shelling proved largely ineffective; many of the heavy rounds from the main guns burst through the trees around the Polish barracks without exploding, while the majority of the fire from the smaller guns (which were designed as anti-aircraft weapons) flew past and into the bay beyond Westerplatte. But one round struck and killed a Polish rifleman, Stefan Jezierski. He was the first casualty of the Second World War.

Despite weeks of heightening tensions, Poland was caught on the back foot. Britain and France had persuaded the Poles to pause early mobilisation as they attempted to extract last-minute concessions from Hitler, so although Poland should have had a force of around 1 million men to deploy against Germany's 1.5 million, huge numbers of troops were nowhere near the front line when war broke out. Efforts to rush them into action quickly descended into chaos, and those who were able to mobilise found themselves outgunned. Germany boasted 2,750 tanks to Poland's 210, 9,000 guns to the Poles' 4,300, and 2,315 aircraft against just 800. Still, the Poles hoped that by throwing the majority of their forces westwards, the German advance could be held off long enough for Britain and France to open a western front. After decades of political manoeuvring and for all of Beck's pragmatic calculations, the Poles never dreamed that, when the hour of war finally arrived, the allies who had guaranteed their security would sit by and watch Poland fall.

When Hitler gave a speech to the Reichstag members that same morning, he didn't use the word 'war' at all. He intended – at least publicly – to portray the German actions as measures necessitated by Polish attacks, and there was little reaction in Berlin or other cities. By contrast, the mood in Poland was bellicose. The commander-in-chief of the Polish Army at the time was the towering, heavy-browed Marshal Edward Rydz, a part-time painter and long-time Piłsudskiite, who gladly added his *nom de guerre*, 'Śmigły' (meaning 'swift' or 'deft'), to his surname. He immediately proclaimed that Poland was fighting a just war against its 'ancient enemy'.[2] Fired up with patriotic fervour, Polish soldiers were full of optimism, and many daubed the sides of their troop trains with the slogan *Do Berlina!* ('Onwards to Berlin!) as they left Warsaw for the front. 'God is with us' was the public refrain; just days earlier, the newly anointed Pope Pius XII had pleaded that a 'peaceful solution' be found to ease German–Polish tensions, and Poles now saw the Germans as 'modern barbarians, threatening European civilisation with their aggression and lust for destruction.'[3]

The first wave of German air attacks targeted Polish airfields, but most Polish planes – particularly the relatively small number of modern aircraft – had already been dispersed in precautionary measures. Elsewhere, German aircraft struck military installations and infrastructure across numerous Polish cities. In Warsaw, people awoke to the clatter of anti-aircraft guns, the droning of aircraft engines, and dull explosions. The attacks on the city – codenamed *Wasserkante* ('Waterfront') – were directed at widespread industrial targets, but low cloud and intermittent fog resulted in many bomber units either failing to find their objectives or simply aborting their missions entirely. The small number of Polish fighters defending Warsaw put up spirited resistance, destroying 15 German aircraft, while a further 35 were shot down across the rest of Poland.[4] Had more Polish fighters been available to defend the capital, they might have inflicted significant losses on the Luftwaffe in the early days of the war.[5] However, numerical superiority meant that the Luftwaffe was able to cause considerable damage, both on the ground and in the air. Across the 30 Polish airfields that were attacked, about 180 Polish planes were lost. Meanwhile, on the ground, civilians leapt into action and joined military personnel digging anti-tank ditches at the city outskirts.

Strategically speaking, the German air campaign was unprecedented in its ambitions. Aside from neutralising the Polish air force, the Luftwaffe was expected to provide coordinated support to the advancing army while quickly eliminating key Polish armament centres, communication hubs, and naval bases from the very first day of the war. Within hours, it became apparent that the air force lacked clear prioritisation between these objectives, and outdated target intelligence meant that many sorties were wasted on 'secondary or even tertiary' – frequently civilian – targets. The numbers of the first day emphasise this: the Germans' 2,700 sorties covered a total of just 30 targets with a loss of 37 aircraft (compared to the Poles' loss of 29 aircraft out of 280 sorties).[6] The future commander of the Home Army, Stefan Rowecki, remarked on the first day's raids over the capital:

> Around 6, an air alarm shook Warsaw. Indeed, several German bombers appeared over Warsaw. During the day, the raids were repeated several times, the largest of about 15 planes around 5–5.30 p.m. The anti-aircraft artillery opened fire, apparently firing inappropriately, too low and too short, but apparently the shells shot down several planes. Parts of the shells fell on roofs and gardens, and a few unexploded shells fell. On the outskirts of the city (so as not to cause fires), our fighters attacked the Germans ... Throughout Poland, bomb and gas raids inflicted some losses, but they lifted the mood, which had been somewhat weakened by mobilisation, and phenomenally increased hatred and anger. Everyone wants to beat the Germans as quickly as possible ... My general

impression of the bombing raids on Warsaw is: weak. These few planes scattered throughout the day did not make a serious impression. It was striking that they could travel around Poland so brazenly.

The Massacres Begin

Rowecki also criticised the lack of forewarning that the raids were incoming.[7] For many Poles, it was the sound of the Stukas' wing sirens or 'Jericho trumpets' that announced the arrival of war on their doorsteps as the Germans began indiscriminate bombing campaigns on civilian population centres. The first major casualty was the town of Wieluń on the frontier with German Silesia; repeated raids devastated the town, destroying over 70 per cent of its buildings and killing hundreds of civilians – despite there being no military units or vital installations in the area. This was confirmed by German reconnaissance aircraft the same day, but the systematic terror raids continued as a means of breaking the will of the Polish population to resist.[8] German airmen soon hardened their attitudes, as one bombardier recalled:

> I had to drop bombs onto a train station in Posen (Poznań) on the second day of the war in Poland. Eight of the 16 bombs fell in the city, right in the middle of houses. I didn't like it. On the third day I didn't care, and on the fourth day I took pleasure in it. We enjoyed heading out before breakfast, chasing individual soldiers through the fields with machine guns and then leaving them there with a few bullets in their backs.[9]

Meanwhile, German ground forces swept across the frontier. In many cases, there was little or no resistance. Hans von Luck was a junior officer in the reconnaissance battalion of 2nd Light Division, soon to be upgraded to 7th Panzer Division, and his division had been deployed near Gleiwitz in late August. The soldiers had been told they were conducting a major field exercise with blank ammunition, but this was replaced on 26 August with live rounds. On 1 September, Luck and his men watched Luftwaffe planes fly towards Poland, and then approached the frontier themselves:

> The frontier was manned by a single customs official. As one of our soldiers approached him, the terrified man opened the barrier. Without resistance we marched into Poland. Far and wide there was not a single Polish soldier in sight, although they were supposed to have been preparing for an 'invasion' of Germany.

> I spread my company out. We advanced on foot along a wide front and came to the first Polish village. Still no Polish soldiers to be seen …
>
> Where were the Polish troops?[10]

Other German units encountered tougher resistance. Luck's 2nd Light Division was part of General Walter von Reichenau's Tenth Army, and another of its units, 4th Panzer Division, crossed the frontier further north with German artillery shells passing overhead. The commander of the division's panzer regiment, Oberstleutnant Heinrich Eberbach, later wrote:

> We advanced only slowly. The road was crowded and the bridge over the Liswarta River had been blown. We splashed across a ford. We took our motorcyclists across on the decks of our tanks. None of our vehicles were left behind. We thrust through Krzepice to Opatów where we came under machine-gun and artillery fire, which we returned with our tanks, and reached Wilkowiecko … II Battalion attacked, destroyed a Polish artillery battery, fought through the villages and advanced to within 400m of the edge of the nearby forest. There, it came under fire from artillery, anti-tank guns and machine-guns. The enemy couldn't be seen. The shots from the Polish anti-tank rifles penetrated our light armour.[11]

Eberbach failed to mention that Polish civilians were expelled from both Krzepice and Opatów and most of the buildings were set ablaze; several of the tanks advancing towards the woodland to the east were partly screened from Polish gunfire by fleeing civilians, who intentionally or otherwise functioned as human shields.[12] Many of the men of the motorcycle battalion that had accompanied the German tanks were killed or wounded and several more were taken prisoner as the Germans made a hasty withdrawal. In the exchange of fire that followed, Polish anti-tank guns forced the German tanks to pull back a short distance and a swift Polish cavalry attack then inflicted further losses on the German infantry that had been left behind. As the Germans attacked again, they encountered an armoured train that opened fire at close range with good effect. By the end of the day, the Germans had driven off the Polish troops opposing them but had suffered substantial losses and a late Polish counterattack caused considerable confusion. Eberbach recorded that his regiment had lost 15 dead, 14 wounded, and had suffered the destruction of 14 tanks; Polish accounts claimed that the division lost about 800 men and at least 50 tanks.[13] The Poles fought hard and, to the dismay of many senior German officers, caused significant confusion and panic in the ranks of their units. The war diary of 4th Panzer Division reflected on the day's events:

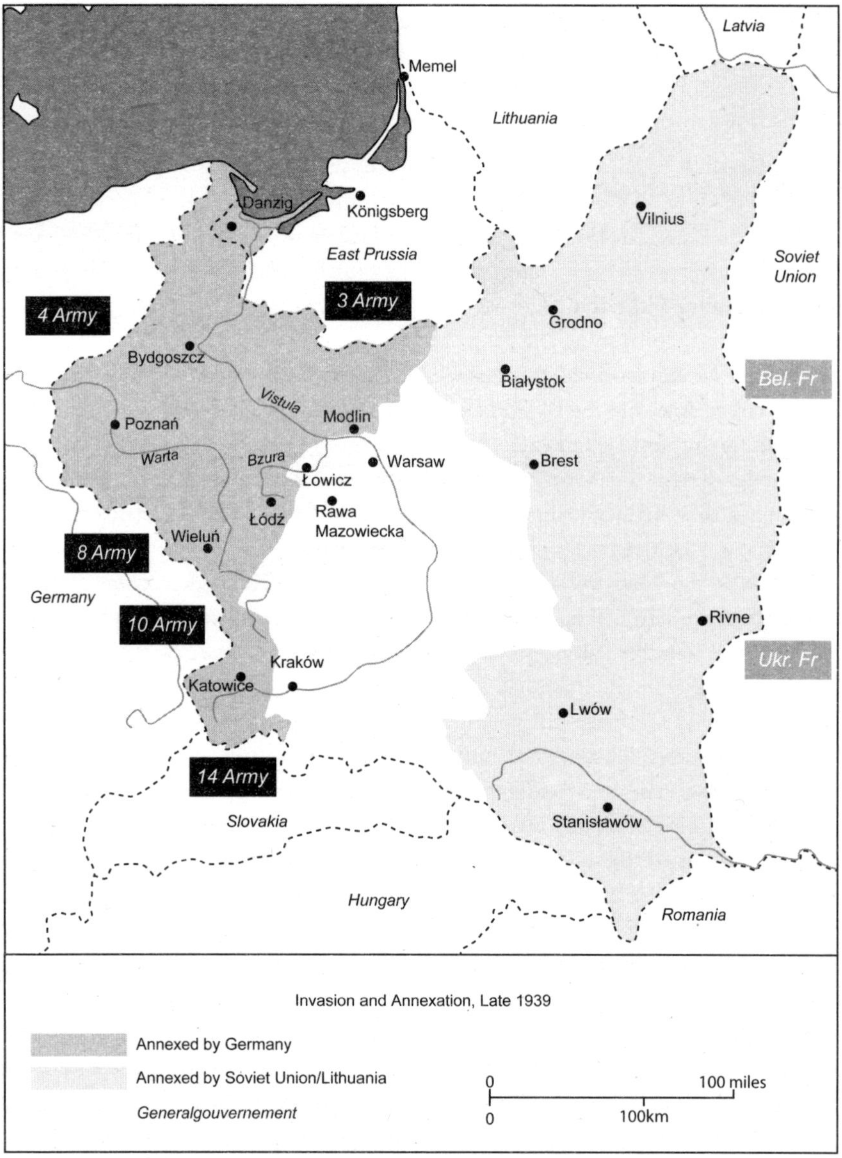

The first day of battle was full of difficulties. Cooperation of different combat formations was inadequate, reporting and command systems poor, partly perhaps because of the preceding weeks of radio silence, but also due to numerous subordinate units that weren't integrated parts of the division. The poor off-road capability of most wheeled vehicles was further exposed by the

> heavy rain of preceding days. The troops were still inexperienced at overcoming terrain obstacles.
>
> The panic during the evening showed the nervousness of men who had been inadequately prepared by all too short a period of training. The first impressions of war are powerful: burning farms, fleeing civilians, huge clouds of dust, the smell of burnt cattle, the first enemy fire, rumours, wounded men, the first losses – sudden, unexpected failures can occur all too easily and then spread.[14]

In Danzig, several hundred German marines were waiting aboard *Schleswig-Holstein*; as the old battleship's guns fell silent, they surged ashore. The attack on the Polish barracks in Westerplatte was expected to be a quick affair, but the marines were driven off by heavy defensive fire. Within minutes, *Schleswig-Holstein* opened fire again, hammering the Polish positions for a further hour. When the German marines – now bolstered by a small group of SS volunteers from the German population of Danzig – tried again, they were once more forced back, leaving about half the force of marines dead or wounded. Elsewhere in Danzig, German police units supported by SS volunteers attempted to seize the city's post office, which was occupied by 58 Poles – many of them civilians. Two attacks in quick succession failed, and a third attempt in mid-morning, reinforced by two German armoured cars, fared no better. During the afternoon, after the Poles had refused to surrender, heavy German artillery fire drove the surviving defenders into the cellar. The Germans then brought up a fuel tanker and pumped gasoline into the basement. As the fuel was set alight, the Poles attempted to surrender but many were gunned down. A few managed to escape, while others were captured; 38 of them were later executed after being classified as non-uniformed guerillas.[15]

The second day of war brought better weather conditions for the invading forces. The Luftwaffe concentrated on providing closer support to the advancing ground offensive, especially around the Warta River. This was, in part, due to Oberstleutnant Joseph 'Beppo' Schmid, head of Luftwaffe intelligence, erroneously assuming that the Polish air force had already been wiped out. The Poles certainly found themselves increasingly stretched, but they still claimed valuable kills over Łódź and Bydgoszcz and tried their best to pick off isolated bombers. Beck described the 'employment of almost the entire German Air Force' as the 'greatest difficulty' facing the Polish defenders and appealed to the west for immediate support, arguing that 'Allied decisions which would tie up a considerable part of the German Air Force are the concern of all' in foreshortening another European war.[16] The bombing of civilian areas was already igniting outrage around the globe, and despite German assertions to the contrary, attacks on non-military targets continued unabated:

> German aircraft, after bombing various localities and ... villages of no military importance whatever, and having fired at peaceful farmers at work in the fields, have again carried out raids on Warsaw, in the course of which they bombed a health resort ... and in particular the villa of the United States Ambassador. This very day, in suburbs of Warsaw ... four private houses have been bombed as well as a lamp factory, and a railway station at the very moment when a Red Cross train was standing there.[17]

As early as 1 September, President Roosevelt condemned the bombardment of civilians and warned both sides against 'this sort of inhuman barbarism' – to no avail.[18] In Britain, Chamberlain announced to the House of Commons that the time had come to 'set our teeth and to enter upon this struggle', but stopped short of declaring war on Germany.[19] Beck pleaded with the Allies to follow through on their promises to support Polish independence, but it was not until 3 September that Britain and France officially entered the war.

In the weeks and months that followed, German propaganda would boldly proclaim the success of the panzer divisions, but in truth they were still learning the difficult art of combined arms warfare. 4th Panzer Division struggled for a second day, this time held up by forested terrain. Artillery support was markedly improved on the first day's fighting, but inexperienced soldiers were prone to nervy moments; at one point, there were panicky reports of the use of poison gas by the Poles, but by evening Generalmajor Georg-Hans Reinhardt, the division commander, cautiously reported that the Polish units to their front had been driven off.

Even at this early stage of the war, German ground troops showed the same disregard for the rules of war that their airborne comrades were displaying. The village of Wyszanów was just 18 miles from the frontier and German troops reached it late on 1 September. All men capable of bearing arms were rounded up and marched away to an internment camp in Germany, and the following day troops from 10th Infantry Division arrived in the village. Men from this division had already been involved in violence against civilians – they had razed a nearby village and shot 16 unarmed Poles, and a further 18 more (and three Polish prisoners of war) were executed on 2 September. As the Germans marched into Wyszanów, a single shot rang out. The Germans immediately suspected they had been attacked by irregular Polish forces, but it is more likely that the gunshot was an accidental shot fired by one of the nervous Germans. The soldiers responded with ruthless violence. They moved through the village, setting fire to buildings and throwing grenades into cellars; in a farm on the edge of Wyszanów, 21 women and children were in a cellar and 16 were killed by grenades. In all, 22 civilians – 11 of them children – were killed.[20]

German filmmaker Leni Riefenstahl had already achieved fame (and a degree of censure) for her propagandistic films *Triumph des Willens* ('Triumph of the Will') and *Olympia* before she donned a quasi-military uniform to accompany German troops into Poland. In the second week of the war, she witnessed the execution of a group of Polish civilians in the town of Końskie. When she protested to the senior German officer present, her complaints were curtly dismissed on the grounds that the Poles – all of whom were Jews – were being shot in revenge for attacks on German troops. In the original German edition of his memoirs, Erich von Manstein – who would end the war with the rank of Generalfeldmarschall and a reputation as one of Hitler's finest operational commanders – wrote that the incident was the result of a 'senseless outburst of shooting because of the nervousness of an anti-aircraft officer, who reached the square just as an unfounded panic erupted there'.[21] This account fails to explain why most or all of the victims were Jews. The officer concerned was eventually court-martialled, something that Manstein described as demonstrating how seriously the army took such matters, but charges were brought only because Riefenstahl raised the matter repeatedly. In any event, the officer was given a one-year sentence, which was rapidly quashed.[22]

PLAN ZACHÓD

Despite serious setbacks, the Polish Army fought on in the hope that the Western Powers would soon intervene. The Polish defensive plan (*Plan Zachód* or 'Plan West') involved fighting as close to the frontier as possible for only a limited period: protracted battles here would risk the destruction of the army in terrain ill-suited for defence, and if Hitler was not satisfied with taking the Polish Corridor, the main battle was to be conducted in central Poland. If necessary, Polish forces would withdraw as far as the Vistula, where they would mount prolonged resistance until the anticipated Western Allied attack drew off enough of Hitler's forces to stop the German advance. Thereafter, once supplies and equipment from Britain and France had arrived to replenish the Polish Army, an offensive phase would begin to drive the Germans back.

But by the end of the first week of the war, this strategy was rapidly unravelling. German units like 4th Panzer Division, which had struggled in the first days of the fighting, were now operating more effectively and taking advantage of the Polish withdrawal from the frontier regions. To the horror of the Poles, the

Western Powers seemed unwilling to help; British planes mounted a few attacks against German shipping, but there was no sign of any major ground offensive. Much of this inaction was based on poor intelligence: it was feared that the German defences facing France were too strong, and that the Luftwaffe would carry out major attacks against British and French cities. In reality, the French outnumbered the modest forces facing them by at least 3:1, and the great bulk of the Luftwaffe was deployed against Poland. A small French attack into the Saar region had no effect on the fighting in the east. Prior to hostilities, the British had hinted – without making any firm commitments – that they would transfer a bomber squadron to Poland and would provide the Polish air force with Hurricane fighters, but despite several requests from Warsaw for these planes, these hadn't materialised.

With the ground forces now gathering momentum, German military planners attempted to facilitate the connection between the resident ethnic German populations along the Vistula and the advancing Wehrmacht. At the same time, suspicion of possible German saboteurs operating behind the front line spread quickly throughout Poland and triggered a number of violent attacks on the *Volksdeutsche*. On 3 September, Polish troops moving through the city of Bydgoszcz – known to the Germans as Bromberg – came under fire from nearby buildings. At this stage, German ground forces were still about 12 miles to the west, and the Polish soldiers realised that the shots had been fired by *Volksdeutsch* irregulars. A sweep of known addresses of *Volksdeutsche* followed; those found to have weapons were executed, while others were badly beaten and taken to a nearby barracks. Estimates of the number of those killed, both during the roundup and in the barracks afterwards, vary between 150 and 400.[23]

There were similar incidents elsewhere. Several young *Volksdeutsche* wrongly concluded that the Polish Army had already withdrawn, donned swastika armbands, and attempted to seize key buildings in Katowice in southern Poland – only to be swiftly rounded up by Polish soldiers. Clare Hollingworth, a British journalist, was in the city:

> I had just returned to the Consulate when everyone ran to the windows. Thirty or forty young men, the oldest not above 20, were marched by under double guard. All wore swastika armbands. Hearing the guns and alarm, they had assumed that the German forces were through. Their long-prepared badges on their arms, they had catapulted on to the streets, yelling '*Heil Hitler!*' Instead of a popular rising, they had found troops to surround and disarm them. A few minutes after this, we heard two lorries crash by. They were full of workmen, their clothes ripped, smeared with blood and dirt. They were crouching in a ring of soldiers, and every time one raised

> a head, a rifle-butt drove it down again. These men had been involved in another Nazi revolt. When I drove to lunch I passed a court ... I saw out of the tail of my eye the improvised sheds, the figures with rifles up, and guessed those others against the wall. The volley sounded as my car took the hill beyond.[24]

Polish countermeasures against armed civilians were no worse – and arguably less arbitrary – than the behaviour of German troops against suspected partisans, but the incidents in Bydgoszcz, Katowice, and elsewhere would be used by the Germans to justify still greater repression of the Poles in subsequent months.

To their chagrin, the German forces attacking the small garrison in Westerplatte, near the port of Danzig, continued to struggle for several days. After the guns of *Schleswig-Holstein* failed to crush the defenders, Stukas attacked on 2 September, with German land-based artillery arriving a day later. Another infantry attack was beaten off, but the Germans gathered their strength and tried again on 7 September; they captured part of the Polish barracks, and after positioning a tanker railcar loaded with fuel they pulled back. With no hope of outside help, the depleted garrison raised a white flag.

Dogged determination

Early on 3 September the Luftwaffe struck Warsaw in greater strength than before. Despite this, and the arrival of refugees from further west, the mood in the Polish capital remained positive, particularly after the announcement that Britain and France had declared war on Germany. In Warsaw, jubilant crowds flocked around the British embassy and the press celebrated the Western Allies now ready to stand 'shoulder to shoulder with Poland'.[25] Polish ambassador Raczyński reported back to Warsaw that although the defeat of Germany was now London's primary objective, the British 'cannot disperse their forces, which are needed for a decisive blow'.[26] Beck was not to expect the extensive air support he so desperately hoped for, nor the opening of a western front to divert German forces.

This was not the story told in the Polish press. On 6 September, the *Express Poranny* ran a story that the French had triumphantly entered the Rhineland (in reference to the abortive mission into the Saar district) and that Polish bombers had completed a raid on Berlin.[27] Polish Radio supplied a steady supply of positive – if suspiciously vague – reports that painted the defence efforts in a glorious light. If this propaganda was intended to keep the spirit of resistance alive, it was only partially successful; the German advance was gaining irreversible momentum, and Varsovians were already witnessing daily destruction first-hand. The American filmmaker Julien Bryan happened to be in Warsaw as war broke out, and his footage captured a much more honest picture of life in a city struggling to come to terms with its new reality during these days: buildings and roads wrecked by bombs; women sheltering underground with babies just hours old; civilians cut down in the middle of picking potatoes; children sitting numb next to the dead bodies of their parents.[28] And although the radio and newspapers continued to give optimistic reports, many doubted their veracity. An officer in Warsaw noted that the *Express Poranny*, reduced often to a single page, was avidly read again and again only because 'one soon understands that one is obstinately seeking some report which would lift the weight from one's heart, and one seeks it in vain.'[29] With little concrete information to go on, Varsovians responded to the constant danger of air attacks with dark humour, as one resident recounted: 'Bombs exploded, houses collapsed in Warsaw, and this chap got a bad attack of hiccups. Finally he begged his friend, "I can't stand these hiccups, just give me a fright, old man."'[30]

The Germans were now clear of the frontier region, and sent the Poles into a chaotic retreat under constant harassment from the air. By dawn of 8 September, 4th Panzer Division had reached Rawa Mazowiecka, 45 miles from the centre of Warsaw, with 1st Panzer Division a short distance to the south. Reinhardt divided his division into two battlegroups and dispatched the first along the main road to Warsaw and by midday the leading elements had seized the vital bridge across the Utrata River. After refuelling, the German tanks pressed on again during the afternoon, but the Poles succeeded in blowing the last bridges before Warsaw at Raszyn. A small group of tanks pushed across the small Raszynka River while German pioneers set to work repairing the bridges; when the division was finally able to cross in strength, it encountered improvised defences with barricades blocking the highway. Polish troops in an airfield just outside Mokotów – now the location of the city's airport – and in barracks in Ochota unleashed heavy fire on 4th Panzer Division. A platoon of German armoured vehicles slipped past the northern edge of Mokotów and approached the city centre. A Polish officer described the moment:

> It happened that among the people, who were running in all directions seeking shelter in the doorways, there was a chauffeur who was a retired NCO of an armoured regiment. He was just going to his garage with a tin of petrol. Seeing the advancing German car, it occurred to him to lie in wait for it at the side of the road, and when the tank passed him he threw the petrol in its track and after it a lighted match. The fire from the exploding petrol ran all over the asphalt and

> enveloped the whole car in flames. The crew jumped out. The people now rushed at the German soldiers who would have been torn to pieces had not some military police arrived to rescue them. The other two tanks retreated from the city on seeing the fire.[31]

Rather than risk penetrating the urban area by night, Reinhardt ordered a temporary halt.

The thrust towards Warsaw had passed to the south of Łódź. To the north of the city, the Bzura River flows east before turning north and joining the Vistula, and a substantial group of Polish units had gathered in the area between the two rivers. The Pomorze and Poznań Armies had united their remaining troops and, fearing that encirclement was imminent, General Tadeusz Kutrzeba decided to counterattack towards the south across the Bzura. It was a bold move, but given the German lunge towards Warsaw, there was at least a possibility of hitting the northern flank of the advance before it could be reinforced, forcing the Germans to pull back from the capital. Concentration of the Polish units was hampered by increasingly effective Luftwaffe attacks; in addition to striking at military columns, the German pilots deliberately bombed and strafed refugees struggling along the roads to add to the general confusion. By dawn on 9 September, Kutrzeba had pulled together sufficient strength to launch an attack. He notified Rydz-Śmigly of his plans, but the Polish commander-in-chief was unimpressed and refused to authorise the operation. Taking advantage of the increasing disruption of communications, Kutrzeba decided to proceed anyway.

In the path of the Polish troops and defending the northern flank of Eighth Army was the German 30th Infantry Division. The attack came as a complete surprise to the Germans and they fell back in disarray, in places up to 12 miles. Over the next few days, in the face of renewed German resistance and under constant air attack, the Polish advance slowed, reaching a line about 15 miles to the north of the centre of Łódź. On the eastern flank, Polish troops attacked Łowicz, recapturing the town in heavy fighting. A Polish officer described the temporary victory:

> Enemy stragglers, lost and wandering in our rear, have been eliminated. German troops trying to hold the southeast end of the town have pulled back. After a misty dawn, morning sunshine floods the liberated town with joyous light. The townspeople fill the streets, showing their happiness in every way they can. There are flowers, buckets of hot and cold drinks, bread, sweets, fruit, and endless joyful cheering.[32]

Varsovian Jew Szmuel Zeldman served in the 14th Kuyavan Infantry Regiment and was involved in Kutrzeba's attack:

> We crossed the Bzura River several times, both ways. On one occasion, I went with six other men to patrol the riverbank. We heard gunshots from the mill. A few Germans, probably also a patrol, convinced that we were going for them, entered the windmill and started shooting at us from there. We threw several hand grenades at the enemy. Then we demanded from a distance that they should surrender. But no one replied. When we approached the mill, after throwing a few more grenades, we saw three German soldiers lying with their mouths shot through. They preferred death to surrender to the enemy.[33]

At first, the Germans hoped that the units already deployed in the area would be sufficient to halt the Polish attack, and Reinhardt's 4th Panzer Division was ordered to resume the advance on Warsaw. But the city's defenders had now established a network of barricades and other obstacles, and the solitary panzer division lacked the strength to seize the centre of the city. Making the best of the situation, the Germans now redirected 1st and 4th Panzer Divisions – reinforced by the newly formed SS-*Leibstandarte Adolf Hitler* regiment – northward to deal with Kutrzeba's strike towards Łódź. As it withdrew, 4th Panzer Division was reduced to just 57 combat-worthy tanks.[34] Attempting to justify their setback, some German accounts claimed that the defenders of Warsaw numbered up to 100,000; even if such a large number had been available, most would have been reservists or volunteers, with little by way of organised military formations.

The Polish defenders of Warsaw were justifiably proud of their efforts but had little idea of events unfolding along the Bzura; they didn't realise that the withdrawal of German forces from the western edge of the city was in fact part of a general regrouping. The officer who described the improvised attack on the leading German tanks using a tin of petrol was with a small group that found themselves isolated by the German thrust into Warsaw before Reinhardt withdrew his division:

> We have no reserves for the time being, except different companies of staff, supplies, ammunition columns, which do not make up any real strength, especially for night fighting in the streets. We must therefore be prepared to be suddenly involved in the battle. Since there is no chance either of breaking through nor of retreat one must look to one's pistol, verify that the magazine is full, and wait quietly for further developments.

> It happened that our batteries soon cut them up. Well-organised and concentrated fire from a few batteries gave the Germans such a hiding that they halted their attack and retreated in great disorder to their former positions. In the morning hundreds of bodies showed the path of their unsuccessful effort.
>
> The repulse of the attack has had an important moral significance for the young soldier. He felt his superiority over the enemy, he saw with his own eyes the bloody losses sustained by his action, he satisfied himself of the weak endurance of the German infantry under fire and its lack of obstinacy and initiative in advancing. A few more such trials by fire and we can be quite sure of the morale of our men.[35]

Many Germans commented on the courage of the Poles; even *Leibstandarte* SS soldiers had praise for their opponents' obstinance. But this respect for worthy foes disappeared when the two sides weren't exchanging fire on the battlefield, and German units falling back under Polish pressure remained committed to Hitler's mandate for waging war with merciless intensity. In many locations, Polish male civilians were herded into buildings that were then deliberately set ablaze, with anyone attempting to escape gunned down. Inevitably, Jews were often singled out; on 18 September, *Leibstandarte* took custody of about 50 Jews who had earlier been rounded up by other German troops and executed them all.[36] Far worse killings lay ahead.

Advance and Exodus

The German columns now moved west from Warsaw towards the eastern flank of Kutrzeba's forces. General Władysław Bortnowski – whose Pomeranian Army, now subordinated to Kutrzeba, had been badly mauled in earlier fighting – proved unable to organise determined resistance. Bortnowski's failure aside – one of his subordinates furiously said, 'If I die, let everyone know that I died because of that son of a bitch'[37] – most Polish units fought bravely, even if overall coordination was lacking. Łowicz, which had been liberated with such jubilation on 12 September, came under heavy German attack just three days later. Janusz Bardziński, a junior officer in a cavalry regiment, held on at the town's bridge over the Bzura to buy time for other units to pull back, and sent a final radio message to higher commands:

> Enemy infantry within range for an assault. I am under mortar and machine-gun fire. Most of the lancers are dead or wounded. I am lightly wounded. Still fulfilling

> my duty, though it is too late for help to arrive. That's all, Colonel. For country and regiment. This is my last message.[38]

With the Luftwaffe now interdicting every attempt to reinforce the units that had crossed the Bzura or that were trying to pull back, the Polish retreat rapidly degenerated into a complete rout. The Italian war correspondent Indro Montanelli was accompanying the German units counterattacking. When he came across the mangled remains of a Polish cavalry unit, with the corpses of men and horses lying entwined, he fancifully imagined how the fighting might have unfolded, inventing a story of repeated charges by lancers on horseback against German armour. The account was picked up first by German newspapers and then elsewhere, giving rise to a completely false legend of how the Poles had attempted to fight against their mechanised enemies.

The Polish counterattack in tatters, the Germans closed in on Warsaw. Inside the city, civilians were already learning to adapt; walls of sandbags had appeared outside public buildings, windows were carefully taped up, trenches dug, and tank traps improvised from torn-up trolley car tracks. Nervous excitement and disbelief simmered amongst a public that had been anticipating war for years. New anti-aircraft batteries had been installed in Warsaw in the late 1930s, and from 1937 the defence ministry organised public air defence courses, which were completed by 150,000 people within a year. A mandatory national reserve system, reserve officer corps, auxiliaries (including women's divisions), paramilitary groups, and shooting clubs proliferated in the lead-up to the war, all of which fuelled an active sense of public duty and patriotic fervour.[39] Of course, the victory of the 'Miracle on the Vistula' – not to mention partition – was still in living memory for plenty of Varsovians, and galvanised their determination to repel another foreign invader. Meanwhile, the Warsaw press continued to paint the Poles' heroic resistance efforts on the border in a glorious light that befitted the nation's historical destiny:

> Vigilant Warsaw! ... how could we [let ourselves be broken], here, when there in Pomerania, in Gdynia … not only do they defend themselves like lions when temporarily cut off from the defences, but are rushing to a victorious attack, they are capturing machine guns, cannon, taking prisoners …
>
> Warsaw made sure that the country's nerves never faltered … We are not frightened by bombing raids. We are not frightened by the echoes of gunfire under the walls. We have known this music for centuries. We have survived and we shall last.[40]

Yet at the same time that the press was encouraging the public to hold fast, the Warsaw government was starting to fear for its security and eyeing an escape. On the night of 4 September, a convoy of limousines and private cars – which were now banned for the general population – slipped east out of the city, carrying President Mościcki's national government towards Lublin and then on to Romania. The exodus took place completely unbeknownst to the Germans, and, until the last moment, the Polish defence ministry. Late on 6 September, Rydz-Śmigly – by now struggling to keep in touch with the field armies – ordered a general withdrawal behind the Vistula. The following day, he and most of the military high command left for Brest, some 120 miles to the east. Colonel Adrian Carton de Wiart, head of the British military mission in Warsaw, joined the convoy as it left Warsaw:

> [We encountered] a slowly moving mass of heart-rending humanity, pushing and pedalling their incongruous forms of transport, clutching their children and their pitiful bundles, and trudging no one knew where.[41]

Retired Lieutenant Colonel Wacław Lipiński, whose brother-in-law was an active colonel in the defence ministry, was awoken in the middle of the night by his panicked sister as she breathlessly related the news. He was horrified by the departure of so many senior figures:

> The evacuation of the government, carried out with such indecent haste, created an atmosphere of panic in Warsaw which has spread like an epidemic. Everyone who holds public office is racing across the Vistula, sped on by a kind of psychosis of fear and terror. I can't understand this, it's beyond my comprehension. Weren't they all, just a few days ago, so heroic and willing to fight and endure? A few bombs, a few explosions, the approach of the Germans has turned these people into a pack of cowards. Are we really worth so little?[42]

Lipiński took it upon himself to help coordinate the government and military leaders that remained in Warsaw. This included General Walerian Czuma, who was handed control of Warsaw defences and for whom Lipiński came out of retirement to serve as propaganda chief. Of course, the evacuation was intended to buy time for the Polish command to regroup, but once the government, military command, and, by mid-month, the Catholic primate of Poland had fled the capital, it fell to those that remained to prevent public panic and bolster morale.

Thousands of Varsovians chose to follow the government out of the city in search of refuge. Able-bodied men – including hundreds of police personnel and firefighters – were ordered to evacuate in the hope that forces could be rallied in the east and prepared for a counterattack.[43] Women, children, and elderly Varsovians watched as the Vistula crossings became snarled with friends, loved ones, and neighbours hurrying to exit the city, leaving behind them a sense of confusion, fear, and despair. Newspaper publisher Aleksander Donat (then known as Michał Berg) said goodbye to his wife, Lena, and his 21-month-old son, Włodek:

> Hundreds of thousands left Warsaw that night. In the pale twilight dawn, a torrent of people with knapsacks headed eastward on foot, bicycles, motorcycles, carts, carriages, automobiles, trucks, and buses. Through the golden shine of the Polish autumn the stream flowed east, or rather crawled. It was our first meeting with war's disorganisation: burning towns, outbreaks of spy and paratroop manias, the despair of unbelievable swift defeat, and the incessant dive-bombing by Nazi Stukas.[44]

Many in the intelligentsia were quick to condemn the government for setting a poor example in choosing to evacuate at a time when 'every industrial labourer, every ordinary citizen of the capital' would rather stand and defend their city.[45] The idea that politicians were leaving to form a government-in-exile was hardly reassuring to the Varsovians left behind, and the evacuation led to Warsaw (unlike Prague, Paris, or Belgrade) being deprived of any intermediary governmental structure with which to deal with German occupiers; Polish civilians were left all the more vulnerable.[46]

THE CITY'S DEFENDERS

One leader who refused to evacuate was Warsaw's mayor, Stefan Starzyński. A former member of Piłsudski's Legions, Starzyński had been appointed by the *Sanacja* regime in 1934, but had earned considerable respect even amongst anti-government critics for his far-reaching financial reforms, urban infrastructure development, and reduction of unemployment. When war broke out, he was serving his second term as mayor and now entered the most pivotal and tragic months of his life. After the government exodus, Lipiński ensured that Starzyński featured frequently on Polish Radio and in the press to keep Varsovians optimistic and engaged. On 7 September, the *Express Poranny* ran an interview with the mayor in which he discussed the sourcing of glass, sorting of debris, and plans to fill in bullet holes as though Warsaw was already preparing to dust herself off from the invasion.[47] This was followed the next day by promises that the prices of vegetables in the city centre were set to drop thanks to supplies from the suburbs, reports that electricity was already being restored in many bomb-stricken districts, and suggestions that access to gas would soon follow.[48] Evidently, the authorities wished to convey the idea that things would soon return to normal to prevent the city spiralling into chaos. But it was becoming hard for Varsovians to shut out the sights and sounds of constant German bombing raids, especially during the long nights of blackout. The poet Maria Dąbrowska described how she sat through the night of 6 September, listening as Polish forces exchanged call signs on the airwaves:

> Night. Complete silence. The silence is terrible. I don't sleep. I keep the radio open all night … At 12 at night I suddenly hear: Blaskota. Blaskota. Bolesław calls to Warsaw. It repeats itself, these words many times, over and over again, lifelessly, menacingly, terribly. Blaskota. Blaskota. Bolesław calls to Warsaw.[49]

As Bryan captured in his film footage, each evening the Germans covered the Warsaw suburbs in fresh incendiary bombs that set the night sky ablaze for hours. Varsovians huddled in their shelters, knowing that their blackout was rendered useless and that the fires around them would rage for hours.

Able-bodied men, police, and other officials poured out of the city and Czuma scrambled to coordinate the city defences while Starzyński continued to do his best to curtail public panic and maintain order. On 8 September, Czuma appointed the mayor as civil commissioner, giving him authority to manage the city's Civil Guard. The Guard was tasked with keeping shops open to ensure the circulation of vital supplies, filling in for the absent police force, guarding state property, and assisting citizens. Starzyński used the press to appeal to the public for support in these efforts, and newspapers duly called upon Varsovians' 'great cohesion and harmony' and 'profound social sense' to help secure their city. Even children had patriotic roles to fill in this narrative:

> Stasio has an innate sense of duty … Daddy, the caretaker of the Czackiego 6 house, has gone to war … Stasio considers himself his replacement. From early morning, he cleans the courtyard, collecting rubbish, sweeping. 'It has to be clean everywhere, like it was in Daddy's time … When Daddy comes back …' A tear turns in the little boy's eye. But he wipes it away quickly … How is it possible to cry? At a time like this? You have to be a man … And he goes back to his work, helps his mother.[50]

It would be naïve to take the press's triumphant tone at face value. The residents of Warsaw were starting to struggle – psychologically, economically, and physically – as the reality of life under siege settled in. Newspapers also reminded civilians not to neglect their personal hygiene – to wash their hands, rinse their mouths, and ventilate their apartments – in order to reduce the risk of infectious diseases. Just over a week after war broke out, General Czuma announced that practically all crimes committed in the area of Warsaw would be processed through military courts, with perpetrators to be 'punished by death by shooting'.[51] Many survivors of this period would proudly recall the 'spontaneous effort' of the population towards the defence of their city, but in other respects Warsaw society fractured, shifted, and transformed in less than a fortnight. Even as Varsovians fled, thousands of refugees arrived from the west, many carrying with them the raw terror of having barely escaped with their lives. One of these refugees was 15-year-old Mary Berg, whose family fled their Łódź home and found themselves drawn into the 'steady flow of humanity toward the capital'. She would soon learn that her neighbours who had instead followed the Polish armies retreating towards Brzeziny 'had been massacred almost to a man by German planes.'[52] Her account reflects the nightmarish devastation that Varsovians had so far been spared:

> When we arrived in Łowicz, the city was one huge conflagration. Burning pieces of wood fell on the heads of the refugees as they forced their way through the streets. Fallen telephone poles barred our path. The sidewalks were cluttered with furniture. Many people were burned in the terrible flames. The odour of scorched human flesh pursued us long after we had left the city …
>
> In Warsaw we found women standing at the doorways of the houses, handing out tea and bread to the refugees who streamed into the capital in unending lines. And as tens of thousands of provincials entered Warsaw in the hope of finding shelter there, thousands of old-time residents of the capital fled to the country.[53]

As Jews, the Berg family would soon number among the Nazis' primary targets for extermination. At the outbreak of war, however, Poles and Jews felt united in their plight as victims of a common enemy. Ghetto historian Emmanuel Ringelblum described an 'easing of tension' between the communities: 'antisemitism disappeared as if at the touch of a magic wand' as the Poles realised that continued antipathy to their Jewish neighbours would mean alignment with their enemy. In Ringelblum's view, the Jew who had long felt himself to be 'a second- or third-class citizen, a pariah to be beaten, kicked, insulted at every turn, eliminated from all office or public position' finally felt accepted as a true citizen of Poland.[54] This would, as Aleksander Donat recalled, be a short-lived idyll, but it is undeniable that Varsovian Jews and Poles saw each other as invaluable allies in those early days of resistance. Jewish newspapers echoed the patriotic calls of their secular counterparts, encouraging readers to throw their weight behind the fight 'for our glorious future, for the freedom of all peoples' and appealing to Jewish congregations to engage in mutual aid initiatives.[55] Rabbis and diverse members of the Jewish community were photographed digging trenches and building barricades alongside their Warsaw neighbours.[56] Władysław Szpilman, a Jewish pianist, found himself working alongside an elderly bearded man wearing a dark kaftan who dug with what Szpilman described as 'biblical fervour'. Szpilman tried in vain to persuade the old man to go home and rest; the man replied with a sob, 'I have a shop,' and continued his labours.[57]

Nevertheless, many Jews still found themselves blocked when they attempted to enlist for military service or take up prominent roles in civic councils and aid committees. One Jewish reservist joined the officers' bureau in Warsaw and left barracks in a company that was 70–80 per cent Jewish; relations between Poles and Jews were 'friendly' to begin with, he recalled, until a non-commissioned officer took over the company and ordered that the Jews be separated and sent on a fruitless search for German paratroopers. When they returned to Warsaw days later, the Jewish troops were disarmed and assigned to labour battalions.[58] Ringelblum attributed this issue to ongoing 'antisemitic tendencies' that had not, indeed, vanished; in many cases, it was an unfortunate hangover from inter-war restrictions on Jewish military school admissions and participation in other civic bodies.[59] It was also yet another symptom of the generalised chaos left in the wake of the leadership exodus that affected the Jewish community as much as it did non-Jewish Poles.

Indeed, the chairman of Warsaw's Jewish community council was amongst those who had fled Warsaw. In the same way that the leadership vacuum drew Lipiński back into public life, it was the Jewish Council's 'overwhelmingly ordinary' deputy chairman who found himself shouldering responsibility for his community. Adam Czerniaków was a 59-year-old engineer, teacher in a vocational school, and dedicated representative in the local Jewish social and political spheres. That he served on the Warsaw city council in the pre-war years – despite mounting antisemitic tensions – testifies to his assimilationist outlook: he was 'too nonobservant for religious orthodoxy', 'too pragmatic to embrace socialism', and too bound to Polish life to lean towards Zionism.[60] On 10 September, Czerniaków recorded in his diary that he had joined the Civil Guard and, just two days later, that a new Jewish Citizens' Committee had been formed. Within the week, the Committee earned Starzyński's formal recognition, though Czerniaków found it noteworthy that Jews were still excluded from the headquarters of the city's Civil Guard.[61] According to Ringelblum, the Committee had negligible impact and lacked popular support, but the Jewish war effort went on regardless; ladies' committees set up refreshment stations for off-duty troops and Jews of all ages helped collect vital medical supplies, beds, and bandages, while Czerniaków himself helped coordinate an impromptu 100-bed hospital.[62]

Ten days into the war, Warsaw was struggling to weather yet more bombing, yet more shortages, and yet more uncertainty. Scenes that would have been unimaginable a month before were now the reality of daily life. Mary Berg recounted her father waiting for hours in line at a bakery for the luxury of bread:

> As he waited there, several German planes suddenly swooped down and strafed the people with machine guns. Instantly the line in front of the bakery dispersed, but one man remained. Disregarding the firing, my father took his place behind him. A moment later the man was hit in the head by a bullet. The entrance to the bakery shop was now free and my father made his purchase.[63]

As Ringelblum noted, 'death from a bomb was preferable to slow death from hunger' – and food was a ubiquitous talking point in the besieged city.[64] The press had begun to praise the qualities of horsemeat, or, as Czerniaków quipped in reference to the famous 18th-century Polish horseman, 'Emir Rzewuski's famous steed'.[65] Meanwhile, more and more Varsovians were displaced from their homes as the unrelenting bombing raids left houses, apartments, and shelters in ruins. Still, they did not yet give up hope that their city would be saved; Szpilman remarked that conditions in the city were deteriorating 'in reverse proportion, you might say, to the increasing courage and determination of its people.'[66]

But despite the general atmosphere of solidarity and camaraderie, Ringelblum saw cracks appearing in Varsovian relations, whether it was the sidelining of Jews in bakery queues, water distribution, or even, as he witnessed, the exclusion of Jews from bomb shelters.[67] Rumours of German paratroopers, spies, and saboteurs were also trickling through the city, adding an extra layer of fear and paranoia to life in packed quarters. Szpilman recalled how an eccentric spinster – who was unfortunate enough to have a German name – refused to retreat to the communal shelter until she had finished her daily music practice; her neighbours concluded that her compulsive piano-playing could only be a means for signalling bombing targets to the Luftwaffe and forcibly shut her up in a cellar.[68]

Above all, the key question remained: when would Poland's allies deal a decisive blow to the German invaders and bring this madness to an end? Many of the city's newspaper publishers had fled the city, but the publications that remained continued to churn out optimistic – and frequently misleading – propaganda: that the British and French were inflicting incredible defeats on an imaginary Western Front, and that the Germans were suffering crippling losses day after day.[69] Even if this messaging succeeded in buoying public morale in the short term, it only 'deepened [the] disappointment later.'[70] With Polish troops pouring back into the capital from the west, it was becoming impossible to suppress news of the German advances.

The cost of the fighting along the Bzura had been heavy. About 18,000–20,000 Polish soldiers were killed and over 30,000 wounded, with the Germans eventually taking 170,000 prisoners as they drove the Poles back to the north. Individually or in small groups, some of Kutrzeba's soldiers managed to slip through the German lines and reached units still fighting further to the east, but most were forced to lay down their arms. Wehrmacht losses had been substantial – 12,000 dead or missing and perhaps 18,000 wounded – but the roads to Warsaw were now clear. At the same time, other German units had advanced from East Prussia and were threatening the Polish capital from the north. Soon, artillery shells as well as bombs began to fall on the city and its ragtag defenders prepared for a renewed German assault. But after their earlier armoured probe, the Germans were in less of a hurry.

By 14 September, Rydz-Śmigly had ordered all Polish troops east of the Vistula to retreat via Lwów to the Romanian bridgehead on the southeastern border. The plan was to regroup and use the swampy terrain to hold off the Germans until the British and the French broke through in the west – as the Poles believed they had been promised. Meanwhile, Brigadier General Thomée, whose operational group was the only one of the Łódź army not to have dissolved in the retreat eastward, led his troops to the Modlin fortress 25 miles northwest of Warsaw and settled in for a final stand. With Polish forces west of the Vistula effectively eliminated and the thrust from East Prussia cutting many of the roads running northeast and east from Warsaw, the capital was effectively isolated. On 16 September, a German officer crossed the front line under a white flag with a demand that the defenders of Warsaw should surrender to avoid pointless bloodshed; the demand was rejected.

Immediately, the Germans resumed air and artillery attacks. Parts of the Royal Castle in the centre of the city were destroyed and much of the ceiling of St John's Cathedral collapsed. Gas, electricity, and water installations were repeatedly hit and fires raged unchecked in many parts of the city. Poland was desperately looking to the west for relief – but attention was already shifting in the east.

CHAPTER 4

A NEW PARTITION

The building is on fire; the flames die back,
And then – look – as they flare up once again
Against the wall I see widows dressed in black
Pushed by armed men –
And now, up on the porch men gather round
And – though I'm blinded by the smoke that's drifting –
I see a thing like a coffin that they're lifting
And ... your piano comes crashing – crashing to the ground!

Cyprian Kamil Norwid, 'Chopin's Grand Piano', 1865
Translated by Bill Johnston[1]

JUSTIFYING AN INVASION

On 2 September, a signal was sent from Moscow to Red Army units on the frontier with Poland, placing all the troops of the Belarusian Military District on a higher level of alert. What might have seemed a logical defensive adjustment during German–Polish tensions was in reality a calculated step towards aggression.

Even as the British and French were declaring war on Germany, Aleksei Alekseyevich Shkvartsev – the new Soviet ambassador in Berlin – was meeting Hitler and Ribbentrop and offering assurances that the Soviet Union would adhere to the non-aggression pact. Both sides knew that such an agreement included abiding by the plan to establish spheres of influence in an area stretching from the Arctic Circle to the Black Sea. After just 21 years, a new partition of Poland was about to take place.

On 4 September, Moscow rejected a request from Poland for the transit of military supplies on the grounds it would risk drawing the Soviet Union into the conflict. Meanwhile, Molotov met with Friedrich Werner Graf von Schulenburg, the German ambassador in Moscow, whom Hitler had tasked with clarifying Soviet intentions now that hostilities had commenced. According to the telegram Schulenburg sent to Berlin, Molotov replied:

> We agree with you that at a suitable time it will be absolutely necessary for us to start concrete action. We are of the view, however, that this time has not yet come. It is possible that we are mistaken, but it seems to us that through excessive haste we might injure our cause and promote unity among our opponents.[2]

When Reinhardt's 4th Panzer Division made its temporary entry into the western suburbs of Warsaw, Molotov sent Schulenburg a telegram congratulating the Germans on their achievement. In actual fact, the speed of this development had blindsided the Soviet high command, and orders were issued urgently for the Red Army to prepare for operations into Poland. On 10 September, Schulenburg sent a further update to Ribbentrop in Berlin:

> In today's conference at 4pm Molotov modified his statement of yesterday by saying that the Soviet Government was taken completely by surprise by the unexpectedly rapid German military successes. In accordance with our first communication, the Red Army had counted on several weeks, which had now shrunk to a few days. The Soviet military authorities were therefore in a difficult situation, since, in view of conditions here, they required possibly two to three weeks more for their preparations. Over three million men were already mobilised.
>
> I explained emphatically to Molotov how crucial speedy action of the Red Army was at this juncture.
>
> Molotov repeated that everything possible was being done to expedite matters …
>
> Then Molotov came to the political side of the matter and stated that the Soviet Government had intended to take the occasion of the further advance of German troops to declare that Poland was falling apart and that it was necessary

> for the Soviet Union, in consequence, to come to the aid of the Ukrainians and the Belarusians 'threatened' by Germany. This argument was to make the intervention of the Soviet Union plausible to the masses and at the same time avoid giving the Soviet Union the appearance of an aggressor.[3]

Discussions between Molotov and Ribbentrop continued on a daily basis, with the former insisting that Soviet military action be framed both domestically and internationally as an intervention to safeguard minorities in Poland – and not as an act of aggression. Therefore, the Red Army would not commence its operations into Poland until Warsaw was either cut off or in German hands – in other words, at a stage when the Polish government could be deemed to have ceased to operate.

There was concern in Berlin about the tone of Soviet statements. The invasion and occupation of eastern Poland by the Red Army was seen both as inevitable and desirable, since it would remove any requirement for German units to advance far to the east to mop up the last elements of the Polish Army; but Moscow's intention to portray this as a move to protect Ukrainian and Belarusian minorities from the dangers of German occupation caused alarm. Ribbentrop suggested an alternative approach; late on 15 September, when the Soviets seemed on the cusp of action, he sent a further telegram to Schulenburg with a suggested joint communiqué:

> In view of the complete collapse of the previous form of government in Poland, the Reich Government and the Government of the USSR consider it necessary to bring to an end the intolerable political and economic conditions existing in these territories. They regard it as their joint duty to restore peace and order in these areas which are naturally of interest to them and to bring about a new order by the creation of natural frontiers and viable economic organisations.[4]

Even Stalin – who had issued statements of breathtaking dishonesty – balked at this, rightly assessing that international and domestic audiences would recognise the flagrant hypocrisy of Germany and the USSR intervening to save Polish territories from chaos that they themselves had inflicted. Instead, Molotov suggested, Moscow would announce that given the collapse of the Polish government, all existing agreements between the USSR and Poland were null and void and that the USSR felt an obligation to protect ethnic Ukrainians and Belarusians – without specifying who was threatening them.

(PRETENCES OF) NEUTRALITY ABANDONED

Early on 17 September, Stalin decided that the moment for intervention had arrived, and the Luftwaffe was requested not to operate over the eastern parts of Poland. Just after 0300, Ambassador Wacław Grzybowski was summoned to Moscow and informed that the Soviets were suspending previous agreements with the Poles since 'Warsaw no longer exists as the capital' and 'the Government no longer shows any signs of life':

> Left to her own devices and bereft of leadership, Poland has become a suitable field for all manner of hazards and surprises, which may constitute a threat to the USSR … the Soviet Government, which hitherto has preserved neutrality, cannot any longer observe a neutral attitude to these facts.
>
> The Soviet Government further cannot view with indifference the fact that the kindred Ukrainian and White Russian people, who live on Polish territory and are at the mercy of fate, are left defenceless.[5]

Grzybowski, with Beck's approval, refused to receive the note. The Poles were outraged by the Soviets' transparent presumptuousness and the ominous implications of their promise to 'extricate the Polish people from the unfortunate war'. The Polish ambassador barely escaped arrest – in part thanks to the intervention of Schulenburg, who had an interest in ensuring German diplomats would be safe from similar reprisals abroad. Forty-five minutes later, Soviet troops began crossing Poland's eastern border.

The Red Army had mobilised two Fronts – or army groups in western parlance. To the north of the Pripyat River was Belarusian Front, commanded by army commander Mikhail Prokofevich Kovalev, consisting of four field armies and a cavalry-mechanised group. To the south was Ukrainian Front, under army commander Semen Konstantinovich Timoshenko, with what effectively amounted to three armies. In total, these forces comprised about 500,000 combatants, backed by nearly 5,000 tanks, a similar number of guns, and between 2,000 and 3,000 aircraft.[6] Using their mobile elements, they were tasked with the capture of Vilnius, Grodno, and Lwów within 48 hours. Any Polish troops they encountered were to be destroyed or forced to surrender, and further attempts by the Poles to withdraw towards the southeast and the Romanian border were to be blocked.

The Polish defence plan had been predicated on the assumption that the Soviets would remain neutral. After mobilisation, somewhere around 12,000 troops had been left to man the 870-mile border with the USSR, organised into 18 battalions of the *Korpus Ochrony Pogranicza* ('Border Defence Corps' or

KOP); the rest of the Polish forces were either heading south towards the Romanian bridgehead, holed up in Warsaw and Modlin, or fighting to escape the Germans further west. The small squads of border guards stood no chance against the sudden Soviet advance. But as was so often the case with Soviet forces – and remains the case in the post-Soviet era – the numerical strength of the Red Army's units was misleading. The purges inflicted on all parts of Soviet society by Stalin had stripped the army of large numbers of senior officers and at almost every level, men were commanding formations one or more steps higher than their rank, training, and experience justified. Spare parts for vehicles were in short supply, and training in the preceding months had been woefully inadequate; the period's pervasive paranoia meant aviation accidents were presumed acts of sabotage until proven otherwise, which severely limited Soviet pilots' flight hours and prevented them from acquiring essential skills. Another historical weakness of the Red Army – inherited from the armies of the tsars – was almost complete neglect of logistic and support services. There was little understanding that modern mechanised warfare demanded precise coordination of fuel, food, and ammunition.

The mobilisation process also proved chaotic. Planning for artillery transport relied on requisitioning tractors from collective farms based on their reported vehicle inventories – numbers which frequently proved to be works of fiction. Officials routinely exaggerated their vehicle counts, both out of fear of the consequences of admitting that vehicles were inoperable due to damage and parts shortages, and as a means of justifying larger fuel supplies that could then be sold on the black market. Uniforms, boots, and even rifles were in short supply; desperate attempts were made to seize items from units that weren't going into Poland with the result that many of the men in the two Fronts were issued with clothing and weapons that were far from new. In many cases, troops received rifles and machine-guns that were different models from those on which they had received (inadequate) training.

Conversely, and despite their numerical disadvantages, the Polish defenders were far from impotent. The border battalions were supported by at least 300,000 Polish troops that had succeeded in withdrawing across the Vistula – though many of these would be needed to hold back the Wehrmacht – and had the benefit of extensive fortifications along the frontier, particularly the *Sarneński Rejon Umocniony* ('Sarny Fortified Area') to the north of Rivne and at Brest. The Poles also had the advantage of fighting in defence of their homeland, while most of the Red Army personnel had little or no idea why they were going to war. But given the pressure already placed upon the Polish Army by the Wehrmacht, the outcome was never in doubt, and the initial reports of Soviet movements caused widespread confusion amongst the Polish command.

When ordered to send an emissary to approaching Soviet units, a *KOP* commander to the southeast of Lwów responded that his men had already destroyed two Soviet tanks, rendering diplomatic contact pointless, and despite repeated demands that he communicate with the Soviet forces, he insisted the continuous air raids prevented him from complying.[7]

Under no illusion that Poland could repel invasion on two fronts, at 0400 Rydz-Śmigły ordered the border units to fall back to join the regrouping forces at the Romanian bridgehead – orders which either never reached many of the eastern commanders or were disregarded. General Orlik-Rückemann rallied his garrison of 4,000 troops in the fortifications near Sarny to push back against the Soviets until the Red Army's superior weaponry and tanks finally forced him to retreat on 20 September. Other units of the *KOP* added local volunteers to their ranks and fought until they were destroyed. But many battalions simply pulled back with little or no attempt to interfere with the Soviet advance; officers followed their orders to withdraw towards Romania, and soldiers of all ranks recognised the futility of confronting mechanised forces without any anti-tank weapons or artillery.

CONFUSION, CONTENTION, AND CUT-OFF

Polish political and military circles were caught off guard by the Soviet action, but the reaction amongst civilians was even more disoriented. A woman in the town of Nowogród, to the northeast of Warsaw, watched columns of tanks, armoured cars, cavalry, and infantry, all heading towards the Polish capital from the east: 'Where was this grey army decorated with stars going? Was it bringing us assistance or final defeat? What was the meaning of all of this?'[8]

For most Poles, confusion quickly turned to alarm and a desire to support or join the ranks of the army – unsurprising, given the long history of Russian occupation and the more recent war with the Bolsheviks. But this was not universal, and some Poles viewed the Soviet advance as a potential bulwark against German aggression. In particular – and although the Soviets had exaggerated their interest in protecting Belarusians and Ukrainians in Poland – it wasn't hard to convince both minorities that the time had come to eradicate these 'enemies of the people', to loot their property, and to fill ensuing power vacuums with Communist committees. Armed members of the *Komunistyczna Partia Zachodniej Białorusi* ('Communist Party of Western Belarus' or *KPZB*) attacked Polish troops in the northeast, while in eastern Galicia members of the Ukrainian *OUN* robbed and killed civilians in the wake of the Polish retreat; members of both groups turned out in the streets, donning red armbands to greet the advancing Soviets with cheers and banners. Hot on the heels of the advancing Red Army came the notorious *NKVD*, which, with the help of local minorities with grudges to settle, wasted no time in rounding up Polish nationalists and fighters. Of particular interest to the *NKVD* was the elimination of the 40,000 *Osadnicy* – Polish military veterans who had settled in the Kresy borderland region in the aftermath of the Polish–Bolshevik War.

Polish troops often responded violently and executed suspect minority resistance groups upon capture, fuelling ethnic tensions that – predictably – expanded to target Jewish communities as well. In the town of Wołkowyska, for example, six Jewish merchants were shot for unspecified hostility towards Poles. Many who attempted to establish friendly relations with the Soviet troops fared little better. When the mayor of Złoczów – to the east of Lwów – made a traditional offering of bread and salt to the commander of a Soviet cavalry unit, the officer responded by kicking him mercilessly and ordering his arrest. He was executed a short while later.[9]

It hardly helped the Polish public that the press remained conspicuously quiet regarding the Soviet invasion. The triumphalist narrative continued unabated, and on 19 September, the *Express Poranny* cited 'German sources' to declare that 'the collapse of the German front in Poland is closer than it might seem'.[10] Days later, the *Kurjer Warszawski* quoted both the French and Swiss press discussing the impossibility of combined Soviet and German military action, even going so far as to suggest that Germany would 'not be able to resist Soviet blackmail' over eastern Polish territories and would 'ultimately be forced to pull the proverbial hot chestnuts out of the fire for Russia.'[11] There was no suggestion whatsoever that the Red Army was already on Polish soil; nor that, by the evening of 17 September, Rydz-Śmigły had issued the order for military forces and remaining government personnel to evacuate to Hungary and Romania and that, by the following dawn, Poland's commander-in-chief himself had crossed the border. This was the man Piłsudski had once described as being amongst the best Polish generals 'in terms of strength of character and will', yet he had – prophetically – doubted his ability 'in the scope of the work of the Commander-in-Chief and his ability to measure not only the military forces, but also those of his own and the enemy's entire state.'[12]

Behind Rydz-Śmigły went President Ignacy Mościcki, Prime Minister Felicjan Składkowski, and Foreign Minister Beck, followed by thousands of Polish troops and virtually all that was left of the Polish air force. The plan was to use Romania's ties with the French to arrange transfer to Paris where the Poles would establish a government-in-exile. To the rear of those escaping across the frontier, fighting raged on in what is now southeast Poland. The remains of several Polish armies fought a desperate battle around Tomaszów Lubelski, between Lublin and Lwów. Some Polish troops managed to slip past the German units and escaped to the south, but most were forced to surrender. Within two days the Red Army had swept down to Stanisławów at the southeastern tip of Poland, closing the Romanian bridgehead off for good.

A NATION FORSAKEN

Like many who fled Warsaw as the Germans approached, the writer Zofia Nałkowska wandered aimlessly, one by one discarding the possessions she had taken with her and attaching herself to a small group that gained and lost members as the days dragged by. Despite her Bolshevik sympathies, she was shocked by the news that the Red Army had entered Poland, and even more horrified that the government and much of the army was trying to escape to Romania:

> O shame, O sorrow! When the whole country is full of bewildered, hungry people pointlessly set in motion, wandering to and fro, with volunteers whom no one is willing to enlist, soldiers abandoned by their commanders and discarding their weapons by the roadsides. When defeat has been unavenged for countless years, when lives are destroyed and ruins and destruction are everywhere. What madness! These tragic masses had been lulled to a deceptive slumber by false reassurances, not warned about anything, deprived of everything, told lies for months on end by the radio and newspapers and now these same heads of state are safe and sound abroad.[13]

Evidence that the Polish population had been badly misled was growing, she noted, but it was hard to challenge the dominant patriotic narrative. 'A person of sober judgement,' she recorded glumly, 'at the very least someone who is reasonable, is immediately considered to be a bad Pole.'[14] With no safe destination available, she and many others decided to retrace their steps to Warsaw.

If the French and British reaction to the German invasion fell short of Poland's expectations, their reaction to the Soviet invasion was even more exasperating. The Polish command immediately notified the Western Allies of the Soviet's contravention of non-aggression agreements, reminding them that 'The Polish government reserve the right to call upon their Allies in regard to the obligations devolving upon them by virtue of the treaties in force'.[15] The French government was, at first, willing to lodge a formal protest against the Soviet incursion, but the British were more cautious. Secretary of State for Foreign Affairs Halifax pointed out that military support for the Poles had only been agreed for cases of German aggression. Perhaps more tellingly, the British were interested in preserving economic ties with the Soviet Union, and even convinced that 'German-Soviet close contact … should lead to a desirable friction' that would put Hitler at a disadvantage.[16] This resulted in pronouncements that were at best vague, and at worst outright insulting to the Poles. In lieu of a formal protest, Prime Minister Chamberlain made a statement that although the intervention '[could] not be justified by the arguments put forward by the Soviet Government', it 'was still too early to pronounce any final verdict on the motives or consequences of the Russian action'; David Lloyd George went further, commending the Soviets for 'liberating their kinsmen from the Polish yoke.'[17] In the end, the British left it to France to approach Moscow, but no commitments were made to aid the Poles. That neither country was willing to equate the Soviet invasion with German aggression signified that they felt relations with Poland came second to those with the USSR.

Meanwhile, the Poles had been granted a few days of breathing space thanks to the dispersal of German troops across the eastern territories, from Białystok in the north down to Lwów. Until the Germans could hand these territories over to the Soviets – as agreed in the Molotov–Ribbentrop Pact – it was up to Küchler's Third Army to cover the entire Warsaw and Modlin area. Around 35,000 Poles were still holding the Modlin fortress and, thanks to intact rail links to the capital, foiling German efforts to encircle Warsaw. These lines of communication were eventually severed on 22 September, but the Modlin forces would fiercely fight on for another week. The Germans to the west of the city and those east of the Vistula were finally starting to tighten the noose on Warsaw, although they were forced to delay further while waiting for artillery reinforcements. Taking into account those who had managed to escape the Battle of Bzura, the Poles mustered around 140,000 troops to defend the capital against the 13 divisions and 920 artillery pieces the Germans were preparing for their assault. Amongst the defenders were the last remnants of the Poznań Army, including two regiments of Uhlans who abandoned their horses and infiltrated through on foot. One of those who made their way from the Bzura battlefields to Warsaw was Kutrzeba, and on reaching the city on 20 September, the first words he said to General Juliusz Rómmel, commander of all Polish forces in Warsaw, were 'I have lost a battle.'[18] He was greeted with sympathy and understanding and became Rómmel's deputy.

THE SIEGE OF WARSAW

While ground forces were regrouping, the Germans continued their onslaught of air and artillery attacks against the capital. The Germans to the east of the city were within artillery range of all bridges across the Vistula, which made communications with the Polish forces across the river in Praga extremely difficult. Probing attacks on the suburbs of Zacisze and Praga didn't amount to much, though on 22 September, Hitler arrived at Third Army headquarters to watch the bombardment of the city from a church tower.[19] In addition to the Royal Castle – outside of which still flew the flag of the evacuated President of Poland – the Germans shelled Warsaw's main waterworks, and civilians resorted to using sand to attempt to control the fires raging across the city.[20] Szpilman, convinced that he was more use to his city as a musician than as a trench-digger, described his journey to work:

> It was more and more difficult for me to reach the broadcasting centre. Corpses of people and horses killed by shrapnel lay about the streets, whole areas of the city were in flames, and now that the municipal waterworks had been damaged by artillery and bombs no attempt could be made to extinguish the fires. Playing in the studio was dangerous too. The German artillery was shelling all the most important places in the city, and as soon as a broadcaster began announcing a programme German batteries opened fire on the broadcasting centre.[21]

Poor weather on 22 and 23 September interrupted the German barrage, though hardly enough to bring Varsovians any significant relief. Yet even enduring days confined to suffocating bomb shelters, gambling for their survival day after day, and fully aware that their military leaders and government had deserted them, the people of Warsaw remained doggedly determined. As Mary Berg recorded, despite everything, public sentiment was not defeatist:

> I shall never forget September 23, the date of the Day of Atonement in 1939. The Germans deliberately chose that sacred Jewish holiday for an intensive bombardment of the Jewish district. In the midst of this bombardment a strange meteorological phenomenon took place: heavy snow mixed with hail began to fall in the middle of a bright, sunny day. For a while the bombing was interrupted, and the Jews interpreted the snow as a special act of heavenly intervention … But later in the day the enemy made up for lost time with renewed fury …
>
> That night hundreds of buildings blazed all over the city. Thousands of people were buried alive in the ruins. But ten hours of murderous shelling could not

> break the resistance of Warsaw. Our people fought with increased stubbornness; even after the government had fled and Marshal Rydz-Śmigly had abandoned his troops, men and women, young and old, helped in the defence of the capital.[22]

On the same day, Szpilman completed his final recital on Warsaw Radio, and, by chance, crossed paths with the mayor of Warsaw. It is hard not to feel for Starzyński, whose utter exhaustion was at complete odds with the optimistic sentiment he was trying so hard to sustain amongst the public:

> I have no idea myself how I reached the broadcasting centre that day … I met Mayor Starzyński at the door … He was dishevelled and unshaven, and his face wore an expression of deathly weariness. He hadn't slept for days. He was the heart and soul of the defence, the real hero of the city. The entire responsibility for the fate of Warsaw rested on his shoulders. He was everywhere: he went along the trenches, he was in charge of the building of barricades, the organisation of hospitals, the fair distribution of what little food there was, the air-raid defences, the fire services, and still he found time to address the population daily. Everyone waited eagerly for his speeches and drew courage from them: there was no reason for anyone to lose heart as long as the mayor had no doubts. Anyway, the situation did not seem too bad. The French had broken through the Siegfried Line, Hamburg had been badly bombed by the British air force and the British army might land in Germany any moment now. Or so we thought.[23]

That evening, the city's loudspeakers, which had delivered the mayor's daily speeches since the war began, fell silent. A recording of Rachmaninov's Piano Concerto in C minor was being broadcast when a German bomb hit the city power station. It was a day of the heaviest shelling to date, and a Polish officer described what he saw as he crossed the city:

> The Teatralny Plac is covered with ruins. At the Town Hall, Vice-Mayor Okolo-Kulak was killed yesterday, but Mayor Starzyński is still administrating from there. The building of the Ministry for Foreign Affairs is burning – they may be able to save it. Flames are coming from the windows of the Kronenburg Palace and in the Art Gallery they are brushing out the cinders of pictures. When we passed the Museum of Industry and Agriculture on Krakowski Przedmieści it was burning … German fire is consuming Polish art and science. At last the major stopped on the corner of Traugut and Czacki Streets. It was not possible to drive further. So many burning beams on the road, so much broken glass, so dark from the smoke that we had to go back … [On foot,] I started an impressive wandering

> through bombed Warsaw. Although it is 10am it is dark from the smoke which hurts one's throat and eyes. One must go round the burning fronts of beautiful shops on the left side of Mazowiecka Street because the heat is too great, and one can't walk on the other side because shrapnel is falling and fragments are flying. I try Jasna Street … but [it] is burning too …
>
> Along Jerozolimska [Jerusalem] Avenue, which is so widely open from the east to the west, the whine of shells is louder than anywhere else.[24]

Several ground attacks took place on 23 and 24 September. Many were repulsed, but elsewhere the Germans seized more parts of the city. A suburb in northeast Warsaw had been captured by the Wehrmacht a few days earlier; Michalina Mazińska, in testimony given after the war, described her experience of the new occupation:

> When the Germans noticed that the [Polish] forces were small, they surged forward and killed or wounded those soldiers who didn't manage to flee. One heavily wounded soldier burst into a house, but the Germans set it on fire and he burned alive.
>
> I was in my flat with my husband and child … and my husband was taken away for execution. My child was crying desperately for its father, and I looked through the window. The Germans got three men, ordered them to put their hands up and executed them by shooting … I went to the basement. As I was going downstairs, I heard the last words of my husband, who said, 'Jesus, Mary, deliver my soul!' Germans yelling, a crack, and a blood-curdling moan. The last moans of the other executed people were also clearly audible …
>
> [A week later] I crawled towards my husband and buried him in the garden … Eighty men were executed then in that district.[25]

Acts of violence against innocent civilians occur in every war and frequently stem from combatants' struggles with the severe pressures of life-or-death situations. But the attacks on Polish civilians both in Warsaw and in other cities were more than the actions of a minority of men dealing with acute stress. A witness named Śliwiński described killings near a school in Targówek; Ješefa Biernacka witnessed the executions of Poles and Jews outside her house; Halina Dziugieł described 'numerous executions' near another school; a man named Szaczykowski recalled that 'one could hear machine-gun shots every morning' as Polish people were executed; Teresa Tyk said that a man was shot for refusing to work for the Germans, and that 'execution salvoes rang out non-stop'; Antonina Miklaszewska remembered that there were so many executions at the school in Targówek, both during the battle for the city and in the weeks that followed, that the Germans dug a huge pit to dispose of the corpses. In some cases, the victims were accused of having hidden weapons. Others were shot for failing to hand over works of art to the Germans. Jews were often killed purely because they were Jews. But countless individuals were shot for no obvious reason at all. The sheer number of such accounts shows the scale of the killing and still leaves thousands more tragedies untold.[26]

Evidently frustrated by the Poles' tenacity, the Germans resorted to dropping leaflets on the city threatening that poison gas would be used if the defenders didn't surrender. The leaflets were ignored, but considering the shortage of available gas masks, there was quiet relief when the attacks failed to materialise. By dawn on 25 September, Göring had ordered the delayed Operation *Wasserkante* to proceed against the capital city. Generalmajor Wolfram von Richthofen – who had been instrumental in the bombing of Guernica during the Spanish Civil War and bombardments elsewhere in Poland – stepped up air raids over the city once again, using his 400 available aircraft to drop around 480 tons of high explosives and 70 tons of incendiaries.[27] In addition to striking defensive positions, German planes attacked power plants, gas works, and targets that had no real military value – the Royal Castle, the parliament buildings, the Cathedral of St John, and the Warsaw Concert Hall were all hit repeatedly. Following weeks of bombardment, Polish anti-aircraft batteries were critically low on ammunition and downed just three aircraft across the entire day, while civilians struggled to find shelter in what remained of their city:

> The dreadful days of 25 and 26 September came. The noise of explosions merged with the constant thunder of guns, penetrated by the boom of nose-diving aircraft like electric drills boring holes in iron. The air was heavy with smoke and the dust of crumbling bricks and plaster. It got everywhere, stifling people who had shut themselves up in cellars or their flats, keeping as far as possible from the street.[28]

The smoke that engulfed the city was so dense that German gunners had difficulty finding their targets. Polish forces fared surprisingly well in repelling German attacks in the suburbs – urban warfare is a great leveller, allowing relatively weak forces to hold off far stronger enemies – but Varsovians were powerless to quell the inferno raging in the city they were fighting so hard to defend. They could do little more than hope that fate would spare them from senseless death for another day:

> From eight to six pm, that is, for ten hours, [which seemed like] ten centuries, you could hear only the whir of engines, the whistle of falling bombs – that maddening, murderous, piercing whine, as if the highest note had suddenly leapt off the scale. And then the blast. You felt relief after the blast. Even though it meant that a

> building had been turned into rubble and that several hundred people had been killed, you then relaxed.
>
> We are still alive. Our turn had not come yet.
>
> A new dawn comes and you wait again. Life's a gamble. Hit or miss. Life or death.[29]

The day that would be remembered as 'Black Monday' amongst the Poles claimed somewhere between 6,000 to 10,000 of the 25,000 Varsovians killed during the entire siege of Warsaw.[30]

The Germans unleashed their ground assault in earnest on 26 September. Fierce fighting erupted in the western district of Wola and the southern district of Mokotów, where the Germans couldn't deploy artillery in close support, and the Polish defenders inflicted significant losses in vicious street battles. Nevertheless, the Germans had the upper hand in numbers and ammunition, and the Poles were inevitably driven back. Sensing the end was drawing near, Rómmel called an emergency meeting of the defence council; commanders agreed that, despite the Army of Warsaw's heroic efforts, it now was only a matter of days until the city fell. With around 10 per cent of the city already razed in the bombing and at least 16,000 soldiers lost, 20,000 dead, and tens of thousands more wounded, it was hard to justify the costs that further resistance would demand of the city's population.[31] Water, bread, and gas supplies were all but exhausted, and the hospitals that were still functional couldn't cope with the volume of casualties. That afternoon, Rómmel sent a request to the Germans for a 24-hour ceasefire to open talks for surrender.

THE FIRST CAPITULATION

At 1300 on 28 September, Kutrzeba arrived at the wrecked Skoda plant in Rakowiec to officially sign the surrender. Their supplies and ammunition virtually exhausted, Thomée's forces in Modlin fortress capitulated shortly afterwards, though not before the SS claimed 50 more Polish lives in a flagrant violation of the ceasefire. Electricity blackouts across the city had quietened the Warsaw press for several days, and in the absence of radio or newspaper updates it was difficult for civilians to ascertain what was going on. As the guns and bombs fell silent and they cautiously crept out of their shelters, Varsovians were confronted by both the hellscape of their ruined city and what it signified for their fate:

> How weird! No whine of falling bombs. No crack of bursting bombs. No swish of shrapnel. Just corpses, corpses, corpses everywhere …

> Rotting and stinking human and equine corpses lying unburied for three weeks. Crows had left them untouched because they too had abandoned this city doomed to annihilation … Over the streets, buildings, and ruins of this once beautiful city there now reigned a single, all-powerful ruler – Death.
>
> She was lurking in the unexploded shells. She was ready to suddenly fall down on you in the form of a brick. Or bury you under a collapsing wall.
>
> You knew this was Her kingdom. Oh, you knew it!
>
> Dante … if he were alive, even he would be unable to render or depict these thousands of corpses – of people, horses, and buildings lying motionless, naked, uncovered, and terrifying in their mute accusation. They all seem to be imploring the Earth and sky with one and the same question:
>
> Why? In the name of what? By what right?[32]

After everything the Varsovians had suffered through and survived, the news of capitulation was devastating. For the city that had celebrated its patriotic resistance, its solidarity, and its unswerving courage, surrender had seemed out of the question, especially to an enemy that – they had been reassured – was itself on the verge of defeat. Yet history had repeated itself, and the citizens of Warsaw found themselves controlled by a foreign nation once more:

> It was the terrifying silence that precedes a great calamity, but I could not imagine anything worse than what we had already been through. Suddenly someone rushed into the cellar with the news that Warsaw had capitulated. No one stirred, but I noticed tears in the eyes of the grownups. I, too, felt them choking in my throat, but my eyes were dry. So all our sacrifices had been in vain. Twenty-seven days after the outbreak of the war, Warsaw, which had held out longer than any other city in Poland, had been forced to surrender.[33]

Mary Berg was not alone in her hopelessness. Socialite Halina Regulska captured the public's despair when she wrote in her diary, 'Could it be that our struggle and suffering had yielded such meagre results? Was it all unnecessary?'[34] Few people understood the Varsovians' sacrifices better than Stefan Starzyński. The week before capitulation, the mayor had sought to rally the city in a moving radio speech that paid homage to the city's unique fate:

> I wanted Warsaw to be great. I believed it would be great. My colleagues and I made plans, drafted the great future of Warsaw. And Warsaw is great. It happened sooner than we thought. Not in fifty years, not in a hundred, but today I see that Warsaw is great.

> Speaking to you now, I see her through the windows in all her greatness and glory, surrounded by clouds of smoke, flames of fire, the wonderful, indestructible, mighty, fighting Warsaw. And although wonderful orphanages have now been replaced by rubble, although barricades covered with corpses have now replaced parks, although our libraries and hospitals are burning – Warsaw is defending its honour at the pinnacle of greatness and glory today, not in fifty years, not in a hundred years.[35]

Starzyński's words were more pertinent than he perhaps realised. Warsaw had set itself on a new historical trajectory distinct from the rest of Poland and its absent government. The city would become an emblem of the continued fight, suffering, and struggle for survival against enemy occupation, and the heart of Polish resistance – and its mayor would go down in history as one of its heroes. Shortly before the surrender, a plane landed in Mokotów bearing orders from Rydz-Śmigły to the Warsaw command, and the pilot offered to evacuate Starzyński to join the exiled government in Romania. Just as he had three weeks earlier, the mayor refused. On 28 September, Starzyński announced the surrender via the *Gazeta Wspólna* ('United Gazette') and conveyed his heartfelt gratitude for the 'boundless heroism and willingness to sacrifice' shown by his fellow Varsovians and their support for his policies 'in spite of these difficult conditions.' Even the absent President Mościcki acknowledged that in holding out long after other regions had fallen, Warsaw had 'saved the honour of Poland'. Both Starzyński and Mościcki vowed that the Varsovian resistance would be 'judged rightly by history', just as Poles now had to look to 'the memory of the heroism of the past Polish generations' for inspiration.[36] This was cold comfort for a population that had fought so hard and lost so much in a matter of weeks.

Fall Weiss claimed the lives of around 66,300 Polish troops and at least 150,000 civilians; about 140,000 Polish troops surrendered at the end of September, and more than 660,000 ended the month as German or Soviet prisoners. The Polish military forces had been decisively neutralised, despite the Polish government technically not having surrendered to the Germans.[37] The exiled leaders set about regrouping in Paris, where Marshal of the Senate Władysław Raczkiewicz replaced Mościcki as President of the Republic and Władysław Sikorski became prime minister. With no formal capitulation, the remaining Polish forces were still recognised under international law as combatants entitled to all the protections of the Geneva Convention; of course, the Germans demonstrated their disregard for any such obligations long before the fighting was over.

The capitulation agreement stipulated that Poles were not to destroy any working military equipment on surrender – not that this stopped many Polish commanders from ordering the destruction or dumping of weapons to prevent them falling into German hands. One regiment threw machine-gun bolts and breech blocks from field guns into the Vistula and many others found hiding places for equipment that would prove invaluable for the resistance.[38] In terms of personnel, officers were to be held in prisoner-of-war camps, while soldiers and NCOs would be released within a few days. Large numbers were forcibly taken to Germany and required to work in factories and farms – with so many German males in uniform, it was impossible for German industry and agriculture to function without such measures. Though some soldiers were permitted to return to their homes in keeping with the surrender agreement, others – and thousands of civilians, especially Jews – faced a much darker future.

The 'Conquering Caesar'

The dust of the siege settled, fires burned out, and Polish uniforms were replaced by those of the Wehrmacht in the streets of Warsaw. German photographer Hugo Jaeger travelled through Poland during the invasion and after the capitulation, capturing snapshots of a country ravaged by war and coming to terms with its strange new reality: burnt-out tanks littering the streets of Warsaw; refugees on bicycles, horses, and farm trucks; and countless graves where Varsovians were left with no option but to bury their dead in the city streets and parks. Juxtaposed against this were the images of Hitler's military parade of 5 October: German troops lining the ruined streets, Nazi flags adorning every lamppost, and the Führer himself saluting the triumphant procession from a platform in Łazienki Park. The Nazis took a number of political hostages in order to guarantee Hitler's safety for the event, including Mayor Starzyński and Janusz Regulski, commander of the *Główna Straż Obywatelska* ('Citizen's Militia' or *SO*). Adam Czerniaków – whom Starzyński had formally appointed Chairman of the Jewish Community before capitulation – also volunteered himself as a hostage but was rejected by the Germans. The ten-year-old son of Starzyński's deputy Julian Kulski watched in astonishment as the foreign invaders claimed his home city for themselves:

> Rolling in perfect formation, row upon row of gleaming tanks were moving down Ujazdowskie Avenue, with black-uniformed troops standing at attention in the open hatches …

> Then came the artillery, followed by goose-stepping, steel-helmeted troops in rows of twelve. I marvelled at how they raised their legs with such perfect precision. The march-past of the magnificent robots continued beneath the long sinuous red flags that were suspended from the light standards on both sides of the boulevard. In the centre of each flag was a white circle with a twisted black cross. Its sense of jagged movement carried with it an inexplicable feeling of fear and foreboding.
>
> The band played on as the last rows passed Belweder Palace, once the home of Marshal Piłsudski. Then I remembered the military parade on Piłsudski Square on the Third of May, 1938 – a glorious parade of different tanks, different colours, and different men.
>
> This was a parade of Germans for Germans. It was not for us. Here in the heart of Warsaw … the pulsating drums of an ancient enemy reached a dreadful crescendo before receding in the autumn dusk.[39]

For Hitler, the parade was long overdue. The Führer had been 'burning to enter [Warsaw] like a conquering Caesar' for days and had planned his first major speech since the beginning of the war for the occasion. The Poles' refusal to surrender earlier had sent him into a 'terrible rage' and forced him to speak in Danzig instead – further fuel for his very particular hatred for the Poles and especially their capital.[40] In Berlin, American journalist William Shirer watched the September invasion with a mixture of incredulity at the Germans' vehemence towards the Poles and astonishment towards the Allies' inaction:

> The [German] maid came in tonight to say how terrible war was.
>
> 'Why do the French make war on us?' she asked.
>
> 'Why do you make war on the Poles?' I said.
>
> 'Hum,' she said, a blank over her face. 'But the French, they're human beings,' she said finally.
>
> 'But the Poles, maybe they're human beings,' I said.
>
> 'Hum,' she said, blank again.[41]

For the Poles, it was impossible to ignore the echoes of history: partition was nothing new, and nor was the sense of having been abandoned by the Western Powers. If the antipathy of the Germans towards Poland was to be expected, the level of apparent apathy displayed by the Allies was not. It is a sad irony that Shirer, hundreds of miles away from Warsaw, expressed what Polish propaganda had prevented the public from understanding until it was too late:

Apparently the war in Poland is all but over. Most of the correspondents a bit depressed. Britain and France have done nothing on the western front to relieve the tremendous pressure on Poland. It begins to look as though in Hitler we have a new Napoleon who may sweep Europe and conquer it.

… after the Anglo-French declaration of a state of war the average German is beginning to wonder if it's a world war after all.[42]

CHAPTER 5

INTELLIGENZAKTION

Those dying here, the lonely
forgotten by the world,
our tongue becomes for them
the language of an ancient planet.
Until, when all is legend
and many years have passed,
on a great Campo dei Fiori
rage will kindle at a poet's word.

Czesław Miłosz, 'Campo dei Fiori', 1943[1]

MEANS TO AN END

Poland's September ordeal, devastating as it was, turned out to be only a prelude to full-scale German brutality. Hitler had made clear his full intentions during a final briefing on the invasion – as General Franz Halder, chief of the German general staff, recorded in his diary:

> Goal: annihilation of Poland, that is, destruction of active power. We are not setting out just to reach a specific line or establish a new frontier, but rather we seek the annihilation of the enemy, which we must pursue in ever new ways …
>
> Means to this end: it does not matter what they are. *The victor is never called upon to vindicate his actions. The question is not one of the justice of our cause, but exclusively of achieving victory* [emphasis in original] …

> Execution: harsh and remorseless. We must steel ourselves against humanitarian reasoning![2]

Beyond permitting – indeed, encouraging – extreme violence on the part of the Wehrmacht, Hitler tasked specialised units with the pre-emptive crushing of resistance. During the annexations of Austria and Czechoslovakia, *Sicherheitsdienst* ('Security Service' or *SD*, the security service of the SS) and *Einsatzgruppen* ('task forces', paramilitary death squads of the SS) units had arrested 21,000 Austrians and 10,000 Czechs respectively; both operations had also been beset by disciplinary problems around German personnel looting personal valuables, prompting Heydrich to issue repeated threats of merciless punishment.[3] Most of those detained were released within a few months, but a significant proportion – especially Jews and political opponents – were interned in the growing concentration camp system.

The task assigned to Heydrich's *Einsatzgruppen* for the invasion of Poland was far larger. Their mission extended beyond the quelling of immediate resistance to the active advancement of Hitler's plan to eradicate Poland altogether – starting with the removal of the nation's social and cultural figureheads. Thus the Polish intelligentsia – teachers, business figures, aristocrats, and clergy – were all targets. The scale of the plan – codenamed *Tannenberg* – was enormous; in 1937, a Gestapo department had started compiling a list of people to be detained under the title of *Sonderfahnungsbuch Polen* ('Special Prosecutions Book Poland'), and by the beginning of the war it included the names and addresses of 61,000 targets. Five *Einsatzgruppen* – later increased to seven – would deploy in Poland, and in recognition of past indiscipline, their orders included strict warnings that sexual relations with non-German women would be punished severely.

Heydrich had been personally selected to lead the *SD* by Reichsführer Heinrich Himmler, head of the SS; the slim, blond, urbane figure was almost the epitome of Himmler's vision of the perfect Nazi. What he lacked in knowledge – he had only minimal experience of intelligence work in the German Navy in the 1920s, and largely bluffed his way through the recruitment process thanks to his knowledge of cheap detective novels – he made up for with determination. He tended to be cautious when it came to leaving incriminating evidence, and so his written orders for the *Einsatzgruppen* urged strict discipline with avoidance of excessive violence and mistreatment; yet in person, Heydrich assured his subordinates on the outset of the invasion that in their mission to 'liquidate' thousands of Polish intelligentsia, 'anything is permissible'.[4] However confident he might have been in ultimate victory for Germany, his actions show that he knew his instructions were questionable at best, and illegal at worst – but like

Himmler he ensured that those he recruited were loyal both to him personally and to the Nazi regime.

The elimination of the Polish intelligentsia under *Tannenberg* was intended to be completed by the end of October 1939.[5] But for all the successes of *Fall Weiss*, not everything went to plan. Polish defence efforts – and especially the Varsovians' defiance – had extended the campaign at least two weeks longer than anticipated. Goebbels' propaganda machine would portray the war as a swift victory achieved by the Wehrmacht against an enemy inferior in technology, tactics, and humanity, but the Germans still lost about 48,000 men killed or wounded. Despite operating immediately behind the front line, the *Einsatzgruppen* were running behind schedule.

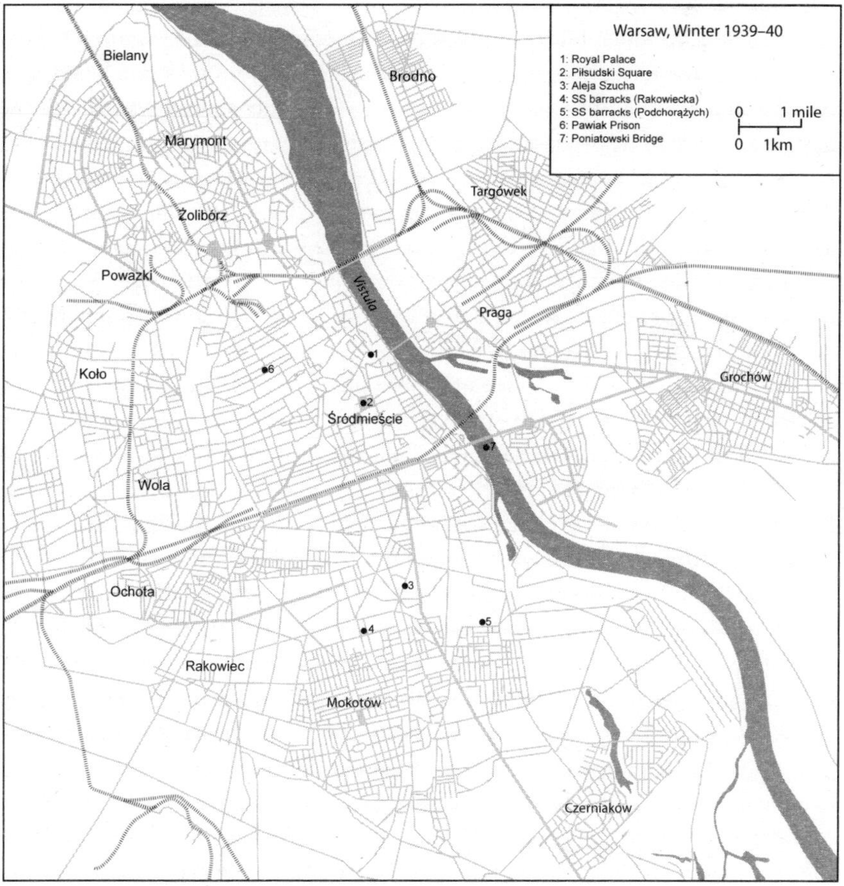

EXPANDING ATROCITY

Heydrich was actively scaling operations before the conflict was a week old. After the Polish repression of *Volksdeutsche* in Bydgoszcz on 3 September resulted in at least 150 ethnic Germans being killed, Himmler immediately approved Heydrich's request to deploy an additional *Einsatzgruppe* under the command of Obergruppenführer Udo von Woyrsch. Woyrsch had been heavily involved in Hitler's purge of the *Sturmabteilungen* ('Assault Squads' or *SA*, the brown-shirted paramilitiaries responsible for much of Germany's political violence) on the Night of the Long Knives in June 1934 and had used the occasion to execute a rival in the SS contrary to orders. Aided by hastily organised groups of *Volksdeutsche*, Woyrsch's men slaughtered hundreds of Poles, particularly Jews; in Dynów, Jews were herded into the synagogue which was then set ablaze.

The degree to which Hitler's orders about the complete annihilation of Poland were passed down the chain of command varied. Numerous commanders balked at the brutality of the SS, but those at lower ranks who were obsessed with the threat of partisan resistance largely approved of anti-Polish 'reprisals'. On 20 September, Generaloberst Gerd von Rundstedt complained that the SS preoccupation with slaughtering civilians over fighting the Polish Army was damaging morale amongst his men. Aware that he was responsible for all actions of German military forces under his command, he ordered that Woyrsch's *Einsatzgruppe* was forbidden from operating in his sector. Almost immediately, this order was countermanded by Berlin.

The Germans rounded up tens of thousands of Poles in a matter of weeks, guided by – but not restricted to – the names compiled in the *Sonderfahndungsbuch Polen*. Those that weren't immediately shot faced brutal interrogation – which frequently ended in death – and deportation to concentration camps across the Reich. As the activities of the *Einsatzgruppen* became more systematic, friction with the Wehrmacht increased – though more out of fear of legal liability than from any moral qualms. On 19 September, for instance, when the army's quartermaster-general Oberst Eduard Wagner met with Heydrich, no objections were raised against Heydrich's general intention to 'deal with' Poland's Jews, clergy, and aristocracy; Wagner's only concern was that the army avoid blame for the crimes. Heydrich conceded that *Einsatzgruppen* activity would be curbed until the end of military administration in the newly conquered territories, and a little later, reluctantly agreed to withdraw Woyrsch's *Einsatzgruppe*, which had attracted particularly heavy criticism.[6] But any hope that this would restrict the activities of the SS relied on Heydrich following both the letter and the spirit of the agreement. Instead, he ordered his men to overburden the military administration with so many prisoners and demands for assistance that they would have little option but to allow the *Einsatzgruppen* to operate without hindrance.

The fall of Warsaw led to renewed protests from field commanders on the conduct of the *Einsatzgruppen*. Eventually, Generaloberst Johannes Blaskowitz – who had led the German Eighth Army during the invasion and was then appointed as commander-in-chief of German forces in Poland as the fighting died down – wrote a report describing the conduct of the SS as 'criminal atrocities, maltreatment, and plundering' by personnel who displayed 'animal and pathological instincts'. He also had several SS officers and men placed under arrest, with some even sentenced to death.[7] When he saw Blaskowitz's memorandum, Hitler angrily rejected what he described as the 'maudlin sentimentality' of old-school army officers, declared an immediate amnesty for all SS and military personnel charged with war crimes in Poland, and removed the SS from the jurisdiction of army courts.

However forcefully Rundstedt, Blaskowitz, and others denounced the actions of the *Einsatzgruppen*, the Wehrmacht's own record was far from spotless. Poland was held under military administration until the end of 25 October, during which time it has been estimated the Wehrmacht was directly involved in up to 60 per cent of atrocities, including the razing of 531 towns and villages, at least 700 organised executions, and the murder of at least 16,300 civilians, most of whom were Polish Christians.[8] To attribute this violence to a generalised 'anti-Slavic' racial sentiment on the part of the Nazis is too simplistic. As historian John Connelly has argued, Hitler wrote of his suspicions of Slavic people in *Mein Kampf*, but in such general terms as to make it difficult to explain the variation in occupation policy towards different Slavic populations; after all, the Poles were subjected to a level and scale of cruelty that, for example, the Czechs and Slovaks were not. There was never any question of establishing a puppet government in Poland. From the very outset of the invasion, Nazi propaganda justified the special treatment of Polish people according to their particularly primitive inhumanity and barbarity, a narrative which was easy to sustain in light of the Poles' fierce resistance to their occupiers. Another senior Nazi, Alfred Rosenberg, gave voice to this view:

> The Poles: a thin Germanic layer, underneath frightful material. The Jews, the most appalling people one can imagine. Towns thick with dirt … if Poland had gone on ruling the old German parts for a few more decades everything would have become lice-ridden and decayed.[9]

As was frequently the case with the Nazis, the unmoderated savagery of individual atrocities belied the highly systematic and pragmatic nature of Hitler's larger programme of extermination. The Führer recognised that eradication of the Poles depended on first rooting out the cultural, political, and social leaders who might otherwise rally significant public opposition. This *Intelligenzaktion* campaign specifically targeted 'designated leaders' and members of the middle classes, including, in Heydrich's words, 'teachers, clergy, gentry, Legionnaires [Piłsudskiites], reserve officers and suchlike.'[10] In a speech to SS officers, Himmler confirmed their objective: 'You should hear this but also forget it again – to shoot thousands of leading Poles.'[11] Heydrich – now head of the *Reichssicherheitshauptamt* ('Reich Main Security Office' or *RSHA*), overseeing the *SD*, Gestapo, and *Kriminalpolizei* – used the *Intelligenzaktion* to justify the expansion of Nazi police infrastructure and to circumvent the Wehrmacht's protests towards his recruitment of 26,000 extra military-age men for the SS. On 27 September, before Warsaw had even signed the capitulation, he briefed police leaders on plans to subdue the occupied population:

> The solution of the Polish problem – already in large part accomplished – varies with regard to the leadership classes (the Polish intelligentsia) and the lower working classes of Polentum. At most three percent of the leadership will remain in the occupied territories, and they are to be brought into concentration camps and rendered harmless ... The goal of all this is: that the Pole becomes and remains a kind of eternal seasonal migrant labourer.[12]

DEUTSCHFEINDLICH GESINNT

The intelligentsia were the ostensible targets of the *Intelligenzaktion*, but the operation was used to legitimise indiscriminate violence and murder. In some cases, when the Germans failed to capture individuals named in their lists, they would arrest – and frequently execute – substitutes taken at random. All Poles were objects of suspicion and had only to appear *deutschfeindlich gesinnt* ('inimically disposed toward the Germans') to be detained, tortured, or killed. In one case near Kościan, two landowners by the German names of Boening and Graeve were arrested and told to sign a declaration that they were *Volksdeutsche*; they refused and paid with their lives for identifying as Polish. Fifty Polish schoolboys were arrested near Gydnia over a broken window in the police station; when their parents refused to whip them, the SS brutally beat the youths, shot ten of the students in public, and forbade the burial of their bodies. In Warsaw, 22-year-old student Elżbieta Zahorska and an older woman, Eugenia Włodarz, were shot 'on the charge of having torn down a German propaganda poster.' The poster in question showed Prime Minister Chamberlain averting his gaze from a ruined Warsaw while a wounded Polish soldier exclaimed, 'England, behold thy work!'[13]

In the lead-up to the war, the *Volksdeutsch* population played a crucial role in feeding intelligence to the German police which was used to compile the original *Sonderfahnungsbuch Polen* lists. Once German troops arrived in Poland, the *Volksdeutsche* were expected to help facilitate the *Intelligenzaktion* and serve as auxiliaries in the general suppression of the Poles. Essentially, this provided the *Volksdeutsche* – whether or not they were involved in official *Selbstschutz* ('self defence') units – with an opportunity to settle scores over any local, racial, political, economic, or religious grievances they held with their Polish neighbours. Once Polish suspects were arrested and tried in *Sondergerichte* ('special courts') – which were entirely performative – their cases became fuel for the sensationalist headlines driving German propaganda on the home front. Offences such as participation in 'anti-German demonstrations', 'denouncing Germans to the Polish authorities', or simply 'offences of an anti-German character' earned the death penalty.[14] Crimes committed directly against *Volksdeutsche* or German personnel were used to justify reprisals on a disproportionate scale, where ten, fifty, or even a hundred innocent civilians were forced to bear 'collective responsibility' for a single German casualty.[15] Still, relations between assimilated *Volksdeutsche* and their Polish neighbours frequently led to complications. In Poniec, older members of the local German population interceded on behalf of 26 condemned Poles with the result that all but three were spared execution. Yet when a German engineer attempted to intervene on behalf of a Polish employee in Łódź, he was strung from a gallows in the city, doused in cold water, and left to die with an inscription describing his crime fastened to his chest.[16] Even ethnic Germans had to walk a fine line in dealing with the irredeemable Polish enemy.

As well as the constant danger of arrest, detention, deportation, and possible execution, the Polish population faced further hardships when the German authorities imposed limits on the food available to non-Germans. Inevitably, this was further adjusted according to ethnicity: whereas ethnic Germans were allotted 2,000 calories per day, Slavic Poles were to be given 1,000 calories; Jews, seen by the Germans as the most inferior part of the population, received just 400 calories. Civilians were able to augment this by working for the occupation authorities or by using their dwindling wealth to purchase more food, but the latter depended both on the availability of money and valuables, and the availability of food to buy. Deprived of all but the most basic rations, Jews became the most active in sourcing additional supplies through unofficial channels, which in turn reinforced longstanding suspicions among segments of the Polish population that the Jews had amassed large quantities of wealth in secrecy prior to the war – a belief the Germans deliberately encouraged in order to feed the pre-existing antisemitism. As a result, there were many occasions when Poles denounced Jews to the authorities and, as soon as they had been arrested, ransacked their homes in search of the fabled treasure.

Northern, western, and southern Polish territories that were to be directly annexed into the Reich endured the harshest anti-Polish persecution in the occupation's first wave. Almost immediately, SS offices were established in major cities like Poznań – now reverting to its German name of Posen – and Danzig, where civilians were screened to determine whether they were ethnically German enough to be permitted to stay. Nearly a million were expelled, though, as was often the case, application of the policy was left in the hands of local officials. In Danzig, for example, *Gauleiter* Albert Forster decided to allow civilians to self-declare their ethnicity, resulting in thousands of Poles being permitted to stay despite objections from rival Nazis including Heydrich. The expulsions were necessary because Hitler was encouraging ethnic Germans in other parts of Europe (and indeed across the world) to return to Germany as part of the *Heim ins Reich* ('Home to the Reich') policy. Over the preceding centuries, large German populations that had migrated across the Baltic region, parts of Russia, and Transylvania were now to be resettled in the land cleared of Poles. In northern Poland, where large parts of Polish territory were to become part of East Prussia, Heydrich sent Otto Rasch to oversee matters, who, after a swift review of the area under his new jurisdiction, concluded that the main problem was that the large numbers of Poles who had been detained included thousands of army officers, and that 'liquidation' of these men should be a high priority. Heydrich agreed on the condition that executions take place as covertly as possible, and Rasch accordingly established a *Durchgangslager* ('transit camp' or *Dulag*) in Soldau (now the Polish Działdowo) from which prisoners were to be shipped further south. Still, hundreds of prisoners were taken away into the surrounding forests and shot.[17]

WARSAW'S NEW REALITY

The execution of *Tannenberg* in these newly conquered territories was far from consistent. Localised discretion was one issue; another was the burgeoning friction between the Wehrmacht and Heydrich's forces, which were pushing for greater influence in the future occupation administration. The swift yet uneven military advance left the SS and *Einsatzgruppen* fully occupied with subduing the native population and unable to focus solely on their intelligentsia targets; disarming and dealing with Polish soldiers became an extra burden, even when many were interred or executed as bandits. But importantly for the Poles, the Germans' disorder bought time for eastward evacuation. Of those unable to flee the country, like Mary Berg's family, many chose Warsaw as their place of refuge, hoping to shelter with friends and family in the city that had become a bastion of resistance. Others, like Aleksander Donat's family, had to weigh up the unknown devil of life under Soviet administration against the immediate danger of staying in the besieged city. Donat's position was particularly precarious as, in addition to being Jewish, he had published numerous exposés on the Nazis; yet even as wave upon wave of refugees arrived from the west bearing 'terrifying' reports of the atrocities they had escaped, Donat's wife Lena remained relatively optimistic: 'the Germans would be vicious,' she reasoned, 'but what could happen to women and children?' The family opted to remain in Warsaw, but her husband would later reflect on the path not taken, writing, 'How many lives might have been saved then, at the beginning of the war, when the Soviet Union opened its gates to refugees from Nazism.'[18]

After capitulation, many of those who had fled Warsaw began to return – not to reclaim their former lives, but to forge an existence from the pieces that remained. The writer Zofia Nałkowska walked back to the city on 8 October and, finding the family apartment in the city largely intact – though the windows were all shattered – she slowly set to work clearing the detritus left by soldiers who had fought from the building. She was soon joined by her sister Hanna and their elderly mother. Hanna's Jewish husband had prudently evacuated Warsaw on the advice of the tobacco company for which he worked, and the two sisters now opened a small tobacco shop of their own. It was a huge downward step for a woman who had been regarded as one of Poland's finest authors before the war; later, the writer and friend Tadeusz Breza dedicated one of his books to her with the words 'To the great Mistress of Polish prose and to the modest owner of a small cigarette shop'.[19] Every morning, the two sisters made the arduous journey across the city to collect tobacco and cigarettes from a warehouse, and in her diary, Nałkowska described the desperate state of affairs they witnessed in one part of Warsaw: '[We saw] pictures of terrible destitution, thin caricatures of people in tattered clothes, bent under heavy burdens, everyone dragging something along on little sledges or simply hauling their loads over the trampled, hard, dirty snow.'[20]

The people the sisters observed were Jews. At this stage, the old Jewish Quarter was still open, but the selective persecution of Jews was already leaving its mark. Szpilman claimed that, incredibly, some in the Jewish community found hope in the idea that 'the Germans could hand Warsaw over to Soviet Russia at any moment, and areas occupied just for the sake of appearances would be restored to Poland as soon as possible.'[21] With Polish newspapers shut down and Polish radio silenced, Varsovians naturally filled the information void with a potent combination of hearsay, rumour, and wishful thinking. Many of Szpilman's neighbours and friends were so convinced that they could escape to the east that they actually packed up and left:

> One of those colleagues came back two days later, bruised and angry, without his rucksack and his money. He had seen five half-naked Jews strung up by their hands to the trees near the border and whipped. And he had witnessed the death of Dr Haskielewicz, who told the Germans he wanted to cross the bend. At pistol point, they had ordered him to walk into the river, further and deeper into the water until he lost his footing and drowned. My colleague had merely lost his belongings and his money, and was then beaten and sent back. But most Jews, although they were robbed and ill-treated, did make it to Russia.*
>
> We were sorry for the poor man, of course, but at the same time we felt a sense of triumph: he would have done better to follow our advice and stay. Our decision was not swayed by any kind of logical consideration. The simple fact is that we decided to stay because of our fondness for Warsaw, although we could not have given any logical explanation for that either.[22]

Warsaw was not properly exposed to *Tannenberg* until after capitulation, but even before Brigadeführer Lothar Beutel's *Einsatzgruppe IV* entered the city on 2 October, Varsovians were anticipating an onslaught of oppression. Mayor Starzyński's deputy Julian Kulski described how for Polish patriots, surrender of the city did not mean defeat, and it was incumbent upon Warsaw to secure 'people and resources for further fighting' whenever the opportunity would present itself. This meant 'erasing [the] past' of Polish patriots, military personnel, and other local leaders to make them less conspicuous targets for the occupying powers. After learning that documents left behind by fleeing leaders at general staff headquarters had fallen into enemy hands, the mayor ordered the

* Although tens of thousands of Polish Jews did flee east into Soviet territory in 1939, the overall pattern was varied, with others diverted to Romania, Hungary, Lithuania, or trapped in other occupied zones.

'cleans[ing] of the public register', taking advantage of the post-siege disorder to dispose of other incriminating records. The fire that sprang up in the Saxon Palace conveniently erased large quantities of military personnel records, but in a city strewn with wrecked buildings, it drew no attention. Other priorities for the city administration included providing support to social organisations that would soon be forced underground and securing cash to fund future resistance efforts. The earlier government exodus had stripped the country of its entire gold reserve, but foreign and domestic currency was divided up between trusted individuals for safekeeping. Kulski himself was 'burdened with such a deposit' of ten thousand *złotys*, which would later be handed over to treasurers of the underground movements.[23]

Even after capitulation, city officials implored the mayor to evacuate for his own safety – not least because society would need his leadership in the fight to come. But as Kulski recorded, Starzyński 'regarded remaining in the position of Mayor of the City in conditions of war with Hitler as remaining at a soldier's post.' The fact that he would not countenance being 'guilty of desertion, even an apparent one' alludes to the bitterness and resentment harboured by the defeated Varsovian population towards their absent leaders.[24] Szpilman described the pervasiveness of this feeling in the days after capitulation:

> At this early stage anger with the government and the army command, both of which had fled, leaving the country to its fate, was in general stronger than hatred for the Germans. Bitterly, we remembered the words of the field-marshal who had sworn that he would not let the enemy have a single button of his uniform – and nor did he, but only because the buttons remained attached to his uniform when he saved himself by escaping abroad.[25]

The Germans weren't wrong in their assessment that the right leaders could galvanise popular resistance, nor that their absence could be devastating for public morale. But what they failed to appreciate and to stifle in the early days of occupation was the particular obstinance of Varsovian society. The siege experience had set the capital apart from the experience of the rest of the country, and, just as the city had held out until the very last moment, just as their mayor refused to abandon his post, so too would Warsaw fulfil its destiny as the epicentre of resistance. In many ways, Starzyński was precisely the breed of 'undisputed social leader' that the *Intelligenzaktion* intended to eliminate, so it is striking that when he and 11 other city leaders were held as hostages against Hitler's visit to the city, the Germans did not automatically add them to their list of intelligentsia targets.[26]

Perhaps judging that it was too soon to risk further inflaming Varsovian resistance, the Germans permitted Starzyński to remain as mayor and to assist with the transfer of power. The benefit of this was that the Germans were able to leverage his influence and popularity to subdue the newly occupied population. When the mayor met with the German military command, he was reminded in no uncertain terms that his priority was to guarantee the safety of the occupiers; he had barely been introduced to the German authorities before being assured that 'if something happens' in Warsaw, 'no stone will be left unturned' in the German reaction.[27] In the weeks that followed, Starzyński continued both his official and secret activities under the Nazis' watchful eyes. As well as provisioning and distributing food to the shell-shocked population, he was tasked with organising efforts to begin clearing and reconstructing the ruined city, which, due to a shortage of glass, was in no shape for the winter that was fast approaching. He also oversaw the creation of translated correspondence forms for the German authorities, and, in a successful gamble on their vanity, suggested the relocation of German command to the Blanka Palace, where they would be kept at arm's length from the Polish administration in City Hall. Kulski praised Starzyński for maintaining an 'external calm' and a 'dignified attitude' in the face of escalating demands while still devoting time to 'touring the city', meeting future resistance leaders, and applying himself to every task with a conscientiousness intended to reduce the occupiers' suspicions.[28] Unlike the Varsovian Jewish leadership, which would later gain notoriety as a 'monstrous organization … bitterly hated' by those it was meant to serve, Starzyński's popularity amongst Varsovians endured even after capitulation.[29] As Kulski described:

> Starzyński could see for himself the scale of the destruction and the losses suffered, but also the great sympathy he enjoyed among the population … Shouts of welcome were heard whenever he was recognised. Warsaw was faithful to its September leader, and only a few saw him as the cause of their misfortunes.[30]

But Starzyński's luck with the Germans didn't last long. When the Germans discovered his covert work involving the transfer of funds to underground social organisations, they challenged him with contravening the terms of capitulation and threatened Gestapo intervention. The subsidies were repaid, but the Poles wrongfully assumed that the Gestapo would adhere to some semblance of legitimacy. When Starzyński's arrest did come, on 27 October, no effort was made to dress up his detainment with any formal charges, and Kulski's attempts to ascertain the reason for arrest and to intercede were stonewalled.[31] Asked by the Germans if they could count on his cooperation, Starzyński's colleague chose to follow the example set by the mayor, to remain in post 'in order to protect the good of the city and its people.'[32] Starzyński was taken to Pawiak prison, where all trace of him disappeared by December 1939. The *Instytut Pamięci Narodowej* ('Institute of National Remembrance') would finally close the case on his death in 2014, determining that he was shot sometime between 21 and 23 December. Yet his spirit of courage, steadfast resistance, and indefatigable honour lived on, inspiring not only Julian Kulski but tens of thousands of Varsovians who had found comfort in his radio speeches and found in him a symbol of hope during the darkest days of the siege.

THE PABST PLAN

Although Starzyński and Kulski were given permission to allocate resources for the repair of the bomb- and shell-damaged parts of Warsaw, the scale of reconstruction fell far short of what was required. From the German perspective, this was deliberate policy: they had no intention of permitting the restoration of the Polish capital. In June 1939, Hitler had visited an architectural exhibition in the town of Würzburg, where one particular item caught his attention: a relatively small exhibit of a proposed new German town that might replace the city of Warsaw. At this time, the Polish capital had a population of about 1.3 million, but the new town would be far smaller, with less than a tenth of this number living in what is effectively the modern city centre, on the west bank of the Vistula. The map that formed the centrepiece of the exhibit showed a neat grid of streets amidst wide-ranging parkland, bounded by the river to the east and the main north–south railway line in the west. Over 90 per cent of the Polish city was to be demolished. In addition to the new city to the west of the Vistula, there would be a smaller settlement to the east of the river, tucked away behind more parkland; this was the location of a work camp of Poles who would serve the needs of the German population. The size of this work camp would vary as German plans evolved, with its proposed population ranging from 30,000 to 80,000 people.[33]

The drawing of the future 'New German City of Warsaw' that caught Hitler's eye had been made by the architect Hubert Gross, and his proposal fitted strongly with the Führer's ambitions to resettle eastern territories. The industrial output of the new city would clearly be far smaller than was currently the case, and would be closely aligned with the needs of the German war machine. The limited reconstruction permitted after the surrender of the city was in keeping with this overall scheme and also influenced by constant German preoccupation with disease. Discussions and reports repeatedly highlighted the risk of contagions arising in areas where non-Germans had been crowded together and then spreading to German areas. Of course, there was no recognition of the fact that the Germans were largely to blame for creating the conditions for such illnesses in the first place.

As the Wehrmacht's responsibility for Warsaw came to an end, Oskar Dengel – who as mayor of Würzburg had commissioned the exhibit about a future German Warsaw – replaced Kulski as head of the city's civil administration. He immediately appointed Gross and about 20 others to develop the plans they had already exhibited, and the team submitted their first formal proposal on 'how and where the urban structure could be given the stamp of a German city with extensive buildings for Party and state functions' in February 1940.[34] Ultimately, the planned redevelopment of Warsaw would become known as the Pabst Plan, named after the architect Friedrich Pabst, even though he played a relatively minor role. But it is typical of the chaotic and often contradictory manner in which German policy evolved that the plan underwent several iterations as rival Nazi factions competed for Hitler's attention and approval.

By the end of October 1939, the structures of occupation were starting to solidify. Whilst the Danzig, Poznań, West Prussian, and Upper Silesian areas were formally annexed into the Reich, the central section of the country – which encompassed around 11.5 million inhabitants and included the cities of Kraków, Kielce, Radom, Warsaw, and Lublin – was to be administered as a separate region. When Warsaw was seized by the Germans in the First World War, they created a *Generalgouvernement Warschau* ('General Governorate Warsaw'), and in 1939 the new rump region of Poland was named the *Generalgouvernement für die Besetzten Polnischen Gebiete* ('General Governorate for the Occupied Polish Territories'), shortened to *Generalgouvernement* in the summer of 1940. As governor-general, Hitler chose Hans Frank, a leading Nazi lawyer (and Hitler's own legal advisor), veteran of the *Freikorps*, and participant in the failed Beer Hall Putsch. Frank's appeal lay less in his creative policymaking or leadership skills than in his shrewdness for navigating legal obstacles and facilitating Hitler's grandiose missions; as he would later testify at Nuremberg, in his 'own sphere', he 'did everything that could possibly be expected of a man who believes in the greatness of his people and who is filled with fanaticism for the greatness of his country, in order to bring about the victory of Adolf Hitler and the National Socialist movement.'[35]

It was Kraków, and not Warsaw, that was named capital of the *Generalgouvernement*, in part because of the Pabst Plan, but primarily because the Nazis believed Kraków to be an *urdeutsche Stadt* ('ancient German city') awaiting re-Germanisation and recolonisation by its ancestral people. While Frank was settling into Kraków, he appointed another Nazi lawyer and longtime ally,

Ludwig Fischer, as chief administrator (and later governor) of the Warsaw District. Like Frank, he had little power over SS and police operations operating within his territory and there was nothing obvious to recommend him for a management role aside from his loyalty to the Reich to the bitter end. But whilst Warsaw's Gestapo leadership would change five times during the course of the occupation, Frank's and Fischer's names would linger in Varsovians' awareness for much longer and render them common targets of resentment, ridicule, and, later, direct violence.

AB-Aktion

Beutel's time as commander of *Einsatzgruppe IV* in Warsaw, on the other hand, proved to be brief. Shortly after arrival in the city, he was arrested on various corruption charges and replaced by an equally unsavoury character, Standartenführer Josef Albert Meisinger. A former police officer, he became a member of the SS in 1933 with specific responsibilities for seeking out opponents of Hitler within the Nazi Party as well as the prosecution of homosexuals, people involved in abortion cases, and those having sexual relations with Jews. Walter Schellenberg, head of the counter-intelligence department of the *SD* and a rising star in Heydrich's inner circle, wrote:

> [Meisinger was] one of the most evil creatures among Heydrich's bunch of thugs and he carried out the vilest of his orders … He was a frightening individual, a large, coarse-faced man with a bald head and an incredibly ugly face. However, like many men of his type, he had drive and energy and an unscrupulous sort of cleverness.[36]

Beutel might have been corrupt, but Meisinger would prove to be a far more murderous commander in Warsaw.

The winter of 1939–40 passed and the scale of repression and mass detention increased. In early May 1940, the Germans conducted the first major sweep through Warsaw, detaining thousands of Poles at random and shipping them off to labour camps from which few ever returned home. Once the military campaign in the west commenced in May, the attention of the world's press to events in Poland – already diminishing – almost disappeared entirely. It was an opportunity for Obergruppenführer Friedrich-Wilhelm Krüger, appointed by Frank as *Höhere SS- und Polizeiführer* ('Senior SS and Police Commander' or *HSSPF*) for all the *Generalgouvernement*, to flex his muscles. With the original *Intelligenzaktion* wrapping up, Krüger presented plans to Frank for a further wave of arrests under the title of *Ausserordentliche Befriedigungsaktion* ('Extraordinary Pacification Action' or *AB-Aktion*). Frank's diary entry of 30 May made clear that even the rudimentary rules that might have applied to date were to be ignored:

> If ... we wish to accomplish our purpose, namely the total subjugation of the Polish people in this territory, we have no time to waste ... At this very moment when, in the west, thousands of Germans are laying down their lives each minute, each second, and the finest German blood is being shed it is our duty as National Socialists to do everything we can to prevent the Poles rallying at the expense of the sacrifices suffered by Germans. It was this that led me to discuss ... this extraordinary pacification programme, the object of which is to hasten the liquidation of seditious politicians, most of whom are in our hands, and other politically suspect individuals, and to put an end to traditional Polish lawlessness. I admit openly that this will cost the lives of some thousands of Poles, mainly the leading figures of the Polish intelligentsia ...
>
> The Führer said to me ... the men capable of leadership whom we have already identified must be liquidated; their successors must be kept under surveillance and eliminated at an appropriate moment. There is no need to burden the Reich or central police agencies with this. There is no need to send these elements to concentration camps, as we would only involve ourselves in additional problems and unnecessary correspondence with their families; we shall settle this issue on the spot and we will do so in the simplest way possible.[37]

The *AB-Aktion* gave the SS and police *carte blanche* to eviscerate any and every aspect of Polish cultural life. In the immediate aftermath of the German conquest, it had been the annexed territories that suffered the most severe oppression as the Nazis unrolled their full operation of 'de-Polonisation' in preparation for German resettlement. But it was Warsaw, along with the rest of the *Generalgouvernement* – which was forced to absorb refugees and, later, astronomical numbers of deportees from the western territories – that felt the full force of the *Intelligenzaktion* and *AB-Aktion*. Over the following days, about 30,000 intellectuals (many of whom had previously been arrested and released) were detained.

DISMANTLING A NATION'S CULTURE

One of the most immediate Polish cultural targets was the Catholic Church, which claimed to serve over 90 per cent of the Polish population – though how many were observant Catholics, and how many merely identified as Catholics, is open to question. In any case, the Germans considered Catholicism – and by proxy, the Church hierarchy – an integral and influential element of Polish national identity. Bishops and priests were arrested on nebulous charges across the country, and if spared immediate execution, prescribed particularly humiliating punishments or deported to concentration camps.[38] In Łódź, priests were ordered to clean the gutters of Piotrkowska Street in the rain. In Warsaw, the Germans immediately detained 330 priests, 80 schoolteachers, and several professors. The city's *Reichskommissar* (the German governor) Dr Helmut Otto told those in prison that they would be released so long as they 'undertake to keep away from politics, and especially avoid the mention of political subjects in sermons, generally refraining from any activity harmful to the German State', but the promise was rarely fulfilled.[39] Protestantism was also particularly concentrated in Warsaw, and, with the exception of *Volksdeutsch* Nazi sympathisers, no less of a target for the occupying powers. The Protestant church in Małachowski Square was destroyed by incendiary bombing during the siege and other buildings, including the seminary of theology, were deliberately reduced to rubble. Two Protestant schools 'well known for their high scholastic standards' were turned into German hospitals, and by October, all but two of the Varsovian Protestant clergy had been arrested.[40]

The Nazis' attack on the Church went beyond cultural and spiritual demoralisation. Having seen how the Church had helped keep Polish identity alive in the 19th century, the Germans sought to make it impossible for Poles to participate in religious life and educational structures that might detract from or directly threaten the total authority of the occupation administration. As with other elements of cultural and social repression, this was only partially successful, largely because overt oppression of leadership figures only had the effect of pushing the 'lay' public underground. The historian Jadwiga Biskupska argues that because 'churchgoers employed in secular professions' were left to fill and reimagine informal religious networks, the Catholic response to Nazism was highly diverse and certainly 'not an institutional one'.[41] In Warsaw, church attendance would actually rise during occupation (not least due to the closure of other institutions) as Poles sought out social and spiritual support networks, and numerous intelligentsia-led groups – such as the *Iuventus Christiana* ('Christian Youth') and *Unia* ('Unity') – emerged underground offering educational, charitable, and even practical support for the resistance.

The Germans sought to dismantle all institutions and social symbols that supported independent Polish thought. In October, they launched their offensive against Warsaw's education systems, starting with the seizure of the Polish

Ministry of Education on Aleja Szucha. Julian Kulski's son, then 11 years old, recalled his personal experience of the Nazi crackdown:

> As I approached the school, I could see some of my classmates standing outside. A notice, SCHOOL CLOSED, was posted on the doors. What good news! We were elated, but curious, since there was no explanation. Then we saw our science teacher, Mr. Lewandowski, coming toward us. He told us that he did not know who had given the order, or why, but that all the other schools are also closed. Mr. Lewandowski said he would get in touch with us and that we should go home.[42]

The youngster's recollection belies the deeply sinister motives behind this development. The Germans made no secret about their aim to convert Poland into 'a community composed only of manual workers, who are to be slaves, deprived of their own culture and national tradition, and forming a reservoir of labour for the benefit of the German Reich.' To this end, Hans Frank declared that Poland could – and should – be reduced to an 'intellectual desert' (*intellektuelle Wüste*), rendering the continued functioning of Polish secondary schools and universities redundant.[43] Himmler believed circumscribing even primary schooling would help in the subjugation and elimination of the less desirable 'alien races':

> A basic issue in the solution of all these problems is the question of schooling and thus the question of shifting and selecting of the young. For the non-German population of the East there must be no higher school than fourth-grade elementary school. The sole goal of this school is to be:
>
> Simple arithmetic up to 500 at the most; writing of one's name; the doctrine that it is a divine law to obey the Germans; and to be honest, industrious, and good. I do not think that reading should be required.[44]

Volksdeutsch schools were, of course, the exception. But Himmler's memorandum added that parents who wished further education for their children would have to make a request to the SS, who would then grant permission depending on 'whether the child is racially perfect and conforming to our conditions'. Those deemed of 'good blood' would be offered relocation to Germany for education, and if the parents chose to remain in Poland, they would be warned against producing any more intelligent offspring to avoid 'the danger of this subhuman people of the East obtaining a class of leaders, which, since it would be equal to us, would also be dangerous for us.'[45] The reality of these policies was even more horrific. Himmler's principle of 'shifting and selecting' the young unfolded as brazen kidnapping with the goal of Germanising desirable children for the Reich. As early as November, official memoranda endorsed the selection of children between the ages of eight and ten, who were thought still malleable enough for indoctrination; on arrival in Germany, the youngsters would be given German names, embedded in German families, and have their ancestry obscured in public records. It is estimated that, by the end of the war, as many as 200,000 Polish children were forcibly displaced under the Nazis' so-called *Lebensborn* ('fount of life') initiative alongside tens of thousands more from across Europe. Less than half learned the truth later in life, and even fewer – perhaps just 20 per cent – were ever reunited with their Polish families.[46]

Where children's education could be configured around broader goals of colonisation and Aryanisation, higher education posed an intolerable threat to Nazi authority. Scores of professors of the University of Warsaw were arrested and transported to concentration camps in the months after capitulation, with those remaining left no choice but to turn to manual work; even Warsaw University's rector, Dr Włodzimierz Antoniewicz, began working as a coachman.[47] Mieczysław Michałowicz, director of the University of Warsaw Children's Clinic, was permitted to continue working but dealt a severe warning by the supervising German doctor: 'should I come across an academic gathering of any sort, I will start shooting.' Nevertheless, Michałowicz and his colleagues were reluctant to give up on what they considered their 'duty of teaching future doctors':

> We did not cease to teach. We carried on, having laid out patients' records on the table to make it look like a purely administrative enterprise. Thus we managed to survive these times. It goes without saying that receiving subscriptions to any magazine and keeping up to date with academia in Poland and worldwide were impossible … When visiting, Dr. Schrempf demanded to see staff registers laid out in writing. Whenever he met someone passing by, he would ask them to present credentials. If they were not employed permanently, dire consequences would ensue, he threatened.
>
> Therefore, what is called contributing to academia would have been thoroughly eliminated had we adhered to the regulations.[48]

Michałowicz was finally arrested in November 1942, and his clinic was requisitioned for the treatment of *Volksdeutsch* children only. Of the 28 intellectuals in his cell at Pawiak prison, just four survived to the end of the war; he attributed the loss of 46 per cent of University of Warsaw professors to *AB-Aktion*, adding that 'certain faculties, for instance the Faculty of Law, were nearly wholly liquidated.'[49]

Academic disciplines associated with Poland's cultural heritage attracted particular scrutiny; institutions for science, history, literature, and the arts were closed in both annexed and *Generalgouvernement* territories, and the buildings that housed them appropriated and looted. In some cases the pillaging was directed by German academics; in others, it was nothing more than impulsive vandalism and theft. German troops stationed in the Warsaw School of Engineering plundered everything from tools to furniture, while at the Radium Institute, invaders carried off 1.5 grams of radium presented to Poland's beloved Maria Skłodowska-Curie.[50] When Michałowicz's children's clinic was seized, the Polish reference books were used to stoke furnaces and all other apparatus was stripped from the labs.[51] National arts and treasures disappeared from the Royal Castle, National Museum, and State Archaeological Museum alongside scores of others, with Poles forbidden access to the collections that remained. Meanwhile, archives were examined for evidence of Germany's historic and cultural claims to Poland, and records relating to the territories newly annexed to the Reich including 'a most valuable collection of records relating to the Teutonic Knights', were exported back to the Reich.[52] Anything that undermined this narrative was disposed of or destroyed. Archivist Adam Stebelski estimated that in Warsaw, where the majority of state records were held, 92.8 per cent of archives were lost during the war. Much of the material that escaped the Nazis' pillaging would not survive the bombing of the city in 1944.[53]

RESHAPING THE URBAN AESTHETIC

The Germans' systematic destruction of Polish cultural icons was visible everywhere in the city and deliberately calculated to shatter the aesthetic fabric of Varsovian life. The Polish authorities were convinced that even the September bombardment had been organised to 'target quarters of the city which were densely inhabited by the middle and working classes and on buildings of historical interest, sparing the fashionable quarter' near the Ujazdowskie Avenue for later German appropriation. One of the most notable losses was the 14th-century Royal Castle, which suffered extensive damage from first incendiary bombing and then structural demolition, leaving the national monument in ruins by February 1940. Elsewhere, the devastation of the rococo *Pałac Raczyńskich* ('Raczyński Palace'), the Warsaw Stock Exchange Building, and the 17th-century heart of the University of Warsaw erased centuries of architectural and cultural history from the cityscape. The gutting of the neoclassical *Teatr Wielki* ('Great Theatre'), *Filharmonia Narodowa* ('National Philharmonia'), and at least seven other theatres left Warsaw's once vibrant opera, music, and ballet scenes homeless. National monuments were also targeted, starting with the Chopin statue in Łazienki Park and the independence fighter memorial in Małachowski Square, and by 1941 including the monuments to Adam Mickiewicz, Jan Kiliński, who had led Poles in the 1793 uprising against the Russians, and General Józef Sowiński, who defended Warsaw against the Russians in 1831.[54] Meanwhile, the elegant – largely intact – downtown villas and flats of Mokotów were swiftly occupied by Germans, rendering the district a no-go area for native Varsovians. As the city around them changed, so too did the names by which it was recognised as the Nazis sought to leave their mark. In 1940, Piłsudski Square was renamed as Adolf-Hitler-Platz in a grand public ceremony, during which an inconveniently placed statue of Napoleonic hero Prince Józef Poniatowski had to be hidden behind a Third Reich banner.

One of the most ominous name-changes was that of Aleja Szucha to Strasse der Polizei ('Police Street'); here, the former Ministry of Religion and Public Education became the headquarters of the *Sicherheitspolizei* and the *SD*. Prisoners arrived in a steady stream and underwent brutal interrogation; many did not survive the ordeal. Other prisoners were taken to SS barracks on Rakowiecka Street and Podchorążych Street, or the headquarters of the *Kriminalpolizei* on Ujazdowskie Avenue. Standartenführer Günther Claassen, who had been appointed *Polizeipräsident* ('police president') of Warsaw, regularly published announcements in the city's German-controlled newspapers listing those who had been executed; on 21 October, for example, one announcement stated that four people – one explicitly described as 'a Jew' – had been found guilty of possession of firearms and ammunition and had been executed.[55] Others were killed with little or no fanfare, and, as was the case in most of the territories occupied by the Germans during the war, violent reprisals could take place anywhere at any time. On 13 November 1939, a Polish policeman serving the Germans was shot by Pinkus Zylberryng, a convict recently released from prison; even though his identity was quickly confirmed, all 53 residents of the house from which he had fired the shot were arrested. Zylberryng's Jewish ethnicity was loudly proclaimed and the Jewish authorities of the city were ordered to pay 300,000 *złotys* for the release of the detainees. The money was hastily raised, but when it was presented to the Germans, the response was that it was too late: the men had been executed. The money was seized anyway.[56]

CULTURAL PRIMITIVISATION

The war on intellectual life in Warsaw wasn't only focused on dismantling institutions. Varsovians of all walks of life became accustomed to the threats of arrest, violence, and even death spilling into the streets of their city and overshadowing their everyday activities. One report described how, during the first roundups, Varsovians mistakenly assumed the Germans were simply recruiting for forced labour:

> The seizure of people in the cafés began as early as the winter of 1939–40; it was applied to both men and women, more or less at random. Then street roundups began, usually affecting whole districts. Lately such a seizure took place all over Warsaw at once … All the streets were closed at the same time by the Gestapo, the military police and the *Selbstschutz* … The trams were held up, and all the Polish men passengers told to alight (Jews were not arrested). The police entered all the shops, cafés, hairdressers, etc., and ordered the men out into the streets. Everyone who attempted to escape or to resist was shot.[57]

It quickly became apparent that intellectuals, both men and women, of the 'ages varying from sixteen to fifty' were in particular danger of disappearing – not to labour projects, but to concentration camps. Varsovians tried to anticipate the patterns of hostage-taking and would steer clear of certain streets, cafés, or trams to reduce their risk of capture, but outmanoeuvring random persecution was an impossible task. As in the universities and the Church, those that evaded arrest were still deprived of their former means of making a living.

Starting in the earliest days of occupation, the *Abteilung für Volksaufklärung und Propaganda* ('Department of Education and Propaganda') issued a steady stream of decrees that clamped down on Polish newspapers, literature, arts, and entertainment. The pre-war Polish press, which had boasted an output of 2,000 different periodicals, plus 250 in various other minority languages, was shut down; a slew of German-approved publications appeared in their place, including *Nowy Kurjer Warszawski* ('New Warsaw Courier'), as the German authorities seized larger publishing houses and distributed smaller shops amongst the *Volksdeutsche* and German colonists. Polish radio was also taken off air, and studios looted, destroyed, or also appropriated for German use. In the words of the Polish Ministry of Information, part of the government-in-exile, the quality of the German outputs was 'extraordinarily low,' their main task being 'to attack England and revile Polish history and the Polish intellectual classes'. It was with good reason that German periodicals swiftly earned a contemptuous nickname amongst Poles: 'The name "reptile press" is given to those papers which treacherously use the Polish language to poison the body of the nation with the venom of their contents. The printed word in those papers is Polish. Their aim is work for Germany.'[58]

Generally treated by the Poles 'with the contempt which they deserve', these were read less for their literary merit than for the – increasingly frequent – public decrees that the German authorities posted in their pages.[59] Meanwhile, pre-war journalists and editors were prime targets for arrest or fell into poverty even if they were able to contribute to the underground Polish press. Of the 1,300 Polish journalists in permanent employment before the war, at least 20 per cent were exterminated during the occupation.

The publication of Polish books was also prohibited. All Jewish lending libraries and scores of bookshops across the *Generalgouvernement* were forced to close for their potential to spread material deemed *deutschfeindlich* ('hostile to Germanism'), or, equally problematic, literature conducive to Polish or Jewish cultural expression. The sale and lending of all English and French books were immediately banned, and by September 1940, around 3,000 specific Polish titles – including works of national icons Sienkiewicz, Mickiewicz, and Copernicus – were explicitly proscribed. According to the *Abteilung für Volksaufklärung und Propaganda*, the only form of artistic expression that was permitted was that which would 'satisfy the primitive need for entertainment and amusement, all the more as it is a question of diverting the attention of intellectual circles, so far as from conspiracy, and even from political discussions which encourage an anti-German attitude.' Only light novels and short stories were cleared for publication, which aside from serving as a vapid substitute for an entire literary culture, were – the Polish Ministry of Information complained – frequently pornographic.[60] A circular issued in June 1940 banned the recital of Polish folk songs or works of national composers, including Chopin; it was decreed that theatre performances were to include only comic operas, revues, or other light, uncontroversial entertainments; and painters, sculptors, and artists were forbidden any allusion to Polish cultural motifs, history, or depictions of the war. At the same time, the occupiers imported German literature, music, arts, and theatre for their own amusement, but these were strictly off limits to the intellectually inferior Polish public.

By mid-1941, as many as 3,500 members of the Varsovian intelligentsia had been murdered – but the persecution of intellectuals did not end with *AB-Aktion*.[61] The Germans continued to root out real and imagined threats to their authority and throughout the occupation carried out particularly harsh reprisals against intellectuals whenever the opportunity arose. Historian Richard Lukas' summary of the numbers reveals the devastating impact of the Nazis' systematic plan of extermination by the end of the war:

> The Nazis were so thorough in their grim work that when Dachau was liberated at the end of the war, there were only 50 Polish physicians, 100 lawyers,

> 50 engineers, and 100 teachers still alive there, in contrast to 5,000 farmers and 3,600 artisans. Testimony of just how successful the Germans were in their resolve is revealed by the fact that during the war Poland lost 45 percent of her physicians and dentists, 57 percent of her attorneys, more than 15 percent of her teachers, 40 percent of her professors, 30 percent of her technicians, and more than 18 percent of her clergy. The majority of her journalists also disappeared – 73 were murdered, 77 died in concentration camps and jails, 50 died in the ghetto, and 12 perished in the Warsaw Uprising.[62]

The impact of the assault on Varsovian culture was complex. On the one hand, although the demolition of historical landmarks pales in comparison to efforts to annihilate the city in 1944, in less than four months Varsovians nonetheless saw their city reduced to a shell of its former self. On the other hand, and despite their brutal efforts, the Germans failed to uproot and eliminate Polish culture. The *Intelligenzaktion* might have decapitated numerous potential sources of resistance, but if it was intended to eviscerate Polish solidarity, subjugate the public, and quell any appetite for resistance at all, it broadly failed. The *Warschauer Zeitung* ('Warsaw Newspaper'), created by the new occupation authorities, seethed in July 1940: 'It would be a great mistake to think that after the notable successes of German policy and of the talented German High Command there has been any disillusionment or revision of view among the Polish population.'[63]

The writer explicitly blamed the Polish intelligentsia for 'poisoning' the occupied population with intractable ideas.[64] What is not mentioned is that the destruction of landmarks and persecution of intellectuals failed to fracture Polish identity because it had the unintended effect of driving cultural leaders and activity underground where they crystallised into more resilient and collaborative expressions of affiliation. Intellectuals, scientists, artists, actors, and other performers who lost access to their former livelihoods were generally forced to turn to manual work, but they still found outlets for their talents in underground organisations, which frequently opened doors to more proactive oppositional activities. The Germans struggled because they were trying to annihilate two distinct targets: the Polish intelligentsia as a class, and Polish culture at large. It was easy to make the connection between the two, but the suffocating of one did not guarantee the extinguishment of the other – especially with an increasingly dynamic and cross-class underground adding fuel to the fire. Importantly, the culture of an occupied people is itself influenced by the experience of occupation – and the Germans were attempting to eradicate a culture with a long-established tradition of defying foreign rulers. As historian John Connelly explains:

> When one views the matter *sine ira et studio*, one sees that Poles of an earlier generation refused to collaborate not because of collective attachment to virtues like personal freedom or liberal democracy but rather out of a supreme devotion to Polish sovereignty – understood to include culture – that made compromises painful to countenance, both for elites and the masses.[65]

At the same time, the occupiers were fighting against the fact that artistic and intellectual activities don't merely function as expressions of specific cultures, but of humanity as a whole. Władysław Szpilman experienced first-hand how even the Germans struggled to separate their cultural sensitivity from their political imperative:

> We were already halfway down Zielna Street, and it began to look as though we would reach our destination safely, when a police patrol suddenly came round a corner. We had no time to retreat or hide. We just stood there in the dazzling light of their torches, each of us trying to think of some excuse, when one of the policemen marched straight up to us and shone his torch in our faces.
>
> 'Are you Jews?' The question was purely rhetorical, since he did not wait for us to answer. 'Right, then ...' There was a note of triumph in this statement of our racial origin ... So this was how we were to die... I heard someone say out loud, 'This is the end.' Only a moment later did I realise that I myself had spoken. At the same time I heard loud weeping and convulsive sobbing. I turned my head, and in the harsh torchlight I saw my father kneeling on the wet tarmac, sobbing and begging the policemen for our lives.
>
> A few moments passed, and a loud voice came through the wall of light.
>
> 'What do you do for a living?'
>
> Henryk [Szpilman's brother] answered for all three of us ... 'We're musicians.'
>
> One of the policemen stationed himself in front of me, grabbed my coat collar and shook me in a final fit of temper, not that there was any reason for it now he had decided to let us live.
>
> 'Lucky for you I'm a musician too!'
>
> He gave me a shove, and I stumbled back against the wall.
>
> 'Get out!'[66]

CHAPTER 6

OPPRESSION AND DEFIANCE

Because I am learning the greatest art of life:
To smile always and everywhere
And to tolerate pain without despair
And not to regret what has passed
And not to be scared of what is to come!

Irena Bobowska, 'Because I Am Learning', 1941[1]

MURDER AT PALMIRY

The ancient Kampinos pine forest sits to the west of Warsaw, stretching between the Vistula and Bzura Rivers to the village of Palmiry. In November 1939, Varsovians saw the first truckloads of detainees disappearing northwards from Aleja Szucha towards the dense woodland, sandy marshes, and treacherous swamps of Kampinos – from which, as one witness recalled, the same trucks would return hours later full only of 'singing German soldiers'.[2]

The factors that had once made locations like Kampinos useful to the Polish military – relative isolation, limited observation, but good rail and road connections – also made them ideal killing grounds for the Germans. In many cases, construction of the military facilities was incomplete when the Germans took control of the area, and the partially excavated foundations of fuel tanks or ammunition stores were repurposed as mass graves. In other cases, killing grounds were selected largely for convenience, their public visibility functioning as a means to further terrorise the occupied population. One such was part of the Parliament Gardens in Warsaw, adjacent to the former *Sejm* buildings which had been appropriated by a German police battalion. Groups of up to 20 Poles at a time were lined up in the gardens close to the Vistula and gunned down, their bodies later removed. Some Polish researchers claimed that up to 1,000 victims died just in this one location.[3] Though mass killings were generally carried out in secluded locations, the Germans made no secret of their magnitude. In an interview published in the virulently pro-Nazi *Völkischer Beobachter* ('People's Observer') newspaper, Frank contrasted the occupation of Poland with that of Czechoslovakia:

> In Prague, for example, large red posters were displayed announcing that seven Czechs had been shot that day. [When I saw them,] I said to myself, if I wanted to put up a poster every time seven Poles were shot, the forests of Poland wouldn't suffice to produce the paper required.[4]

The scale of murder in Poland was so great that it necessitated careful systematisation. Everything – from the selection of killing sites to the preparation of mass graves – became almost routine, giving shape to protocols the Germans would later deploy and refine during their advance into the Soviet Union. Workers from nearby camps – at this stage mainly Germans from the *Reichsarbeitsdienst* ('Reich Labour Administration' or *RAD*) – were notified a day or two in advance to prepare trenches and pits. Prisoners in Warsaw were told that they were being taken to concentration camps and were permitted to bring personal baggage; in most cases, personal documentation was also returned to them to add to the illusion that they were being resettled. By the time the prisoners realised the truth, it was usually too late to attempt to escape. Some tried to drop personal items and valuables in the hope that they would later be found, but when they arrived at the killing ground, they were led to the trenches and shot.

As the killings proceeded, there were attempts to improve the efficiency of the process. Prisoners were ordered to lean back against a long bar which was removed after they were shot so bodies would fall neatly into the trenches to facilitate more efficient 'stacking' of corpses. Once the killings were complete, the ground was carefully restored with a final carpet of moss and pine needles and saplings were planted throughout the area.[5] Despite these measures, Varsovians were aware of most of the execution sites and methods, thanks to both the intelligence networks of the growing underground resistance and local witnesses to the murders. Local foresters attempted to identify killing grounds by marking trees with notches in the hope that one day, the graves would be exhumed.

Several prominent figures featured amongst the thousands of Polish lives claimed by the *AB-Aktion*. The peasant activist and former Polish president Maciej Rataj, *PPS* representative, former member of the *Sejm* and *Robotnik* editor Mieczysław Niedziałkowski, and the Olympic gold medallist athlete Janusz Kusociński – all of whom had been involved in underground conspiracies – were executed. One of the reasons the Germans sought to conceal the precise identities of their victims was to cultivate fear and uncertainty; from late 1941, this policy was formalised through Hitler's *Nacht und Nebel* ('Night and Fog') decree, which was originally targeted at France, Belgium, the Netherlands, Luxembourg, and Norway, but was then rapidly applied to other parts of Europe.[6] Himmler issued new orders to the Gestapo throughout the occupied territories:

> The Führer is of the opinion that, in such cases, penal servitude or even a hard labour sentence for life will be regarded as a sign of weakness. An effective and lasting deterrent can be achieved only by taking measures which will leave the family and population uncertain as to the fate of the offender.[7]

The military was also expected to conform. Acting on verbal instructions from Hitler, Generalfeldmarschall Wilhelm Keitel, head of *Oberkommando der Wehrmacht* ('Armed Forces High Command' or *OKW*), ordered that 'efficient, enduring intimidation can only be achieved either by capital punishment or by measures by which the relatives of the criminals do not know the fate of the criminal'. To this end, prisoners who had been detained for more than a week and had not been executed were to be handed over to the Gestapo or *SD*, who would see to it that they would 'vanish without trace'.[8] On top of the killing grounds around Warsaw, the authorities had numerous concentration camps at their disposal. In May 1940, about 1,500 prominent Polish prisoners were taken to Sachsenhausen where almost all of them died in the following months. Amongst the first to perish was Brigadier General Bolesław Roja, a prominent officer in the Polish Legions during the First World War. Gabriel Zych, another prisoner, described his death:

> When the war broke out, Roja was seriously ill. Nevertheless in March 1940 Gestapo officers … took the General off to the Pawiak …
>
> The arrival of a Polish general in the camp [in Oranienburg] was an unusual attraction for the guards. '*Wo ist der polnische General?*' ['Where is the Polish general?'] they kept coming and asking. The visits went on incessantly and after each one Roja was closer to death since none of the Nazi 'knights' could forego the pleasure of administering a few hefty kicks at the old general lying in a corner

> of the barrack. After a few days of this, Schubert, bored by the helpless old man's dying so long, beat him to death.[9]

Large numbers of prisoners were taken to Auschwitz and used as slave labour until malnutrition, disease, injuries, exposure, mistreatment, or so-called medical experiments took their lives. With everything shrouded in secrecy, many victims' families only learned what befell their loved ones during post-war investigations. On 20 June 1940, the day that Rataj and Niedziałkowski were shot, Halina Karśnicka received a note from her brother, who had been imprisoned for political conspiracy, telling her not to worry as he was being deported for agricultural work. When Karśnicka requested information from the Gestapo on her brother, she was told first that he was deported, and later that he had died in prison; only when she learned about the mass murder in Palmiry did she suspect the truth – that her brother had been shot alongside Rataj and Niedziałkowski – but she, like thousands of others, was denied true closure.[10]

The Warsaw Death Ring

The German apparatus of death maintained such a relentless pace throughout 1940 and 1941 that Palmiry alone could no longer accommodate the slaughter around Warsaw. Deportations to concentration camps had also increased, but more immediate – and less logistically demanding – solutions were required to deal with those sentenced to death. In May 1942, a Wehrmacht unit was deployed in Sękociński Forest near the village of Magdalenka, to the south of Warsaw, to excavate three substantial ditches. A few nights later, when a group of Pawiak prisoners were driven from their cells, they immediately suspected the worst: transports to concentration camps usually departed during daylight. Amongst the selected inmates were two women, Janina Mardej-Zamajska and Janina Górska, who were both seriously ill, and despite protests from other prisoners, they were loaded into the waiting trucks on stretchers. Together with about 200 men and 20 other women they were taken to Sękociński Forest and shot by a mixture of Germans and Ukrainians.[11] According to at least one account, some of the prisoners tried to resist:

> The Ukrainian guards who attended the execution gleefully described their exploits as they washed the blood off their boots. It appeared from their story that one of the groups of prisoners flung themselves on the SS-men carrying out the murder. Of course, bare fists were of no avail against machine-guns: they died fighting.[12]

Others named the leader of those who resisted as Roman Kukiełło, a major in the army. The identities of the victims were successfully uncovered by Polish resistance groups and many were named in the clandestine newsletter *Informacja Bieżąca* ('Current Information') within a few weeks. When the mass graves were exhumed after the war, there were signs that some of the dead had suffocated – they were still alive when they were buried.

Not far from the Sękociński Forest was another wooded area, Kabaty Wood, which became another site of mass executions between early 1940 until at least September 1943; yet another was the cemetery and nearby woodland at Wólka Węglowa, to the northwest of Warsaw. Collectively, these would later be remembered as the 'Warsaw Death Ring', a network of sites around the capital whose names were synonymous with massacre. Upon exhumation of the mass graves in Palmiry alone, Władysław Bartoszewski – who fought in the ranks of the resistance, was imprisoned in Auschwitz, and wrote extensively about the occupation – estimated a total of 1,793 people were shot over the course of 21 mass executions, including members of the intelligentsia, Jews, women, and children.[13] A forensic expert present at the exhumations described how prisoners would be lined up along a six-and-a-half-foot-wide pit in a specially prepared clearing, shot, and pushed into the pit even if they were still alive; scattered bullet holes on the trees showed where panicked prisoners had broken away from the execution clearings and tried to escape.[14]

Pawiak prison and Aleja Szucja

One of the most notorious names in the occupied city landscape was Pawiak, a former tsarist prison renamed *Gefängnis Warschau* under the Gestapo. The prison had been used to incarcerate Polish independence fighters during partition, so it was only too fitting that it once again became a focal point of the Varsovian occupation experience. The true horror of life inside can only be reconstructed through fragmentary survivor testimonies and underground records, and it is clear that operations evolved through the occupation. Varsovians of all ages, classes, and religions passed through Pawiak (and Serbia, the women's prison next door) on charges ranging from political sedition to denunciation to illicit study. Although the building's original architectural plans stipulated a capacity accommodation for 428 prisoners, as many as 2,000 would be crammed into Pawiak at any one time under the Nazis; detainees were constantly transferred onward to concentration camps or disappeared elsewhere, but the prison could barely cope with the dual pressures of growing public resistance and impulsive arrests.[15]

Prisoners were subjected to violence from their moment of arrival at the prison. Newcomers were shaved, stripped, beaten, and quarantined for 14 days in the prison basement before being inducted to regular prison life. Zygmunt Śliwicki, arrested in September 1940, spent nearly four years in Pawiak serving as prison physician; he would recall the pitiful rations, forced exercise, and strict rules that shaped everyday prison life – all of which was overshadowed by the constant threat of physical and mental brutalisation:

> The following methods were being used in Pawiak in order to force statements: bestial beatings with whips containing a wire inside, with rubber truncheons, with chairs or chair legs, and kicking. Some prisoners were tortured to death …
>
> Sometimes the Gestapo men would not allow us to provide the tortured prisoners with any medical aid. At the end of 1941, they forbade us to admit sick Jews to the hospital or to provide them with any medical aid. We had to do it secretly …
>
> In order to force statements, apart from beating, the Germans were using the dark cell or reducing the food ration by half … for up to 10 days. Those cells were in a damp basement … The prisoner was not being taken to the toilet at all. I remember that some major of the Polish Army was kept in the dark cell for over three months, in winter, without so much as a mattress or a blanket. Medical appeals to the prison commander to give this major at least a blanket, as it was very cold in his cell, were to no avail.[16]

Violence against Pawiak inmates was both a tool for extracting information and an exercise in casual, randomised brutality. Śliwicki himself received a lasting injury to his back from a passing knock from a rifle butt. Another Varsovian recalled witnessing the torture of a 72-year-old priest, who was ordered by guards to jump three feet in the air and beaten every time he failed to comply.[17] Stanisława Sroka, a nurse at Pawiak-Serbia, recalled watching a German officer push a usually bedridden woman down a flight of stairs for not moving quickly enough.[18]

The most barbaric interrogation torture, however, was saved for No. 25 Aleja Szucha: the former Ministry of Religion and Public Education, a fine neo-classicist building with Art Deco interiors. As soon as the *SD* moved in, it became a detention centre, its extensive basements converted into prison cells for the Gestapo and its upper floors transformed into a network of interrogation rooms. Every imaginable form of torture was used on prisoners, as one Polish labourer recounted:

> I saw people who were in good health when entering the building and who no longer looked like themselves when leaving it. I saw people crawling the stairs on their knees. Those who, because of the brutal torture to which they had been subjected, were unable to walk were beaten and kicked by Gestapo men. People suffered excruciating torture and it was next to impossible to stand their screams. There is no way of describing the scenes which took place there.[19]

Perhaps the most haunting testimonies come from the basement cells themselves, where prisoners scratched messages on to the walls; one of the most poignant read:

> It is easy to talk about Poland
> More difficult to work for her
> Still more difficult to die
> But it is most difficult to suffer.[20]

Prisoners knew what to expect when they were dispatched to Aleja Szucha or Pawiak. In many instances, detainees attempted to poison themselves en route to avoid compromising loved ones and colleagues – or simply to escape the excruciating torture they knew lay ahead. One of the only other chances of reprieve was if a prisoner was deemed too sick for interrogation or an infection risk to the rest of the prison population – typhus being an especially big concern – in which case there was a possibility of transfer to a hospital elsewhere. Otherwise, ill health was not enough to guarantee mercy; when one young boy was judged too sick to survive a beating, the SS arrested his mother and tortured the 50-year-old woman in view of the dying boy to force him to speak.[21] Felicjan Loth – an arrestee-turned-prison surgeon – witnessed the Germans' indiscriminate (and frequently fatal) violence towards prisoners suffering from dementia, the mentally impaired, and even pregnant women, deeming it proof 'that the most basic human feelings were completely foreign to the Germans.'[22] Another labourer in Szucha, Stefan Sokołowski, recalled seeing people throw themselves – or being pushed – out of windows during interrogations. He was desperate to leave the job because he 'could not endure psychologically':

> I saw many times those who had been interrogated being led out … I often saw that they had bruised faces, that they were covered in blood, and some were being led arm in arm by their fellow victims, as they could not walk by themselves. I also saw once the arrestees taking an unconscious woman out on a stretcher. She was about 30 years old …

> I remember that a 6–7 year old girl was walking by the stretcher, and she was calling out 'mummy' to the unconscious woman.

When Sokołowski attempted to resign, the Nazis gave him a choice: continue working for the Gestapo, or go to Auschwitz.[23]

THE MACHINERY OF MURDER

In the early years of occupation, the Germans were heavily dependent on Polish labour throughout the Warsaw prison system. Many pre-war guards remained at Pawiak, meaning that it was often Polish guards who were meting out punitive violence outside of interrogations. Still, they were more likely to offer sympathy than the German authorities and were frequently open to bribes. However, in November 1940, the sealing of the surrounding ghetto and escalation of *AB-Aktion* triggered a reassessment of Pawiak management and the SS formally took over all guard duties. Poles like Śliwicki and Loch continued to work in the prison's hospital, but they couldn't help but notice how the direct intervention of SS deputies made Pawiak even more hellish. Particularly notorious was Oberscharführer Franz Bürkl, a prison deputy who took a sadistic pleasure in the torture and murder of prisoners and, it was rumoured, had been assigned to Pawiak for precisely such 'special tasks'. Bürkl's reputation made him universally feared and loathed by occupants of the prison: he always had a German shepherd dog at his side and was the master of pedantic inspections (known amongst prisoners as *udziwienia*, or 'oddities') where prisoners would repeatedly be forced to empty their cells into the corridor and then retrieve everything; he also had a penchant for forcing prisoners to walk or crawl over red-hot cinders from the boiler house, and was an unscrupulous murderer known to shoot or hang prisoners on the slightest whim.[24] Unfortunately for Bürkl, his degeneracy turned him into a prime target for the Polish underground.

The atmosphere of Pawiak changed once again when, in March 1942, the remaining Polish prison staff were replaced by *Volksdeutsch* recruits and Ukrainian *Hilfswillige* ('voluntary helpers' or *Hiwis*) who began dispensing their own system of arbitrary savagery. In some cases, this stemmed from desires for revenge – many recruits harbouring grudges from the 1930s oppression of minorities – while in others, the growing casualness of violence was simply a reflection of the brutalising effects of war and the manner in which it was being conducted. Historian Christopher Browning describes how ordinary policemen, mobilised into battalions that were deployed for 'security' purposes in the occupied territories, were gradually exposed to increasing cruelty against civilians. They typically knew little about their task in advance and were first assigned to guard those who had been rounded up; volunteers were then requested to escort small groups of prisoners to selected killing grounds and to take part in firing squads.[25] Crucially, although peer pressure might have resulted in mockery and disapproval, there was no punishment for men who chose not to volunteer. After the war, many Germans and *Hiwis* would claim that they only took part in atrocities out of fear of punishment, but there are few recorded cases of anyone being formally reprimanded for refusing to take part in killings. By the time they arrived in Warsaw, most *Hiwis* and *Volksdeutsche* had been exposed to – or actively participated in – mass executions.

The commencement of Germany's war with the Soviet Union in June 1941 shifted Hitler's broader ambitions of warfare and mass murder further east. Populations in western Ukraine and the Baltic States, long suspicious of the USSR, offered fertile ground for Heydrich and others to nurture anti-Soviet sentiment. An integral part of this was to promote the German view that Bolshevism and Jewishness were effectively indistinguishable; in the Baltic States in particular, Jews were often seen to have collaborated with the Soviet authorities after the forcible annexation of the region and many of the resistance groups in Ukraine had strongly antisemitic views. These groups therefore proved all too willing to function as auxiliaries in the huge wave of killings that took place before the end of 1941, and, later, for redeployment to other regions such as Poland.

THE BLUE POLICE

But the Germans needed collaboration in areas other than the prisons and killing grounds. With ambitious arrest targets and limited SS and Gestapo personnel assigned to Warsaw, carrying out *Tannenberg*, *AB-Aktion*, and other killings while maintaining a semblance of public order relied on a substantial civilian police force. Thousands of Polish state police (*Policja Państwowa*) remained in Warsaw even after the government ordered evacuation, and by the end of 1939 the Germans had inducted them into a new auxiliary force, the *Granatowa policja* – or 'Blue Police', according to the colour of their uniforms. Strictly subordinated to the German police, this force was charged with day-to-day street policing and dealing with petty crimes involving non-Germans. By the end of 1942, the Blue Police force across the *Generalgouvernement* numbered around 14,300, of which 3,000 were stationed in Warsaw.[26]

The Polish underground resistance hoped that the pressganging of pre-war police officers into German collaboration would work to the advantage of the population. Unfortunately, as historian Jan Grabowski's damning examination of the Blue Police's *Generalgouvernement* operations has revealed, this was far from the case. Even excusing the fact that they were functioning under German directives, the Blue Police were often viewed with suspicion for being self-serving, 'brave associates in murder', theft, pillage, and general brutality towards their compatriots, and were known to act on their own initiative to wage localised campaigns of persecution for their own profit.[27] Emmanuel Ringelblum went further, claiming that the Blue Police capitalised on the defencelessness of Jews, implying that the very act of continuing to refer to them as 'the Blue or uniformed police' was simply a means of masking the less than palatable record of 'Polish' policemen in carrying out antisemitic persecution. The force was, in his view, 'an enthusiastic executor of all German directives regarding the Jews', and he pointed out that policemen were incentivised with 'a reward for every Jew caught, namely one third of his property.'[28]

As in many cases of collaboration under occupation, the truth is more nuanced. On the one hand, the Blue Police were instrumental in the formation of Polish ghettos, the rounding up of 'undesirables', and the preparation of deportees for resettlement – and there are countless anecdotes to confirm their cooperation in these operations. In March 1941, the Blue Police willingly carried out an order to execute a number of Jews in the Warsaw Ghetto for smuggling; in the winter of the same year, they carried out two mass executions in the yard of Gęsiówka prison on top of their daily dispensation of violence; and in 1943 the Blue Police supported the Germans in crushing the Ghetto Uprising.[29] In the aftermath of the failed uprising, the policemen looked on as Jews such as Mietek Pachter were packed into trains bound for concentration camps:

> We see the Polish 'Blue' policemen. They stand by, watching this parade of death. A few of them stand farther away from the Germans and quietly say: 'Throw us your diamonds and money, you won't need them anymore.' Who could possibly be more vulgar than these leeches? I cannot contain myself and I shout: 'Don't think you are safe! Your moment shall also come – be damned!' I can only damn them from the bottom of my soul … A few others started swearing at the police; the marching crowd was riled up by the policemen, while the policemen's impudence and greed reached its peak. But, after all, what could one expect? Why should the collaborators be any better than their masters? They work together so well.[30]

The Directorate of Civil Resistance, created to coordinate various branches of resistance activity, had created a set of underground courts to administer justice. It was for such crimes as those described above that these courts sentenced Blue Police Lieutenant Roman Leon Święcicki to execution, followed by at least 38 more policemen in 1943.[31] On the other hand, it is telling that the Germans remained sceptical of the indigenous force, complaining that 'policemen not only do not fulfil their obligations adequately, but outright facilitate criminal behaviour' by obstructing arrest efforts.[32] The first commander of the Blue Police, Marian Kozielewski (brother of resistance courier Jan 'Karski' Kozielewski), attempted to use his power to support and protect the occupied population while sabotaging the Nazis, but by the summer of 1940 the Germans' suspicions were aroused and he was sent to Auschwitz. Kozielewski was replaced by Aleksander Reszczyński, who, by way of contrast, offered words of encouragement to his subordinates during mass executions: 'Keep your chin up, boys! Be strong!'[33]

It is difficult to ascertain exact numbers, but the Blue Police counted hundreds of members of the underground amongst its ranks who were variously involved in training resistance fighters, distributing intelligence, acquiring 'Aryan' documents, delivering supplies, and even neutralising unwelcome informers in the Polish community. Some played a role in enabling would-be arrestees to escape, either by alerting targeted individuals in advance or else fumbling the arrests themselves, making 'plenty of noise by shouting on the streets and breaking doors to give enough time for some people to escape or hide.'[34] Numerous policemen were shot by the Germans for refusing to carry out executions or showing sympathy for the underground. For the most part, the most reprehensible behaviour towards fellow countrymen – and even Jews – was less a sign of ideological alignment with the Nazis than an instinct for exploiting the occupation for their own gain. Moreover, it is striking that for all the acrimony they provoked, the Blue Police were still less detested than the Jewish Ghetto Police.[35]

Invisible Intelligence-Gathering

Police infiltration was just one mechanism the Poles leveraged to undermine German models of repression; another was penetration of the prison system. From November 1939, the head of the Information and Propaganda Department of the *Służba Zwycięstwu Polski* ('Polish Victory Service' or *SZP*) Warsaw Headquarters, Zygmunt Hempel, set out to establish intelligence networks that penetrated every one of the city's prisons. There were two hospital wards in the prison, one for each sex, and the Polish medical staff in each were enlisted to establish and maintain contact with prisoners, enabling the Polish underground to maintain relatively accurate records of who was imprisoned, deported, or executed. Intelligence on key SS personnel, meanwhile, would later facilitate various assassination attempts.

In the early years of occupation, these networks of activity were chaotic and inconsistent. Before the surrounding ghetto was enclosed, for example, prisoners could throw *grypsy* (clandestine notes) through the prison windows where they could be picked up by civilians. After the sealing of the ghetto, however, communication became harder, and prisoners had to bribe guards or use underground contacts to help smuggle messages out and food supplies in. Prison staff and labourers were crucial here, too; dentist Anna Sipowicz-Gościcka spent 'some three or four years' working in Pawiak 'engaged in the large-scale smuggling of messages to the families of prisoners', which also meant shouldering the burden of passing on news of execution or deportation to families denied any information from the Germans.[36] Messages were smuggled from the outside into the prison, too, keeping members of the resistance up to date with developments on the street. After his arrest one morning in February 1940, underground activist Stefan Korboński recalled a moment in Pawiak when he 'was munching a roll when I started to choke and felt something strange in my throat'. His wife had sent him a scrap of paper explaining his detention – he was being held hostage for the duration of Frank's visit to Warsaw.[37] Yet where high-profile political prisoners were concerned, prison staff were powerless to intervene in any meaningful way. As Nurse Stanisława Sroka recalled:

> At the beginning of December 1939, the former president of the city, Starzyński, was brought to the prison. He was kept in absolute isolation, so that even when he was allowed to go to the toilet or to get some water, the corridors had to be empty. His cell was guarded by the Gestapo men only. As for food, Starzyński received only bread and water, the same amount of bread as other prisoners. He did not receive soups. Only after five days or a week, upon appeal from the chief of the female ward, Klunderowa, did he begin to receive soups. He could not receive any packages from his family. He was also forbidden to walk. Also thanks to Klunderowa, he could use baths and books. He was taken for a bath quite often, as it provided an opportunity to slip him some chocolate or other dry foods through the Polish prison guard, but only in such quantities as he could safely conceal in his pocket ... When someone suggested to him asking the German authorities for permission to receive dinners from home, he answered that he was not going to ask Germans for anything.[38]

Sympathetic staff could only bear witness to the cruelty to which beloved community leaders, former politicians, and resistance fighters were subjected – and report back to the underground. If the Germans believed sequestering key members of the intelligentsia would dampen resistance, they had not counted upon the Poles' underground networks being quite so far-reaching.

Escape from prison was incredibly difficult but not altogether unknown. Fearing that he could not stand up to ongoing torture in Pawiak, photographer Stanisław Tomaszewski – arrested for attempting to document Nazi atrocities – asked his underground allies to smuggle him some poison. His request was denied, and he was instead sent to the prison dentist, who intentionally infected him with typhus as a means of justifying his transfer to a hospital for infectious diseases. A feigned bout of appendicitis, a mock operation, and the replacement of his body with a corpse completed his extraordinary escape.[39] According to his father, 17-year-old Olgierd Wilczewski (also a member of the underground) managed to escape three times; twice through bribes, and once from a train en route to the camps.[40] Generally, escape was usually a matter of chance that not everyone was prepared to take: most were aware that failure could lead to disastrous consequences for co-conspirators, fellow prisoners, or loved ones outside the prison.

These systems of incarceration, torture, and slaughter would have been impossible to sustain without the particular talents of inhumanity and psychopathy that the Nazi regime so favoured. One such role model was the corpulent Josef Meisinger, who after inheriting command of *Einsatzgruppe IV* during 1939, became *Kommandeur der Sicherheitspolizei und des Sicherheitsdienstes* ('Commander of the Security Police and the *SD*' or *KdS*) for the Warsaw District. In this role, he oversaw the Warsaw Death Ring operations, enthusiastically collecting large numbers of hostages in response to acts of resistance and then executing them if perpetrators failed to surrender. In December 1939, 107 Poles were shot on his orders in retaliation for the deaths of two Germans. Even Heydrich commented that his methods were 'extremely radical', and Meisinger quickly became known as the 'butcher of Warsaw' amongst both Poles and Germans – a title that he would share with several other Germans.[41] In his admittedly self-serving memoir, Schellenberg described him as committing 'bestial acts', and that after reading a file regarding Meisinger's conduct, Himmler intended to have Meisinger arrested and shot. He was saved by an intervention by Heydrich, who in April 1941 appointed his protégé as police liaison officer and special representative of the *SD* in Tokyo. That Meisinger faced prosecution for cruelty when such treatment of occupied populations was officially sanctioned underlines the extraordinary level of his barbarity.

Meisinger's replacement as *KdS* in the Warsaw District was Sturmbannführer Johannes Müller, and then Sturmbannführer Ludwig Hahn, a veteran of *Tannenberg* and the *AB-Aktion* in Kraków, who remained in Warsaw until the Germans abandoned the city in 1945. Hahn's merciless campaign against resistance was documented in post-war investigations which uncovered 29 public notices where he announced the execution of more than 1,500 hostages in retaliation for anti-German actions.[42] Records from the Gross-Rosen and Stutthof concentration camps showed that in addition to dispatching large numbers of prisoners to these facilities, he also ordered the murder of specific individuals. His actions met with the approval of his superiors and Obergruppenführer Ernst Kaltenbrunner – who replaced Heydrich after the latter was assassinated in 1942 – advocated for Hahn's promotion, describing him as 'an old, tried, and tested National Socialist and an energetic SS leader who always rose to the occasion … he was particularly distinguished by his wide-ranging experience, meticulous working methods, and organisational skills.'[43]

The Germans' persecution of Polish cultural identity represented just one facet of the comprehensive eastern colonisation strategy which gradually took shape between 1939 and 1942. Compiled jointly by the *Reichssicherheitshauptamt* ('Reich Security Main Office' or *RSHA*) and the *Reichskommissar für die Festigung deutschen Volkstums* ('Reich Commissioner for the Consolidation of German Nationhood' or *RKFDV*), the *Generalplan Ost* ('General Plan East') – as the plan became known – detailed the systematic removal of Slavs, Jews, and other 'undesirable' populations in readiness for German expansion. The scale of what was intended was both horrific and enormous: more than 60 million people were to die, through execution, being worked to death, or famine. About 80 million Russians would be pushed east beyond the Ural Mountains into Siberia where they were expected to 'fend for themselves' – a euphemism for inevitable starvation.[44] At the same time, Nazi racial theorists devised elaborate racial categorisations of people in Eastern Europe to decide which groups could be sufficiently 'Germanised' to be incorporated into the Reich for much-needed labour. The implementation of *Generalplan Ost* was divided into two phases: the 'small plan', which would proceed as soon as territories were conquered and included operations such as the *Intelligenzaktion* and *AB-Aktion*, and the 'large plan', which would commence after the end of the war and would necessitate mass killing on an even greater scale. In Poland, *Generalplan Ost* required the 'removal' of at least 20 million people – more than 80 per cent of the population – within 15–20 years to make way for millions of German settlers. About 2 million Poles would be 'Germanised' and a rump population of up to 4 million would be left as slave labour, forbidden to marry or to receive medical care, thus slowly fading away. In the meantime, experiments on concentration camp prisoners were used to investigate the practicalities of mass sterilisation, which would have been rolled out as part of the 'large plan'.[45]

The Germans therefore saw little reason to invest in or manage the welfare of an occupied Polish population whose days they considered numbered. But at the same time, it would be impossible to extract labour from a starved populus, and dealing with a disease-riddled, poverty-stricken public would put the occupiers themselves in greater danger. Fear of contagion was a recurring theme in the occupied territories of the east, though German public health officials would always blame illnesses on what they described as the lower level of social development of inferior races rather than reconsider the policies that were the true cause. In any case, the Germans didn't block the work of native charitable welfare organisations across the *Generalgouvernement.* In September 1939, Mayor Starzyński oversaw the establishment of the *Stołeczny Komitet Sampomocy Społecznej* ('Capital Social Welfare Committee' or *SKSS*), which was permitted to continue coordinating transport, health, supplies, youth welfare, labour affairs, and the care of refugees across the city. From 1940, the *SKSS* worked alongside the *Rada Opiekuńcza Miejska* ('City Welfare Council' or *ROM*), the Warsaw branch of a larger *Generalgouvernement* group, and the *Rada Główna Opiekuńcza* ('Central Welfare Council' or *RGO*) responsible for acquiring resources and liaising with authorities. As in the previous war, American donations through the Polish Red Cross and Commission for Polish Relief provided significant support, but, in addition to public collections and even official funding from the occupation regime, the *RGO* also received clandestine donations from the Polish government-in-exile and benefited from close ties to the Polish underground. Alongside sanitation, one of the most pressing issues for the occupied city was food aid and the creation of community kitchens; in total, around 26 million meals were distributed to Varsovian adults and 17 million to children, with total monthly beneficiaries reaching 200,000.[46] Members of the intelligentsia, former soldiers, officials, and activists turned to these organisations for employment, and the remarkable resilience of these groups against unsympathetic authorities was at least partly attributable to the influential social standing of their leaders. Even so, by early 1940, the *SKSS* was increasingly burdened by German surveillance and interference, with treasurer Wacław Fabierkiewicz frequently hauled away for questioning with the Gestapo. In February of 1941, Fischer ordered the liquidation of the *SKSS*, but Varsovian and national welfare efforts survived in various forms right through to December 1944.

Meanwhile, the closure of schools across Poland resulted in a major fall in children undergoing any education; by 1941, elementary school attendance across the *Generalgouvernement* was barely half the pre-war level.[47] Even this was better than the annexed parts of Poland, where all classes were conducted in German and Polish was banned. But as in other Polish responses to German repression, the experiences of the partition decades were put to good use: in 1882, when tsarist Russia made a new attempt to 'Russify' Congress Poland and imposed similar bans on education in any language other than Russian, secret classes were organised in private houses in Warsaw. These were eventually merged into a single structure that became known as the *Uniwersytet Latający* (literally 'Floating University', usually translated as 'Flying University') which provided courses for students of both sexes and classes that relocated regularly to avoid detection. Over the following two decades, a large number of leading Polish intellectuals contributed to the Flying University to the benefit of about 5,000 students – including twice Nobel Prize-winner Maria Skłodowska-Curie.[48] In the same vein, October 1939 saw the creation of the *Tajna Organizacja Nauczycielska* ('Secret Teaching Organisation' or *TON*) which sought to organise primary-level education across the *Generalgouvernement*. Within a few months, it increased its scope to cover secondary education and was also involved in the printing and distribution of Polish-language books. By the end of the German occupation, this had evolved into a new incarnation of the Flying University, covering education from elementary to university level, with many from the dwindling ranks of Polish teachers and academics taking part. It is estimated that even as early as 1942, over 1.5 million students had benefited from its activities, with groups operating not only in Warsaw but also in Lwów, Vilnius, and Kraków, and smaller 'branches' in other cities.[49]

Another element of former life under partition that enjoyed a revival was the underground press. The Poles' thirst for information was heightened by their isolation under Nazi occupation; war was raging across Europe while their own government was sitting in exile thousands of miles away, and the Germans were waging a concerted campaign to deprive them of reliable news. The pages of German publications such as the *Nowy Kurjer Warszawski* were filled with tales of victories for the Reich, cowardliness on the part of the Allies, and gushing testaments to the Führer's superiority. The purpose of the 'reptile press' was purely propagandistic, not to foster Polish loyalty towards the German authorities so much as to convince them of the finality of defeat; as far as facts were concerned, Polish readers had read between the lines to glean insights into the Nazis' outlook and their current preoccupations. This left a vacuum waiting to be filled by Polish journalists who felt they had a duty in 'informing society, inspiring and regulating the behaviour of the masses, and setting out future prospects'. Feminist activist and journalist Jadwiga Krawczyńska described how the majority of press workers spared by the *Intelligenzaktion* abhorred the idea of registering to work for the Germans.

Instead, groups of writers met in secret, in the Blikle Café on Nowy Świat Street, the Social Committee canteen on Smolna Street, or the *Pomoc Gospodarcza* ('Economic Aid') cooperative grocery store, lamenting their lost livelihoods, bemoaning their new menial occupations, and dreaming of intellectual escape through ambitious resistance projects.[50] One of the first to act was career scout leader and member of the *Związek Walki Zbrojnej* ('Union for Armed Struggle' or *ZWZ*), Aleksander Kamiński. On 31 May 1940, Kamiński published the first edition of *Biuletyn Informacyjny* ('Information Bulletin') in Warsaw: four pages of unbroken text under the mysterious instructions, '*biuletyn zniszcz osobiście*' – 'destroy bulletin personally'.[51] Each weekly edition was packed with international developments, news of the Polish military forces and government abroad, stories from across Poland, and evidence to contradict the propaganda being pushed by the Germans. Nevertheless, this indigenous press had its own agenda. From naming Gestapo informants to denouncing unpatriotic behaviour, reporting on trials held by the underground Directorate of Civil Resistance to offering advice on how to inconvenience the occupiers, *Biuletyn Informacyjny* fuelled Varsovian solidarity while providing a framework for acceptable and non-acceptable behaviour under occupation. As more than a source of news, the paper kept the public – and not just the intelligentsia – engaged in constant, democratised habits of resistance. In November 1940, Kamiński explained that although 'insurgent action and sabotage of a military nature' were 'inadvisable' for the present, everyone – 'men, women, children, members of organisations and people still unaffiliated must take part in the action of *mały sabotaż* ["petty" or "minor sabotage"]':

Here are examples of *mały sabotaż*:

1. Dragging out the time of work carried out to the order of the occupier in his own occupation
2. Various 'mistakes' made in the work ordered by the Germans
3. Falsely informing Germans asking for directions (losing them fuel and time)
4. Responding: 'I don't understand' to any attempts to make contact, not accepting any German services e.g. in trains, trams (creates a feeling of unkindness, hostility)

> 5. Disregarding all German regulations, negligent execution of them, putting them off until the last minute, etc.
> 6. Various types of 'dog tricks' (anonymous denunciation to the Gestapo of some zealous Volksdeutsche …)
>
> A moment's reflection will allow each of us to expand and complement the examples given here with ever new ideas … [to] make the enemy's stay in the occupied area burdensome and unpleasant.[52]

At its height, *Biuletyn Informacyjny* boasted a circulation of 43,000–50,000 copies, each of which was likely shared, passed on, and re-read both within and outside Warsaw.[53] Although it was one of the most popular underground newspapers to last the course of occupation, it was certainly not the only option for information-starved Poles. Jadwiga Krawczyńska was recruited to help in the production of *Dziennik Radiowy* ('Radio Diary'), which compiled news from intercepted radio transmissions and monitoring across Europe. This work was fraught with danger and relied on an improvised network of technicians, liaison officers, and couriers to circumvent the confiscation of radio receivers. When Krawczyńska suspected her maid was spying on her on behalf of the Gestapo, she took to scattering her desk with 'some hastily cobbled together pseudo-sentiment novel' as a precautionary cover of her real work. Unlike *Biuletyn Informacyjny*, *Dziennik Radiowy* was not intended for public consumption and instead served the paramilitary and conspiratorial interests of the *ZWZ*, the Government Delegation (representing Polish civilian government), and the Home Army; as Krawczyńska would later discover, however, the journal was secretly copied and circulated far beyond its original audience.[54] Soon there emerged a proliferation of titles from political groups and denominations across the spectrum, scouting organisations, women's groups, cultural associations, and professional circles. The format, frequency, and target audience varied, but the appeal of cultivating solidarity through shared narratives remained the same. Warsaw was the centre of these operations, housing, at peak, some 200 clandestine publishing presses that produced 700 different publications.[55]

Publishers were under no illusion that their papers would not fall into German hands, and, at times, took the opportunity to goad their occupiers in their search for intelligence:

> Publishing a successful underground newspaper required men who were thoroughly trained and competent, not merely to produce effective journalism but to make sure that nothing of importance was revealed to the enemy ...

> The editors of many of these papers took pleasure in sending copies directly to Gestapo headquarters in Warsaw, usually with a message: 'We are sending you a copy of our paper to facilitate your research, to let you know what we think of you, and to keep you informed of our plans for you.'[56]

Still, the distribution of these publications through the city was carefully controlled. The underground drew upon the 'three-system' – created by former Piłsudski ally and president of Poland Stanisław Wojciechowski, who had been a clandestine editor and printer under the tsarist regime – according to which everyone involved in the circulation of a paper only knew 'one man behind and one man ahead' in the chain so authorities would struggle to trace any publication back to its source.[57] The public improvised ingenious methods to circulate the publications, which became yet another element of the seamless ebb and flow between conspiracy and subservience that characterised daily life under occupation:

> Newsboys on the streets of Warsaw and Kraków sold the German local papers … No Pole bought these papers, unless the boy smilingly said to him:
>
> '*Today* you have extraordinary news about German victories … buy it.' And handed him a copy. The passer-by knew the copy was worth buying, for it was stuffed. Between the pages full of German dispatches describing incredible successes of the swastika-bearing flag, he found a hidden copy of his underground paper.
>
> A butcher would say to a woman customer, while wrapping her steak:
>
> 'Put it on ice *immediately* when you reach home, will you?'
>
> And she would know that the paper was wrapped inside.[58]

The 10,000 metre gold medallist Janusz Kusociński – who was killed during *AB-Aktion* – worked as a waiter in a Warsaw café at the time of his arrest, where he would slip underground newspapers under patrons' plates.[59]

The expansion of underground communication channels beyond the capital significantly bolstered credibility and morale for the resistance. The wife of Stefan Korboński, Zofia, stumbled almost by accident across an intercepted message alluding to 'a secret underground radio station broadcasting daily in the Polish language at 8am and 7pm.' Stefan and Zofia were astonished, for despite being involved in the clandestine transmission of broadcasts to London, they weren't aware of any other channels broadcasting on the Poles' behalf besides the BBC. A telegram from General Władysław Sikorski, Supreme Commander of Polish Forces in London, cleared the mystery up: the radio station known as *Świt* ('Dawn') was masquerading as a station inside Poland to 'confuse' and 'harass' the occupying forces while actually being broadcast from the safety of an Allied country. The international credibility of *Świt* as an authentic player in the Polish underground depended on it receiving a steady stream of up-to-date news from life under occupation, so the Korbońskis set to work compiling stories and Stefan roamed the streets of Warsaw collecting German execution lists, decrees, and gruesome anecdotes to raise awareness amongst the foreign audience.[60] But the broadcasters also revelled in the fact that the occupiers were obsessively monitoring the station and puzzling over its provenance, and invented ingenious 'ways of making fools of the Germans'. On one occasion, Korboński managed to acquire early galley proofs of the latest edition of the Germans' *Nowy Kurjer Warszawski*, and, selecting the most laughable propagandistic excerpts, forwarded them to the *Świt* team with 'a single word of instruction: "Ridicule".'[61] In other cases, the Warsaw team used the radio station to intimidate the listening German authorities and to call out the executors of particularly horrific atrocities. Thus Korboński frequently issued instructions with brutal specificity:

> Broadcast a threat to Geyer, head of the German police in Kielce, who personally killed two village officials and the wife and two daughters of the village secretary during a reprisal expedition to Samsonowo. Broadcast a threat to Gestapo agent Witek in Lagow Kielecki for burning several families alive in a barn, and to railway official Vogt in Jedrzejow, who shot a passenger and railway worker Kudera without provocation …
>
> Keep repeating the following announcement: 'The Gestapo has recently embarked upon a new wave of terror … The Poles cannot be intimidated by such senseless and cruel activity. In reprisal for this kind of terror, additional retaliatory measures will be taken by the underground.'[62]

Świt celebrated efforts of resistance, Polish martyrdom, and the justice meted out by the underground courts. According to Korboński, the Germans didn't realise it was broadcasting from abroad until 1944, by which time it had gained national and international momentum – and the Gestapo had wasted considerable resources on rooting it out.[63]

The information war was not bound to the printed word and airwaves. Poles everywhere understood that the silence over their country's fate had to be shattered and the full horror of German barbarism exposed to the light of day; unless they could make their voices heard, their government-in-exile stood little chance of influencing Allied Powers who had already failed to come to the country's aid and internal resistance movements would struggle in oblivion. This challenge produced a particular breed of underground activist: couriers, inconspicuous agents willing to endanger their lives travelling across Poland and Europe for the sake of trafficking information.

Perhaps the most famous Polish courier was Jan 'Karski' Kozielewski, a former secretary in the Ministry of Foreign Affairs who, like many couriers, had extensive travel experience, spoke several languages, and felt it his duty to serve the underground when his pre-war career (divided between study and military service) became impossible. He was born in Łódź but drawn to Warsaw by family and friends – including his brother Marian, the conspiratorial chief of the Blue Police – and found himself recruited into the *SZP* by an old friend. The violinist Leon Dziepątowski had accompanied Karski during his university days when he had toured the Lwów provinces giving 'rousing lecture[s] on history, Polish literature, hygiene, or the co-operative movement'; whilst Karski sought to 'bring about a rapprochement between the intelligentsia and the peasants', Dziepątowski's role was to make the lectures 'a trifle less tedious' by rewarding those who stayed to the end with his musical talent.[64] In any case, Dziepątowski had obviously picked up on Karski's deep social conscience and empathy for Poles in all classes. When the pair reunited during occupation, Karski shared his sense of powerlessness; 'I know that the Allies will win the war sooner or later,' he told his friend, 'but, meanwhile, we have to live here. Conditions and the inability to do anything affect people. It is only natural.' Dziepątowski regarded his friend and thought for a moment before replying. 'Jan,' he said, lowering his voice slightly and speaking very slowly, 'not every Pole has resigned himself to fate.'[65]

After completing several initiation missions for the resistance, Karski was dispatched to France in early 1940 to connect with General Sikorski, who communicated to him the 'Doctrine of the Polish Underground': the order that all resistance groups – regardless of their political outlook – were to work together within the underground state.[66] Karski's work demanded the transgression of social boundaries as well as national borders. In preparation for his foreign reports, he undertook complex – and highly dangerous – research missions across Warsaw, interviewing Poles, Jews, Zionists, and Bundists, and even visited the Bełżec death camp to formulate a nuanced picture of experiences under occupation. Armed with thousands of pages of printed material – recorded on microfilms no larger than a couple of matchsticks and secreted within the handle of a razor – he travelled to Great Britain and the United States where he delivered reports on the Polish situation to the government-in-exile, the Allied governments, Jewish community leaders, and Polish exiles.

On arrival in London, General Sikorski awarded Karski the Cross of the Virtuti Militari, Poland's highest military honour, for his services. The reception he received from the Western Allies, however, was variable. Karski's meeting with future British prime minister Anthony Eden left a mark on him, not least because, as a student, he had idolised Eden's work in the League of Nations Council; but Eden ultimately disappointed him, stating that since Great Britain had already accepted 100,000 Polish refugees, further support would not be forthcoming.[67] Karski's overall impression was that occupied Poland was still an afterthought for the Western Allies:

> Poland's contribution to the war effort was a far different thing in a cold, conspiratorial meeting place than the world saw it from remote London. In London, our effort meant some hundreds of thousands of Polish soldiers, a handful of ships, a few thousand Polish aviators who were hailed for their heroic feats in the Battle of Britain but soon became lost in the overwhelming mass of Allied air power. Our efforts meant the brief September campaign and some echoes of obstinate resistance.
>
> In London these things bulked small. London was the hub of a vast military wheel, the spokes of which were made up of billions of dollars, armadas of bombers and ships, and staggering armies that had suffered great losses. Then, too, people asked where did Polish sacrifice rank next to the immeasurable heroism, sacrifice, and suffering of the Russian people? What was the share of Poland in this titanic undertaking? Who were the Poles?[68]

Even the exiled Polish officers and politicians Karski encountered struggled to understand the plight of their compatriots under occupation. Many failed to understand Poland's place in the war beyond the exiled Polish Army; others feared that Karski's discussions of Jewish persecution risked derailing support for the national cause.

Former artilleryman Jan Nowak-Jeziorański followed in Karski's footsteps in advocating for the Polish resistance cause in London, but in 1941 the 27-year-old started his couriering journey trafficking a very different type of information. The Home Army cell to which he was assigned, *Akcja N* ('Action' or 'Section N' – N being short for *Niemcy*, Polish for 'Germany'), was dedicated to the production of various German-language propaganda materials intended to shake the convictions of Third Reich civilians, *Volksdeutsche*, Wehrmacht troops, and even senior occupation officials. The key was to make these publications – fluent in German war slang and Gothic lettering – appear as though they were being produced by anti-Hitler groups within the Reich itself. The result was an array of literature catering to different parts of the German population and bearing pithy titles such as *Goldfasanen* ('golden pheasants', slang for 'party bigwigs'), *Etappenschweine* ('pigs in gold braid'), or the ominous *Kennst Du die Wahrheit?* ('Do You Know the Truth?').[69] Couriers like Nowak took the papers on trains across the German frontier where they were mailed across the Reich, slipped into restaurant menus, or even dropped straight into soldiers' knapsacks.[70] In early 1943, Nowak turned his focus to coordinating distribution through the Gydnia and Gdańsk ports; from here, he sought to push clandestine materials not only onto German warships and U-boats, but also onto ships bound for neutral Sweden, where he hoped the defeatist messaging might create a 'journalistic sensation and considerable public stir.'[71]

Couriering was a risky business for everyone involved. The couriers themselves knew to expect torturous interrogations if they fell into the hands of the German police and dreaded the idea of being forced to betray their underground colleagues. As Nowak admitted, 'no one who has never undergone police interrogation and torture can be sure how he will behave when water is being poured through his nostrils, or when he is hung by his hands from a beam with his feet off the floor, or when his genitals are being pounded with a metal bar.'[72] Moreover, couriering was only possible thanks to a complex network of guides, hosts, and other loose allies who, on the one hand, added potential points of compromise to every operation, but on the other, endangered themselves each time they provided assistance. When, on one occasion, Karski and his guide were discovered sheltering in a peasant's safe-house and arrested by German gendarmes, he only blamed himself:

> Across the room, I could see the guide undergoing a similar beating and questioning. At one point, his face streaming with blood, he looked up at the peasant, not in anger or hate, but in deep, resigned sorrow.
>
> 'Why did you do it?' he asked reproachfully.
>
> The peasant shook his head inarticulately and blinked painfully as tears ran down his plump, coarse-grained cheeks. I did not believe he was a traitor … Franek, the missing guide, must have been arrested. Under torture, he had probably revealed the complete route and all the stopping points. My guide's forebodings had been warranted. This was the bitter result of his adherence to me out of a sense of duty and loyalty, despite the clarity with which he had foreseen our dangers. I could have wept with shame. How could I have pressured him like that? Why hadn't I kept on going until the end of our journey?
>
> As we were dragged out of the house, I kept shouting to him over and over: 'I am sorry! … I am sorry!'
>
> I could see him smile weakly at me as if granting my plea and urging me to keep up my courage and faith. We were separated on the spot and dragged off in opposite directions. I never saw or heard of him again.[73]

With the Germans systematically targeting Polish military-aged men, it fell to women and youngsters to step into the roles of couriering, guiding, and liaising. *Łączniczki*, or liaison girls, took advantage of gender stereotypes to mask their clandestine activity, pushing strollers and lugging grocery bags to camouflage the transport of illegal materials. Compared to agents like Karski and Nowak, the *łączniczki* were 'completely exposed'; the underground held the girls under constant surveillance and demanded their homes – and lives – be placed at the disposal of resistance efforts. Once captured – which, according to Karski, was more or less an inevitability – they were trained to expect no chance of escape and to poison themselves rather than succumb to the particularly bestial torture the Gestapo reserved for such cases. Karski recalled one 22- or 23-year-old who was arrested in a trolley car bearing compromising documents; she failed to swallow her poison, but a message smuggled out of the prison described her fate – 'When they carried her away, the lower half of her body was in shreds.'[74] One of the saddest aspects of the *łączniczki* girls' stories is that the majority fought, made sacrifices, and suffered in obscurity. In Karski's words, 'their lot was the most severe, their sacrifices the greatest, and their contribution the least rewarded. They were overworked and doomed. They neither held high rank nor received any great honours for their heroism.'[75]

As the journalist Krawczyńska described, the 'hunger for information' was 'one of the most severe occupation hungers' intended to isolate the Poles and crush their morale, so underground communication, in its various forms, constituted a powerful force of public resistance. Considering the number of intellectuals who had already lost their lives, faced imprisonment, or suffered the annihilation of their professional legacies, the very act of mobilising against German proscription became more than just a duty for the intelligentsia; it was an opportunity for intellectual reinvigoration, comradery, and, however fleeting, for hope:

> Our lovely liaison officers would sometimes come to me outside the morning round of the obligatory collection of the 'Diary' typescript to warm themselves by the electric lamp, the so-called 'sun', which gave the illusion that something was warming us … These conversations with the young people were good, the beautiful atmosphere of their nobility in the surrounding world of horror, terror, misery … I think of them often … and their lively, young voices. Of the three, Dorota … was soon to die.[76]

Of course, information wasn't the only clandestine cargo in circulation. The siege of Warsaw had crippled supply chains of food, medicine, and other vital resources, and the occupation authorities showed little interest in seeing them restored. The black market that sprang up became an open secret and, like the native charitable organisations, fulfilled a function that the occupiers were unwilling to shoulder themselves. Smuggling and distribution of prohibited goods carried the most severe of penalties, but this didn't deter those eager to profit from their desperate compatriots. Szpilman observed:

> Unexpectedly, all these people – people without a roof over their heads, without work, with the gloomiest of prospects – realized that large sums of money could be made with great ease by circumventing German decrees. The more decrees were issued, the higher the chances of earning.
>
> Two lives began to go on side by side: an official, fictional life based on rules which forced people to work from dawn to dusk, almost without eating, and a second, unofficial life, full of fairy-tale opportunities to make a profit, with a flourishing trade in dollars, diamonds, flour, leather or even forged papers – a life lived under constant threat of the death penalty.[77]

Prices of bread and potatoes were 30 times higher than they had been in 1939 and a luxury like bacon was 60 times more expensive. But according to Karski, the black market profiteering was generally not a cause for resentment; it was thanks to the disinterest of the occupying authorities that 'everyone was left to his own devices', so 'any trick that would get someone more food was moral.'[78] Smuggling and illegal exchange were unavoidable in occupied life, and the ingenuity of those involved demonstrated Polish capacity to develop 'talents equal to their inhuman sufferings.'[79] One story circulated about a 'legendary pig that was conveyed in a railway compartment dressed up as a peasant woman, with a shawl covering its dead snout', which even elicited a laugh from the normally humourless gendarmes.[80] Women played a major role in the distribution of clandestine food supplies too, from producing bread in illegal bakeries, to secreting bags of supplies under their clothes, to resisting arrest or attempting daring escapes from the authorities. It is impossible to quantify the scale of black market operations, but certainly the majority of the population benefited or were in some way involved in these informal networks of exchange. Another popular joke ran:

> Question: How could the Allied armies land on the continent in such a way that the Germans would not notice?
> Answer: Entrust the Polish black market with the task … and rest easy.[81]

Despite the daily horrors, the struggle for survival, the personal losses, and the unfathomable scale of German brutality, the Poles' appetite for resistance only grew. Like Szpilman, Krawczyńska described a duality of existence split between the immediate terror of occupation and the dynamic life of the underground: 'real life reigned here,' she wrote, 'human, cultural, professional and social energies developed in many ways, and substitute forms of normal existence were created.'[82] There would always be individuals willing to sell out their neighbours or to profit from the occupation regime, but the mood across Poland, and in Warsaw in particular, was one of quiet determination. For the Germans, establishment of a collaborationist regime in Poland was impossible not only – as is commonly assumed – because of the unacceptability of permitting the racially inferior Poles to set up a government, but also because the Poles were staunchly resistant to the idea in the first place. This oppositional attitude extended far back to the pre-war years when the Poles rebuffed Hitler's advances time and again over Danzig and the Polish Corridor. To quote Connelly, 'Poland was the first country to say no to Hitler'; what triggered the Germans' particular vehemence against Poland 'was not [purely] a deeper Nazi ideological animus against Poles but Polish refusal to cooperate.' Poles spoke less of 'collaboration' versus 'resistance' than of 'treason' versus 'the underground' because conspiracy became synonymous with national identity under occupation.[83] That the idea of substantive collaboration never arose singles Poland out as one of the most hostile victims of German occupation – something the Allies either failed to understand or disregarded:[84]

> In Warsaw the perspective had been different. There, Polish participation meant accepting the challenge of the most formidable and ruthless war machine that ever existed, while all Europe was passive or compromising.
>
> ... the outside world could not comprehend the two most important principles of Polish resistance. It never could understand or estimate the sacrifice and heroism entailed in our nation-wide refusal to collaborate with the Germans. It could not estimate the fact that our unyielding attitude had prevented a single Quisling from arising, nor imagine what this attitude was like.[85]

Resistance, for the average Varsovian, did not always constitute daring acts of sabotage or counter-intelligence. It could be as simple as reminding each other of better times. Under the shadow of occupation, the smallest intimacies became treasured moments, chances to preserve pre-war memories and hold on to scraps of familiarity from a way of life lost forever. In her unheated tobacco shop where she continued to scrape a living, Zofia Nałkowska took every opportunity to engage with her customers, keeping notes on her regulars that together offer a vivid picture of life under occupation. A 'handsome man' always came with carefully combed hair, wearing one of two suits, but Nałkowska noted that he became thinner as time passed. An elderly man in ragged clothes would shelter from the rain; an equally elderly flower seller would leave her flowers in the shop overnight; another old woman told Nałkowska that her home had been destroyed and she now lived in a haystack on the edge of the city, walking into the centre daily in her worn-out cloth shoes in search of food or to beg. One man who now worked as a hairdresser came almost every morning:

> [He is] full of jokes and conversational skills. He confesses that before the war he 'played in the theatre' … [He] closes the door from the street and with a carrying, splendid tenor voice sings away until the window panes shake. As soon as a new customer appears, he falls silent at once … and that little extract from a former life disappears like a hallucination.[86]

CHAPTER 7

THE WARSAW GHETTO

Non omnis moriar …
So let your hands rummage through Jewish things,
You, Chomin's wife from Lvov, you mother of a volksdeutscher …
Let them drink all night and at daybreak
Begin their search for gemstones and gold
In sofas, mattresses, blankets and rugs.
Oh how the work will burn in their hands!
Clumps of horsehair, bunches of sea hay,
Clouds of fresh down from pillows and quilts,
Glued on by my blood, will turn their arms into wings,
Transfigure the birds of prey into angels.

Zuzanna Ginczanka, '*Non omnis moriar*', 1942
Translated by Nancy Kassell and Anita Safran[1]

JEWS AS *UNTERMENSCH*

The word 'ghetto' was first used to describe an area where Jews were required to live in the city of Venice in 1516. The nature of Jewish ghettos varied; in Venice, for example, the area was home to affluent Jewish merchants, but in other cities the ghetto was synonymous with poverty. Nazi Germany would add an entirely new layer of meaning to the word.

Nazi ideology saw Jews as the lowest form of humanity but even within this there existed a hierarchy of discrimination between different Jewish groups.

The Jews of Eastern Europe were regarded as particularly primitive and distasteful, and the constant fear of contagion from this inferior population added to the urge to sequester them. The first city ghetto was created in Piotrków Trybunalski in early October 1939; this was followed by the first major city ghetto in Łódź in April 1940, and in Warsaw in October. In total, 280 ghettos were created across Poland with populations ranging from a few hundred Jews to nearly half a million in Warsaw.

The Nazi concept of 'Jewish Bolshevism' quickly gained ground amongst anti-Soviet groups in Eastern Europe. Stories circulated of how the Jews had welcomed the arrival of Soviet rule, and the high percentage of Jews in administrative positions under the Soviet administration was leveraged as proof of their criminality.[2] This collaboration – real or perceived – contributed to a rise in Polish antisemitic sentiment through the war, which the Germans were only too willing to exploit; even the Polish government-in-exile quietly feared that Jews would be prone to serious reprisals from Poles for their cooperation with the Soviets.[3] During the first days of the invasion of the Soviet Union the Germans unleashed a wave of shocking violence which was then used to justify the creation of ghettos – the only way further violence could be prevented, they insisted, was if the Jews were confined to distinct areas. But in the case of Poland, despite widespread antisemitism in the 1920s and 1930s, there were few such pogroms. Instead, the Jews were told that they had to be confined in ghettos because of Jewish participation in sniper attacks and looting – though no evidence of this was ever presented.

THE VARSOVIAN JEWS

In Warsaw, most Jews had lived in Muranów, Powązki, or the old part of Praga on the east bank of the Vistula. The Jewish population had peaked in the early 1930s at about 330,000 people but then declined as the post-Piłsudski regime became increasingly hostile towards Jews. Just before the outbreak of war, there were about 270,000 Jews living in the city, but the influx of refugees from the west would have raised this number by the end of 1939. Varsovian Jews, along with the majority of Polish Jews, were in a precarious economic situation even before the war arrived. The last years of *Sanacja* had seen Jews forced out of specific professions – including teaching, civil service, and enterprise management – with the result that the Jewish population became highly stratified across the occupations left open to them; a list that ranged from doctors and lawyers, to owners or staff in small shops, tailoring, furriers, leather workshops, residential real estate down to street peddling, rag-picking, and portering.[4] Once the Germans arrived and began attacking intellectuals, looting and confiscating Jewish property, and liquidating or requisitioning Jewish businesses for

Volksdeutsch use, it didn't take long to fracture the already fragile Jewish economy. Moreover, though Poles and Jews had a long history of living side by side, Polish Jews were arguably far less assimilated than their European neighbours in other countries. According to a 1931 census, the vast majority – around 80 per cent – considered Yiddish their native tongue and described their nationality as Jewish; many did not speak Polish, and sent their children to Yiddish and Hebrew schools, and as many as 40 per cent were sympathetic to Zionist causes.[5] That there already existed significant social, cultural, and economic divides between Poles and Jews worked to the Germans' advantage and made it easier for them to identify and isolate their prime targets for extermination.

The repression began immediately. Jews were particularly likely to be rounded up and held as hostages to ensure compliant behaviour, and, as already described, were frequently executed for little or no reason. Even before the fall of Warsaw, Heydrich sent orders to the commanders of his *Einsatzgruppen* that wherever Jewish communities existed in the future *Generalgouvernement*, a *Judenrat* ('Jewish Council') was to be established to take responsibility for ensuring compliance with the edicts of the occupation authorities:

> The Council is to be composed of 24 male Jews …
>
> It is to be made *fully responsible* (in the literal sense of the word) [emphasis in original] for the exact execution … of all instructions released or yet to be released.[6]

The order threatened the *Judenräte* with the severest consequences for any acts of disobedience or sabotage.

In Warsaw, engineer Adam Czerniaków had held a number of political posts in the 1920s and 1930s and was recognised by many – both Jews and non-Jews – as a prominent voice of the Jewish community. When the siege of Warsaw commenced, he was already serving on a committee representing Jews, and in early October he was appointed chair of the new *Judenrat*. The Germans began making demands straightaway, starting with the provision of labourers to clear rubble and for other menial tasks; in return, Czerniaków was promised worker compensation and humane treatment, but these assurances proved entirely false. He was also tasked with producing a detailed census on Warsaw's Jewish population and gathering money to pay the SS for a variety of purposes: for the meagre rations made available, for ransoms for hostages, and not infrequently for entirely spurious reasons. The result was a gradual diminution of funds available to the Jews, both individually and collectively, to buy food.

On 26 October, the first decrees against Jews began to circulate, beginning with the prohibition of Kosher butchery. Over the coming months, Varsovians became accustomed to the steady stream of decrees designed to make the Jewish community feel ever more culturally, socially, and economically exposed. By early November, German restrictions on Jewish bank accounts were already undermining the *Judenrat*'s efforts to support the community. Czerniaków recorded in his diary:

> 2 November: *Devisenstelle* [currency office] in the morning. As of now, no permission has been granted for unfreezing the money paid into the Discount Bank. I have no money to pay the staff's salaries, the expenses of the census, the labour battalion, etc ... Yesterday I received a delegation from the orphanage which was just denied a municipal subsidy ... under the pretext that the Community should assume complete financial responsibility for the institution.[7]

The orphanage in question was run by Henryk Goldszmit, a paediatrician also known by his pen-name, Janusz Korczak. In 1912, supported by wealthy philanthropists, Korczak helped create a Jewish orphanage at 92 Krochmalna Street. Many Varsovians were astonished that Korczak – whose writing career and medical practice had both flourished – chose to spend most of his time and energy caring for Jewish orphans. He justified his decision by explaining that as a paediatrician he had concentrated purely on children in poor health, whereas he could now care for them in every respect. In many respects, he was a visionary; his Declaration of Children's Rights stated that all children had the right to be loved, respected, and given the best conditions in which to grow and thrive.

Many of the Krochmalna Street orphans emigrated to Mandate Palestine and Korczak visited them in the mid-1930s; according to one source, he was tempted to migrate himself but felt it his duty to stay in Warsaw to ensure the care of the next generation of children.[8] When war broke out a few months after his 61st birthday, his application to serve in the army was turned down and he continued his work in the orphanage, which was later relocated to Śliska Street in the ghetto. Its Jewish population made it especially vulnerable to the Germans, and with far less money coming from his previous benefactors Korczak had no choice but to turn to Czerniaków – only to find that the *Judenrat* was powerless to help him.

Polish Jews' history of non-assimilation had taught them to be resourceful in recruiting support from across the international Jewish community. One example of this was the New York-based America Jewish Joint Distribution Committee (JDC), which from 1914 had provided material and monetary support for the relief, rescue, and renewal of Jewish communities around the world. In 1932, a Galician-born Jewish historian had joined the committee from his adoptive city of Warsaw; seven years later, the same man was in Geneva attending the 21st World Zionist Congress when he and his fellow Varsovian delegates learned of the German invasion and decided, rather than emigrate to Palestine, Europe, or the United States, to return immediately to Warsaw. Within days, the man, 39-year-old Emmanuel Ringelblum, was back at his JDC desk in Warsaw, where he threw himself at once into emergency relief activities. Ringelblum was a tall, slim man, admired for his humour and gregariousness, both of which were stretched to breaking point as he tirelessly worked to coordinate various Jewish organisations and source food, clothing, and shelter for refugees.[9] Towards the end of September 1939, Ringelblum met Jewish journalist Rokhl Auerbach, to whom he disclosed his desire 'to employ as many members of the Jewish intelligentsia as possible' in his community efforts. He tasked Auerbach with setting up a soup kitchen at 40 Leszno Street where she managed operations for almost three years:

> We rummaged through the apartments of shopkeepers and looked for cooking utensils, dishes, and food ... the very day that Hitler came to Warsaw to review the victory parade on Saxon Square, I was making my way with Piotr Sulin, the Polish janitor of the retail association, through the rubble of a side street that we were forced to use so as not to interfere with the German military. I was carrying a packet of blank forms to set up the paperwork as well as a box of dried prunes to start cooking. Piotr lugged a half-full sack of rice on his shoulders. The day before we had received several packages of dried saltwater fish.
>
> That's how it began ... The first day we served fifty meals. The last meals were served at the end of July 1942, during the Great Deportation ... That whole time I kept working in the same kitchen; I was one of those people who seemed to be able to hang on no matter what ... I found myself at the epicentre of Jewish troubles, in the front lines of the battle against hunger, as close as one could get to the suffering of the Jewish masses.[10]

By late 1939, Ringelblum, fluent in German, was entreating the occupation authorities to allow for the extension of welfare provision for Varsovian Jews – to no avail. Cut off from their international connections and, gradually, from their Polish neighbours, it was becoming clear that Varsovian Jews could expect little help in the months to come.

CREATING THE OTHER

Decrees came thick and fast through the end of 1939. On top of the existing restrictions on commercial bank accounts, Jewish private accounts with more than 2,000 *złotys* were blocked and the paltry food stamp system forced Jews to either spend their dwindling financial resources on extra supplies or work for the occupiers. Jews aged 12 or over were required to wear white armbands and forbidden from public transport, while Jewish businesses had to mark themselves as such with large Stars of David.[11] The indefatigable Ringelblum quipped, 'Nalewki Street looks like Hollywood nowadays – wherever you go you see a star!'[12] With these visual identifiers, the social dislocation of Polish-Jewish communities would have been all but complete except that it was unclear exactly who was to wear an armband. In the immediate aftermath of the announcement, many assimilationist Jews took advantage of the vague and contradictory messaging of the decree to avoid wearing them. According to Jewish-born statistician and member of the underground Ludwik Landau, wearing or not wearing the Star of David became a catch-22 for Varsovian Jews: 'not wearing armbands makes them susceptible to imprisonment, or more often, necessitates recourse to bribery. By wearing them they are likely to be beaten up and subjected to mugging.'[13] Jewish lawyer Mieczysław Maślanko later blamed Governor Fischer for the particularly arbitrary implementation of the armband regulation in Warsaw compared to the rest of the *Generalgouvernement.* As Maślanko pointed out, the decree was only announced in the Polish-language paper *Nowy Warszawski Kurjer* (at a time when the majority of Polish Jews spoke Yiddish as their first language), and in addition to the stipulated armbands being 'two centimetres wider than stated by the general regulation', the Varsovian ruling applied to children from ten years old instead of 12.[14] It's unlikely these discrepancies were a deliberate ploy to catch Jews out, but it added to the sense of confusion, fear, and paranoia that security depended on the discretionary whims of the occupying authority. Moreover, it wasn't until August 1940 that the Nazis codified their definition of 'Jewishness' across the *Generalgouvernement* in line with the 1935 Nuremberg Laws – though even this did not fully quell arguments amongst the Jews. Zionist Chaim Kaplan felt it his duty to wear the badge of the Jewish nation, even if it was at the behest of the Nazis; another Varsovian tentatively agreed that 'armbands were worn with pride but only when we were not scared of being beaten up.'[15]

It was no secret that the decrees were a prelude to formal segregation. The authorities had already raised the establishment of a ghetto in discussions with the *Judenrat*, and Czerniaków was increasingly concerned that the area described was far too small for its intended population. On 17 November 1939, there seemed to be a reprieve – the Germans informed the *Judenrat* that the establishment of the ghetto was delayed by several months – but signs were to be erected around the edges of the Jewish parts of Warsaw warning '*Achtung Seuchengefahr. Eintritt verboten*' ('Alert: danger of epidemics. Entry forbidden').[16] Next came the prohibition of communal prayers, also under the guise of preventing the spread of disease.[17] 'Community activity has completely ceased,' Ringelblum lamented on 1 January 1940; 'Everyone looks after himself, first and foremost.'[18]

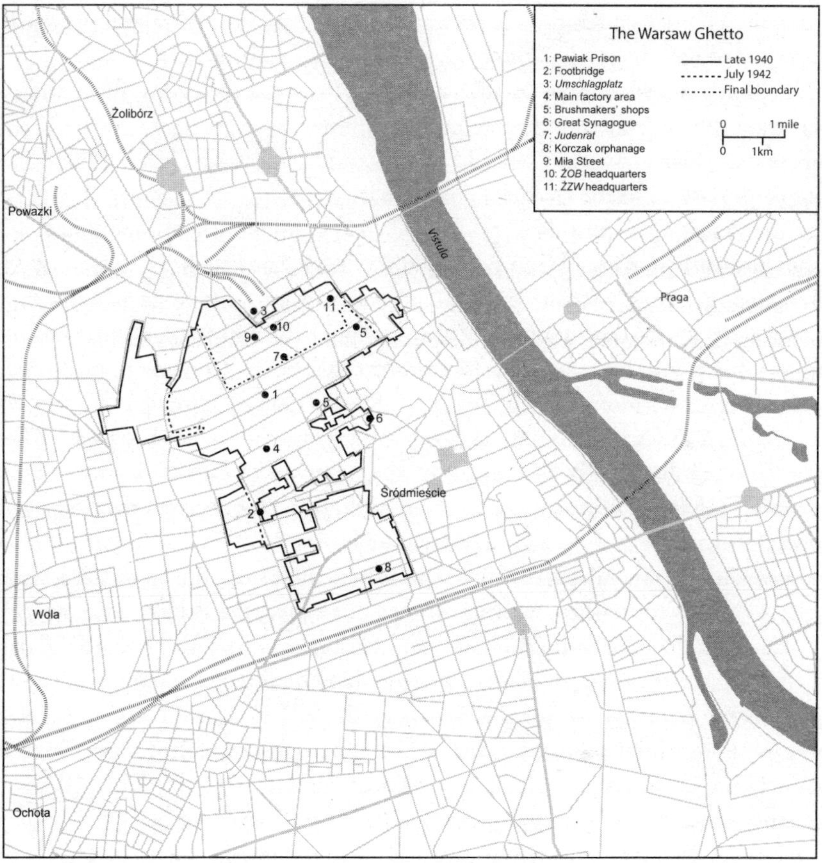

THE POLISH RESPONSE

It was impossible for non-Jewish Varsovians not to notice the Nazis ramping up their persecution of the Jews. Whether in the pages of German-controlled newspapers or plastered on walls across the city, the decrees – always couched in terms of maintaining public order – became a familiar sight. At the same time, the Germans unleashed a propaganda campaign that played on familiar antisemitic tropes with the intention of driving a wedge between Poles and Jews. Newspaper articles, leaflets, posters, newsreels, and loudspeakers mounted on street corners proclaimed the greed, laziness, and cunning of Jews to stoke suspicion and fear; conversely, attacks on Jews and Jewish property – frequently committed by the Nazis themselves – were depicted as acts of Polish antisemitic frustration towards their degenerate neighbours. In stoking resentment on both sides, the Germans attempted to portray themselves as the neutral intermediaries and civic peacemakers, the '*Kulturträger* ('bearers of culture') to the "Wild East"'. Ringelblum described how, in Warsaw as well as in the provinces, this narrative was carefully cultivated in photographs and films for export back to the Reich, where German citizens would be reassured of the Nazis' boundless humanitarianism in the face of savage barbarity.[19]

The Polish reaction to Nazi propaganda was complex. There is no doubt that from the earliest days of occupation, some Varsovians took advantage of the Germans' presence to loot, pillage, and report their Jewish neighbours; but, particularly in the early months of the war, pre-existing social resentments and opportunism were bigger motivators than Nazi narratives. Conversely, many Poles found it easier to side with their Jewish neighbours than their foreign invaders and saw through the Nazis' antisemitic smears and slander for what they were. When 11-year-old Julian Kulski – the son of the Starzyński's former deputy – came across an interview in which the German health director declared that Varsovian Jews, as carriers of typhus, had to be separated from the rest of the population, he reacted with commendable disdain: 'This is incredible – do the Germans actually believe their own propaganda? They surely don't expect the Poles to swallow it!'[20]

Nevertheless, the indiscriminate persecution against Jews, coupled with a crumbling social order, gave rise to a particularly detested character in occupied Poland: the *szmalcownik* (or 'blackmailer', derived from the German *schmalz* and the Polish *smalec*, both words for lard and connoting lubrication). True to their name, *szmalcowniki* gained notoriety for denouncing and extorting Jews or anyone who offered them aid. They emerged at all levels of occupied society, from street criminals to members of the Blue or Jewish Police, underground spies to members of the Jewish Gestapo, or within *Sonderkommando* (literally, 'special commando') work brigades. But *szmalcowniki* were generally defined by their materialistic ambitions rather than ideological conviction, and it wasn't uncommon for Jews to collaborate with *szmalcowniki* if it meant saving themselves at the expense of others. As one Jew, Maximilian T, recorded on his arrival in Warsaw:

> Hunting for Jews and blackmailing them became a lucrative business … These hyenas, working hand in glove with Jews who, for the price of letting them live when they were themselves discovered, cooperated with the *szmalcowniki*, supplying them with addresses and other details about Jews living in hiding as Aryans …[21]

Maximilian T went on to describe a close escape with three *szmalcowniki*, whom he managed to bribe with 500 *złotys*, copious vodka, and some homemade sandwiches. His generosity paid off more than he had hoped when the next day, to his astonishment, one of the blackmailers returned to his apartment bearing his full list of Jewish targets living in Warsaw under Polish names. Maximilian persuaded the *szmalcownik* to burn the list, and also extracted from him the names of Jewish informants who had assisted in putting it together:

> I was stunned to learn that, among others, there were two colleagues of mine … They both came from so-called good Jewish families, and who would have believed that they could have been the source of information given to blackmailers, by which they betrayed a Jew, their fellow classmate?[22]

Szmalcowniki appeared almost as soon as the Germans arrived. In the early days of occupation – before Jews were forced to wear armbands – they helped Germans identify Jews who might otherwise have escaped immediate notice; to quote Ringelblum, 'thus was the first bond sealed between Polish antisemites and the Nazis.'[23] As the Germans set about appropriating Jewish businesses and looting property, the *szmalcowniki* obliged in fulfilling the role of intermediary as a 'local element acquainted with the terrain … giving information as to which homes and shops belonged to wealthy Jews.'[24] From guiding Germans and taking part in the pillaging, Ringelblum explained, it was an easy step for ambitious informants to become committed collaborators either assisting the Gestapo or, later, as full-time members of auxiliary police forces. To repeat, not all *szmalcowniki* were ardent antisemites; many were simply unscrupulous Poles who were happy to deflect German violence away from themselves. Stefan Orczykowski, then aged 11, described one such instance:

> Another assault next to our house took place at the 'Chiquito' bistro, where a brawl broke out. As the clients were leaving the premises and were near the entrance to our stairway, somebody shouted, 'That one is a Jew!', and then the other revellers fell upon him. Some SS-men were just passing by and they pounced on the man, who was almost on the ground. They wore heavy studded boots with metal heels, and with these boots they kicked this man in the face, torso, and head … The Germans told the policeman to inspect the victim's pockets, and he found a band with a star. The Germans and the Poles who had beaten him smiled with evident satisfaction because they had found a Jew who insolently dined at a restaurant where only Germans were allowed … the Germans were adamant and they wanted him taken where he could be finished off. The policeman said he agreed and promised to carry out the order, and that he was now taking him to the Jewish cemetery.[25]

As the net drew tighter around the ghetto, the *szmalcownik* gangs became even more powerful in exploiting the mounting desperation of their victims. Remarkably, *szmalcowniki* were not exclusively non-Jewish; there was the infamous Josef Ehrlich, nicknamed 'Josele Kapota' for his long Hasidic coat, who served as a willing middleman between the German and Jewish police and extorted privileges from the *Judenrat* at every opportunity. There was also the notorious Regina Judtowa, branded 'a whore' by Ringelblum and a 'repulsive witch' by Czerniaków, who had had a relationship with a German officer during World War I and leveraged her connections to extract a theatre licence, jobs, and other luxurious concessions from the council. By February 1942, Czerniaków had finally put his foot down and barred the so-called 'Miss Ghetto' from entering the *Judenrat* offices.[26]

ANSWERING THE 'JEWISH PROBLEM'

On 1 April 1940, Governor Fischer finally ordered the construction of walls around most of the Jewish areas west of the Vistula. The 36-year-old Waldemar Schön was appointed head of a new *Umsiedlungsabteilung* ('Resettlement Department'), responsible for moving Jews into the ghetto area. The area's 113,000 non-Jewish Varsovians were evicted to make space for around 138,000 Jews from Praga and other parts of Warsaw, plus the influx of thousands more refugees from other regions. By this time, Jews accounted for at least 30 per cent of the population of Warsaw and had been allocated less than 3 per cent of the city's area. The intended population density of the ghetto would inevitably open the door to humanitarian disaster – which largely aligned with Schön's plans. As an 'attritionist' – an advocate of Jewish extermination through artificial famine and starvation – he frequently came into conflict with Ludwig Leist, Fischer's deputy in the city administration; in particular, Leist and others objected to the severity of Schön's ghettoisation policies on the grounds that they unnecessarily disrupted the Jewish workforce, resulting in loss of productivity.

Of course, it fell to the Jews to build their own prison, and Czerniaków was required to organise work parties to dig the wall foundations. He found excuses to delay work for several days until he was threatened with arrest. To make matters worse, the Germans insisted that because – in their opinion – the walls were being built to protect the Jews from attack, the cost of materials should be levied from the Jewish community. Even before the walls were complete, the ghetto was being sealed off from the rest of the city; Czerniaków noted in his diary on 4 April that the closure of Krochmalna Street resulted in several thousand people being unable to get food, since Jews were forbidden from entering or leaving unless as part of work parties.[27]

Like many other ghettos, the Warsaw Ghetto was divided into two zones, with a larger northwestern ghetto separated by Chłodna Street from the small ghetto. Logistically, this made it easier for the Germans to isolate segments of the population – such as the elderly – in a smaller area, from which they could be transferred for immediate execution or internment elsewhere. The population of the large ghetto could then be redistributed between the two zones. Besides segregating the Jews, the ghetto also became a manufacturing hub, housing factories that produced various items – especially leather and fabrics – for sale to Polish businesses and even to the Wehrmacht. German entrepreneurs took advantage of the skilled labour to scale up industrial production under loose confederations such as the *Judische Produktionsgesellschaft GMBH* ('Jewish Production Company Ltd'); Jews actively tried to get work in factories of this group as working conditions were generally better than elsewhere – particularly compared with the work parties forced to labour outside of the ghetto. In other cases, however, the German supervising staff turned their enterprises into their own private theatres of cruelty. Aleksander Donat described being recruited off the street in the spring of 1940 to work in a motor pool repair shop:

> It differed from other such labour impressment places in that people were usually held as long as a week rather than for a single day's work. It was a place notorious for torture and people were killed there daily by the head sadists and executioners, Schultz and Krüger. These two were especially fond of personally torturing Jews who still wore the old-fashioned caftan or those who were well-dressed and prosperous-looking.
>
> … The Germans made a pious Jew work all day wearing his phylacteries [small leather boxes containing Hebrew texts, worn on the forehead during prayers], and at the end of the day Schultz played William Tell with him, using the phylactery headpiece as the apple. He took careful aim and was delighted whenever his pistol shot hit the bull's eye; whenever he missed, the Jew was beaten. There were other such games as well. One crew of Jews was set to pushing a heavily loaded truck and another crew a light passenger car. Both crews had to move their vehicles at exactly the same rate of speed and were beaten when they failed to do so.[28]

Jewish accounts of this period describe the constant fear of being picked up off the street and press-ganged into forced labour units. Rumours abounded of sickly work registrants being shot on the spot, and of Jews being subjected to the filthiest and most humiliating tasks imaginable – in one workplace, 'workers [were] ordered to beat one another with their galoshes' and 'a rabbi was ordered to shit in his pants'.[29] The Nazi newspaper *Völkischer Beobachter* gloated in November 1939:

> It gives us particular pleasure to use the beloved gentlemen of Abraham's seed for carrying straw and setting up camps. Their hollow excuses were of no avail. We simply go through the streets, collecting them, and whoever, despite a friendly request, thought he had no time, was soon taught better. During a war there is no time to waste, and there are – thank God! – plenty of ways of dealing with recalcitrant Jews.[30]

Violence against Jews was becoming normalised in every area of city life. In his diary, Ringelblum noted in February 1940 that a Polish woman had taken to walking the streets in and around the ghetto area with a large stone in her glove; she would use this to strike Jews on the face or head. She claimed that this was because Jews had killed her brother in Grodno, but many Jews recognised her as a prominent antisemite from before the war – and knew she had never had a brother. Meanwhile, though some of the Jewish women working in newly established Gestapo and SS brothels did so voluntarily, many were forced into prostitution. When challenged over the brothels on the grounds that sexual relations with Jews would violate Nazi conventions of racial purity, one Gestapo officer replied, 'this is war and theories are dead for the time being.'[31]

Unlike the ghettos of earlier centuries – which were regarded as at least semi-permanent Jewish quarters – the Nazi ghettos were only supposed to be temporary. But although Hitler had never made any secret of his intention to clear Europe of any Jewish presence, the precise means of annihilation remained undecided. During the 1930s, German attention had been focused on the Polish lands around Lublin and Nisko. It was a far from ideal location for settling hundreds of thousands – perhaps millions – of Jews considering there were few significant towns and the region was swampy and unfertile. But when Artur Seyss-Inquart – briefly Austrian chancellor during the 1938 crisis – visited the region shortly after it was occupied by the Wehrmacht, he reported favourably on the poor state of the land, concluding it would be conducive to the rapid decimation of any Jewish population.[32] Trains of Jews from the Silesian region arrived before the onset of winter to find that no preparations had been made for them, and their first task was to scrape together materials to build makeshift huts. Several thousand died of disease, exposure, and malnutrition before the

'Nisko-Lublin Reservation' was abandoned in the spring of 1940. A different solution to the 'Jewish Problem' had to be found.

Meanwhile, the Germans recalled that tentative discussions between France and the Polish governments had taken place in 1937 regarding the creation of a Jewish homeland on the French-administered island of Madagascar. The scheme had been abandoned after initial research suggested that it would be impossible to accommodate more than a few thousand Jews, but in 1940, with the Nisko reservation looking less feasible and France facing defeat, the Germans set about formulating their own *Madagaskarplan* ('Madagascar Plan').[33] Obersturmbannführer Adolf Eichmann, working for Heydrich, drew up a document describing how European Jews could be resettled at a rate of about a million per year; at this pace, the report estimated, Europe would become *Judenfrei* ('free of Jews') in four years. Of course, there were more than 4 million Jews in Europe, so the unstated assumption was that the rest would die of malnutrition, disease, exposure, or executions during this period.[34] Once a Jewish colony had been established on Madagascar, Eichmann concluded, it would remain under strict SS control.[35]

After the surrender of France on 22 June, implementing the *Madagaskarplan* depended on bringing war with Britain to a conclusion in order to open sea lanes to the Indian Ocean. In anticipation of this, existing plans for the Jews of Europe were suspended. Back in Kraków, Frank was growing frustrated with the ceaseless influx of Jews into the *Generalgouvernement* and was now able to secure agreement for further deportations to be stopped on 10 July. Six days later, work was suspended on construction of the walls around the Warsaw Ghetto.[36] The relocation of millions of people would undoubtedly be an expensive undertaking, but the German planners decided it could be paid for using the assets of the Jews themselves. A bank was to be created specifically for the purpose of pooling these resources, and after the relocation was complete, would act as an intermediary between Madagascar and the rest of the world – since Jews would be forbidden from engaging in any international transactions directly. Shipping for the relocation would be seized from Britain after a successful invasion in the second half of 1940.[37] But by mid-August, with the Luftwaffe failing to establish air superiority over southeast England, immediate defeat of Britain looked less likely. Even if Britain could be worn down through the interdiction of shipping by U-boats, this wouldn't be until late 1941 at the earliest. Work on ghettos in Warsaw and elsewhere was therefore resumed.[38]

In any case, Frank had decided that the clearance of Jews from Kraków and other areas couldn't wait for the Madagascar Project, which was now dropped. Several thousand Jews had already left Kraków for Warsaw and compulsory deportations commenced in August. Other towns along the lower Vistula were also to expel their Jewish populations. The result was a steady stream of Jewish refugees into Warsaw; they were permitted to take only 25 kilograms of possessions each, and most arrived with few or no resources to supplement their inadequate official rations. Czerniaków and the *Judenrat* had spent most of 1940 struggling to secure sufficient funds from German-controlled bank accounts for their existing costs and now had to deal with the burden of feeding and housing spiralling numbers of refugees. To date, Jews living in Warsaw outside the ghetto had not been compelled to move, but a proclamation issued on 7 August declared that any Jew who had to change address could only do so if they moved to the ghetto. Adding to the chaos was the fact that the official ghetto area remained open to debate, often because non-Jewish Varsovians refused to leave streets where they insisted they were in the majority; in giving up their homes, they were expected to resettle elsewhere in the city while the best sectors were reserved for *Volksdeutsche*. When Czerniaków expressed concern at the overcrowding, he was told that up to 20,000 Jews would soon be removed from the ghetto and sent to labour camps elsewhere.[39]

ASSISTANTS IN REPRESSION

Despite Czerniaków's best efforts, food shortages in the ghetto were reaching critical levels, the numbers of people starving and perishing of hunger steadily growing. As Ringelblum noted in his diary on 23 September, several children from Korczak's orphanage were amongst the dead: 'At the funeral for the small children from the … orphanage, the children from the home placed a wreath at the monument with the inscription: "To the Children Who Have Died from Hunger – From the Children Who Are Hungry."'[40]

Czerniaków's diary for this period is dominated by exasperating meetings with different German agencies as he struggled over the release of funds, the release of prisoners, and the escalating workforce quotas. Part of the problem was that the various German agencies had overlapping responsibilities; this often resulted in contradictory orders being given to the *Judenrat*, and was also an opportunity for the Germans to deny almost any request from Czerniaków on the grounds that he was consulting the wrong person. Struggling with headaches and back pain, the chairman trudged wearily from one meeting to another, often finding that the person who had demanded the meeting was absent or unable to provide him with any information or help; 'ghetto and more ghetto!' he recorded with exasperation in his diary.[41] The bald, dapperly dressed man, familiar to Jews and Gentiles alike in Warsaw from his pre-war life as a teacher and local politician, looked increasingly worn down by the relentless pressure: 'The moment I arrived at the Community at 8am I was surrounded by a group of women, mothers of the workers in the camps. Weeping and shouting. Recriminations why I am not obtaining their releases.'[42]

Like other ghetto administrators, he was aware of the charges of collaboration being levelled at him by other Jews – yet he remained convinced that refusal to cooperate would only lead the Germans to find a more compliant replacement. One moment towards the end of January 1940 exemplified the hopelessness of his situation: on top of mounting fines for Jews caught not wearing armbands, the Germans were levying a hefty penalty for the purported beating of an ethnic German woman, threatening to shoot a further 100 Jews in retaliation if the *Judenrat* failed to pay. At his wits' end, Czerkianów 'asked the SS to be released from the chairmanship' since he found it 'impossible' to manage the community under what he euphemistically described as 'abnormal conditions'. The response was as threatening as it was vague: it was 'inadvisable' for him to resign.[43] He consoled himself with the hope that at least he was able to mitigate the worst of the German intentions, but knew he could not please everyone. One elderly community worker in the ghetto commented that Czerniaków was 'picking up the smell of the Gestapo'.[44]

If many Jews were prepared to give Czerniaków the benefit of the doubt, the *Judenrat* as a whole garnered no such sympathy. The council was tasked with managing every aspect of Jewish community life, from administering health and police operations to issuing passes for Jews to cross to the 'Aryan' side of the city, registering labour and managing food rations, exemption certificates, and all the other bureaucratic paraphernalia of life under occupation. Once the ghetto was established, *Judenrat* operations multiplied five-fold to employ a total of 9,030 people by July 1942.[45] Many of those who took up employment in the council were assimilationist Jews or members of the Polish-speaking intelligentsia, which did not endear them to the more traditional Jews. Stuck between the German authorities and a starving, impoverished Jewish population, the council became an emblem of spineless subservience, treachery, and unforgiveable incompetence.

Instances such as the infamous Kott affair only deepened this sentiment. On 14 January, 20-year-old Kazimierz Kott was arrested for his involvement in the underground *Polska Ludowa Akcja Niepodległościowa* ('Polish People's Independence Action' or *PLAN*). After three days of brutal interrogations at Aleja Szucha, Kott spotted his chance for escape when a guard uncuffed him for a visit to the toilet and leaped out of the nearest window. The following day, when the Germans learned of the absconder's Jewish heritage, they retaliated with mass arrests across the Jewish community. One witness described how these arrests were expedited thanks to the armbands that made Jews readily identifiable, and that, as in the broader *Intelligenzaktion*, detainees were chosen according to their occupations, 'mostly attorneys, doctors, engineers, teachers, rabbis and other intelligentsia representatives.'[46] Czerniaków was held hostage by the SS for six hours while the first arrests were made and kept in the dark as to their fate over the following days. On 22 January, the chairman was informed that 100 of the detainees had been shot, with the intimation 'that further executions will take place.'[47] Families of the arrestees desperately petitioned for his intervention, and according to Maślanko, many were reassured that the arrestees were still alive and had been sent to concentration camps.[48] 'There is nothing I can do for them,' Czerniaków wrote in his diary.[49] Unbeknownst to him, the Gestapo had already executed all but two of the arrestees – 253 Jews in total.

The Kott affair was just one of many incidents that served as lightning rods for public resentment against the council and significantly undermined the idea it could be trusted to work in Jewish interests. As Jewish policeman Stanisław Gombiński described:

> All the evils that have befallen Jews in Warsaw: forced labour, roundups, arrests, the Kott affair, beatings on the street, muggings, confiscations of goods, furniture, clothing, being forbidden to help the arrested, no news from them – for all this it was the *Judenrat* that was responsible. The atmosphere of dislike meant that many people preferred to keep away from it, limiting their contacts to personal matters or social help issues.[50]

To Varsovian Jews, the fact that the *Judenrat* was powerless, and little more than a 'blind executor of German orders' did not excuse its failure to protect them.[51] When, in the spring of 1940, it was decreed that Jewish men between the ages of 12 and 60 and women between 14 and 45 were to be registered for two years 'educative' labour in concentration camps, Szpilman spoke for many in the Jewish community in his evaluation: 'To spare themselves the trouble, the Germans were handing the job over to the Jewish Council ... We were to assist at our own execution, preparing for our downfall with our own hands, committing a kind of legally regulated suicide.'[52] The community rankled against being repeatedly press-ganged into forced labour, against the inefficiencies of obtaining the correct documentation, and against the perceived inequalities in the labour exemption system, where members of the intelligentsia, assimilated Jews, and those with deep pockets seemed the most likely to escape work in the camps.

Rokhl Auerbach was one such fortunate member of the intelligentsia who secured community employment, but her work as a kitchen director did not spare her the public's resentment:

> The directors of the Jewish 'government' surrounded themselves with gatekeepers and hid in offices and corridors. But the manager of a public kitchen was also reckoned to be part of the 'government' and became the easiest target for people who needed to unload their anger, pain, and despair at the injustices of the world, at this historical cataclysm that played itself out in an infinite number of individual variations. The kitchen director found herself on the receiving end of the deep resentment a declassed person felt after losing everything except that daily bowl of soup, that identification card, that ticket to the kitchen: the sum total of disaster broken down into tiny bits of small change.[53]

Equally controversial were the German-sanctioned *parówki* (steam bath disinfections) of households to curb the putative typhus epidemic. Ringelblum repeatedly complained that the rich and privileged could pay to be exempted, and deemed the entire operation as nothing more than a 'swindle' since the sulphur used in the steaming process was too weak to kill lice anyway.[54] In one house on Muranów Street, he claimed, there were 15 cases of typhus, but the building had not been quarantined 'because the doctor is getting 800 *złotys* a day' in bribes.[55] Meanwhile, those unable or unwilling to pay for exemption had to face their households being cordoned off and sprayed, while they – along with their belongings – were turfed out into the street at the mercy of opportunistic looters; after disinfection, Jews would be lucky to find their homes in any habitable shape. The fact that most sanitation workers – as in other areas of *Judenrat* operation – tended to be members of the affluent or acculturated intelligentsia only enhanced the sense of social inequality.[56] Then from June 1940, the *Judenrat*'s desperate financial situation gave rise to yet another point of indignation: a bread tax was to be levied from ration cards for all Jews except the most destitute. This became one of over 40 taxes imposed upon ghetto inhabitants that pushed more and more into absolute poverty; by March 1942, a report from the Polish underground claimed over 20,000 bread ration cards remained uncollected because Jews lacked the funds to pay for them.[57] To make things worse, the actual rations of bread for Jews had already been substantially cut by spring of 1940, meaning that a ration card afforded a Jew just 200 grams of bread compared to the 570 grams allotted for Christian Poles; a year later, Jews would qualify for just 10 per cent of the food rations afforded to German citizens.[58]

Ghettoisation

Despite all this, during the first year of occupation, life for the Jewish community settled into a rhythm that alternated between crushing lows and moments of quiet hope. On the one hand, antisemitic violence was a persistent threat, frequently stoked by the Germans, but also revealing deeper divisions lurking within Polish society. Incidents such as the Easter Pogrom of 1940 saw mass attacks on Jewish property and Jews caught out on the streets; witnesses described crowds of teenagers armed with daggers, knives, and sticks swarming on Jewish victims, looting Jewish stalls, and parading around with stolen wares.[59] Later analysis would reveal the pogrom was stoked by right-wing Polish activists, but German involvement could not be ruled out, given that the Germans took the opportunity to film the violence, and that the attacks suddenly stopped – as if on command – eight days later.[60] On the other hand, Varsovians, Jewish and non-Jewish alike, anticipated the spring would bring news of a long-awaited Allied offensive that would knock the wind out of the Germans; tenuous as these expectations might have been in the wake of the September invasion, they were enough to convince the majority of the population that hope was not yet lost.[61] As the Netherlands and Belgium fell in May 1940, attention turned to Poland's old ally France to quell Hitler's momentum, but despair was starting to set in.[62] One month later, when news of the French surrender reached Warsaw, public morale plummeted. Szpilman captured the Jews' particular sense of dread: 'Intoxicated with victory and stopping for a moment to draw breath, the Germans now had time to think of us again, although it cannot be said that they had forgotten us entirely during the fighting in the west … Now there was worse to be expected.'[63]

The Jews waited anxiously as rumours swirled about the closing of the ghetto – or potential deportations to some unknown destination. Ringelblum noted the effect: 'There were Jews who said they'd rather be poisoned with gas than tortured so' – an ominous observation, in view of what was to come.[64] Mary Berg's family was amongst the Jewish refugees who had just escaped ghetto enclosure in Łódź and the 'massacre' that had followed, and they feared the same thing would occur in Warsaw.[65] Others hoped that the establishment of a ghetto would protect them from antisemitic persecution at the hands of Poles and *Volksdeutsche*. Medical doctor Henryk Makower described how many were tired of living in fear of looting and 'marauding gangs' and resigned themselves to segregation: '"let them go ahead and close us in … Things couldn't possibly get worse than they are right now" people said.'[66] Others reasoned that it would be easier to face hardship if all Jews 'would be surrounded by family, friends, people

As German ground forces swept across the Polish frontier, Warsaw endured relentless bombing raids by the Luftwaffe. Each evening, the Germans covered the Warsaw suburbs in fresh incendiary bombs that set the night sky ablaze for hours. (Getty Images)

American filmmaker Julien Bryan happened to be in Warsaw as war broke out, and his footage captured a much more honest picture of life than the stories told in the Polish press. This photo shows a boy and his mother, who was killed in a field as the Germans approached the city. (Getty Images)

Hitler salutes the triumphant victory procession from a platform in Łazienki Park, 5 October 1939. Julian Kulski's ten-year-old son recalled: 'Then came the artillery, followed by goose-stepping, steel-helmeted troops in rows of twelve. I marvelled at how they raised their legs with such perfect precision … This was a parade of Germans for Germans. It was not for us.' (Getty Images)

The repression of the Jews began immediately after the arrival of the Germans. Jews were particularly likely to be rounded up and held as hostages to ensure compliant behaviour, and were frequently executed for little or no reason. (Getty Images)

On 1 April 1940, Governor Fischer ordered the construction of the walls which would surround the ghetto. Despite Jews accounting for at least 30 per cent of the population of Warsaw by this time, they were allocated less than 3 per cent of the city's area; the extreme population density resulted in an inevitable humanitarian disaster. (Getty Images)

The Warsaw Ghetto was divided into two zones: the 'large ghetto' and the 'small ghetto'. The two halves were separated by Chłodna Street, which was reserved for the 'Aryan' population. A footbridge was built in 1942 to connect the two sides without disrupting the traffic below; today, a monument marks where the footbridge used to stand on the otherwise unrecognisable junction. (Getty Images)

By mid-1942, the *Umschlagplatz* ('Exchange Place') became the holding area for Jewish deportees bound for Treblinka and a site of horrors in its own right. Unknown numbers were executed, beaten, and raped in and around the railyard whilst awaiting transport. On some days, as many as 12,000 Jews could be deported from here. (Getty Images)

The camp at Pruszków was established during the first week of the Warsaw Uprising to process refugees before transporting them elsewhere; by September, it was rumoured that all Varsovians were being sent on to concentration camps. The railway halls became critically overcrowded and were a hotbed for disease, leading to spiralling mortality rates. (Getty Images)

The later weeks of the Ghetto Uprising are remembered as the 'battle of the bunkers', with guerrilla skirmishes and frantic escapes as the Germans choked the remaining life out of the ghetto. The image of this boy raising his hands, photographed for Stroop's self-congratulatory report, became a recurring motif in the paintings of Samuel Bak, a survivor of the Vilnius Ghetto. (Getty Images)

Initially, Stroop was ordered to preserve workshop premises as far as possible, but the Jews' resistance frustrated progress enough to warrant the indiscriminate razing of property. By 25 April, fires were widely sanctioned, and troops received this order: 'if any resistance is encountered or if dugouts cannot be reached, the buildings are to be burnt down.' (Getty Images)

In Warsaw, men and women from across the social spectrum found themselves swept into resistance groups such as the *ZWZ* or the *AK*. Thousands of Varsovian teenagers, too young to have fought in 1939 but filled with youthful energy and a sense of immortality, joined the Uprising, as did a number of Jewish fighters who had survived the Ghetto Uprising. (Getty Images)

On 27 September 1944, Polish rebels in Mokotów tried to escape their encircled position via the sewer system, only to emerge straight into German hands. Jerzy 'Zbroja' Umiński, pictured, was captured and taken to a POW camp; around 120 others were shot on Dworkowa Street. (Getty Images)

The Red Army moved into Warsaw on 17 January to find that about 85 per cent of the city had been utterly destroyed. Between 2,000 and 3,000 so-called 'Robinson Crusoes' survived by hiding in these ruins; one of them was Władysław Szpilman. (Getty Images)

Zofia Nałkowska was a Polish writer, activist, and diarist. She ran a tobacco shop in Warsaw with her sister to survive, which was a huge downward step for a woman who had been regarded as one of Poland's finest authors before the war. (Public domain via Wikimedia Commons)

Stefan Starzynski was mayor of Warsaw from 1934 to 1939 and gave daily radio speeches to boost morale. Władysław Szpilman described him as 'the heart and soul of the defence, the real hero of the city.' (Public domain via Wikimedia Commons)

El-mole-rachmim by Bronisław Wojciech Linke, painted in 1956. Linke was forced to flee Warsaw in 1939 and returned to the devastated city in 1946. In this series of paintings (*Kamienie krzyczą* or 'Screaming Stones'), he tried to find traces of the murdered people in the ruins as well as the heroic spirit of their struggle. (National Museum in Warsaw)

who wish each other well, people of the same faith and brothers in unhappiness.'[67] The Germans, meanwhile, sought to prohibit the use of the word 'ghetto', insisting instead that the proper term for their forthcoming project was a 'Jewish quarter' with no connection to medieval precedents.[68] This was hardly convincing, and in any case, it didn't diminish the Jews' foreboding. 'Everyone was kept guessing, on edge,' wrote Aleksander Donat. 'This demoralising uncertainty was kept up right down to the last minute before the ghetto was actually established.'[69]

By early October 1940, the precise boundaries of the ghetto still remained uncertain. But at a meeting with several senior German figures on 3 October Czerniaków was informed that once it was formally set up, anyone leaving the ghetto would require a delousing certificate. Czerniaków interpreted this as meaning that whilst Jews would have to live in a confined area, they would be in an 'open ghetto'.[70] Finally, on 12 October, Schön shared definitive information:

> [Schön said] that in the name of humanity and in conformity with higher authority, a ghetto is to be established. I was given … a map of the ghetto. It turns out that the ghetto border streets have been allocated to the Poles.
>
> I was ordered to form a Jewish militia of 1,000 men. Until 31 October the resettlement will be voluntary, after that compulsory. All furniture must remain where it is. When I raised objections with respect to the financial problem, I was told that the militia could be [unpaid] volunteers and again that there were enough material resources within the ghetto itself.[71]

To the chairman's exasperation, a public proclamation published two days later included a different map of the ghetto area with three more streets removed. Meanwhile, most of the remaining Jews in Praga decided to move before the deadline and thousands began to arrive in the ghetto area, where accommodation had to be allocated to them by the hard-pressed *Judenrat*. Czerniaków was stonewalled by Leist when he protested the boundary changes; a telephone call to Frank's offices in Kraków confirmed the amendments had been ordered by the governor-general himself. The only concession that Czerniaków was able to secure was a postponement of the deadline for Jews to move into the ghetto by 15 days so that incoming Jews could negotiate apartment swaps with Poles obliged to move out of the ghetto area; this was further extended until the end of November, but only verbally – Czerniaków waited in vain for written confirmation. Instead, on 4 November, German soldiers arrived at the offices of the *Judenrat* and savagely beat Czerniaków and several other members of the *Judenrat* before taking them away in a truck to Pawiak. They were told that they were accused of making insulting remarks about the SS, but released a day later.

Once again, the landscape of Warsaw underwent tumultuous upheaval; around a quarter of a million Varsovian residents were expected to relocate in less than a month.[72] Despite Czerniaków's efforts to stall and structure the relocation process, it was impossible to prevent the public panic that followed. Jews were forced to abandon homes, businesses, and other property as they moved to the ghetto, leaving behind livelihoods and generations of memories. Moving vans were hijacked by opportunistic hoodlums, or else Jews trusted their 'finest possessions to Gentile acquaintances either to be returned to them later, or not at all'; meanwhile, those living on the ghetto boundaries, on Waliclow, Ceglana, Zlota, and Sienna Streets, were left guessing as to whether or not they had to move, and 'literally sat on their suitcases waiting to learn their fate.'[73] Donat recorded:

> The streets of Warsaw looked like the genius of chaos ruled ... The two-way shift of populations, Poles and Jews, was macabre and explosive with panic and hatred. Thousands, half-crazed because they no longer had roofs over their heads, stormed the housing bureaus of the *Judenrat* and the Warsaw municipal authorities ... The *Judenrat* sent inspectors out to list empty living quarters and apartments that could hold more people. Some families willingly allowed others to share their apartments to avoid having to accept unknown tenants later on. Unscrupulous individuals, some of whom worked in the housing bureaus, did a lively business in bribes.[74]

Czerniaków still hoped that the ghetto would be 'open', but Frank announced its separation from the rest of Warsaw on 15 November, after which time Jews would no longer be able to negotiate apartment swaps. Varsovians from the Polish district could still enter the Jewish district – provided they weren't carrying parcels or luggage – but large numbers of German police took up positions to check that Jews leaving the ghetto had appropriate passes. Even Czerniaków himself had difficulty getting the right pass with the right endorsements so he could attend meetings with the German officials who summoned him.

Jews grew to dread the ordeal of passing through the ghetto gates for the myriad punishments and humiliations the German gendarmes would inflict on them. To travel between the large and small ghettos, Jews had to line up on the corner of Żelazna and Chłodna Streets and wait for gendarmes to stop traffic to allow them to cross. One diarist described how this crossing became notorious for German cruelty, with Jews frequently ordered to perform exercises with bricks, climb walls, lie in the mud, dance with strangers, run as fast they could – or else be beaten.[75] But this didn't deter Jews from crossing to procure vital supplies that were cheaper outside the main ghetto. Even later, when shootings became an everyday occurrence at the ghetto gates, desperate Jews still attempted to smuggle contraband supplies through via the crossing. Elsewhere, barbed wire was spread across streets where walls had not yet been finished, and the Germans doled out lashings to their press-ganged labourers who didn't work fast enough. Observing this, the young Mary Berg was reminded of the Biblical slavery of the Jews in Egypt; 'but,' she asked, 'where is the Moses who will release us from our new bondage?'[76]

THE JEWISH ORDER POLICE AND THE THIRTEEN

Meanwhile, recruitment began for Czerniaków's mandated 'militia', which became known as the Jewish Order Police or Jewish Ghetto Police. From its inception, employment in the Jewish Police was highly sought after, not least because it offered reprieve from labour round-ups, but also – for the less scrupulous – the opportunity to wield power and influence over neighbours. One diarist described how the price of buying a position in the force was a typical listing on the 'ghetto stock exchange', and it was a widely accepted fact that the well-connected were most likely to be recruited.[77] Consequently, it was former members of the professional middle classes – merchants, industrialists, and especially lawyers – who were most commonly recruited for a force that, at its peak, counted around 2,000 in its ranks. Subordinate to the Polish Blue Police, the Jewish Police were primarily tasked with maintaining public order: clearing street obstructions, facilitating traffic, preventing loitering, and overseeing the cleanliness of public areas, courtyards, and staircases. The force had no authority to deal with criminal cases and found itself – like the *Judenrat* in general – critically underfunded, ill-equipped, and underprepared to deal with the complex challenges of smuggling and sanitation endemic to the ghetto.

As in the Blue Police, some Jewish Police officers used their power to try to help their neighbours. Policemen were often privy to advance information about labour round-ups, assisted victims of the *szmalcowniki*, interceded on behalf of housing committees, and generally took steps to keep their families and immediate neighbours safe. One former lawyer-turned-policeman, Stanisław Gombiński, who would go on to distinguish himself for his assistance of Jews and criticism of his police colleagues, described the tentative trust that characterised attitudes to the Jewish Order Police in its earliest days: 'the Jewish population welcomed the appearance of the functionaries on the streets of the ghetto with a smile of kindness. Associated with this smile was a mixture of light irony: for every Jew a real policeman was still a Polish policeman.'[78]

Unfortunately, it didn't take long for the Jewish Police to become a particularly detested symbol of corruption, self-interest, profiteering, and German collaboration – the most abhorrent form of assimilationism imaginable. Both in Warsaw and in other ghettos, there were many examples of ghetto police rigorously searching work parties to prevent food smuggling and showing little or no mercy, either beating their victims or handing them over to the Germans; in other cases, they simply seized food or other contraband for themselves or extorted money and valuables from their fellow ghetto dwellers. Some demanded sexual favours from Jewish women in return for food; others were known collaborators with – or were themselves – *szmalcowniki* prepared to blackmail vulnerable members of the ghetto public. The fact that the police commander, Józef Szeryński, was a Jewish-born Catholic convert undermined the idea that the force truly empathised with the Jewish situation. There were probably very few other converts in the ranks of the Jewish Police, but it was tempting for a resentful public to blur assimilationists, Polonised Jews, and converts into one homogenous, collaborationist enemy, 'separate from the community of "real" Jews, who, therefore, would not bear the responsibility for their behaviour.'[79] They were commonly seen as key actors in the disintegration of the Jewish social fabric, 'the moral decay, the amorality, and the radical blunting of people's moral sense.'[80] Szpilman described how 'men with whom we used to shake hands, whom we had treated as friends, men who had still been decent people not long ago' seemed to be overcome with the 'Gestapo spirit' when they donned their police uniforms and picked up their rubber truncheons. When one of his less popular relatives joined the force, 'it merely confirmed his bad reputation' in the eyes of the rest of the family.[81] Reporter Stanisław Różycki went further, describing how the lack of trust actively fed into the sense of lawlessness in the ghetto streets, where 'everything is forbidden and everything is allowed':

> [It is] difficult to find justification for our police force, which as a rule settles all criminal cases solely through bribery … You can count neither on justice, nor on courts, nor on the 'order service' to actually keep order, nor on the public organs' protection of private property. What can one do? Where ransom or bribe will not do, there the sad, macabre, bloody act of lynching takes place to provide satisfaction for vengeance and to satisfy people's sense of justice. Our police walk indifferently past such scenes as they will not extort anything from a beggar. So why would they trouble themselves to take him to the police station?[82]

Just outside the ghetto's northern boundary stood the *Umschlagplatz* ('Exchange Place'), the only authorised site for exchanging goods between the ghetto and the outside world. The hub gave the Germans easy control over the movements of supplies, with guards and other officials able to extort arbitrary payments on the side. In early 1941, Schön leveraged the opportunity to implement the 'attritionist' vision of the ghetto, applying strict limits to the importation of food to create an artificial famine. The consequence was an as yet unprecedented rise in death rates from malnutrition, disease, and exposure; other German authorities reliant on labour from the ghetto complained that it was impossible for them to function with such malnourished workers. Schön was removed from his post in the spring, and his attritionist policies rapidly dismantled in favour of making the ghetto more self-sufficient.[83]

In the meantime, Jews sought every opportunity to smuggle goods out of the ghetto and, more importantly, food into the ghetto. Those who had already been living in the ghetto area – particularly the wealthy – had been able to keep most or all of their possessions and thus coped best with the widespread shortages. Jews who had been forced to move to the ghetto from other parts of Warsaw often succeeded in bringing at least some of their valuables with them, and were also able to alleviate some of the difficulties they faced. Both of these groups had contacts outside the ghetto; black marketeers were happy to put antisemitic leanings aside if given the chance to make a profit or undermine German authority. The risks of smuggling were high, and those caught faced beatings, imprisonment, or execution, but lives were almost certainly saved – or at least, prolonged – thanks to their efforts. Pre-war attorney Leon Berenson, one of the founders of the Jewish Police, was rumoured to have joked that 'a monument to the unknown smuggler should be one of the first monuments to be erected after the war.'[84]

German demands that the *Judenrat* clamp down on smuggling came to nothing. In most cases, Czerniaków and his colleagues were powerless; in others, they deliberately turned a blind eye or even accepted bribes from the smugglers. At the end of 1940, the Germans lost patience and established a new authority, the *Wirtschaftspolizei* ('Economic Police'), to deal with the problem. Its leader was Abraham or Chaim Gancwajch, a Jew who was linked with the *SD* from early on in the occupation and spent his time in the Zionist *Hashomer Hatzair* (literally, 'Young Guard') movement as an informer, handing weekly reports to his German masters.[85] Convinced that the Germans would win the war, he believed that the Jews' only chance of survival was to cooperate in the hope that the *Madagaskarplan* or some similar scheme might come to fruition – but his main motive appears to have been self-enrichment. His new green-hatted police force, based at 13 Leszno Street – to which they owed their nickname, *Trzynastka* ('The Thirteen') – was widely despised. They became renowned for extorting bribes from smugglers and black marketeers, and Gancwajch repeatedly attempted to undermine Czerniaków, who described him in his diary as a 'despicable, ugly creature'. Ringelblum concurred, declaring 'There are three currencies in the Ghetto: hard, soft, and Gancwajch.'[86]

THE *ERSATZ* COMMUNITY

Gancwajch and The Thirteen weren't the only ones challenging the authority of the *Judenrat*. There was a long tradition of Jewish welfare organisations and volunteer work that rapidly coalesced in the ghetto; officially known by several different names, almost everyone referred to the largest group as the *Aleynhilf* ('Self-Help'), but there existed a complex hierarchy of welfare arrangements down to the immediate neighbourly level. The old Jewish quarter of Warsaw comprised blocks of apartments arranged around courtyards, usually with only one or two archways that gave access; each courtyard had its own hierarchy, with the poorest accommodation being in the cellars or lower floors, and larger apartments in higher floors. There was a general custom of blocks organising their own welfare groups, with everyone making financial or other contributions according to their means. When Jewish refugees began to arrive in Warsaw, many blocks arranged rotas for the destitute families to be fed in turn by the permanent block residents. One of the many functions of the *Aleynhilf* was to coordinate its activity with the 'house committees' that represented the blocks, a difficult task because of the wide variations between these committees. Some were elected and had elaborate constitutional rules, while others – perhaps most – were organised in a more ad hoc manner. The abilities of those on the committees also varied greatly. Ringelblum played a major role in this liaison work, often raging in impotent fury at the growing corruption of the more venal house committee members.

Led by a coalition of left-wing intellectuals, rabbis, and committed Zionists, the *Aleynhilf* attracted many members of Warsaw's Jewish intelligentsia to welfare work. Thanks to the Yiddish Culture Organisation (*IKOR*), the more Polonised *Aleynhilf* recruits were encouraged to learn Yiddish in order to connect better with the general Jewish public in Warsaw – an effort which neither the Ghetto Police nor the *Judenrat* proved willing to emulate.[87] Others dedicated themselves to underground cultural and social action in the ghetto community. Perhaps the most famous example of this was the *Oneg Shabbat* ('Joy of the Sabbath' in Hebrew) group led by Emmanuel Ringelblum, which embarked on an ambitious clandestine mission to document and archive Jewish life in Warsaw and beyond. Alongside Rokhl Auerbach, Ringelblum recruited leftist ally Hersh Wasser, Zionist activist Eliyahu Gutkowski, and the writer Israel Lichtenstein for the project, as well as many other committed contributors, financial supporters, and 'yet others who collected placards (often ripping them down from walls), announcements, and communiques; who recorded eyewitness accounts, wrote reports, and noted incidents; who conducted research, studied, investigated, and described what was happening during the occupation.'[88] To quote Auerbach, the historian in Ringelblum had 'sensed that "real history" was beginning' from the earliest days of the war, and felt compelled to record the Jews' plight for posterity.[89] In accordance with their name, the *Oneg Shabbat* group met together on Friday evenings and began weaving a rich archival tapestry of stories on ghetto life, statistical analysis, surveys, and essays, but also pieces of fiction, poetry, songs, sketches, and diaries from people who felt their heritage and cultural existence slipping away into oblivion.

Actors, singers, and musicians performed in the ghetto – either to scrape together their own means of subsistence or to raise funds for *Aleynhilf* initiatives. Venues such as the Femina on Leszno Street, the Cameral on Nowolipki Street, or the Azalel on Nowolipie Street drew huge crowds with their homages to Yiddish and Polish music and drama, comedic revues, operettas, and biting satire – of which Czerniaków and Gancwajch were frequent targets. *IKOR* was instrumental in coordinating these underground artistic endeavours and also propagated cultural education through lecture series on Jewish history. As outside the ghetto, underground newspapers sprang up to quench the thirst for information and distraction. One librarian, Basia Berman, established a secret lending library of children's books in Yiddish and Polish. By mid-1941, professional, industrial, and handicraft schools, courses, and youth clubs proliferated, testifying to the Jews' resourcefulness and community dynamism even as conditions were worsening; Mary Berg's sister, Anna, took a course in children's clothing, repurposing old hats (for lack of leather) to produce shoes for children in the orphanages. Auerbach described how, for many, the simplest acts of expression restored meaning to life under occupation:

> How can one explain the extraordinary intensity of cultural and civic life in the ghetto? The explanation is simple: every positive initiative served to protect life, to provide strength and the will to live. To that end the fight against despair was just as important as the battle against hunger.[90]

Still, she acknowledged, participation in these cultural activities was a luxury available 'to those of us who were physically weakened but not yet totally crushed' – a proportion of the population that was diminishing with each passing month.

And indeed, for all their strength of spirit, Auerbach's words underlined the precariousness of material survival in the ghetto – something that Schön's artificial famine had made devastatingly clear. Even the most affluent Jews were caught in a strange state of existential limbo, hardly knowing what to expect in the days, let alone months to come; even for the most culturally active and intellectually engaged, there was no hiding the fact that their hopes, dreams, and plans for the future had disappeared under occupation. In pretty much every ghetto, diarists alluded to a sense of surreality; Benjamin Murmelstein of the Theresienstadt *Judenrat* labelled his ghetto an 'as if' town with 'as if coffee, as if meals, as if a job.'[91] All the other civic institutions of the ghetto – from the *Judenrat* itself to the Jewish Order Police – fulfilled parody roles where their power was constrained by arbitrary rules set by the occupiers. Różycki described feeling surrounded by '*ersatz*' paraphernalia that emblemised the futility of life in the ghetto:

> I buy cigarettes … All 'made in the ghetto'. I get back a 50-grosz coin in change – a primitively and sloppily falsified piece of tin … Bread is sprinkled with talcum powder to make it whiter. Saccharine is added to rolls to make them sweet … Tobacco – cut, home-grown leaves, often mixed with hay. Not long ago you could buy wedges of cheese in yellow packaging. It was quite tasty. Its fakes appeared on the market after a week. They looked original but tasted awful and upset your stomach. Honey, candy, marmalade, soap – whenever a decent substitute appears on the market, its fakes make the most of its popularity. It is the irony of our life that the orgy of substitutes means nothing. For an original substitute is a valuable thing nowadays. The real problem is that we are sinking under a wave of fake ersatzes.[92]

Jews laboured, smuggled, and struggled for subsistence, but in strange and seemingly pointless patterns where existence became an end in itself. Habits of exchange, consumption, and cultural expression had become devalued in ways that not even those members of the Jewish community with time and money to spend could reverse.

DESTITUTION

Amongst the worst off were Jews who had been forced to move to Warsaw from other regions. They found themselves in a strange place, friendless and with few possessions to trade for extra food, without which they faced starvation; refugee shelters were chronically overwhelmed and left thousands fighting for survival in the street. These were the Jews that shared the ghetto with the dressed-up theatre-goers, the 'fashionable crowd' that met at the Café Sztuka on Leszno Street, and the social elite who gathered to hear Władysław Szpilman and Andrzej Golfeder play at Café Pod Fontana – but there the similarities between the groups ended.[93] Różycki wrote how on the busiest streets of the ghetto, the likes of Dzika, Dzielna, Karmelicka, Leszno, Żelazna, Grzybowska, and Ciepła, one felt as if one had 'entered a beehive or a wasp nest', being immediately swarmed by clingy, pushy beggars, street hawkers, and other 'dirty, unkempt people'.[94] Begging, prostitution, theft, and shameless violence became facts of daily street life to which the most destitute were most vulnerable; the typical attacker would '[stop] and [look] into the eyes of his (would-be) victim without any embarrassment, as if there were nothing out of the ordinary', while bystanders would elect not to notice, let alone intervene.[95] It wasn't uncommon to find corpses in the street – most frequently the results of starvation, exposure, or suicide – nor to encounter filthy, skeletal children as young as three or four years old begging for alms.[96] Różycki saw this moral decay of the street as synonymous with the degradation of Varsovian Jewish society – one that could not completely be excused away by the occupation.[97] Ringelblum, however, took a more sympathetic view in noting the rise of streetwalking and other desperate activity in the streets: 'necessity drives people to anything.'[98]

Alongside refugees, it was Jewish children who suffered some of the most heart-breaking hardship in the ghetto. Józef Gitler-Barski, secretary-general of the American Children's Relief Committee in Warsaw, explained after the war:

> The children in the ghetto were in a particularly dire situation because they had lost their relatives. Parents were regularly taken to camps from the very beginning and the children were orphaned very early on, so the number of orphans, which stood at 1,200 before the establishment of the ghetto, reached 6,000, and these children quickly filled the orphanages we set up in the ghetto. The other children, half-orphans from emigrant stations, loitered in the streets and inspired horror in whomever found himself in the streets of the Warsaw ghetto: lying there next to each other were turgid, hungry, ulcerated children pleading for help.[99]

Around 20 per cent of the ghetto population was less than 17 years old, of which, according to Gitler-Barski, only around 300 survived the war. His committee tried to deter children from begging in the streets but largely failed since this was one of the few options to find subsistence, and children were liable to be exploited by siblings or family members to play on the mercy of passersby. Those who were enticed off the street for hot meals would be shut into the committee's kitchens, which doubled as clandestine schools for the hungry youths.[100] On top of the efforts made by Jewish aid committees, the government-in-exile and the underground resistance sanctioned their own Catholic Council to Aid Jews, known as *Żegota*, whose children's division succeeded in caring for and trafficking scores of Jewish youngsters out of the ghetto. Former city council worker Irena Krzyżanowska-Sendler smuggled supplies of food, money, and false documents into the ghetto and, together with the likes of the Father Badouin Orphanage, helped ensure the children that escaped the district found shelter – if not homes – with Polish families or convents.[101] Not all children were so lucky; many took part in smuggling goods through the ghetto walls or the sewers, places where adult bodies might not fit, knowing that capture meant death regardless of their age. Others were simply abandoned in the street, or else on the doorsteps of the Jewish police headquarters or *Judenrat* offices by adults who had no means to provide for them.[102] If children managed to exit the ghetto on smuggling trips, they were often sheltered by non-Jewish Varsovians; one such child spent more than one night in Zofia Nałkowska's tobacco shop.[103] The young Stefan Orczykowski helped his Jewish friend and former playmate, Heniek, scavenge for food and supplies for his family whenever he could escape the ghetto. One summer day, he met Heniek for what he realised would be the last time; the boy who had shared his prized bicycle with Stefan a few years before was now wasting away:

> One day, Heniek showed up, swollen … He was dirty. I took him to the toilet in the yard, where there was running water … We had the key because we used to hide there, playing. Heniek was cleaning himself up and I dashed from door to door, asking the neighbours for anything to eat for him. Eventually, with difficulty and having to hear a lot of excuses about the danger from the Germans, I somehow managed to fill Henio's sweater with plenty of modest handouts. Miss Oleńka brought to the cupboard a good barley soup which had been cooked for the Germans. Heniek was forced to eat some – he could not eat as much and as fast as on his previous visits … It turned out that he could barely carry the gifts, and he took potatoes, biscuits, some bread, and vegetables … As he was about to leave, he thanked me, shook my hand … 'Goodbye, Stefan,' he said, like he had never said before. What was that supposed to mean?
>
> I would like to leave these awkwardly sketched images for others. I want them to know the story of the friendship of two boys, aged 11 or 12, who helped each other and also helped others; of kids who stuck together when things were good but also through hardships.[104]

The German authorities showed no leniency to Jewish children – nor did they suffer any less than their elders from starvation, typhus, scabies, or the other dangers of ghetto mortality. The testimony of 14-year-old Fryda Koch lays bare the nightmare these youngsters were forced to live through:

> Daddy was taken away and killed. Mommy did not tell us for a few days. Our uncle, a pharmacist, gave Mommy three measures of a poison. Mommy wanted us to take the poison immediately, but me and my brother did not want to, and we said to Mommy that she had no right to do it to us because maybe Daddy was still alive somewhere. But at the end of May the Germans took my Mommy and my brother, and then I wanted to kill myself.[105]

As the days slowly lengthened in 1941, more Jews arrived: 8,000 were deported from Vienna and brought to Warsaw by train at the end of February, and the *Judenrat* was left with the almost impossible task of housing them. Those who owned substantial properties were now required to give up rooms to house those without anywhere to live. By late spring, the incidence of typhus was beginning to rise alarmingly. There had been a surge in cases in early 1940, but the number of reported cases had peaked at fewer than 400 per day; by June 1941, it was over 1,000 and still rising. Meanwhile, the overall ghetto death rate topped 1,000 in February, 2,000 in April, and surged to over 3,800 in May.[106] Heinz Auerswald, who had replaced Schön as the commissar in overall control of the ghetto, commented in a report that 'a quantum leap in deaths for May ... showed that the food shortage had already grown into a famine' – clearly identifying the root cause of the deteriorating health of ghetto inmates.[107] Unlike his 'attritionist' predecessor Schön, the 'productionist' Auerswald was not in favour of imposing a starvation regime on the ghetto and recognised the economic value of its occupants as workers. Acknowledging that 'the amount of legally delivered food is utterly insufficient effectively to counter the famine situation existing in the Jewish district', Auerswald indicated that policies to curb smuggling – which accounted for up to 80 per cent of the food consumed in the ghetto – could be quietly relaxed.[108] This did not, however, extend to Jews leaving the ghetto in secrecy, in case the epidemic should spread through Warsaw, and in mid-November, a number of Jewish smugglers caught outside the ghetto gates were sentenced to execution.[109]

Normally, typhus would be expected to spread more rapidly in winter, but increasing malnutrition, terrible overcrowding, and lack of facilities for washing provided ideal conditions for lice in the warmer months too. During 1941, the epidemic accounted for perhaps 100,000 deaths. Of these, only 20,000 were attributed directly to typhus, but the rest – mainly classified as deaths from malnutrition – had typhus as at least a contributory factor.[110] Given the conditions in the ghetto, other illnesses like tuberculosis and dysentery were also rife. As one report described, 'starvation-related exhaustion' made people increasingly indifferent to maintaining their personal hygiene; just 4,630 Jews used community showers in June compared to the 12,305 in May.[111] Extreme overcrowding, particularly of recently arrived refugees from the countryside, only accelerated transmission, as one witness recorded:

> Walking down the street, I saw peasants' shaky carts passing by, filled with people worn out by the hardships of travel; I thought that those were the classic conditions for the onset and development of an epidemic.
>
> It was not until I started working in a shelter for refugees at Dzika Street 3 that my fears were confirmed … In not even ten rooms some 500 people had been placed … I knew that once plague sets in, it would not leave the house until the last of its residents was afflicted. And from there, through the *punktowcy* [refugees], who were spilling into the entire district, it would spread across the city. It was not only the overcrowded rooms and poor sanitary and material conditions that seemed to me a dangerous factor, but also the state of mind of the residents. That entire cluster of people had been thrown to the bottom of life within just a few days; robbed of their previous existence, they were overcome with despair and misery.[112]

The outbreak only corroborated German stereotypes, lending apparent credibility to their 'Jews–Lice–Typhus' propaganda and rationalising the community's segregation according to their 'uncleanliness'. Attempts to increase steam bath sanitation continued to be undermined by the corruption of sanitation workers, insufficient chemicals, and doctors acting as vectors for the disease who sought to profit on illegal home visits. It didn't help that Jews were deterred from reporting positive cases for fear of being forced into quarantine or seeing their food supplies destroyed – nor that louse-ridden clothing of the dead was frequently reappropriated.

Yet remarkably, typhus cases peaked in early autumn 1941 and then declined rapidly. Several factors contributed to this. Firstly, Auerswald permitted ration increases for working Jews; this benefited the entire ghetto in that smuggling continued unabated and the extra rations therefore increased the total amount of food entering the ghetto. Secondly, it is hard to overstate the work of Jewish microbiologist Ludwik Hirszfeld in curbing and tackling the epidemic that had come close to overwhelming the ghetto. Resettled in Warsaw in February of

1941, Hirszfeld had spent the winter tracking the disease and, with a group of other physicians in the ghetto, formed an underground 'health council' to spread awareness on detecting and preventing typhus. The group introduced a series of programmes that addressed issues of basic hygiene, social distancing, and sanitation, and organised several educational courses that ranged from public lectures to what amounted to an underground medical school.[113] These efforts were complemented by the *Aleynhilf* – whose work was in turn bolstered by close ties to the American JDC – and house committees organising a network of communal kitchens to make more efficient use of the available food. The much-maligned *Judenrat* played a role in this too, as did almost every agency working in the ghetto.

Still, the ghetto was slowly choking, and Jewish life fading into a shadow of what it had been. The Varsovian Jews made every effort to make the most of their new reality, but in truth, every aspect of their experience – from cultural activity to religious practice to social community – was rendered a sad reflection of its former self or irrevocably broken in some way. A vibrant community with centuries-deep roots in Warsaw's history was being sealed off from the outside world and suffocated. Looking for an apt way to describe this apocalyptic rupture, Różycki imagined guiding a visitor 'who has been asleep since 1 September 1939' through the Warsaw Ghetto:

> My untimely awoken guest blinks his eyes because he cannot believe that there is a wall cutting the street lengthwise and crosswise into big sections … He glances at people – miserable, thin, depressed, scared, with white bands on their right arm. Only Jews. No Poles … Ulcerated and swollen bodies. Skinny legs. Sallow, half-dead faces. Ghastly skeletons, whose only connection with the material world is the physical existence of lice, rags, skin, bones, and their ability to moan. Is it an image from Dante's *Inferno*? …
>
> But wait … this can be neither the Middle Ages nor some fantastic world as his senses are working normally …
>
> Only one thing is not right. This Romantic image lacks one important element: chivalry … Jews have not been permitted direct participation in the war. They have not had the honour.[114]

CHAPTER 8

ENDLÖSUNG AND THE GHETTO UPRISING

We, the slain, will stand up and stare at you,
stare at you mutely in our anguish,
and, staring at you, devour you in silence:
we'll cling to your very bones ...

May the earth in her great fury and in her hatred
spit you out of her mouth with loathing
and let you lie dead in the streets, like us, like us,
huddled together with your wife and child ...

Yitzkhok Katznelson, 'Woe unto You', 1942[1]

RIPPLES FROM WANNSEE

Once home to the painter Max Liebermann, the elegant Wannsee villa sits in the suburbs of Berlin, hemmed in by tranquil gardens and an old birch grove that stretches down to the lake. By noon of 12 January 1942, a bitterly cold day, 15 high-ranking officers of the SS, Nazi Party, and German government had converged on the villa – now the *RSHA* headquarters – at the behest of Reinhard Heydrich. The conference for which they had been summoned would go down in history as one of the darkest moments in European history. In reality, it merely formalised plans that had already been set in motion. Calls for an '*Endlösung* [final solution] of the Jewish question' had been growing louder since the German invasion of the Soviet Union the previous summer, but execution – and especially the question of timing – remained confused. Policy continued to oscillate between two imperatives: eliminating Jews during food shortages versus exploiting their labour when workers were scarce.[2] However, food and labour issues served as temporary modulations to the overall attitude to Jews; in the long run, nothing short of complete annihilation would satisfy Hitler.

At the end of July 1941, Heydrich received a letter from Reichsmarschall Göring commissioning him to prepare a '*Gesamtlösung* [general solution] of the Jewish question within the area of German influence in Europe.'[3] By the end of that year, the sheer volume of Jews in the eastern territories was overwhelming the Nazis' existing mechanisms of forced emigration, resettlement, or manual murder – a problem that would be compounded further if the Germans penetrated deeper into the Soviet Union. At Wannsee, Heydrich summarised the change in policy in characteristically euphemistic terms:

> Emigration has now been replaced by evacuation of the Jews to the East, as a further possible solution, with the appropriate prior authorisation by the Führer.
>
> However, this operation should be regarded only as a provisional option; but it is already supplying practical experience of great significance in view of the coming final solution of the Jewish question.[4]

In fact, the SS had already begun experimenting with more efficient and systematic methods of exterminating the Jews in 1941. The 'Holocaust by bullets' – the mass shooting of hundreds of thousands of Jews across the captured regions of the Soviet Union – was intended to make space for Jewish populations from further west who would be worked to death in the eastern territories. By the end of 1941, around 500,000 Eastern European Jews had already been murdered.[5] But the failure to defeat the Soviet Union before the end of the year left Germany facing a protracted war, and it was therefore impossible to proceed as planned. In any case, mass shootings were themselves problematic, and some questioned the use of so much ammunition at a time when front-line troops were suffering from supply shortages. Even Himmler expressed horror at the likely psychological effect of involvement in mass murder on the perpetrators and raised fears about how they might struggle to return to civilian life. A 'better' way was needed.

Earlier in 1941, experiments in Lublin had tested a new killing method: Jews were locked in crudely insulated buildings and gassed by fumes of a Russian submarine engine. From early December, 31 miles north of Łódź, Jews from the city ghetto were already being killed at Chełmno using mobile gas vans whose exhaust systems were redirected to the rear compartment.[6] But the SS documented two issues with the vans: many victims survived prolonged gassing, and dealing with the corpses was stressful for the personnel involved. Gaseous cyanide and carbon monoxide – tested on Soviet prisoners of war – proved more promising; death was swift, and the gases were more suitable for use in mass killing than exhaust fumes from vehicles, for which fuel was always in short supply.

As a result, Wannsee represented less a turning point in policy than a commitment to scale these operations across the occupied territories. During the conference, Heydrich estimated that the solution of the European Jewish question must take into account approximately 11 million Jews, of which nearly 2.3 million were based in the *Generalgouvernement*; the Polish Jewish question, then, was to be particularly prioritised:

> Secretary of State Dr. Bühler [Hans Frank's deputy] put on record that the Government-General would welcome it if the final solution of this problem *was begun in the Generalgouvernement* [emphasis in original], as, on the one hand, the question of transport there played no major role and considerations of labour supply would not hinder the course of this *Aktion*. Jews must be removed as fast as possible from the *Generalgouvernement*, because it was there in particular that the Jew as carrier of epidemics spelled a great danger, and, at the same time, he caused constant disorder in the economic structure of the country by his continuous black-market dealings. Furthermore, of the approximately 2½ million Jews under consideration, the majority were in any case *unfit for work* …
>
> He had only one request: that the Jewish question in this area be solved as quickly as possible.[7]

The plan sanctioned the establishment of three specialised death camps – Treblinka, Bełżec, and Sobibór – where mass gassing could be effected more efficiently. The officers entrusted with managing the camps – such as *Kriminalkommissar* Christian Wirth, Obersturmführer Irmfried Eberl, and Hauptsturmführer Franz Stangl – had been heavily involved in the murder of more than 70,000 disabled Poles, Austrians, and Germans under the *T4-Aktion* euthanasia programmes between 1940 and 1941.[8]

The new operation was to be headed by Brigadeführer Odilo Globočnik, former *Gauleiter* of Vienna. Nicknamed 'Globus', the heavily built Globočnik was the son of a railway worker from Slovenia, and for much of his life endured mockery for his Slavic name. He became involved in far-right Austrian politics in the early 1920s; perhaps seeking to dodge questions about his ancestry, he embraced extremist pro-German policies and readily transferred his anti-Slavic hostility to the Jews. His ambitious proposals – such as the deportation of Jews to Siberia – astonished other senior figures in Germany, as Rudolf Höss, the infamous commandant of Auschwitz-Birkenau, described after one meeting:

> He developed fantastic plans to establish camps as far away as the Urals ... He dismisses all objections with a wave of his hand. He wants to liquidate the Jews in this area immediately, right here, unless they are needed for work in 'his' camps ... He said this in a relaxed, conversational tone in his Viennese dialect in the evening by the fireplace, as if it were the most harmless of tales ... Globočnik couldn't get enough [Jews deported from further west], because he absolutely wanted to be at the forefront with extermination policies.[9]

Whatever others thought of Globočnik's plans, Himmler was deeply impressed with Globočnik's energy. Once resettlement – either in Siberia or Madagascar – was abandoned, Globočnik held meetings with Philipp Bouhler and Viktor Brack, who had also been involved in the *T4-Aktion*. Like many others, he wasn't averse to taking full personal advantage of the destruction of European Jewry. His adjutant Ernst Lerch later described seeing large 'bags of money' appearing in the basement of Globočnik's residence after major clearances, and he was also involved in black market activities in Lublin; Szama Grajer, a Jewish collaborator, was a regular accomplice, and when rivals in the SS began to urge investigations, Globočnik had Grajer killed.[10] After the Wannsee Conference, units of the SS, Gestapo, and Order Police were put at his disposal for the prodigious task of deporting Poland's Jewish population. With German manpower increasingly tied up on the active fronts, Latvian, Ukrainian, and Lithuanian *Hilfswillige* would once more provide important support in these operations.

That summer, construction of death camps began as part of a shift towards industrialised mass killing. During the autumn, when a railway worker asked some SS personnel who were surveying the site of a new camp what was being planned, she was told that she would soon find out – and that it would be 'a good laugh'.[11] Globočnik had already created a labour camp at Bełzec, not far from Lublin, and after Wannsee he authorised the construction of a gas chamber using an engine dismounted from a truck tuned to produce carbon monoxide. As they arrived, Jews were told that they were to strip and have showers before being issued new work clothes. They then endured a sham medical examination designed to identify those with gold fillings, their backs were marked with chalk to make identifying the corpses easier. Finally, they were sent into the gas chamber.

But the instigator of the *Endlösung* would not live to see it implemented, for in June 1942, Heydrich was the victim of an assassination attempt by

British-trained Czech resistance fighters. He was injured by shrapnel from a grenade thrown into his car, and when one of the assassins attempted to fire on him, the weapon jammed; but Heydrich collapsed just as he was drawing his weapon to fire back. One of his abdominal wounds was contaminated with horsehair from the car's upholstery and he developed peritonitis, dying in great pain on 4 June. Vengeance was swift. The assassins were betrayed and cornered in a church, where some chose suicide rather than capture. Hitler demanded the execution of 10,000 Czech civilians, but agreed to scale down his plans when local Nazi officials reported it would be to the detriment of industrial output in the region. After wrongly implicating civilians from nearby villages Lidice and Ležáky, the Germans shot 172 Lidice males and completely razed both settlements – even digging up cemetery graves. All Ležáky adults were executed; most Lidice women were sent to Ravensbrück, where four underwent forced abortions. Children deemed 'Germanic' went to German foster families, while 81 others were gassed at Chełmno. Ultimately, the Germans killed at least 1,300 Czech civilians in revenge for Heydrich's death.[12] They also gave his name to the Jewish extermination programme, which was now known as *Aktion Reinhard*.

BAD OMENS

News of the *Endlösung* did not arrive immediately in the Warsaw Ghetto. However, thanks to the Polish underground, word-of-mouth reports from escapees or refugees, and other informal information networks across Poland, rumours of new and more terrible modes of persecution abounded. The Jewish underground had already brought news of mass shootings in Lithuania, Belarus, and Ukraine – reports that were greeted with a mixture of horror and disbelief. Although it was almost impossible to separate fact from fiction amidst the constant bombardment of hearsay, catastrophising rhetoric, and unverifiable suspicions, many of the stories circulating in early 1942 foreshadowed horrors that were about to become commonplace – as Ringelblum recorded:

> On April 12 rumours were thick that an extermination squad had come to Warsaw and had begged permission to go on a rampage through the Ghetto for just two hours. But permission was not granted. Auerswald wouldn't agree … This rumour is associated with the fact that there are various foreign contingents in Warsaw, such as Lithuanians and Ukrainians, and they're just waiting for the right moment to start a pogrom. Besides, one is always hearing reports about extermination squads that are wiping complete Jewish settlements off the face of the earth.

> One hundred sixty-four of the German Jews who came to Warsaw a few days ago, the cream of the young people, including a large number of *chalutzim* [pioneer settlers] preparing to migrate to Palestine, were sent to the penal camp at Treblinki, near Sokolow, where most of them were exterminated in a short time. In three weeks, out of 160 Jewish young people from Otwock only 38 were left.[13]

Stories of deportations trickled in from the Łódź Ghetto, where tens of thousands of Jews were shipped out in late 1941. 'Some took this news very much to heart,' Szpilman recalled, 'with others it went in one ear and out the other. After a while people stopped talking about Łódź and began on Lublin and Tarnów, where apparently the Jews were being poisoned with gas.'[14] Mary Berg's uncle left Lublin just in time to escape the 'resettlement actions' that started there in mid-March: 'about half of the ghetto population was murdered,' he related in a letter, 'and a considerable number were deported to an unknown destination. About two thousand Jewish people remained of the original forty thousand. These two thousand were taken to the Majdanek camp near Lublin. Even today the streets of the Lublin Ghetto are drenched in blood and the victims have not yet been picked up.'[15] From Zamość came stories of Jewish children being forcibly removed from their parents; from Warthegau, claims that Jews were paying the *Judenrat* to avoid being sent to their 'last stop' at Chełmno; from the east, tales of windowless trucks – or *dushegubki* ('people killers') – and further mass shootings.[16] What recurs in Varsovian diarists' accounts of early 1942 is a sense of foreboding accompanied by unwillingness, or inability, to accept the rumours as fact. 'We were terribly shaken but not entirely certain that this was really happening,' Auerbach noted.[17] At the same time, the ghetto residents, by now finely attuned to the Germans' habitual modes of persecution, sensed that a change was imminent. As Szpilman declared, the sudden cessation of 'human-hunting' and random street round-ups in early 1942 could only be 'because they had thought up another and better idea for tormenting us.'[18]

No one foresaw the coming catastrophe more clearly than Czerniaków. On 19 January, one day before the Wannsee Conference, he was perturbed by news that Auerswald had been called to Berlin; 'I cannot shake off the fearful suspicion,' he wrote, 'that the Jews of Warsaw may be threatened by mass resettlement.'[19] His diary also alludes to scores of male Jewish prisoners being sent to Treblinka in early 1942 where, unbeknownst to him, the internees of the Treblinka I work camp were tasked with constructing the new death camp that would become Treblinka II. The beleaguered chairman struggled on, spread ever more thinly between impossible demands, all the while 'spitting blood' from his ceaseless – and, more often than not, fruitless – efforts.[20] Amidst the daily battles with the

German authorities recorded in his diary, it is hard not to sense his mounting pessimism – his unshakeable feeling that 'the future looks grim for the Jews.'[21]

Life in the ghetto was becoming ever more claustrophobic and oppressive. On the night of 17 April, the entire district was paralysed by rumours of an imminent pogrom; on what would become known as 'Bloody Friday', 52 Jews were hunted down in their homes, arrested, and shot. The victims included welfare workers, bakers, printers, and underground activists, but also several known collaborators, *szmalcowniki*, and associates of the notorious Thirteen. In the aftermath of the massacre, Czerniaków was ordered by the Germans to issue a statement declaring the action would not recur so long as the Jewish community remained compliant.[22] Of course, not everyone was convinced. Citing a pattern of arrests and shootings across the *Generalgouvernement*, Ringelblum assumed the Germans had embarked on a deliberate campaign to 'terrorise the Jewish populace'. 'Probably this is in connection with the spring campaigns,' he reasoned, 'they want their rear to be secure.'[23]

When viewed with the knowledge of the deportations to come, it becomes apparent that the Germans used the first half of 1942 to extract as much economic value, labour, and propagandistic material from the ghetto as possible. On top of the labourers sent to the camps, over 1,000 Varsovian Jews were put to work at the Többens firm at 12 Prosta Street, repairing German uniforms and, from late 1941, preparing winter clothing to support the campaign in the Soviet Union.[24] During the winter, decrees were issued across the entire *Generalgouvernement* requiring Jews to surrender their fur coats. Unsurprisingly, this gave rise to people smuggling valuable clothing out of the ghetto, affluent Jews paying off the *Judenrat* for exemptions, and, once again, the poorest bearing the brunt of the suffering through the cold winter. When the requisitioned furs failed to satisfy the Germans, Czerniaków was tasked with funding and producing more items, and furriers in Gęsia Street worked around the clock to hit impossible targets. By the end of January, a total of 181,788 fur items had been collected, at significant cost to the Jewish community; 'for the rest,' Czerniaków commented, 'we will have to tear our guts out.'[25] Adult Jews threw themselves into work, hoping that proving themselves as valuable labourers might spare them the terrible fate of the Jews of Łódź and Lublin. Auerbach noted the ensuing 'shop panic', where both real and bogus workers donned any work uniform or clothing they could find 'as a kind of body armour [that] gave them more hope of survival than a mere shop ID card.'[26] As Ringelblum had observed regarding the fur coat saga, 'the popular fantasy is rich and quickly reacts to everything that happens in the street'; Varsovian Jews created rules and rituals for themselves in the hope that they could influence their fate when, more often than not, it was already far beyond their control.[27]

In May 1942, ghetto life was interrupted by another unprecedented occurrence. 'The Germans have decided to make a film of life in the ghetto,' Berg recorded; though naturally, as the film's title – *Asien in Mitteleuropa* ('Asians in Central Europe') – suggested, it was to be a very contrived depiction.[28] Michał Zylberberg, headmaster of a vocational school on Nowolipki Street, was ordered to ensure children come 'elegantly dressed' and 'bring oranges' for a lavish breakfast to be filmed the following day.[29] Shop windows were stuffed with long-forgotten luxuries, elaborate dinner parties staged between well-dressed Jews pulled off the street, and men and women forced to bathe naked in a public bath. In Czerniaków's office, a nine-armed candlestick was placed on the chairman's desk for pantomime meetings with rabbis and Jewish leaders. On Smocza Street, a crowd was driven together, and a German policeman filmed intervening just in time to stop a Jewish policeman from beating a fallen straggler.[30] Every sequence was carefully staged to reinforce the German narrative; scenes of abject poverty, starvation, sickness, and suffering were not recorded unless they could be construed as evidence of the Jews' moral perversity towards their own people. The ghetto populace watched on with a mixture of fascination and bafflement. Only after the fact could Szpilman remark: 'The Germans were making these films before they liquidated the ghetto, to give the lie to any disconcerting rumours if news of the action should reach the outside world. They would show how well off the Jews of Warsaw were – and how immoral and despicable they were too.'[31]

Others speculated that the Germans' latest propaganda effort was intended to serve as ideological reassurance to German civilians in light of recent setbacks in the east. In actual fact, the film did represent a slight shift in the Germans' propaganda around Jews. Where earlier propaganda had served to justify the Reich's antisemitism, historian Anja Horstmann has shown that ghetto films created in and after 1942 were 'intended to be archived for the future and only used once the "Jewish policy" had been completed.' *Asien in Mitteleuropa* was therefore carefully curated to show 'a community that must perish not through external violence but through an internal dynamic'; in other words, to paint for future generations of the Reich a picture of the Jews as victims of nothing but their own depravity, doomed to self-destruction.[32]

GROSSAKTION WARSCHAU

The answer to the question on every Varsovian Jew's mind – 'When will it be our turn?' – finally arrived in July 1942.[33] In the middle of the month, Czerniaków mentioned in his diary, 'rumours about the deportation of Jews from the Quarter, with 120,000 to be left behind'; his entries over the following days noted other scraps of ominous hearsay as panic spread in the ghetto.[34]

The first members of the SS team that would oversee Operation *Reinhard* arrived in mid-July, headed by Hauptsturmführer – soon promoted to Sturmbannführer – Hermann Höfle, a close associate of Globočnik. He imposed strict secrecy, requiring all his subordinates to sign declarations that photography of the coming events was prohibited and that the 'process of the evacuation of the Jews' was a classified secret to be kept even after men returned to civilian life.[35] On 21 July, 60 *Judenrat* officials and other community leaders were arrested as hostages to ensure ghetto cooperation, and the following morning, the chairman received the orders he had been dreading:

> We were told that all the Jews irrespective of sex and age, with certain exceptions, will be deported to the East. By 4pm today a contingent of 6,000 people must be provided. And this (at the minimum) will be the daily quota.
>
> We were ordered to vacate a building at 103 Zelazna Street for the German personnel who will be carrying out the deportation …
>
> The most tragic dilemma is the problem of children in orphanages, etc. I raised this issue – perhaps something can be done…
>
> Sturmbannführer Höfle … asked me into his office and informed me that for the time being my wife was free, but if the deportation were impeded in any way, she would be the first one to be shot as a hostage.[36]

Judenrat officials and their relatives were exempted, as were other civic workers, hospital staff, enterprise employees, and members of the Ghetto Police. Deportees were permitted to bring with them 15 kilograms of luggage and food rations for three days, as well as valuables, jewellery, and money; they were being sent east, they were told, to be settled in barracks and put to work in German factories. As Jews gathered around the posters announcing the initiation of the *Grossaktion* – as the operation was codenamed – their first reactions were mixed. Many reasoned that it was only those unfit for employment who would suffer – perhaps 20 per cent of the population. Donat explained this point of view: 'True, Nazi brutality spoke in every line of the ghetto decree, there would be shootings, victimisation of the weak, and beatings, but still everyone reassured himself, it *was* a resettlement'; as for the less fortunate 20 per cent, 'well, weren't they the inevitable victims of war?'[37] This was an especially seductive narrative for those who considered themselves 'productive' members of the ghetto, and one that the Nazis worked to reinforce by using 'othering' language that divided those that brought economic value from the 'unfit' and the 'unproductive'. When the first day's deportation quota included inmates pulled out of the Gęsiówka prison, refugees from the overcrowded shelters, and beggars from the street, plenty of Jews felt assured in this reasoning. One survivor claimed to have heard from a cemetery superintendent that the Germans had unloaded several elderly Jews rounded up for deportation in the cemetery and executed them over pre-dug graves; perversely, this act of brutality was supposed to reassure Jews that so long as they were fit to work, they would not have to fear for their lives.[38]

But more observant Jews noticed something more sinister about the posters announcing the deportation. 'For the first time,' Szpilman noted, 'a decree did not carry the signature of the chairman of the Jewish Council.'[39] Indeed, Czerniaków had refused to sign the decree he considered a death sentence for his community. His diary, in which he diligently recorded all the bureaucratic nightmares he faced but little in the way of personal reflection, ends abruptly on 23 July 1942: aware of the mass deportations from the ghetto in Lublin and the disappearance of its Jews into Bełzec and Sobibór, and realising that similar fates awaited the Jews of Warsaw, he committed suicide in his Grzybowska Street office. After all the satire and criticism directed towards him from the more cynical Jewish populace, the man who had tried so hard to moderate the Nazis' brutal antisemitism refused to be a part of transporting his people to their deaths. Whatever his faults, to the very end he tried to be a beacon of hope for the community, a shield between them and their tyrannical occupiers:

> Because of the panic I drove through the streets of the entire Quarter. I visited three playgrounds. I do not know whether I managed to calm the population, but I did my best. I try to hearten the delegations which come to see me. What it costs me they do not see. Today I took two headache powders, another pain reliever, and a sedative, but my head is still splitting. I am trying not to let the smile leave my face.[40]

But it was impossible to quell the anguish amongst a ghetto population who, upon hearing of his suicide, felt utterly deserted. He had 'failed to summon his people to resistance,' Donat wrote. 'His suicide only intensified our fear and panic.'[41]

During the first days of the *Grossaktion*, round-ups continued to prioritise the most vulnerable in society, and, as promised, the police generally exempted those with correct work documentation. When the Germans posted a decree that Jews who volunteered for emigration would earn three kilograms of bread and three kilograms of jam per person, plenty took up the offer. However, it wasn't long before the *Grossaktion* descended into violence and randomised brutality. Under the notorious Colonel Józef Szeryński, Captain Jakub Lejkin (nicknamed 'Little Napoleon' by the Germans for his tyrannical tendencies), and Captain Josef 'Kapota' Ehrlich, the Jewish Police played a major role in rounding up their neighbours, intimidating and extorting from those desperate for exemption. Jews scrambling to secure work that would protect them from deportation found themselves ensnared in Kafka-esque bureaucracy whose rules were highly discretionary. To quote Donat, the acquisition of work documents gave Jews 'false confidence' and was just another 'illusion that led thousands to their deaths.'[42]

As the old and infirm disappeared, the ghetto population became accustomed to a new pattern of terror: buildings would be surrounded, exits and alleys cut off, and the inhabitants dragged out into the courtyards to have their documents checked. Those sentenced to deportation would be dragged onto horse-drawn carts and taken to the dreaded *Umschlagplatz*, 'crammed into trucks and dispatched into the unknown.'[43]

Numerous diarists, including Szpilman, recall the arrival of the Ukrainian and Lithuanian auxiliaries who were deployed alongside the Jewish Police:

> They were just as venal as the Jewish police, although in a different way. They took bribes, but as soon as they had received them they killed the people whose money they had taken. They liked killing anyway: killing for sport, or to make their work easier, as target practice or simply for fun. They killed children before their mothers' eyes and found the women's despair amusing. They shot people in the stomach to watch their torments. Sometimes several of them would line their victims up in a row and throw hand grenades at them from a distance to see who had the best aim. Every war casts up certain small groups among ethnic populations: minorities too cowardly to fight openly, too insignificant to play any independent political part, but despicable enough to act as paid executioners to one of the fighting powers. In this war those people were the Ukrainian and Lithuanian Fascists.[44]

Panic mounted across the ghetto as it became harder to deny the Germans' true intentions. *Judenrat* staff were perplexed by German demands for 'reinforced crates, 150 by 70 cm, for storing necessary items', until they learned that these would be used for the collection of deportees' valuables, gold teeth, and other personal possessions on arrival at Treblinka.[45] Even civilians spared deportation witnessed first-hand the increasingly indiscriminate cruelty of the round-ups. Donat watched a young mother who had stepped out for some milk for her baby get dragged away when she failed to produce her papers; Zygmunt Warman looked on in horror as the Germans 'killed on the spot' his neighbours who failed to come down the staircase quickly enough when called.[46] Another *Judenrat* official, Stanisław Adler, ran out onto some stairs and 'had to wade ankle deep through blood', passing 'a lock of hair with a piece of brain stuck to a wall'; he described how 'old people began shaving off their heads to hide grey hair from the sight of their butchers. A father voluntarily followed a child that was caught for transport', and 'daughters exempted on some basis gave up staying and left together with their "resettled" mother.'[47] On 5 August, ghetto residents watched as Janusz Korczak led the children out of his orphanage for the last time:

> He had spent long years of his life with children, and now, on this last journey, he would not leave them alone. He wanted to ease things for them … He told them to wear their best clothes, and so they came out into the yard, two by two, nicely dressed and in a happy mood.
>
> The little column was led by an SS man who loved children, as Germans do, even those he was about to see on their way into the next world. He took a special liking to a boy of twelve, a violinist who had his instrument under his arm. The SS man told him to go to the head of the procession of children and play – and so they set off.
>
> When I met them in Gęsia Street the smiling children were singing in chorus, the little violinist was playing for them and Korczak was carrying two of the smallest infants, who were beaming too, and telling them some amusing story.[48]

Korczak had refused offers from the underground organisation *Żegota* to smuggle him out of the ghetto. 'You do not leave a sick child in the night,' he insisted, 'and you do not leave children at a time like this.'[49]

THE *UMSCHLAGPLATZ* AND BEYOND

By mid-1942, roads into the *Umschlagplatz* were blocked and regular traffic to the compound had long ceased; the area had become yet another black spot in the occupied territory, a place that existed at the edges of consciousness for the ghetto's Jews and associated with the most horrifying acts of cruelty. To the south of the compound was a large oval space which became the holding area for deportees until they were herded 'like cattle' into waiting trucks on the north side of the station. Railcars intended for goods or livestock were doused in lime between transits and packed with as many as 150 Jews at a time.[50] Deportees would be forced to lie on top of each other in the suffocating trucks without access to food or water, and frequently locked inside hours or even days before the train was ready to depart. Those that survived the *Grossaktion* shared terrifying memories of the *Umschlagplatz*; corpses of men and women of all ages littered the outskirts of the compound, with children killed on the spot for crying, adults shot for getting in the way of German guards, and women openly sexually abused by the police. Using what little money and valuables they still had, some desperately bargained for their lives with the Jewish policemen assigned to guard the compound; others resigned themselves to awaiting their fate in the baking summer heat, sensing that the end – whether from dehydration, starvation, or murder – was just hours away.[51] When the German police swept through the holding area to pick out the young and strong for labour, those desperate for one last chance of reprieve would jostle and fight to be selected. Finally, the moment for loading would arrive and the Jewish Police, together with the *Hilfswillige* and SS, would close in on the remaining crowd and press them towards the eye-watering stench of chlorine that surrounded the waiting railcars. Despite their efforts, the Germans could not stop the truth about the deportations filtering back to the ghetto:

> The fugitives, mainly people who had been responsible for sorting out clothes in Treblinka, told us about the Germans delivering speeches to those who arrived, announcing the beginning of a new era: from now on they would be employed working productively on the land; then, they would receive their own farms. At the beginning, they were to take off all their clothes and have a bath; then, they would receive new clothes for the continuation of the journey. The alleged bath was a gas chamber, in which the victims of that atrocity would die in torment after 15 minutes. Terror descended upon the quarter.[52]

Szpilman was rescued from deportation at the *Umschlagplatz* at the last possible moment – just as his family stepped onto the train. Distraught and devastated, he watched the carriages bearing his loved ones start off from the station at the same moment he overheard an SS officer remark to a Jewish policeman, 'Well, off they go for meltdown!'[53]

The deportations continued through the summer of 1942, with transports numbering 12,000 Jews on some days. The volumes of victims being sent to Treblinka rapidly exceeded the capacity of the gas chambers and the Germans and their auxiliaries instead resorted to shooting large numbers of Jews as they arrived. One survivor described seeing 'hundreds of bodies lying around' the railway lines, and another recalled that 'the camp yard was littered with corpses, some still in their clothes and some naked, their faces distorted with fright and awe, black and swollen, the eyes wide open, with protruding tongues, skulls crushed, bodies mangled.'[54] Some escaped death by being selected for camp labour, which usually meant clearing the gas chambers of the dead. One such selectee described his arrival in Treblinka: 'After we left the wagon the Germans and Ukrainians, whips in their hands, drove us into a courtyard, where they ordered us to lie down with our faces to the ground. Then they walked through and shot us in the back of the head.'[55]

The disorder in Treblinka owed its roots to the manner in which so many in the Nazi system competed to demonstrate their zeal. In this case, Irmfried Eberl, an Austrian psychiatrist who had been an enthusiastic proponent of the *T4-Aktion* to kill those with mental disabilities and was now running Treblinka, was the culprit. Hans Hingst, a relatively junior SS NCO guard, described how Eberl tried 'to reach the highest possible numbers [of victims] and exceed all the other camps.'[56] With Jews now being killed in the railway yards, there were more opportunities for escape, and therefore returning to the ghetto to tell others what was happening. As news of the chaos at Treblinka percolated up the German chain of command, Hauptsturmführer Franz Stangl was dispatched to investigate. Despite his experiences in the *T4-Aktion* and a spell running the Sobibór camp, he was shocked by the sight of hundreds of corpses putrefying in mounds by the railway tracks. Eberl was dismissed and after a pause – during which Jewish labourers were forced to bury the rotting corpses – Stangl resumed operations in a more 'efficient' manner. Eberl was arrested in January 1948 but hanged himself in his cell before he could be brought to trial.

THE CAULDRON

Early in August, residents of the small ghetto were forced to relocate to the main quarter as the Germans drew their net tighter. What fragile equilibrium had existed in ghetto society was crumbling fast. The turmoil of rampaging police and mass round-ups caused shops and bakeries to close, which disrupted both the distribution of rations and smuggling operations. The threat of starvation rose to such an extent that hundreds more were lured into voluntary deportation by the promise of food, while those who refused sensed it was only a matter of time until their luck ran out. In September, the operation changed gear once again; the authorities began blockading workshops and factories that had thus far been spared and selected workers for deportation. On 6 September, the ghetto awoke to a new order: all remaining residents were to gather in a designated area bounded by Smocza, Gęsia, Zamenhof, and Szczesliwa Streets and Parysowski

Square by 10am. Everyone was to bring food for two days, residences were to be left unlocked, and anyone who did not comply would be executed. So began the most terrible selection so far: *kocioł na Miłej* – the 'Cauldron' or 'Trap' on Miła Street. A total of 32,000 Jews received numbered cards that secured their right to work in the ghetto; the rest, the Germans declared, were to be deported. Antoni Szymanowski reported on behalf of the Polish underground:

> Anyone who did not see this procession will never understand the menace it represented. A huge crowd, stunned, stupefied, and at the same time still teeming with fear and anxiety, moved slowly toward the gates that had been constructed where the selection took place …
>
> Many still had bundles with them, food. The incorrigible property instinct! I saw terrifyingly horrific things there – above all the separation of children from their parents …
>
> Another woman who, despite permission for herself only to leave, wanted to smuggle out her little son. The German separated them and before the eyes of everyone began to beat her with his whip, kick her, punch her in the face and head. When he finally let her go and she came round, the child was gone. I saw her eyes, when she was looking around for the child. I won't forget. An old Jew, perhaps eighty years old, probably a grandfather, bowed to the SS man, who was a twenty-year-old youth: he wanted to beg for the life of the boy he was leading. The German laughed. I won't forget.
>
> The patients from the hospital were deported along with the medical personnel. Adina Blady-Szwajger, a doctor in the Bersohn and Bauman's Children's Hospital, which had been moved to Stawki Street, gave the children morphine, so that they could die in their beds and escape the horrors of deportation.[57]

Thousands opted to hide rather than present themselves for certain death at Miła Street. The Germans raked through unlocked apartments to root out these would-be escapees and, as promised, dealt with them severely. Others attempted to run from the police, hoping to find a safe spot to wait out the *Grossaktion* or a means to escape to the 'Aryan' quarter. Thirteen-year-old Samuel Eisen recounted:

> When the action began, my father and I started to run, but Daddy was hit and he crumpled at our feet. We did not stop and kept running into the field. Next day, we found Daddy, but he was already naked, as were all the corpses around. The administrator allowed us to bury our Daddy, he gave me and my brother shovels, and we dug a pit and buried Daddy naked. We had no clothes to dress him in.[58]

To go, to hide, or to run; it was an impossible dilemma, and making the right choice required 'more luck than brains'. Still, some, like Auerbach, were incredibly fortunate: hiding in a tiny coal cellar with ten other people, she escaped detection only because a fire broke out in the neighbouring apartment, and the firemen became so preoccupied with looting the surrounding apartments that they didn't think to check under the rugs that masked the hideout entrance.[59] According to Szymanowski, the Cauldron resulted in 2,648 people shot, 54,269 deported, 60 suicides, and over 300 other deaths in just two days. In addition to the Jews who had obtained number cards, around 25,000–30,000 escaped the action and remained in the ghetto illegally.[60]

Selections generally dropped off in the aftermath of the Cauldron, but the Germans weren't yet finished. In the second half of September, the Jewish Police were ordered to reduce their numbers from 2,400 to 380 men. The final deportation of 2,196 Jews included hundreds of police officers and long-time collaborators with the Nazis such as the detested 'Little Napoleon' Lejkin, and the *Umschlagplatz*'s loathsome 'hangman with the whip', Mieczysław Szmerling.[61] Despite their best efforts, these collaborators were always expendable and considered a liability the longer they were involved in the occupiers' operations. As Ringelblum had remarked in disgust earlier in the year, 'The Gestapo beast devours its own progeny,' just like 'beasts that devour their young.'[62] At the end of the month, the Germans announced the end of the *Grossaktion*. Since its initiation in July, the population of the Warsaw Ghetto had been reduced by around 300,000. The change was clearly visible from outside the ghetto, prompting Zofia Nałkowska to write of 'that dead town. That place of terror and torment. All the windows and balconies, once so full of overcrowded people – are empty today.'[63]

In early 1943 a telegram to Eichmann in Berlin listed the achievements to date. The message gave details of the deportations to the death camps in the course of *Reinhard*, with the camps identified by initials: L (Lublin, i.e. the nearby Majdanek) received 24,733 deportees; B (Bełżec) received 434,508; S (Sobibór) received 101,370; and T (Treblinka) received 713,555.[64] These numbers included Jews and others who were taken to camps from all locations – not just the Warsaw Ghetto. German communications of this kind were encrypted using an Enigma machine prior to transmission, but by this stage of the war the British had no difficulty decoding them. Unfortunately, however, the significance of the telegram was not understood at the time; codebreakers and most of those who read the decryption wouldn't have been aware of the weight of references to Operation *Reinhard*, nor the gruesome significance of the initials and numbers.[65]

Processing the Unimaginable

Following the *Grossaktion*, the downsized ghetto essentially functioned as a 'huge labour camp'.[66] Workers were subjected to back-breaking work in the factories and workshops on ever-diminishing wages – from which they were taxed for food during working hours – and, in some cases, were branded as the property of their employers. The blocks of larger shops became miniaturised ghettos in themselves, with their own – typically filthy and overcrowded – workers' accommodation, stores, and synagogues; other workers were employed outside the shrunken ghetto and had to march miles under supervision every day. Those who had escaped deportation illegally lived under the constant fear of discovery. The remaining ghetto population watched as the Germans – with units of Jewish labourers – stripped apartment buildings of valuables, furnishings, and family treasures as they themselves faced starvation, yet again unable to shake the fear that their reprieve from death was only temporary.

Many non-Jewish Varsovians would later claim that it wasn't until the *Grossaktion* that they realised the true extent of the Germans' murderous intent towards the Jews. Biskupska argues that 'Jewish "inaction" nevertheless fed antisemitic Polish stereotypes', but the same was probably true in reverse: Polish inaction towards the ghetto augmented the Jews' sense of isolation, to which Ringelblum gave voice when he declared that 'Polish Fascism and its ally, antisemitism, have conquered the majority of the Polish people.'[67] Considering Ringelblum himself was rescued numerous times by the Polish underground and sheltered by a non-Jewish Pole, this was not an entirely fair assessment; his words testify more to the Jews' sense of helplessness and alienation than to any verifiable claim that 'hundreds of thousands of Jews … could have been saved despite the Germans.'[68] No doubt there were antisemites, blackmailers, and other Poles who did not actively help the Jews, but considering the existential threat Poland as a whole faced it is difficult to judge their reaction to an unprecedented holocaust on Ringelblum's terms. Lukas instead highlights the remarkable resilience and generosity of spirit displayed by thousands of non-Jewish Poles who knowingly endangered themselves by offering aid: 'The wonder is not how few but how many Jews were saved.'[69] Of the 12,681 people awarded the status of 'Righteous Among the Nations' by the Yad Vashem institute, there are more Poles – 4,478 or 35 per cent of the total – than people of any other nationality.

Indeed, support for the Jews came from many quarters, some more surprising than others. The writer Zofia Kossack-Szcucka, for instance, was a vocal antisemite and considered Judaism incompatible with the Roman Catholic spirit of Poland, yet she was also a cofounder of the *Żegota* relief council for Jews. In response to the events of the summer of 1942, she penned a leaflet, *Protest!*, which explained her nuanced attitude towards Polish–Jewish relations; maintaining her ideological and religious opposition to the Jews, she decried the silence of the Western Powers – as well as the Poles – towards the German atrocities, and underlined the Catholic and patriotic imperative for Poles to be more than 'Pilates washing their hands.'[70] Kossack-Szcucka was instrumental in recruiting Irena Krzyżanowska-Sendler, the Catholic social worker who helped smuggle around 2,500 children out of the ghetto.[71] There was also Reverend Marceli Godlewski, who worked within the ghetto with Jewish Catholic converts and helped transport children to his orphanage outside; then there were all the Polish acquaintances, ex-colleagues, friends, and former neighbours of Jews who helped smuggle resources across the ghetto wall and hid refugees. Kossack-Szcucka was not the only one who chose to sideline personal and political convictions in the pursuit of what she considered her duty of protection. One rescued Jew recalled:

> In the small houses in Warsaw's Żoliborz district inhabited mostly by the Polish intelligentsia there were hidden many Jews who had escaped from the ghetto. I was in such a home which belonged to a known prewar Endek [member of the antisemitic *Endecja* movement]. Having learned that he was sheltering two Jewesses I asked with surprise: 'You who before the war were an antisemite are now harbouring Jews in your home???' He replied: 'We have a common enemy and I am fighting in my way. They are Polish citizens and I have to help them.'[72]

The pervasiveness of Polish support for the Jews was reflected in the September 1942 decree imposing the death penalty for Varsovians caught aiding Jews. In few other German-occupied territories were such severe laws implemented. Elsewhere, civilians who helped Jews were usually liable to face imprisonment or fines; only in the eastern territories did these people – and by extension, their families – risk execution. The decree rendered those sheltering or assisting refugees all the more vulnerable to *szmalcowniki*, blackmailers, and other collaborators, prompting the Polish underground to respond via the Directorate of Civil Resistance in March 1943 with an announcement that 'every case of such blackmail will be recorded and punished with all the severity of the law, whenever possible now, and at all events in the future'.[73] This was a case of the underground taking justice into its own hands on issues of social morality at the heart of the occupation experience. The declaration lived up to its promise: a number of Varsovians were sentenced to death by the underground courts as a result of the decree, including one corporal of the Blue Police.[74]

It was during this period that underground courier Jan Karski was smuggled into the ghetto in preparation for his report to the Western Allies. Wrapped in an old, shabby coat and accompanied by a representative of the socialist Bund movement and a member of the Jewish underground, Karski stepped into the 'city of death', a 'new world utterly unlike anything that had ever been imagined':

> These were still living people, if you could call them such. For apart from their skin, eyes, and voice there was nothing human left in these palpitating figures. Everywhere there was hunger, misery, the atrocious stench of decomposing bodies, the pitiful moans of dying children, the desperate cries and gasps of a people struggling for life against impossible odds … From time to time we passed a well-fed German policeman who looked abnormally bloated by contrast with the meagreness of those who surrounded him …
>
> We passed a miserable replica of a park … Children, every bone in their skeletons showing through their taut skins, played in heaps and swarms.
>
> 'They play before they die,' I heard my companion on the left say, his voice breaking with emotion.
>
> Without thinking – the words escaping even before the thought had crystallised – I said: 'But these children are not playing – they only make believe it is play.'[75]

Karski witnessed first-hand the quotidian horrors of the ghetto to which the rest of the world was blind. He watched a 'rosy-cheeked' German shoot dead a Jew for amusement; he passed countless corpses of Jews in the street, stripped naked by their families to avoid paying an unaffordable burial tax; he noted the ominous absence of elderly Jews.[76] Whatever nightmares he had anticipated, nothing could have prepared him for the reality of the ghetto. One Jewish resident must have sensed his distress; 'You came to see us?' she asked. 'It won't do any good. Go back, run away. Don't torture yourself any more.'[77]

Karski could hardly have done more to raise awareness about the plight of the Poles and, in particular, Polish Jews – but the Western Allies simply refused to accept the level of horror he described. In May 1943, he delivered his report in the presence of President Roosevelt and the US Supreme Justice, Felix Frankfurter – himself a Jew – who would go down in history for uttering the damning dismissal that probably summed up the feelings of many Allied leaders: 'I did not say this young man is lying. I said I am unable to believe him. There is a difference.'[78] To any Pole in Karski's shoes, the feeling of being disregarded on the international stage yet again must have been devastating. As historian Andrew Roberts put it, 'To have utterly vital information, but to be ignored or disbelieved, must be almost as terrible as to be interrogated for information one doesn't possess.'[79] The ghetto resident Karski had met was correct. It didn't do any good.

REHEARSING RESISTANCE

In the same way that the Polish underground state had been growing and mobilising since the invasion of the city, the Jewish community had developed its own array of conspiratorial groups and resistance elements. These were also spread across the political spectrum and struggled to coalesce in any robust form until 1942. During the *Grossaktion*, social activist Yitzhak Zuckerman, leftist Mordechai Anielewicz, Bundist Marek Edelman, and a range of other centrist leaders rallied together to form the *Żydowski Komitet Narodowy* ('Jewish National Committee' or *ŻKN*), a political coalition designed to mirror the Polish underground state within the ghetto. At the end of the summer, the *ŻKN* launched its military wing, the *Żydowska Organizacja Bojowa* ('Jewish Fighting Wing' or *ŻOB*), which, under the command of Anielewicz, set about planning an armed uprising in earnest. At the same time, a more right-leaning affiliation of Zionists and radical youth groups formed their own militant wing under the *Żydowski Związek Wojskowy* ('Jewish Military Union' or *ŻZW*). Members of all groups were involved in impromptu skirmishes with the Germans during the summer of the *Grossaktion* but found their impact limited so long as they operated in isolation from each other.

Another major challenge for the Jewish underground resistance was the procurement of arms. As with most goods in the ghetto, smuggling was the solution, but this was dependent on having willing partners and suppliers on the outside. The largest resistance force in the city, the *Armia Krajowa* ('Home Army' or *AK*), was itself struggling with severe weapons shortages and therefore reluctant to help. But logistics and resources weren't the only issues giving the *AK* pause; at a time when the Polish underground state and the *AK* were trying to use their military value to galvanise western support, they judged that the ghetto Jews 'had nothing to offer' in this broader picture.[80] Such arguments overlooked the desperation of the Jewish situation by late 1942, where resistance was no longer a question of 'politics or tactics' but one of principle – of protesting against annihilation. In September, Julian Kulski, by now a 13-year-old member of the Polish underground, was also smuggled into the ghetto and spoke with young Jewish resistance leaders. 'What we need now is arms and ammunition, so that we can start an Uprising,' one told him. 'We know that we should have been training as your Underground Army has been doing.'[81] As the Jewish leaders explained to Jan Karski, surely now was the time 'that the earth must be shaken to its foundations, the world must be aroused':

> 'We are organising a defence of the ghetto … not because we think it can be defended, but to let the world see the hopelessness of our battle – as a demonstration

and a reproach. We are even now negotiating with your commander for the arms we need. If we get them, then, one of these days, the deportation squad is going to get a bloody surprise.'

'We shall see,' the Zionist concluded, 'whether we Jews can still obtain the right to die fighting and not – as Hitler has ordered – to die suffering.'[82]

The occupied population received an unexpected morale boost at the close of 1942. No matter how hard the Germans tried, they could not suppress the news of Allied victories in North Africa and the catastrophic encirclement of the German Sixth Army at Stalingrad. For the Poles, this optimism was to be short-lived, and by the middle of January 1943, the Gestapo stepped up their *łapanka* (round-ups) to the extent that many non-Jewish Varsovians sought refuge inside the Warsaw Ghetto itself.[83] Around 700,000 Poles across Warsaw and the rest of the *Generalgouvernement* were detained in less than a week – then the Germans redoubled their actions against the Jews.[84]

On 18 January, German military and auxiliary troops once more poured into the ghetto. The new operation was intended to cleanse the city of illegal non-productive residents, but many feared the ghetto was about to be liquidated once and for all. Thousands of residents who had spent the winter securing bunkers and hideouts for just such eventualities barricaded themselves in from the German police, which caused the latter to resort to indiscriminate arrests on the streets. Meanwhile, the *ŻOB, ŻZW*, and Jews unaffiliated to specific groups decided that the moment had come for concerted resistance. Around a dozen members of the *Hatzomer Hatzair* youth movement and the *ŻOB* joined the crowd being herded to the *Umschlagplatz* and, on Mordechai Anielewicz's signal, opened fire on the Germans. Fierce fighting broke out on the corner of Miła and Zamenhof Streets in which around 12 Germans were shot dead; hundreds of Jews managed to escape deportation in the chaos that ensued. In the end, the resistance fighters paid a heavy price for their desperate attack, with around 1,200 Jews losing their lives – one account claimed only Anielewicz and one girl survived from the original insurgents.[85] There were scattered skirmishes elsewhere, with resistance fighters like Yitzhak Zuckerman firing on German police from their bunkers and hideouts. This 'baptism of fire' was an instructive experience for the Jewish resistance; Marek Edelman wrote, 'It turned out that fighting in the streets cost us too much – we weren't prepared. We weren't properly armed. We moved underground.'[86] But the attack rattled the Germans, who succeeded in rounding up only 5,000 of the planned 8,000 Jews for deportation and suspended further actions and searches for the time being. As fighter Zivia Lubetkin declared, 'Evidently it did not seem to them befitting for Germans to pay with their lives for the death of the Jews.'[87] The Jews had proved to themselves that they could indeed choose how they faced their deaths, even if they stumbled on this realisation tragically late; 'it required a quarter of a million Jews to give their lives,' recalled diarist Szmuel Winter, 'for the remainder to understand the reality of the situation and come to the right conclusions.'[88]

This surge of Jewish resistance came as much of a surprise to the Poles as it did the Germans. The clandestine press paid tribute to the ghetto's 'sense of honour' and credited the Jews for leaving a 'deep and widespread impression' on their persecutors.[89] What boosted the Jews' public appetite for defiance in January was their – mistaken – belief that they were about to be liquidated; had the population been anticipating a more minor deportation action, the resistance movement might not have gained so much support. Ghetto resident Israel Gutman would later attribute the unique strength of the Varsovian Jewish resistance movement to its youth and to the extent of existential terror amongst the public, writing that 'in the time between the first mass expulsions and the final destruction of the ghetto, the resolve of the fighters and the distrust of other ghetto residents hardened. The Jewish masses saw no grounds for hope except through fighting.'[90]

In the aftermath of the January Uprising, Jews who had any chance of escaping the ghetto to find refuge in the Aryan quarter of the city continued to do so, while those that remained doubled down on building shelters and stockpiling equipment for survival in hiding. Jews grouped together to dig bunkers under the cover of night, hiding excavated earth in empty cellars to avoid attracting attention. The most sophisticated constructions were supplied with water, electricity, and even tunnels leading across or out of the ghetto; Gutman remarked, 'Seemingly overnight, the ghetto, particularly the central area, had become a city on two levels – houses above ground, and cellars and tunnels below.'[91] A significant amount of effort was also directed to acquiring and setting aside already precious foodstuffs, medications, and other resources. Łazarz Menes noted that aside from food, 'the things that were in the greatest demand at that time were: 1) firearms and ammunition, 2) cyanide pills.'[92]

Meanwhile, the resistance organisations had come to the realisation that unity was their best weapon against the occupiers. Between January and April, the *ŻOB*, *ŻZW*, and other youth groups came together to plan for the 'inevitable struggle' to come, knowing that its timing was out of their hands.[93] The groups divided themselves into squads with defined command addresses at which they gathered for training and discussion. In general, this marked a moment of unprecedented solidarity between the ghetto Jews of all political backgrounds; it is telling that commanders were selected according to their seniority and experience, rather, as had been the case in the past, according to their ideological or intellectual standing. By April, the *ŻOB* counted around 700 men, women, boys, and girls amongst its ranks, and the *ŻZW* around 250 more. Their plan of resistance drew heavily upon the lessons learned in January:

> The organisation's strategy was based on the reality of the situation. The houses in the ghetto were almost of equal height, between three and five stories, topped with tiled roofs that formed triangular attics. Between the roofs, passages were formed with ladders. At first, this route allowed for surreptitious movement from house to house. Over time, these passages were improved and became an element in the action plan. It was possible to appear at posts near the attics or the upper stories without moving about in the streets and to withdraw without being seen by the forces in the street. Clearly, in the familiar alcoves, on the narrow ladders, in the corners and crevices, the fighters had a marked advantage over the Germans, who feared entering the dark and little-known maze.[94]

One thing was conspicuously absent from the *ŻOB*'s plan: an exit strategy. This was no accident; unlike their non-combatant relatives, friends, and neighbours, resistance fighters did not involve themselves in the preparation of bunkers for long-term hiding. They were under no illusions that they could inflict a decisive defeat on the Germans, but nor were they hoping to escape; instead, they had elected to 'fight and fall in the streets and the neighbourhoods', to die with honour and courage rather than as helpless victims.[95] But as they awaited their hour of reckoning, they took steps to deal with German informants. Several were identified, detained, and killed, including Alfred Nossig, a sculptor who had been a member of Czerniaków's *Judenrat*; after he was shot in February 1943, a Gestapo identity card and a dossier on Jewish resistance groups were found either on his person or amongst his possessions.[96]

'*JUDEN HABEN WAFFEN!*'

The Jews were right in assuming that their time was running out. On 16 February, Himmler sent an order to Obergruppenführer Krüger:

> For reasons of security I herewith order that the Warsaw ghetto be pulled down after the concentration camp has been moved: all parts of houses that can be used, and other materials of all kinds, are first to be made use of.

> The razing of the ghetto and the relocation of the concentration camp are necessary, as otherwise we would probably never establish quiet in Warsaw, and the prevalence of crime cannot be stamped out as long as the ghetto remains.
>
> An overall plan for the razing of the ghetto is to be submitted to me. In any case we must achieve the disappearance from sight of the living-space for 500,000 *Untermenschen* that has existed up to now, but could never be suitable for Germans, and reduce the size of this city of millions – Warsaw – which has always been a centre of corruption and revolt.[97]

Even in early 1943, the total annihilation of the Jews was by no means a foregone conclusion for all German organisations. In particular, the Wehrmacht relied on Jewish labour in munitions factories and workshops across the occupied territories, of which Polish Jews accounted for almost one third.[98] As a compromise – and an acknowledgement of the impact that the eradication of Jewish workers could have on the Reich's war effort – it was decided that larger Varsovian factory operations were to be relocated to camps at Poniatowa and Trawniki in the Lublin area. Firm manager Walter Többens was put in charge of organising the transfer operations and took responsibility for persuading Jewish workers that they were indeed bound for work camps, and not the gas chambers. This proved extremely difficult: in March, just 280 of 1,600 clothing workshop labourers presented themselves for transport; from the brush workshops, just 30 out of 3,600 came forward.[99] The *ŻOB* issued proclamations to workers advising them not to leave, and that the labour transfers could only mean the Germans planned to liquidate the rest of the ghetto. Sure enough, despite Többens' promises, the Varsovian Jews moved to Poniatowa and Trawniki were slaughtered in the massacre of *Aktion Erntefest* ('Operation *Harvest Festival*') in November 1943.

Late on 18 April – two days before Passover, which fell on the same day as Hitler's birthday – rumours trickled into the ghetto that the walls were being surrounded. During the night, a small number of Jews succeeded in making a final escape while the rest of the population rushed into hiding, set about barricading entryways, and prepared their arms in anticipation of their final stand. At 2am, *ŻOB* sentries reported that Ukrainian *Hilfswillige* and SS troops had tightened the cordon, rendering further escape impossible. The entire quarter fell eerily quiet, 'like a ghost town.'[100] In the following hours, the Jews watched German convoys converging on the centre of the ghetto: streams of troops 'marching without end', followed by tanks, cars, guns, Ukrainians, and hundreds of SS men on bicycles. 'What is our strength against this armed and well-equipped army,' one fighter thought, when 'we merely have pistols and at best, hand grenades?'[101] It was immediately noticeable that the Germans, too, had learned from the January Uprising. The forces assembled for the April operation were noticeably more substantial – numbering over 2,000 – than those deployed for previous actions. The Jewish force of 750 were armed with assorted handguns, with just 10–15 rounds of ammunition and four or five – usually homemade – hand grenades allocated per person, plus a few thousand Molotov cocktails, a few rifles, and a couple of submachine-guns stolen from the Germans. Their enemy combatants arrived with '1,174 rifles, 135 submachine guns, 69 light machine guns, and 13 heavy guns, a cannon, a flamethrower, and three armoured cars.'[102] Still, the Jews held fast, and at around 6am struck from their positions around Nalewki, Gęsia, Zamenhof, and Miła Streets. Fighter Tuvia Borzykowski's account captures the fierce determination of the first attack:

> We did not wait for the enemy to be the first to start the slaughter, and from all our posts we showered a hail of bullets and hand-grenades and bombs. Well, our home-made efforts were not so disappointing; they went off as they should and did their work well, leaving many slain and wounded Germans on the streets.
>
> It was our first confrontation, and the bursting bombs proclaimed and told everyone that the uprising has begun! ... the first moments of shock passed and the German response was not long in coming. Under the open skies, they were exposed to our fire. As for us – the wall was our refuge and protection.[103]

The Germans were caught completely off-guard by the ambush. According to their own report, 12 men were lost as the troops found themselves unable to take cover in the barricaded buildings.[104] One Jewish fighter claimed to hear their astonished cries, '*Juden haben Waffen!*' – 'The Jews have arms!'[105] The Germans withdrew temporarily and the Jews rejoiced at their early success.

At the time the Ghetto Uprising broke out, the commander of the SS and police in the Warsaw District was Oberführer Ferdinand von Sammern-Frankenegg, who had also overseen the *Grossaktion* of the previous summer. However, Himmler must have had reason to doubt his leadership, for in the days leading up to the April action he dispatched Brigadeführer Jürgen Stroop to Warsaw. Stroop certainly arrived in the city with the perfect credentials for the job, having earned a name for himself suppressing the independence movement in Czechoslovakia, quashing partisans in Galicia, and commanding the Posen *Volksdeutscher Selbstschütz* – at whose hands at least 2,000 Poles were massacred – during the invasion. According to Stroop, Sammern-Frankenegg came to him at 7.30am on 19 April declaring 'everything is lost', and announced that he was calling for air support from Kraków. Reminding him of the urgency of the liquidation action, Stroop promptly seized command from Sammern-Frankenegg and coordinated a new attack on the ghetto.[106]

This time, the Germans advanced in full expectation of opposition, determined to comb out the resistance fighters from their bunkers. Stroop's report on this first day of action describes the successful breaking of resistance hotspots and the rooting out of numerous dugouts, but the Jews celebrated moments of triumph too. In Muranowski Square, next to their headquarters, the *ŻZW* halted the German assaults with machine-gun fire while Jewish and Polish flags flew from the roof of their hideout – a sight that would stay etched in the minds of survivors on both sides. Over the following days, Stroop's troops discovered that thousands of Jews were holed up in German-managed workshops and factories, and set about trying to round up able-bodied labourers for transportation to work camps in order to 'get the way free at last for cleaning out the Ghetto.'[107] Firm managers at the workshops were charged with preparing their personnel for transportation, but once again, of the thousands of Jewish workers, only a handful came forward. Stroop quickly realised that resistance fighters were using factories and workshops to produce homemade explosives; in the brushmakers' blocks, the Jews barricaded themselves in so defiantly that, when a flamethrower failed to push them out, Stroop 'resolved to destroy this shop the next day by fire'. Regardless of the unprecedented nature of this resistance, the Germans didn't expect the fighting to rumble on for weeks; according to Stroop's report, it actually took 'a few days' for the Germans to accept that 'the Jews no longer had any intention to resettle voluntarily.'[108] He was also astonished by the 'military emancipation' of Polish women he encountered in the Warsaw Ghetto and beyond, whose fearless contributions to insurgency and sabotage stood in stark contrast to the Nazi concepts of the ideal *Hausfrauen* at home.[109] The Germans had majorly miscalculated the Varsovian Jews' capacity for defiance.

The Germans also gradually came to realise the extent of the labyrinthine cellars, dugouts, and passages that connected to the ghetto sewers, facilitating 'undisturbed subterranean traffic' that gave the numerically inferior Jewish forces the advantages of speed, invisibility, and mobility in the urban environment.[110] Stroop's force adjusted their tactics to force the Jewish fighters into the open where their revolvers and light explosives stood little chance against the occupiers' heavy weapons.[111] On the second day of fighting, the Germans successfully overran the flag-bearing buildings near Muranowski Square and killed *ŻZW* commander Leon Rodal. Raiding parties began storming through the Jews' dugouts, hauling out survivors in their hundreds for deportation. The Germans also attempted to flood the ghetto sewers to prevent escape to the Aryan quarter, but according to Stroop, 'the Jews frustrated this plan to a great extent by blowing up the turning off valves'; nor did the lowering of smoke candles or spreading of creosote in the sewer waters 'have the desired effect'.[112] Scores of Jews also escaped the Germans on hearses laden with corpses bound for the Jewish cemetery, from which they crossed the ghetto boundaries. By 23 April, however, the resistance in the brushmakers' block was finally broken when the building was set ablaze:

> Those Jews whom we had not been able to find … left their hideouts under the roofs, in the cellars, and elsewhere, and appeared at the outside of the buildings, trying to escape the flames. Masses of them – entire families – were already aflame and jumped from the windows or endeavoured to let themselves down by means of sheets tied together or the like. Steps had been taken so that these Jews as well as the remaining ones were liquidated at once. During the whole night there were shots from buildings which were supposed to be evacuated. We had no losses in our cordoning forces. 5,300 Jews were caught for the evacuation and removed.[113]

Stroop had earlier been ordered to preserve workshop premises as far as possible, but the Jews' resistance frustrated progress enough to warrant the indiscriminate razing of property. By 25 April, the fires were widely sanctioned: 'if any resistance is encountered or if dugouts cannot be reached, the buildings are to be burnt down,' was the order. 'This is the only and final method,' Stroop recorded, 'which forces this trash and subhumanity to the surface.'[114] Inside the hideouts, thousands of non-combatants tried to hold out for as long as possible as they felt the walls, earth, and air around them heating up:

> We can think of nothing but a breath of air. The heat in the bunker is unbearable. This is not simply a burning heat. The seething walls exude odours, as if the mildew of decades was released …
>
> I sit with my mouth open and everyone around me does likewise, with the illusion and effort that we are swallowing air. One does not talk in the bunker. When one talks, it is even more difficult to breathe. But from time to time there is shouting, quarrels, nervousness and tension without end, and generally the quarrels are nonsensical. We have not eaten now for twenty-four hours … All the food supplies have been spoiled. The mouldy smell has seeped into the food and it cannot be used …
>
> This afternoon, an argument started which implicated almost everyone in the bunker. Someone went to the entrance, moved the hidden cover, and started to swallow the fresh air coming in from outside. To do this in the middle of the day was like committing suicide. The Nazis above us are poking around and looking for us – at any moment they may be just above our heads.[115]

After the first few days of furious attacks, the uprising transformed into what would be remembered as the 'battle of the bunkers': weeks of guerrilla skirmishes and frantic escapes as the Germans gradually choked the remaining life out of the ghetto.

Non-Jewish Varsovians had seen Germans and Ukrainians converging on the ghetto in preparation for the liquidation action. Now they saw the ghetto engulfed in smoke and fire; they heard the whistles of light artillery shells, gunfire, and explosions that told them the Jews had not gone to their deaths willingly; they smelt the embers and the 'sweet, putrid smell of burning human flesh' that belonged in nightmares.[116] In late April, a large poster appeared on the signboard of Bonifraterska Street:

> POLES, CITIZENS, SOLDIERS FOR FREEDOM!
>
> ... Amid the smoke of the fires, the dust and the blood of the murdered Warsaw Ghetto: We, the prisoners of the Ghetto, send you brotherly, heartfelt greetings. We know that you are with us in the battle which for many days now we have been waging with the cruel Occupier ...
>
> Know that we breathe, just as you do, with wishes for reprisals and punishments for all the crimes of our common enemy!
>
> ... Death to the executioners and torturers! Long live the fight for our life and for death to the Occupier![117]

The poster was signed by the *ŻOB*. It spoke of a 'brotherhood of arms and blood' that never fully materialised during the Ghetto Uprising. In February, the commander of the *AK*, General Stefan Rowecki, had issued an order to district commanders to provide Jews inside the ghetto with arms for self-defence and authorised attacks on the ghetto perimeter in the case of a Jewish uprising.[118] In the first days of the fighting, Polish groups did stage a number of minor attacks on German units around the ghetto walls, but failure to coordinate with the Jewish fighters rendered these skirmishes largely inconsequential. Unfortunately for the Jews, the appointment of General Tadeusz 'Bór'-Komorowski as Rowecki's successor in March 1943 was not to their advantage. Where Rowecki had supported the Jewish cause and, according to Zimmerman, manifested an 'intolerance for anti-Jewish excess' that 'undoubtedly impacted the rank-and-file underground fighter', Komorowski's political outlook was rooted in the right-wing, antisemitic nationalist movement that considered the Jews as marginal to the interests of the Polish underground.[119] Upon his accession, he reversed Rowecki's policies and refused to provide support for the Jewish resistance. Months after the liquidation of the Warsaw Ghetto, when pressed by the London government-in-exile to provide arms for Jews still fighting the Germans, Komorowski made his attitude quite clear:

> There can be no place for more aid to the Jews for the following reasons:
>
> 1. The population treats Jews as a foreign element (*element obcy*) and in many cases as being inimical to Poland as documented by their actions during the Soviet occupation …
> 2. Armed Jews in large numbers appear in bands of robbers and communists that plague the country …
> 3. Societal opinion as well as the rank and file of the underground would not be amenable to greater assistance to Jews as they would see this as a depletion of their own resources and thus contrary to the interest of Poland.
> 4. Jews attempt to inform the world … about the enormity of their armed resistance against the Germans, which in reality was only expressed in the Warsaw ghetto and on the part of several thousand people who fought courageously for their lives in the face of the total passivity of the remaining Jewish masses.[120]

These statements, made in August 1943, hardly justify the decision not to come to the Jews' aid during the Warsaw Ghetto Uprising. The Jews never had any hopes of successfully repelling the Germans, but nor had they ever pretended otherwise; Komorowski's unflinching antisemitism allowed him to gloss over questions of morality and humanity when aid was most needed. To quote historian Joseph Lichten:

> Two standards – one white and red, the other white and blue [the Polish and Zionist flags respectively] – hung on the walls of the ghetto gave the sign of the uprising. These two standards fluttering next to each other expressed with the eloquence of a symbol the judgment of history against those who … were unable to rise to a level of humanity.[121]

WALECZNYM

The battle of the bunkers dragged on into May. German progress was slowed by the laborious hunt for dugouts whose entrances were virtually invisible; sound-detecting devices and dogs were used to detect those in hiding, and Jewish captives were frequently forced to reveal the location of their neighbours. Numerous survivors claimed that the Germans used asphyxiating gas to force them into the open, though Stroop strongly denied these allegations.[122] But however frustrated Stroop was that the liquidation action was taking far longer than anticipated, the remaining resistance fighters knew that they were running out of time. They marked May Day with a 'holiday action' against the Germans and buoyed themselves with renditions of the 'Internationale', but dwindling ammunition and the rupturing of communications with suppliers outside the wall lent their efforts an increasingly tragic tone. Two days later, the Germans unearthed one of the bunkers at 30 Franciszkanska Street which housed many of the *ŻOB* fighters from the brushmakers' block. According to Marek Edelman, the ferocious fighting that ensued claimed the lives of half of the remaining *ŻOB* forces in the ghetto.[123] The next crippling blow came on 8 May, when German and Ukrainian troops converged on the *ŻOB* headquarters at 18 Miła Street – a space designed for a few dozen people that by this time housed around 300 Jews. Underground courier Vladka Meed recounted how, when the Jews refused to come out, the Germans pumped poison gas into the bunker and tossed in hand grenades. The Jews returned fire as long as they were able, until one of the leaders, Jurek 'Arieh' Wilner, shot himself, and 'the rest followed suit'; another fighter, Lejb Rotlblat, shot his mother and sister before turning the gun on himself. 'Thus ended the lives of people who incited the Jews of the ghetto to rebel with fearless determination,' Meed wrote. The *ŻOB* was critically weakened, this time counting 24-year-old commander Mordechaj Anielewicz amongst the losses.[124] A year later, the *AK* honoured their memory by posthumously awarding Anielewicz and Wilner the Cross of Valour, a bronze medal inscribed with a single word: *Walecznym*, 'brave'.[125]

But the Germans could not yet claim victory. Over the following week, Stroop's forces continued to comb through bunkers, extracting thousands of Jews for deportation, shooting hundreds and murdering unascertainable numbers through incendiary and artillery attacks. On 10 May, some Jewish combatants managed to escape in broad daylight, emerging from the sewers and jumping into trucks that set off deep into the Aryan quarter; some of these escapees would go on to join other Jewish refugees in fighting under the *ŻOB* banner during the 1944 Warsaw Uprising. The brazen escape hardened Stroop's resolve to root out resistance elements – whom he always referred to as 'bandits' or 'partisans' – and crush the ghetto once and for all. What little of the ghetto was still standing was to be reduced to rubble, building by building. Finally, on 16 May, Stroop ordered the destruction of the Great Synagogue of Tłomackie Street to mark the end of the liquidation 'in a suitably artistic manner.'[126]

Given that the synagogue had already been bombed and stood outside the current ghetto limits, this choice of target was more symbolic than it was strategic – a reflection of the Germans' desperation to save face after an embarrassingly frustrating campaign. Six years later, Stroop would find himself sharing a jail cell with *AK* soldier Kazimierz Moczarski, to whom he related the sense of jubilation when, 29 days after the start of the uprising, the explosion of the synagogue lit up the evening sky:

> The operation took ten days to prepare. The synagogue was solidly built, and demolishing it at one go, in accordance with Krüger's wishes, involved considerable work …
>
> What a marvellous sight it was. A fantastic piece of theatre … I glanced over at my brave officers and men, tired and dirty, silhouetted against the glow of the burning buildings. After prolonging the suspense for a moment, I shouted, 'Heil Hitler' and pressed the button. With a thunderous, deafening bang and a rainbow burst of colours, the fiery explosion soared toward the clouds, an unforgettable tribute to our triumph over the Jews. The Warsaw Ghetto was no more. The will of Adolf Hitler and Heinrich Himmler had been done.[127]

By Stroop's final reckoning, a total of 56,065 Jews were caught during the action – a number he relished for its 'perfect symmetry'.[128] Of these, 7,000 were 'exterminated' within the ghetto itself, a further 7,000 at Treblinka, tens of thousands transported to Majdanek and other camps, and somewhere in the region of another 5,000–6,000 killed in the destruction of the ghetto.[129] Stroop reported German casualties improbably at 110, including 17 dead. Moreover, these numbers fail to take into account the truth that the dramatic destruction of the Great Synagogue did not, in fact, bring an end to the fighting. In any case, this was hardly of concern to Stroop, who received the Iron Cross First Class from Krüger for his services before promptly delegating management of the area to *Schutzpolizei* Major Otto Bundtke. Blue Policemen – tasked with supporting Bundtke after the campaign's ostensible culmination – claimed to have heard SS personnel talking about the 'hundreds of Jews [still] … hiding in the underground haunts and ruins.'[130] The remaining Jews struggled to find water, food, and a chance to escape from the devastated ghetto, and engaged the occupation authorities in scattered skirmishes through the summer of 1943. By autumn, total Jewish losses probably totalled closer to 71,000.[131]

Any embarrassment the Germans felt towards the Jewish resistance and its unexpected ferocity was sidelined by bigger strategic debates between the Reich leadership. While many lamented the loss of the Jewish workforce, Fischer pointed to an additional blow: the destruction of ghetto property meant that 'the possibility of erecting industrial enterprises here has gone forever.'[132] He also feared the uprising could inspire further dissent amongst the Varsovian public and across Poland more widely. 'Lately there have been a series of murderous attacks in the city of Warsaw,' he wrote on 13 May. 'The same force stands behind these attacks as those who hope one day to bring to this country the bloody rule of Bolsheviks.' Blurring the boundaries between 'Communist and Jewish agents' had always made perfect sense to the Germans looking to reinforce common antisemitic stereotypes, but now it also deprived Jewish fighters in the Warsaw Ghetto Uprising of any sense of historical autonomy.[133] The Reich leadership had to walk a fine ideological line between emphasising the inhumanity of the Jews – especially 'when they have weapons in their hands' – and simultaneously acknowledging military setbacks in a way that would frame the eventual suppression of the Jews as an even greater heroic achievement.[134] Hence why, in his post-war discussions of the subject, Stroop was willing to accept that German authorities had 'obviously misjudged' Jewish capabilities; the fact that he had to comb through 631 bunkers was a 'tribute to the *ŻOB*'s organisational ability' but, more importantly, to his troops' hard-won victory.[135]

The liquidation action and its aftermath did not mark the end of tragedy in the ghetto. Reduced to a 'brick and stone-strewn desert', the area became the ideal location for executing Pawiak prisoners – with fewer logistical concerns and risks of detection than other Warsaw Death Ring sites. As Ludwig Hahn (now promoted to Obersturmbannführer) explained to Stroop, 'With so many Jewish bodies scattered about, and more to come, if we chuck in a few thousand Polish corpses, who's to know the difference?'[136] Varsovians were not so easily fooled. By the end of the occupation, as many as 20,000 detainees had been murdered in the ruins of the former ghetto, frequently hundreds at a time. The brother of Stroop's Polish cellmate and confidant, Jan Morczarski, was one of them; so too was Emmanuel Ringelblum.[137]

'THE CONSCIENCE OF THE WHOLE WORLD'[138]

The question that survivors, descendants, and historians constantly rake over is an agonising one: were the Varsovian Jews abandoned to their fate, and could more have been done to help them? On the Polish side, there is no denying that whilst the *AK* and the government-in-exile spoke out against the atrocities being committed in the ghetto, no widespread support for the Jewish resistance ever took shape. Part of this can be attributed to the logistical limitations of the

Polish underground, but antisemitism – in the case of Komorowski – and concerns about compromising the national resistance effort also factored in.

In the west, the Allies had not yet come to terms with the true scale of Jewish persecution and how it fitted into the broader landscape of war. In this regard, the Poles were far ahead of the western governments – and even western Jewish organisations – in their assessment of German antisemitic ambitions, and were advocating for stronger reprisals long before the Nazis implemented the *Endlösung*. In 1940, the government-in-exile produced a pamphlet titled *Persecution of Jews in German-Occupied Poland*; this was followed up by the *Black Book of Poland* in January 1942, a catalogue of German oppression since the invasion and their unmistakably genocidal operations against both Poles and Jews. The *AK* produced a volume entitled *Liquidation of the Warsaw Ghetto* later the same year. At the same time, Jan Nowak, Jan Karski, and Szmul Zygielbojm – a Jewish member of the National Council of the government-in-exile – delivered a constant stream of first-hand reports to western politicians that underlined the urgency of the situation, but these efforts did not translate into the response they hoped for. When the American Federation for Polish Jews published its own *Black Book of Polish Jewry* in 1943, the true scale and barbarity of the Holocaust were watered down – generally omitting references to death camps, gas chambers, and mass deportations – for the sake of appealing to an American readership.[139]

The Allies' reluctance to speak openly about Nazi crimes was the inevitable result of a more general unwillingness to take action. The government-in-exile took the lead in mustering an inter-allied conference of nine countries occupied by the Germans in January 1942, which unanimously passed a resolution to prosecute Germans found guilty of unlawful violence against civilians; the United States and Britain refused to sign the declaration, citing insufficient evidence of atrocities having been committed. If one were to give the Allies the benefit of the doubt, the Nazis' systematic brutality presented an unprecedented challenge in terms of litigation; it wasn't clear whether 'the body of law relating to war crimes would also apply in such cases, or whether these actions by the Germans and their collaborators were so serious – and indeed horrific – that they warranted the classification of a new crime in international law.'[140] Another concern was that the mistakes of the previous war might be repeated, whereby many rumours of German atrocities turned out to be falsifications. Further complicating the Nine-Power Declaration, as it was known, was the question of whether the genocide against Jews constituted a separate crime to the Nazis' persecution of other ethnic minorities and nationalities – an issue which not only divided supporters of the Jewish cause from those suspicious of 'Zionist propaganda', but also threatened to undermine the credibility of claims coming out of Poland.[141] In any case, the logistical question of how to deal with German criminals after the war was still to be determined, and inevitably took a back seat to priorities seen crucial to securing that victory in the first place – such as alliance with the Soviet Union.

Polish Jews had no visibility of this. They could not fathom how, despite the consistent flow of reports and photographic evidence to the west from 1942 onwards, the Allies continued to prevaricate. It is easy to understand why, to quote Ringelblum, Varsovian Jews found it easy to accuse 'the Polish liaison men of deliberately keeping our tragedy quiet, so that their tragedy might not be thrown into the shade.'[142] In June, as the Polish Bund's report on the persecution of the Jewry aired on British radio, Ringelblum graciously conceded: 'Now for the first time we understood why they kept silent. London simply didn't know what was happening in detail; hence the silence.'[143] But even if the London public was only just being made aware of the extent of German atrocities, politicians on both sides of the Atlantic had been collecting mounting evidence from the Polish government-in-exile for nearly two years. The turning point Ringelblum hoped for in terms of sympathy for the Jewish cause never arrived. In July 1942, head of the Directorate of Civil Resistance Stefan Korboński telegrammed London with news that 'the Germans ha[d] begun the slaughter of the Warsaw Ghetto', but it was another month before this news reached BBC radio airwaves. 'Your messages were disbelieved,' he was later informed by a government emissary. 'They said you were exaggerating for the sake of anti-German propaganda.'[144]

To the Jewish community within and beyond Poland, the sense that nothing was being done on the international stage to stop the 'greatest crime in human history' was a wound far worse than grief.[145] Long before Karski arrived in the west, Szmul Zygielbojm had tried repeatedly and in vain to convince the Americans and the British of the urgency of the situation for Polish Jews. When even the news of May 1943 – that the Warsaw Ghetto Uprising had been crushed and Varsovian Jews liquidated – failed to move the Allies to action, Zygielbojm lost hope entirely. Amongst the 13,000 Jews slaughtered in the suppression of the uprising were his wife, Manya, and his 16-year-old son, Tuvla. On 11 May, Zygielbojm took a fatal overdose in London. His suicide note left no illusion as to his feelings towards the Western Allies and all those who had let the Warsaw Ghetto burn:

> Responsibility for the crime of murdering the entire Jewish nation in Poland falls primarily on the perpetrators, but also indirectly on the whole of humanity, the

people and governments of the Allied states, who to this day have not taken any concrete action to put an end to this crime …

Perhaps I shall be able by my death to contribute to the arousing from lethargy of those who could and must act in order that even now, perhaps at the last moment, the handful of Polish Jews who are still alive can be saved from certain destruction.

My life belongs to the Jewish people of Poland, and therefore I hand it over to them now.[146]

CHAPTER 9

RESISTANCE

Day and night, mother, father, I'll endure
in the rifle-fire, I, soldier, poet, dust of time.
I'll go on – this I have from you: I do not fear
death, as I bear desires like burned roses in my arms.

Krzysztof Kamil Baczynski, 'To my parents', 1943
Translated by Bill Johnston[1]

BUILDING AN UNDERGROUND STATE

The outbreak of war in 1939 found Brigadier General Michał Tokarzewski-Karaszewicz, a former Polish Legion officer, in Pomerania, where he commanded two infantry divisions during the fighting on the Bzura. On 27 September, with German and Soviet troops advancing towards each other, he was given a new role. Poland was facing defeat but would not formally surrender; even after the country was occupied, resistance was to continue in every way possible. The title chosen for the first iteration of the resistance organisations – *Służba Zwycięstwu Polski* ('Polish Victory Service' or *SZP*) – was a clear statement of strategic aims, and Rómmel appointed Tokarzewski as its commander.[2] From the outset, the *SZP* combined both military and political functions.

Polish politicians had crossed the frontier into Romania late on 17 September 1939 expecting free passage onwards to France, but the Romanian government suddenly declared this would only be possible if they renounced their positions in the Polish government. When they refused, they were interned. Aware of the urgent need to establish a government-in-exile, President Mościcki's suggested candidate was vetoed by members of the *Sanacja* Party who were already in Paris. In the end, it was Władysław Raczkiewicz who became president with strong support from the French government; despite his links to *Sanacja*, Raczkiewicz understood the importance of a unified government – not least because he was suffering from leukaemia and knew that he might not be able to continue in office – and appointed several members of other parties to his cabinet. Amongst these, General Sikorski became both prime minister and commander-in-chief of Poland's armed forces.

A long-time opponent of the *Sanacja* regime, Sikorski had spent much of the preceding decade in France but remained well regarded amongst pro-democracy groups in Poland. 'He was the kind of man whom Poles call a "European",' Karski recalled, 'slightly Gallicised' in his manners but a 'great general' and 'convinced liberal'.[3] Amongst the Allied Powers, however, he earned a reputation for a forthrightness that bordered on arrogance. The American ambassador to the Polish government, Drexel Biddle, explained:

> While he is a thoroughly honest, sincere and courageous character, he has gained, during the past few months, an inordinate ambition, a thirst for publicity. He pictures himself on the one hand as the leader of post-war Poland, on the other hand, now that France has disappeared as a dominant influence on the continent, the leader of continental Europe.[4]

This evaluation does not do justice to the nuance of Sikorski's foreign policy perspective. Unlike Beck, Piłsudski's bellicose foreign minister, Sikorski did not conceive of Poland as a great power and viewed the pattern of events that led to its defeat in 1939 as proof of its problematic geographic and diplomatic isolation. Rather than advocating for the full restoration of Poland's pre-war borders, Sikorski aimed to extract guarantees for territories of strategic and economic importance – an approach that drew the ire of those fearful of ceding too much ground to the Soviet Union. In any case, political tensions and divisions plagued the government-in-exile from its earliest months. Fearing that the *SZP* was too close to *Sanacja*, Sikorski ordered its disbandment in mid-November 1939 and established in its place a new organisation, *Związek Walki Zbrojnej* ('Union of Armed Struggle' or *ZWZ*). Its overall commander was General Kazimierz Sosnkowski, who had fought outside Lwów during the invasion and had escaped to France via Hungary; but communication with those still in Poland proved almost impossible and it was January before a clandestine emissary arrived in Warsaw.

Tokarzewski and others were informed that the new *ZWZ* was to have no political role and was to prepare for a time when it would conduct an armed uprising when regular Polish troops entered the country.[5] However, the resistance landscape within Poland was proving difficult to control, as Tokarzewski wrote to Sikorski:

> Polish territory is teeming with new organisations modelled on the Polish Military Organisation. Some allegedly emerge on your orders, others on that of the old government. I am liquidating these organisations or incorporating them into the *SZP* [by then the *ZWZ*]. I am asking for further orders regarding those organisations acting in your name. Here, in the country, only one organisation can represent our government and Polish interests.[6]

The problem Tokarzewski highlighted was one that would plague the exiled leadership for months to come: the success of resistance hinged on the consolidation of competing groups – or at least alignment between their causes.

Meanwhile, underground administration within Poland was split between two Government Delegations – one for the territories annexed to Germany, and the other for the *Generalgouvernement* – each of which coordinated with and was intended to mirror the government-in-exile. In February 1940, the latter Delegation's political arm, the *Polityczny Komitet Porozumiewawczy* ('Political Consultative Committee' or *PKP*) came into being, uniting four of the most prominent parties in the pre-war Polish political scene: the Socialist Party, the National Party, the People's (Peasant) Party, and the Christian Labour movement. Jan Karski noted that after years of being politically sidelined under the *Sanacja* regime, these parties found their defining moment under occupation:

> These parties had no place in the government that ruled Poland in the years preceding the present war. Interior political conditions did not permit them to take any action or to enter the elections. Those in power at the time held it to be a primal necessity that the structure of Polish politics be in conformity with the 'strong' regimes of its powerful eastern and western neighbours ...
>
> Paradoxically, while the Underground was a continuation of the Polish nation, at the same time it broke away from this prewar tradition and returned to the still older traditions of Polish parliamentary democracy. The political parties in the Underground had more power and freedom and were able to increase their activity beyond anything that was possible in prewar Poland.[7]

As Karski conceded, the *PKP* did not represent all the diverse groups across the occupied territory – and nor did the four primary parties always see eye to eye in their plans for resistance; 'from prewar times these parties distrusted the state administration,' he wrote. Yet it was he who was appointed 'father confessor for each party', responsible for transmitting 'important secrets, plans, internal affairs, and points of view of all four of the political parties to their own representatives' in exile.[8] The Government Delegation also oversaw the formation of the Directorate of Civil Resistance which, under the leadership of Stefan Korboński, was tasked with establishing the underground courts of justice, managing sabotage, sourcing armaments, registering German crimes, and – critically – coordinating with the armed resistance.

Taking account of the realities in Poland, the *ZWZ* was also to function as two separate commands. In the areas occupied by Germany, it would be commanded by Colonel (later General) Stefan Rowecki; in the Soviet zone, by Tokarzewski. Almost immediately, these arrangements ran into problems. Tokarzewski was arrested by the *NKVD* in March 1940 as he attempted to cross from the German zone into the Soviet zone with fake documents; unaware of his identity, the Soviet authorities sent him to a labour camp in the far north and he was eventually permitted to join the Polish forces being raised in the Soviet Union. In the wake of his disappearance, Sikorski sent instructions that Rowecki was to become commander of the *ZWZ*. Aided by large numbers of Polish officers who had escaped capture, Rowecki rapidly set up a comprehensive command structure with Poland divided into six separate areas, each subdivided into districts. The Warsaw Area consisted of four such subdivisions; in addition to districts for Łódź and Kielce–Radom, there were two districts for Warsaw covering the urban area and the surrounding countryside respectively.

The organisation remained the *ZWZ* until February 1942, when Sikorski renamed it the *Armia Krajowa* ('Home Army' or *AK*). In an attempt to distinguish the group from irregular partisans who were subject to summary execution by the Germans, Sikorski explicitly stated that all members of the *AK* were on active service in the Polish homeland.[9] This claim was of questionable value; given that most *AK* personnel weren't in uniform, protection under the Geneva Conventions was limited – and, in any case, completely dependent upon the Germans respecting their status as legal combatants. The occupation authorities ignored such distinctions in nearly every incident prior to 1944; captured *AK* soldiers were likely to face mistreatment, followed by dispatch to concentration camps or immediate execution.

The *AK* was organised into five sections dealing with personnel matters, intelligence, operations and training, logistics, and communications. Two further departments were responsible for information and propaganda, and finances; finally, the *Kierownictwo Dywersji* ('Diversion Directorate' or *Kedyw*) was created to oversee combat operations.[10] Like the *ZWZ*, the *AK* was first organised by region, but in 1943 it was restructured into formations resembling the pre-war Polish Army in a further effort to assert its legitimacy as a combatant force.

As early as February 1941, senior Polish figures in London were considering plans for a general uprising against the occupying German and Soviet forces. The first plan – which was rapidly overtaken by events – was documented in Operational Report 54, which called for an uprising across all of Poland and the transfer of up to 16 squadrons of aircraft formed from personnel currently serving in the Royal Air Force (RAF). In addition, at least three special battalions were to be raised in the west and parachuted into Poland immediately before the uprising. These *Cichociemni* ('Silent Ones') as they were known were broadly analogous to the modern concept of special forces, and around 300 were parachuted into Poland for various operations over the course of the war. But implementing such a far-reaching plan remained impossible until Germany had been brought closer to defeat; and for that situation to arise, circumstances would have to change radically.

The first drastic shift arrived on 22 June 1941 with the commencement of Operation *Barbarossa* – the German invasion of the Soviet Union. At first, this new phase of the war heralded further German victories, the Wehrmacht's rapid advance catching Stalin off-guard as it swept over the Baltic States, Belarus, and much of Ukraine. But towards the end of the year, a combination of winter weather, lengthening supply lines, growing casualties, and the improving performance of the Red Army brought the Germans to a halt just a few miles from Moscow. In the north, Leningrad was besieged, and in the south the leading German units briefly occupied Rostov on the lower Don River before being forced to make a tactical retreat.

Suddenly, an uprising seemed more feasible for the Poles. Following US entry into the war in late 1941, Churchill spoke with Roosevelt about the Polish plans and suggested that a European land invasion might align with uprisings in Poland and beyond. To the disappointment of the Poles, the newly established Joint Chiefs of Staff (JCS) committee – consisting of senior British and American military figures – was unenthusiastic. Another new organisation, the British Special Operations Executive (SOE), showed more interest, and Sikorski hoped that, with their help, the JCS might be persuaded to change its opinion. In July 1942, however, Major Peter Wilkinson's report *Third Front* informed SOE chief Major General Colin Gubbins that given the JCS's lack of interest in the proposal, establishing a 'third front' alongside a European landing would fall solely to the SOE.[11]

UNEASE IN THE EAST

At this stage of the war, it seems that Sikorski's understanding of the full consequences of the new anti-German alliance – which included the Soviet Union – was limited. While Stalin professed a commitment to restoring Europe's pre-war borders, his understanding of what that entailed was deeply problematic. On the one hand, he declared that the agreements made with Germany in 1939 were now invalid; on the other, he refused to countenance a post-war Poland regaining all its territories in the east. In July 1941, the Poles came under intense pressure from the British to accept the Soviet Union as an ally in the war against Germany, with British foreign minister Anthony Eden telling Sikorski that 'whether you wish it or not, the [alliance] treaty must be signed.'[12] Sikorski grudgingly accepted reality. The Sikorski–Mayski Agreement, as it became known – Ivan Mikhailovich Mayski being the Soviet ambassador in London – was signed at the end of July. Diplomatic relations between the government-in-exile and Moscow were re-established; all Polish prisoners held by the Soviet Union since 1939 were to be released, and a Polish army – later known as the Anders Army after its commander, Lieutenant General Władysław Anders – was to be raised in the Soviet Union. These diplomatic games cost Sikorski dearly: three ministers resigned in protest from his government, including Sosnkowski, who commanded significant respect amongst the Polish Army and *Sanacja* officers. Even Sikorski's relationship with General Anders would be complicated by the fact that recruits for the new army were largely derived from the very same territories Sikorski was said to be considering ceding to the Soviets in exchange for territorial gains in the west.[13] At this stage, the Poles had no knowledge of the thousands of Polish officers massacred by the Soviet Union.

Former cavalry brigadier Władysław Anders had been captured by the Soviets after the Romanian bridgehead was cut off in 1939. Now commissioned with establishing a Polish army, he submitted to the Soviet authorities a list of Polish officers for recruitment. The response was obfuscation and prevarication. Stalin and his associates knew that most of the men had been killed near Katyn and elsewhere, but they cited administrative and bureaucratic problems, telling Anders they were struggling to locate the men in the huge Soviet prison camp system. Painter and former pacifist Józef Czapski was tasked with investigating the fate of the nearly 15,000 men – including 8,000 officers – who had disappeared from Soviet camps at Starobilsk, Kozelsk, and Ostashkov; between 1941 and 1942 he interviewed thousands of prisoners and was stone-walled by scores of *NKVD* officials across the Soviet Union as he tried to ascertain the truth. 'At the time it never entered our heads that such a huge number of prisoners of war could have been murdered,' he later wrote.[14] He unearthed rumours that the men had been exiled further north to Franz Josef Land, and more ominously, that prisoner barges had been deliberately sunk in the White Sea. But he remained quietly hopeful: 'when the first rumors came of their mass extermination in cold blood by the Bolshevik authorities,' he explained, 'we refused to take them seriously.'[15]

The new Polish Army in the Soviet Union was to consist of about 30,000 men, and Stalin deliberately limited food rations to prevent further expansion. In fact, food supplies rarely met these requirements, and still around 70,000 Polish soldiers now joined the ranks. Thousands of civilian Poles who had been imprisoned in the Soviet Union had reached the camps where the army was being trained near Tashkent and the soldiers shared their meagre rations with the starving women and children. By early September, sufficient recruits had been gathered from prison camps to commence the creation of two infantry divisions; ultimately, three such divisions based on the Red Army model and a further three based on the British model would be created. At this stage, the tensions that already existed between the Poles and the Soviets around the whereabouts of missing officers were exacerbated by arguments about nationality. Contrary to the clause in the Sikorski–Mayski treaty that declared any Soviet agreements with Germany null and void, the Soviets now insisted that Poles who had lived in the eastern parts of Poland were Soviet citizens – particularly those of Belarusian, Lithuanian, or Ukrainian heritage – and therefore out of bounds for recruitment to Anders' army.

Meanwhile, Stalin was keen to restrict the scope of native Polish resistance. Rightly surmising that the *AK* was likely to oppose Soviet interests, Stalin insisted that the British scale back their support for the organisation. British support to date had been modest, and though London was unwilling to forsake the *AK* – and, by extension, the government-in-exile – it was equally compelled to ensure cooperation with the Soviet Union against Germany. The result was a continuation of the general approach of 1939, whereby British officials gave their Polish counterparts imprecise and vague assurances for future support.

For their part, the Poles continued to draw up plans for an uprising in the faith that this support would indeed materialise. In late 1942, Sikorski's staff produced a new Operational Report 154 with the support of SOE. Acknowledging the difficulties of supporting Sikorski's plans – given the shortage of long-range aircraft – but also recognising the number of fighters that the *AK* could potentially deploy, Gubbins wrote:

> The strategic benefits of being able to create an additional army of fresh troops in the German rear at a crucial moment of the war cannot be overestimated. If the

> most urgent Polish requests were approved, the forces diverted from the main theatre would be infinitesimally small, and the impact on the preparations of the *AK* and morale in Poland would be priceless.[16]

The general argument put forward was accepted by the JCS, but they stipulated that further action remained contingent on further German defeats. The additional – largely unspoken – reason for reluctance was concern as to how Stalin would likely react. In the months that followed, Sikorski was frustrated to see that British support – including that of the SOE – was largely confined to supporting the *AK* to carry out acts of sabotage. By February 1943, even the SOE was expressing doubts, pointing out that the Polish proposals would require an average of over 100 transport aircraft being dispatched to Poland every day for a substantial period of time. Nevertheless, Sikorski pressed on with preparations, confident that even a slight shift in circumstances could alter British and American views.

Allied support was finally and decisively put to the test in 1943 when long-simmering tensions with the Soviet Union finally boiled over. In March 1940, the Soviet Politburo had authorised the execution of Polish prisoners classified as counterrevolutionaries or Polish nationalists, and in a matter of weeks about 22,000 Poles – including the men Czapski was searching for – were shot in forests near Katyn and two other locations.[17] It was only in early 1943 that German troops in the region discovered the mass graves and an intelligence officer sent a coded report back to Berlin; British intelligence officers in Bletchley Park decoded the report and passed it to the British government. Goebbels sought to use the mass graves to drive a wedge between the Soviet Union and the Western Allies, broadcasting news of the discovery to the world and inviting the Red Cross to send a committee to confirm the findings. Moscow's evasiveness regarding the whereabouts of Polish officers had already aroused Sikorski's suspicions and he now demanded a full enquiry. Stalin responded by acknowledging that the dead men had at one time been prisoners of the Soviet Union, but asserted they had been captured by the Germans, who used them for forced labour before executing them. On the basis of the intercepted German signals, British and American officials knew that this was untrue, but the necessities of *Realpolitik* and the need to ensure ongoing Soviet cooperation meant that they had to accept the Soviet version of events. The same did not apply to Sikorski, who refused to cooperate further with Moscow. The Soviet Union hit back, declaring that the *AK* units operating in Poland were 'white Poles' or German collaborators, and ordered its own partisans in the eastern Polish territories to attack the *AK*.[18] Over the following months, there were over

200 such clashes.[19] Throughout the war, but particularly after the rift caused by the Katyn discoveries, Communist partisan groups in eastern Poland energetically portrayed the *AK* as *Sanacja*-linked Fascists.

The Katyn revelations happened to coincide with Jan Karski's visit to the United States – the same trip during which Justice Frankfurter dismissed Karski's ghetto report with damning disbelief. Karski and Polish ambassador Jan Ciechanowski had hoped the trip would shore up western support for the resistance, which made the reticence over the Katyn massacre – on top of Frankfurter's scepticism – bitterly disappointing. Sir William Strang, British Assistant Under-Secretary of State for Europe, encapsulated the attitude of the Allies: 'It is better that Russia should dominate Eastern Europe,' he wrote, 'than that Germany should dominate Western Europe.'[20] Karski and Ciechanowski left Washington with little more than paltry words of assurance from the president: 'Tell [the Polish resistance fighters] that we are going to win this war, and tell them that they have a friend in the White House.'[21]

THE MANY FACES OF RESISTANCE

These diplomatic blows did not stem the appetite for resistance in Poland itself, however. Underground military groups were undergoing gradual democratisation, steadily but surely evolving from elite and intelligentsia-led movements to mass movements. Despite formalised command structures, the armed resistance often seemed more of a conglomeration of elements from all parts of the political spectrum – ranging from hard right-wing nationalists to Communists (not all of whom were pro-Soviet) – than a rigid military organisation. On the right were the *Organizacja Wojskowa Związek Jaszczurczy* ('Military Organisation of the Lizard Union' or *OWZJ*) and the *Narodowa Organizacja Wojskowa* ('National Military Organisation' or *NOW*); these adhered to the ethnocentric concepts of pre-war Polish nationalism and idealised the restoration of an independent Poland as free of Jews, Communists, and ethnic minorities as it was of foreign occupiers. As a result, they questioned the authority of the *ZWZ* and *AK* to monopolise resistance in the Polish public interest, and by 1942, the *NOW*, *OWZJ*, and a number of other right-wing groups had merged with the Catholic National Party to form the *Narodowe Siły Zbrojne* ('National Armed Forces' or *NSZ*). The signing of the Sikorski–Mayski Agreement and the *AK*'s attempts to unite underground groups into a single force of resistance only spooked the right-wing radicals further; they feared Poland would be overrun with Communism if resistance was in any way reliant on Soviet support or complacent towards Stalin's ambitions. Unsurprisingly, the *NSZ* was more active in the eastern borderlands than in Warsaw itself, but its members remained a constant thorn in the side of the underground state and were known to kill Polish leftists and *AK* officers suspected to have Communist leanings.[22]

On the left of the resistance scene was the non-Communist *Polska Ludowa Akcja Niepodległościowa* ('Polish People's Independence Action' or *PLAN*), which, established in October 1939, numbered university students and other Polish-Jewish intellectuals like Kazimierz Kott amongst its numbers. Kott's escape from Pawiak in January 1940 and the ensuing fallout spelled the end for *PLAN* and similar groups by laying bare a number of inherent weaknesses. Firstly, these early resistance groups were prime targets for the *Intelligenzaktion* which, in the case of *PLAN*, forced their dispersal by early 1940. Secondly, intelligentsia-led violence, even against the detested occupying authorities, was not always welcomed by a public living in fear of reprisals. One of the earliest and most notorious instances of collective punishment took place in the neighbourhood of Warsaw in December 1939 in response to the murder of two German policemen by two well-known Polish bandits. The occupation authorities organised a show trial that found 114 men guilty of conspiracy and led to 107 being shot dead, including a bank official of German extraction, a number of teenagers, and at least one 60-year-old.[23] The massacre in turn catalysed retaliation against the authorities and even spawned a new youth resistance movement that, under the name *Wawer*, carried out around 150 acts of sabotage against the Germans.[24] But at the same time, the incident – alongside countless other reprisals and the ever-present threat that 'Polish people will answer for it' – inflicted deep scars on the public psyche and left the population feeling dangerously exposed.[25]

In 1943, Soviet successes in Stalingrad inspired the remaining *PLAN* survivors and other emergent Communists to regroup as the *Polska Armia Ludowa* ('People's Polish Army' or *PAL*), under the leadership of Varsovian Henryk Borucki. Unlike the radical right, the *PAL* was open to potential Soviet material support, to subordination to the government-in-exile, and to joining forces with the *AK* in an organised uprising. Moreover, despite the group's intelligentsia roots, it managed to bring together more diverse parts of the population. Villages and towns throughout Poland had established groups geared more towards immediate and economic self-defence than to active political or military antagonism against the Germans. These grassroots organisations gradually coalesced under the leadership of the Peasant Party – and training from other groups – to form the *Bataliony Chłopskie* ('Peasants' Battalions' or *BCh*) in 1943, which was closely allied to the *PAL*. By the time the *BCh* joined forces with the

AK in 1944, it boasted around 150,000 recruits, making it one of the largest alternative militant groups.[26]

The relationship between Jewish and non-Jewish resistance elements was a complex and often controversial issue. Although Polish politics had been coloured by antisemitic views before the war, not everyone subscribed to them; and the percentage of Jews in the ranks of the *AK* was lower than might have been expected from the percentage of Jews in the overall population of Poland for several reasons. Firstly – and most obviously – the ghettoisation of Jews made it much more difficult for Jews to join the *AK*. Secondly, although Jews and Poles had lived side by side in large numbers for centuries, the two populations largely kept to themselves.[27] The separation of the two populations during the German occupation bred new resentments: Poles regarded the Jews in their ghettos as being protected from deportation to work in German factories; Jews saw that however difficult life was for non-Jewish Poles, it was still better than that in the ghetto.

In some units of the *AK* – particularly in the eastern parts of Poland – pre-existent antisemitism combined with suspicion of Jewish–Soviet collaboration to result in open hostility towards Jews. Following the German invasion of the Soviet Union, Moscow authorised the creation of the *Gwardia Ludowa* ('People's Guard' or *GL*), and later the *Armia Ludowa* ('People's Army' or *AL*); both organisations attracted support from supporters of left-wing political groups and significant numbers of Jews. Accurate numbers are impossible to determine; one study shows that of the first nine *GL* units raised in and around Kielce in 1942–43, three were exclusively Jewish, one had a Jewish majority, and two others had large Jewish minorities.[28] Ultimately, about 30 Jewish partisan units were created, either as elements of the *GL* and *AL* or as independent groups.[29] Throughout eastern Poland, there was mutual suspicion and often conflict between the *AK* and the *AL*/*GL* and its affiliates, but in other parts of Poland, *AK* units welcomed Jewish recruits and on occasion took action to aid Jews. As the Jews learned – to their detriment – during the Ghetto Uprising, changes in the leadership of the *AK* played a major role in shaping its attitude towards them.[30]

The number of fighters recruited into the ranks of the *AK* varied over the course of the war, and the very nature of the organisation makes verification of its true strength a difficult matter. When it was first formed, it numbered perhaps 100,000; regardless of its starting strength in 1942, its membership more than doubled in the following year, reaching its peak shortly before the uprisings of 1944. By this stage, its strength was somewhere between 200,000 and 500,000.[31] This higher number would include both combatants and all people involved in helping the *AK*, but even the lower estimate shows that by 1944, the strength of the *AK* exceeded the numbers in the resistance forces of all other fully occupied nations and matched the estimated numbers of partisans fighting behind the lines in the Soviet Union. However, throughout the war, the fighting strength of the Polish resistance movement was far less than its numbers suggested; a British report of November 1941 stated that while the *ZWZ* claimed to have 121,000 soldiers – including nearly 4,000 officers – it possessed sufficient firearms for just 35,000.[32]

These weapons were obtained from a variety of sources. As it was being overrun by the Wehrmacht in 1939, the Polish Army succeeded in hiding stockpiles of guns and ammunition with future resistance in mind; but these were buried hastily, often with little opportunity to ensure protection from water, and of 33,000 rifles, 6,700 pistols, and 1,800 machine-guns in these caches, only a third were usable when they were recovered.[33] The Poles had no choice but to become more resourceful and to procure arms elsewhere – including, if necessary, directly from the enemy. *AK* groups frequently raided German barracks, supply depots, and transports purely to capture weapons. Alongside garrison troops – whose numbers dwindled as the Wehrmacht faced increasing strain – various German occupation agencies, including the SS, Gestapo, and paramilitary police, were tasked with civil and military engineering duties across the occupied territories. Even those with the most rudimentary military training were typically armed for self-protection and for guarding their barracks, and inevitably some Germans proved to be willing to sell 'mislaid' weapons and ammunition to Polish groups. Armed personnel from countries allied to Germany – such as the paramilitary units from Ukraine and the Baltic region, and small units from Romania, Hungary, Italy, and Slovakia – proved particularly willing to part with their weapons.

In an attempt to make more of the cached weapons from 1939 usable, the *AK* also organised several units – an engineering section in one of its divisions, a 'productions department' in another – to make replacement parts. This rapidly expanded into the manufacture of complete weapons and explosives; in Warsaw alone, there were five small 'factories' – including one Pruszków pencil factory, which was simultaneously producing stretchers and coffins for the Wehrmacht – that added about 700 *Błyskawica* (a version of the British Sten submachine-gun), thousands of hand grenades, 900 flamethrowers, and a variety of mortars to resistance stockpiles.[34] To the southeast of the city, in a forest near Józefów, a firing range was created to test and train with these home-made firearms.

Finally, even if their support left much to be desired, the Western Allies also contributed materiel via airdrops. In the aftermath of 1939, many soldiers, sailors, and airmen reached France and Britain and formed the nucleus of Polish units that continued to fight against Germany – including 16 squadrons of the RAF. Leaving aside air operations during the Warsaw Uprising of 1944, about

485 such missions were flown – roughly half of them by Polish servicemen – delivering about 600 tons of guns, ammunition, explosives, signals equipment, and other items.[35] On several occasions, usually at the urging of Gubbins and SOE, the British government made requests to Moscow for aircraft carrying out such airdrops to land in the Soviet Union, where they could load further supplies for a second drop on their way back to the west; Stalin refused permission on every occasion.

A generation of Columbuses

It was seasoned military men and politicians who first conceived the underground movement, but its rank and file crossed all generational, political, and denominational boundaries. In Warsaw, men and women from across the social spectrum found themselves swept into the *ZWZ*, the *AK*, or one of the myriad other clandestine resistance groups. The so-called Columbus Generation of Poles born after independence found themselves coming of age during a new existential crisis, their abrupt transition to adulthood mirrored in their country's struggle for its very soul. Some, like Jan Karski, were inducted by friends. For others, like 16-year-old Zbigniew Dębczyński, it was something that ran in the family; when his mother, a close associate of the underground high command, was shot during a Gestapo raid on their apartment, Dębczyński's escape down a drainpipe marked his entry into the resistance.[36] Thousands of Varsovian teenagers, too young to have fought in 1939 but filled with youthful energy and a sense of immortality, joined resistance activities through organisations like the *Związek Harcerstwa Polskiego* ('Polish Scouting and Guiding Association' or *ZHP*), which had been established in 1916 as Poland's equivalent to the international scouting movement. Units of girl guides operated in parallel, serving as nurses, smugglers, and liaisons. When the Germans banned the *ZHP*, their leader, Florian Marciniak, converted his scouts and guides into a new clandestine group codenamed the *Szarych Szeregów* ('Grey Ranks'), who trained under a programme named *Dziś, Jutro, Pojutrze* ('Today, tomorrow, the day after tomorrow').[37] The 'today' section referred to current acts of resistance, covering the full range of activity from intelligence-gathering through assisting refugees to acts of sabotage; 'tomorrow' was concerned with preparations for formal combat against the Germans in anticipation of a nationwide uprising that would bring the occupation to an end; and 'the day after tomorrow' referred to ensuring education in subjects that would be of use to a liberated Poland that would face the formidable challenges of rebuilding itself.[38]

With Varsovians of all ages involved in the underground in various forms, many diarists described how neighbours, friends, and family members instinctively adopted a discretionary policy of 'don't ask, don't tell' to avoid any potential exchange of compromising information. Korboński painted a picture of mothers across Poland watching their children transform into resistance fighters, powerless to protect them from their fate:

> They were more affectionate and more solicitous for their mother, but they were rarely at home. They went their own ways, grave and thoughtful. The mother did not know, but suspected, and cried quietly, without asking questions and without attempting to stop them. She yielded to the power which took her children away from her, perhaps, one day soon, forever. That power was Underground Poland.[39]

Still, as Korboński recalled with exasperation, there were always some who needed reminding of the need to stay inconspicuous:

> Men had a special predilection for strong top-boots, but unfortunately the Germans soon suspected any who had adopted this fashion and many a young man or boy risked arrest because of it. Nevertheless, the youngsters of the Underground Army paraded in such boots all day long disdaining the risks involved. One of my friends, who is now pining away in a prison in Poland, happened to be arrested by a German police agent in mufti while waiting at a bus stop … he only got out by bribing the agent, who seemed to be a *Volksdeutsche*. When asked by my friend why he had arrested him the agent replied:
>
> 'Why the hell do you walk about in top-boots? Don't you know what sort of people wear such boots nowadays?'[40]

Newly initiated recruits were reminded that consequences would be fatal should they betray the underground. Operational cells were typically limited to five members so that, were any member to be caught and interrogated, only the immediate group of acquaintances would be at risk of exposure. All members of the underground operated under assumed pseudonyms to protect their identity. 'Some select theirs from history or literature,' Kulski explained. 'Others use biblical or foreign names, or pick one at random from the names of animals, places, and battles.' Kulski chose for himself the name 'Chojnacki', in memory of an uncle taken prisoner by the Germans in 1939.[41]

One of the leaders of the Grey Ranks was Jan Bytnar, who operated under the codename 'Rudy'. His small cell carried out various minor acts of resistance – such as painting graffiti – but on 23 March 1943 he was arrested, taken to

Pawiak, and subjected to daily interrogations at Aleja Szucha.[42] Fearing that Bytnar would be forced to reveal the identities of other members of the Grey Ranks, a rescue attempt was organised under the codename *Meksyk* ('Mexico'), but the planned ambush was called off when his would-be rescuers failed to obtain permission from higher resistance authorities.[43] Undeterred, the Grey Ranks planned a more detailed second attempt, including organising a car to help Bytnar escape and setting up an improvised medical station for both Bytnar and any rescuers who might be wounded. A total of 28 members of the Grey Ranks were deployed in two groups; one to carry out the rescue attempt, and the other to prevent any German patrols in the area from intervening.

Meksyk II took place on the afternoon of 26 March. When the Grey Ranks attempted to stop the truck carrying Bytnar, the driver took evasive action, only to run into another group of attackers. The cab was set ablaze with a Molotov cocktail but Gestapo guards in the rear of the truck fired back; two prisoners who attempted to overpower them were shot and injured. The rescuers exchanged shots with both the Germans in the truck and a few Polish police officers, and the two Gestapo guards were soon killed or wounded. A total of 21 prisoners escaped from the wrecked vehicle; Bytnar was unable to walk and had to be carried to a waiting car. Four Gestapo guards were left dead, and a further nine guards – two of whom were Polish policemen – injured. One prisoner and two rescuers were also killed, while another was captured and executed by the Germans. Bytnar was taken to safety but died from the injuries he had sustained during his interrogation.

As anticipated, the Germans responded with brutality: the day after the rescue, 140 prisoners in Pawiak were executed in the courtyard. Fearing further reprisals against their families, a few of the prisoners who had escaped from the truck surrendered to the Germans, who sent them all to concentration camps; few survived. Due to the location of the attack, *Meksyk II* would become known as *Akcja pod Arsenałem* ('Arsenal Action'). The ability and willingness of young Poles (the average age of those involved in the rescue was 21) to take part in such daring attacks showed the defiance and resilience of resistance in Warsaw, despite all the attempts of the Germans to crush it.

AKCJA GŁÓWKI

If anything, the acts and ambitions of Polish underground resistance grew in proportion with the Germans' brutality. Secret courts had already been set up in the early days of the German occupation to try those charged with breaches of military law, and their jurisdiction increased when, in the summer of 1940, the government-in-exile authorised hearings against common criminals, informants, collaborators, and other persecutors of Polish citizens. By late 1943 a list of some of the worst perpetrators of crimes against Polish citizens had been drawn up for a programme of assassinations. The operation was known as *Akcja Główki* ('Action Little Heads') – a sardonic reference to the *Totenkopf* (or 'skull', literally 'dead man's head') badges worn by the SS. But the resistance was carrying out assassinations – like that of Blue Policeman Roman Leon Święcicki – even before *Akcja Główki* commenced. Ultimately, the *AK* would claim to have assassinated nearly 6,000 Germans, though many of these were low-ranking soldiers killed during raids to capture supplies and weapons.[44] Obersturmführer Herbert Schultz, one of Jan Bytnar's torturers, was shot and killed in May 1943; Rottenführer Ewald Lange, his colleague, was killed a few days after.[45] Later that year, the underground courts examined the cases of those named on the lists drawn up for *Akcja Główki* and resistance units were authorised to carry out assassinations. Not all were successful, but at least 11 prominent figures were killed. These included Anton Hergel, who was responsible for the German-run newspapers in Warsaw; Franz Bürkl, the notorious monster of Pawiak; and Brigadeführer Franz Kutschera, who became *SSPF* ('SS and Police Commander') for the Warsaw District in September 1943 and oversaw the deaths of at least 5,000 Poles.

Oberscharführer Franz Bürkl exemplified how it was often brutality, not rank, that determined punishment; his horrifying record was more than sufficient to condemn him to death. During the summer of 1943, the *Anty-Gestapo* ('Anti-Gestapo' or *Agat*) cell of the *AK* began monitoring shift changes at Pawiak and easily identified Bürkl because he was almost always accompanied by his dog. On 5 September, the seven-man Polish team took up their positions of Marszałwska Street, and despite the presence of more German soldiers than anticipated, carried out their attack in broad daylight. Two men walked up behind Bürkl – who was accompanied by his wife pushing a pram – and shot him at close range. A brief but fierce exchange of fire left several more Germans dead or wounded, but the Poles escaped without any casualties.[46] In revenge, the Germans executed 36 prisoners in Pawiak.

Brigadeführer Franz Kutschera, on the other hand, was seen as being responsible for large-scale street executions and deportations of forced labourers. The first step was to identify him – there were no photographs of Kutschera, and he even signed documents with just his rank and title. After his death sentence was passed in November 1943, his city address was identified with the help of Ludwik Żurek, who worked for the Polish criminal police and had access to official documents. Following an abortive attempt in January 1944 – when Kutschera had left Warsaw for a conference – a second assassination attempt was organised on 1 February, involving 12 *AK* personnel.[47] On this occasion, Kutschera's staff car appeared as expected; the Poles blocked the road with a car and machine-gunned Kutschera at short range, before dragging him – still alive – from his vehicle; they then rifled through his briefcase to ascertain his identity and left him to die on the street. Four other Germans were killed in the ensuing gunfight; four of the Poles were killed and a further two wounded.[48] In the days that followed, the Germans executed about 300 Poles and a substantial fine was levied on the city's population for failure to fulfil its 'obligations to fight criminal elements'.[49] As the executions continued, the *AK* decided that the civilian population was paying too high a price for its activities. In a note to Frank in Kraków, Fischer – himself a target of a failed assassination attempt – noted:

> In December 1943, 50 Germans were murdered [in Warsaw], but in January 1944, only five. The number of wounded also decreased significantly; while in December 1943 56 Germans were wounded, this number fell to 20 in January 1944. The number of attacks across Warsaw district also decreased markedly, to a level not recorded for several months. This clearly visible improvement in security is largely the result of harsh but necessary measures taken in consultation with me by the *SS- und Polizeiführer*, Brigadeführer Kutschera. Therefore, it is particularly tragic that he, who did so much for the safety of the Germans living here, fell victim to a Polish attack at the end of this reporting period.[50]

The Kutschera assassination had a strange aftermath. His partner, the Norwegian Jane Lillian Gyertsdatter Steen, was pregnant, and Himmler wanted to ensure that the child would not be born to an unmarried mother, so a wedding ceremony was held with Steen standing beside Kutschera's open coffin. More importantly for the Varsovians, Kutschera's death brought an end to randomised round-ups and executions.

Every assassination attempt cost dozens of lives of Polish prisoners in inevitable reprisals. In other occupied areas of Europe, the principle of 'collective responsibility' was at least partially effective in deterring attacks on the Germans and their auxiliaries; in Poland, the killing of civilians was so indiscriminate that the threat of retributive executions did not always carry the impact the Germans hoped. But the *AK* was not blind to its responsibilities to the public. When the BBC broadcast reports – often embellished – of 'heroic' acts of sabotage, Rowecki sent an urgent message to the government-in-exile asking it to intervene; the reports, he said, were resulting in large numbers of civilians being detained and often killed.[51] In the second half of 1941, Sikorski had advised Rowecki to reduce the level of activity across much of Poland; all efforts were to concentrate on disrupting traffic to the east. This had a direct military significance, and the risk of reprisals against civilians could be justified, whereas operations elsewhere in Poland were unlikely to bring German defeat significantly closer. But when Rowecki organised a unit codenamed *Fan* to operate in eastern Poland, he found that it was frequently attacked by pro-Soviet groups. Its losses were so high that the group was disbanded in late 1942.[52]

SABOTAGING BOTH SIDES

Public awareness of the underground movement stemmed from sources beyond the visible street violence and retributive crackdown. The underground press was instrumental in helping the resistance permeate popular consciousness, publishing thrilling accounts of both real and fictional operations. *Biuletyn Informacyjny* editor Kamiński published a novella, *Stones for the Rampart*, which drew heavily on the adventures of Tadeusz Zawadzki, a scout insurgent who helped break Jan Bytnar out of Pawiak prison. Kamiński's novella centred on a plucky group of young resistance fighters, 'Wojtek', 'Czarny', 'Stach', and 'Antek', all of whom were orphaned by the *Intelligenzaktion*; from acts of minor sabotage, the group progressed in their revenge against the Germans to armed resistance and assassinations. No doubt the story mirrored the experience of countless children of the intelligentsia, but Kamiński's choice of narrative points to a very deliberate effort to inspire – and even radicalise – his younger audience with a sense of patriotic duty and a yearning to follow in the protagonists' footsteps.

Moreover, sabotage wasn't limited to acts of violence. Thousands of Poles answered Kamiński's calls for *mały sabotaż* with enthusiasm: workers rendered machinery inoperable, slogans and symbols of resistance were daubed on walls across Poland, and foul-smelling gases were piped into cinemas broadcasting German films. Even German propaganda was subtly altered for satirical effect: posters proclaiming the likes of 'Germans are winning on all fronts' became 'Germans lie on all fronts'. With the example set by the Grey Ranks and Kamiński's own *Wawer* group (a smaller group within the Grey Ranks) this activity was particularly energetic in and around Warsaw. When the Germans moved a statue of Jan Kiliński, Maciej Dawidowski – a young leader of the Grey Ranks and one of those killed in the operation to rescue Jan Bytnar – daubed the empty plinth with a declaration: 'People of Warsaw – I am here. Jan Kiliński'.[53] One *AK* member, known as 'Jan', was fluent in German and would strike up conversations with German soldiers in bars and at railway stations; when the opportunity arose, he would drop a louse from a matchbox behind the collar of his victim. These lice were often infected with typhus, and acts by people like 'Jan' resulted in hundreds of Germans being infected.[54] Meanwhile, when chemistry student Jan Rosinski abandoned his studies to join the *AK*, he embarked on a personal mission to contaminate the Germans' beer supply with whatever he could scavenge from the university laboratory: some uranium salts, alkaloids, and a kilogram of morphine. 'Maybe they'll glow,' he joked to a classmate.[55]

The scale of sabotage operations across Poland is difficult to determine with any certainty, but one *AK* report estimated that from the beginning of 1941 until the eve of the Warsaw Uprising in the summer of 1944, nearly 7,000 locomotives and 19,000 railcars had been damaged; 38 railway bridges had been destroyed; and over 100 military warehouses had been set ablaze.[56] In October 1942, as Germany attempted to increase the flow of supplies to its troops fighting in and around Stalingrad, Warsaw was shaken by a series of powerful explosions. Many Varsovians took shelter, fearing that the city was under aerial attack, but the detonations were in fact the result of Operation *Wieniec* ('*Wreath*') mounted by seven *AK* squads – two of which were exclusively female. All rail traffic heading east was paralysed for several days while railway tracks were repaired. Although the *AK* personnel suffered no losses, the Germans executed about 40 civilians in revenge.[57]

German records show that as the war progressed, there was increasing concern about the security of railway lines running across Poland which were vital for supplying the armies fighting in the Soviet Union. By 1943, they resorted to assigning large numbers of armed guards to the trains and avoiding journeys during the night wherever possible. General Siegfried Haenicke, in command of the military units stationed in the *Generalgouvernement*, sent an exasperated message to all his formations in late 1943, warning that soldiers 'do not seem to have realised that when they find themselves in the *Generalgouvernement*, they are not in the Fatherland, but in a region where the majority of the population is hostile to us and opposes us with violence'.[58]

In addition to the casualties suffered in the field – through a mixture of clashes with Germans and pro-Soviet groups, or betrayals – the *AK* was hit by significant losses in its higher ranks. A key player in one of the most devastating leadership casualties was Ludwik Kalkstein, who was just 19 when the war broke out. In January 1940 he joined the intelligence department of the *ZWZ* in Warsaw; he was soon promoted and received a medal for stealing German maps and for formulating a new aluminium alloy, but in so doing became a prominent target for the Gestapo. After arresting his parents, the Germans seized Kalkstein in April 1942 and persuaded him to switch sides. He was then released from Aleja Szucha in October with documentation for two fake identities while at the same time, information was leaked to the *AK* that he had been executed.

Kalkstein now revived his intelligence network, which included his brother-in-law Eugeniusz Świerczewski and a young woman named Blanka Kaczorowska, whom he married shortly after. The trio fed critical intelligence about numerous *AK* members and Poles to the Gestapo; one calculation attributes the subsequent capture of over 500 people directly to their betrayals.[59] Their most important victim was Rowecki, who was living under an assumed name in Warsaw. The Gestapo captured the head of the *AK* on 30 June 1943, and after a brief spell in Aleja Szucha transferred him to Berlin. Here, he was invited to cooperate with the Germans, who were exploring possibilities of at least some elements of the *AK* fighting alongside the Germans against the Soviet Union; he refused, and was sent to Sachsenhausen concentration camp, where he spent much of his time in isolation.[60] His replacement in Poland was Brigadier Tadeusz Komorowski, who operated under the codename Bór. Whereas Rowecki had worked assiduously to ensure that the *AK* accepted all Poles into its ranks regardless of their ethnicity, Komorowski's tenure marked a shift in policy that resulted in the *AK*'s inaction during the 1943 Ghetto Uprising.

Kalkstein, Świerczewski, and Kaczorowska continued working for the Gestapo for several months after Rowecki's arrest, but the escalating arrests forced the *AK* to become more aggressive in their counter-intelligence investigations. Both Kalkstein and Świerczewski were unmasked in late 1943; Świerczewski was tried, sentenced to death, and hanged in June 1944, while Kalkstein escaped arrest and was sheltered by the Germans, even joining the SS. After the war, he lived under a series of assumed names until his arrest in 1953 when he was finally tried for collaborating with the Germans. Despite his family's claim that he died in France in the 1980s, he was hounded by *AK* veterans until his actual death in 1994. Blanka Kaczorowska, who survived the war under Gestapo protection and divorced Kalkstein in 1945, was sentenced to death *in absentia* by the *AK*. She was finally arrested in 1952 and sentenced to life imprisonment but released in 1958, having spent her prison years informing on her fellow inmates.

Rowecki wasn't the only major Polish casualty suffered in 1943. That summer, Sikorski flew to the Middle East to meet the men of the Anders Army who were re-forming their units following their transfer from the Soviet Union. It wasn't a happy meeting; Anders was vehemently opposed to any territorial concessions in Stalin's favour, insisting the Soviet leader simply couldn't be trusted, particularly in light of the Katyn revelations. Sikorski, his chief of staff, and seven others boarded a Liberator bomber to fly back to Britain, landing at Gibraltar to refuel on 4 July before taking off shortly before midnight. Less than a minute later, it crashed into the sea. Only the pilot survived.[61]

Sikorski's body was recovered after the crash. The official report on the incident stated that the plane became unstable after cargo shifted towards the tail, but almost immediately there emerged a number of alternative theories of conspiracy. Perhaps the most controversial was a suggestion that the air crash was deliberately staged, and that Sikorski and several others had already been murdered after a meeting with Mayski in Gibraltar as part of an attempt to reset relations with Moscow.[62] His remains were interred in Newark, but were exhumed in 1993 and returned to Poland where they were buried in a crypt in Wawel Castle. In 2008, he was exhumed once more to try to settle the arguments around his death. The final report excluded death by shooting, strangling, or poisoning, and confirmed earlier findings of multiple skeletal and organ injuries consistent with an air crash.

Sikorski had combined the roles of prime minister and military commander-in-chief. His replacement in the former role was Stanisław Mikołajczyk, the leader of the Peasant Party and Sikorski's deputy. The new military commander was Kazimierz Sosnkowski, under whose orders Jewish soldiers had been confined to an internment camp near Warsaw in 1920; most agreed that the former *Sanacja* ally had great intellectual and analytical skills though he lacked decisiveness.[63] Still a vocal opponent of the Sikorski–Mayski Agreement, he quickly launched a forceful diplomatic campaign to rally western support, condemning what he saw as the high-handed attitude of British and American leaders towards Poland and protesting the exclusion of the government-in-exile from critical decisions about the nation's future.

In some ways, the prospect of an organised Polish uprising felt as distant at the beginning of 1943 as it had in 1939; the ranks of committed resistance fighters had grown substantially within Poland, but their ambitions remained constrained by the whims of foreign allies. However, slowly yet surely, the Germans were beginning to feel the strain. As Rosinski explained, it was not the underground state's activity in London, negotiations in Moscow, or the fraught manoeuvres of resistance commanders that staved off a collapse in public morale; it was the tangible and ubiquitous presence of resistance 'on the streets of Warsaw and other cities'. Its power lay not just in its active acts of sabotage, but in the 'psychological lift' it provided to Varsovians who still looked for light at the end of the long, dark tunnel of occupation.[64] Four and a half years after the September invasion, Kulski remained convinced that 'everyone refuses to consider the possibility that we will not regain our freedom'.[65]

One of the most revealing illustrations of this phenomenon emerges from an act of resistance that never actually occurred – and may have been little more than urban legend. According to Rosinski, on 5 October 1939, the day that Hitler received the victory parade in Warsaw, the Poles had placed a high-explosive device under the main podium 'that would have removed the Führer and the top army command, as well as Joseph Goebbels, from history':

> However, at the last minute an order apparently was issued that the bomb was to be removed or defused and the team involved ordered to move to a new location for some other operation. Hitler departed Warsaw later that afternoon, unaware of how close he had come to being killed ... How history might have turned dramatically ...[66]

Was this true? And if so, what on earth would have compelled Polish resistance fighters to back down at such an opportunity? These questions ignore the real significance of this story: the Poles were prepared to believe it. They deemed their resistance fighters worthy of such mythology, and were only too willing to share these tantalising stories as allusions to a victory within their reach. Because even after suffering years of German brutality, they believed their luck could change at any time, and they would once more seize control of their destiny.

CHAPTER 10

BURZA

They taught you, little son, to know by heart your land of birth
as you were carving out with tears of iron its many paths.
They reared you in the darkness and fed you on terror's bread;
you traveled gropingly that shamefulest of human roads.

And then you left, my lovely son, with your black gun at midnight,
and felt the evil prickling in the sound of each new minute.
Before you fell, over the land you raised your hand in blessing.
Was it a bullet killed you, son, or was it your heart bursting?

Krzysztof Kamil Baczynski, 'Elegy for a Polish Boy', 1944
Translated by Bill Johnston[1]

EYEING INDEPENDENCE

By autumn 1943, the final defeat of Germany no longer seemed so distant. Preparations for an invasion of France were progressing – even if Stalin and others in Moscow were suspicious of the delays and could not shake the idea that it suited the purposes of the Western Allies for the Soviet Union and Germany to bleed each other to death while they took their time. On the Eastern Front, the fighting was inching closer to Polish territory, and as diplomatic sands settled in the wake of the Katyn revelations, the thoughts of the Poles returned to their long-established hopes of an uprising that would reassert national independence.

Sikorski's death brought the Polish government-in-exile no closer to reconciling their nationalist ideals with the brutal logic of *Realpolitik*. It was evident that, regardless of their fine words, the British and Americans would not be prepared to fight to restore Poland's eastern frontiers to their 1939 status; the best the Poles could hope for was that the Western Powers would apply sufficient pressure on Moscow to secure their independence after the war. With this in mind, Mikołajczyk was coming to realise that intransigence towards the Soviet regime was no longer tenable. But Sosnkowski, now commander-in-chief of all Polish forces, continued to insist on nothing less than the full restoration of the status quo of 1939; 'the final aim of the Soviet Union,' he declared, 'is to transform Poland into a vassal Communist republic or simply into the 17th Soviet republic.'[2] Ultimately, he thought a confrontation between the Western Powers and the Soviet Union was inevitable – in which case, the question of Poland's status would provide as good a pretext as any. Needless to say, Sosnkowski and Mikołajczyk were left at loggerheads.

British aid to the *AK* remained modest. The British claimed – with some justification – that they lacked the resources to send more weapons at a time when most long-range bombers were committed to battering German cities, but here too *Realpolitik* – or, to be precise, Stalin – was a problem. However much Sosnkowski and others might wish otherwise, the reality was that the Red Army was going to reach Poland long before any other of the nations arrayed against Germany might be in a position to do so. Trying to face reality, Mikołajczyk's government issued instructions on how the *AK* was to conduct itself when this happened: if Polish–Soviet relations had not been normalised when Soviet troops arrived, the *AK* was to continue military action against the Germans, but to avoid clashes with the Red Army. In the meantime, it was to remain underground and await further instructions. Sosnkowski regarded these orders as unworkable and decided simply to ignore them. Instead, he – and Komorowski in occupied Poland – set about drawing up a far more proactive plan.

Rowecki had also harboured deep suspicions towards Soviet intentions. Before his betrayal and capture, he had developed a three-phase uprising strategy whereby the *AK* would free Polish cities before Soviet forces arrived: the first would take place in the east, centred on Lwów and Vilnius, as the Red Army approached; this would be followed by general fighting in the eastern parts of Poland that had been occupied by the Soviet Union in 1939; and finally, the rest of Poland would rise up against the occupiers. With the support of Sosnkowski in London, the *AK* leadership in Poland continued planning in the same vein – and in defiance of the instructions issued by Mikołajczyk.

So long as the *AK* could seize major towns and cities from the retreating Germans, they reasoned, they could deny the Red Army the privilege of describing themselves as liberators – and the claims to power that would be sure to follow. Instead, when Soviet units reached the newly freed towns, the *AK* units were to make contact and offer to help the Red Army's pursuit of the Germans. These plans, known as *Akcja Burza* ('Operation *Tempest*'), completely overlooked the hostility of the Soviet authorities towards the *AK* following the Katyn accusations.

The feasibility of a general uprising had always hinged upon the weakening of the German forces. This was especially the case now that the Poles couldn't count on forthcoming Allied support, and so Sosnkowski's plan demanded that Reich forces be on the verge of complete collapse. Plus, with limited resources, the *AK* units would have to wait until the Red Army arrival was imminent or the Germans would crush any attempt to seize towns and cities. But if the *AK* waited too long, the Red Army would take control of these areas before the Poles could assert their independence. Another concern was the potential toll on civilians caught up in uprisings; Komorowski originally sought to exclude the largest towns and cities from the plan 'in an effort to spare the defenceless population and safeguard historical buildings', but this would have rendered other uprisings almost meaningless.[3] Eventually, a decision was made in March 1944 to exclude only Warsaw, but this too was soon reversed.

In the meantime, liaison with the government-in-exile in London and the Allies continued, but it was clear that not everyone was on the same page. On 23 November 1943, Cordell Hull – Roosevelt's secretary of state – sent the president a telegram after a meeting with Mikołajczyk's government: 'A rising in Poland against Germany is being planned to break out at a moment mutually agreed upon with our Allies either before or at the very moment of the entry of Soviet troops into Poland.'[4]

Given the growing divergence between Mikołajczyk's intentions and those of both Sosnkowski and Komorowski, the possibility of any plans being 'mutually agreed' – and most importantly, drawn up in collaboration with Soviet authorities – was remote. For the military leaders, any such alignment was seen as almost impossible given their lack of trust in Stalin and their doubts about the willingness of the British and Americans to uphold Polish interests. Mikołajczyk continued to hope – with little real justification – that the Western Powers would be able to agree some sort of deal with Stalin that would protect Poland. Few shared his optimism.

AKCJA BURZA

The first major test of Soviet–*AK* relations came before any consensus had been reached. On 4 January 1944, Soviet troops reached what had been the old eastern frontier of Poland in the region of Volhynia, close to Sarny. Over the following weeks, local *AK* units reorganised themselves into the 27th Volhynian Home Army Infantry Division under the command of Colonel Jan Kiwerski, and on 4 March the first contact was made with the leading Red Army units. Two weeks later, Kiwerski's fighters encircled and disarmed a German company near Kowel. The Germans responded forcefully and clashes took place over the next few days, with particularly heavy fighting along the Turia River. To Kiwerski's disappointment, the Soviet units did little to help the *AK* division, which was surrounded by German units in mid-April. He was killed in the fighting that followed, but many of his men managed to escape the encirclement and retreated towards Lublin.[5]

Around the same time, the Poles in London made another shocking discovery: their allies had effectively surrendered eastern Poland to the Soviet Union at the Tehran Conference in late 1943. On 25 April, Zygmunt Berezowski, a member of the government-in-exile, and General Stanisław Tatar, the deputy chief of staff of the *AK*, met Churchill. Berezowski told the British prime minister that the Poles continued to have confidence that Britain would support them in asserting their pre-war frontiers. Churchill replied that whilst he remained resolutely supportive of Polish independence, the best he could promise was the 'Curzon Line' – something closely resembling the demarcation line that the Germans and Soviets had agreed in 1939. This meant ceding substantial territories to the Soviet Union, but in return Churchill promised that Poland would gain land in the west at the expense of Germany. The dismayed Berezowski insisted that his nation had to include its eastern territories, and that Poles would fight to achieve this. Churchill's response was of little comfort. 'Obviously, a decision to resist, regardless of the consequences, is the privilege of every nation, and cannot be denied even to the weakest'; but he made no commitment to support it.[6] Similarly, when Mikołajczyk met Roosevelt in June, he was offered only US 'moral support' in his efforts to reach an understanding with Moscow. Yet unlike Berezowski and Tatar, Mikołajczyk saw reason for hope in the fact that the president had declined to enter into detailed discussions with Stalin at the Tehran Conference: Churchill might have been content to settle for the Curzon Line, but Roosevelt might not.[7]

In the summer of 1944, the soldiers of the Western Powers stormed ashore on the beaches of Normandy, opening the long-heralded second front. As promised at the Tehran Conference, Stalin ordered his commanders to draw up plans for a major concurrent offensive to prevent Germany from moving troops from one front to another. Accordingly, the Red Army prepared to launch Operation *Bagration*, its largest and most ambitious assault to date. Four Fronts – equivalent to the army groups of the Western Allies – would attack the German Army Group Centre in Belarus. The lessons learned so painfully over several years were to be exploited in full: surprise; coordination between tanks, infantry, and artillery; adequate logistic support; and a level of command flexibility that would have been far beyond the skills of the Red Army in its earlier operations. When it began on 22 June, *Bagration* proved to be every bit as effective as Stalin had hoped. Casualties were very high – the Red Army lost 2.2 men for every German soldier killed, wounded, or captured – but the Soviet Union could afford such losses. The Germans could not – and lost over 400,000 men. Varsovians greeted the Allies' advances with a mixture of excitement, relief, and trepidation. On the one hand, they hoped that the 'beginning of the end' to which Churchill had alluded in late 1942 was finally coming to pass.[8] On the other, they knew all too well what this could mean for their occupied nation, as the elder Julian Kulski reminded his son: if 'they [the Germans] ever have to leave Poland, they will first make sure they leave no one alive here.'[9] As the Soviet spearheads raced across Belarus and closed in on the old Polish frontier, the *AK* faced their moment of truth: the launch of *Burza*.[10]

Vilnius, the ancient capital of Lithuania, was at the heart of a uniquely intricate anti-German resistance network. In addition to the *AK*, the city was home to many Jewish resistance fighters – some of whom were pro-Soviet – as well as modest numbers of Soviet partisans. With the Red Army advancing, the Germans tried to come to terms with the *AK*; there were tentative discussions in early 1944 between Colonel Aleksander Krzyżanowski, the regional *AK* commander, and Seidler von Rosenfeld, an officer in the *SD*, about fighting together against the Soviet forces, but Krzyżanowski refused to cooperate. Nonetheless, the Germans deliberately left weapons and ammunition in poorly guarded locations hoping the *AK* would put them to use against the Red Army.[11]

On 7 July, shortly before the Red Army reached the city, Krzyżanowski ordered the implementation of *Ostra Brama* ('*Gates of Dawn*', a famous Vilnius landmark) – the local version of *Burza*. Having faced similar insurgencies elsewhere, the Germans weren't caught off-guard, and the *AK* – numbering no more than 8,000 lightly armed combatants – failed to make any gains. The Poles fought on against the Germans over the following week while avoiding any significant contact with the Red Army. When Vilnius was firmly in Soviet control, Krzyżanowski was ordered to evacuate his men from the city and, with assurances that his men would receive supplies from the Red Army without any preconditions, he led his remaining combatants to the nearby Rūdninkai Forest.

To date, the relationship between the Red Army and the *AK* had been at best ambiguous, but everything changed on 14 July when Stalin sent Directive 220145 to General Ivan Danilovich Cherniakhovsky, commander of 3rd Belarusian Front; the Red Army was ordered to take 'immediate and energetic action against Polish armed underground formations.'[12] An envoy was sent to Krzyżanowski in the forest, inviting him to Cherniakhovsky's headquarters and on arrival, Krzyżanowski and his senior officers were arrested by the *NKVD*. In the days that followed, many of Krzyżanowski's soldiers were also captured. One of those who managed to escape was an officer named Maciej Kalenkiewicz, who had been parachuted into Poland in 1941 after undergoing training in Britain. He had been injured in June 1944, resulting in the amputation of one hand, and he gathered about 2,000 Poles in the forest and attempted to slip away from the Red Army. He and his men were later surrounded and overrun by the *NKVD*, but not before he managed to send a radio signal to London informing his superiors that the Soviets were systematically disarming and destroying *AK* units. The Soviets clearly had no intention of supporting the *AK*, he added, suggesting that any future uprisings should include the capture of airfields so that Polish air squadrons currently deployed in Britain could move to Poland. The unstated – and unjustifiably optimistic – implication was that the British and others would agree to this, and would provide adequate logistic support to make it happen.

The Vilnius incident turned out not to be an isolated occurrence. In other cases, the Red Army deliberately paused to allow *AK* units and German units to fight each other before moving forward. It was becoming increasingly clear that the Soviets were not interested in recognising the *AK* as the official army of Poland and that the hopes of those in London that *Burza* would consolidate Polish sovereignty were not going to be fulfilled. Yet even this didn't curtail plans for a major uprising in Warsaw. Many in the *AK* hoped that, being further west than places like Lwów and Vilnius, it would be easier for British and American aircraft to support an uprising there; Polish paratroopers could be dropped into the city from England, and the capture of an airfield would permit the transfer of Polish RAF squadrons. Moreover, any further delay increased the risk of the arriving Soviets branding the *AK* as Nazi collaborators. A statement by Komorowski on 12 July laid bare the threat approaching from the east: 'We must be prepared for an open collision between Poland and the Soviets, and for our part we must fully demonstrate in such a collision the independent position of Poland.'[13] Komorowski was keen to emphasise that even if the Red Army had shown little interest in supporting or recognising the *AK* units it had encountered further east, it could hardly disregard a Polish uprising that succeeded in liberating the capital.

At the same time, this meant keeping Soviet-sanctioned Communist support at arm's length to avoid compromising Polish autonomy. Hence why, for example, the suggestion that the *AK* be merged into the Stalin-backed *AL* – who were positioning themselves to install members of the Communist underground in power after the war – was rejected outright.[14] In his memoirs, Komorowski would go to great lengths to highlight the moral divergences between the *AK*'s 'military organisation which permeated every section of national life and was directed by a centralised single command' on the one hand, and the Communist 'partisans' who 'never took the safety of the Polish population into consideration' on the other.[15] This comparison glosses over the fact that the *AK*'s record on 'collective responsibility' was far from spotless, but Komorowski was highlighting a more prescient point: that to the average non-initiate of the Polish public, it could be hard to differentiate between the myriad resistance groups – let alone to know which to trust.

Ideological divisions were deepening in the civic sphere, too. When Polish underground leaders began assembling a pre-emptive post-war government in April, the newly appointed deputy prime minister, Jan Janowski, named a Council of Ministers featuring representatives from the three primary political parties – the Peasants, Socialists, and Nationalists – but not the Communists. Nor had they been included in the formation in January 1944 of a Council of National Unity, which controlled all political decisions affecting the Polish underground. These omissions demonstrated the extent to which Komorowski and other leaders in Poland and behind Sosnkowski in London and were already deviating from Mikołajczyk's plans to ameliorate relationships with the Soviets.

DISINTEGRATION VERSUS IMPATIENCE

Preparations for the Warsaw Uprising fell to two figures who were determined to prove to the world that Poland had the right to assert its independence. Major General Tadeusz Pełczyński had made a vital contribution to the war even before hostilities commenced in 1939: it was thanks to his recommendation that Poland passed its knowledge of German Enigma cyphers to the British and French, which became the focal point of the British decryption effort at Bletchley Park.[16] Having fought with the Warsaw *Kedyw* section of the *AK* through the war, he was a staunch advocate of the Sosnkowski approach towards the Soviet Union. He was partnered with Leopold Okulicki, who, having commanded Polish resistance units in the Soviet-occupied sector in late 1940, had been arrested and tortured by the *NKVD* before being released as part of the Sikorski–Mayski Agreement. He had then made his way west with the Anders Army before finally parachuting back into Poland, where he joined the *AK* command. On 21 July, amid growing reports of German retreat and chaos, Komorowski gave the two men permission to start putting their plans in motion.

By this time, the *AK* had spent years quietly accumulating armaments and supplies and, where they struggled, improvising impressively resourceful networks of procurement. As well as stealing arms from the occupiers and producing weapons in their own factories, the underground circulated blueprints for both standard weapons and new arms – including timebombs, incendiary bombs, railway bombs, and detonators – that would be invaluable in resistance warfare. Manufacturing these more technical arms and procuring parts meant using German-controlled factories and Polish technicians to produce contraband weapons either during their night shifts or, by modifying factory work plans, in the open during their day shifts. Materials and parts were stolen, traded, or bought from German plants, and even, on occasion, sourced directly through the factory supply chains; thanks to Polish factory directors deliberately over ordering and diverting materials to the resistance cause, German companies such as Magdeburg Werke, Zeiss of Jena, Bruhn-Werke of Brunswick and Stock of Berlin became unknowing suppliers to the Polish underground.[17] On top of this, and despite a number of pauses, the RAF airdropped in excess of 300 tons of supplies during the two years leading up to the Uprising, including British anti-tank PIAT guns, small arms, medical provisions, and uniforms. One of the corollary challenges for members of the Polish underground was storing these supplies without German detection. Weapons were divided among trusted resistance fighters and their families and allies, or else secreted in unlikely locations; in one case, at the edge of the notorious killing fields of the Kampinos Forest.[18] When the Germans succeeded in unearthing a number of these hidden caches during the spring of 1944, they were baffled by both the quantity and variety of what they found and offered substantial bribes to captured Polish personnel for information on how the *AK* was acquiring its weapons – to little effect. Komorowski interpreted this as a sign that the Nazis were not only 'foreseeing possible defeat and war on their own territory', but that they also 'wished to prepare themselves for underground activity and to profit from our experience.'[19]

The long-awaited uprising finally looked to be within reach as key conditions began to converge. Firstly, the shattered state of retreating German units was clear for all to see. The survivors of the German Army Group Centre – three of its armies having been destroyed in the course of *Bagration* – passed through Warsaw, and Varsovians were astonished at the difference between these bedraggled, exhausted, often weaponless men and the triumphant units that had marched through the city in 1939. Alceo Valcini, an Italian journalist, was staying in the Venice Hotel in Warsaw, where he looked down at the Poniatowski Bridge in the centre of the city. He described the men streaming back from the east:

> They were no longer soldiers. They were the remnants of human beings, tired, frightened, apathetic, visibly depressed, both physically and morally. They were sweating, hungry, encrusted from head to foot with mud … They were unshaven, glancing around with lifeless eyes … a horde of defeated soldiers.[20]

The Germans had tried their best to repress reports of the disaster that had engulfed Army Group Centre; even the BBC's reports were cautious about the results, largely because they were so dramatic that many in London doubted the accuracy of Soviet information. But there was no hiding the fact that the Wehrmacht had been critically wounded. Varsovians crowded the sides of the roads running west from the river, 'greedy to feed their eyes on the sight of the defeated Germans', mockingly waving goodbye to the retreating troops and exchanging furtive smiles in the July sunshine.[21] Discipline amongst the mixture of rear area units and shattered combat formations was rapidly unravelling, and surely, the Poles reasoned, the German units in the Warsaw area would be unable to deal with an uprising – any formations with combat strength would have to deploy to face the Red Army, and the rest clearly had no stomach for further fighting. And it wasn't just the soldiers of Army Group Centre who were leaving. The exodus of troops confirmed to Varsovians the 'symptoms of disintegration and fear' they had already detected amongst their occupiers; German personnel began selling up their requisitioned properties in Warsaw and loading up whatever stolen furniture, art, and other valuables they could cart off to the west, with thousands of *Volksdeutsche* following suit.[22] Ludwig Fischer, governor of Warsaw, fled west on 23 July. The *AK*, meanwhile, capitalised on the occupiers' demoralisation to purchase weapons and ammunition from Ukrainian paramilitaries – and even from German police officers.[23]

The next critical factor that accelerated the uprising plans emerged not from developments within Poland but from events at Hitler's headquarters in Rastenburg. On 20 July, Oberst Claus Schenk Graf von Stauffenberg stepped out from a conference with the Führer to take a telephone call. He left behind a briefcase that sat under the conference table next to Hitler, but another officer moved the briefcase aside, putting it behind one of the thick table legs. The case contained a bomb that detonated shortly after. Originally, it had been intended to contain two explosive charges, but Stauffenberg, badly maimed in North Africa where he lost his right hand and two fingers of his left hand, was unable to arm both devices. Moreover, the conference had been moved from its usual location, a concrete bunker, to a wooden building, because the bunker was being repainted. If any of these three factors had not occurred – the moving of the briefcase, the failure to arm both explosive charges, and the move of the conference to a wooden building that burst outwards, thus dissipating a blast that would have been lethal in an enclosed concrete bunker – Hitler and most of the others in the conference would surely have been killed. Instead, four of those in the conference room died and several others were wounded; Hitler's trousers were scorched and shredded and one eardrum was perforated, but he survived.

Stauffenberg flew to Berlin to join his fellow conspirators who had put in place a plan to seize control of Germany. When news of Hitler's survival began to circulate, the conspiracy rapidly disintegrated, but it was a momentous development and the enemies of Nazi Germany watched with bated breath. In Warsaw, Komorowski and his fellow *AK* commanders took the entire plot as further evidence of the growing chaos and disaffection in the German regime that would surely work in their favour.

In actual fact, the real consequences of the failed plot were entirely detrimental to the planned uprising. As the war progressed and the tide turned against Germany, Hitler grew increasingly wary of his senior army officers, having always been aware that these men – largely drawn from traditional Prussian backgrounds – had little love for the Nazis in general. Following the failed Moscow offensive in 1941, the Führer tended to deflect blame on to his generals for the setbacks rather than recognise his own substantial contributions to Germany's growing list of defeats. The disaster that engulfed Army Group Centre during *Bagration* was a case in point: senior officers had warned of an imminent assault, and when the Soviet operation began, most field commanders demanded a rapid switch to mobile warfare, where their tactical advantages over their Soviet counterparts would give the Wehrmacht a chance to stop the advance. But Hitler insisted that Army Group Centre had to hold firm, and refused permission for retreats until it was too late.

The July Plot, which involved many senior officers, seemed to confirm Hitler's suspicions that the army could not be trusted. Henceforth, he would place far more confidence in the SS. Himmler was given control of the *Ersatzheer* ('Replacement Army'), the organisation that oversaw men undergoing training prior to deployment – and which the conspirators had intended to use to seize control of Germany. The Nazi salute was made compulsory in all army units, and all formations from battalions upward were ordered to designate *Nationalsozialisticher Führungsoffiziere* ('National Socialist Leadership Officers' or *NSFO*s). This role, broadly similar to the Soviet political commissar, had been created the previous year, but many units had not implemented it. Now, they were obliged to have *NSFO*s who were responsible for ensuring political indoctrination of all ranks. Moreover, senior army officers who had previously been disdainful of the Nazi 'riff-raff' now showed unprecedented zeal in trying to prove their loyalty to Hitler, if only to avoid closer scrutiny of their flirting with the anti-Hitler conspirators in the past.

IMPERFECT OMENS

Bagration had greatly exceeded expectations, but it was impossible to sustain the advance indefinitely. As they approached Warsaw, Red Army formations were over 420 miles from their start line, and wherever possible the Germans had destroyed railway lines, bridges, and other infrastructure in an attempt to slow the Soviet advance. As many units were reduced to shadows of their establishment strength, momentum stalled. If the Germans could catch their breath and bring up reinforcements, they might be able to stop the advance before it reached Praga, on the right bank of the Vistula.

At the head of the 1st Belarusian Front advancing towards the Polish capital was Marshal Konstantin Konstantinovich Rokossovsky. Of mixed Polish–Russian parentage, Rokossovsky fell foul of Stalin's purges in the late 1930s and was arrested after another prisoner denounced him – almost certainly in a desperate attempt to avoid further beatings. Rokossovsky himself insisted on his innocence even in the face of brutal questioning – most of his teeth were knocked out by his *NKVD* interrogators – and he was released in time to take part in the fighting against the Germans in 1941. Thereafter, he repeatedly demonstrated his skill in mobile operations. At the outset of *Bagration*, his Front formed the southern part of the assault on Belarus. The front line in this part of the Soviet Union was effectively divided in two by the widespread swamps of the Pripyat region; units south of the marshes started their offensive after *Bagration* was underway, swept past Lwów to reach the Vistula, and established a substantial bridgehead near Sandomierz. Others turned north to clear the east bank of the river and approached Praga from the southeast at the same time as other units of Rokossovsky's Front were advancing from the east.

The Soviets had pinned their hopes on capturing – or at least interdicting – the river crossings in Warsaw. Most important were the bridges over the Narew River at Serock, a little to the north, which, if taken, would leave the remaining formations of the German Army Group Centre completely isolated. The Germans were of course well aware of this and rushed whatever reinforcements could be spared from other sectors to this battlefield. Like all German commanders, Generalfeldmarschall Walter Model – who now commanded Army Group

Centre – was a skilled exponent of powerful counterattacks to defeat enemy advances and he sensed an opportunity to inflict sufficient damage on the already depleted Soviet units while buying some precious breathing space. The armoured units needed for such a counterattack were slowly assembling, and the stage was set for the sort of swift-moving battle in which German officers still showed greater expertise than their Soviet equivalents.

The Red Army had come a long way from its defeats of 1941. Whereas German officers had to deal with ever greater suspicion and micromanagement from above, Stalin was granting his trusted commanders – who were of a far higher calibre than before – increasing leeway. One of these was Colonel-General Semen Ilyich Bogdanov, who was leading Second Tank Army towards Praga. Having shown great energy and skill in driving past the southern edge of the Pripyat region, he was then ordered to secure the city of Lublin, where Stalin sought to establish a pro-Soviet Polish government that could rival the government-in-exile. Bogdanov was badly wounded by a German sniper as his troops approached the city; the bullet smashed his shoulder, forcing him to endure a lengthy spell in hospital. His replacement was Major General Aleksei Ivanovich Radzievsky, Bogdanov's chief of staff – another experienced officer, albeit short of the high standard set by Bogdanov. As his army turned north and northwest to follow the Vistula towards Praga, its subunits became dangerously strung out.

This proved crucial to what became known as the Battle of Radzymin. Reinforced by several divisions, Model struck at the Soviet spearheads, badly mauling them and driving them back in disarray. The consequence was that an early Soviet advance to the outskirts of Warsaw became impossible, but when they heard the thunder of artillery growing louder to the east, Varsovians naturally assumed the opposite. Whilst many – particularly in the ranks of the *AK* – had decidedly mixed feelings about the reliability of the Soviet Union as an ally, they agreed that if an uprising was to be staged to seize control of Warsaw, the moment was rapidly approaching.

TALENTS OF SAVAGERY

The implications of Operation *Bagration* for the *AK* threatened to penetrate far deeper than the immediate military reversals. The rear area behind the German front line across the Soviet Union was a mess of overlapping agencies and individuals taking full advantage of Hitler's encouragement of competition to expand their influence. Amongst these were numerous SS units involved in the murderous campaign being fought against pro-Soviet partisans. After a difficult start, the partisan movement had burgeoned, reinforced first by Red Army stragglers left behind in 1941, then by trained personnel who were infiltrated through the front line or brought in by air. The brutal German occupation policies could almost have been designed to encourage the civilian population to take up arms, and the widespread forests of Belarus in particular became a huge battleground. The Germans threw more and more troops into their campaigns to suppress the partisans; these were a mixture of SS, Wehrmacht, and paramilitary formations, and the sweeps through the swamps and woodland became exercises in mass slaughter. The Germans would triumphantly report thousands of 'partisans' killed in these operations, yet the haul of captured weapons was consistently far lower; most of the victims were simply civilians who were caught up in the action.

Anti-partisan warfare is almost always a dirty business; in German hands, it became an exercise of particular savagery and merciless repression. The officers involved would rank as some of the worst war criminals in the German armed forces. One of the most senior was Erich von dem Bach-Zelewski, a Pomeranian with part-Kashubian heritage; he grew up speaking Polish and Kashubian at home, and added 'von dem Bach' to his name – after one of his ancestors – to make his name sound more Germanic. After Hitler's accession to power, he removed 'Zelewski' entirely, though he would – ironically – reclaim it in post-war years as he attempted to distance himself from his Nazi record. Perhaps because of his Kashubian ancestry – or because all three of his sisters married Jewish men – he became a virulent party supporter and was appointed SS and police chief in Silesia in 1937. After the conquest of Poland, he was instrumental in the conversion of Polish barracks in the town of Oświęcim into the Auschwitz concentration camp, and after the invasion of the Soviet Union he became SS and police chief in Belarus. Here, he oversaw the mass shooting of Jews by *Einsatzgruppe B*, boasting proudly about the numbers slaughtered.[24] But like several others involved in such crimes, he didn't emerge unscathed; in 1942, he spent a spell in hospital suffering from intestinal problems brought on by opiates he had been taking to escape the memories of the mass executions. Ernst-Robert Grawitz, a senior SS medical officer, wrote that Bach 'screamed at night and was beset by hallucinations, and was haunted by the ghosts of his guilt'.[25] Nonetheless, he returned to duty and, promoted to Obergruppenführer, he was tasked with overseeing anti-partisan operations in Belarus.

After Heydrich's assassination in 1942, Bach was nominated as his replacement, but Himmler insisted that he remain in Belarus where his 'expertise' in anti-partisan operations was more in demand. Just how effective he was at suppressing the partisans is debatable. Hundreds of thousands of people were slaughtered under his authority – of the pre-war Belarusian population of about 9 million, at least 2 million perished during the war – but any reduction in partisan activity was only temporary, and attacks on isolated German outposts, bridges, railway lines, and other targets continued to rise. However, the suave, jovial Bach, with his dimpled smile and impressive physique, continued to rise in Himmler's esteem. Others had perhaps more realistic opinions of a man who seemed able to adopt almost any point of view to ensure his promotion and success. Walter Schellenberg, chief of the *SD*, wrote: 'He has the kind of personality that can't differentiate between truth and lies. He gets himself so much into the whole thing that he can't differentiate … Originally, it was not the truth, but he so convinces himself – he's ready to die for it.'[26]

Bach was stationed in an appropriated palace in the city of Mogilev – perilously close to the front line – when the Red Army surged into Belarus in the summer of 1944. He hastily fled west, first to Minsk and then to Poznań. This so-called expert in anti-partisan operations was therefore both unemployed and conveniently located for Hitler and Himmler to call upon if there was any major unrest in Poland.

Whilst Bach succeeded after the war in passing himself off as a genial, sophisticated officer whose less-than-palatable career had been shaped by the whims of his superiors, his subordinates numbered amongst the most repulsive figures to rise to prominence in Nazi Germany. The sharp-faced, sunken-eyed Oskar Dirlewanger would be remembered as a foul, brutal personification of evil. Born in 1895, he was wounded in the First World War and, like many other survivors of that conflict, left both physically and mentally scarred by his experiences; although he does not appear to have had any criminal record prior to the war, he was repeatedly in trouble in the years that followed. He was frequently involved in violent episodes – sometimes fuelled by alcohol or amphetamines – and despite obtaining a doctorate in political science in Frankfurt and being the executive director of a Jewish textile company in Erfurt, he faced investigation and arrest on multiple occasions. Matters came to a head in 1934 when he was accused of sex with a minor; he was dismissed from his job, expelled from the Nazi Party, stripped of his doctorate, and sent to a concentration camp. But as was often the case in Nazi Germany, an old friend came to his aid. He was rescued by a wartime comrade, Gottlob Berger, who had become head of the *SS-Hauptamt* ('SS Main Office', responsible for SS recruitment) and was a close friend of Himmler.

After serving with the Condor Legion in the Spanish Civil War, Dirlewanger joined the SS and was sent to Poland, where he once more found himself in trouble. Georg Konrad, a lawyer in the SS, charged him with numerous crimes – sex with a Polish woman; rape of children of both sexes; the torture and genital mutilation of prisoners from the Lublin Ghetto; stripping female prisoners naked and whipping them for the sake of entertainment at his evening parties; and injecting Jewish women with strychnine so that he could watch them suffer and die.[27] Once more, higher authorities – this time Himmler himself – intervened to suppress any investigation into Dirlewanger's 'eccentric character'.[28]

Dirlewanger's unit was then sent to Belarus, where it was expanded into a 'poacher' brigade with particular talents for savagery.

> I said to Dirlewanger: Listen, find yourself suitable men among thugs incarcerated in our concentration camps and among professional criminals. The regime in the regiment is naturally often, let's say, a medieval one, with beating etc. Also, if any of them doubts whether we will win this war, then he falls dead at the table, he is dropped by someone on the spot. One cannot handle this sort of people any other way.[29]

Indeed, Dirlewanger treated his men brutally and encouraged his subordinates – many of whom were released from prison purely to serve in *Sonderkommando Dirlewanger* – to commit atrocities, urging them to rape women indiscriminately before executing them. His unit rapidly gained notoriety, with some senior German figures complaining that the atrocities were merely encouraging Belarusians to support the anti-German partisans. Wilhelm Kube, the *Generalkommissar* of *Weissruthenien* (the term used by the Nazi government for Belarus), sent an angry report to Berlin:

> In the war of annihilation he wages pitilessly against an unarmed population, [he] deliberately refuses to consider political necessities. His methods, worthy of the Thirty Years War, make a lie of the civil administration's assurances of their wish to work with the Belarusian people. When women and children are shot *en masse* or burned alive, there is no longer a semblance of humane conduct of war.[30]

It should be pointed out that Kube had no problem with the mass killing of Jews – it was purely the non-Jewish Belarusians that he wished to keep as a labour force. Other Nazis might have found Dirlewanger distasteful, but regarded him as a useful asset. He also had a particularly close relationship with Bach.

With the German front line in Belarus disintegrating during *Bagration*, several anti-partisan units came together under the command of Brigadeführer Curt von Gottberg; alongside Dirlewanger's *Sonderkommando*, this ad hoc group included the former *Volksheer-Brigade Kaminski* ('People's Army Brigade Kaminski'). Bronislav Vladislavovich Kaminski was a Belarusian who had been arrested during Stalin's purges and had been released just a few weeks before the German invasion of the Soviet Union. When German forces reached Bryansk, where he was living, he volunteered to help them set up a local administration and police force, resulting in the creation of a poorly disciplined militia that was heavily involved in anti-partisan operations.[31] In 1943, as the Germans retreated to Belarus, Kaminski's brigade suffered heavy losses, worsened by hundreds deserting to join the partisans – despite Kaminski personally killing several would-be defectors. Renamed *Waffen-Sturm-Brigade RONA* ('Armed Assault Brigade of *Russkaya Osvobditelnaya Naerodnaya Armiya* or the Russian People's Liberation Army'), it was part of the force that Gottberg attempted to deploy to defend Minsk from the Soviet advance. Gottberg had been placed under the command of General Dietrich von Saucken's XXXIX Panzer Corps; Saucken was the epitome of the East Prussian officer, an austere career soldier who took few measures to hide his disdain of the Nazis, and Gottberg resented being subordinated to someone outside the SS. Like so many who had spent the war massacring civilians, his men proved to be no match for the Soviet units attacking them, and when his group was redeployed, Gottberg immediately informed his new commander that his men were too badly weakened to remain in the front line. He then headed west to Lida, gathered further police units to reinforce the survivors of his group, and retreated further west. The result was that *Bagration*, which had carried the Red Army almost to the gates of Warsaw, simultaneously pushed German units who had 'distinguished' themselves in bloody anti-partisan operations – along with their brutal commanders – closer to the Polish capital.

MISREADING THE SIGNS

But the Poles, utterly consumed in their uprising plans, were already taking Soviet successes at face value. By the final weeks of July, Komorowski was coordinating daily conferences at *AK* headquarters in Pańska Street during which underground officers and government delegates examined the latest intelligence on Soviet and German movements. Around 21 July, the underground monitoring service intercepted a German message reporting the decisive rout of Fourth Panzer Army at Zamość. That the call was uncoded signified the extent of the Germans' desperation, and the news that Russian forces had reached and crossed the Vistula appeared to confirm to the Poles that their long-awaited moment of liberation was fast approaching.[32] Komorowski concluded from these reports that the Germans faced complete defeat in the east unless they were able to deploy fresh forces and reported so to London. Around the same time, the occupation authorities issued an order that German women were to leave Warsaw for their own safety, which caused what remained of the occupiers' community to descend into chaos as troops, police, and intelligence officials rushed to exit the city. Within days, the city had apparently emptied of Germans.

That Komorowski found it necessary to justify his assumption of German defeat in his post-war memoirs suggests some awareness of its contentiousness. He claimed that his assessment was later proven accurate according to 'official documents', citing the Nuremberg testimony of General Heinz Guderian – who had been chief of the German general staff at the time – who described the Eastern Front forces as 'hardly more than an agglomeration of the remains of our armies' when they attempted to withdraw to the Vistula.[33] What Komorowski fails to mention is that not all the *AK* leaders shared in his conviction. During the meeting on 21 July, just as Chief of the Information and Propaganda Bureau Colonel Jan Rzepecki declaimed the disappearance of Germans from the city streets, Chief of Intelligence Colonel Kazimierz Iranek-Osmecki spoke up with information that ought to have given the *AK* pause. According to unverified sources, fresh panzer units had materialised in the forests between Wyszków and Jabłonna, on the right bank of the Vistula, while elements of the *Hermann Göring* panzer division had been withdrawn from the Italian front for transport to Warsaw.[34]

Time and again in the final week of July Osmecki would put forward unsettling intelligence – that the Germans were loading trains bound for Warsaw with armaments, and that Wehrmacht forces were rallying to the north of the city – and on every occasion Rzepecki and Okulicki would dismiss them. Osmecki was trying to make the point that to trigger the uprising too early and before the Soviets were within safe distance would make liberating the city from the Germans far more difficult, especially if they were already on the front foot for a counteroffensive in the north. For much the same reasons, Chief of Operations Janusz Bokszczanin was warning that the Poles needed to be careful not to take the Soviets' arrival as given, and only to act when absolutely sure that liberation was within reach. Rzepecki disagreed, stating that whilst an early uprising could be problematic, starting it too late would risk being 'condemned for good' under Soviet authority.[35]

Having planned and waited so long for the uprising, it seems almost incredible that Rzepecki and Okulicki were so willing to call the Germans' bluff and risk gambling away Warsaw's liberation at the final moment. But by this time, they, like Komorowski, were swept up in the cultural mythology of the resistance that they had spent months cultivating. On 30 July, the courier Jan Nowak arrived back in Warsaw and advised Komorowski that, in any case, an uprising would never succeed 'in terms of its intended effect on Allied governments and public opinion', and that on the world stage it would amount to little more than a 'tempest in a teacup'. Even this information – delivered just 14 months after the Allies failed to intervene in the catastrophic Ghetto Uprising – failed to deter the *AK* leaders. Komorowski later told Nowak that his warning 'would have been taken into account had it been received a week earlier.'[36] The problem, he claimed, was that plans had already developed a momentum of their own:

> The general lust of revenge for the years of tragedy and humiliation suffered under the Germans was overwhelming and practically impossible to check. The whole town was waiting breathlessly for a call to arms, and the vast majority of the population would have considered a passive attitude as a betrayal of the Polish cause. In an atmosphere of such intensity there was grave danger of an outbreak of less disciplined elements, whether through deliberate provocation or merely some accidental circumstance, leading to the unleashing of an unplanned uprising.[37]

Whether there really was a danger that the *AK* would be unable to keep the lid on Polish resistance or whether these arguments – redolent of Polish patriotism and chauvinism – simply served to justify the dismissal of Osmecki and Bokszczanin's warnings is beside the point. As historian Alexandra Richie underlines, the *AK* leadership had a choice whether to move forward with the uprising immediately or to wait a little longer; ultimately, it was the Varsovian public who would pay the price for their decision.[38]

On 25 July, Komorowski notified London that, in accordance with his judgement of the situation, he was placing resistance forces on stand-by. The government-in-exile felt they had little choice but to entrust the final decision to the leadership on the ground, and Mikołajczyk signalled his acquiescence to the delegate in Warsaw; 'if possible, advise us beforehand' was his only request.[39] The *AK* sprang into action to mobilise and prepare their forces across the city in readiness for the command to attack. Arms that had been hidden or buried had to be retrieved, cleaned, and distributed in complete secrecy. Resistance troops hurried to kit themselves out in rough and ready uniforms from the things they had to hand; some 'borrowed' helmets from the crosses over the graves of Polish troops who had died defending the city in 1939, while others requisitioned SS combat jackets from local factories. Polish girls took charge of making red and white armbands which were to become an emblem of the uprising as 'the only standard part of [an] otherwise crazy mixture of civilian and military outfits of all ages, styles, and colours.'[40] As elsewhere in underground operations, young female messengers played an instrumental role in distributing information so that the fighters knew where to assemble at the commencement of the uprising. The *AK*'s chain of command was inevitably slowed by the need for secrecy so long as the enemy still occupied the city. Yet despite the logistical challenges, the leadership determined that – thanks to the by now well-oiled machinery of underground liaisons – they were in a position to trigger the uprising with just 24 hours' notice.[41]

But the *AK* weren't the only ones mobilising. News reached Warsaw that the Soviets had officially declared both the government-in-exile and the underground civic authorities illegal – and, even more dismissively, 'ephemeral and of no consequence at all.'[42] Instead, the Soviets had succeeded in establishing their own *Polski Komitet Wyzwolenia Narodowego* ('Polish Committee of National Liberation' or *PKWN*) in Lublin that was to become the *de facto* Polish government upon liberation. At the same time, the Communist-leaning People's Army was starting to make noises about its own uprising, and Soviet radio stations *Kościuszko* and *Moskva* filled the clandestine airwaves with calls-to-arms in Polish:

> Warsaw … hears … the … guns [of the] Polish Army … trained in the USSR, now joined by the People's Army to form … the Polish Armed Forces … Its ranks will be joined tomorrow by the sons of Warsaw. They wipe out the Hitlerian vermin … Poles, the time of liberation is at hand! Poles, to arms![43]

Stalin had continued raising troops under a Polish banner even after the departure of the Anders Army from the Soviet Union. Whilst many of the recruits were from the eastern parts of Poland – mainly men who had been conscripted into the Red Army between the Soviet occupation of the region and the German invasion of 1941 – others, particularly the officers, were non-Polish Soviet citizens. The new formation was commanded by General Zygmunt Berling, a veteran of Poland's independence struggle. He had been discharged from the Polish Army in the summer of 1939 and was arrested by the *NKVD*, but was released to join the Anders Army; he refused to leave with the rest of the army and commanded Polish units within the Red Army that developed into the First Polish Army. Stalin was aware of the symbolic importance of Poles leading the Red Army into Poland, and First Polish Army was inserted into Rokossovsky's 1st Belarusian Front as it approached the Vistula. The *AK* knew that to delay much longer was to risk allowing the city to be liberated by Berling's troops, which would indeed render any concept of future Polish independence 'ephemeral'. There were, to quote Korboński, 'two plans for an uprising in Warsaw': one Polish, one Soviet, and it was critical that the 'realisation of the Polish plan forestalled the realisation of the Soviet plan.'[44] In fact, the *AK* leadership were so committed to this that they dismissed any idea of establishing direct contact with the Soviet High Command, presuming instead that Soviet and Polish efforts would mesh seamlessly together once the uprising began. To make such assumptions on the part of Stalin would prove to have terrible consequences.

After their initial panic, there were signs that German resolve was hardening, too. Just four days after he had evacuated the city, Governor Fischer reappeared in Warsaw and issued an order for 10,000 Varsovian men to begin digging trenches and fortifying the city. The *AK* ordered Varsovians not to comply, and only a 'handful' of men – mostly invalids and elderly not affiliated to the resistance – responded to the announcement.[45] Fearing the damage that could be inflicted on the *AK* forces if the Germans chose to round men up by force, local *AK* commander Colonel Antoni 'Monter' Chruściel called for the uprising to be brought forward and issued the order for final mobilisation without consulting other *AK* leaders. As it happened, the Germans did not press the Polish public, most likely because they were well aware they were sitting on 'a volcano on the point of eruption', and the order for mobilisation was quickly cancelled.[46] But it was too late: the Poles had taken another irrevocable step towards the uprising. Thousands of men and women had already hurried to their designated stations in the belief that the fighting was about to begin; the false start only succeeded in frustrating the *AK* rank and file further while compounding the pressure on Komorowski. As Richie explains, 'to cancel the mobilisation order a second time, he felt, would have a disastrous impact on morale.'[47]

Moreover, in their concern for protecting the able-bodied men in their ranks, the *AK* leadership failed to heed the Germans' broader motive for fortifying Warsaw. In the final days of July, SS and Gestapo personnel began to fill the city once more, pillboxes and barbed-wire barricades sprang up around key locations, armed cars moved through the streets, and Germans who had left the city illegally were arrested. The reason for this came from the Führer himself. Hitler was furious that German forces had fled Warsaw and ordered them to reverse their retreat. Warsaw, he decreed, was to become a 'fortress city': it was to hold out against the Soviets at all costs and Germans were forbidden to withdraw without his authorisation. He appointed Generalleutnant Rainer Stahel, who had been awarded the Knight's Cross for his defence of Vilnius, to oversee the defence of the city. Even if the Poles had no way of knowing all of this, the signs were plain to see that the Germans weren't about to abandon Warsaw without a fight – and that their return to the city streets had drastically shifted odds against the *AK*.

'Nothing we can do'[48]

Still, the resistance leadership pressed on. Soviet propaganda calling for an uprising was reaching fever pitch, and Komorowski chose to read into this that the 'Russians judged the situation ripe for the beginning of our fight'. Again, that the *AK* were prepared to place so much blind trust in Soviet signals seems extraordinary. Even Komorowski acknowledged that the Soviets' proclamations 'were nothing new', so to attribute the final call for mobilisation to particular instances of propaganda seems completely illogical.[49] Indeed, during early meetings on 31 July, the *AK* leadership generally concluded that the time was still not right to guarantee victory over the German forces. During a late afternoon conference, however, Colonel Chruściel arrived with intelligence that reignited Komorowski's optimism: 'Soviet tanks were already approaching the suburb of Praga,' he announced, and 'a number of localities in the immediate vicinity of the capital – Radość, Miłosna, Okuniew, Wołomin, and Radzymin – were already in Soviet hands.'[50] There was no time to lose if the *AK* was to lead the city's liberation before the Soviets arrived. With government delegate Jan Jankowski's approval, Komorowski gave the order to Chruściel: 'tomorrow, at 1700 hours precisely, you will start operations in Warsaw.'[51]

Almost immediately after runners were dispatched to prepare the order for distribution across Warsaw, Komorowski received an unwelcome shock. Outside of the meeting room, he ran into Osmecki, who had not been present when the final decision was taken. The chief of intelligence arrived bearing the worst possible news: 'I have the latest dispatches from my people on the ground. There is no doubt that the Praga bridgehead has not been broken,' he told Komorowski, 'The Germans are preparing a counterattack.'[52] This time, Komorowski did not dismiss the intelligence because he did not believe it; it had simply arrived too late. The conversation with Osmecki is conspicuously absent from the general's memoirs, as is the fact that he refused to countenance reversing the order to mobilise. In fact, it had taken at least an hour for Chruściel to issue the mobilisation order, as it had to be coded before being distributed; very few, if any, *AK* units would have received the command before the German-enforced curfew forced the runners to retire for the night at 8pm. Logistically speaking, it is possible that Komorowski could have rescinded the order, or at least tried to do so. From other accounts it is clear he certainly realised the significance of his error, but felt – or decided – there was nothing more he could do.[53]

This incident cut to the heart of the controversy surrounding the uprising and its timing. It was convenient for the *AK* to ascribe events to the inevitability of fate, and to justify the order to mobilise as something that was largely out of their control – whether due to public restlessness, the approach of the Soviets, or signs of German defeat. In deciding to take their cues from these external factors, they wilfully overlooked key pieces of intelligence that didn't sit comfortably with their plans. Jan Rosinski recounted in his memoirs another incident that demonstrated the almost dogmatic intransigence of the *AK* command:

> Three days before the uprising, I was summoned to an *AK* meeting called by *AK* commanders in the city. I and the others assembled there were told that the uprising would achieve great things. Our success, they said, would enable us to join with the allies to defeat the Germans, who were now fighting on two fronts. The briefer, a young lieutenant, continued to voice his optimistic predictions, and I could no longer hold my growing frustration: 'The Germans will simply destroy us! The *Hermann Göring* Division is poised on the outskirts of the city. They will burn Warsaw to the ground! We will not meet up with any allies or the Russian army because we will not exist.' There was stony silence in the room … The officer turned to me and finally could only say, 'Well, we must fight the best we can.' 'Fight with what?' I asked. He replied, 'We just need to launch the uprising.'
>
> 'I'm for action, but not suicide,' I almost shouted back. 'We need to survive this occupation to be the new leadership for Poland after the war, after Germany is defeated. We can't do that from the grave. This is nothing but suicide. Are those orders for people without arms?' I spoke without regard to rank or status, and I was the only one present to do so. No one else voiced any objections. Finally in exasperation, I blurted out, 'Did you all lose your minds?'
>
> As events turned out, that was my last meeting with my AK commanders … Perhaps I was no longer regarded as important, as I learned of the [mobilisation] order indirectly by word of mouth.[54]

Osmecki's intelligence was correct. After a month of breathless advances, the Soviets were facing major setbacks. The Germans deployed around 450 tanks and self-propelled guns near Praga in an attempt to halt the Red Army's progress and by 31 July, just as the *AK* resolved to start the uprising, the advantage turned in the Wehrmacht's favour.

The first day of August dawned a humid, cloudy, and drizzly day. Beneath the surface of everyday street life – people attending Mass, shopping, and visiting neighbours – the city was electric with excitement. Women hurried through the streets carrying bundles and bags as they transported weaponry to waiting *AK* units; young men faced the summer heat in heavy trench coats concealing arms and ammunition; nearly everyone, Komorowski observed, seemed to be laden with conspicuous baggage that risked attracting attention from the constant German patrols.[55] Underground courier Leokadia Rowińska remarked that there were so many suitcases being ferried around the city it was as though everyone in Warsaw 'had decided to take their vacation at the same time and were on their way to their chosen vacation spots'; those that looked as though they were skiing were in fact 'medics bringing stretchers to their designated medical stations'.[56] The day was marked by thousands of Varsovians meeting loved ones, friends, and neighbours, praying and enjoying final meals together before saying their goodbyes with a mixture of excitement and terror. Others slipped away silently to take up their posts, either because they preferred not to stand on ceremony or because they could not face the heartbreak of uncertain farewells. Irena Orska had joined the *AK* alongside her two brothers and two sisters as a nurse, but her worst fears were realised on the day of mobilisation when she learned her 13-year-old daughter was also involved:

> 'I got to tell you something, Mummy,' said Barbarka ... 'I can't stay home this afternoon. I have to go ... to work.'
>
> 'To work? Barbarka, what are you talking about?'
>
> 'Well, to my post.'
>
> 'At what time?'
>
> I heard my voice then, it sounded calm. Yet I could feel my heart pounding.
>
> 'At five o'clock I have to be there,' Barbarka spoke evenly, without hesitation, and her own brown eyes looked straight into mine.
>
> I knew that I could not fail her then. The frail human hope of saving a life that was dearest above all no longer mattered.
>
> 'I'm going too,' I heard my voice saying. It was still calm ... I felt it then, this miracle of Barbarka's life that I, myself, was ready to bring in a supreme sacrifice to the German bullets ... It was not my hand that was cold this time. It was my heart.[57]

Given their lack of training, experience in urban warfare, and, critically, armaments, the *AK*'s practical objectives for the uprising were highly ambitious. In the first place, the resistance was to target key communication hubs, logistical sites, and administration centres to dismantle the Germans' apparatus of power across the city, with German police and soldiers disarmed and neutralised along the way. Once the city was liberated from the occupiers, the *AK* planned to establish two defensive cordons around the eastern sector of the city – one to the east of Praga, and the other from Bielany down to Siekierki on the west bank of the Vistula – to insulate the area from further German reinforcements. One significant problem was that having committed themselves so fully to the idea that the Germans would be easily overcome, the *AK* leadership failed to draw up detailed contingency plans in case their forces faced serious opposition – or defeat. Another was that the initial intentions for the uprising had been defined by Rowecki, who had worked under the assumption that the Poles would benefit from aid from the Allies and reinforcement from Polish troops arriving from the west.

When the moment actually arrived, the *AK* stood alone. The Poles had approached the British SOE in late July with six key demands for support during the uprising: an increase in airdrops; the bombing of German-controlled airfields around Warsaw; Polish fighter squadrons to be transferred to the city as soon as the resistance had captured the airfields; the Polish parachute brigade to be dispatched; the Polish *AK* to be recognised as an official component of the Allied fighting forces; and an Allied military mission to be sent to Komorowski's aid. It was General Stanisław Tatar who presented these demands, evidently unaware that the combined chiefs of staff stationed in London had decided it was more prudent to '[urge] the Poles not to arm their secret army, but to concentrate on sabotage of communications.'[58] The prospect of deploying the parachute brigade was dismissed as a logistical nightmare, and diverting more aircraft from operations in the west was met with resistance by the RAF. The result was that, despite assurances from both SOE and Churchill that the resistance would be supported, the only demand that was fulfilled was the recognition of the Poles' combatant status – and this not until the very end of August. Of course, the Poles had been forewarned that they couldn't necessarily rely on Allied support. When Nowak parachuted into Warsaw on 30 July, he explicitly informed the *AK* leadership that the parachute brigade was unlikely to materialise. Moreover, Sosnkowski had been complaining to SOE since autumn of 1943 of the insufficiency of their arms airdrops, in terms of both the frequency and quality of supplies; he warned the Allies that further dereliction of this duty to Poland would 'prevent the Secret Army [*AK*] from carrying out not only its conspiratorial activities and intelligence work, but also the destruction of German lines of communication.'[59] His words had little effect, but he was proven correct almost as soon as the uprising began.

It is hard to quantify the true numbers of resistance fighters available for mobilisation on 1 August, but the figure likely sat somewhere between 28,000 and 35,000 men, plus around 4,200 women. What is clear is that the supply of weaponry was so 'deplorable' that at the start of the uprising only around one tenth of insurgents carried guns, and that there was only enough ammunition to last a week at the very most.[60] Others carried stones, improvised weapons, or were expected to collect the guns off the corpses of their fellow fighters who died in action. Many of their weapons were in such poor repair as to render them useless if not downright dangerous; Julian Kulski was armed with an old Polish rifle that had been buried in 1939 and was so rusty that he was almost killed the very first time he fired it.[61] Then there was the issue that resistance troops had generally been trained to launch their attacks at night, and were not prepared for the extra exposure that came with operating in broad daylight.

Warsaw had already suffered terribly during the course of the war, but its greatest ordeal was about to begin. The *AK* leadership were stuck in a position where there were no longer any good choices available. If they did nothing, the Red Army would 'liberate' the city and crush any groups deemed to be anti-Soviet; if they triggered the Uprising, they faced huge odds. Their only hope lay in receiving substantial help from the outside world. The failure of this help to arrive doomed Warsaw and its inhabitants to an episode of concentrated horror and destruction.

CHAPTER 11

TRAGEDY

We await you
We're waiting for you, O scarlet plague
To save us from the Black Death:
Waiting for a salvation
To be welcomed with disgust
By a country that's already hanged and quartered ...

We are waiting whilst you delay and delay.
We know very well that you fear us.
That you'd prefer us to be killed.
So you are waiting, too – for our extermination.

Józef Szczepanski, 'The Scarlet Plague', 1944
Translated by Norman Davies[1]

GODZINA W

Godzina W ('W-Hour', as the start time of the Uprising was codenamed) had been chosen so that resistance units could make their final preparations under the cover of heavy city traffic as office and factory workers thronged homewards. The plan was to capitalise on the remaining daylight to take the Germans by surprise and seize enemy positions before the occupiers had a chance to organise any significant opposition. In the final hours before the appointed time, members of the *AK* took up their stations in chosen buildings around key targets – railways, barracks, stores, or public works departments – requisitioning flats and apartments from civilians who 'did their best to help in every way and offered their best food.'[2] The mobilisation was by no means perfect, with the combination of short notice and precarious communications networks leaving a number of units stationed outside of the city unable to cross the German and Soviet lines in time to join the Uprising. Overall, though, that tens of thousands of fighters were assembled according to plan in less than a single day testifies to the Varsovians' appetite for the coming fight:

> The soldiers brought out their arms and put on white-and-red armbands, the first sign of a Polish Army on Polish soil since the occupation. For five years they had all awaited this moment. Now the last seconds seemed an eternity. At five o'clock they would cease to be an underground resistance movement and would become once more Regular soldiers fighting in the open.
>
> At exactly five o'clock thousands of windows flashed as they were flung open. From all sides a hail of bullets struck passing Germans, riddling their buildings and their marching formations. In the twinkling of an eye, the remaining civilians disappeared from the streets. From the entrances of the houses, our men streamed out and rushed into the attack. In fifteen minutes an entire city of a million inhabitants was engulfed in the fight. Every kind of traffic ceased. As a big communications centre where roads from north, south, east and west converged, in the immediate rear of the German front, Warsaw ceased to exist. The battle for the city was on.[3]

The fighting that raged around Radzymin is beyond the scope of this work.[4] The terrain – a mixture of low hills and patches of dense woodland, with few good roads running through it – resulted in a series of confused battles. To add to the problems for the Germans, there were units from three different military commands involved: the regular army, the SS, and the Luftwaffe, the latter in the form of the *Hermann Göring* panzer division, a personal vanity project of the head of the Luftwaffe. There were constant disagreements and attempts to blame other services for errors or failures, but the confusion was even greater on the Soviet side. Major General Aleksei Ivanovich Radzievsky lost control of the disparate corps of his Second Tank Army advancing along the Vistula valley from the south; with the formations unable to provide mutual support, the Germans were able to pick them off in turn. At the same time, the units of Rokossovsky's 1st Belarusian Front were exhausted and badly weakened by their advance from the east and the Germans were able to fend them off long enough to conduct their counteroffensive. Varsovians could still hear the thunder of artillery and tank fire but had no way of knowing that far from heralding the arrival of the

Red Army, it represented the end of the Soviet advance and the German retreat – albeit for just a few months. The Warsaw Uprising started at the very moment that the possibility of the arrival of friendly – or at least German-hostile – forces dropped almost to zero.

Contrary to official plans, fighting broke out over three hours before *Godzina W* in the northern district of Żoliborz. The *Żniwiarz* ('Reaper') group were ferrying arms from a weapons warehouse to Krasiński Street when they crossed paths with a German patrol whose suspicions were aroused by the Poles' heavy winter clothing. 'There was a moment when we were clearly observing each other,' the platoon leader and former journalist Zdzisław Sierpiński later recalled, 'it was obvious that the Germans were making some kind of profit and loss calculation.' Deciding it wasn't worth waiting for the German reaction, Sierpiński

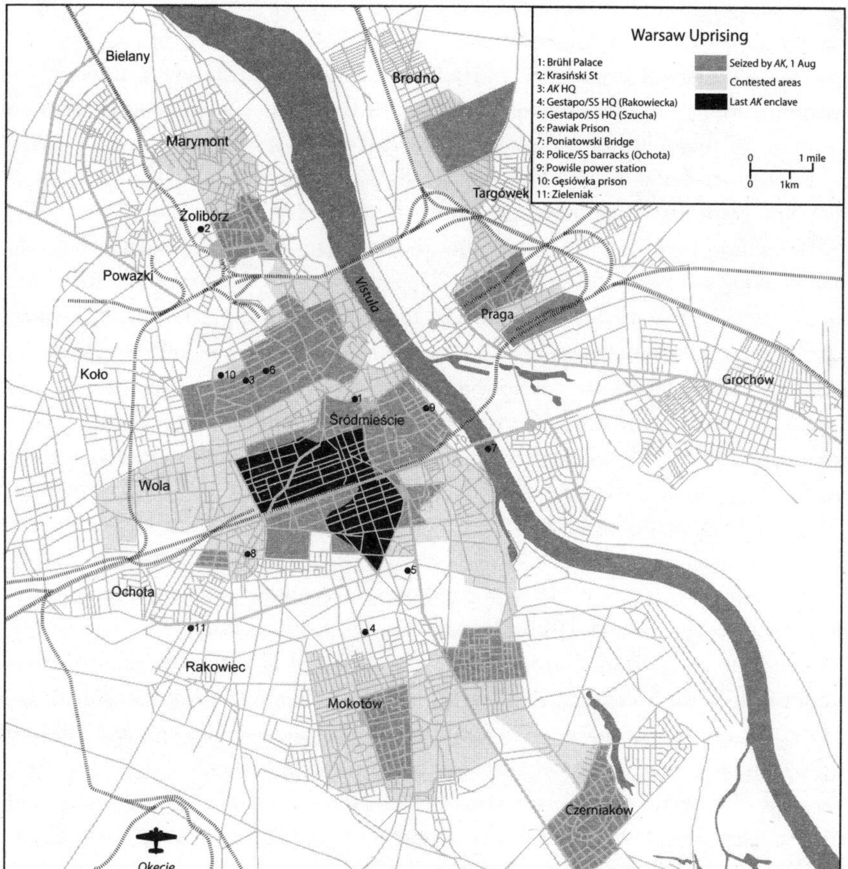

drew his gun, shouting, 'Halt! *Hände hoch*!' and fired the first shot of the Warsaw Uprising.[5] Kulski, whose unit was patrolling down the street, was also drawn into the chaotic attack:

> A German patrol truck drove quite slowly down Krasiński Street. Seeing the column, the Germans brought the vehicle to a screeching halt and opened fire on the men in the middle of the boulevard.
>
> 'Świda' [Sierpiński] responded with his Sten gun; one of his men pulled a light machine gun out of a sack, took up position and, after firing a short salvo, uttered a curse: his gun was stuck. At that moment, 'Wilk' and 'Horodeński' entered the action.
>
> The Germans, surprised by the fire on their flank from the other side of Krasiński Street, turned around. This gave the opportunity to the 'Świda' group to withdraw to Kochowska Street.[6]

The insurgents succeeded in finding cover and hurriedly distributed their weapons. The Germans soon returned with two truckloads of SS. By the time *Godzina W* rolled around, German tanks had taken up positions on the main boulevard intersections around Kulski and his comrades, and the fighters in Żoliborz could hardly cross the street for all the gunfire.

The start of the Uprising didn't go quite to plan for Komorowski either. He had chosen to situate his command headquarters in the Kammler furniture factory which sat next door to a tobacco factory housing a garrison of SS troops. On his arrival in the afternoon of 1 August, Komorowski was informed that the situation with regard to their neighbours wasn't looking good; against the Germans' newly-reinforced 50 men and two machine-guns, the *AK* had around 33 men, 'fifteen rifles, forty grenades, and a few *filipinki* [home-made hand grenades].'[7] If the Germans' suspicions were already aroused, they were soon confirmed when they spotted armed Polish sentries. The Kammler factory and surrounding streets came under such heavy fire that the *Kedyw* Battalion sent to protect Komorowski was delayed for hours and finally reached him only by blasting through the attics of buildings from Okopowa Street.[8]

The abnormal traffic around the city prior to *Godzina W* hadn't gone unnoticed by the Germans, and by 4pm Stahel had issued a general alert to his forces. An hour later, many units hadn't received the order, allowing the Poles to take some German positions in a state of unpreparedness, if not complete surprise. The occupation authorities quickly turned on the loudspeakers around the city, declaring that operations to suppress the insurgents were about to begin and that anyone found in the street would be fired upon. Amongst the first insurgent casualties was the 15-year-old 'Sadovski', who was burned by a German flamethrower on Flora Street; also the 30-year-old nurse, Krystyna 'Danuta' Krahelska, who as well as penning the popular Uprising song, 'Fix bayonets, lads', once posed as a model for one of Warsaw's mermaid statues. She was shot as she rushed to the aid of a wounded soldier.[9]

VAINGLORY AND VENGEANCE

In general, however, the long wait for the Uprising, the last-minute scramble to mobilise, and the chaotic, uneven outbreak of fighting culminated in an evening of vainglorious optimism for the *AK* forces. Key targets including a German garrison, the Prudential Building, the Post Office Savings Bank, and the Town Hall were seized by Polish forces, and red and white flags unfurled against the evening sky; 'for the first time in five years', Komorowski wrote, 'the Polish colours were once more floating defiantly over the city.' As he gazed upwards at the banners and the 'glare over the city, the smoke rising from burning houses', he and other Varsovians shared the conviction that 'all these should be visible to the forward Soviet troops on the Warsaw bridgehead.'[10] Damage to the *AK* Command's radio equipment during the bombardment on the Kammler factory meant Komorowski couldn't alert London that the Uprising had begun until the following day. 'Arrange immediately for ammunition and arms to be dropped' were his demands; 'we ask for Soviet help to be supplied by an immediate attack from the outside.'[11] Such expectations were to be profoundly disappointed.

The early days of August saw the civilian population swept up in the spirit of resistance and throwing themselves into the Uprising in a manner that, they probably thought, would have made their Varsovian ancestors proud. Those not engaged in combat showed great inventiveness and resourcefulness in supporting the insurgents, coordinating shelters, and building barricades. Diarist Miron Białoszewski described:

> People began organising. Block leaders. Duty tours. Digging cellars. Tunnelling underground passageways. Barricades … Meetings and conferences in the courtyards. Assignments: who, what …
>
> The first barricades, wooden, weren't worth anything. The tanks rode right over them. Shells set them on fire in an instant … So people started tearing up the concrete slabs from the sidewalks, the cobblestones from the streets … The trolley drivers had prepared iron crowbars and pickaxes for the Uprising. They handed them out to the people …

> Everything was done stealthily, at a run, under cover of the barricades. At the intersection the trolley wires were torn and twisted from the crossfire; someone had hung a portrait of Hitler on them and this infuriated the Germans. They were shooting at that intersection.[12]

As one member of the *AL* recorded in his diary, the fighters were grateful to receive aid from Varsovians of all ages:

> The enemy has been attacking all day with short breaks. The troops are tired. It is the thirst that is most nagging. If only one could get some water from somewhere. Then all of a sudden a ten-year-old kid appears out of the blue with a can full of delicious cold lemonade. You have to keep quiet at the outpost; otherwise, the boy would have been greeted with a roar of joy. The boy receives his dreamt of prize: he is allowed to hold a real rifle, a rifle bigger than himself, in his hand for a few minutes.[13]

Many civilians died during the first hours of fighting, cut off from their homes or, like Eugenia Kowalewska's husband, caught in the crossfire as the Germans began 'shooting at anyone they could see'.[14] Others were sought out more deliberately and made to pay for the insurgents' actions in brutal reprisals. On Hutnicza Street, three *AK* fighters broke into Aleksandra Biegaj's house just 15 minutes after the Uprising's commencement; minutes later, a tank-load of drunken Germans rolled down the street and ordered all residents out into the courtyard. Ten men, including Biegaj's husband and the three insurgents, were separated from the women and children and marched to the Gley factory a few hundred yards away in Targówek. 'After desperate pleas from the women the Germans promised to set the men free after checking their papers,' Biegaj testified, 'but after a few minutes shots could be heard. All the men were killed.'[15] These early executions were a sign of things to come, whereby the Germans indiscriminately targeted able-bodied Polish men whether or not they were involved in the resistance. On Ziemowita Street, Maria Winiarska's son was taken and shot in what she assumed was 'revenge' for insurgents throwing grenades at Germans, even though, 'in all probability, the throwing of grenades was intended to be a signal of sorts, for at the time there had been no German soldiers in the street.'[16] A little later, Stanisław Mączka was returning home from work with his wife and four-year-old son when they hurried into a shelter to avoid approaching German tanks; he ended up separated from his family and was shot with 16 other men accused of being 'bandits' in the centre of Cyryla i Metodego Street.[17] In most, if not all, of these cases, the Germans' restrictions on movement meant that families were unable to retrieve and bury the bodies of their loved ones for days after they were murdered.

Some *AK* units fought more effectively than others. About 100 men of the 'Stag' battalion, a mixture of former servicemen and new recruits, made a foolhardy frontal attack on German bunkers on the edge of the police district. Their pistols made little impression on the German defenders, who gunned down all but seven of the attackers. By contrast, when a group of fighters of the pro-Communist People's Army came under attack by Tiger tanks and panzergrenadiers from the *Hermann Göring* division, the *Parasol* battalion succeeded in drawing off the German force from the flank and rear and forced it to retreat. Shortly after, the battalion captured three armoured cars and a considerable quantity of guns and ammunition. Casualties, while not negligible, were not disproportionately high.[18]

The Poles' brazen assault bought them significant control of the city, but not the strategic advantages that would be vital for them to be able to hold out. In the first days alone, the Poles suffered around 2,000 casualties to the Germans' 500, and an ongoing failure to concentrate on taking key landmarks meant their gains were largely superficial.[19] This was not for lack of ambition; Chruściel had drawn up an extensive list of targets across the city, including the four Vistula bridges, Warsaw's two airports at Bielany and Okęcie, the Gestapo headquarters on Rakowiecka Street and Aleja Szucha, the SS barracks in Mokotów and Ochota, and other major complexes and railways stations – the majority of which eluded capture at great cost to the *AK*. Komorowski praised the insurgents' 'impetuous fervour', 'drive', and 'enthusiasm' in the first onslaught of attacks, but these were no match for the Germans' discipline, experience, and weaponry. As the general himself conceded, 'this enthusiasm had its disadvantages also. It was impossible to impose strict discipline in the use of ammunition; one solitary German would attract a hail of bullets.'[20] Nor did it help that as many as 5,000 insurgents resorted to their old underground tactic of retreating into the forests around Warsaw to regroup, which was especially baffling in the context of trying to wrest the city from enemy control.[21] The Poles' patriotic bravado frequently bordered on the theatrical, and certainly didn't always reflect the 'organised military operation' Komorowski claimed to have put into motion. On the second day of the Uprising, 18-year-old Zbigniew Dębczyński was amused to see 'an old man with a fine pair of whiskers and beard holding a naked sabre in his hand' alongside a group of his *AK* comrades; 'Very 1863,' was his remark, in reference to the ill-fated January uprising against the Prussians.[22]

Of course, the failure of the *AK* to seize so many of their pre-defined targets was probably less because of tactical errors than the fact that they faced such impossible odds in the first place. The inconsistency of mobilisation, the dire shortage of arms and ammunition, and the tenuousness of underground strategy makes successes – such as the seizing of two German tanks (dubbed the 'Wacek Panzer Platoon'), the capture of the Powiśle power station after a 19-hour siege, and the securing of large swathes of the Wola district – all the more notable. Elsewhere, the *AK* seized the nightmarish Gęsiówka prison, the concentration camp built on the ruins of the ghetto where Jews from across Europe were interned before being deported to the death camps. Under the supervision of Battalion *Zóska*'s Wacław 'Wacek' Micuta, a Polish cavalry veteran, fighters commandeered one of the captured German tanks to storm the walls surrounding the camp; Micuta's superiors had dismissed the mission as hopeless, but his crew managed to take the Germans by surprise and succeeded in freeing hundreds of emaciated Jewish prisoners whose only hope of escape had been death. Even more astonishing was Micuta's discovery of a group inside the camp who stood to attention and presented themselves as a Jewish battalion ready to join his ranks.[23] Some of these men, like Henryk Lederman, had fought in the Ghetto Uprising 14 months previously and had been confined to Gęsiówka ever since; the majority of them would perish in the 1944 Uprising.

Dozens of *ŻOB* members who had escaped after the Ghetto Uprising regrouped into a new platoon under the leadership of Yitzhak Zuckerman, Zivia Lubetkin, and Marek Edelman, and prepared themselves to join the general Uprising. However, relations between the general resistance leadership and the ghetto fighters remained strained, and when the Jews' approaches to join the *AK* as a unit were rebuffed, they turned instead to its pro-Soviet rival, the *AL*. At least 500 individual Jewish men and women joined the ranks of the *AK*, but usually under assumed names or as acculturated Catholic converts.[24] It is a sad truth that over the previous year, prevailing undercurrents of antisemitism combined with fears of further alienation had left many Jews unwilling to reveal their true identities to the Varsovians they hoped to fight alongside. Once the Uprising began, some, like 16-year-old Krystyna Bierzyńska, were so fully accepted by the *AK* as irreproachable Polish patriots that they felt safe enough to drop their assumed identities. Unfortunately, not all were so lucky; there were incidents when *AK* commanders had to intercede to help Jews who were exposed within their units, and others where Jews were even murdered by their fellow fighters. Even if, as has been claimed, these accounted for only 30 of the 4,500 Jewish deaths over the course of the Uprising, it is a damning reminder of the divisions still present in Polish society, and that the *AK*'s claim it was 'reclaiming Warsaw as the capital of a democratic, independent Poland' meant very different things to different members within its own ranks.[25]

CIVILIAN MOBILISATION

If the *AK*'s prospects of success didn't look the best, they would have been far worse without popular support across Warsaw. The public appetite for resistance was buoyed by the sight of red and white flags around the city, by the long-absent sound of the Polish national anthem on the streets, by the boom of Soviet guns in the distance, and by the optimistic newspaper headlines of the early days. The underground weekly *Biuletyn Informacyjny* began publishing every day from 2 August and by the end of August, 15 newspapers circulated across the various isolated Warsaw districts; perhaps more than ever, the clandestine press played a significant role in informing and influencing the mood of Varsovian civilians as city life around them collapsed. These papers spread stories of the 'exemplary punishment' meted out to the German oppressors while amplifying announcements from the *AK*'s command and highlighting developments – albeit selectively – on the Eastern and Western Fronts.[26] Bartoszewski has shown how this was only made possible through the dogged efforts of editorial staff, writers, photojournalists, typesetters, copiers, and distributors who 'did not leave their posts in the most critical situations' but 'dug up buried machines and printing boxes from the rubble, took equipment out of burning houses and moved it from place to place, stood by the radios [and] … tirelessly sought paper and ink'.[27] At the same time, the Poles managed to recapture the *nur für Deutsche* Palladium Cinema and began airing *AK* newsreels documenting insurgent and civilian successes to boost public morale.

Another remarkable element of civilian resistance was the postal service, which was staffed by the ten- to 15-year-old boys and girls of the Grey Ranks scout movement. From the first week of the Uprising, these youngsters helped establish communications between the liberated districts of the city to keep families, friends, and allies in touch with each other. Messages were limited to 25 words and subject to censorship for reasons of military security, but use of the service was entirely free and was well received: on 13 August, correspondence peaked at 10,000 messages delivered in a single day. At first, rudimentary postmark stamps were fashioned out of linoleum, rubber, and even potatoes cut in half and carved with the Scouts' lily emblem, but when the postal service was officially incorporated into the *AK* in September, these were replaced by specially created 'Army Postal Service' stamps.[28] These insurgency stamps – which came in five variations in honour of the five liberated city districts – were for some time sought out by German intelligence officers to prove to their superiors that they had, beyond any doubt, infiltrated enemy territory and that their reports were credible.[29]

It is just one of the tragic ironies of the situation in which the Poles found themselves that at the same time that the *AK* and Varsovian public were holding out for Red Army support they were still grappling with the repercussions of Soviet crimes committed years before. The Katyn massacre had drastically diminished the ranks of Polish doctors and medical personnel available to support the Uprising; young students and nurses stepped up in their stead, many having come up through the Flying University courses under occupation, frequently with minimal practising experience. Both civilian and *AK* medics worked tirelessly in deteriorating conditions, supported in procuring resources, transporting the wounded, and burying the dead by hundreds more volunteers. Irena Zgrych's house on Furmańska Street was transformed into a first-aid post staffed largely by young girls and scouts; the improvised clinic housed around 40 patients at a time, the majority of whom were wounded not in direct combat but by a sniper who preyed on the neighbourhood from a nearby rooftop.[30] Nurse Irena Orska swept through the wrecked city streets in the wake of *AK* skirmishes to attend to the wounded, carrying them to shelter or else tending to their wounds on the crumbling pavement. She watched as civilians crept out of hiding bearing pitchers of water for the fighters, 'scared to death, yet … stuck to their errands of mercy,' and how the women bathed their handkerchiefs in the blood of the 'martyrs' – 'grim mementoes for those who would live happily in the days to come in a Free Poland.'[31] The *AK* member who had spoken out against the Uprising, Jan Rosinksi, attached himself to the Maltanski Hospital and helped with the collection of medicines, vitamins, blankets, and bandages from across the city. On one occasion, the abrasive 27-year-old struck a Polish colonel who refused to hand over supplies to the civilian hospital; 'Look Colonel, I don't care if I'll be hanged or not – by you, Russians, or Germans,' Rosinski stormed, handing over his name and address in case the wronged officer wanted to court-martial him. 'I'm supposed to deliver bandages, so I'll deliver bandages, and you will not stop me!'[32]

As in every iteration of resistance through Polish history, the Uprising couldn't claim to have unanimous and unwavering public support. Some, like Rosinski, remained highly sceptical and only expected the conflict to hasten another Varsovian catastrophe. 'Now it begins, they will kill us all!' he lamented to a close friend, 'the Russians won't help us at all.'[33] Others – like Zygmunt Skarbek-Kruszewski – saw the Uprising as just the latest in a long line of Polish insurgencies doomed to failure; any victory, he believed, would be a pyrrhic one thanks to the unresolved divisions in Polish society and the contentiousness of Poland's national identity on the world stage. He perceptively explained the contradictions to an aspiring insurgent:

> 'We are all speaking about independence, about free Poland, but in reality we are thinking about a system of government which suits us best. For you, independence

means Christian bourgeois democracy; for other radicals – it is the People's Republic. To reach the desired aim some will welcome the help of England, others the help of Russia ...

'Can we say with a clear conscience that we all aspire to the one goal? Do you think that General Bór-Komorowski, Chief Commander of *AK*, has coordinated his military strategy with General Berling, Chief Commander of *AL*? And that Prime Minister Mikołajczyk his political ideas with Prime Minister Osóbka-Morawski? Already for three days Warsaw has been fighting and bleeding and at this time they are bartering in Moscow about Poland's future government.

'Our history,' I continued, 'gave us many sad examples in the so-called "aspiration of common aim". Just as well that this time our emigrant leaders found some support with foreign allies, otherwise Poles would now be fighting each other. Is there just the one common cause? Independence? Democracy? Those are just words, not the real issue. Why should we deceive ourselves? In Poland before 1939 did the words independence and democracy have the same meaning for a landless peasant as for the wealthy mine owner? For whose independence are we fighting?'[34]

Politics aside, many Varsovians were simply exhausted by five years of life under occupation. They worried that the insurgency would not justify another wave of hardship, food shortages, and, if things did not go to plan, German reprisals. Even away from the immediate fighting, the reality of living under bombardment was taking its toll; families and friends were divided, basic amenities fast disappearing, and the entire city cut off from the outside world. Nevertheless, lack of enthusiasm for the Uprising did not tend to translate into outright opposition to it; after all, Varsovians hardly had any alternative. The Germans made no attempt to prise civilian sympathy away from the *AK*, and, even if they had, years of oppression and brutality had left an irrevocable rift between the occupiers and the occupied. In any case, things were about to get much, much worse for the Poles.

SETTING AN EXAMPLE

In Berlin, the first reports of unrest in Warsaw were dismissed with the assumption that local German forces would be able to restore order quickly. The mood changed as the seriousness of the situation became clear. In a fit of angry vengeance, Himmler sent orders to Sachsenhausen concentration camp, where Rowecki was being held; the former leader of the *AK* was killed by his guards, probably on 2 August. Hitler had been enraged by the precipitate flight of German officials from Warsaw, and his anger now transferred to the insurgents, but Himmler pacified him by pointing out the potential advantages of what was happening:

> *Mein Führer*, the timing is unfortunate, but from a historical perspective, the action of the Poles is a blessing. After five or six weeks we shall leave. But by then Warsaw, the intellectual capital of the former nation of 16–17 million Polish people, who have blocked our eastward path for seven hundred years ... will have ceased to exist. After this, the Polish problem will no longer be a great historical issue for the children who come after us, nor indeed for us.[35]

The German plan for Warsaw had always envisaged the destruction of the Polish city and its replacement with a modest German settlement, supported by a slave labour camp in Praga. At a time when it was clear to almost everyone that Germany could not win the war, Himmler was still committed to this agenda. To add to the surreal nature of the situation, Himmler himself had doubts about 'final victory' and was taking tentative steps to try to secure a separate peace with the Western Allies, deluding himself that they would see him as an acceptable prominent figure – perhaps even leader – of a post-war Germany.

Impressed by Himmler's words, Hitler suggested that German forces should withdraw from Warsaw and that all available aircraft should then be directed to the city to bomb it flat. It was an utterly absurd suggestion. Even if the Luftwaffe had been able to spare any planes from the Eastern Front, attempts to destroy London and Leningrad had already demonstrated that it lacked the fleets of heavy bombers used to such devastating effect by the British and Americans; the fuel shortages plaguing all parts of the German war machine would have made such an operation impossible to execute anyway. Instead, Hitler issued a new order: every citizen of Warsaw – including women and children – was to be killed. The city would be levelled, 'in order to set a terrifying example to the rest of Europe'.[36] It seems that the instructions to kill all women and children were added – probably by Himmler – a few days after the directive was issued; consequently, the first few days saw the slaughter of men who were actual or potential *AK* members, but other civilians were largely spared.

One of the *AK*'s targets for the first day of the Uprising was the capture of the Brühl Palace, now home to Stahel's headquarters. The Germans managed to beat off the attack, but the building was effectively cut off and it became almost impossible for Stahel to organise his forces. In fact, both sides faced great difficulties in coordination during the first days of the Uprising; the various parts of the city seized by the insurgents were separated from each other and the Germans controlled the major highways through Warsaw, but numerous German garrisons were trapped in isolated buildings. Almost immediately, the Germans adopted a stratagem that would become a signature tactic of the Uprising: Polish civilians were used as human shields, forced to advance in front of German troops or positioned in front of their defences. Stahel also implemented this brutal method of defence in the Brühl Palace and ordered his men to execute all Polish males who were actual or potential insurgents.[37] Meanwhile, he contacted Brigadeführer Paul Geibel, the *SSPF* in Warsaw, demanding that he fight his way from the police district to the Brühl Palace. The attack was supported by several armoured vehicles, but was beaten off by a rain of Molotov cocktails.

Stahel then contacted the headquarters of the German Ninth Army with a request it take steps to restore order. But even if General Nikolaus von Vormann had been inclined to help, he had no troops to spare. Generalfeldmarschall Walter Model, the cold-eyed commander of Army Group Centre, also dismissed any suggestion that precious front-line resources be diverted to deal with the Uprising. Aware that turmoil in a large city immediately behind his combat units would endanger the timely arrival of supplies and reinforcements, he told Gruppenführer Heinz Reinefarth, the *SSPF* of the western parts of Poland that had been annexed by Germany, to create sterile zones up to a kilometre on either side of the main highway through the city. 'Show no consideration,' he ordered. 'Otherwise we will be unable to fight our way through.'[38] Reinefarth hastily scraped together various units and set off for Warsaw.

As these and other snippets of information filtered through German channels, Hitler decided that restructuring command in the city was now unavoidable, particularly given Stahel's entrapment in the Brühl Palace. On 2 August, he appointed Bach as commandant of all units in Warsaw with orders to suppress the Uprising and to oversee the destruction of the city – and with the promise of a Knight's Cross for his efforts. Bach would later claim that he did not assume command until mid-August, but this is patently untrue. From the perspective of Hitler and Himmler, Bach's record in Belarus had shown his ability to be utterly ruthless and he was clearly the man to carry out the destruction of Warsaw. Nearly all the forces that he would command in the fighting were from the SS – it would be the largest military operation to be conducted under SS command, using almost exclusively SS troops, in the entire war.

The regular German units in Warsaw were strong enough to prevent the *AK* from taking complete control and succeeded in recapturing most of the parts of the city seized by the *AK* on the east bank, but they were too weak to restore control of the entire city, let alone to carry out the destruction demanded by Hitler.

While Reinefarth's SS and police units were hurrying in from the west, attention turned to two of the SS units that had been withdrawn from the front line during *Bagration*. The Dirlewanger brigade was in Lyck, in East Prussia, and Himmler ordered it to move to Warsaw; to increase its strength, it was assigned a battalion of men from Azerbaijan, former Red Army soldiers who had been captured by the Germans and had volunteered to serve their captors to escape the harsh conditions of prison camps. An advance guard of the brigade set off immediately for Warsaw, reaching the city on 4 August. Their commander, on the other hand, showed little sense of urgency, and disappeared to attend a wild party in Berlin. It is a measure of Dirlewanger's standing with Himmler that this resulted merely in a reprimand; 'I must express my displeasure,' he wrote, 'that despite having been warned to proceed immediately to your regiment on the aeroplane that was reserved for you, you spent several more hours in Berlin. I am used to prompt and immediate obedience.'[39]

In southeast Poland, the survivors of Kaminski's *SS-Sturmbrigade RONA* were also recuperating. The band of hardened killers – recently reinforced by fresh drafts of former Soviet soldiers and violent criminals – was ordered to proceed to Warsaw as quickly as possible. The choice of Kaminski's and Dirlewanger's brigades for the operations in Warsaw was partly because almost no other significant units were available after the disaster that had engulfed Army Group Centre in the course of *Bagration*, but was also partly due to the unique mission that lay ahead. This was not simply a mission to restore order and to suppress the Uprising; it was intended from the outset to result in the complete destruction of Warsaw – both its buildings and its inhabitants. The two brigades – with the grim reputations they had earned in Belarus – were just the blunt instruments Himmler sought for the job. Bach's euphemistic description of Dirlewanger's men reveals it wasn't only Himmler who recognised their value:

> Although their moral qualities left much to be desired, their fighting ability was extremely high. This brigade was composed exclusively of released criminals who were offered a pardon if they showed valour in battle. They had nothing to lose and everything to win. They exposed their lives without hesitation for this reason. They knew that they were respected neither by their own officers nor the enemy. They gave no mercy in battle and did not expect any.[40]

To harden the men's resolve, Reinefarth ordered his officers to circulate stories of *Volksdeutsche* who had been killed by the *AK*. The soldiers were told that the conduct of the Polish fighters – and the support shown for them by civilians – justified the killing of all Poles. The prevailing mood was that the Poles had brought German vengeance upon themselves, and some even rebuked civilians before killing them; one raged that the Poles had attacked the Reich even though Hitler was trying to protect them from Bolshevism.[41]

The East Falls Silent

The night of 3 August brought another worrying new omen for the Poles: Soviet guns across the Vistula had fallen silent. Rokossovsky's offensive had ground to a halt against the German counterattack, and at first the Soviet commander thought it would be just a matter of a couple of weeks before he could resume his advance. He anticipated being able to eliminate German positions on the east bank of the Vistula by the third week of August; then, he would launch a new offensive either side of the Polish capital. But German reinforcements continued to arrive, and the plans faced further delays. Political reasons also began to play a part. Like the Western Allies, the Soviets had no intelligence officers within Warsaw and were keen to size up the situation of the Uprising before getting directly involved. Reports from the Communist *AL* were wildly optimistic, self-congratulatory, and out of touch with Stalin's reticence towards the Polish insurgency. Moreover, to the Soviets, the question of when and how to secure Warsaw was tied less to the microcosmic issues of Polish liberation than to grander designs of reaching Berlin, and, even more broadly, securing the post-war Soviet sphere of influence across Eastern Europe. Unlike the Poles, they had little to lose by biding their time.

The arguments over what the Red Army could have done to assist the Uprising continue to this day. Regardless of intervention on the ground, Soviet air power could have had a transformative impact on the Uprising's success. Soviet aviation was designed to operate from comparatively unprepared fields, and although logistic constraints meant that it took time to bring forward fuel, munitions, and other essentials before new airfields could be created, this had rarely prevented the Red Army from maintaining fighter patrols over its advancing units. German bombers attacked Warsaw almost from the beginning of the Uprising and Soviet fighters did little or nothing to stop them. The Stuka dive-bomber, the iconic symbol of the Luftwaffe's ground support operations, was obsolescent even in the early stages of the war and was almost ineffective in the west in 1944 – US and British fighters had little difficulty in dealing with any Stukas that appeared – but remained a potent weapon in the east. Operating from airfields close to the front line, Luftwaffe pilots could carry out several attacks per day, often reaching their targets and returning before Soviet fighters could intervene. Compared to their German or western counterparts, Soviet fighter pilots showed less initiative, typically limiting their operations to escorting bombers or intercepting enemy planes that had already been identified by ground controllers. But even with these limitations, the aircraft of Sixteenth and Eighteenth Air Armies – the aerial assets of 1st Belarusian Front – were conspicuous by their absence. No attacks were made on the German airfield at Okeçie (now the location of Warsaw Chopin Airport) and German air crews operated with almost complete impunity throughout the Uprising.

Communications between the insurgents, their government-in-exile, and their allies were still dogged by delays, conflicts of diplomatic interest, and clashes of personality. In late July, Prime Minister Mikołajczyk had arrived in Moscow to try to bring about a thaw in relations with Stalin. He was 'ostentatiously snubbed' from the moment he landed and told that Stalin was too busy to meet with him directly, while the British ambassador advised Mikołajczyk that his best chances of winning over the Soviets depended on purging his government of 'anti-Soviet' and 'reactionary' elements, agreeing to the Curzon Line as the basis for future negotiations, accepting Soviet conclusions on the Katyn massacre, and cooperating with the *PKWN*, the Soviet-appointed provisional Polish government.[42] By the time Stalin deigned to receive the Polish premier on 3 August, Warsaw was already engulfed in the Uprising, and the Soviets remained intransigent. Stalin declared that the Red Army would be unlikely to reach the city during the following days as planned, but refused to elaborate further on the 'small delay'.[43] As Karski later wrote, this diplomatic disaster 'revealed the extent to which all calculations on the Uprising had gone wrong'; far from strengthening the credibility of the government-in-exile, the insurgents' failure to liberate the city on their own not only left Mikołajczyk on the back foot in Moscow but actively played into Stalin's hands, transforming the Polish premier into a supplicant reliant on 'indispensable help that might or might not be granted.'[44] Mikołajczyk's attempts to connect with the *PKWN* proved equally fruitless when its representatives flatly denied that there was any fighting in Warsaw and said so to Stalin. In the end, the prime minister left Stalin with a vague impression that he might be open to working with the *PKWN*, but departed Moscow on 9 August with no guarantees of Soviet material support.

As for the Western Allies, it was only on 3 August that President Raczkiewicz could pass on to Churchill Komorowski's request for air assistance, emphasising that without 'giving this operation priority for tonight (3 to 4 August) it may fail to take place [and] my Nation … would never forget that it was left unaided at a most critical moment by its British ally.'[45] However, the British showed little urgency. The question of the *AK*'s combatant status was still without resolution, and the RAF's general outlook remained that air support to Poland was contingent on the success of the Soviet advance. With the Red Army nowhere to be seen, and with Stalin's opinion of Mikołajczyk leaving much to be desired, the Poles' only hope of breaking the deadlock was that Britain and the USA would apply enough pressure on Moscow to force Soviet cooperation. On 4 August, Churchill telegraphed Stalin to notify him that the British were dropping 60 tons of equipment on Warsaw and mentioned that the Poles were also appealing for Soviet assistance; Stalin's response scornfully dismissed the Uprising as 'a few detachments [of] misnamed divisions' incapable of capturing the city, but he did not directly countermand Churchill's plan.[46] Sure enough, though poor weather rendered flights impossible on 3 August, two Halifax bombers appeared in the smoke-filled skies over Warsaw the following evening. Only half of the containers delivered to the besieged city fell into *AK* hands – 'a drop in the ocean' considering what the insurgents needed – but the airdrop lifted the Varsovians' spirits and suggested that they were not, after all, fighting alone.[47] The insurgents would soon learn that the mission had cost the RAF five aircraft, leading Bomber Command to conclude that Warsaw operations were too risky. Further flights to the city were abandoned for the time being.

THE WOLA MASSACRE

By 5 August, the Germans had sufficient troops to seize the initiative; to date, they had largely been passive, defending the ground they held and waiting for reinforcements, aside from the brief attempt to lift the siege of the Brühl Palace. Vormann was growing increasingly worried about the threat to the lines of communication of his Ninth Army and urged a swift resolution. Accordingly, the SS formations were ordered to thrust into Warsaw from two directions. Kaminski's *RONA* brigade was in Ochota, in the southwest part of Warsaw, and it was to advance along Jerusalem Avenue to the Poniatowski Bridge over the Vistula. At the same time, Reinefarth's forces, now numbering about 4,000, would attack the Wola district to the north of Ochota in three groups, with Dirlewanger's men on the southern flank.

The Varsovians expected a tough fight, but the suddenness and viciousness of the German assault took many by surprise. From the outset, Reinefarth made clear his intentions to follow Himmler's orders to the letter. As his group pressed into Wola, he watched crowds of civilians being led to the rear. Irritated by the time it was taking, he commented to officers watching with him, 'Look at this, gentlemen, these refugees are our biggest problem. We don't have enough ammunition to kill all of them.'[48] But they certainly tried their best: Reinefarth would later claim that on 5 August alone – or 'Black Saturday' as it came to be known – the SS took the lives of around 10,000 Varsovian men, women, and children. Other estimates put the number between two to three times higher.[49] By the following Saturday, somewhere between 40,000 and 50,000 Poles had been murdered in the district – over twice as many civilians as were killed during the month-long siege of the city in 1939.

The advance through the dense working-class neighbourhoods of Wola saw the Varsovians subjected to a whole new level of atrocity. Shortly after dawn, German bombers began the assault by dropping high-explosive and incendiary bombs across the district; then came the savage assault of the SS, Dirlewanger, and *RONA* Brigades. As in the ghetto, the Reich forces resorted to setting fire to buildings as a means of expediting murder and depriving the Poles of any hopes of shelter, hurling grenades into basements and firing indiscriminately at occupants of burning buildings. But the German attack on 5 August fell short of its objectives. The thrust into Wola advanced perhaps a mile, and although the overwhelming advantage that the Germans enjoyed in firepower ensured they suffered fewer losses than the *AK*, the realities of urban warfare rapidly imposed themselves. There was always plentiful cover for snipers, and barricades and anti-tank ditches significantly stalled the advance – as did the house-to-house slaughter of civilians with grenades and gunfire. Seeking to accelerate the assault, Reinefarth issued orders that Varsovians were to be pushed to the rear – where they could be executed by other units – so the combatant formations could concentrate on pushing forward.[50]

Polish residents were herded out of the flaming housing blocks in their thousands, divided into smaller groups in the street, and shot, group by group, their bodies adding to piles of corpses that grew to around six and a half feet high.[51] When one woman asked why civilians were being executed, she received the response, 'German women and children are dying owing to you, so you must also die.'[52] Wanda Lurie, eight months pregnant, was forced out of her flat with her three children and escorted to the Ursus factory yard, one of the sites being used for executions. Her account is all too typical on this day of horror and speaks for the thousands who did not survive to record their own testimonies:

> There were about 20 people in our group, mostly children of 10 to 12. There were children without parents, and also a paralysed old woman whose son-in-law had been carrying her all the time on his back. At her side was her daughter with two children of 4 and 7. They were all killed. The old woman was literally killed on her son-in-law's back, and he along with her …

> I begged the Vlasov men around me to save me and the children, and they asked if I had anything with which to buy my life. I had a large amount of gold with me and gave it them. They took it all and wanted to lead me away, but the German supervising the execution would not allow them to do so … I held my two younger children by one hand, and my elder boy by the other. The children were crying and praying. The elder boy, seeing the mass of bodies, cried out: 'They are going to kill us' and called for his father. The first shot hit him, the second me; the next two killed the two younger children. I fell on my right side. The shot was not fatal. The bullet penetrated the back of my head from the right side and went out through my cheek. I spat out several teeth; I felt the left side of my body growing numb, but I was still conscious and saw everything that was going on around me.
>
> … Thus it went on with group after group until late in the evening. It was already quite, quite dark when the executions stopped. In the intervals between the shootings the murderers walked on the corpses, kicked them, and turned them over, finishing off those who still gave any sign of life, and stealing valuables. (They took a watch from my wrist, but I did not give any sign of life) … I lay quite numb for a long time in a pool of blood, the dead weighing on me …[53]

Lurie lay for days under the pile of the dead, hardly daring to move. On the third day, she felt her unborn child begin to move and, delirious with sickness, stole out of the factory yard; miraculously, she gave birth on 20 August. She estimated that between five and seven thousand Varsovians were killed there in the Ursus yard, including all 200 from her block of flats. Scenes like these were repeated thousands of times over in other improvised execution sites that became black spots in less than 24 hours: the tram depot at Młynarska Street; a macaroni factory at 60 Wolska Street; the railway viaduct at 15 Górczewska Street; the Franaszek factory; and Sowiński Park.

The term 'Vlasov men' refers to General Andrei Andreyevich Vlasov, the former commander of the Soviet Second Shock Army. When his army was surrounded by the Germans near Leningrad in 1942, he was captured and then turned against Stalin, becoming head of the *Russkaya Osvoboditelnaya Armiya* ('Russian Liberation Army' or *ROA*, not to be confused with Kaminski's *RONA*) into which thousands of former Red Army soldiers were incorporated. They didn't see action on a large scale until November 1944, but it is commonplace for many accounts – Polish, Soviet, and others – to describe any former Soviet personnel fighting for the Germans as 'Vlasovites'. Similarly, many Polish accounts describe the non-Germans fighting for the SS in Warsaw as 'Ukrainians'; although many were, there were also large numbers of men from other parts of the Soviet Union. Ryszard Piekarek, who was 15 years old, gave a characteristic eyewitness account of the murder of a woman who was struggling to carry a suitcase of money as well as her child, describing the perpetrator as 'a Ukrainian with Mongolian cheekbones in an SS uniform'.[54]

Many of the police units hastily despatched to Warsaw from Poznań and elsewhere had no experience of urban warfare, and their reluctance to advance across streets covered by Polish snipers also reduced the rate of advance. Of all the German units attacking Warsaw on 5 August, the hardened killers of the Dirlewanger brigade were the most energetic, throwing themselves at Polish defences with almost complete disregard for their losses. Matthias Schenk, an 18-year-old Wehrmacht sapper who had been assigned to one of the assault brigades deployed in Warsaw, described the arrival of a detachment from the Dirlewanger brigade – hard-looking men with few or no rank insignia, smelling of vodka, who used Polish women and children as human shields on their tanks – and their commander, a sinister man in a black leather coat who was raging at his men from the back. When a girl emerged from the ruins of a building and raised her hands, the small group of regular Wehrmacht soldiers lowered their weapons, but Dirlewanger's men pushed them aside and beat her to death.[55]

Dirlewanger's and Kaminski's men perpetrated not only wholesale massacre but also systematic sexual violence to the extent that numerous German soldiers recorded their horror at the sight of mutilated women and children. There was also widespread looting, with Stahel later admitting that he ordered no action to be taken against plunderers on the grounds that it was impossible to stop it from happening – and in any case, it seemed irrelevant in a city that was going to be completely destroyed. The killing, rapes, and looting all compounded the Germans' slow progress. Over the next few days, the fighting continued in much the same way, with the Germans' capacity for brutality showing no limit:

> From Kercelli Place the Insurgents were firing towards Towarowa Street. The Germans who were going into the fighting stopped us and made of us a living barricade, under threats of being shot … ordering us to lie down across the street from one side to the other. With our backs turned to the Insurgents, we knelt or crouched and the Germans placed themselves on the ground behind us, or knelt on one knee, firing over our heads towards Kercelli Place. There were 23 of us including two children, mostly young women. It is difficult to describe what we felt during the two hours the fighting lasted. We were all prepared to die and said the Rosary aloud. Bullets whistled over our heads, or past our ears. The noise of the German guns nearly deafened us. As if by some miracle, the bullets only hit

> the Germans. When the first German fell we were paralysed with fear. My mother told me: 'If I am shot remember not to shed one tear; do not complain, preserve the dignity of a Polish woman. Show no weakness in their presence.' Only the children wept bitterly and were greatly afraid.
>
> The Germans were bewildered by the fact that only they were falling. They ordered the men to drag the bodies aside. We thought they would take their revenge on us. Stupefied and astonished they looked towards the insurgent posts, and then at our quiet, resigned attitude; and the children clinging to their mothers.
>
> At last, they let us go.[56]

UNLEASHING HELL

On 9 August, the Dirlewanger brigade finally reached Stahel's isolated garrison in the Brühl Palace. In the neighbouring Piłsudski Square – renamed Adolf-Hitler-Platz by the Germans – soldiers from various formations gathered to watch Dirlewanger's men as they dragged naked nurses, some with blood running down their legs, to a makeshift gallows. Some were hanged, with Dirlewanger personally kicking away the stools; others were suspended by their feet and shot in the stomach, hanging in agony until a soldier from a regular Wehrmacht unit shot them in the head.[57] Matthias Schenk was nearby. 'We were calling him "the butcher",' he recalled of Dirlewanger – but well out of hearing, 'because in his units the way to the rope was short.' Schenk witnessed many of the brigade's savageries first-hand, and his account of the Uprising shows it wasn't only the Poles who found the horror almost too much to bear:

> We were sleeping in cellars. In the quarters, between attacks, we drank a lot of vodka; we talked a lot, too. 'Maybe tomorrow I will be wounded and return home', we were saying.
>
> We had nightmares. I screamed in my sleep. Then my companions were waking me up with cold water saying 'Bubi, *Du hast den Warschaukoller*' (Kid, you have the Warsaw madness).
>
> We slept in clothes, continuous alarms; *Raus! Raus*! [Oberleutnant Bernhard] Fels yelled. More than once we could hear the Poles on the other side of the wall. Once they even sang a lively song. Sometimes I cried. When you attack you are not afraid, but in the quarters you shake. We drank a lot. [58]

Schenk's recollections also paint a picture of the savage, sadistic cruelty that reigned within the brigade itself. The young sapper was tricked into signing up to the Warsaw operation after being promised an easy job driving trucks, and the horrors to which he bore witness during his month in the city would scar him for the rest of his life. He recalled how Dirlewanger always stayed to the rear of his troops, shooting those who lagged behind; how the 'butcher' unflinchingly ordered his men to open fire on a school full of children as they raised their little hands in the air, then to break their heads with blows from their rifle-butts to save bullets; how one of the brigade slit open the stomach of a young Polish woman as he raped her; and how he himself narrowly escaped court-martial – and likely execution – when Dirlewanger caught him offering water to an *AK* fighter in German uniform. Belgian-born Schenk would go on to receive the Iron Cross Second-Class for his service in Warsaw, survive the war and, in the 1980s, organise relief assistance to Poland – but his memories of the Uprising never faded. 'Back then we had no idea that those killed will never die, that they will always be with us,' he would recall. 'Sometimes in a half-dream I see killed people in front of me. Sometimes I am trying to count those I killed myself, but I can't.'[59]

The mass killing of civilians by Reinefarth's men was a huge crime, and the added rape and sadism of the Dirlewanger brigade added a further layer of horror. But the attack by Kaminski's *RONA* brigade was even worse. The orders issued for the assault on 5 August required Kaminski to drive through to the Poniatowski Bridge from the south through the Ochota district, which was defended by about 400 *AK* fighters. Outnumbered and massively outgunned, the majority of insurgents pulled back late the same day, but some were left defending two positions. Most of the initial fighting was done by about 400 German police; Kaminski's men, numbering about 1,700, stopped almost as soon as the attack began, to indulge in pillaging, rape, and drinking. Unlike Dirlewanger's troops, largely made up of the dregs of German prisons, the *RONA* brigade consisted of Russians and Belarusians who had few illusions about ever being able to return to their homelands. They saw the current operation as an opportunity to seize loot as a reward for all they had done for the Germans, and growing up in the Soviet Union, most had never seen the levels of wealth and opulence that they now encountered in this fashionable district of Warsaw. The advance slowed to a crawl. Reinefarth and Dirlewanger might have organised the mass murder of Varsovians in a more rigorous and effective manner, but Kaminski's men indulged in a brutal orgy of violence that drew particular attention from other German units. According to his memoirs, Hans Thieme – a Wehrmacht officer who helped publicise Reinefarth's crimes after the war – tried to call out the *RONA* Brigade's brutality. After detaining two brigade members who had been harassing a Polish woman, he attempted to hand them over to an SS officer, whose indifference to their shameful behaviour astonished him: 'it is good that the Poles would once get a good taste for the Asiatic hordes from whom we were protecting them,' was the response he received.[60] Another Wehrmacht officer, Oberleutnant Eberhard Schmalz, also complained to the SS about the murder of innocent civilian bystanders; he was advised in no uncertain terms that it was none of his concern and that he ought to keep his stories to himself if he didn't want to find his situation becoming 'not too pleasant'.[61]

Some of the worst savagery took place in the hospitals in Wola, where helpless patients and medical staff were killed on the spot. When Kaminski's brigade overran the Radium Institute founded by Maria Skłodowska-Curie in 1925 for the treatment of cancer patients, they raided the pharmacy for anything containing alcohol and then rampaged through the building, looting everything from watches and jewellery to lighters and fountain pens. The Institute's patients and staff were marched to a nearby camp where they were repeatedly raped over the following days. Neither terminally ill women nor young patients as young as 13 or 14 were spared sexual abuse. Those too weak to rise from their beds were either shot where they lay or burned alive as their mattresses were set on fire. Very few survived; one woman who managed to crawl from her bed with severe burns managed to escape immediate death, only to be shot when the brigade returned to raze the Institute 11 days later. One survivor claimed to have heard a German officer summing up the massacre: 'it is of no importance if several old women with cancer perish – the most important thing is to win the war.'[62]

Still, several Poles made miraculous escapes. One patient at Wola Hospital was being lined up for execution when he turned to a guard and claimed, in his best German, that he was *Volksdeutsch.* He spent the night in a nearby German first-aid station and watched line after line of Poles being pushed towards the entrance of a burning building and shot, overwhelmed by the frightful smell of burning human flesh.[63] Maria Kamińska was a patient in a shelter in the Lazarus Hospital:

> It was already dark when several soldiers rushed into the shelter, separated the hospital staff from the others, and took this group with them. They drove the mobile patients and civilians into the courtyard. I was led into the courtyard by two soldiers who grabbed me under my arms, and joined the group standing by the wall. I stood next to Wiesława Chelmińska, whom I had recently met; she was there with her mother.
>
> I saw soldiers throwing grenades and shooting in the direction of the windows of the shelter, where the seriously wounded and sick had stayed. After a while, they ordered several people from our group to go down to the basement adjacent

> to the one from which we had been removed ... When it was my turn, I knew, going down the stairs, why I was being led down there ... Through the open doors of three wards I could see corpses lying on the floors. Armed soldiers were standing at the doors. The three persons walking in front of me stepped on the corpses, and the soldiers at the door shot them in the backs of their heads. Seeing that it was an execution, I began to scream and resist. A soldier took me and a woman following me by the arms and pushed us both into the first ward in the basement ... I fell down right at the doorstep, without being wounded. I felt the other woman fall on my legs. After that, the people following were coming in, being shot right afterwards. There were several corpses lying on me ... There could have been approximately 50 corpses in the ward. At some point I heard footsteps. Two soldiers poured some liquid over the corpses lying by the door, and then set fire to them. The fire erupted. The wounded men rushed to escape. The soldiers chased them ...
>
> I took advantage of the fact that there were no German soldiers around; together with a wounded man who had stayed in there, I jumped over the burning corpses. The man rushed into the yard, I rushed into another ward in the basement ...
>
> The next day ... I met Chełminska, who had also survived the execution, and a wounded Russian man who died just afterwards.[64]

For several days, the two women tried to hide from the Germans in the hospital; eventually, they were caught and sent to a labour camp near Wrocław. Physician Stanisław Trojanowski, on the other hand, survived a bizarre encounter with a *RONA* soldier largely thanks to the latter's drunkenness. 'We will finish off all the Poles for starting the Uprising,' the soldier hollered at Trojanowski as he aimed his revolver at him, 'and preventing the Kaminski Brigade from getting to the Western Front, where the Brigade planned to join the British.' The physician grabbed his hand and rebuked him, which seemed to sober the man up, and Trojanowski escaped with his life.[65]

Anxious to avoid wasting time that could be spent on looting and rape, the *RONA* brigade men herded civilians to Zieleniak, a large farmers' market on Opaczewska Street. Here they were searched for valuables and confined within the walled area; before long, 20,000 Varsovians were gathered, with no running water and little food. Anyone attempting to escape in search of supplies risked being shot. At one point, a herd of cows was driven into Zieleniak, and many were killed as the terrified animals stampeded. A doctor who helped a woman give birth was killed by guards who then smashed her baby to death against a fence; other infants were bayoneted.[66] There was the constant threat of random execution, and women – including young girls and *Volksdeutsche* – were dragged away and violently raped in the surrounding potato fields. By 11 August, the majority of those still alive in the market yard were packed into trains bound for Pruszków.

Senior German officers showed little inclination to stop atrocities on humanitarian grounds, but Bach and Vormann were angered that such behaviour was holding up the elimination of the *AK* units still blocking Poniatowski Bridge from the south. Eventually, backed by air attacks and artillery, the assault resumed on 11 August and one of the two strongpoints still held by the *AK* was overrun. With Kaminski's men unwilling or unable to tackle the other, Ukrainian paramilitary police were deployed and fought their way forward through the rubble until the position was taken. These men were later transferred to the *SS-Waffen-Grenadier-Division Galizien*, which had been shattered by the Soviet advance to Lviv; as a result, it is sometimes erroneously assumed that this division fought in Warsaw.

Suddenly, the massacres of civilians dropped off. After the war, Bach would claim that he had acted unilaterally to stop the killings: when Reinefarth protested that he had received explicit orders not to take prisoners and that civilians were not to be spared, Bach allegedly overruled him. Yet Bach's consistent record of moral indifference and unwavering obedience to superiors makes it inconceivable that he would have done so without first securing permission from Himmler. It is possible that, facing the growing certainty of defeat, Himmler was anxious to curry favour with the future victors. In the past, he had been concerned about the psychological impact of mass murder on SS soldiers, and even at this late stage of the conflict there remained a pressing need for workers in the armaments factories of the Reich. Regardless of the reasons, the mass slaughter that marked the first days of the German onslaught came to an end. Killings continued, but at a lower rate. Incidences of rape, however, remained unchecked.

As the final *AK* positions in Wola were eliminated, clashes erupted between Kaminski's drunken marauders and the regular German soldiers assigned to provide support to the *RONA* brigade. Around 9 August, Bach confronted Kaminski in Zieleniak and ordered him to appear before the German commander in his headquarters in Ożarów to account for the poor performance of his brigade; he remained defiant even here, claiming that his men were merely securing compensation for their previous service. He was ordered to bring his men under control to no avail, and finally, on 19 August, Bach succeeded in having him removed from command. His replacement was Major Ivan Denisovich Frolow, a former Red Army officer captured by the Germans early in the war. Kaminski left Warsaw laden with stolen goods but was detained in Łódź, where, at Bach's instigation, Himmler had him charged with looting and failing to pass on items to government bodies. The atrocities that had taken place under his supervision were simply ignored, but he was sentenced to death and killed around 20 August. The official German line was that Kaminski and others had been ambushed and killed by Polish partisans – though even the staging of the corpses around a wrecked vehicle failed to allay Frolow's suspicions around his predecessor's fate.

Regardless of who was in command, the *RONA* brigade was clearly incapable of contributing anything useful to the elimination of the *AK* forces in Warsaw. It was withdrawn from the city before the end of August and sent to Truskaw, to the northwest of the city. Here, it came under heavy attack by *AK* fighters late on 2 September and was almost completely destroyed.

The assault on Wola came to an end on 11 August. The *AK* had captured a few tanks and put them to good use, but their last vehicle was lost now in the fighting. As they pulled back towards the old city centre, the *AK* fighters were dismayed by the latest orders from Chruściel, according to which civilians were to be discouraged from leaving their homes. On the one hand, the resistance command feared that their stories of German savagery would incite panic, and on the other, they believed that *AK* soldiers would fight harder if they had to hold their positions to protect civilians. At first, most of the civil population had supported the Uprising, but now the mood began to change as – despite Chruściel's orders – tales of atrocity started to spread. Meanwhile, the Germans combed through the ruins of Wola, executing most males and bundling women and children off to a transit camp further west. A number of Jews who had survived the liquidation of the ghetto in hiding were now rooted out by the search parties and killed. Heaps of corpses lay everywhere, and Himmler ordered Standartenführer Ludwig Hahn – who had worked closely with Globočnik in the extermination of Jews under Operation *Reinhard* – to deal with the dead. He and Bach created new units named *Verbrennungskommandos* ('cremation squads') consisting of Polish prisoners to handle the dirty work of moving and cremating the bodies. Most of those in the *Verbrennungskommandos* were themselves executed and burned; only a few survived.

Any sign of hesitation or weakness in the *Verbrennungskommandos* could result in immediate death. The commander of one group, Obersturmführer Thieschke, told his workers that they should be grateful that he had saved their lives by giving them an opportunity to perform 'honest, decent work'.[67] In the Franaszek factory, the Poles found thousands of corpses already rotting in the summer heat. 'As far as I could see,' one later recalled, 'there were just bodies.

They must have squeezed them in, as many as possible, and then thrown grenades ... There were thousands of fat flies everywhere, everything was coated in a kind of stinking jelly with the noise of thousands of flies.'[68] Copying a technique perfected at Treblinka for the efficient cremation of Jewish gas chamber victims, Polish prisoners were ordered to construct pyres with alternating strata of wood and corpses before dousing the structure in gasoline and setting it alight. Amongst their worst ordeals was the clearance of the Wolski Hospital; signs of the violent atrocities committed by Dirlewanger's men were everywhere, and with the staircases in ruins, the *Verbrennungskommandos* were forced to throw the bodies from windows.

After a pause – for rest, regrouping, and more pillaging – the Germans were ready to renew their offensive on the remaining Polish enclaves. The next objective was Old Town, the historic centre of Warsaw. Reinefarth optimistically estimated that it would take just a week to seize the area. But unlike Wola, the area was heavily fortified and the two Polish commanders, Jan Mazurkiewicz and Karol Ziemski, were amongst the most capable in the ranks of the *AK*. By this time, refugees from all over the city had converged on Old Town and as many as 170,000 Varsovians were now packed into an area intended for half as many people. Compared to the rest of the city, Old Town had been largely spared in previous bombing raids, and the densely packed buildings, narrow streets, and networks of medieval cellars and passages played to the *AK*'s strengths over the Germans' heavy armaments. When they began their assault on 11 August, the Germans were dismayed to encounter serious resistance. The ferocious fighters repeatedly retook key positions and Polish snipers continued to exact a heavy toll on any Germans unwise enough to spend too long in the open. The following day, Reinefarth tried again but once more made almost no progress, even when the Germans resumed using human shields. The Dirlewanger brigade suffered particularly significant casualties as its commander repeatedly threw his men into bloody frontal assaults. The tight streets, innumerable barricades, and determined resistance led to rapidly rising losses; morale amongst the Germans plummeted.

His frustration mounting, Hitler ordered the deployment of ever heavier artillery. On top of the constant air raids, the Poles also became acquainted with the *Nebelwerfer*, multiple rocket launchers nicknamed '*krowy*' ('cows') by the Varsovians on account of the lowing sound they made. Miniature Goliath tanks were used to blast through the Poles' barricades in the narrow streets, and at least one armoured train kept Old Town and Zoliborż under a constant barrage of shelling that prevented the *AK* from re-establishing a link between the districts. The Germans didn't have any scruples about resorting to more subversive tactics either, as Komorowski recalled in one incident in Old Town:

> I heard a tank clattering along the street to the accompaniment of shouts and cheers. I leaned from the second-floor window to see a German tank flying a Polish flag and manned by a Polish crew.
>
> 'Another tank captured,' I thought with satisfaction, noticing the skill with which the driver negotiated the barricade. Men, women, and children crowded round, shouting gaily and cheering the crew. Suddenly there was a terrific explosion and the scene was blotted out by clouds of smoke and dust. The force of the blast flung me back from the window as if I had been a feather … When the dust had settled, I could see the results of the explosion. Of the tank crew not the slightest trace remained. The explosion killed about eighty people … human bodies were flung as high as the roofs of the nearby houses … It was our first encounter with a German booby trap. The tank had been loaded with explosive, fitted to a delayed-action fuse and left within tempting reach of our positions.[69]

The Uprising was now two weeks old. The *AK* command still held out hope that the Red Army would advance; any day, they believed, Moscow Radio would announce that Soviet troops were on their way to support the Poles. On 13 August, the radio silence was broken, but it was not the news the *AK* command had been waiting for: the *Telegrafnoye agentstvo Sovetskogo Soyuza* ('Soviet News Agency' or *TASS*) was at pains to stress that the claim made by the government-in-exile that the insurgents had coordinated their Uprising with the Soviet command was 'either a misunderstanding or a libel' against the Soviet Union; 'the only people responsible for the events in Warsaw,' it declared, 'are the Polish émigré circles in London.' In other words, Stalin was washing his hands of the Varsovians' plight. Communist propaganda continued to circulate the idea that only the Soviet-backed *AL* was fighting for liberation while Polish leaders in both Warsaw and London were simply exaggerating the contributions of the *AK* for their own cynical gain. The sense of betrayal cut deep amongst the besieged population: firstly because the *AK* leadership clung to the conviction that their timing of the Uprising had been entirely justified by the Communists' calls to arms in late July; and secondly because the Poles were being blamed for a lack of coordination when it was widely known that members of the *AK* were being disarmed, arrested, and frequently executed by the *NKVD* in the wake of the Soviet advance. In any case, the resistance leadership were forced to accept the fact that they could not count on Soviet air support. 'If we were to hold on,' wrote Komorowski, 'we had only our own strength to rely upon now.'[70]

THE SIEGE OF OLD TOWN

On 13 August, Old Town was cut off from the other *AK* sectors. Hemmed in by endless bombardment, the Varsovians had to become more resourceful than ever. The problem of food was quickly becoming critical, especially because the military authorities had only anticipated the fighting to last seven to ten days at most. In principle, the hospitals and the *AK* fighters were the main provisioning priorities, but owing to the mass displacement of civilians across the city, tens of thousands of refugees and homeless had to be provided for, too. The insurgents managed to seize control of various German storehouses which, together with cooperatives run by civilian authorities, made it possible for large numbers of Varsovians to be fed by improvised communal kitchens. Where various districts ran short of supplies, groups of volunteers carried food and medicine through labyrinthine subterranean passages and sewers or risked their lives crossing streets under fire. Small amounts of food were even smuggled in with the help of peasants from surrounding villages such as Wilanów, Piaseczno, Rzeszno, and Pruszków via the Kampinos forest. Water was an equally – if not more – desperate issue because the Germans controlled the municipal water works. The Poles had no choice but to dig wells in their courtyards – though this work was often delegated to German prisoners captured by the *AK*. As in the siege almost five years earlier, countless Varsovians lost their lives as they queued for supplies, caught once again in the impossible dilemma of dying from shelling or perishing from starvation and thirst.

The Polish fighters and civilians were forced to spend much of their time underground, where hundreds of basements were now connected in a tunnel network that extended across almost the entirety of Old Town. In his memoir of the Uprising, Miron Białoszewski describes in photographic detail his convoluted journeys through this subterranean maze: 'Never has Warsaw – although it is four times larger now than it was then – seemed so large and complicated, so endless.'[71] Cellars were transformed into hospitals, latrines, kitchens, places of worship, and tightly packed places of rest; Varsovians of all creeds and classes were forced to endure together, sharing last supplies, bickering over stove space, and grumbling about the overcrowding. The survival of tens of thousands of civilians had been reduced to a never-ending exodus from cellar to cellar in search of safety, of food, and of a few hours' precious sleep. Many spent their waking hours making final confessions in acceptance of their fate; for others, the dark, claustrophobic underground world that had become home offered 'psychic compartments and distances' from the horrors being waged on the streets above, and, of course, cohabitation bred comfort. As Białoszewski recalled:

> People lost each other as suddenly as they found each other. They'd be close for quite some time. Then others became close. Suddenly these were lost and new people became important. That was common. A matter of herd instinct. It didn't make any difference what herd you belonged to, as long as you were in a herd. Everyone was always flitting about, as happens (in any case) at such hours of death, people couldn't find a place for themselves. The people from one cellar went to the one next door, and the people from next door went over to the first … Because anywhere else was better. And even if it occurred to someone that it was the same everywhere, that didn't help at all.[72]

Irena Orska was one of the nurses who faced a stomach-churning, three-and-a-half-hour journey through the city sewers to provide relief for the overworked medical personnel in Old Town. On arrival, she found about a hundred nurses 'swaying on their feet' from exhaustion.[73] The scarcity of water and overcrowding caused a spike in dysentery, and new casualties – both civilian and insurgent – poured in by the hour. Orska spent 58 hours working virtually non-stop to keep pace with the wounded – including one 15-year-old boy who had helped capture a tank in the first days of the Uprising, whose entire face had been burned by an incendiary bomb and body ripped apart by shrapnel; he could only smile with his eyes as she touched his hand on the one spot that was not covered by a dressing. Towards the end of her shift, Orska broke down, succumbing to the fear that virtually every other living Varsovian must have felt at this point: 'I felt terribly afraid that I should die without seeing the day of freedom for which I had waited these five horror-filled years.'[74]

The mobility of medical personnel like Orska, of *AK* troops, of food supplies, ammunition, and other provisions between the cut-off districts would have been impossible without Warsaw's sewer system. One of the most used tunnels during the Uprising ran underneath the Gestapo headquarters, and the irony was not lost on the Poles that the underground owed its survival to now being literally underground.[75] The Varsovians quicky learned the dangers of navigating the sewers, where unexpected strong currents could wash them into the Vistula, and where they had to avoid passing manholes under German guard as much as possible. Routes were devised and tested by volunteers willing to venture into the darkness and risk their lives to secure lines of communication. The knowledge of Henryk Lederman and the other Jewish Gęsiówka escapees was crucial in clearing the underground routes from Old Town to Zoliborż; their commander and rescuer Micuta remarked that thanks to their experience in the Ghetto Uprising, they numbered amongst the few people who 'had a very good sense of direction down there.'[76] Womens' units and liaisons – nicknamed *Kanalarki* (after the Polish for sewer, *kanal*) – also played an important part in maintaining the sewer routes and helping others navigate through them. Captain Stanisław Jankowski recalled how he and his men were put to shame in the sewers by their young guide:

> The people who would probably know the most about the sewers were the girls that used the sewers to move about. One of those young women travelled from the middle of the city to the old part of the city in 18 hours flat.
>
> ... We were summoned by 'Wachnowski'. When we arrived he told us the following: 'You've travelled through the sewers already, now you will move to the middle city with an update for General "Bór". This is Basia, she will take you to see your guide for the passage through sewers.' We then replied: 'We don't need a guide because we've travelled enough through the sewers.'
>
> Nevertheless we went with the guide. She was a petite unknown girl who was introduced to us by Basia once we reached the sewer entrance. We went into the sewer. I wasn't afraid of the Germans, I wasn't afraid of the mud either, the only thing that scared me were the bricks. The sewer was 120 cm by 60 cm (3.9 ft by 1.9 ft) in cross section. The person was surrounded by bricks from all sides. It was a horrible feeling of enclosure and claustrophobia ... After a few falls into the mud I told the girl I wasn't going any further. I asked my friends if they wanted to go ahead in front of me. They didn't want to go further either. We decided to turn back.
>
> When we were coming out from the sewers our guide wanted to console us on our weakness during the journey, she told us: 'Nobody has yet tried to pass this way with a machine gun on their back.'[77]

The Poles' weak wireless sets were generally useless when it came to connecting district commanders within the city, but they were capable of transmitting and receiving messages from higher-power radio stations, including those in London. This produced another irony in the Polish situation whereby news about sewer routes was transmitted between the city districts via the British capital. Hundreds of messages were passed in this way, communicating newly established routes or tunnels to be avoided where the Germans had thrown gas canisters, mines, or hand grenades down the manholes.[78] One more unlikely overground liaison route was established by a ten-year-old boy, Wacek, and his goat, Basia. The boy explained to Komorowski that he and Basia frequently passed through the gardens between Old Town and Żoliborz without trouble from the Germans and volunteered to make the journey with a hidden message slipped into Basia's halter. Sure enough, thanks to 'the calm of both and the excellent appetite shown by Basia at the patches of grass between the allotments', Wacek and his companion made the journey without arousing suspicion. When they set out for a second trip, however, they did not return.[79]

The battle for Old Town raged on, and despite the *AK* capturing record numbers of German weapons, the Poles' ammunition situation was becoming desperate. For their part, the Germans, were ramping up their use of heavy artillery to try to minimise their casualties, so the ever-resourceful Varsovians increased their efforts to recover and recycle materials from unexploded ordnance. Special units of sappers were tasked with removing fuses from the bombs, the heaviest of which could yield as much as 660 pounds of high-quality explosive that could be used to produce *filipiniki*. The Goliath robot tanks became valuable prizes too, and the *AK*'s Ordnance Service circulated a manual detailing how to disable the machines and extract their 110 pounds of compressed dynamite. The insurgents also became adept at fashioning larger weapons out of the limited materials they had to hand: fire hoses were transformed into flamethrowers, water pipes into grenade launchers; one group created a rudimentary 'anti-tank' catapult out of a large pitchfork mounted in a heavy iron base that could be used to launch explosives around 70 or 80 feet.[80] 'We ought to send this "secret weapon" to our Allies,' one of its creators grumbled bitterly, 'It might hasten their coming to our rescue.'[81]

While Dirlewanger's brigade ground into Old Town from the south and southeast to cut the enclave off from the Vistula, Reinefarth's other two brigades attacked from the north and west. But progress remained painfully slow, and, increasingly fearful about how this would reflect on his own reputation, Bach changed course on 18 August. An emissary was sent across the front line under a flag of truce demanding the *AK* end its 'senseless and suicidal resistance'.[82] Unsurprisingly, Komorowski rejected the demand, not least because the German atrocities in Wola had left many in the Polish camp with the view that death in battle was preferable to what might await them if they surrendered to the enemy. But the Poles were running out of everything – food, water, and ammunition – and waited hopelessly for the Western Powers to drop supplies. Aircraft from Italy continued to try to reach Warsaw, but the Germans had positioned air defence resources in their path. Some 250 Allied airmen were killed during the attempted operations – roughly one for every ton of supplies dropped over the city. Many of the canisters landed in German sectors; on some occasions, Soviet anti-aircraft guns opened fire on the planes. Meanwhile, Stalin persisted in blocking the Allied planes from refuelling at Soviet airfields on the grounds that their supply drops were providing more aid for the Germans than the Poles.

The role played by Churchill at this juncture is controversial. On the one hand, he had shown a 19th-century attitude to drawing up borders without any regard for the people concerned, and many Poles felt betrayed by his failure to defend their rights. But on the other hand, he alone of the leaders of the Western Powers continued to demand more action from Stalin. The Tehran Conference in late 1943 left President Roosevelt confident that he had established a good relationship with Stalin, so he refused to support the British position; preparations were in hand for another conference, to be held in early 1945, and Roosevelt was anxious to ensure Soviet support for his plans for a post-war world order. Finally, perhaps after further demands from Churchill – he hinted that the aid convoys running from Britain past northern Norway to the Soviet Union might be stopped – Stalin conceded to allow refuelling. A mixture of poor weather and further delays meant the first mission carried out by US aircraft didn't take place until 18 September, and immediately the Soviet authorities brought the arrangement to a halt, claiming that 90 per cent of supplies had landed in German areas. The true percentage was about 75 per cent, but it wasn't until the end of the month that permission was granted for operations to resume; by then, the deteriorating weather and further German advances made the airdrops almost meaningless.

The reckless frontal attacks by Dirlewanger and the fierce defence by the *AK* had left the SS badly in need of reinforcements. The mixture of men scraped together by Himmler revealed the desperate straits to which Nazi Germany was being reduced: Dirlewanger received more former Soviet soldiers from Azerbaijan, Kuban, and the Caucasus, and about 1,500 prisoners who had been in concentration camps or punishment battalions. The combined strength of the ground forces arrayed against Old Town now exceeded 13,000 men and was backed by heavy artillery and aircraft that continued to operate with impunity. On 19 August, after a particularly heavy bombardment, the renewed attack began. Over the next few days, the tenacious *AK* units were slowly driven back and their positions pulverised. Attempts to link up with the resistance enclave in Żoliborz resulted in heavy losses, and on 27 August the SS attacked a large block that had housed the Polish mint before the war. Fighting continued in the ruins for a day, with each floor contested in turn; having finally secured control of the building, the Germans killed all their prisoners and the wounded Poles they found in the basement. Realising that the end was near, the *AK* leadership decided it was time to evacuate Old Town; in particular, men like Komorowski had to be kept out of German hands. He left on 25 August via the sewers.

It was a significant day for another reason too. The news spread like wildfire through the ruined city that after a six-day battle, Paris had been liberated from the Nazis. Any sense of solidarity the Varsovians might have had for the occupied French people was tempered by a sudden stab of 'unmitigated envy'. Civilian 'forbearance began to wear thin', erupting more frequently into hostile and wrathful outbursts towards the *AK* soldiers they crossed paths with underground.[83] The will to endure was being eroded with every blow to their means of survival: first, the waterworks had been lost; then the Powiśle power station was pounded to rubble on 4 September; and finally, the food warehouses on Stawki Street were captured by Germans – a catastrophe for those holed up in Old Town.[84] The French success only compounded the Poles' sense of isolation and hopelessness; if nothing else, the Varsovians were looking for someone to blame for their failure to pull off what Paris had managed in less than a week. Perhaps it was for the best that the Varsovians had no way of knowing about General Charles de Gaulle's negotiations with the Americans to divert military aid to the liberation, or they would have felt even more stung by Allied reticence towards their own city. When, one month later, similar news trickled in about the use of airborne forces – including the Polish Parachute Brigade – at Arnhem, Białoszewski described feeling 'cut … to the quick.'[85]

A final attempt by the *AK* to break out towards the south ended in failure, but some fighters managed to escape capture against almost impossible odds. Many of the insurgents were wearing SS uniforms – seized from a warehouse captured in the early days of the Uprising – with only a red and white armband to indicate their true nationality. Captain Andrzej Romocki – the commander of a small unit cut off behind German lines – ordered his men to remove their armbands; then, making no attempt to hide themselves, the men marched through the German lines back to the Polish side. As they approached the *AK* lines, they shouted to their comrades not to open fire and thus evaded capture, at least for the moment.

The remaining *AK* personnel in Old Town dropped through a manhole on Krasiński Square to slip away through the sewers in groups of 50. Worried that a civilian exodus would alert the Germans to the escape, *AK* leaders deliberately withheld news of the evacuation from the huge crowds of ordinary Varsovians trapped in the district. When the time for abandoning Old Town arrived, there were disagreements about whether the wounded should be taken through the sewers – which would slow the escapees – or whether they should be left behind. The trip was a dark and dangerous one, with troops shuffling as a human chain for four hours through 'waist-deep sludge and poisonous fumes'. All were by now so weakened from exhaustion that to lose footing meant drowning in the deeper channels of muck:[86]

> The acrid air was asphyxiating and brought tears to the eyes. The size of the passages varied. The smallest which could be negotiated were three feet high and two wide. Sharp debris, such as broken glass, strewed the semicircular floor of the passages, making hand support impossible when crawling. The most superficial scratch would have caused septicaemia. Two sticks had to be used as supports and progress was made in short jumps, rather like the motion of a kangaroo ... One of the routes leading from Stare Miasto [Old Town] to the centre of the city through one of the narrowest tunnels took as long as nine hours to negotiate, although the distance was no longer than a mile. To advance along a narrow passage of this sort in pitch darkness, with mud up to the shoulders, often caused stark terror ... The feeling of panic was increased by the difficulty of breathing in the foetid atmosphere and that it was impossible to turn round. If an immovable obstacle was encountered, the only course was to back out ... The horror of the sewers was increased by the echoes of moans and cries from the wounded and the hysterical laughter of those whose nerves had given way under the experience ... The gas given off by the corpses decomposing below endangered the sight of anyone who had to stay down for any length of time.[87]

The lucky escapees made it to the city centre close to the Vistula. Further German shelling buried the Krasiński Square manhole under rubble and cut the escape route on 2 September, but by this time most of the *AK* combatants had reached the relative safety of the riverside enclave.

Reinefarth's troops – followed by Bach – moved through the corpse-strewn Old Town later that day. Bach ordered the 35,000 Varsovians and 7,000 Polish wounded still sheltering in cellars to be taken to Pruszków for 'processing': those capable of labour would be sent to camps; the rest, and anyone suspected of being a member of the *AK*, were to be executed. German soldiers who had been wounded and captured were being treated in the same makeshift hospitals as Polish casualties, and in many cases these wounded men persuaded their SS liberators not to kill everyone in the wards. But things changed when Dirlewanger's brigade moved into the area. Once again, those too frail to be evacuated were killed in their beds, and the buildings burned to the ground. By the time the Germans had fully neutralised the district to their satisfaction, Warsaw's 700-year-old Old Town lay in ruins; of many of the city's most historic landmarks – the Church of Our Lady, the Treasury Printing Building, and the Saint John of God Hospital, amongst many others – only craters and rubble remained. Taking one last look across the ruined area, Komorowski tried to place where he had seen such a view before: 'Then I remembered. It was in some photographs of Stalingrad.'[88]

FORSAKEN AGAIN

On 4 September, representatives of the Polish Red Cross met the Germans to discuss the protection of civilians. Komorowski had generally regarded previous approaches from the Germans with suspicion, so his approval on this occasion alludes to the depth of depression felt amongst the *AK* leadership as the Uprising entered its second month. During the brief ceasefire that followed, hundreds of Poles were permitted to cross enemy lines for internment – they were assured – in refugee camps. That relatively few Varsovians chose to leave indicates that 'their mistrust of the Germans was stronger than their horror of the infernal conditions in which they were existing'.[89] This contact between the combatants also laid the foundation for the capitulation talks Komorowski was beginning to realise were an inevitability – but he had reason to delay just a little longer.

For around this time, the Red Army finally received orders to seize Praga. It would take at least a week to prepare, and – always aware of the political dimension of any military operations – Stalin ensured that the First Polish Army would play a major role. Despite its title, the army included many non-Poles in its ranks, particularly amongst its officers. The assault began on 10 September and the Red Army units smashed their way through the German defences. Vormann was wary of being drawn into a battle that he couldn't win and secured permission from Georg-Hans Reinhardt – now promoted to Generaloberst, and who had replaced Model as commander of Army Group Centre – to abandon Praga. The German units slipped away on 14 September, blowing the bridges across the Vistula, and the Red Army took full control of the district the following day. Of course, Hitler blamed his generals for the setback. Vormann – who had inherited command of Ninth Army in the midst of the chaotic retreat across Belarus in the summer and managed to reorganise its battered remnants into a fighting force – was dismissed.

The Soviet troops now approached the Vistula shore opposite the last *AK* enclaves. Bach was ordered to secure the rest of Warsaw as quickly as possible before Soviet units could cross the river. The Czerniaków enclave was defended by about 600 *AK* soldiers – including many who had escaped from Old Town through the sewers – though their ammunition was fast running out.

On 11 September, the Germans once again opened their new operation with a heavy bombardment, then three battlegroups pressed into the enclave as Dirlewanger's brigade attacked from the north. The Poles were briefly buoyed by the news that the Red Army was finally in Praga and fought back with renewed determination, bringing the advance to a standstill. General Smilo von Lüttwitz, Vormann's replacement at the headquarters of Ninth Army, reluctantly released a panzergrenadier regiment from 25th Panzer Division to support the assault. Only a miracle could save the Poles.

On 14 September, it seemed as if their prayers were answered. At last, Soviet aircraft intervened in the battle. The Polikarpov Po-2 biplane was obsolete by any sensible standard, but had been used to great effect in roles ranging from liaison and reconnaissance to nuisance bombing missions; operating from short, improvised airstrips right behind the front line, Po-2s could fly several times per night, switching off their engines to glide over German lines. They then dropped small bombs that did little physical damage but caused great irritation by disturbing sleeping soldiers. Now, several Po-2s appeared over Warsaw and dropped supplies to the *AK*. Flights continued over the following days, dropping canisters at low level. To avoid the airdrops drifting over German areas, the canisters were not fitted with parachutes, but this resulted in many of the items within being damaged beyond repair. Most of the ammunition that was salvaged turned out to be useless anyway, since Russian bullets weren't compatible with the German and British guns used by the *AK*. But more important than the materiel received was the boost to morale brought by the drops, for sentiment amongst the starving, thirsty, vermin-riddled Varsovian public was reaching breaking point.[90] Still, despite every setback, the *AK* – a 'crowd of workers, artisans, college students and civil servants, which in one day had turned into a fighting army' – fought on.[91]

The following day, there was an even more startling development. An astonished Jan Mazurkiewicz met a young officer in Red Army uniform – a man from 3rd Polish Rifle Division, part of the First Polish Army. He had traversed the Vistula and informed Mazurkiewicz that a major crossing was planned for the coming night. Sure enough, shortly before dawn on 16 September, soldiers splashed their way across the river to the south of the ruined Poniatowski Bridge under a modest and relatively ineffective artillery bombardment, and the *AK* fighters greeted the small unit with joy. Larger groups attempted to cross to the south, but here they ran into heavy fire. German searchlights swept across the river and *AK* soldiers watched helplessly as mortar shells raised fountains of water and machine-guns hammered any boats that were spotted. Over 2,000 men tried to cross, but only about 900 made it to the west bank. Unable to support the small bridgehead, the commander of the division, Brigadier General Stanisław Galicki, ordered his men back to the east bank. More than half of those who had succeeded in crossing the Vistula were killed, with the survivors pulling back on 19 September. It is estimated that nearly 5,000 men from Galicki's division perished.[92]

Considering the huge resources available to the Red Army, this brief intervention was surprisingly small and ineffective. Not long after, General Zygmunt Berling was dismissed from command of First Polish Army, later claiming that he had initiated the crossing without authorisation from above. Given the strict control imposed at almost every level of the Red Army – and with First Polish Army fully integrated into the overall forces deployed against the Germans – it seems highly unlikely that Berling would have been able to show such independence. Moreover, of his units, 3rd Rifle Division was the least experienced, having seen little action to date, so whilst it was still numerically strong, its soldiers proved ill-prepared for the realities of urban warfare. It is more likely that the half-hearted attempt was planned at a local level by Berling and others in a desperate attempt to come to the aid of their fellow Poles, but they must have received approval from above. Indeed, the entire operation – including the airdrops by the Po-2s – may have been calculated as the minimum that Stalin needed to do to placate criticisms directed at him from London. Several prominent newspapers and periodicals had taken up Churchill's demands for greater action by the Red Army; there was even growing awareness in US circles that Stalin's reluctance to help the *AK* owed more to political calculations than operational difficulties, and pressure was mounting on Roosevelt to take a firmer line. In any case, the Varsovians were generally more appreciative of Berling's good intentions than they were resentful of his failure. After all, his intervention, 'however weak and futile, coming when all was lost', was still more substantive than anything else Stalin had offered thus far. Of course, the widespread belief – inaccurate as it may have been – that Berling had acted on his own initiative only compounded the Varsovians' belief that the 'official policy of Stalin [was] to let the Germans annihilate the best of the Polish nation'.[93]

No doubt fearing further attempts by the Red Army to cross the Vistula, the Germans redoubled their efforts. On 18 and 19 September, the Dirlewanger brigade stormed several key locations. As in Old Town, surviving *AK* troops escaped through the sewers, this time making for Mokotów. Others continued to cling to their positions in the hope that Berling would try again to support them. Finally, with their ammunition exhausted, the last men tried to slip away while the Germans moved through cellars executing anyone they regarded as a wounded *AK* fighter. Occasionally, there were moments of mercy; one German soldier sat on a hospital bed and drunkenly lamented, '*Schade, schade ich bin nicht Pole, ich wäre auch Partisan*' ('Such a pity I'm not a Pole, I would also have been a partisan'), before leaving without further comment.[94] Some soldiers helped Polish medical staff move their patients. Others were less merciful. Bed-bound Stanisław Likiernik watched as two Germans pulled a Pole – barely alive – from a burning house; 'Look at that,' one of them remarked, pointing to the man's shoulder, 'a sniper. Shoot him.'[95] As always, Dirlewanger's men were amongst the least scrupulous, killing almost everyone they found. When they stormed a paint factory, they found 122 people alive; all the women were raped and everyone was slaughtered. One, a priest, was hanged with his own cassock. From Bach's perspective, his subordinate had performed admirably; he proudly reported how 'heavy fire did not hold SS Oberführer Dirlewanger back. Again fighting at the front line, inspiring his men through daredevil acts and bravery … even though there were heavy losses amongst themselves, the banks of the Vistula were completely clean.'[96] By contrast, most eyewitness accounts describe Dirlewanger as standing behind his men, urging them forward and threatening any who hesitated.

The Poles who attempted to cross the Vistula to the east bank generally lost their lives in a hail of bullets before they ventured far into the stream. By dawn on 23 September, the entire west bank area was in German hands. By this stage, official German policy towards civilian survivors had been altered multiple times. At the outset of the Uprising, Himmler had intended all Varsovians to be killed, but had changed this in the last week of August. Facing growing demands for workers from German industry, he had told Bach to send adult prisoners to work camps; Polish children would be given to childless Germans. But in a forlorn attempt to persuade Poles to join the Germans in the war against the Soviet Union, Bach issued fresh instructions on 9 September that civilians were to be treated as ordinary prisoners. When, on 13 September, he heard that he'd been added to the Allies' list of war criminals, he was outraged. 'What an honour!' Bach scoffed in his diary, 'And this for Warsaw, the very place where I can consider my humanitarianism extended to extreme limits to be a virtue before God!' – leaving one to wonder how a less-humanitarian Bach might have behaved.[97] Meanwhile, German-controlled newspapers decried – in both German and Polish – the cynical behaviour of Stalin and the failure of the British to stand up for their 'First Ally' in the war. It is a measure of the self-delusion of Himmler and other Nazis that they even considered it a possibility that Poles would put aside the years of brutal repression and the more recent horrors of Wola to pay any heed to such messaging.

THE BEGINNING OF THE END

By the third week of September, *AK* control extended to just three parts of the city: Mokotów; Żoliborz, north of the city centre; and Śródmieście, the city centre itself. Two – Mokotów and Śródmieście – were within easy reach of Soviet support, but none was forthcoming. The charade of offering a small degree of support was over. It would have been a simple matter for Soviet guns and tanks to deploy on the east bank, from where they could fire at German positions at a range of less than 650 feet; instead, they remained silent. Nor did Soviet aviation make any serious attempt to stop Luftwaffe assaults.

Mokotów was the first target for the Germans, and Lüttwitz released 19th Panzer Division from his operational reserve to speed up the operation, which was meant to be completed in two days. On 24 September, German aircraft and artillery commenced a now familiar pattern of attacks and shortly after, 19th Panzer Division's tanks advanced into Mokotów from the west. The first assault was halted by Lieutenant Colonel Karol Rokicki's soldiers, but at the cost of heavy and unsustainable losses. To Bach's dismay, many of the reinforcements he had sent to replace Dirlewanger's casualties proved unwilling to replicate their predecessors' reckless attacks and it became clear that the two-day deadline would not be achieved. A brief two-hour ceasefire was hastily arranged to permit civilians to leave; some 9,000 Varsovians took the opportunity to cross the front line and were taken to Pruszków. When they resumed their attacks, the Germans made better progress as the depleted ranks of the *AK* began to run out of ammunition. The flight of so many civilians had a bad effect on morale, which was already sinking with the certainty of defeat. Having lost three quarters of his men, Rokicki sent a message to Chruściel that he was going to try to evacuate the survivors via the sewers. Chruściel demanded that he continue the fight, but his message failed to reach Rokicki, who escaped with about 600 others on 27 September. One group lost its way in the sewers and emerged in a German-held area; the men were pulled from the manhole quickly before they could warn those behind them and 140 were executed on the spot. The last 5,000 civilians in Mokotów emerged cautiously, fearing mistreatment, but Generalmajor Günther Rohr, who was overseeing the last phase of the operation, ensured that – with the exception of a few who fell into the hands of the Dirlewanger brigade – both civilians and *AK* personnel received better treatment than before. The defenders of Mokotów were to be treated as prisoners of war rather than *Partisanen*.

From Mokotów, the Germans switched their attention to Żoliborz. In mid-September, a limited German attack overran the northern edge of the city, but thereafter ground attacks ceased. Instead, the entire area was subjected to repeated air and artillery attacks, and in the days that followed much of the quietly prosperous suburb was slowly reduced to a field of smoking rubble and uptorn trees. The Polish defenders – numbering fewer than 2,000 and including a small number of men from First Polish Army who had not evacuated to the east bank – were led by Lieutenant Colonel Mieczysław Niedzielski. In the last days of September they found themselves grappling with the well-armed veterans of 19th Panzer Division; the initial determined resistance was broken, and faced with certain death if he fought on, Niedzielski secured Komorowski's permission to surrender on 30 September. The surviving *AK* men formed up outside his headquarters and, as agreed with Generalleutnant Hans Källner, commander of 19th Panzer Division, marched into captivity the following morning. Many must have doubted the assurances that they would be treated as proper prisoners of war, and almost immediately several Gestapo officers appeared; to the relief of the Poles, the officers of the panzer division curtly turned them away. The Polish fighters, together with about 15,000 civilians, were also marched to Pruszków.

To date, Bach had been chafing under constant criticism for the slowness in suppressing the Uprising. 'Warsaw is hanging like a millstone around my neck,' he wrote in mid-September.[98] The relatively swift capture of Mokotów and Żoliborz came as a great personal relief. In truth, this owed little to his leadership and far more to the firepower of 19th Panzer Division, which was able to make good use of the wide boulevards of the two districts. For many months, Bach had resented the lack of the recognition that he felt he deserved, and was therefore particularly pleased when he was informed that Hitler had awarded him the Knight's Cross. His sense of satisfaction was only slightly marred by the news that Reinefarth, who was already a Knight's Cross holder, had been awarded the Oak Leaves to the Knight's Cross.

All eyes were now on Śródmieście, the last remaining *AK* enclave. The area's narrow medieval streets were divided into two by the German-controlled Jerusalem Avenue, though they remained linked by underground tunnels. Some 250,000 Varsovians were crowded into Śródmieście, and from mid-September the area suffered the same bombardment that had brought destruction to other parts of Warsaw. Casualties rose rapidly in the overcrowded buildings, overwhelming the last remaining medical facilities. As for those still fighting, it is hard to overstate the sheer physical and mental exhaustion they were suffering by this point. Many were delirious with overtiredness and hunger, rendering their efforts of resistance ever more desperate. In the last days of September, Julian Kulski was overcome with fever but refused to countenance withdrawal. As his unit moved through the city ruins, he was charged with firing a PIAT at several German tanks. He recalled how, for once, he was blessed by an 'ample supply of missiles', and it was ultimately his body that gave out first: 'finally, I could no longer pull the spring and collapsed, utterly exhausted.'[99] With no food or ammunition supplies left to speak of, the situation was clearly hopeless. Just a short distance away, Soviet forces sat in silence as German bombs and shells blasted the city centre.

ANOTHER SEPTEMBER TRAGEDY

Early on 28 September, Komorowski sent Lieutenant Colonel Zygmunt Dobrowolski across the front line under a flag of truce. The Polish representatives were driven to Bach's headquarters at Ożarów; they were made to wait – presumably to impress upon them that Bach was a busy, important person – and finally met the SS commander, who launched into a longwinded, pompous speech. After boasting about his personal status both as a military officer and as a politician, he told the Poles that he personally bore no blame for the atrocities committed in the city. He claimed that he had only taken up his post in the second week of the Uprising, and that the German forces arrayed against the *AK* had varied greatly in quality, adding:

> The unusually difficult conditions were made worse here because of the specific conditions of the Warsaw Uprising during which civilian involvement in combat, and confusion over uniforms, and all such things made it difficult for the German soldier to keep calm, and that is why some very unpleasant things took place, things which should not occur between two cultured nations.[100]

It was a bare-faced lie. Bach had been in command from the outset and at no stage did he make any attempt to rein in Dirlewanger or Kaminski – his previous experience in Belarus can have left him with no doubt how they and their men would behave, and he only took action against Kaminski for looting, not for the atrocities that he and his men were committing. But in the discussions that followed, Bach agreed to Dobrowolski's requests: all *AK* soldiers were to be treated as prisoners of war and civilians would be protected from further harm. Dobrowolski returned to Śródmieście in the early afternoon and briefed Komorowski and other senior figures about Bach's proposals. Chruściel, whose only son had already been killed in the Uprising, was determined to continue the fight. Few shared his conviction, yet still hoping that even at this late stage Stalin would authorise intervention by the Red Army, Komorowski played for time. He requested – and was granted – a visit to Pruszków by a Polish delegation to confirm that conditions were satisfactory. Finally, late on 30 September, a ceasefire was arranged to take effect at 5am the following morning, and civilians would be evacuated to Pruszków. On 1 October, the exhausted, fearful civilians began to leave Śródmieście.

All that remained was to negotiate the final surrender of Komorowski's fighters. Talks dragged on through the morning of 2 October and the final document was signed that evening. The triumphant Bach immediately telephoned Berlin and informed the repulsive Gruppenführer Hermann Fegelein, Himmler's liaison officer in the headquarters, of the development. Fegelein was dismayed that Bach had agreed to almost all of Komorowski's demands, and there was every chance that the agreement would be rejected. To date, the identity of the *AK* commander was largely unknown – the Germans knew him only by his *nom de guerre*, Bór – but for once, fate was kind to the Poles. Fegelein, who had represented Germany in equestrian events before the war, demanded to know Bór's real name. Gerhard von Jordan, who had been a civilian administrator in Warsaw and was now acting as an interpreter, later recalled:

> Bach said, 'Oh, didn't you know? He's the famous showjumper, Count Komorowski. You must know him.' 'Ah, him,' replied Fegelein. 'A fantastic fellow! That changes everything. Please wait a moment.' … After a few moments, Fegelein passed on Hitler's acceptance of the terms of surrender.[101]

In Warsaw, word was passed down the *AK* chain of command. Even if the surrender came as no surprise, it was nonetheless greeted with dismay. A member of the *Parasol* battalion wrote in his diary on 3 October:

> The ceasefire has been agreed for sure. We have the details. There is official confirmation that we are Allied soldiers. We will leave with our guns and banners. We are to be exclusively in Wehrmacht custody; prisoners of war under the Geneva Convention …
>
> Weird atmosphere in our battalion. The last food supplies were distributed for a decent meal. Our cash was also distributed … The guns are a big issue. We have to hand them to the Germans. I can't contemplate saying goodbye to my Sten. I imagined it would end differently.[102]

Despite the bitter taste of capitulation, this time, the city's defenders marched out with their heads held high. 'Although they were such a wretched sight beside their conquerors,' remarked Władysław Szpilman, who had survived the Uprising in hiding, 'you felt it was not they who were defeated.'[103] After weeks of surviving on little more than adrenaline, the *AK* men queued for a chance to wash and shave. On 4 October, with German news cameras recording the moment, Chruściel and Komorowski led their fighters out for the last time. 'We had to remind the Germans what kind of soldiers they had been fighting during the last two months,' Kulski explained.[104] Krystyna Bierzyńska, who was also amongst the marching column, recalled how Poles outside the city greeted the defeated fighters as heroes:

> Civilians and peasants were lining up on our right. There was the road, then a ditch, and then these people standing there waving to us, crying, and throwing us apples and bread and sausage. At this point, I heard someone say, 'if you want to get out, do it now. Jump into the ditch and you'll be fine.' Some of the girls got away. And no one got shot. I don't think the Germans really cared. There were some Wehrmacht officers watching us. The people were throwing us bread. I got an apple or something. The Germans were telling them to go away, but the Poles kept coming back. They were awed by us![105]

And indeed, the Germans' rhetoric of earlier weeks – describing the insurgents as lawless bandits – was replaced by a profound respect for the Poles who had fought so hard for their city. Leutnant Peter Stolten, a Wehrmacht soldier in one of the units that assisted the SS formations in the battle, wrote in a letter home:

> Let's not deceive ourselves. Warsaw fell because of the concentration of our heavy weapons, not because of the courage of our units … Despite everything, the most heroic fighting, given the conditions, was done by the insurgents themselves … The insurgents really should be treated like soldiers. What could they do when they lost their nation and didn't have their own [regular] army? I wouldn't have liked to live under German administration either … The Poles marched in rows of four abreast, avoiding the tear-stained and pain-filled faces of the women, dressed wherever possible in remnants of Wehrmacht or other uniform, with their weapons ready to be surrendered. All done without despair, unbreakable in their national pride.[106]

CHAPTER 12

THE DEVASTATED CITY

… My pen is lighter
Than a hummingbird's feather. This burden
Is too much for it to bear.
How can I live in this country
Where the foot knocks against
The unburied bones of kin?

I hear voices, see smiles. I cannot
Write anything; five hands
Seize my pen and order me to write
The story of their lives and deaths.
Was I born to become
a ritual mourner? …

Czesław Miłosz, 'In Warsaw', 1945[1]

INTO CAPTIVITY

Four months before war broke out in 1939, foreign affairs minister Józef Beck made an impassioned speech to the *Sejm* against Hitler's demands in the Polish Corridor:

> Peace is a precious and a desirable thing. Our generation, bloodied in wars, certainly deserves peace. But peace, like almost all things of this world, has its

> price, a high but a measurable one. We in Poland do not know the concept of peace at any price. There is only one thing in the lives of men, nations and countries that is without price. That thing is honour.[2]

The end of the Warsaw Uprising marked the close of a tragic and at times surreal period of history – but it did not herald the peace that the Poles had dreamed of. In the words of the historian Norman Davies, 'in the western half of the city, a residual community of half a million people were being forced to surrender themselves to Nazi captivity, while in the eastern half, the largest army in the world pretended not to be there'.[3] Jan Rosinski, the estranged *AK* member who spent the Uprising sourcing medical supplies, stepped out of the Maltanski Hospital on 3 October and cried unashamedly as the Germans lowered the Polish flag flying outside. He knew that on the back of the *kapitulacja* came 'a life-altering choice: remain in Warsaw to confront the Russians or become prisoners of war in Germany.'[4]

For most Varsovians who endured these moments, there was little doubt where the blame lay for their defeat. The Western Allies might have done more, but the force that could have done the most to help them had – aside from a brief effort with a fraction of its resources – done nothing. On 5 October Prime Minister Churchill addressed the House of Commons to commend the 'heroic stand' of the Varsovians and acknowledged that the city had suffered to an extent 'unsurpassed even in the miseries of this war'; less comforting to the Poles was his declaration that their defeat came 'despite all the efforts of the Soviet Army.'[5] Even the most superficial visit to Warsaw shows the dishonesty of this. From the east bank of the Vistula, the Soviet units were within rifleshot of the west bank and could easily have provided far more support for the Uprising.

Komorowski was driven to Bach's headquarters, where he was subjected to a typically bombastic welcome. Bach suggested that the real enemy of both Germans and Poles lay to the east and enquired whether Komorowski was prepared to order the *AK* in other parts of Poland to join the Germans in the fight against the Soviet Union; Komorowski bluntly refused.[6] He also rejected Bach's offer of a meal and hospitality, preferring to remain with his men. Further approaches followed, but Komorowski and his senior officers remained adamant. However much they hated the Soviet Union, they would not fight alongside the Germans.

The camp at Pruszków – or *Durchgangslager 121* (usually abbreviated to *Dulag 121*), as it was known – was established only during the first week of the Uprising but quickly gained notoriety. Its sole purpose was the processing of Varsovian refugees before further transport to Germany or elsewhere in the

Generalgouvernement, though by September it was rumoured that all Varsovians were being sent on to concentration camps.[7] Pruszków residents watched in alarm as, on 7 August, a few thousand evacuees of Wola – mostly women and children, for few able-bodied men had been spared – were herded into the town's abandoned railway workshops. Over the following days, wave after wave of prisoners arrived 'in various clothes, some barefoot and wearing underwear only, hungry, thirsty, terrified and utterly terrorised', having been forced to march the nine miles from Warsaw; those that arrived on trains frequently had to step over the corpses of companions who had suffocated in the tightly-packed carriages.[8] It wasn't long before the improvised railway halls were critically overcrowded and had become a hotbed for dysentery, typhus, and diarrhoea. Things descended into chaos as it became apparent the Germans were wholly unprepared for the volume of refugees arriving and had only one method for asserting control: 'to shoot'.[9] Around 10 August, the camp administration was formalised under the 'cold, composed, and taciturn' Sturmbannführer Hans Diehl, the drunken and sadistically cruel Sturmbannführer August Polland, and the slightly more 'old school' Oberst Bernhard Sieber, under whom the process of segregating and deporting evacuees accelerated. Polland in particular took 'bestial pleasure' in tearing families apart, confiscating pets, and requisitioning the refugees' last paltry possessions.

Meanwhile, the responsibility of providing food and medicine to the refugees was delegated entirely to the Pruszków Central Welfare Council and Red Cross. However, even with the support of local volunteers it was impossible to keep pace with the endless arrivals and spiralling mortality rates. Welfare Council worker Władysław Mazurek described how deaths noticeably spiked amongst civilians from the worst-hit areas in the Uprising; those from Wola, Zieleniak, Old Town, and Czerniaków had spent so long in fetid conditions or confined underground that they were usually the fastest to succumb to disease in the camp. When, in early September, the International Red Cross sent a delegation to inspect conditions in the camp, Diehl forced the town's Welfare Council to sign a declaration to the effect that the food, medical care, and freedoms afforded to the camp population were beyond reproach, and that they '[had] not been the victim of any abuses.'[10] Failure to comply, Diehl made it clear, would result in all Polish personnel providing aid to be ejected from the camp – which would have spelt disaster for an already dire humanitarian situation.

Given how few Poles and Germans spoke the language of the other side, the authorities in Pruszków had to rely on a relatively small band of Polish interpreters to sort out who was fit for work and therefore suitable for transfer to labour camps. The translators took advantage of this to invent answers on behalf of the prisoners, but it soon became apparent that the best chance of escaping forced labour was on medical grounds. Realising this, Polish physicians and nurses worked hard to secure exemptions for thousands of refugees by requesting their transfer to hospitals, taking care to diversify their purported illnesses to reduce suspicion. This became significantly harder in mid-August, when all such recommendations became subject to vetting by German physicians or were arbitrarily rejected by the Gestapo, though the Polish medics carefully coached the prisoners on appropriate symptoms and signs.[11] Given the German preoccupation with the spread of disease – particularly typhus – some of the Polish staff deliberately transferred lice to their 'patients', who were then usually released without further ado. Stefan Cichoński was one of the lucky internees who escaped deportation thanks to the intervention of Dr Julia Bielecka – but he was in such a terrible state that his own mother, a Pruszków resident, did not recognise him when he arrived on her doorstep.[12]

The first prisoners of war entered the camp after the fall of Mokotów in late September. Amongst their numbers were children as young as eight to ten years old, all of whom were uniformed and bore the red and white armbands of resistance. In spite of the terms of surrender, the *AK* prisoners were frequently singled out for violent punishment. Mazurek recalled several occasions where the resistance fighters were led behind a vegetable warehouse to be beaten or disappeared into Diehl's ominous 'green wagon' for interrogation.[13] This became a point of contention between Diehl's SS on the one hand, and Sieber on the other, who insisted that the prisoners of war were the Wehrmacht's responsibility. In any case, the fighters were kept strictly separated from the rest of the camp population and denied visits from the bishop, Antoni Szlagowski, who had taken upon himself the pastoral care of the camp population. Many fighters expected nothing less than execution from the Germans, and unknown numbers were indeed murdered before they left the transit camp. The majority, however, were herded on to trains like their civilian counterparts and dispatched to prisoner of war camps in the west. As Julian Kulski boarded the train out of Pruszków on 5 October, the resistance fighters were addressed by a commander of the same panzer division they had faced in Żoliborz: 'He said he was proud that his division had had the chance to fight against such courageous soldiers'; once he finished speaking, these same 'courageous soldiers' were unceremoniously pushed on board the wooden cattle railcar in which they would be confined for three days.[14]

Ultimately, about 55,000 Varsovians were sent from Pruszków to concentration camps, including 13,000 to Auschwitz. As the Red Army poured across the Reich in the last winter of the war, concentration camp inmates were marched along snowbound roads from one camp to another, and stragglers shot; tens of thousands perished in these 'death marches'. A further 150,000 Varsovians were dispatched to labour camps. The relatively lucky ones found themselves assigned to local households as servants, but others were forced to work in factories and mines or in the construction of defences. Even those fortunate enough to be released – about 350,000 – faced the grim prospect of finding accommodation in Poland's towns and villages where resources were already critically scarce. Most of the Varsovians had only the summer clothes they were wearing at the time of their capture.

After the majority of civilians had departed, Pruszków served as a processing centre for male prisoners, many of whom were kept as a source of labour for the ongoing destruction of Warsaw. A final round-up of Varsovians in the last days of the German occupation boosted the population slightly, but the camp's official closure was announced in November, and from then on the remaining internees were slowly liquidated. When Pruszków fell to the Red Army in January 1945, there were still 700 inmates.

THE CITY OF ROBINSON CRUSOES

Back in Warsaw itself, between 2,000 and 3,000 civilians remained in hiding after capitulation.[15] Clinging to life amid the ruins of the city, these survivors became known as the 'Robinson Crusoes', comprising both Poles and Jews who managed to evade immediate capture in October 1944. Amongst their numbers was the pianist Władysław Szpilman; by October, he recalled, he could hardly talk, having spent four months in silent solitude:

> I was alone: alone not just in a single building or even a single part of a city, but alone in a whole city that only two months ago had had a population of a million and a half and was one of the richer cities of Europe. It now consisted of the chimneys of burnt-out buildings pointing to the sky, and whatever walls the bombing had spared: a city of rubble and ashes under which the centuries-old culture of my people and the bodies of hundreds of thousands of murdered victims lay buried, rotting in the warmth of these late autumn days and filling the air with a dreadful stench.[16]

Szpilman survived almost entirely in isolation except for the intervention of a German officer, Hauptmann Wilm Hosenfeld, who secreted provisions to his hiding place above a commando unit. On 12 December, Hosenfeld visited for the last time, assuring Szpilman that the Red Army was on its way: 'If you and I have survived this inferno for over five years,' he told the pianist, 'it's obviously God's will for us to live. Well, we have to believe that, anyway.'[17] Hosenfeld would die a Soviet prisoner in 1952. Szpilman, who petitioned for his rescuer's release after the war, returned to an illustrious music career which lasted until his death in 2000.

As the Germans combed through the gutted city, they became aware that they were not alone. They hounded the survivors by poisoning their well water, tossing grenades into cellars, and setting up elaborate ambushes; even when they remained undetected, the Robinsons had to contend with German and Ukrainian troops looting their last remaining supplies, or, as in Szpilman's case, inadvertently sharing their accommodation. Some, like Jan Kostański, found intact bunkers capable of housing large groups of people, and created improvised communities amongst the starving, dehydrated, vermin-covered survivors – with all the friendships and betrayals this entailed. On one occasion, Kostański's group killed and cooked a German dog to make matzo ball soup; on another, he watched through binoculars as a group of Germans unearthed one of his previous bunkers and executed a group of 24 Jews on the spot.[18] In mid-November, a group of Robinsons was rounded up and joined one of the final transports to Pruszków; incredibly, some of its members lasted the bitter winter through to the arrival of the Soviets on 17 January. The majority eked out their desperate existence in complete secrecy knowing that, having survived so much, they could still be killed at any moment. However, a few continued their open opposition of the Germans. One, known by his moniker 'Ares' – after the Greek god of war, and with which he signed his acts of arson – grew into an urban legend amongst the Robinson community. Survivors shared stories of Germans being sabotaged with explosive devices, terrorised in their barracks, and confronted with a hanging effigy of Hitler labelled 'kaput'. Ominous slogans appeared around the city threatening death to all Germans who remained in Warsaw and declaring the immortal spirit of Polish resistance: 'Ares is spirit, not matter – you have no reason to look for it.'[19]

Even as the guns fell silent, the demolition of what remained of Warsaw began. It was one of the most pointless and vindictive acts of the Nazi regime. Warsaw had been declared a 'fortress', and the Wehrmacht was expected to hold it at all costs when the next Soviet offensive began. Despite the experience of such fortresses in preceding months, Hitler – and to his discredit, Guderian, the chief of the general staff – continued to hope that a chain of fortresses would hold up the Soviet drive towards Berlin long enough for mobile units to counterattack and restore the line. But if Warsaw was to function as a fortress, its ruined buildings should have been left untouched as they would have provided excellent cover for its garrison. Flattening them removed any possibility of the city being held for any length of time. On the other hand, according to the diary of Hosenfeld, Szpilman's rescuer, the Führer's intentions to see the city razed to the ground had been common knowledge for some months. Hosenfeld wrote with a deep sense of disillusionment and despair towards the Reich, but his judgement of the Germans' wanton destruction alludes to a truth that few Nazis would have been prepared to admit, even this late in the war. In the first half of August, he had written:

> All the streets liberated in the uprising are being destroyed by fire. The inhabitants have to leave the city, and are going westward in crowds of many thousands. If the news of this decree is true then it's clear to me that we have lost Warsaw, and with it Poland and the war itself. We are giving up a place we held for five years ... Monstrous methods were used here. We acted as if we were the masters and would never go away. Now we can't help seeing that all is lost, we're destroying our own work, everything of which the civil administration was so proud – it saw its great cultural tasks as being here and wanted to prove their necessity to the world. Our policy in the east is bankrupt, and we are erecting a final memorial to it with the destruction of Warsaw.[20]

Nonetheless, Hitler's orders – restated on 9 October – had to be obeyed. Small squads moved through the deserted streets, dynamiting any substantial structures that remained and lighting innumerable fires. Varsovians being held in Pruszków were often pressganged into these *Brandkommandos* and were forced to help destroy their own city. At the same time, other groups under the control of Oberst Wilhelm Rodewald's *Räumungsstab* ('Clearance Staff') systematically removed any remaining valuable items from the city. Various German agencies scrambled to take part: in Łódź, *Gauleiter* Greiser ordered the police units he had dispatched to Warsaw to earmark large quantities of loot for him; Frank issued similar instructions from Kraków; and individual ministries in Berlin demanded their share of the spoils.[21] Over 23,000 railcars loaded with loot left Warsaw in the first half of October. Thereafter, the gathering of booty slowed but continued until the last week of November.[22]

HISTORICAL INJUSTICE

On 12 January 1945, after extensive preparations, Soviet forces erupted from their bridgeheads at Sandomierz and Magnuszew and established a new bridgehead across the Vistula north of Warsaw. German resistance collapsed almost immediately as the Soviet columns raced across the frozen landscape. With the leading tank columns already far to the east, the Red Army moved into Warsaw on 17 January to find that about 85 per cent of the city had been utterly destroyed. Georgy Gavrilovich Semenov, a staff officer, was ordered to take a small group of officers into the city to assess the state of the roads:

> We drove in two vehicles along the highway where units of Forty-Seventh Army had recently advanced. At the end of the day, after running the risk of setting off German mines, we made our way with great difficulty to the northern part of Warsaw.
>
> The city was quiet. The scale of destruction was astonishing. All buildings were reduced to ruins. Piles of broken bricks littered the streets. The few surviving residents emerged from the basements. With tears of joy in their eyes, they hugged and kissed us, warmly greeting every Soviet and Polish soldier.[23]

Just how warm the welcome was is open to question. Many of the Robinsons who had evaded the German attempts to clear the city had perished from cold and starvation, but those still alive would have been perfectly aware that their 'liberators' had barely lifted a finger to help them during the Uprising. Any doubts were surely extinguished when the *NKVD* immediately began screening the remaining Varsovians to identify former *AK* fighters, and promptly dispatched those with resistance connections to the east. By 1945, it is estimated that the *NKVD* had already arrested over 60,000 Poles and deported at least 50,000, including thousands of *AK* soldiers. A further 100,000 would be arrested in Poland over the following year on political grounds, and by 1949 the Soviet military courts would have handed down 50,000 sentences – at least 4,000 of which were death sentences.[24]

Needless to say, Hitler's fortress city plans for Warsaw proved utterly futile and there was no serious attempt to defend the ruined city. Outflanked to north and south, commander of the XLVI Panzer Corps General Martin Fries took advantage of the confusion of orders between Hitler, the army group, and Ninth Army to withdraw towards the west. Without the support of the formations of this corps, Generalleutnant Friedrich Weber's city garrison hadn't the slightest chance of holding on and managed to secure permission from Guderian's staff to withdraw. All of these retreats took place without the explicit permission of Hitler, whose rage was all-consuming. Oberst Bogislaw von Bonin, the chief of operations in Guderian's headquarters, was arrested; Fries was dismissed, as were Lüttwitz (commander of Ninth Army) and Weber. All were court-martialled for abandoning Warsaw, but Lüttwitz bravely took full responsibility, producing documents to show that both Fries and Weber had withdrawn under his orders. Despite the demands of many – including Keitel, the weak-willed head of *OKW* and one of Hitler's innermost circle – that someone should face the death penalty for failing to defend Warsaw, Lüttwitz and Fries were acquitted; they then slipped away and surrendered to the Western Powers to avoid being re-arrested. Weber, though, was slightly less fortunate. As a fortress commandant, he was directly answerable to Hitler and was found guilty of failing to follow orders. His three-year prison sentence was altered to probation and he too managed to make his way to the west as Germany collapsed. Bonin too was found guilty and sent first to Flossenburg concentration camp, then to Dachau and finally to Niederdorf in north Italy, where he was held together with family members of some who had been arrested following the failed July Plot to kill Hitler.

The *AK* was officially disbanded when the Soviet forces occupied Warsaw. On 19 January, Brigadier General Leopold Okulicki, who had taken command after Komorowski's surrender, issued a final order:

> Soldiers of the Home Army!
>
> The rapid advance may lead to occupation by the Soviet Army in a short space of time. This is not the triumph of our just cause, for which we have fought since 1939 …
>
> We do not wish to fight the Soviets, but we will never accept life in anything less than a free, independent Poland that supports social justice …
>
> Soldiers of the Home Army: I give you my last order. Continue to work and act with the aim of restoring full independence of the country. In this, each of you must be his own commander … I hereby release you from your oath of allegiance and declare the Home Army to be dissolved.
>
> On behalf of the service, I thank you for your sacrifices to date. I believe deeply that our Holy Cause will prevail and that we will meet in a truly free and democratic Poland.[25]

It would be another 44 years before Okulicki's final words came true, but he did not live to experience it, nor the state that arose under strict Soviet control after the war. A group of 16 senior officers, including Okulicki, were told that they were to be flown to London for consultations – with assurances of safe passage. But when they appeared before the Soviet authorities in late March, they were arrested and dispatched to the Lubyanka prison in Moscow. British foreign minister Anthony Eden raised the issue of their arrest with Molotov at the inaugural United Nations conference in San Francisco in May and lamely accepted Molotov's response that they were awaiting trial for conducting hostile operations against the Red Army. The 16 officers were finally put on trial in June after several months of often brutal interrogation. Most had been forced to sign confessions; charges were dropped against four, and the rest were sentenced for terms of between four and ten years. Okulicki died the following year, either through mistreatment or as a consequence of a hunger strike.[26] Jan Jankowski, the delegate of the government-in-exile in Warsaw during the Uprising, was sentenced to eight years' imprisonment. He died in captivity just two weeks before he was due for release, probably murdered by his guards.[27]

The government-in-exile's hopes for independence were decisively extinguished shortly after the Red Army's seizure of Warsaw when Stalin, Roosevelt, and Churchill met in Yalta. The so-called 'Big Three' powers decided that Poland would lose its former eastern territories, receiving in compensation Silesia, Pomerania, and the southern part of East Prussia – once again, with little regard for the German populations who called these regions their home. With the Red Army in firm control of Poland, there was no possibility of the Western Powers insisting on the government-in-exile playing a major role in post-war Poland. The Lublin government, scrupulously loyal to Stalin, would take control, though the Soviets promised that there would be free and fair elections. In his memoirs, Józef Czapski comments on the collective failure of the Poles – and the Allies – to take seriously the threat from the east:

> Why did I not think about what might lie ahead of us after the defeat of Germany? What stopped me from considering a new threat, of Soviet occupation this time? Faith in 'historical justice'? A typically Polish 'somehow it'll work out' attitude? That too, but above all the hope for change for the better after the war, all over the world, including Russia. Above all, overestimation of the moral strengths of the 'great democracies.' We chronically believed – how very few incisive, reticent pessimists there were among us – in all the promises, treaties, and Atlantic Charters. Words, words like Roosevelt's declaration that 'Poland is the inspiration of nations,' seemed to us a guarantee that once the war was won, we weren't going to be treated like just another card to swap in a game with the Soviets.[28]

THE PRICE OF PEACE

The casualties suffered by both sides during the Uprising are inevitably disputed, not least because so many people were buried in the ruins and their bodies were never recovered; nor did the Germans keep any records of the thousands that they massacred. One Polish government account of the fighting gives the military losses as 10,000 *AK* fighters killed, 6,000 wounded, and 5,000 missing; German losses are put at 10,000 killed, 9,000 wounded, and 7,000 missing.[29] When he was interrogated after the war, Bach estimated that total German casualties numbered 20,000. Other accounts give far lower numbers for German losses, but matters are complicated by the different ways that the various agencies – Wehrmacht, SS, and police – recorded both their losses and the time periods in which they took place. The number of civilians who died is even harder to estimate, with a maximum estimate approaching 200,000. Davies has pointed out that this is equivalent to an event the magnitude of the 9/11 attack on New York happening every day of the Uprising.[30] To these numbers should be added tens of thousands of Varsovians who died in concentration camps and work camps in the months that followed. The total number of Varsovians who died during the war exceeded 700,000; by comparison, 450,000 British citizens – civilians and soldiers combined – were killed in the entire conflict.

Of all the countries involved in a war that spanned the globe, Poland lost a larger percentage of its population than any other, with more than one in five killed: shot, starved or worked to death, left to succumb to disease, or gassed in the mechanised slaughter of *Aktion Reinhard*. The devastation inflicted upon Warsaw is a concentrated example of what unfolded across the entire country. As was the case everywhere that the Nazi regime carried out mass murder, the Jews suffered the most, and across all of Poland, Jews made up roughly half the total killed. Barely one in ten of the 3.3 million Jews who lived in the country in 1939 survived. Similarly, the Jewish population of Warsaw – swollen by refugees fleeing the German advance, and then further increased by the forcible movement of Jews into the Warsaw Ghetto from nearby towns – was almost completely wiped out, with some estimates suggesting that only one in 50 survived.[31] The numbers are so large that the human mind struggles to comprehend the scale of killing. Every one of those who died – between 6 and 7 million Poles – represents a tragedy: a life story lost, a future unlived, dreams unfulfilled.

For the brutalised survivors of Poland, there was the added ordeal of finding their homeland reduced to ruins. Warsaw was almost completely destroyed; other cities became battlegrounds as the Red Army drove towards Berlin; and the retreating Germans demolished bridges, railway lines, roads, power stations, and anything else that the advancing Soviet forces might conceivably find useful. But whilst the damage all across the country was severe, nowhere was it worse than in Warsaw, where, even on the eve of the Soviet advance across Poland from the Vistula, German demolition teams were still at work. This created a particularly pressing problem: it was important to establish a new civil administration in

Poland – even if it was to be the Soviet's *PKWN* puppet – but Warsaw was in no state to be the centre of government.

Consequently, even as Soviet troops approached the Oder River on their way to Berlin, the Lublin government moved to Łódź, in western Poland. The Germans had been forced to abandon the city in haste as Soviet units approached but it was largely intact. The sheer scale of damage to Warsaw was so great that there was serious consideration to moving the capital permanently, either to Łódź or to Kraków – which, in addition to its role in the *Generalgouvernement*, had been the capital of Poland in the 11th century and again from 1138 to the beginning of the 17th century. There were even proposals not to rebuild Warsaw, but to create a huge memorial to the suffering of Poland in the war. But even though many in the pro-Soviet government distrusted Warsaw as the hotbed of the pro-western *AK*, the emotional importance of the city to the Polish nation was too great to ignore. Perhaps thinking that he should offer the British and American leaders a crumb of comfort, Stalin announced at the beginning of the Yalta Conference that the Communist government had passed a resolution that Warsaw was to be rebuilt.

In any case, people were voting with their feet. Varsovian residents started to return within weeks of the Soviet advance into and beyond Warsaw. Together with thousands of refugees from other parts of Poland, they started clearing rubble and began to think about piecing their lives back together. In the last week of January 1945, 12,000 returned to the city; 67,000 followed in February; and a further 77,000 in March.[32] With the final defeat of Nazi Germany in May 1945, prisoners from concentration camps and labour camps also began to make their way home. Most had to improvise shelter amidst the sea of ruins. Zofia Nałkowska, the author who had eked a living running a tobacco shop, had fled from Warsaw at the beginning of the Uprising, but returned to the city as soon as she could, and was there in May when Warsaw was lit up by flares and tracer rounds as people celebrated the German surrender. The ruins were 'still a city and are still Warsaw', she wrote.[33] Others struggled to see past and would never escape the mental trauma of more recent events. One nurse who had worked with the *AK* during the Uprising was often haunted by nightmares that left her screaming in the middle of the night; another simply refused to think about the Uprising, fearing the memories it would bring back.[34]

SELECTIVE RECONSTRUCTION

On 14 February, the *Biuro Odbudowy Stolicy* ('Office for the Reconstruction of the Capital' or *BOS*) was formed under the leadership of distinguished architect Roman Piotrkowski. The task was daunting. First, the team created a catalogue of what had survived. Next came discussions on what should be rebuilt, and how. All across Europe, cities that had been wrecked by the war were slowly rising again, and in most cases a conscious decision was made to reconstruct only a limited part of what had been there before. In many locations, it was seen as an opportunity to remove old buildings and monuments that had outlived their purpose, and Piotrkowski was in favour of extensive modernisation. But Jan Zachwatowicz, who had been appointed head of the Department of Historic Architecture of the *BOS*, soon found himself in opposition to Piotrkowski:

> The significance for the nation of the monuments of the past has been dramatically highlighted by the experience of recent years, when – wanting to destroy us as a nation – the Germans demolished our monuments. Because the nation and its cultural monuments are indivisible. We cannot agree to having our cultural monuments torn away from us and we will reconstruct them, rebuilding them from their foundations, so that we can pass on to future generations, if not the authentic originals, then at least the exact replicas of these monuments … Whole pages of our history, written in the stone syllables of architecture, were torn out deliberately. Our responsibility towards future generations demands the reconstruction of what was destroyed.[35]

Zachwatowicz and his team drew up ambitious plans for a huge reconstruction of Warsaw that inevitably had to be reduced in scale; even if funding for such a scheme had been available, the modern needs of the city dictated the construction of new roads and connections that had not existed before. As a result, most of the reconstruction centred on Old Town and the most historic buildings, but even here there were omissions. The Saxon Palace and neighbouring Brühl Palace – where Stahel had ordered his men to use civilians as human shields during the Uprising – were subsequently levelled and the site remains the subject of fierce debate to this day. The *BOS* managed to find documents from the 1930s about planning proposals that provided insights into what had existed before, but details of many old buildings and monuments had to be gathered from other sources, ranging from photographs to oil paintings by Canaletto. Meanwhile, the steady stream of Varsovians who were returning to the city and trying to build homes in the rubble were also causing difficulties. In an attempt to prevent such activity from interfering with official restoration plans, authorities installed approximately 800 *akcję czerwonych* ('red plaques') throughout the city, designating sites of national historical significance where unauthorised building was explicitly prohibited.[36] Thousands of volunteers helped, contributing old illustrations and postcards and labouring on the ruins.

It was the ultimate repudiation by ordinary people of the plans of Hitler and Himmler to erase the city, but it proved to be a harrowing experience. Workers unearthed countless remains of those who had died in the Uprising or been executed in the former ghetto. In Wola, a huge pile of ashes was discovered in what had been a children's playground; two tons of ash were found in Ujazdowskie Avenue. These and other sites were all that remained of those who were heaped onto pyres by forced labourers. Identification of the remains was impossible, and the authorities could only issue approximate estimates of the number of dead. On 6 August 1946, the ashes were interred in a crypt. Thousands of Varsovians – and also the soldiers arrayed along the road as a guard of honour – wept as they threw flowers on the trucks that carried 100 plain coffins to their final resting place.

Reconstruction was also marred by the heavy hand of Soviet influence. Moscow's demands for 'Social Realism' after 1949 found their most enduring expression in the ostentatious Palace of Culture and Science, whose construction required the destruction of numerous 19th-century buildings. From the moment it was built, it became the focus of resentment and ridicule towards Stalinist imposition: the poet Władysław Broniewski named it *koszmarny sen pijanego cukiernika* ('the drunken confectioner's nightmarish dream'); others called it the *Ruski tort* ('Russian cake'); perhaps the pithiest nickname was *chuj Stalina* ('Stalin's dick'). The building remains controversial, an imposing intrusion on Warsaw's skyline, and calls for its demolition continue to this day.

THE FATE OF THE PERPETRATORS

The people who played important roles in the tragedies that unfolded in Warsaw in the war had different fates. By the end of the conflict, many were already dead. Heydrich was assassinated in 1942, Kaminski was shot by the Germans before the Uprising was over, and some of those involved in the long years of repression and murder took their own lives as their dreams of a Nazi future turned to dust. Hitler shot himself in Berlin as the Red Army closed in, and Himmler swallowed a cyanide capsule after he was captured by the British. Odilo Globočnik – who oversaw *Aktion Reinhard* and was described by one historian as 'the vilest individual in the vilest organisation ever known' – was sent to Trieste after his duties in Warsaw were completed; there, he and his men tortured and killed thousands of Italian partisans and Jews.[37] At the end of the war, he attempted to hide in Austria with a group of other prominent Nazis but was captured by the British. Like Himmler, he took cyanide before he could be interrogated. Obergruppenführer

Friedrich-Wilhelm Krüger, the *HSSPF* of the *Generalgouvernement* who oversaw the liquidation of the Warsaw Ghetto, narrowly escaped an attempt by the *AK* to assassinate him in 1943 and then served with *SS-Gebirgsdivision Prinz Eugen* in Yugoslavia, where he was involved in further atrocities. He ended the war in Austria, where he shot himself on the eve of the final surrender.

Some died of other causes before they could face justice. Otto Rasch, heavily involved in the *Intelligenzaktion*, was one of those charged in the 'Einsatzgruppen Trial' in Nuremberg in 1947, but proceedings against him were dropped as he was suffering from Parkinson's Disease. He died a year later. Hermann Höfle – who had effectively been Globočnik's deputy during *Aktion Reinhard* – was with his former commander when the British arrested them in 1945, but was released after two years' interrogation. The Polish government requested his extradition in 1948 but he escaped to Italy where he lived under a false name for three years before returning to Austria and then moving to West Germany. It is inconceivable that the Western Allies were ignorant of his past, but there is a clue in his later employment in West Germany: he worked as an informant for the intelligence arm of the US Army. Like many Nazi criminals, he was considered an asset in the Cold War conflict with the Soviet Union and his crimes were ignored. In 1961, when the Eichmann trial in Jerusalem effectively forced other nations to take action against Nazi criminals, authorities finally arrested him in Salzburg. Two months after Eichmann was executed, Höfle hanged himself in his cell before he could face trial.

In a few cases, justice caught up with the criminals in brutal form. After his brigade's savage rampage through Warsaw, Dirlewanger was sent to Hungary, where the Red Army was threatening Budapest. His brigade of rapists and murderers might have been effective at fighting poorly armed resistance fighters and civilians, but it proved no match for the battle-hardened troops of the Red Army; it rapidly disintegrated, followed by the entire German defensive line. Budapest was besieged for seven weeks before it fell in an orgy of violence and rape as the Soviet units demonstrated that they too were capable of appalling atrocities. Fighting near Guben with his surviving troops – newly designated as the 36th SS-Waffen-Grenadier Division – Dirlewanger sustained a chest wound, adding to his remarkable tally of 12 wartime injuries. In the days after, he disappeared from the military hospital but was arrested in June by French occupation forces. Official French records stated that shortly thereafter, he suffered a heart attack and died, but other sources give a more likely account: the French handed him over to a group of Poles – either former forced labourers or soldiers – who beat him to death.[38]

Only a few of those who were involved in appalling crimes faced prosecution. Josef Meisinger, the former deputy commander of *Einsatzgruppe IV* and later police commander in Warsaw, faced corruption charges before being sent to Japan, where he became a drinking companion of journalist and Soviet agent Richard Sorge. He surrendered to the authorities in September 1945 and was extradited to Poland the following year. Together with Ludwig Fischer, the former governor of the district of Warsaw, he was put on trial for numerous crimes. He was found guilty and was executed in March 1947. Fischer joined him on the gallows.

Having overseen the systematic destruction of the ghetto, Jürgen Stroop produced a self-congratulatory report of his activities entitled *Es gibt keinen jüdischen Wohnbezirk in Warschau mehr!* ('There is no longer a Jewish quarter in Warsaw!') – the details of which proved invaluable to prosecutors at Nuremberg. After he left Warsaw, he ordered the summary execution of nine US airmen who had been captured after being shot down. At the end of the war, he donned a regular Wehrmacht uniform and surrendered to the Americans under the name of Hauptmann Josef Straup, but two months later, was forced to reveal his true identity. He was tried for the execution of the US airmen and, having been found guilty, was sentenced to death; however, the Polish authorities applied for his extradition and he was put on trial in Warsaw in July 1951. In his judgement, the court president was scathing:

> [Stroop's] attitude and his twisted explanations not only indicate a total lack of repentance but actually confirm he retains his Nazi view of the world … His actions show that he is a being devoid of human feeling, a Fascist hangman who tracked his victims with cold and relentless cruelty, an executioner who must be removed from the society of man.[39]

Eight months later, he was hanged, having refused to express any remorse for his actions. In that respect, his behaviour was identical to almost every other senior Nazi figure who appeared in court. Ludwig Hahn, commander of the security police and *SD* in Warsaw, had worked closely with Globočnik during *Aktion Reinhard* and was Stroop's deputy during the suppression of the Warsaw Ghetto Uprising. He served in a variety of roles after leaving Warsaw and was captured by the British in April 1945, but escaped days later. After living under a false name for several years, he resumed his real name in 1949; a year later, his wife falsely claimed that he had been taken prisoner by Soviet troops and had disappeared thereafter. It was only in 1960 that journalists uncovered his past, and in 1972 he was finally charged with war crimes, eventually sentenced to life imprisonment, but granted early release due to cancer; like his former superior Stroop, he never showed any regret for his acts.

Reiner Stahel, Hitler's favourite fortress commander, was captured in August 1944 by Romanian soldiers who had turned against the Axis Powers and handed over to the *NKVD*. After lengthy interrogations, he was finally charged with war crimes in 1951. He would have been executed in other circumstances, but the Soviet Union had (briefly) abolished the death penalty and he was sentenced to 25 years' imprisonment. He died in captivity in 1955.

Hans Frank, the ruler of the *Generalgouvernement*, was captured by US troops in May 1945. After two attempts to kill himself, he appeared as a defendant in the International Military Tribunal in Nuremberg. There, he handed over several volumes of documents to his captors in the belief that they would be used against others and that this would count in his favour, only to find that the evidence was used against him. In some respects, he showed a degree of remorse, though only insofar as assigning guilt to all Germans rather than just himself. He was hanged in October 1946.

For every Nazi war criminal brought to justice, there were several more who escaped punishment for their actions in Warsaw. One of the most prominent perpetrators of crimes in the city, Erich von dem Bach, commanded several SS field formations in the last weeks of the war. He tried unsuccessfully to leave Germany after the final surrender and was arrested by US forces in August 1945. He also agreed to appear as a prosecution witness at the International Military Tribunal in exchange for not being prosecuted himself, and gave evidence at the trial of Fischer in Warsaw. In 1951, he was sentenced to ten years' imprisonment for involvement in the murder of Nazi political opponents in the 1930s, but the court decided that, on account of time already spent in captivity, he would be permitted to undergo house arrest only. He was later charged with further crimes from the 1930s and his sentence eventually increased to life imprisonment, but he was never charged for atrocities committed in Poland or Belarus. In 1972, he was paroled on grounds of ill health and died a year later.

Reinefarth, who as Bach's deputy was involved in the mass murder of thousands of civilians during the Warsaw Uprising – and infamously complained that he lacked the ammunition to kill more – fared even better. In January 1945, he was appointed fortress commander in the town of Küstrin on the Oder River, but in March defied Hitler's order to hold the town to the last man and ordered a retreat. He was sentenced to death but in the chaotic last days of the Reich he remained in command of his troops and succeeded in making his way west to surrender to the British. The Polish authorities requested his extradition, but he was one of the many Nazi war criminals who were working assiduously to persuade western intelligence agencies that they were useful in the growing climate of tension between the USSR and the west. He enjoyed a successful career as a local politician in northern Germany and then as a lawyer, and to add insult to injury the West German government granted him a general's pension on retirement as he had not been found guilty of any crimes. He died in 1979. Finally, in 2014, the Schleswig-Holstein government passed a resolution that it 'deeply regrets that after 1945 it was possible for a war criminal to become a member of the state parliament in Schleswig-Holstein'.[40] A plaque was unveiled in Westerland, where he had been mayor, to mark the seventieth anniversary of the Warsaw Uprising. It bears the inscription:

> The Nazis murdered over 150,000 people in 63 days. Westerland's ex-mayor Heinz Reinefarth, as commander of a battlegroup, was responsible for these crimes. In shame, we bow before the victims and hope for reconciliation.[41]

Fate was not kind to the prominent figures in the Polish government-in-exile and the *AK*. Trying to make the best of a bad situation, Mikołajczyk returned to Warsaw after the war and accepted the post of deputy prime minister and minister for agriculture. He re-established the *Polskie Stronnictwo Ludowe* ('Polish People's Party' or *PSL*, originally created in 1905), but despite the assurances offered at Yalta, Stalin had no intention of permitting a democratic state to be created. A referendum on constitutional reform in June 1946 returned falsified results even though Mikołajczyk and his allies won about two thirds of the vote. The Soviet Union ramped up persecution of his political party and other opponents so that by the time elections were held in January 1947, thousands of candidates who would have run against pro-Soviet figures were behind bars. The outcome was blatant fraud: the pro-Soviet Democratic Bloc recorded a 394-seat win while the *PSL* secured just 28 seats. Mikołajczyk resigned in protest and, fearing arrest, left the country. His short-lived attempt to cooperate with the new regime alienated many other Poles and he emigrated to the United States where he died in 1966, a largely forgotten figure.

Komorowski rejected several German approaches for cooperation against the Red Army and was finally liberated by US soldiers near Innsbruck. When he returned to London on 12 May, he was greeted with great ceremony. He remained active in the government-in-exile, serving as its prime minister from 1947 to 1949, despite having no recognition from most other nations. With no prospect of securing meaningful political and diplomatic support, he took employment as an upholsterer. He died in London in 1966.

Konstantin Rokossovsky, the half-Polish commander whose 1st Belarusian Front failed to provide any meaningful support during the Warsaw Uprising, was sent to Poland by Stalin to ensure close conformity with the Soviet Union.

He became defence minister in Warsaw in 1949 and deputy chairman of the Council of Ministers in 1952, but found it difficult to gain much support from Poles, complaining bitterly that 'in Russia they treat me as a Pole, and in Poland they treat me as a Russian.'[42] He remained a determined Stalinist, implementing a brutal regime of labour battalions in which up to 200,000 men – found guilty of being socially or politically unreliable, sometimes simply for having family members in the west – were forced to work in quarries and mines. In many respects, the system was almost indistinguishable from the forced labour imposed by the German occupiers during the war. He authorised the deployment of troops to put down civil protests in Poznań in 1956, resulting in the deaths of at least 74 people, but he lost influence following Stalin's death and Krushchev refused to support his demands for further military suppression of dissent. He then returned to the Soviet Union, where he held a number of military posts before dying in Moscow in 1971.

LEGACY

Given its long history of struggling for independence against foreign powers, it is unsurprising that Poland remained restless during the Cold War. Władysław Gomułka – seen by many as a 'moderate' Communist – came to power after the death of Stalin, but economic difficulties led to protests first in 1968 and then in 1970. Attempts to improve living standards faltered in the 1970s, leading to further protests in 1976, and two years later an event in Rome added to the rising pressure on the Communist government when Cardinal Karol Wojtyła was elected as Pope John Paul II. Despite over three decades of Communist rule, Poland remained a devoutly Catholic country and the papal visit in 1979 was greeted by huge crowds. In 1980, further industrial unrest led to the creation of the trade union *Solidarność* ('Solidarity') in the Gdańsk shipyards. The government declared martial law in 1981, but with the relaxation of the Soviet grip on Eastern Europe after Mikhail Gorbachev became the Soviet leader, political tides were finally shifting. *Solidarność* gained political momentum to the point that the trade union was able to transform itself into a political party, and in the 1989 elections, won all 161 seats that it was permitted to contest. A further 299 seats were 'reserved' for the pro-Communist *Patriotyczny Ruch Odrodzenia Narodowego* ('Patriotic Movement for National Rebirth'), but although the Communists remained in power, it was clear that their claim to legitimacy was gone. Following further protests Tadeusz Mazowiecki, a member of *Solidarność*, became prime minister, and the last vestiges of pro-Soviet power were swept away when leader of *Solidarność* Lech Wałęsa became president in 1990. The government-in-exile – which had continued its forgotten existence in London – finally returned to Warsaw and presented Wałęsa with the official seals of government that had been smuggled out of the country in 1939.

The terrible wounds inflicted upon Poland during the war and the country's subsequent dislocation meant it was inevitable that a great deal of mythology would arise in the years that followed. As with many post-war accounts, the various memoirs and histories that have emerged often tell only part of the story. Many Jewish accounts highlight the persecution and murder of Poland's Jews, emphasising the disproportionate death toll suffered by the community. These narratives frequently draw attention to Polish antisemitism, which was of course a major problem in Poland both before and during the war. But they often do not mention that although for some Poles, antisemitism was expressed as a dislike or even hatred of Jews, those who considered Jews irrevocably incompatible with Polish society had more in common with Zionists – who sought a separate homeland for their people – than they might have thought. Soviet-era accounts – both in Poland and across the Eastern Bloc – deliberately exaggerated antisemitism in *AK* ranks, and the legacy of these misleading and frequently fabricated versions of history lingers on today. Meanwhile, accounts written by ethnic Poles often concentrate on the heroism of the *AK*, endowing the Warsaw Uprising with hallowed status; in this context, evidence of tension between the *AK* and Jewish resistance groups is sometimes downplayed or even ignored completely. It is understandable that many writers concentrated on the suffering of their own communities; after all, it is sometimes more convenient – or at least, less uncomfortable – to portray the past from the perspective of victimhood rather than to accept that history is rarely so black and white.

An added problem was the rigid imposition of pro-Soviet historiography that dominated for almost half a century after the war. Histories of this sort either fail to mention Stalin's collaboration with Hitler to partition Poland in 1939 or else portray the Soviet Union as coming to the aid of Poles, Belarusians, Ukrainians, and others as the Polish state collapsed. Nor was this bias purely academic, as events at the International Military Tribunal in Nuremberg revealed. The existence of the secret protocol to the Molotov–Ribbentrop Pact – which effectively divided up Eastern Europe into spheres of German and Soviet influence – was known to the Western Powers shortly after the war and surfaced during the tribunal. Yet the Soviets' own chief prosecutor, Roman Andreyevich Rudenko, was not informed of the secret protocol, which raised serious difficulties: after all, Ribbentrop, who had helped draw up the agreement, was one of the defendants, and it was inevitable that the protocol would be discussed in court. Despite their best attempts, the Soviet team was unable to prevent the existence of the protocol being confirmed, though this would not stop them denying all knowledge until 1989.[43] The protocol has since been condemned by Gorbachev and others, but was more recently described by Vladimir Putin as 'a necessary evil'.[44] Using comparisons that were first aired during the Soviet era, Putin has suggested that the entire agreement – including the secret protocol – was no worse than the Munich Agreement between Germany, France, and Britain.

The massacres of Polish prisoners at Katyn and elsewhere were also subjects of contention for the Soviet Union. Anxious to keep Stalin within the anti-Nazi alliance, Roosevelt and Churchill had quietly acquiesced to the Soviet declarations that the killings had been carried out by the Germans, even though they had sufficient information to know that this was a lie. But as preparations for the International Military Tribunal began, US, British, and French prosecutors feared that it would be impossible to prove German involvement and that if, as was most likely, the defendants could pin the atrocity on the Soviet Union, the credibility of all proceedings would be undermined. As the case unfolded, it became clear that the Soviet team had expected the tribunal to function much like Soviet courts – the verdict would be decided in advance and defence witnesses limited in number, or absent entirely. Repeated attempts to prevent such witnesses from speaking failed, yet when the charge was considered, neither side came out on top: Soviet lawyers managed to cast doubt on German claims that the killings had taken place before the Wehrmacht moved into the Katyn area, but the evidence of their witnesses was shown to be flawed. Ultimately, the judges set the charge aside and deliberately avoided mentioning it in their judgement.[45]

Inevitably, as a satellite state of the Soviet Union, the post-war Polish government officially accepted the Soviet version of events. All mentions of Katyn were strictly censored. But although the KGB destroyed many documents relating to the killings in the 1950s, there remained plenty of files documenting this destruction. Finally, in 1989, Gorbachev admitted that the *NKVD* had killed Polish prisoners at Katyn, Mednoye, and Piatykhatky. In later years, the Katyn massacre remained a source of friction. An official Russian investigation concluded in 2005 that whilst Soviet officials were guilty of the killings, all those involved were dead and that there was therefore no further basis for judicial proceedings. The investigation had compiled 183 volumes of evidence, but 116 were deemed to contain state secrets and were not released, and despite numerous requests, many of these volumes remain sealed. In more recent years, many Russian news channels and other agencies have reverted to the Soviet-era view that the killings were carried out by the Germans.

The revision of the Soviet historiography of Poland that began in the 1980s didn't only reframe events in the east. It is certainly true that the crimes of the

Soviets – including, but not limited to Katyn – were exposed to new levels of scrutiny, and the very fact that they had been occluded by decades of Soviet censorship lent them a unique sense of reanimation in Polish memory. At the same time, the historian Andrzej Szpociński claims, references towards Germany were increasingly 'aimed at building a tradition of reconciliation', even going so far as to 'obscure the fact that Germans were the perpetrators.'[46] This cuts to the heart of the fluidity and ambivalence that has continued to characterise Polish memory of the war even as it passes out of living memory. Polish identity was a fractious and contentious thing long before 1 September 1939, and, whilst this may have been true for other nations, no others suffered the trauma of simultaneous yet distinct experiences of prolonged enemy occupation, nor such flagrant obfuscation of public memory in the immediate aftermath of the war. To quote the writers Barbara Szacka and Marjorie Castle, 'the abyss between the official, "bureaucratic" memory of the war and the divided social memory made it difficult or even impossible to reconcile these and create a socially agreed upon common collective memory.'[47]

On the one hand, for at least two centuries the Polish concept of collective memory has closely been intertwined with Romantic and Catholic ideas of victimhood and martyrdom, and the events of 1939–45 reinforced this narrative of heroic – if tragic – resistance. On the other, the narratives of victimhood and suffering during the war and after became so diversified, so fraught by intellectual, political, ethnic, and religious rivalries, that reconciling them remains difficult and painful for those closest to them. As sociologist Jeffrey Alexander has noted on cultural trauma, 'social groups can, and often do, refuse to recognise the existence of others' trauma, and because of their failure they cannot achieve a moral stand.'[48] The truth is that two perspectives can be true at once, and understanding another group's pain need not detract from one's own. The Polish population as a whole suffered, both statistically and psychologically, some of the worst Nazi atrocities; within that population, there were groups – especially, but not solely, the Jews – singled out for horrors that reflected the absolute worst of humanity.

Against this backdrop of shifting narratives, of a centuries-old legacy of victimhood, of unprecedented ideological persecution, and of a sense of isolation on the world stage, the city of Warsaw has its own, distinct story to tell. The same city that turned the tide of a Communist advance in 1920 was the first European capital to fall once war finally broke out in 1939; however terrifying the violence of that September siege, it would pale in comparison to the brutality that would be waged against the city five years later during the Uprising. But the sentiment of Varsovian society as a whole was never defeatist, and certainly not collaborationist. In her analysis of the 'Miracle on the Vistula', historian Ewa Ochman has described how even Polish events of 'glory, pride and … triumph' are transposed into the dominant 'continuum of suffering'; in the same way, many Varsovians felt a sense of fatalistic honour in being at the epicentre of Nazi persecution and, more importantly, of a tragic and doomed resistance.[49] Miron Białoszewski, for instance, felt 'disconsolate' that his parents had evacuated him out of the city in 1939 to escape the siege. Hence his reflection during the Uprising:

> So a person wanted to escape from that hell by some miracle. But here something else popped into one's head from the start. A new mood. All over again. And I know, just as surely as I know myself and every average Varsovian, that I would have wanted to return immediately from that miraculous salvation outside of Warsaw to this hell.[50]

Some, like Julian Kulski and his fellow members of the Columbus Generation, came of age just as the nation around them was being torn apart – the same nation their fathers and grandfathers had rankled under generations of occupation to see born. In August 1939, Kulski wrote, tens of thousands of these youngsters considered it their duty and honour to follow in their footsteps; 'If there is going to be a war,' Kulski wrote in August 1939, 'I do not want to miss it.'[51] He started the war as a child. Five and a half years later, the 15-year-old Kulski had been imprisoned and interrogated in Pawiak, witnessed first-hand the unspeakable horrors of the Warsaw Ghetto, participated in some of the fiercest fighting of the 1944 Uprising, and ended the war as a prisoner of war. Yet for every Kulski, there were thousands of children, teenagers, men, and women who suffered the same and far worse, and whose dreams of patriotic fatalism – dreams for which, surely, no children should ever be asked to lay down their lives – only ended in tragedy. For every Stefan Starzyński, Maciej Rataj, Mieczysław Niedziałkowski, or other high-profile murder at the hands of the Nazis, thousands more died in total obscurity, their disappearance left unexplained, and their graves unmarked for years. For every Szpilman, who survived by the slightest of margins, and whose story bears witness to the very best and worst of humanity, thousands of Jews went to their deaths with the silence of the Western Allies ringing in their ears.

The systematic destruction of Varsovian society and culture under occupation – compounded by decades of Soviet heavy-handedness – has left us with little in the way of official statistics and records during the war period. Yet the fact we are left with such rich and vivid material in the diarist tradition surely says something about Varsovians' sense of identity, their instinct for cultural self-preservation, and their historical consciousness. Of course, the memoirs to which we have access shine a disproportionate amount of light on members of the intelligentsia – people like the diplomat-turned-courier Jan Karski, the journalist and politician Stefan Korboński, or, inside the ghetto, writer Rokhl Auerbach. More often than not, the diarists were literary-minded people who either understood the significance of what they were recording or were in a privileged enough position to do so, or both. This is not to imply that these members of the intelligentsia did not suffer as much as the non-intelligentsia population of Warsaw – on the contrary, the weight of their influence made them the Germans' prime targets in the *Intelligenzaktion* – but rather to reinforce the fact that their experience cannot be assumed to be universal. Some parts of Varsovian society left very little, if any, written record, and sometimes it is only through the throwaway details and anecdotes of our writers that we get a glimpse into the lived reality of the poor, the marginal, and the non-literate. It is this that makes the seemingly mundane details – like Miron Białoszewski's stream-of-consciousness remembrances of the Uprising bunker communities, and Auerbach's interactions with the Jewish poor in her soup kitchen, and Nałkowska's conversations with her shop customers – all the more poignant. We are fortunate to have access to caches of material such as the Ringelblum Archive, which – despite not having been fully recovered – comprised everything from cultural essays to poetry, letters to reports, songs, diary entries, and other testimonials from across Jewish society. As in the case of any contemporary record, the choice of what is included for posterity is as telling as – and sometimes even more so than – the content itself.

Warsaw was not the only European capital to suffer Nazi occupation, but what one notices from historiography on the subject is that the Poles place a heavy emphasis on distinguishing themselves as non-collaborators. This sentiment was already deeply engrained during the war, and in 1945, one Polish journalist described the population as 'the most purely moral among all nations that had to live under [Nazi] occupation.'[52] After the war, the Soviets deliberately blurred the lines between resistance and Fascist collaboration to suit their purposes of repressing social and political enemies, but in so doing reinforced the Poles' sense of patriotic exceptionalism – and victimisation. But whilst it is true that Poland never established a native collaborationist administration in the mould of Norway or France, claims of unanimous non-cooperation break down as soon as we actually question the definition of collaboration. Symbols of the most blatant, self-interested collaborationism – such as the Blue Police, the Ghetto Police, the *szmalcowniki*, and the *Volksdeutscher Selbstschutz* – conveniently mask the fact that cooperation was, to varying degrees, a necessity for Poles across the social spectrum. Bribery was rife, as was the leveraging of powerful acquaintances, and in most cases Poles attributed these subversive behaviours to an instinct for self-preservation rather than condemning them as exploitation of privilege. At the highest levels of Varsovian society, the likes of Mayor Stefan Starzyński and his successor Julian Kulski felt compelled to cooperate with the Germans if only to try to moderate their impact on city life. But the deeper one looks into these arrangements, the harder it becomes to differentiate self-interested cooperation from inadvertent collaboration, especially when the occupiers named the terms of the exchange. The most blatant example of this was the Warsaw *Judenrat*; for all Adam Czerniaków's intervention and soul-searching, the council ended up facilitating the annihilation of the very people it was intended to protect.

Today, Warsaw is a thriving, bustling city that bears little resemblance to what was there before: in 1939, it was one of the most densely populated urban spaces on the planet, whereas now it is one of the most spacious cities of Europe. The memories of the past are at once invisible and omnipresent, and travelling along the new boulevards, crossing the leafy parks, and navigating the new blocks of glass and steel, it is easy to forget that an entire city of ruins still lies beneath. But when one looks closer, it becomes impossible not to notice the indelible traces of war: the *Tchorek* plaques that mark execution sites; the ghetto boundary markers that once demarcated whether one might live or die; the splatter of bullet holes on buildings that survived the Germans' final destruction. If the modern sprawl feels far removed from the cramped, winding streets of the former city, it is the inevitable result of post-war urban planning – but it is also a mark of everything Warsaw lost in the war, and that no amount of restoration will ever bring back. Today's Varsovians learn the tragic, heroic history of their predecessors at school, but as a tour guide explained to the authors, they have their own dreams and worries; for them, constant remembrance of the past would simply become overwhelming.

From Leningrad and Stalingrad to Berlin and Cologne, cities across Europe saw huge damage and suffering during the war. Warsaw was in many respects unique. Unlike these other cities – which became battlegrounds for land armies – the devastation inflicted upon Warsaw was primarily an unequal struggle between the German occupiers and the poorly equipped people who resisted, both in the Ghetto Uprising and the Warsaw Uprising. It was the only metropolis to experience Hitler's policy of near-total annihilation to make way for his vision of the Thousand Year Reich. Yet reading the accounts of those who cowered in cellars as bombs and shells devastated the buildings above, those who simply wanted the violence to end, it is impossible to distinguish their memories from those of Berliners who waited with exhausted desperation for the same thing, or of the citizens of dozens of cities caught in similar nightmares. Ultimately, however courageously the *AK* and Jewish resistance fighters fought against their oppressors, however vocal their leaders and commanders at home and abroad, the price – as in cities around the world – was paid by ordinary people.

As far as Poland was concerned, the outcome of the war was a clear victory for the Soviet Union. Having declared war on Germany in response to Hitler's invasion of Poland, Britain and France failed to deliver on their promises of upholding Polish independence; measured in these terms, the nature of their victory becomes rather more problematic. Considering the evidence presented to them – of the Warsaw Ghetto, concentration camps, Katyn, and countless other atrocities – it is difficult to argue that the Western Powers succeeded in positioning themselves entirely on the right side of history. To quote historian Timothy Snyder, telling the truth about their decisions means seeing the war as 'an alliance with one totalitarian power against another, not a triumph of democracy.'[53] Both Churchill and Roosevelt – with varying degrees of reluctance – treated Poland as little more than a bargaining chip in their negotiations with Stalin, even if, given the cold reality of the situation, there was little else that they could do. It is hardly surprising that the Soviet leader showed no inclination to honour the agreements that he grudgingly made and instead ensured that Poland was tightly bound to the Soviet empire; it is equally unsurprising that VE Day – which heralded 44 more years of occupation – tends not to be celebrated as a big affair in Poland.

Still, the Western Allies were convinced that Yalta had been a success. In the words of one American advisor, 'we were absolutely certain that we had won the first great victory of peace, and by "we" I mean all of us, the whole civilised human race'; the Poles would have begged to differ.[54] It took a German officer to see the growing divide between the Allied ambitions for what it was; 'The Warsaw Uprising,' Oberst Hermann Teske wrote in 1952, 'was the beginning of the Cold War between East and West.'[55] The Treaty of Versailles and its ensuing 'stab in the back' myth had put Europe on a collision course decades before; now it was Yalta – at least in the east – that became synonymous with western betrayal over the next half century.

Not for the first time, Poland was simply the stage upon which the international powers enacted their political theatre of competing egos and performative diplomacy. Not for the last time, the price would be paid for generations to come. In 1944, Churchill promised 'when the final Allied victory is achieved, the epic of Warsaw will not be forgotten'; around the same time, George Orwell issued a prescient warning to those in the west: 'Don't imagine that for years on end you can make yourself the boot-licking propagandist of the Soviet regime, or any other regime, and then suddenly return to honesty and reason.'[56] Oppman's mermaid is visible on numerous monuments and plaques around modern Warsaw, still watching over her city; and writing at a time when the fate of another nation in Eastern Europe is the subject of negotiations involving Moscow, it is well to remember the cynical bad faith of politicians of an earlier era.

GLOSSARY

Polish

Akcja Burza	'Operation *Tempest*', a campaign of Polish uprisings from late 1943 in anticipation of Soviet arrival
Akcja Główki	'Operation *Little Heads*', the assassination programme of SS personnel sentenced by the underground courts
Akcja N	'Action N' or 'Section N'; sabotage and counter-propaganda campaign of the Polish underground
Anty-Gestapo (*Agat*)	Anti-Gestapo group
Armia Krajowa (*AK*)	Home Army
Armia Ludowa (*AL*)	People's Army
Bataliony Chłopskie (*BCh*)	Peasants' Battalions
Biuro Odbudowy Stolicy (*BOS*)	Office for the Reconstruction of the Capital
Centralny Komitet Narodowy w Warszawie (*CKN*)	Central National Committee of Warsaw
Endecja	The National Democracy Movement founded by Roman Dmowski
Główna Straż Obywatelska (*SO*)	Citizen's Militia
Granatowa policja	The Blue Police, the municipal police of the *Generalgouvernement*
Hatzomer Hatzair	Labour Zionist youth movement
Kierownictwo Dywersji (*Kedyw*)	Diversion Directorate
Kocioł na Miłej	The Cauldron on Miła Street, a mass roundup during the 1942 July *Grossaktion*
Komitet Narodowski Polski (*KNP*)	Polish National Committee

Korpus Ochrony Pogranicza (KOP)	Border Defence Corps
Łączniczki	Underground couriers
Łapanka	German roundups
Mały sabotaż	'Petty sabotage' encouraged by the underground
Narodowa Organizacja Wojskowa (NOW)	National Military Organisation
Narodowe Siły Zbrojne (NSZ)	National Armed Forces
Obóz Narodowo-Radykalny (ONR)	National-Radical Camp
Organizacja Wojskowa Związek Jaszczurczy (OWZJ)	Military Organisation of the Lizard Union
Patriotyczny Ruch Odrodzenia Narodowego	'Patriotic Movement for National Rebirth'
Policja Państwowa	Pre-war Polish state police
Polityczny Komitet Porozumiewawczy (PKP)	Political Consultative Committee
Polska Armia Ludowa (PAL)	People's Polish Army
Polska Ludowa Akcja Niepodległościowa (PLAN)	Polish People's Independence Action
Polska Organizacja Wojskowa (POW)	Polish Military Organisation
Polska Partia Socjalistyczna (PPS)	Polish Socialist Party
Polski Komitet Wyzwolenia Narodowego (PKWN)	Polish Committee of National Liberation, or Lublin Committee
Polski Stronnictwo Ludowe (PSL)	Polish People's Party
Rada Główna Opiekuńcza (RGO)	Central Welfare Council
Rada Opiekuńcza Miejska (ROM)	City Welfare Council
Sanacja	Ruling regime of 'Sanitation' 1926–39, first instigated by Piłsudski for the sake of political 'healing' but increasingly associated with authoritarian and antisemitic overreach
Służba Zwycięstwu Polski (SZP)	Polish Victory Service
Stołeczny Komitet Sampomocy Społecznej (SKSS)	Capital Social Welfare Committee
Świt	Polish radio station popularly believed to be broadcasting from within occupied Poland but actually based in England

Szarych Szeregów	Grey Ranks, a clandestine group of scouts and guides
Szmalcowniki	Blackmailers and collaborators who profited from threatening to report on Jews or their rescuers in occupied Poland
Tajna Organizacja Nauczycielska (TON)	Secret Teaching Organisation
Trzynastka	The Thirteen, Jewish collaborationist unit based at 13 Leszno Street and associated with Abraham Gancwajch
Tymczasowa Rada Stanu (TRS)	Provisional State Council
Uniwersytet Latający	Literally 'Floating University', usually Flying University
Umschlagplatz	'Exchange Place'; the only authorised site for exchanging goods between the Jewish ghetto and the outside world
Żegota	Council to Aid Jews, formally integrated with the Polish underground
Związek Harcerstwa Polskiego (ZHP)	Polish Scouting and Guiding Association
Związek Walki Zbrojnej (ZWZ)	Union for Armed Struggle
Żydowska Organizacja Bojowa (ŻOB)	Jewish Fighting Wing
Żydowski Komitet Narodowy (ŻKN)	Jewish National Committee
Żydowski Związek Wojskowy (ŻZW)	Jewish Military Union

GERMAN

Abteilung für Volksaufklärung und Propaganda	Department of Education and Propaganda
Abwehr	German Military Intelligence
Ausserordentliche Befriedigungsaktion / AB-Aktion	Extraordinary Pacification Action
Durchgangslager (Dulag)	Transit camp
Einsatzgruppen	SS paramilitary death squads
Gauleiter	Leader of Nazi Party in a region (*Gau*) of Germany

Gefängnis Warschau	German name for Pawiak prison
Generalgouvernement für die Besetzten Polnischen Gebiete	General Governorate for the Occupied Polish Territories
Generalplan Ost	'General Plan East', the Nazis' resettlement plan for Eastern European territories
Hilfswillige	'Willing help', pro-German auxiliary volunteers from Eastern Europe
Judenrat	'Jewish Council' – body of prominent Jews in ghettos responsible for enforcing German instructions
Kaiserlich und Königliche (k.u.k.)	'Imperial and Royal' Austro-Hungarian Army
Nacht und Nebel	'Night and Fog' policy of deliberate obfuscation around the fate of Nazi political prisoners
Oberkommando der Wehrmacht (OKW)	Armed Forces High Command
Reichsarbeitsdienst (RAD)	Reich Labour Administration
Reichskommissar für die Festigung deutschen Volkstums (RKFDV)	Reich Commissioner for the Consolidation of German Nationhood
Reichssicherheitshauptamt (RHSA)	Reich Security Main Office
Selbstschutz	Ethnic-German 'self-protection' paramilitary groups
Sicherheitsdienst (SD)	'Security Service', effectively the intelligence arm of the SS
Sicherheitspolizei	Security Police
Sonderfahnungsbuch Polen	Special Prosecutions Book Poland, a list of Polish cultural and intelligentsia targets compiled before the invasion
Sonderkommando	'Special unit', work brigade of camp prisoners usually tasked with corpse disposal or military unit with 'special' tasks
SS-Hauptamt	SS Main Office
SS- und Polizeiführer (SSPF)	SS and Police Leaders
Totenkopf	'Dead Person's Head', the insignia associated with the SS and especially those staffing concentration and death camps

Waffen-Sturm-Brigade RONA	Armed Assault Brigade of the *Russkaya Osvobditelnaya Naerodnaya Armiya* (Russian People's Liberation Army)

RUSSIAN

Narodnyy Komissariat Vnutrennikh Del (*NKVD*)	People's Commissariat for Internal Affairs

OTHER

Aleynhilf	Short for *Yidishe Sotsyale Aleynhilf*, the Jewish 'self-help' organisation designed to provide aid to camp prisoners and ghetto residents
Oneg Shabbat	'Joy of the Sabbath', the name given to Emmanuel Ringelblum's archival project
Orhanizatsiia Ukrainskykh Natsionalistiv (*OUN*)	Ukrainian Nationalist Organisation

NOTES

INTRODUCTION

1 A. Zamoyski, *Poland: A History* (HarperCollins Publishers, 2015), p.13
2 I. Gieysztorowa, 'Pierwsze zniszczenie Warszawy i jej odbudowa po potopie 1655–1696' in *Mówią Wieki* (Warsaw), No. 11 (1962)
3 K. Piechura, 'Voltaire's Interpretation of the International Rivalry in the Eastern Baltic Region' in *Journal of Baltic Studies* (Routledge, Milton), Vol. 16 No. 4 (Winter 1985), p.361
4 A. Storozynski, *The Peasant Prince: Tadeusz Koskiuszko and the Age of Revolution* (Tomas Dunne, New York, 2009), p.211
5 M. Brandys, *Kozietulski i inni* (Iskry, Warsaw, 1982), p.146
6 J. J. Rousseau, *The Government of Poland* (Hackett, Indianapolis IN, 1985)
7 B. Porter, *When Nationalism Began to Hate: Imagining Modern Politics in Nineteenth-Century Poland* (Oxford University Press, 2000), p.16
8 J. Lelewel, *Polska, dzieje i rzeczy jej* (Poznań, 1851–68), as cited by A. Walicki, *Między filozofią, religią, i polityką* (Państwowy Instytut Wydawniczy, Warsaw, 1983), p.215
9 J. Janowski, *Krótki Katechizm Polityczny* (Trzcionkami Juliana Duillot, Agen, 1834)
10 A. Mickiewicz, *Księgi narodu polskiego i pielgrzymstwa polskiego* (Księgarnia Luxemburgska, Paris, 1866), pp.33, 35, 45, 47, and 49
11 G. Brandes, *Poland: A Study of the Land, People, and Literature* (Heinemann, London, 1903), pp.11–12
12 T. Weeks, 'A City of Three Nations: Fin-De-Siècle Warsaw' in *The Polish Review* (Polish Institute of Arts and Sciences of America, New York), Vol. 49 No. 2 (2004), p.752
13 L. Jaśkiewicz, 'Książę Aleksander Imeretyński o społeczeństwie Królestwa Polskiego w przededniu wizyty cara Mikołaja II (memoriał z 24 lipca/5 sierpnia 1897)' in *Przegląd Historyczny* (Dwumiesięcznik Naukowy, Warsaw, 2005), p.464
14 Brandes, *Poland*, pp.5–6
15 Ibid., p.38
16 Ibid., p.17
17 A. Kraushar, quoted in T. Weeks, 'A City of Three Nations: Fin-De-Siècle Warsaw' in *The Polish Review*, Vol. 49 No. 2 (2004), p.763

18 D. Crowley, 'The Symbolism of the Ruin in Warsaw after 1944' in *Journal of Modern European History* (University of Chicago Press), Vol. IX No. 3 (2011), pp.353–54
19 Ibid., pp.351–52

CHAPTER 1: THE REBIRTH OF A NATION

1 A. Mickiewicz (trans. J. Zawadzki), '*Oda do młodość*', 1820, Internet Archive, CC BY-SA 3.0, https://creativecommons.org/licenses/by-sa/3.0/
2 *Chicago Daily Tribune* (Tribune Publishing, Chicago IL), 16 May 1935, p.10
3 I. Protassewicz (trans. H. Zawadski), *A Polish Woman's Experiences in World War II* (Bloomsbury, London, 2019), p.73
4 A. Jarry (trans. B. Keith and G. Legman), *Ubu Roi* (Dover, New York, 2003), p.1
5 T. Weeks, 'A City Of Three Nations: Fin-De-Siècle Warsaw' in *The Polish Review*, Vol. 49 No. 2 (2004), p.248
6 Ibid.
7 P. Kropotkin and J. Bealby, 'Warsaw' in *1911 Encyclopedia Britannica*, Vol. 28, available at https://en.wikisource.org/wiki/1911_Encyclop%C3%A6dia_Britannica/Warsaw
8 J. Piłsudski, *The Memories of a Polish Revolutionary and Soldier* (AMS, New York, 1971), p.11
9 *Robotnik* (Vilnius, 1898), 13 February 1898
10 Y. Ro'i, *Jews and Jewish Life in Russia and the Soviet Union* (Routledge, 1995), p.138
11 E. Mendelsohn, *The Jews of East Central Europe Between the World Wars* (Indiana University Press, Bloomington, 1984), p.41
12 W. Sobieski and K. Tymieniecki, *Dzieje Polski* (Wydawnictwo Antyk – Marcin Dybowski, Komorów, 2010, 3 volumes), Vol. III, p.131
13 M. Kukiel, *Dzieje Polski Porozbiorowe* (Świderski, London, 1961), p.561
14 B. Dmytryshyn (ed.), *Imperial Russia: A Source Book, 1700–1917* (Holt, Rinehart & Winston, Fort Worth TX, 1990), p.512
15 A. Tanikowski, K. Zieliński, and M. Silber, *Jew, Pole, Legionary: 1914–1920* (Museum of the History of Polish Jews, Warsaw, 2014), p.124
16 I. Boerner, 'Z Pamiętnika' in *Kalendarium* (Uniwersytet Jagielloński, Kraków) No. 1 (1938), p.407
17 J. Mankoff, 'The Future of Poland, 1914–1917: France and Great Britain in the Triple Entente' in *The International History Review*, Milton), Vol. XXX No. 4 (2008), p.745
18 Quoted in J. Korbel, *Twentieth Century Czechoslovakia: The Meaning of its History* (Columbia University Press, New York, 1977), p.142
19 A. Kramer, *Dynamic of Destruction: Culture and Mass Killing in the First World War* (Oxford University Press, 2007), p.151
20 M. Biskupski, 'The Origins of a Relationship: The United States and Poland, 1914–1921' in *The Polish Review*, Vol. 54 No. 2 (2009), p.148

21 W. Wilson, *Peace Without Victory* speech, 22 January 1917. 64th Cong., 23 Sess., Senate Document No. 685: *A League for Peace*, available at https://web.mit.edu/21h.102/www/Wilson%20Peace%20Without%20Victory.htm
22 M. Dąbrowska, *Dzienniki 1914–1965. T. 1, 1914–1925* (Komitet Nauk o Literaturze, Warsaw, 2009), p.46
23 Ibid., pp.49–50
24 B. Kutsher (trans. G. Marcus), *Once There Was Warsaw* (Syracuse University Press, New York, 2024), p.71
25 S. Filasiewicz, *La Question Polonaise Pendant la Guerre Mondiale* (Section d'Études et de Publications Politiques de Comité National Polonais, Paris, 1920), p.151
26 W. Wilson, *Joint Address to Congress Leading to a Declaration of War Against* Germany, 2 April 1917, available at https://www.archives.gov/milestone-documents/address-to-congress-declaration-of-war-against-germany
27 President Wilson's Message to Congress, 8 January 1918; Records of the United States Senate; Record Group 46; Records of the United States Senate; National Archives
28 E. Gerson, *Woodrow Wilson and the Rebirth of Poland, 1914–1920: A Study in the Influence on American Policy of Minority Groups of Foreign Origin* (Archon, Hamden CT, 1972), p.84 note 71
29 E. House, *The Intimate Papers of Colonel House* (Ernst Benn, London, 1928), Vol. III, p.239
30 M. Lubomirski, *Pamiętnik Księżnej Marii Zdzisławowej Lubomirskiej 1914–1918* (Wydawn. Poznańskie, Poznań, 1997)
31 Dąbrowska, *Dzienniki 1914–1965*, pp.168–69
32 J. Piłsudski, *Monitor Polski* (Drukarnia Państwowa w Warszawie, 1922), R.1, No. 206 (18 November 1918), p.1
33 J. Schoenfeld, *Jewish Life in Galicia under the Austro-Hungarian Empire and in Reborn Poland, 1898–1939* (Ktav, Hoboken NJ, 1985), p.201
34 Zamoyski, *Poland: A History*, p.298
35 *New York Times* (19 January 1919), p.2
36 E. D'Abernon, *The Eighteenth Decisive Battle of the World* (Hodder & Stoughton, London, 1931), p.39
37 H. Hoover, *The Memoirs of Herbert Hoover: Years of Adventure, 1874–1920* (Kessinger, Whitefish MT, 2010), p.356
38 W. Wilson, quoted in B. Weissman, *The American Relief Administration in Russia, 1921–1923: A Case Study in the Interaction Between Opposing Political Systems* (PhD dissertation, Columbia University, 1968), p.37
39 V. Kellogg, 'Review of The Children of Warsaw', 14 August 1919, Vernon Kellogg Papers, Box 1, Folder 11, Hoover Institution Archives (Stanford CA)
40 Ibid.
41 H. Hoover, *An American Epic* (Regnery, Chicago, 1964, 4 volumes), Vol. IV, *The Guns Cease Killing & the Saving of Life from Famine Begins*, p.144
42 Ibid., p.43
43 *Minorities Treaty between the Principal Allied and Associated Powers (The British Empire, France, Italy, Japan, and the United States) and Poland, signed at Versailles*

(28 June 1919), Article 2, available at http://www.forost.ungarisches-institut.de/pdf/19190628-3.pdf

44 B. Jezierski, 'Paderewski and the Treaty of Versailles' in *Polish American Studies*, Vol. 11, No. 1/2 (January–June 1954), pp.44–46

45 Paderewski, quoted in ibid., p.47

46 W. Churchill, quoted in M. Gilbert, 'Churchill and Poland' in *Politeja* (Uniwersytet Jagielloński, Kraków), No. 13 (2010), p.10

47 Ibid.

48 E. D'Abernon, quoted in P. Stachura, *Poland, 1918–1945: An Interpretive and Documentary History of the Second Republic* (Routledge, Milton, 2004), p.43

49 *Kurier Poranny* (Białystok), 10 September 1920, p.3

50 J. Szapiro, 'Poland and Pilsudski' in *Journal of the Royal Institute of International Affairs* (Oxford University Press), Vol. 8 No. 4 (1929), p.5

51 Ibid., p.7

52 Ibid., p.1

53 *Kurier Poranny*, 10 May 1926

54 J. Piłsudski, quoted in C. Dawson, 'Pilsudski's Seizure of Power in Poland' in *Current History* (University of California Press, Oakland CA), Vol. 24 No. 4 (1926), p.590

55 A. Garlicki, *Historia 1815–1939 Polska i* świat (Warsaw, 2003), p.370

56 Dąbrowska, *Dzienniki*, p.17

57 M. Muller, quoted in Z. Gąsiorowski, 'Joseph Piłsudski in the Light of British Reports' in *The Slavonic and East European Review* (Manney, Leeds), Vol. 50 No. 121 (1972), p.566

58 Szapiro, 'Poland and Pilsudski', p.381

59 Ibid., p.385

60 H. Seton-Watson, *Eastern Europe Between the Wars, 1918–1941* (Cambridge University Press, 1946), p.389

61 J. Beck, quoted in A. Cienciala, 'The Foreign Policy of Józef Piłsudski and Józef Beck, 1926–1939: Misconceptions and Interpretations' in *The Polish Review*, Vol. 56 No. 1/2, 'Commemorating Józef Piłsudski' (2011), p.116

62 See for example J. Beck, *Dernier Rapport: Politique Polonaise 1926–1939* (Editions de la Baconnière, Zurich, 1951), p.66; L. Moczulski, *Wojna Prewencyjna: Czy Piłsudski Planowal Najazd na Niemcy?* (Bellona, Warsaw, 2017)

63 J. Lemański, 'Generalizacja Zobowiązań Mniejszościowych' in *Sprawy Narodowościowe* (Instytut Slawistyki PAN, Warsaw) Vol. 8 No. 5–6 (1934), p.527; W. Zaleski, quoted in K. Czechowska, 'The Polish Minority Treaty and the Polish Idea of Generalisation of Minority Protection Commitments Within the League of Nations' in *Przegląd Zachodni* (Instytut Zachodni. Instytut Naukowo-Badawczy im. Zygmunta Wojciechowskiego w Poznaniu, Poznań), Issue 2 (383) (2022), p.164

64 Czechowska, 'The Polish Minority Treaty', p.165

65 B. Raczyński, quoted in Czechowska, 'The Polish Minority Treaty', p.171

66 Cienciala, 'Foreign Policy', p.129

67 *Kurjer Warszawski,* 13 May 1935, r.1 no. 130, p.1
68 *Kurjer Warszawski,* 17 May 1935, r.1 no. 134, p.1
69 I. Móscicki, Warsaw, Zamek, 12 May 1935, quoted in *Warsaw Weekly,* 17 May 1935, Vol. 1 No. 19, p.2

CHAPTER 2: *LEBENSRAUM*

1 A. Hitler, *Mein Kampf* (Hurst & Blackett, London, 1939), Vol. II, p.438
2 Quoted in A. Roberts, *Churchill: Walking with Destiny* (Allen Lane, London, 2018), p.106
3 A. Tooze, *The Wages of Destruction: The Making and Breaking of the Nazi Economy* (Penguin, Harmondsworth, 2006), p.26
4 Zamoyski, *Poland: A History*, p.311
5 D. Buzinkai, 'Poland and the League of Nations, 1934–1939: A Political Analysis' in *The Polish Review*, Vol. 10 No. 4 (1965), p.57
6 J. Beck, quoted in ibid., p.58
7 Cienciala, 'Foreign Policy', p.129
8 A. Hitler, quoted in *Official Documents Concerning Polish-German and Polish-Soviet Relations, 1933–1939: The Little White Book* (Hutchinson, London, 1940), p.47
9 A. Hitler, quoted in ibid., p.46
10 J. Beck, quoted in Buzinkai, 'Poland and the League of Nations', p.66
11 M. Litvinov, quoted in ibid.
12 *Kurjer Warszawski,* 12 March 1938, r.118 no. 70, p.2
13 For a full account of the Sudetenland Crisis and the Munich Agreement, see D. Faber, *Munich: The 1938 Appeasement Crisis* (Simon & Schuster, London, 2008); E. Goldstein and I. Lukes, *The Munich Crisis 1938: Prelude to World War II* (Weidenfeld & Nicholson, London, 1967)
14 Point XIII, *President Woodrow Wilson's Fourteen Points,* available from https://avalon.law.yale.edu/20th_century/wilson14.asp
15 Quoted in D. Schenk, *Hitlers Mann in Danzig: Gauletier Forster und die NS-Verbrechen in Danzig-Westpreussen* (Dietz, Bonn, 2000), p.53
16 J. Beck, quoted in *Little White Book*, p.48
17 G. Weinberg, *The Foreign Policy of Hitler's Germany: Starting World War II, 1937–39* (University of Chicago Press, 1980), p.627
18 Schenk, *Hitlers Mann in Danzig*, p.103
19 German government memorandum to the Polish government, *Little White Book*, p.81
20 J. Beck, quoted in M. Kornat, 'Choosing not to Choose: Poland's Assessment of the Nazi-Soviet Pact' in *The International History Review*, Vol. 31 No. 4 (December 2009), p.779
21 W. Hubatsch (ed.), *Hitlers Weisungen für die Kriegsführung* (Dörfler, Utting, 2000), pp.17–19
22 W. Michalka, *Deutsche Geschichte 1933–1945: Dokumente zur Innen- und Aussenpolitik* (Fischer Taschenbuch Verlag, Frankfurt am Main, 1994), pp.165–66

23 Quoted in Schenk, *Hitlers Mann in Danzig*, p.106
24 *Archiwum Narodowe w Krakowie Oddział w Tarnowie*, Tarnów, 33/226, sig. V141
25 *Bundesarchiv*, Berlin, R9350/774
26 *Little White Book*, p.103
27 A. Nekrich, A. Ulam, and G. Freeze, *Pariahs, Partners, Predators: German-Soviet Relations, 1922–1941* (Columbia University Press, New York, 1997), p.110
28 Sebag Montefiore, S., *Stalin: The Court of the Red Tsar* (Vintage, London, 2004), p.40
29 W. Shirer, *The Rise and Fall of the Third Reich: A History of Nazi Germany* (Simon & Schuster, London, 1990), p.537
30 A. Ulam, *Stalin: The Man and His Era* (Allen Lane, London, 1974), p.513
31 W. Grzybowski, quoted in Kornat, 'Choosing not to Choose', p.784
32 Kornat, 'Choosing not to Choose', p.783; J. Lipski, to Łubieński, 16 June 1939, in S. Żerko (ed.), *Polskie Dokumenty Dyplomatyczne 193*, (Warsaw, 2005), Vol. I, p.350
33 *Kurjer Warszawski*, 22 August 1939, r.119 no. 231, p.1
34 J. Beck to Lukasiewicz and Raczynski, 22 August 1939, *Akta dyplomatyczne polskie odnoszące się do rokowań brytyjsko-francusko-sowieckich w okresie przed wybuchem drugiej wojny światowej* (London, 1955), pp.17–18
35 Kornat, 'Choosing not to Choose', p.789
36 J. Beck, quoted in ibid., p.791
37 *New York Times*, 28 August 1939, p.11
38 J. Noakes and G. Pridham (eds), *Nazism 1919–1945* (University of Exeter Press, 2000, 3 volumes), Vol. III, p.743
39 J. Böhler, *Der Überfall: Deutschlands Krieg Gegen Polen* (Eichborn, Frankfurt am Main, 2009), p.70
40 M. Lebovic, '80 Years Ago, How a Very Different Schindler's 'List' helped ignite WWII', *Times of Israel*, 30 August 2019, available at https://www.timesofisrael.com/80-years-ago-how-a-very-different-schindlers-list-helped-ignite-wwii/
41 Hitler's speech to the commanders in chief (22 August 1939), *German History in Documents and Images*, available at https://germanhistorydocs.org/en/nazi-germany-1933-1945/hitler-s-speech-to-the-commanders-in-chief-august-22-1939
42 A. Hitler, quoted in L. Lochner, *What About Germany?* (Dodd, Mead & Co., New York, 1942), pp.1–4

CHAPTER 3: *FALL WEISS*

1 A. Mickiewicz (trans. B. Johnston), '*Do Matki Polki*', 1830. Used with permission.
2 *Express Poranny* (Dom Prasy, Warsaw), 2 September 1939, p.1
3 *Kurjer Warszawski,* 1 September 1939, r.119 no. 242, p.3
4 J. Cynk, *The Polish Air Force at War: The Official History* (Schiffer, Atglen PA, 1998, 2 volumes), Vol. I, p.74

5 'If the raids on Warsaw had been opposed by 100 Polish fighters instead of 20–30, the German bombers would likely have suffered a real drubbing. Furthermore, had the Poles received even a single squadron of Hurricanes in spring 1939, the Bf 110Cs would have faced a more serious challenge in the initial aerial battles over Warsaw.' See R. Forczyk, *Case White: The Invasion of Poland 1939* (Bloomsbury, London, 2019), p.155
6 Ibid.
7 S. Rowecki, *Wspomnienia i notatki autobiograficzne (1918–1939)* (Czytelnik, Warsaw, 1988), p.141
8 Ibid.
9 Lieutenant Pohl, bombardier on an He 111, II./KG 26, quoted in S. Neitzel and H. Welzer, *Soldiers: German POWs on Fighting, Killing, and Dying* (Random House, New York, 2012), p.202
10 H. von Luck, *Panzer Commander* (Cassell, London, 2002), p.28
11 H. Schäufler, *So Lebten und so Starben Sie: Das Buch vom Panzerregiment 35* (Kameradschaft ehemaliger Panzer-Regiment 35 e.V, Bamberg, 1983), p.15
12 M. Bielski, *Grupe Operacyjna Piotrków 1939* (Bellona, Warsaw, 1991), p.462
13 H. Stańczyk, J. Smoliński, T. Panecki, M. Sikora, J. Żak, and P. Gotowiecki, *Polskie Siły Zbrojne na Zachodzie po II Wojnie Światowej: Klęska Zwycięzców* (Oficyna Wydawnicza Rytm, Warsaw, 2016), p.158
14 J. Neumann, *Die 4. Panzerdivision 1938–1943* (Verlag & Antiquariat für Zeitgeschichte, Bad Dürkheim, 1985), p.32
15 D. Schenk, *Die Post von Danzig: Geschichte eines Deutschen Justizmords* (Rohwohlt, Hamburg, 1995), pp.61–67
16 J. Beck, quoted in *Little White Book*, p.137
17 Note Verbale from the Ministry of Foreign Affairs transmitted to the Royal Netherlands Legation, ibid., p.132
18 Appeal of Mr. Roosevelt, President of the United States, in regard to bombing of open towns, ibid., p.128
19 Address by Neville Chamberlain, Prime Minister, in the House of Commons, 1 September 1939, available at https://avalon.law.yale.edu/wwii/gb1.asp
20 A. Galiński (ed.), *Zbrodnie Wehrmachtu w Wielkopolsce w Okresie Zarządu Wokskowego (1 Września-25 Paźsziernika 1939)* (Instytut Pamięci Narodowej, Kalisz, 1986), p.49
21 Quoted in M. Melvin, *Manstein: Hitler's Greatest General* (Thomas Dunne, New York, 2011), p.129
22 O. von Wrochem, *Erich von Manstein: Vernichtungskrieg und Geschichtspolitik* (Brill Schöningh, Leiden, 2009), p.47
23 T. Chinciński and P. Machcewicz (eds), *Bydgoszcz 3–4 Września 1939: Studia i Dokumenty* (Instytut Pamięci Narodowej, Warsaw, 2008), pp.266–68
24 C. Hollingworth, *The Three Weeks' War in Poland* (Duckworth, London, 1940), pp.19–20
25 *Kurjer Warszawski*, 4 September 1939, r.119 no. 244, p.2
26 Count Raczyński to Beck, *Little White Book*, p.139

27 *Express Poranny*, 6 September 1939, no. 246, p.1
28 *Siege*, directed by J. Bryan (RKO Pictures, 1940), available at https://www.youtube.com/watch?v=eMcF7Cszz6s
29 S. Ordon (trans. F. Anstruther), *Fire over Warsaw* (Ksiażnica Polska, Glasgow, 1942), pp.20–21
30 W. Bartoszewski, *1859 dni Warszawy* (Znak, Kraków, 1984), p.30
31 Ordon, *Fire over Warsaw*, p.8
32 M. Wojewoda and J. Wojewoda, *Bitwa nad Bzura: Pierwsza Wśród Wielkich Bitew II Wojny Światowej* (Bellona, Warsaw, 2016), p.30
33 S. Zeldman, quoted in T. Epsztein, J. Majewska, and A Bańkowska (eds), Sara Arm et al. (trans.), *Archiwum Ringelbluma, Vol. XV, Wrzesień 1939. Listy kaliskie. Listy płockie, Wydawnictwo ŻIH/Wydawnictwo UW*, p.60
34 Schäufler, *So Lebten und so Starben Sie*, p.18
35 Ordon, *Fire over Warsaw*, p.17
36 R. Moorhouse, *First to Fight: The Polish War 1939* (Vintage, London, 2020), pp.160–62
37 Ibid., p.144
38 Quoted in P. Bauer, *17 Pułk Ułanow Wielkopolskich im Króla Bolesława Chrobrego* (Oficyna Wydawnicza Ajaks, Pruszków, 1994), p.56
39 J. Biskupska, *Survivors: Warsaw under Nazi Occupation (Studies in the Social and Cultural History of Modern Warfare)*, (Cambridge University Press, 2022), p.26
40 *Kurjer Warszawski,* 6 September 1939, r.119 no. 246, p.3
41 A. Carton de Wiart, *Happy Odyssey: The Memoirs of Lieutenant General Sir Adrian Carton de Wiart, VC, KBE, CB, CMG, DSO* (Pen & Sword, Barnsley, 2007), p.157
42 Quoted in Z. Gluza and M. Markowska, *Rok 1939: Rozbiór Polski* (Fundacja Ośrodka Karta, Warsaw, 2009), p.108
43 Biskupska, *Survivors*, p.34
44 A. Donat, *The Holocaust Kingdom: A Memoir* (Holocaust Library, New York, 1978), p.3
45 Z. Zaremba, *Żeby chociaż świat wiedział* (Bellona, Warsaw, 2010), pp.66–67
46 Biskupska, *Survivors*, p.36
47 *Express Poranny*, 7 September 1939, no. 247, pp.1–2
48 *Express Poranny*, 8 September 1939, no. 248, pp.1–2
49 Dąbrowska, *Dzienniki 1914–1965*, p.262
50 *Kurjer Warszawski,* 11 September 1939, r.119 no. 251, p.1
51 Ibid.
52 M. Berg, *The Diary of Mary Berg: Growing up in the Warsaw Ghetto* (Oneworld, 2006), p.27
53 Ibid., pp.29–30
54 E. Ringelblum, *Polish-Jewish Relations During the Second World War* (Northwestern University Press, Evanston IL, 1992), pp.24–25
55 Quoted in J. Lichten, *Notes on the Assimilation and Acculturation of Jews in Poland 1863–1943* (Blackwell, Oxford, 1986), p.124; *Haynt*, 1 September 1939, p.10

56 K. Person, *Assimilated Jews in the Warsaw Ghetto, 1940–1943* (Syracuse University Press, New York, 2014), p.24
57 W. Szpilman, *The Pianist: The Extraordinary Story of One Man's Survival in Warsaw 1939–1945* (Picador, London, 2019), pp.34–35
58 Z. Kawa in *Archiwum Ringelbluma*, Vol. XV, pp.28–29 and 30
59 Ringelblum, *Polish–Jewish Relations*, p.32
60 A. Czerniaków, R. Hilberg, and S. Staron, *The Warsaw Diary of Adam Czerniaków: Prelude to Doom* (Ivan R. Dee, Chicago, 1999), pp.26–27
61 Czerniaków et al., *The Warsaw Diary of Adam Czerniaków*, p.74
62 Ringelblum, *Polish–Jewish Relations*, p.28; ibid.
63 Berg, *The Diary of Mary Berg*, p.30
64 Ringelblum, *Polish–Jewish Relations*, p.36
65 Czerniaków et al., *The Warsaw Diary of Adam Czerniaków*, p.73
66 Szpilman, *The Pianist*, p.35
67 Ringelblum, *Polish–Jewish Relations*, pp.35–36
68 Szpilman, *The Pianist*, p.36
69 *Express Poranny*, 14 September 1939, no. 254, p.1
70 Berg, *The Diary of Mary Berg*, p.30

CHAPTER 4: A NEW PARTITION

1 C. Norwid (trans. B. Johnston), '*Fortepian Szopena*', 1865. Used with permission.
2 Telegram 264, Schulenburg to Foreign Office Berlin, 05/09/1939, available at https://avalon.law.yale.edu/20th_century/ns062.asp
3 Telegram 317, Schulenburg to Foreign Office Berlin, 10/09/1939, available at https://avalon.law.yale.edu/20th_century/ns069.asp
4 From Telegram 360, Ribbentrop to Schulenburg, 15/09/1939, available at https://avalon.law.yale.edu/20th_century/ns072.asp
5 Text of the Russian note by M. Potemkin to M. Grzybowski, *Little White Book*, p.189
6 S. Zaloga, *Poland 1939: The Birth of Blitzkrieg* (Osprey, Oxford, 2002), p.80; G. Krivosheev, *Rossiya I SSSR v Voynach XX Veka: Poteri Vooruzhennyich Syl. Statystycheskoe Issledovanye* (Olma, Moscow, 2001), pp.242–44
7 Moorhouse, *First to Fight*, pp.176–77
8 Quoted in J. Gross, *Revolution from Abroad: The Soviet Conquest of Poland's Western Ukraine and Western Belorussia* (Princeton University Press, Princeton NJ, 2002), pp.21–22
9 Moorhouse, *First to Fight*, p.179
10 *Express Poranny*, 19 September 1939, nr. 259, p.1
11 *Kurjer Warszawski*, 21 September 1939, nr. 261, p.2
12 M. Cieplewicz, 'Generalowie polscy w opinii J. Piłsudskiego' in *Wojskowy Przegląd Historyczny* (Ministerstwo Obrony Narodowej), nr. 1 (37) (1966), pp.327 and 330

13 Quoted in Bartoszewski, *1859 dni Warszawy*, p.49
14 Z. Nałkowska, *Dzienniki* (Czytelnik, Warsaw, 1976–96, 4 volumes), Vol. IV, p.54
15 Note presented by the Polish ambassador in Paris to the French Foreign Office, 18 September 1939, *Little White Book*, p.190
16 Telegram (no. 292), from Moscow to FO, 17 September 1939. PROF037I/23Io3 CI4003
17 L. Woodward, *British Foreign Policy in the Second World War* (HMSO, London, 1970, 5 volumes), Vol. I, p.12; Forczyk, *Case White*, p.308
18 Moorhouse, *First to Fight*, p.197
19 W. Gorlitz (ed.), *In the Service of the Reich: The Memoirs of Field Marshal Keitel* (Cooper Square Press, New York, 2000), pp.66–68
20 Czerniaków et al., *The Warsaw Diary of Adam Czerniaków*, p.75
21 Szpilman, *The Pianist*, p.36
22 Berg, *The Diary of Mary Berg*, p.31
23 Szpilman, *The Pianist*, p.37
24 Ordon, *Fire over Warsaw*, p.47
25 Testimony of Michalina Mazińska, available at https://zapisyterroru.pl
26 All of these accounts are available at the online archive at https://zapisyterroru.pl
27 Forczyk, *Case White*, p.314
28 Szpilman, *The Pianist*, p.38
29 Unnamed, quoted in *Archiwum Ringelbluma*, Vol. I, p.6
30 Forczyk, *Case White*, p.314
31 *Gazeta Wspólna* nr. 3, 29.IX.1939
32 Unnamed, quoted in *Archiwum Ringelbluma*, Vol. I, p.8
33 Berg, *The Diary of Mary Berg*, p.33
34 H. Regulska, *Dziennik Z Oblężonej Warszawy* (PAX, Warsaw, 1978), p.115
35 S. Starzyński, quoted in J. Kulski, *The Color of Courage: A Boy at War: The World War II Diary of Julian Kulski* (Aquila Polonica Publishing, Los Angeles CA, 2014), pp.9–10
36 *Gazeta Wspólna* nr. 2, 28.IX.1939; *Kurjer Warszawski*, 28 September 1939, nr. 268, p.1
37 Forczyk, *Case White*, p.332; Biskupska, *Survivors*, p.44
38 Forczyk, *Case White*, p.316
39 Kulski, *The Color of Courage*, pp.18–21
40 W. Shirer, *Berlin Diary: The Journal of a Foreign Correspondent 1934–1941* (Alfred A. Knopf, New York, 1941), p.216
41 Ibid., p.209
42 Ibid., p.207

CHAPTER 5: *INTELLIGENZAKTION*

1 C. Miłosz, 'Campo dei Fiori', 1943, in *The Collected Poems, 1931–1987* (The Ecco Press, Hopewell NJ, 1988), pp.33–35
2 F. Halder, C. Burdick, and H.-A. Jacobsen, (eds), *The Halder War Diary 1939–1942* (Presidio, Novato CA, 1988), p.31
3 *Bundesarchiv*, Berlin, R581/256, f.90
4 *Bundesarchiv*, Berlin, R58/241, f.169, *Richtlinien für den Auswärtigen Einsatz der Sicherheitspolizei und des SD*; K.-M. Mallmann, J. Böhler, and J. Matthäus, *Einsatzgruppen in Polen* (Wissenschaftliche Buchgesellschaft, Darmstadt, 2008), p.121
5 *Bundesarchiv*, Berlin, *Protokoll der Amtschefbesprechung* 07/09/1939, R58/825
6 E. Wagner, *Der Generalquartermeister. Briefe und Tagebuchaufzeichnungen des Generalquartermeisters des Heeres General der Artillerie Eduard Wagner* (Olzog, Munich, 1963), p.134
7 G. Gross, E. Hansen, K.-V. Neugebauer, H. Potempa, and W. Rahn, *Das Zeitalter der Weltkriege – Völker in Waffen* (Oldenbourg, Berlin, 2009), p.365
8 R. Lukas, *Forgotten Holocaust: The Poles Under German Occupation 1939–1944* (Hippocrene Books, New York, 2012), p.42
9 J. Connelly, 'Nazis and Slavs: From Racial Theory to Racist Practice' in *Central European History*, Vol. 32 No. 1 (1999), p.14
10 Quoted in Biskupska, *Survivors*, p.49
11 *Nazi Conspiracy and Aggression, Office of the United States Chief of Counsel for Prosecution of Axis Criminality ("Red Series")*, (Office of United States Chief of Council for Prosecution of Axis Criminality, 1947), Vol. I, p.1029
12 Quoted in Biskupska, *Survivors*, p.49
13 Polish Ministry of Information, *Black Book*, pp. 29, 34, 30, and 54
14 Ibid., pp.59 and 67
15 See ibid., p.48
16 Ibid., pp.35 and 44
17 S. Friedländer, *Nazi Germany and the Jews: The Years of Extermination 1939–1945* (HarperCollins, New York, 2007), p.40
18 Donat, *The Holocaust Kingdom*, p.4
19 Quoted in J. Robertson, *From Corsets to Communism: The Life and Times of Zofie Nałkowska* (Scotland Street Press, Edinburgh, 2019), p.159
20 Nałkowska, *Dzienniki*, Vol. IV, p.116
21 Szpilman, *The Pianist*, p.45
22 Ibid., pp.45–46
23 J. Kulski, *Stefan Starzyński w mojej pamięci* (Państwowe Wydawnictwo Naukowe, Warsaw, 1990), pp.105–06
24 Ibid., p.105
25 Szpilman, *The Pianist*, pp.43–44
26 Kulski, *Stefan Starzyński*, pp.87 and 108
27 Ibid., p.111
28 Ibid., pp.116 and 106

29 Donat, *The Holocaust Kingdom*, p.5
30 Kulski, *Stefan Starzyński*, p.106
31 Ibid., p.118
32 Ibid., p.120
33 S. Jankowski and A. Ciborowski, *Warszawa 1945 I dziś* (Wydawnictwo Interpress, Warsaw, 1971), p.23
34 Quoted in H. Steidle, 'Die Zerstörung Warschaus auf dem Reissbrett' in *Meeviertel Anzeiger* (Würzburg), No. 3 (2010)
35 Testimony of Hans Frank, 18 April 1946, Nuremberg, available at http://law2.umkc.edu/faculty/projects/ftrials/nuremberg/franktest.html
36 W. Schellenberg, *The Labyrinth: Memoirs of Walter Schellenberg, Hitler's Chief of Counterintelligence* (Da Capo, Boston MS, 1956), pp.160–61
37 S. Piotrkowski, *Dziennik Hansa Franka* (Wydawnictwo Prawnicze, Warsaw, 1957), pp.344–45
38 Polish Ministry of Information, *Black Book*, p.325
39 Ibid., pp.355 and 358
40 Ibid., pp.401–02
41 Biskupska, *Survivors*, p.193
42 Kulski, *The Color of Courage*, p.68
43 Polish Ministry of Information, *Black Book*, p.444
44 Quoted in Noakes and Pridham, *Nazism 1919–1945*, Vol. III, p.933
45 *Nazi Conspiracy and Aggression*, Vol. V, p.35
46 B. D. Dyck, 'Hitler's Lebensborn Children: Kidnappings in German-Occupied Poland' in *WWII History*, Vol. XII No. 7 (December 2013)
47 Polish Ministry of Information, *Black Book*, p.455
48 Testimony of Mieczysław Michałowicz, available at https://zapisyterroru.pl
49 Ibid.
50 Polish Ministry of Information, *Black Book*, p.477
51 Testimony of Mieczysław Michałowicz
52 W. Dworzaczek, 'Polish Archives War Losses' in *Slavonic and East European Review*, Vol. 24 No. 63 (January 1946), p.189
53 A. Stebelski, *The Fate of Polish Archives During World War II* (Państwowe Wydawn. Naukowe, Warsaw, 1964), p.51
54 Polish Ministry of Information, *Black Book*, pp.459–63
55 W. Bartoszewski, *Warsaw Death Ring 1939–1944* (Interpress, Warsaw, 1968), p.21
56 Bartoszewski, *Warsaw Death Ring*, p.24
57 Polish Ministry of Information, *Black Book*, p.96
58 *Biuletyn Informacyjny*, 9 January 1941, p.1
59 Polish Ministry of Information, *Black Book*, p.498
60 Ibid., p.503
61 Ringelblum, *Polish-Jewish Relations*, p.6
62 Lukas, *Forgotten Holocaust*, p.9
63 Polish Ministry of Information, *Black Book*, p.458

64 Ibid.
65 J. Connelly, 'Why the Poles Collaborated so Little: And Why That is no Reason for Nationalist Hubris' in *Slavic Review*, Vol. 64 No. 4 (Winter 2005) p.775
66 Szpilman, *The Pianist*, pp.51–52

CHAPTER 6: OPPRESSION AND DEFIANCE

1 I. Bobowska (trans. K. Johnson), '*Bo ja się uczę*', 1941
2 Testimony of Zygmunt Juchniewicz, available at https://zapisyterroru.pl
3 S. Datner, J. Gumkowski, and K. Leszczyński, *Genocide 1939–1945* (Wydawnictwo Zachodnie, Warsaw, 1962), pp.48–50
4 Piotrkowski, *Dziennik Hansa Franka*, p.321
5 Bartoszewski, *Warsaw Death Ring*, pp.40–41
6 R. Huhle, 'Nacht und Nebel: Mythos und Bedeutung' in *Zeitschrift für Menschenrechte* (Wochenschau Verlag, Frankfurt am Main), Vol. VIII No. 1 (2014), p.121
7 Quoted in E. Crankshaw, *Gestapo: Instrument of Tyranny* (Putnam, London, 1956), p.215
8 K. Bracher, *The German Dictatorship: The Origins, Structure and Consequences of National Socialism* (Penguin, Harmondsworth, 1978), p.418
9 G. Zych, *Oranienburg* (Ksiżka i Wiedza, Warsaw, 1962), pp.51–52
10 Testimony of Halina Karśnicka, available at https://zapisyterroru.pl
11 A. Czuperska-Śliwicka, *Cztery Lata Ostrego Dyżuru, Wspom ienia z Pawiaka, 1940–1944* (Czytelnik, Warsaw, 1989), pp.216–17
12 S. Płoski, *Wspomnienia Więźniów Pawiaka* (Polska Akademia Nauka, Warsaw, 1964), p.138
13 W. Bartoszewski, *Palmiry* (Wyd. Książka i Wiedza, Warsaw, 1969), pp.12–13, 28–37, 40–42, and 47
14 Testimony of Wiktor Grzywo-Dąbrowski, available at https://zapisyterroru.pl
15 Biskupska, *Survivors*, p.86
16 Testimony of Zygmunt Śliwicki, available at https://zapisyterroru.pl
17 Testimony of Maria Przyborowska, available at https://zapisyterroru.pl
18 Testimony of Stanisława Sroka, available at https://zapisyterroru.pl
19 Testimony of Antoni Podgórski, available at https://zapisyterroru.pl
20 Bartoszewski, *Warsaw Death Ring*, pp.5–6
21 Testimony of Felicjan Loth, available at https://zapisyterroru.pl
22 Ibid.
23 Testimony of Stefan Sokołowski, available at https://zapisyterroru.pl
24 Testimonies of Leon Wanat, Maria Kopeć, Felicjan Loth, Zygmunt Śliwicki, Marcela Skrzypińska, and Maria Adamczyk, all available at zapisyterroru.pl
25 C. Browning, *Ordinary Men: Reserve Police Battalion 101 and the Final Solution in Poland* (Harper Perennial, New York, 1993), pp.55–77
26 Ringelblum, *Polish-Jewish Relations*, p.133

27 Leon Najberg, quoted in J. Grabowski, 'The Polish Police Collaboration in the Holocaust', United States Holocaust Memorial Museum, Ina Levine Annual Lecture, 17 November 2016, p.19, available at https://www.ushmm.org/m/pdfs/20170502-Grabowski_OP.pdf
28 Ringelblum, *Polish-Jewish Relations*, pp.133–34
29 Grabowski, 'The Polish Police Collaboration'; T. Piotrowski, *Poland's Holocaust: Ethnic Strife, Collaboration with Occupying Forces and Genocide in the Second Republic, 1918–1947* (McFarland, Jefferson NC, 1998), p.109
30 M. Pachter, *Umierać też trzeba umieć* (Stowarzyszenie Centrum Badań nad Zagładą Żydów, Warsaw, 2015), p.81
31 S. Korboński, *Fighting Warsaw* (Pickle Partners Publishing, Halstad MN, 2016) p.75; Lukas, *Forgotten Holocaust*, p.72
32 Major Franciszek Przymusiński, quoted in ibid.
33 Grabowski, 'The Polish Police Collaboration', p.6
34 Z. Klukowski, *Diary From the Years of Occupation, 1939–44* (University of Illinois Press, Urbana IL, 1993), p.215
35 A. Hempel, *Pogrobowcy Kleski: rzecz o policji "granatowej" w Generalnym Gubernatorstwie, 1939–1945* (Państwowe Wydawn. Nauk., Warsaw, 1990), p.174
36 Testimony of Waleria Szymańska, available at https://zapisyterroru.pl
37 Korboński, *Fighting Warsaw*, p.77
38 Testimony of Stanisława Sroka, available at https://zapisyterroru.pl
39 P. Kenney, *Dance in Chains: Political Imprisonment in the Modern World* (Oxford University Press, New York, 2017), p.152
40 Testimony of Władysław Wilczewski, available at https://zapisyterroru.pl
41 E. Harich-Schneider, *Charaktere und Katastrophen. Augenzeugenberichte einer Reisenden Muskierin* (Ullstein, Berlin, 1978), p.203
42 Bartoszewski, *Warsaw Death Ring*, p.434
43 Quoted in Bartoszewski, *Warsaw Death Ring*, p.435
44 P. Giaccaria and C. Minca (eds), *Hitler's Geographies: The Spatialities of the Third Reich* (University of Chicago Press, Chicago IL, 2016), pp.189 and 213; J. Zimmerer, *From Windhoek to Auschwitz? Reflections on the Relationship between Colonialism and National Socialism* (De Gruyter Oldenbourg, Berlin, 2023), p.314
45 G. Weinberg, *Visions of Victory: The Hopes of Eight World War II Leaders* (Cambridge University Press, 2005), p.24
46 S. Tazbir, *W obronie dzieci i młodzieży w Warszawie, 1939–1944* (Państwowy Instytut Wydawniczy, Warsaw, 1975), pp.28–29
47 Lukas, *Forgotten Holocaust*, p.10
48 Porter, *When Nationalism Began to Hate*, p.85
49 N. Davies, *God's Playground: A History of Poland* (Oxford University Press, 2005, 2 volumes), Vol. II, pp.340–44
50 J. Krawzcyńska, 'Wspomnienia z prasy podziemnej 1939–1944' in *Rocznik Historii Czasopiśmiennictwa Polskiego* (Komisja Prasoznawcza, Wrocław), Vol. I,
51 Biskupska, *Survivors*, p.146
52 *Biuletyn Informacyjny*, 1 November 1940, p.1

53 Biskupska, *Survivors*, p.146
54 Krawzcyńska, 'Wspomnienia', pp.334 and 336
55 Biskupska, *Survivors*, p.148
56 J. Karski, *Story of a Secret State: My Report to the World* (Penguin, Harmondsworth, 2019), p.288
57 Ibid., p.293
58 Ibid.
59 Ibid.
60 Korboński, *Fighting Warsaw*, pp.202–03
61 Ibid., p.204
62 Ibid., p.205
63 Ibid., p.209
64 Karski, *Story of a Secret State*, pp.63–64
65 Ibid., p.65
66 Ibid., p.135
67 Ibid., p.414
68 Ibid., p.415
69 J. Nowak, *Courier from Warsaw* (Wayne State University Press, Detroit MI, 1982), p.78
70 Ibid., pp.85 and 86
71 Ibid., p.108
72 Ibid., p.176
73 Karski, *Story of a Secret State*, p.156
74 Ibid., pp.304–05
75 Ibid.
76 Krawzcyńska, 'Wspomnienia', pp.334–35
77 Szpilman, *The Pianist*, p.48
78 Karski, *Story of a Secret State*, p.271
79 Ibid., p.275
80 Korboński, *Fighting Warsaw*, p.218
81 Karski, *Story of a Secret State*, p.275
82 Krawzcyńska, 'Wspomnienia', p.325
83 Connelly, 'Why the Poles Collaborated so Little', pp.773–74
84 Korboński, *Fighting Warsaw*, p.450
85 Karski, *Story of a Secret State*, p.415
86 Robertson, *From Corsets to Communism*, pp.163–64

CHAPTER 7: THE WARSAW GHETTO

1 Z. Ginczanka (trans. N. Kassell and A. Safran), '*Non omnis moriar*', 1942. Used with permission. Originally published by AGNI (2006), available at https://agnionline.bu.edu/poetry/non-omnis-moriar/
2 Lukas, *Forgotten Holocaust*, p.32

3 Ibid., p.34
4 Czerniaków et al., *The Warsaw Diary of Adam Czerniaków*, p.34
5 Lukas, *Forgotten Holocaust*, p.36
6 I. Trunk, *Judenrat: The Jewish Councils of Eastern Europe under Nazi Occupation* (University of Nebraska Press, Lincoln NE, 1996), p.2
7 Czerniaków et al., *The Warsaw Diary of Adam Czerniaków*, pp.86–87
8 https://blog.nli.org.il/en/januszkorczak/
9 J. Sloan (ed.), *Notes from the Warsaw Ghetto: The Journal of Emmanuel Ringelblum* (Normanby Press, London, 2015), pp.10–13
10 R. Auerbach (trans. S. Kassow), *Warsaw Testament* (White Goat Press, Amherst, 2024), pp.96–98
11 J. Grzesik, *Holocaust – Zagłada Żydów 1939–1945* (Liber Duo, Lublin, 2011), pp. 43, 44, and 54
12 Sloan, *Notes from the Warsaw Ghetto*, p.54
13 Person, *Assimilated Jews in the Warsaw Ghetto*, pp.25–26
14 Testimony of Mieczysław Maślanko, available at https://zapisyterroru.pl
15 Person, *Assimilated Jews in the Warsaw Ghetto*, p.26
16 Czerniaków et al., *The Warsaw Diary of Adam Czerniaków*, pp.90–91
17 Trunk, *Judenrat*, p.191
18 Sloan, *Notes from the Warsaw Ghetto*, p.40
19 Ringelblum, *Polish-Jewish Relations*, pp.44–46
20 Kulski, *The Color of Courage*, p.95
21 J. Schoenfeld (ed.), *Holocaust Memoirs: Jews in the Lwów Ghetto, the Janowski Concentration Camp, and as Deportees in Siberia* (KTAV Publishing House, Hoboken NJ, 1985), p.240
22 Ibid., pp.241–42
23 Ringelblum, *Polish-Jewish Relations*, p.38
24 Ibid., p.42
25 Testimony of Stefan Orczykowski, available at https://zapisyterroru.pl
26 Sloan, *Notes from the Warsaw Ghetto*, p.328; Czerniaków et al., *The Warsaw Diary of Adam Czerniaków*, p.326
27 Czerniaków et al., *The Warsaw Diary of Adam Czerniaków*, p.136
28 Donat, *The Holocaust Kingdom*, p.18
29 Sloan, *Notes from the Warsaw Ghetto*, p.37
30 Polish Ministry of Information, *Black Book*, pp.231–32
31 Polish Ministry of Information, *Black Book*, p.226
32 L. Yahil, I. Friedman, and H. Galai, *The Holocaust: The Fate of European Jewry 1932–1945* (Oxford University Press, 1991), pp.160–61
33 C. Browning, *The Origins of the Final Solution: The Evolution of Nazi Jewish Policy, September 1939–March 1942* (University of Nebraska Press, Lincoln NE, 2004), p.82
34 Ibid., p.87
35 I. Kershaw, *Hitler: A Biography* (Norton, New York, 2008), p.577
36 Czerniaków et al., *The Warsaw Diary of Adam Czerniaków*, p.174

37 Browning, *Origins of the Final Solution*, p.88
38 P. Longerich, *Holocaust: The Nazi Persecution and Murder of the Jews* (Oxford University Press, 2010), p.165
39 Czerniaków et al., *The Warsaw Diary of Adam Czerniaków*, p.190
40 Sloan, *Notes from the Warsaw Ghetto*, p.66
41 Czerniaków et al., *The Warsaw Diary of Adam Czerniaków*, p.201
42 Ibid., p.201
43 Ibid., p.111
44 Sloan, *Notes from the Warsaw Ghetto*, p.70
45 Czerniaków et al., *The Warsaw Diary of Adam Czerniaków*, p.41
46 Testimony of Mieczysław Maślanko
47 Czerniaków et al., *The Warsaw Diary of Adam Czerniaków*, pp.108–09
48 Testimony of Mieczysław Maślanko
49 Czerniaków et al., *The Warsaw Diary of Adam Czerniaków*, p.110
50 Person, *Assimilated Jews in the Warsaw Ghetto*, p.59
51 Testimony of Łazarz Menes, available at https://zapisyterroru.pl
52 Szpilman, *The Pianist*, p.54
53 Auerbach, *Warsaw Testament*, p.105
54 Sloan, *Notes from the Warsaw Ghetto*, pp.68, 70, 205, and 233
55 Ibid., p.75
56 Person, *Assimilated Jews in the Warsaw Ghetto*, p.61
57 Ibid., p.62
58 Sloan, *Notes from the Warsaw Ghetto*, p.74
59 https://www.jhi.pl/en/articles/the-easter-pogrom-1940,354
60 T. Szarota, *U progu Zagłady. Zajścia antyżydowskie i pogromy w okupowanej Europie* (Wydawnictwo Sic!, Warsaw, 2000), p.70
61 Szpilman, *The Pianist*, p.56
62 Berg, *The Diary of Mary Berg*, p.44
63 Szpilman, *The Pianist*, p.57
64 Sloan, *Notes from the Warsaw Ghetto*, p.111
65 Berg, *The Diary of Mary Berg*, pp.39 and 45
66 Person, *Assimilated Jews in the Warsaw Ghetto, 1940–1943*, p.28
67 Ibid., p.28
68 Sloan, *Notes from the Warsaw Ghetto*, p.118; Szpilman, *The Pianist*, p.58
69 Donat, *The Holocaust Kingdom*, p.25
70 Czerniaków et al., *The Warsaw Diary of Adam Czerniaków*, p.204
71 Ibid., p.206
72 Person, *Assimilated Jews in the Warsaw Ghetto, 1940–1943*, p.28
73 Donat, *The Holocaust Kingdom*, p.26
74 Ibid., p.27
75 Unnamed, quoted in *Archiwum Ringelbluma*, Vol. I, p.54
76 Berg, *The Diary of Mary Berg*, p.53

77 K. Person, *Warsaw Ghetto Police: The Jewish Order Service during the Nazi Occupation* (Cornell University Press, Ithaca NY, 2021), p.37
78 Ibid., p.106
79 Ibid., p.114
80 https://cbj.jhi.pl/documents/1025424/77/
81 Szpilman, *The Pianist*, pp.77–78 and 108
82 https://cbj.jhi.pl/documents/1025424/63/; https://cbj.jhi.pl/documents/1025424/77/
83 C. Browning, 'Nazi Ghettoization Policy in Poland: 1939–41' in *Central European History* (Cambridge University Press) No. 4 (1986), pp.353–54
84 L. Berenson, quoted in *Archiwum Ringelbluma*, Vol. I, p.55
85 W. Rubinstein, *The Left, the Right, and the Jews* (Routledge, London, 2017), p.136
86 Czerniaków et al., *The Warsaw Diary of Adam Czerniaków*, p.330; Sloan, *Notes from the Warsaw Ghetto*, p.236
87 S. Kassow, *Who Will Write Our History?: Rediscovering a Hidden Archive from the Warsaw Ghetto* (Penguin Group, London, 2009), p.116; Person, *Warsaw Ghetto Police*, p.33
88 Auerbach, *Warsaw Testament*, p.208
89 Ibid., p.207
90 Ibid., p.277
91 Person, *Warsaw Ghetto Police*, p.70
92 S. Różycki, quoted in *Archiwum Ringelbluma*, Vol. I, p.64
93 Berg, *The Diary of Mary Berg*, p.76
94 Różycki, *Archiwum Ringelbluma*, Vol. I, p.68
95 Ibid., p.78
96 Ibid., p.173; Sloan, *Notes from the Warsaw Ghetto*, p.167
97 Ibid., p.77
98 Sloan, *Notes from the Warsaw Ghetto*, p.153
99 Testimony of Jósef Gitler-Barski, available at https://zapisyterroru.pl
100 Testimony of Jósef Gitler-Barski
101 Testimony of Irena Sendler, available at https://zapisyterroru.pl
102 Sloan, *Notes from the Warsaw Ghetto*, p.173
103 Robertson, *From Corsets to Communism*, p.169
104 Testimony of Stefan Orczykowski
105 Testimony of Fryda Koch, available at https://zapisyterroru.pl
106 Browning, 'Nazi Ghettoization Policy in Poland', p.360
107 C. Browning, 'Genocide and Public Health: German Doctors and Polish Jews, 1939–41' in *Holocaust and Genocide Studies* (Oxford University Press), No. 3 (1998), p.24
108 Browning, 'Nazi Ghettoization Policy in Poland', p.360
109 Czerniaków et al., *The Warsaw Diary of Adam Czerniaków*, p.298
110 L. Stone, D. He, S. Lehnstaedt, and Y. Artzy-Randrup, 'Extraordinary Curtailment of Massive Typhus Epidemic in the Warsaw Ghetto' in *Science* (American Association for the Advancement of Science, Washington DC), No. 6 (2020), p.7

111 https://cbj.jhi.pl/documents/1025424/176/
112 https://cbj.jhi.pl/documents/1025424/395/
113 H. Feldmeier, 'Typhus in the Warsaw Ghetto 1940–1942: How an Epidemic Increased Exponentially, was Abated and Eventually Disappeared' in *One Health and Implementation Research* (OAE Publishing, Los Angeles CA), No. 1 (2021), pp.51–55, http://dx.doi.org/10.20517/ohir.2021.03
114 https://cbj.jhi.pl/documents/1025424/95/

CHAPTER 8: *ENDLÖSUNG* AND THE GHETTO UPRISING

1 Y. Katznelson (trans. R. Whitman and M. Rothstein), '*Vey Dir*', 1820, Poetry in Hell, CC BY-SA 3.0, https://creativecommons.org/licenses/by-sa/3.0/
2 T. Snyder, *Bloodlands: Europe Between Hitler and Stalin* (Vintage, London, 2011), p.263
3 H. Arendt, *Eichmann in Jerusalem: A Report on the Banality of Evil* (Penguin Classics, New York, 2006), p.83
4 https://www.yadvashem.org/docs/wannsee-conference-protocol.html
5 Biskupska, *Survivors*, p.116
6 Arendt, *Eichmann in Jerusalem*, p.87
7 https://www.yadvashem.org/docs/wannsee-conference-protocol.html
8 Browning, *Origins of the Final Solution*, p.191
9 J. Sachslehner, *Zwei Millionen Ham'ma Erledigt: Odilo Globočnik – Hitlers Manager des Todes* (Styria Premium, Vienna, 2014), p.162
10 Ibid., pp.236–38
11 J. Schelvis, *Sobibor: A History of a Nazi Death Camp* (Berg, Oxford, 2007), pp.26–27
12 I. Kershaw, *Hitler: 1936–1945: Nemesis* (W. W. Norton, New York, 2000), p.519
13 Sloan, *Notes from the Warsaw Ghetto*, pp.300–01
14 Szpilman, *The Pianist*, p.82
15 Berg, *The Diary of Mary Berg*, p.156
16 Donat, *The Holocaust Kingdom*, p.50; Auerbach, *Warsaw Testament*, p.149
17 Auerbach, *Warsaw Testament*, p.149
18 Szpilman, *The Pianist*, p.75
19 Czerniaków et al., *The Warsaw Diary of Adam Czerniaków*, pp.316–17
20 Ibid., pp.323–40 and 328
21 Ibid., p.320
22 https://1943.pl/en/artykul/bloody-friday-17-18-april-1942/
23 Sloan, *Notes from the Warsaw Ghetto*, p.307
24 Ibid., p.307
25 Czerniaków et al., *The Warsaw Diary of Adam Czerniaków*, p.321
26 Auerbach, *Warsaw Testament*, p.152
27 Sloan, *Notes from the Warsaw Ghetto*, p.295

28 Berg, *The Diary of Mary Berg*, p.164
29 Testimony of Michał Zylberberg, available at https://zapisyterroru.pl
30 Berg, *The Diary of Mary Berg*, p.164; Szpilman, *The Pianist*, p.81; Czerniaków et al., *The Warsaw Diary of Adam Czerniaków*, p.348; Sloan, *Notes from the Warsaw Ghetto*, p.309
31 Szpilman, *The Pianist*, pp.81–82
32 A. Horstmann, 'Judenaufnahmen fürs Archiv – Das dokumentarische Filmmaterial "Asien in Mitteleuropa", 1942' in *Medaon* (Hatikva, Dresden), No. 4 (2009), pp.6–7, available at https://www.medaon.de/de/artikel/judenaufnahmen-fuers-archiv-das-dokumentarische-filmmaterial-asien-in-mitteleuropa-1942/
33 Auerbach, *Warsaw Testament*, p.150
34 Czerniaków et al., *The Warsaw Diary of Adam Czerniaków*, p.380
35 Y. Arad, *Belzec, Sobibor, Treblinka: The Operation Reinhard Death Camps* (Indiana University Press, Bloomington IN, 1987), pp.18–19
36 Czerniaków et al., *The Warsaw Diary of Adam Czerniaków*, p.385
37 Donat, *The Holocaust Kingdom*, p.58
38 Testimony of Michał Zylberberg
39 Szpilman, *The Pianist*, p.89
40 Czerniaków et al., *The Warsaw Diary of Adam Czerniaków*, pp.381–82
41 Donat, *The Holocaust Kingdom*, pp.60–61
42 Ibid., p.62
43 Szpilman, *The Pianist*, p.90
44 Ibid., p.92
45 Testimony of Zymunt Warman, available at https://zapisyterroru.pl
46 Donat, *The Holocaust Kingdom*, p.62; Testimony of Zygmunt Warman
47 Testimony of Stanisław Adler, available at https://zapisyterroru.pl
48 Szpilman, *The Pianist*, pp.95–96
49 K. Brown, *The Sound of Hope: Music as Solace, Resistance and Salvation During the Holocaust and World War II* (McFarland, Jefferson NC, 2020), p.144
50 Testimony of Łazarz Menes, available at https://zapisyterroru.pl
51 Person, *Warsaw Ghetto Police*, p.172
52 Testimony of Stanisław Adler
53 Szpilman, *The Pianist*, p.107
54 R. Evans, *The Third Reich at War* (Penguin, Harmondsworth, 2009), p.290; J. Wiernik, *A Year in Treblinka: An Inmate Who Escaped Tells the Day-to-Day Facts of One Year of his Torturous Experience* (American Representation of the General Jewish Workers' Union of Poland, New York, 1944), p.8
55 Quoted in Snyder, *Bloodlands*, p.267
56 Friedländer, *Nazi Germany and the Jews*, p.432
57 A. Szymanowski, 'Likwidacja getta warszawskiego. Reportaż' in W. Bartoszewski, *Tryptyk polsko-żydowski* (Rada Ochrony Pamięci Walk i Męczeństwa, Warsaw, 2003), p.34
58 Testimony of Samuel Eisen, available at: https://zapisyterroru.pl

59 Auerbach, *Warsaw Testament*, pp.164–65
60 Szymanowski, 'Likwidacja getta warszawskiego. Reportaż', p.40
61 Sloan, *Notes from the Warsaw Ghetto*, p.355
62 Ibid., p.326
63 Nałkowska, *Dzienniki*, Vol. IV, p.239
64 *National Archives*, Kew, HW16/23, decode GPDD 355a
65 R. Hanyok, *Eavesdropping on Hell: Historical Guide to Western Communications Intelligence and the Holocaust, 1939–1945* (Dover, Mineola NY, 2005), pp.89–90
66 Berg, *The Diary of Mary Berg*, p.201
67 Biskupska, *Survivors*, p.121; Ringelblum, *Polish-Jewish Relations*, p.247
68 Ringelblum, *Polish-Jewish Relations*, p.247
69 Lukas, *Forgotten Holocaust*, p.140
70 Z. Kossak, quoted in M. Szczepaniak, "*Protest!" – 75 years Ago Zofia Kossak Condemned the Holocaust*, https://sprawiedliwi.org.pl/en/news/protest-75-years-ago-zofia-kossak-condemned-holocaust
71 Biskupska, *Survivors*, p.124
72 Piotrowski, *Poland's Holocaust*, p.112
73 Korboński, *Fighting Warsaw*, p.253
74 Ibid.
75 Karski, *Story of a Secret State*, pp.362 and 357
76 Ibid., pp.357–58
77 Ibid., p.361
78 Ibid.
79 A. Roberts, in ibid., p.449
80 Biskupska, *Survivors*, p.126
81 Kulski, *The Color of Courage*, pp.199–200
82 Karski, *Story of a Secret State*, pp.355–57
83 Szpilman, *The Pianist*, p.128
84 Biskupska, *Survivors*, p.127
85 B. Engelking and J. Leociak, *Getto warszawskie: przewodnik po nieistniejącym mieście* (Wydawn. IFiS, Warsaw, 2001), p.711; C. Lubetkin, *Zagłada i Powstanie, Żydowski Instytut Historyczny* (Książka i Wiedza, Warsaw, 1999), pp.88–89
86 W. Bartoszewski and M. Edelman, *I była dzielnica żydowska w Warszawie: wybór tekstów* (Literatura Faktu PWN, Warsaw, 2010), p.252
87 Engelking and Leociak, *Getto warszawskie*, pp.720–21; Gutman, *Resistance*, p.236
88 B. Mark, *Dziennik Szmuela Wintera. Ważny dodatek do dokumentacji przedpowstaniowej* (Kwartalnik Historii Żydów, January 2019), p.79
89 Gutman, *Resistance*, p.237
90 Ibid., p.239
91 Ibid., p.249
92 Testimony of Łazarz Menes, available at https://zapisyterroru.pl
93 Gutman, *Resistance*, p.249
94 Ibid., pp.250–51

95 Ibid., p.251
96 A. Klien, 'Alfred Nossig, Jewish Intellectual and Jewish Traitor' in *The Jewish Magazine* (available at jewishmag.org), May 2009
97 H. Himmler, Journal No. 38/33/43 g. 16 February, 1943. *Secret!* available at https://www.jewishvirtuallibrary.org/himmler-orders-the-destruction-of-the-warsaw-ghetto
98 Gutman, *Resistance*, p.245
99 Ibid., pp.245–46
100 Testimony of Łazarz Menes; Gutman, *Resistance*, p.257
101 Gutman, *Resistance*, p.258
102 Ibid., p.257
103 T. Borzykowski, *Tsvishn falendike vent* (Ghetto Fighters House, Israel, 1976), pp.51–52
104 https://www.jewishvirtuallibrary.org/german-battle-diary
105 Gutman, *Resistance*, p.259
106 K. Person, *Testimony of Jürgen Stroop Given on the Second Day of the Trial, 19 July 1951, Jürgen Stroop Speaks: The Trial of the Warsaw Ghetto Uprising Liquidator before the Warsaw Provincial Court*, p.370, available at https://www.zagladazydow.pl/index.php/zz/article/view/822/794
107 https://www.jewishvirtuallibrary.org/the-stroop-report-may-1943
108 Ibid.
109 K. Moczarski, M. Fitzpatrick, J. Stroop, *Conversations with an Executioner* (Englewood Cliffs NJ, 1981), p.131
110 https://www.jewishvirtuallibrary.org/the-stroop-report-may-1943
111 Ibid.
112 Ibid.
113 Ibid.
114 Ibid.
115 Gutman, *Resistance*, pp.282–83
116 Kulski, *The Color of Courage*, p.237
117 Ibid., pp.229–30
118 J. Zimmerman, 'The Polish Underground Home Army (AK), and the Jews: What Postwar Jewish Testimonies and Wartime Documents Reveal' in *East European Politics and Societies*, Vol.XXXIV, Issue 1 (February 2020), p.208
119 Ibid.
120 Ibid., pp.209–10
121 J. Lichten (trans. H. Segel), 'The Warsaw Ghetto Uprising: Legend And Reality' in *The Polish Review*, Vol. 8 No. 3 (1963), p.69
122 Gutman, *Resistance*, p.299
123 M. Edelman, *The Warsaw Ghetto Uprising*, available at https://libcom.org/article/warsaw-ghetto-uprising-marek-edelman
124 Gutman, *Resistance*, p.304; Edelman, *The Warsaw Ghetto Uprising*
125 Moczarski et al., *Conversations with an Executioner*, p.162
126 Ibid., p.164

127 Ibid.
128 Ibid., p.166
129 https://www.jewishvirtuallibrary.org/the-stroop-report-may-1943
130 Gutman, *Resistance*, p.309
131 Moczarski et al., *Conversations with an Executioner*, p.167
132 Gutman, *Resistance*, p.319
133 Ibid.
134 Ibid.
135 Moczarski et al., *Conversations with an Executioner*, pp.176–77
136 Ibid., p.173
137 Ibid., p.175
138 The Last Letter From Szmul Zygielbojm, The Bund Representative With The Polish National Council In Exile, available at https://www.yadvashem.org/docs/zygielbojm-letter-to-polish-national-council-in-exile.html#:~:text=I%20cannot%20continue%20to%20live,them%2C%20to%20their%20mass%20grave.
139 M. Fleming, *Auschwitz, the Allies and Censorship of the Holocaust* (Cambridge University Press, New York, 2014), pp.191–93
140 J. Fox, 'The Jewish Factor in British War Crimes Policy in 1942' in *The English Historical Review*, Vol. 92 No. 362 (January 1977), p.83
141 *National Archives*, F.O. C7839/6i/i8, 309I7, Lias to Roberts, 6 August 1942
142 Sloan, *Notes from the Warsaw Ghetto*, p.342
143 Ibid., p.343
144 Lukas, *Forgotten Holocaust*, p.185; Korboński, *Fighting Warsaw*, p.252
145 Gutman, *Resistance*, p.287
146 The Last Letter From Szmul Zygielbojm

CHAPTER 9: RESISTANCE

1 K. Baczynski (trans. B. Johnston), 'To my parents', 1943. Used with permission.
2 L. Bartelski, *AK* (Tekst, Warsaw, 1990, 2 volumes), Vol. I, p.5
3 Karski, *Story of a Secret State*, p.131
4 H. Kochanski, *The Eagle Unbowed: Poland and the Poles in the Second World War* (Penguin, London, 2013), p.325
5 Korboński, *Fighting Warsaw*, p.31
6 Biskupska, *Survivors*, p.232
7 Karski, *Story of a Secret State*, pp.142–43
8 Ibid., pp.145–46
9 M. Ney-Krwawicz, 'Organizacja Prac Nad Powstaniem Powszechnym w Kraju w Sztabie Naczelnego Wodza na Obczyźnie. Zarys Problemu' in *Kwartalnik Historyczny* (Warsaw), Vol. 102 (1995), pp.197–208
10 A. Prazmowska, *Civil War in Poland 1942–1948* (Palgrave Macmillan, London, 2004), p.10

11 G. Bines, *The Polish Section of the Special Operations Executive 1940–1946: A British Perspective* (Doctorate Thesis, University of Stirling, 2008), p.96
12 Quoted in Lukas, *Forgotten Holocaust*, p.41
13 Kochanski, *The Eagle Unbowed*, p.326
14 J. Czapski (trans. A. Lloyd-Jones), *Inhuman Land – Searching for the Truth in Soviet Russia, 1941–1942* (NYRB Classics, 2018), p.58
15 Ibid., p.63
16 A. Szuiecki and T. Piotrowski, *The Polish Deportees of World War II: Recollections of Removal to the Soviet Union and Dispersal Throughout the World* (McFarland, Jefferson NC, 2004), p.97; Quoted in J. Tebinka and A. Zapalec, *Polska w Brytyjskiej Strategii Wspierania Ruchu Oporu. Historia Sekcji Kierownictwa Operacji Specjalnych (SOE)*, (Neriton, Warsaw, 2021), p.77
17 B. Łojek, *Muzeum Katyńskie w Warszawie* (Polska Fundacja Katyńska, Warsaw, 2001), p.174
18 B. Musiał, *Sowjetische Partisanen in Weissrussland: Innenansichten aus dem Gebiet Baranoviči 1941–1944: Eine Dokumentation* (Oldenbourg, Munich, 2013), pp.84–86 and 134
19 Ibid., p.225
20 A. Richie, *Warsaw 1944: Hitler, Himmler, and the Crushing of a City* (William Collins, London, 2013), p.163
21 Karski, *Story of a Secret State*, p.453
22 Biskupska, *Survivors*, p.243
23 Piotrowski, *Poland's Holocaust*, p.25; Testimony of Jósef Wasilewski, available at https://zapisyterroru.pl
24 Piotrowski, *Poland's Holocaust*, p.25
25 Testimony of Stanisļaw Kruoka, available at https://zapisyterroru.pl
26 Biskupska, *Survivors*, p.241
27 Mendelsohn, *The Jews of East Central Europe Between the World Wars*, pp.29–30
28 M. Elkins, *Forged in Fury* (Ballantine, New York, 1971), p.182
29 S. Krakowski, Y. Bauer, and O. Blaustein, *War of the Doomed: Jewish Armed Resistance in Poland, 1942–1944* (Holmes & Meier, New York, 1984), p.3
30 For a comprehensive study of this subject, see J. Zimmerman, *The Polish Underground and the Jews, 1939–1945* (Cambridge University Press, 2015)
31 R. Leslie, *The History of Poland Since 1863* (Cambridge University Press, 1983), p.234; S. Salmonowicz, *Polskie Państwo Podziemne* (Wydawnictwa Szkolne i Pedagogiczne, Warsaw, 1994), p.317
32 https://web.archive.org/web/20250213100032/https://elitadywersji.org/armia-krajowa/
33 Korboński, *Fighting Warsaw*, p.63
34 F. Pogonowski, *Podziemna Zbrokownia* (Wydawnictwo Ministerstwa Obrony Narodowej, Warsaw, 1975), pp.30–44
35 M. Peszke, *The Polish Underground Army, the Western Allies, and the Failure of Strategic Unity in World War II* (McFarland, Jefferson NC, 2005), p.183
36 Z. Czajkowski, *Warsaw 1944: An Insurgent's Journal of the Uprising* (Pen & Sword, Barnsley, 2013), p.2

37 For a comprehensive history of Marciniak and the Grey Ranks, see S. Broniewski, *Florian Marciniak naczelnik Szarych Szeregów* (PWN, Warsaw, 1988)
38 M. Binasiak, *Dziś, Jutro, Pojutrze* (Muzeum Harcerstwa, Warsaw 2009), pp.9–19
39 Korboński, *Fighting Warsaw*, p.163
40 Ibid., p.9
41 Kulski, *The Color of Courage*, pp.156–57
42 S. Broniewski, *Akja pod Arsenałem* (Iskry, Wrocław, 1993), pp.24–26
43 Ibid., p.54
44 M. Ney-Krwawicz, *Armia Krajowa: Siła Zbroina Polskiego Państwa Polskiego* (Wydawnictwa Szkolne I Pedagogiczne, Warsaw, 1993), p.214
45 T. Strzembosz, *Akcję Zbrojne Podziemnej Warszawy 1939–1944* (Państwowe Wydawnictwo Naukowe, Warsaw, 1983), p.497
46 Ibid., pp.343–46
47 P. Stachiewicz, '*Parasol*'. *Dzieje Oddziału do Zadań Specialnych Kierownictwa Dywersii Komendy Głownej Armii Krajowej* (Instytut Wydawniczy Pax, Warsaw, 1984), p.329
48 Ibid., pp.350–51
49 M. Dylawerska, E. Dziembowskia, Z. Gąsior, and D. Kaczyńska, 'Akcja na Kutscherę' in *Wojskowy Przegląd Historyczny* (Wojskowe Biuro Historyczne, Warsaw, 1959), p.116
50 L. Fischer, *Raporty Ludwiga Fischera, Gubernatora Dystyktu Warszawskiego 1939–1944* (Wydawnictwo Książka, Warsaw, 1987), pp.731–32
51 Lukas, *Forgotten Holocaust*, p.67
52 A. Suchcitz and E. Maresch (eds), *Armia Krajowa w Dokumentach, 1939–1945* (Instytut Pamięci Narodowej-Komisja Ścigania Zbrodni Przeciwko Narodowi Polskiemu, Warsaw, 2015, 2 volumes), Vol. II, pp.342–45
53 J. Einhorn, *Recollections of the End of an Era: Poland 1919–1945* (Author House, Bloomington IN, 2005), pp.128–29
54 Suchcitz and Maresch, *Armia Krajowa w Dokumentach*, Vol. II, p.36
55 J. Rosinski and R. Hile, *The Warsaw Underground: A Memoir of Resistance, 1939–1945* (McFarland, Jefferson NC, 2014), p.29
56 Lukas, *Forgotten Holocaust*, p.67
57 Bartoszewski, *Warsaw Death Ring*, p.140
58 J. Haestrup, *European Resistance Movements, 1939–1945: A Complete History* (Meckler, Westport CT, 1981), p.423
59 P. Dubiel and J. Kozak, *Polacy w Il Wojnie Światowej: Kim Byli, Co Robili* (Oficyna Wydawnicza Rytm, Warsaw, 2003), pp.66–67
60 A. Kunert and J. Szyrmer, *Stefan Rowecki. Wspomnienia I Notatke Autobiograficzne 1906–1939* (Spółdzielnia Wydawnicza Czytelnik, Warsaw 1988), pp.5–14
61 T. Kisielewski, *Zamach: Tropem Zabójców Generała Sikorskiego* (Rebis, Poznań, 2005), pp.169–70
62 https://nto.pl/historyk-general-sikorski-zostal-zamordowany/ar/4092281
63 A. Zięba, 'Kazimierz Sosnkowski (1885–1969)' in *Polski Słownik Biograficzny* (Polska Akademia Nauk I Polska Akademia Umiejętności, Krakow, 2001, 52 volumes), Vol. XL, pp.524–39

64 Rosinski and Hile, *The Warsaw Underground*, p.30
65 Kulski, *The Color of Courage*, p.296
66 Rosinski and Hile, *The Warsaw Underground*, p.28

CHAPTER 10: *BURZA*

1 K. Baczynski (trans. B. Johnston), '*Elegia O Chłopcu Polskim*', 1944. Used with permission.
2 Quoted in Richie, *Warsaw 1944*, p.163
3 T. Komorowski, *The Secret Army: The Memoirs of General Bór-Komorowski* (Frontline Books, Barnsley, 2011), p.202
4 Quoted in N. Davies, *Rising '44: The Battle For Warsaw* (Macmillan, London, 2003), p.206
5 J. Sziling and K. Minczykowska (eds), *Akcja Burza: Materiały z XXIV Sesji Naukowej w Toruniu w Dniu 18 Listopada 2014 Roku* (Fundacja General Elżbiety Zawackiej, Torún, 2015), pp.38–40
6 J. Ciechanowski, *The Warsaw Rising of 1944* (Cambridge University Press, 1974), p.48
7 Ibid., p.53
8 W. Churchill, Speech At The Lord Mayor's Day Luncheon At The Mansion House, London, 10 November 1942, available at https://winstonchurchill.org/resources/speeches/1941-1945-war-leader/the-bright-gleam-of-victory/
9 Kulski, *The Color of Courage*, p.303
10 For a comprehensive account of this operation, see P. Buttar, *Bagration 1944: The Great Soviet Offensive* (Osprey, Oxford, 2025)
11 Piotrowski, *Poland's Holocaust*, pp.88–89
12 M. Paul, *A Tangled Web: Polish-Jewish Relations in Wartime Northeastern Poland and the Aftermath* (Perfina Press, Toronto, 2021, 2 volumes), Vol. II, p.36
13 Kulski, *The Color of Courage*, p.305
14 Ibid., p.303
15 Komorowski, *The Secret Army*, pp.170–71
16 W. Kozaczuk, *Enigma: How the German Machine Cipher was Broken, and How it was Read by the Allies in World War II* (University Publications of America, Frederick MD, 1984), p.64
17 G. Bruce, *The Warsaw Uprising: 1 August–2 October 1944 (Major Battles of World War Two)*, (Hart Davis, London, 1972), p.92
18 Kulski, *The Color of Courage*, p.306
19 Komorowski, *The Secret Army*, p.154
20 A. Valcini, *Il Calvario di Varsavia, 1939–1945* (Garzanti, Milan, 1945), p.202
21 Korboński, *Fighting Warsaw*, p.341
22 Ibid.
23 Richie, *Warsaw 1944*, p.138
24 P. Blood, *Hitler's Bandit Hunters: The SS and the Nazi Occupation of Europe* (Potomac Books, Sterling VA, 2006), p.58
25 R. Lifton, *Ärzte im Dritten Reich* (Ullstein, Berlin, 1998), p.188

26 Quoted in L. Goldensohn and R. Gellately, *The Nuremberg Interviews: Conversations with the Defendants and Witnesses* (Pimlico, London, 2007), p.423
27 F. MacLean, *The Cruel Hunters: SS-Sonderkommando Dirlewanger, Hitler's Most Notorious Anti-Partisan Unit* (Schiffer, Atglen PA, 1998), p.61
28 H. Himmler, Speech made at a meeting of NSDAP district leaders, 3 August 1944, Poznań
29 Ibid.
30 C. Ingrao, *The SS Dirlewanger Brigade: The History of the Black Hunters* (Skyhorse, New York, 2013), p.26
31 C. Winchester and I. Drury, *Hitler's War on Russia* (Bloomsbury, London, 2011), p.343
32 Komorowski, *The Secret Army*, p.207
33 Ibid., pp.207–08
34 Iranek-Osmecki, *Powołanie I Przeznaczenie*, p.420
35 Richie, *Warsaw 1944*, p.170
36 Korboński, *Fighting Warsaw*, p.170
37 Komorowski, *The Secret Army*, p.204
38 Richie, *Warsaw 1944*, p.171
39 Korboński, *Fighting Warsaw*, p.170
40 Kulski, *The Color of Courage*, pp.310–11
41 Komorowski, *The Secret Army*, p.209
42 Ibid., p.173
43 Kulski, *The Color of Courage*, p.311
44 Korboński, *Fighting Warsaw*, pp.171–73
45 Kulski, *The Color of Courage*, p.312
46 Korboński, *Fighting Warsaw*, p.342
47 Richie, *Warsaw 1944*, p.174
48 Iranek-Osmeckie, *Powołanie I Przeznaczenie*, p.413
49 Komorowski, *The Secret Army*, p.213
50 Ibid., p.215
51 Ibid.
52 Richie, *Warsaw 1944*, p.178
53 Bruce, *The Warsaw Uprising*, p.132
54 Rosinski and Hile, *The Warsaw Underground*, pp.104–05
55 Komorowski, *The Secret Army*, p.215
56 L. Rowińska, *That the Nightingale Return: Memoir of the Polish Resistance, the Warsaw Uprising and German P.O.W. Camps* (McFarland, Jefferson NC, 1999), p.75
57 I. Orska, *Silent is the Vistula: The Story of the Warsaw Uprising* (Longmans, Green and Co., Toronto, 1946), pp.9–10
58 E. Harrison, 'The Special Operations Executive and Poland' in *The Historical Journal* (Cambridge University Press), Vol. 43 No. 4 (Dec. 2000), pp.1082–83
59 Quoted in ibid., p.1081

60 Ciechanowski, *The Warsaw Rising of 1944*, p.87

61 J. Kulski, *Warsaw Rising: The Forgotten Soldiers of World War II* (Documentary), CNN Presents, 2 June 2004, available at https://archive.org/details/warsaw-rising-the-forgotten-soldiers-of-world-war-ii

CHAPTER 11: TRAGEDY

1 J. Szczepanski (trans. N. Davies), 'The Scarlet Plague', 1944. Used with permission. Available at https://www.sppw1944.org/poezja/poezja_szczepanski_eng.html#:~:text=Professor%20Norman%20Davies.-,The%20Scarlet%20Plaque,for%20our%20thousands%20of%20wounded

2 Komorowski, *The Secret Army*, p.216

3 Ibid., p.216

4 For a detailed account of the battle, see Buttar, *Bagration*, pp.373–412. An exhaustive history is D. Nash, *From the Realm of a Dying Sun. Volume I: IV. SS-Panzerkorps and the Battles for Warsaw, July–December 1944* (Casemate, Havertown PA, 2020)

5 *Zdzisław Sierpiński. The Man Who Started the Warsaw Uprising. Listen to His Memories*, Polskie Radio, available at https://polskieradio24.pl/artykul/2348832,Zdzislaw-Sierpinski-czlowiek-ktory-rozpoczal-Powstanie-Warszawskie-Posluchaj-jego-wspomnien

6 Kulski, *The Color of Courage*, p.314

7 Komorowski, *The Secret Army*, p.218

8 Ibid., p.221

9 Davies, *Rising '44*, p.279

10 Komorowski, *The Secret Army*, pp.221–22

11 Ibid., p.222

12 M. Białoszewski, *A Memoir of the Warsaw Uprising* (Ardis, Ann Arbor MI, 1977), pp.22–23

13 *Muzeum Powstania Warszawskiego* (Warsaw), 'Armia Ludowa 27'

14 Testimony of Eugenia Kowalewska, available at https://zapisyterroru.pl

15 Testimony of Aleksandra Biegaj, available at https://zapisyterroru.pl

16 Testimony of Maria Winiarska, available at https://zapisyterroru.pl

17 Testimony of Bronisław Mączka, available at https://zapisyterroru.pl

18 Stachiewicz, *Parasol*, pp.467–98

19 Lukas, *Forgotten Holocaust*, p.223

20 Komorowski, *The Secret Army*, p.225

21 Lukas, *Forgotten Holocaust*, p.226

22 Czajkowski, *Warsaw 1944*, p.27

23 W. Micuta, *Warsaw Rising: The Forgotten Soldiers of World War II* (Documentary), CNN Presents, 2 June 2004, available at https://archive.org/details/warsaw-rising-the-forgotten-soldiers-of-world-war-ii

24 B. Holmgren, *Warsaw is my Country: The Story of Krystyna Bierzyńska, 1928–1945* (Academic Studies Press, Boston, 2018), p.72
25 Ibid., pp.77 and 72
26 *Biuletyn Informacyjny,* 2 August 1940, p.1
27 W. Bartoszewski, *Prasa Powstania Warszawskiego: Zarys Historyczno-Bibliograficzny* (Państwowy Instytut Wydawniczy, Warsaw, 1972), p.319
28 Z. Bokiewicz, *The Scouts' Postal Service During the Warsaw Uprising of 1944*, available at https://warsawuprising.org/paper/postservice.htm
29 K. Iranek-Osmecki, *Drogi Cichociemnych* (Bellona, Warsaw, 1993), p.282
30 Testimony of Irena Zgrych, available at https://zapisyterroru.pl
31 Orska, *Silent is the Vistula*, pp.41 and 36
32 Rosinski and Hile, *The Warsaw Underground*, pp.111–12
33 Ibid., p.108
34 Z. Skarbek-Kruszewski, *Bellum Vobiscum: WWII Memoirs*, available at https://www.warsawuprising.org/witness/skarbek1.htm
35 T. Sawicki, *Rozkaz: Zdławič Powstanie – Siły Zbrojne III Rzeszy w Walce z Powstaniem Warszawkim 1944* (Dom Wydawniczy Bellona, Warsaw, 2001), p.25
36 *Bundesarchiv-Militärarchiv*, Freiburg, H 12-9/9
37 A. Przygoński, *Powstanie Warszawskie w Sierpniu 1944* (Państwowe Wydawnictwo Nauowe, Warsaw, 1988), p.241
38 Quoted in Richie, *Warsaw 1944*, p.232
39 MacLean, *The Cruel Hunters*, p.179
40 Quoted in Bruce, *The Warsaw Uprising*, p.198
41 Quoted in Richie, *Warsaw 1944*, p.258
42 Karski, *The Great Powers & Poland, 1919–1945: From Versailles to Yalta* (University Press of America, Maryland, 1985), p.537
43 S. Mikołajczyk, *The Rape of Poland: Pattern of Soviet Aggression* (Whittlesey House, New York, 1972), p.74
44 Karski, *The Great Powers & Poland*, p.538
45 Quoted in Davies, *Rising '44*, p.294
46 *Stalin's Correspondence with Churchill, Attlee, Roosevelt and Truman, 1941–45* (Lawrence & Wishart, London, 1958), doc. 311, p.248; Davies, *Rising '44*, p.297
47 Komorowski, *The Secret Army*, p.240
48 Quoted in W. Lewandowska and B. Martin (eds), *Powstanie Warszawskie 1944: Praca Zbiorowa* (Wydawnictwo Polsko-Niemieckie, Warsaw, 1999), p.272
49 T. Sawicki, *Rozkaz Zdławić Powstanie: Niemcy i ich Sojusznicy w Wwalce z Powstaniem Warszawskim* (Bellona, Warsaw, 2010), p.31
50 Lewandowska and Martin, *Powstanie Warszawskie 1944*, p.269
51 Przygoński, *Powstanie Warszawskie*, p.297
52 Record No. 80 available at https://www.warsawuprising.org/witness/atrocities3.htm
53 Record No. 63, available at https://www.warsawuprising.org/witness/atrocities4.htm
54 Drozdowski, Maniakówna, and Strzembosz, *Ludność Cywilna*, Vol. I, p.272
55 M. Schenk, W. Nowak, and A. Kuźniak, *My Warsaw Madness. The Other Side of the Warsaw Uprising*, *Gazeta Wyborcza*, 27 August 2004, available at https://warsawuprising.org/witness/schenk.htm

56 Record No. 117, available at https://www.warsawuprising.org/witness/atrocities7.htm
57 Richie, *Warsaw 1944*, p.302
58 Schenk, Nowak, and Kuźniak, *My Warsaw Madness*
59 Ibid.
60 H. Thieme, available at https://www.warsawuprising.org/witness/thieme.htm
61 E. Schmalz, available at https://www.warsawuprising.org/witness/schmalz.htm
62 Record No. 45 / II, available at https://www.warsawuprising.org/witness/atrocities2.htm
63 Record No. 80, available at https://www.warsawuprising.org/witness/atrocities3.htm
64 Testimony of M. Kamińska to the Commission for the Investigation of German Crimes, 1946, available at https://zapisyterroru.pl
65 Testimony of Stanisław Trojanowski, available at https://zapisyterroru.pl
66 L. Ujazdowska (ed.), *Zagłada Ochoty: Zbiór Relacji na Temat Zbrodni Hitlerowskiej Dokonanej na Ludności Ochoty w Czasie Powstania Warszawskiego* (Fronda, Warsaw, 2022), p.89
67 Quoted in Richie, *Warsaw 1944*, p.382
68 T. Klimaszewski, *Verbrennungskommando Warschau* (Czytelnik, Warsaw, 1984), pp.50–51
69 Komorowski, *The Secret Army*, p.256
70 Ibid., pp.267–68
71 Białoszewski, *A Memoir of the Warsaw Uprising*, p.74
72 Ibid., p.78
73 Orska, *Silent is the Vistula*, pp.74–77
74 Ibid., p.88
75 Komorowski, *The Secret Army*, pp.268–69; Orska, *Silent is the Vistula*, p.296
76 W. Micuta, *From Old Town to Zoliborz*, in A. M. Kobos, *Kanaly w Powstaniu Warszawskim. Zeszyty Historyczne*, No. 109 (Instytut Literacki, Paris, 1994), available at https://www.warsawuprising.org/witness/micuta1.htm
77 S. Jankowski, *From Old Town to Zoliborz*, in ibid.
78 Komorowski, *The Secret Army*, p.300
79 Ibid., pp.282–83
80 Ibid., pp.268–69; Orska, *Silent is the Vistula*, p.103
81 Orska, *Silent is the Vistula*, p.104
82 Quoted in Richie, *Warsaw 1944*, p.418
83 S. Likiernik, *By Devil's Luck: A Tale of Resistance in Wartime Warsaw* (Mainstream Publishing, Edinburgh, 2001), pp.126–27
84 Białoszewski, *A Memoir of the Warsaw Uprising*, p.61
85 Ibid., p.222
86 Kulski, *The Color of Courage*, p.374
87 Komorowski, *The Secret Army*, pp.268–269 and 302
88 Ibid., pp.304–05
89 Ibid., p.336
90 J. Zawodny, *Nothing But Honour: The Story of the Warsaw Uprising, 1944* (Hoover Institution Press, Stanford CA, 1978), p.185

91 Komorowski, *The Secret Army*, p.334
92 Likiernik, *By Devil's Luck*, p.144
93 Ibid., p.142
94 Ibid., p.144
95 Ibid.
96 Quoted in MacLean, *The Cruel Hunters*, p.194
97 E. Bach, quoted in *Muzeum Powstania Warszawskiego* (Warsaw)
98 Ibid.
99 Kulski, *The Color of Courage*, p.398
100 Drozdowski, Maniakówna, and Strzembosz, *Ludność Cywilna*, Vol. II, p.502
101 A. Kunert, *Generał Tadeusz Bór-Komorowski w Relacjach I Dokumentach* (Ofycina Wydawnicza RYTM, Warsaw, 2000), p.138
102 Czajkowski, *Warsaw 1944*, pp.165–67
103 Szpilman, *The Pianist*, p.166
104 Kulski, *The Color of Courage*, p.402
105 Holmgren, *Warsaw is My Country*, pp.82–83
106 Quoted in Lewandowska and Martin, *Powstanie Warszawskie 1944*, p.268

Chapter 12: The Devastated City

1 C. Miłosz, 'In Warsaw', 1945, in *The Collected Poems, 1931–1987* (The Ecco Press, Hopewell NJ, 1988), pp.76–77
2 J. Beck, quoted in R. Kunźniar, *Poland's Foreign Policy After 1989* (Wydawnictwo Naukowe Scholar, Warsaw, 2009), p.19
3 Davies, *Rising '44*, p.433
4 Rosinski and Hile, *The Warsaw Underground*, p.123
5 W. Churchill, *Warsaw Epic (Tribute to Polish Nation),* HC Deb 05 October 1944, Vol. 403 cc1139-40
6 Sawicki, *Rozkaz*, p.186
7 Davies, *Rising '44*, p.437
8 Testimony of Helena Kałuska, available at https://zapisyterroru.pl
9 Testimony of Władysław Mazurek, available at https://zapisyterroru.pl
10 Testimony of Władysław Mazurek
11 Testimony of Julia Bielecka, available at https://zapisyterroru.pl
12 Testimony of Stefan Cichoński, available at https://zapisyterroru.pl
13 Testimony of Władysław Mazurek
14 Kulski, *The Color of Courage*, p.408
15 Davies, *Rising '44*, p.509
16 Szpilman, *The Pianist*, p.167
17 Ibid., p.180
18 *Oral history interview with Jan Kostański*, The Jewish Holocaust Museum and Research Centre, Melbourne, Australia, 1997, available at https://collections.ushmm.org/search/catalog/irn507221

19 M. Tychmanowicz, *Robinsonowie z wyspy gruzów*, 14 January 2010, available at https://web.archive.org/web/20120429063100/http://www.focus.pl/historia/artykuly/zobacz/publikacje/robinsonowie-z-wyspy-gruzow/strona-publikacji/2/nc/1/
20 Szpilman, *The Pianist*, pp.207–08
21 Drozdowski, Maniakówna, and Strzembosz, *Ludność Cywilna*, Vol. II, pp.580–82
22 Richie, *Warsaw 1944*, p.622
23 G. Semenov, *Nastupayet Udarnaya* (Voyenizdat, Moscow, 1986), p.193
24 B. Szacka and M. Castle, 'Polish Remembrance of World War II' in *International Journal of Sociology* (Taylor & Francis, London), Vol. 36 No. 4, 'Collective Memory and Social Transition in Poland' (Winter 2006/2007), p.11
25 *Biuletyn Informacyjny*, 19 January 1945, p.1
26 A. Applebaum, *Iron Curtain: The Crushing of Eastern Europe 1944–56* (Penguin, Harmondsworth, 2012), p.142
27 Prazmowska, *Civil War in Poland*, p.117
28 Czapski, *Inhuman Land*, p.356
29 *Polskie Siły Zbrojne w Drugiej Wojnie Swiatowej* (Instytut Historyczny im. Gen. Sikorskiego, London, 1951, 3 volumes), Vol. III, pp.819 and 824
30 N. Davies, *Warsaw Rising: The Forgotten Soldiers of World War II* (Documentary), CNN Presents, 2 June 2004, available at https://archive.org/details/warsaw-rising-the-forgotten-soldiers-of-world-war-ii
31 G. Paulsson, *Secret City: The Hidden Jews of Warsaw, 1940–1945* (Yale University Press, New Haven CT, 2002), p.1
32 Richie, *Warsaw 1944*, p.641
33 Nałkowska, *Dzienniki*, Vol. I, p.47
34 Richie, *Warsaw 1944*, p.648
35 J. Zachwatowicz, 'Program I Zasady Konserwacji Zabytków' in *Biuletyn Historii Sztuki I Kultury* (Zakład Architektury Polskiej I Historii Sztuki Politiki, Warsaw), No. 8 (1946), p.49
36 J. Zachwatowicz, 'Ochrona I Konserwacja Zabytków Warszawy' in *Kultura Warszawy* (Państwowe Wydawnictwo Naukowe, Warsaw, 1979), p.347
37 G. Kranjc, *To Walk with the Devil: Slovene Collaboration and Axis Occupation, 1941–1945* (University of Toronto Press, 2013), p.124
38 *Arolsen Archives* (Bad Arolsen), *Hohes Kommissariat der Republik Frankreich, Kartei der Verfolgten in der Französischen Besatzungszone und von Franzosen in Anderen Zonen* Bilt 77330504, 77867470; W. Laquer and J. Baumel, *The Holocaust Encyclopaedia* (Yale University Press, New Haven CT, 2001), p.150
39 Moczarski et al., *Conversations with an Executioner*, p.265
40 Resolution of the Schleswig-Holstein Government 18/2124, 7/7/2014, available at https://www.landtag.ltsh.de/infothek/wahl18/drucks/2100/drucksache-18-2124.pdf
41 *Fluter* (Bundeszentrale für Politische Bildung, Bonn, 31 July 2014)
42 W. Białkowski, *Rokossowski – na ile Polak?* (Alfa, Warsaw, 1994), p.326
43 M. Biskupski and P. Wandycz, *Ideology, Politics, and Diplomacy in East Central Europe* (Boydell & Brewer, Martlesham, 2003), p.147

44 *Daily Telegraph* (London, 6 November 2014)
45 For an excellent and detailed account of both the Secret Protocol and the Katyn Affair at Nuremberg, see F. Hirsch, *Soviet Judgment at Nuremberg* (Oxford University Press, 2020)
46 Quoted in Szacka and Castle, 'Polish Remembrance of World War II', p.15
47 Szacka and Castle, 'Polish Remembrance of World War II', p.12
48 J. Alexander, 'Toward a Theory of Cultural Trauma' in J. Alexander, R. Eyerman, B. Giesen, and N. Smelser (eds), *Cultural Trauma and Collective Identity* (University of California Press, Berkeley CA, 2004), p.1
49 E. Ochman, 'Why is Poland Unable to Celebrate Victories? The Miracle on the Vistula, a Century Later' in *The Polish Review*, Vol. 64 No. 2, 'Collective Suffering in the Polish Lands' (2019), p.120
50 Białoszewski, *A Memoir of the Warsaw Uprising*, p.51
51 Kulski, *The Color of Courage*, p.34
52 K. Małcużyński, quoted in K. Friedrich, 'Collaboration in a "Land without a Quisling": Patterns of Cooperation with the Nazi German Occupation Regime in Poland during World War II' in *Slavic Review*, Vol. 64 No. 4 (Winter, 2005), p.714
53 T. Snyder, in Czapski, *Inhuman Land*, p.21
54 Karski, *The Great Powers & Poland*, p.614
55 Quoted in Richie, *Warsaw 1944*, p.475
56 Churchill, *Warsaw Epic*; G. Orwell, 'As I Please', *Tribune* (1 September 1944)

BIBLIOGRAPHY

Arolsen Archives, Bad Arolsen
Bundesarchiv, Berlin
Bundesarchiv-Militärarchiv, Freiburg
Hoover Institution Archives, Stanford CA
Muzeum Powstania Warszawskiego, Warsaw
National Archives, Kew
National Archives and Records Administration (Washington DC)

Biuletyn Historii Sztuki I Kultury (Zakład Architektury Polskiej I Historii Sztuki Politiki, Warsaw)
Biuletyn Informacyjny (Warsaw)
Central European History (Cambridge University Press)
Chicago Daily Tribune (Tribune Publishing, Chicago IL)
Current History (University of California Press, Oakland CA)
Daily Telegraph (London)
East European Politics and Societies (Sage, London)
English Historical Review (Oxford University Press)
Express Poranny (Dom Prasy, Warsaw)
Fluter (Bundeszentrale für Politische Bildung, Bonn)
Gazeta Wspólna (Czas, Warsaw)
Holocaust and Genocide Studies (Oxford University Press)
International Journal of Sociology (Taylor & Francis, London)
Journal of Baltic Studies (Routledge, Milton)
Journal of Modern European History (University of Chicago Press)
Journal of the Royal Institute of International Affairs (Oxford University Press)
Kalendarium (Uniwersytet Jagielloński, Kraków)
Kultura Warszawy (Państwowe Wydawnictwo Naukowe, Warsaw)
Kurier Poranny (Białystok)
Kurier Warszawski (Warsaw)
Kwartalnik Historyczny (Warsaw)
Medaon (Hatikva, Dresden)

Meeviertel Anzeiger (Würzburg)
Mówią Wieki (Warsaw)
New York Times
One Health and Implementation Research (OAE Publishing, Los Angeles)
Polish American Studies (UI Press, Champaign IL)
Politeja (Uniwersytet Jagielloński, Kraków)
Przegląd Historyczny (Dwumiesięcznik Naukowy,Warsaw)
Robotnik (Vilnius)
Rocznik Historii Czasopiśmiennictwa Polskiego (Komisja Prasoznawcza, Wrocław)
Science (American Association for the Advancement of Science, Washington DC)
Slavic Review (Cambridge University Press)
Sprawy Narodowościowe (Instytut Slawistyki PAN, Warsaw)
The Historical Journal (Cambridge University Press)
The International History Review (Routledge, Milton)
The Jewish Magazine (jewishmag.org)
The Slavonic and East European Review (Manney, Leeds)
The Polish Review (Polish Institute of Arts and Sciences of America, New York)
The Warsaw Weekly (Warsaw)
Wojskowy Przegląd Historyczny (Ministerstwo Obrony Narodowej)
WWII History (Warfare History Network, McLean VA)
Zeitschrift für Menschenrechte (Wochenschau Verlag, Frankfurt am Main)

1943.pl
avalon.law.yale.edu
forost.ungarisches-institut.de
histdoc.net
jewishvirtuallibrary.org
jhi.pl
kolekcje.muzeumwarszawy.pl
nli.org.il
russianhistory.org
sprawiedliwi.org.pl
ushmm.org
warsawuprising.org
winstonchurchill.org
yadvashem.org
zagladazydow.pl
zapisyterroru.pl

Akta dyplomatyczne polskie odnoszące się do rokowań brytyjsko-francusko-sowieckich w okresie przed wybuchem drugiej wojny światowej (London, 1955)

Alexander, J., Eyerman, R., Giesen, B., and Smelser, N. (eds), *Cultural Trauma and Collective Identity* (University of California Press, Berkeley CA, 2004)

Applebaum, A., *Iron Curtain: The Crushing of Eastern Europe 1944–56* (Penguin, Harmondsworth, 2012)

Arad, Y., *Belzec, Sobibor, Treblinka: The Operation Reinhard Death Camps* (Indiana University Press, Bloomington IN, 1987)

Arendt, H., *Eichmann in Jerusalem: A Report on the Banality of Evil* (Penguin Classics, New York, 2006)

Auerbach, R. (trans. Kassow, S.), *Warsaw Testament* (White Goat Press, Amherst, 2024)

Bartelski, L., *AK* (Tekst, Warsaw, 1990, 2 volumes)

Bartoszewski, W., *Warsaw Death Ring 1939–1944* (Interpress, Warsaw, 1968)

Bartoszewski, W., *Palmiry* (Wydawnictwo Książka i Wiedza, Warsaw, 1969)

Bartoszewski, W., *Prasa Powstania Warszawskiego: Zarys Historyczno-Bibliograficzny* (Państwowy Instytut Wydawniczy, Warsaw, 1972)

Bartoszewski, W., *1859 dni Warszawy* (Znak, Kraków, 1984)

Bartoszewski, W. and Edelman, M., *I była dzielnica żydowska w Warszawie: wybór tekstów* (Literatura Faktu PWN, Warsaw, 2010)

Bauer, P., *17 Pułk Ułanow Wielkopolskich im Króla Bolesława Chrobrego* (Oficyna Wydawnicza Ajaks, Pruszków, 1994)

Beck, J., *Dernier Rapport: Politique Polonaise 1926–1939* (Editions de la Baconnière, Zurich, 1951)

Berg, M., *The Diary of Mary Berg: Growing up in the Warsaw Ghetto* (Oneworld, 2006)

Białkowski, W., *Rokossowski – na ile Polak?* (Alfa, Warsaw, 1994)

Białoszewski, M., *A Memoir of the Warsaw Uprising* (Ardis, Ann Arbor MI, 1977)

Bielski, M., *Grupe Operacyjna Piotrków 1939* (Bellona, Warsaw, 1991)

Binasiak, M., *Dziś, Jutro, Pojutrze: Harcerki I Harcerze w Służbie Polskiego Państwa Podziemnego: Wystawa w 70-lecie Szarych Szeregów* (Muzeum Harcerstwa, Warsaw, 2009)

Bines, G., *The Polish Section of the Special Operations Executive 1940–1946: A British Perspective* (Doctorate Thesis, University of Stirling, 2008)

Biskupska, J., *Survivors: Warsaw under Nazi Occupation (Studies in the Social and Cultural History of Modern Warfare)*, (Cambridge University Press, 2022)

Biskupski, M. and Wandycz, P., *Ideology, Politics, and Diplomacy in East Central Europe* (Boydell & Brewer, Martlesham, 2003)

Blood, P., *Hitler's Bandit Hunters: The SS and the Nazi Occupation of Europe* (Potomac Books, Sterling VA, 2006)

Böhler, J., *Der Überfall: Deutschlands Krieg Gegen Polen* (Eichborn, Frankfurt am Main, 2009)

Borzykowski, T., *Tsvishn falendiḳe venṭ* (Ghetto Fighters House, Israel, 1976)

Bracher, K., *The German Dictatorship: The Origins, Structure and Consequences of National Socialism* (Penguin, Harmondsworth, 1978)

Brandes, G., *Poland: A Study of the Land, People, and Literature* (Heinemann, London, 1903)

Brandys, M., *Kozietulski i inni* (Iskry, Warsaw, 1982)

Broniewski, S., *Florian Marciniak naczelnik Szarych Szeregów* (PWN, Warsaw, 1988)

Broniewski, S., *Akja pod Arsenałem* (Iskry, Wrocław, 1993)

Brown, K., *The Sound of Hope: Music as Solace, Resistance and Salvation During the Holocaust and World War II* (McFarland, Jefferson NC, 2020)

Browning, C., *Ordinary Men: Reserve Police Battalion 101 and the Final Solution in Poland* (Harper Perennial, New York, 1993)

Browning, C., *The Origins of the Final Solution: The Evolution of Nazi Jewish Policy, September 1939–March 1942* (University of Nebraska Press, Lincoln NE, 2004)

Bruce, G., *The Warsaw Uprising: 1 August–2 October 1944 (Major Battles of World War Two)*, (Hart Davis, London, 1972)

Buttar, P., *Bagration 1944: The Great Soviet Offensive* (Osprey, Oxford, 2025)

Carton de Wiart, A., *Happy Odyssey: The Memoirs of Lieutenant General Sir Adrian Carton de Wiart, VC, KBE, CB, CMG, DSO* (Pen & Sword, Barnsley, 2007)

Chinciński, T. and Machcewicz, P. (eds), *Bydgoszcz 3–4 Września 1939: Studia i Dokumenty* (Instytut Pamięci Narodowej, Warsaw, 2008)

Ciechanowski, J., *The Warsaw Rising of 1944* (Cambridge University Press, 1974)

Crankshaw, E., *Gestapo: Instrument of Tyranny* (Putnam, London, 1956)

Cynk, J., *The Polish Air Force at War: The Official History* (Schiffer, Atglen PA, 1998, 2 volumes)

Czajkowski, Z., *Warsaw 1944: An Insurgent's Journal of the Uprising* (Pen & Sword, Barnsley, 2013)

Czapski, J. (trans. Lloyd-Jones, A.), *Inhuman Land – Searching for the Truth in Soviet Russia, 1941–1942* (NYRB Classics, 2018)

Czerniaków, A., Hilberg, R., and Staron, S., *The Warsaw Diary of Adam Czerniaków: Prelude to Doom* (Ivan R. Dee, Chicago, 1999)

Czuperska-Śliwicka, A., *Cztery Lata Ostrego Dyżuru, Wspom ienia z Pawiaka, 1940–1944* (Czytelnik, Warsaw, 1989)

D'Abernon, V., *The Eighteenth Decisive Battle of the World* (Hodder & Stoughton, London, 1931)

Dąbrowska, M., *Dzienniki 1914–1965. T. 1, 1914–1925* (Komitet Nauk o Literaturze, Warsaw, 2009)

Datner, S., Gumkowski, J., and Leszczyński, K., *Genocide 1939–1945* (Wydawnictwo Zachodnie, Warsaw, 1962)

Davies, N., *Rising '44: The Battle for Warsaw* (Macmillan, London, 2003)

Davies, N., *God's Playground: A History of Poland* (Oxford University Press, 2005, 2 volumes)

Dmytryshyn, B. (ed.), *Imperial Russia: A Source Book, 1700–1917* (Holt, Rinehart & Winston, Fort Worth TX, 1990)

Donat, A., *The Holocaust Kingdom: A Memoir* (Holocaust Library, New York, 1978)

Drozdowski, M., Manianówna, M., and Strzembosz, T. (eds), *Ludność Cywilna w Powstaniu Warszawskim* (Panstwowy Instytut Wydawniczy, Warsaw, 1974, 3 volumes)

Dubiel, P. and Kozak, J., *Polacy w Il Wojnie Światowej: Kim Byli, Co Robili* (Oficyna Wydawnicza Rytm, Warsaw, 2003)

Einhorn, J., *Recollections of the End of an Era: Poland 1919–1945* (Author House, Bloomington IN, 2005)

Elkins, M., *Forged in Fury* (Ballantine, New York, 1971)

Engelking, B. and Leociak, J., *Getto warszawskie: przewodnik po nieistniejącym mieście* (Wydawn. IFiS, Warsaw, 2001)

Evans, R., *The Third Reich at War* (Penguin, Harmondsworth, 2009)

Faber, D., *Munich: The 1938 Appeasement Crisis* (Simon & Schuster, London, 2008)

Filasiewicz, S., *La Question Polonaise Pendant la Guerre Mondiale* (Section d'Études et de Publications Politiques de Comité National Polonais, Paris, 1920)

Fischer, L., *Raporty Ludwiga Fischera, Gubernatora Dystyktu Warszawskiego 1939–1944* (Wydawnictwo Książka, Warsaw, 1987)

Fleming, M., *Auschwitz, the Allies and Censorship of the Holocaust* (Cambridge University Press, New York, 2014)

Forczyk, R., *Case White: The Invasion of Poland 1939* (Bloomsbury, London, 2019)

Friedländer, S., *Nazi Germany and the Jews: The Years of Extermination 1939–1945* (HarperCollins, New York, 2007)

Galiński, A. (ed.), *Zbrodnie Wehrmachtu w Wielkopolsce w Okresie Zarządu Wokskowego (1 Września-25 Paźsziernika 1939)* (Instytut Pamięci Narodowej, Kalisz, 1986)

Garlicki, A., *Historia 1815–1939 Polska i* świat (Warsaw, 2003)

Gerson, E., *Woodrow Wilson and the Rebirth of Poland, 1914–1920: A Study in the Influence on American Policy of Minority Groups of Foreign Origin* (Archon, Hamden CT, 1972)

Giaccaria, P. and Minca, C. (eds), *Hitler's Geographies: The Spatialities of the Third Reich* (University of Chicago Press, 2016)

Gluza, Z. and Markowska, M., *Rok 1939: Rozbiór Polski* (Fundacja Ośrodka Karta, Warsaw, 2009)

Goldensohn, L. and Gellately, R., *The Nuremberg Interviews: Conversations with the Defendants and Witnesses* (Pimlico, London, 2007)

Goldstein, E. and Lukes, I., *The Munich Crisis 1938: Prelude to World War II* (Weidenfeld & Nicholson, London, 1967)

Gorlitz, W. (ed.), *In the Service of the Reich: The Memoirs of Field Marshal Keitel* (Cooper Square Press, New York, 2000)

Gross, G., Hansen, E., Neugebauer, K.-V., Potempa, H., and Rahn, W., *Das Zeitalter der Weltkriege – Völker in Waffen* (Oldenbourg, Berlin, 2009)

Gross, J., *Revolution from Abroad: The Soviet Conquest of Poland's Western Ukraine and Western Belorussia* (Princeton University Press, 2002)

Grzesik, J., *Holocaust – Zagłada Żydów 1939–1945* (Liber Duo, Lublin, 2011)

Gutman, I., *Resistance: The Warsaw Ghetto Uprising* (Houghton Mifflin Harcourt, Boston, 1994)

Haestrup, J., *European Resistance Movements, 1939–1945: A Complete History* (Meckler, Westport CT, 1981)

Halder, F., Burdick, C., and Jacobsen, H.-A. (eds), *The Halder War Diary 1939–1942* (Greenhill, Novato CA, 1988)

Hanyok, R., *Eavesdropping on Hell: Historical Guide to Western Communications Intelligence and the Holocaust, 1939–1945* (Dover, Mineola NY, 2005)

Harich-Schneider, E., *Charaktere und Katastrophen. Augenzeugenberichte einer Reisenden Muskierin* (Ullstein, Berlin, 1978)

Hempel, A., *Pogrobowcy Kleski: rzecz o policji 'granatowej' w Generalnym Gubernatorstwie, 1939–1945* (Państwowe Wydawn. Nauk., Warsaw, 1990)

Hirsch, F., *Soviet Judgment at Nuremberg* (Oxford University Press, 2020)

Hitler, A., *Mein Kampf* (Hurst & Blackett, London, 1939)

Hollingworth, C., *The Three Weeks' War in Poland* (Duckworth, London, 1940)

Holmgren, B., *Warsaw is my Country: The Story of Krystyna Bierzynska, 1928–1945* (Academic Studies Press, Boston, 2018)

Hoover, H., *An American Epic* (Regnery, Chicago, 1964, 4 volumes)

Hoover, H., *The Memoirs of Herbert Hoover: Years of Adventure, 1874–1920* (Kessinger, Whitefish MT, 2010)

House, E., *The Intimate Papers of Colonel House* (London, 1928, 3 volumes)

Hubatsch, W. (ed.), *Hitlers Weisungen für die Kriegsführung* (Dörfler, Utting, 2000)

Ingrao, C., *The SS Dirlewanger Brigade: The History of the Black Hunters* (Skyhorse, New York, 2013)

Iranek-Osmecki, K., *Drogi Cichociemnych* (Bellona, Warsaw, 1993)

Jankowski, S. and Ciborowski, A., *Warszawa 1945 I dziś* (Wydawnictwo Interpress, Warsaw, 1971)

Janowski, J., *Krótki Katechizm Polityczny* (Trzcionkami Juliana Duillot, Agen, 1834)

Jarry, A. (trans. Keith, B. and Legman, G.), *Ubu Roi* (Dover, New York, 2003)

Karski, J., *The Great Powers & Poland, 1919–1945: From Versailles to Yalta* (University Press of America, Maryland, 1985)

Karski, J., *Story of a Secret State: My Report to the World* (Penguin, Harmondsworth, 2019)

Kassow, S., *Who Will Write Our History?: Rediscovering a Hidden Archive from the Warsaw Ghetto* (Penguin Group, London, 2009)

Kenney, P., *Dance in Chains: Political Imprisonment in the Modern World* (Oxford University Press, New York, 2017)

Kershaw, I., *Hitler: 1936–1945: Nemesis* (W. W. Norton, New York, 2000)

Kershaw, I., *Hitler: A Biography* (Norton, New York, 2008)

Kisielewski, T., *Zamach: Tropem Zabójców Generała Sikorskiego* (Rebis, Poznań, 2005)

Klimaszewski, T., *Verbrennungskommando Warschau* (Czytelnik, Warsaw, 1984)

Klukowski, Z., *Diary From the Years of Occupation, 1939–44* (University of Illinois Press, Urbana IL, 1993)

Kochanski, H., *The Eagle Unbowed: Poland and the Poles in the Second World War* (Penguin, London, 2013)

Komorowski, T., *The Secret Army: The Memoirs of General Bór-Komorowski* (Frontline Books, Barnsley, 2011)

Korbel, J., *Twentieth Century Czechoslovakia: The Meaning of Its History* (Columbia University Press, New York, 1977)

Korboński, S., *Fighting Warsaw: The Story of the Polish Underground State, 1939–1945* (Pickle Partners Publishing, Halstad MN, 2016)

Kozaczuk, W., *Enigma: How the German Machine Cipher was Broken, and How it was Read by the Allies in World War II* (University Publications of America, Frederick MD, 1984)

Krakowski, S., Bauer, Y., and Blaustein, O., *War of the Doomed: Jewish Armed Resistance in Poland, 1942–1944* (Holmes & Meier, New York, 1984)

Kramer, A., *Dynamic of Destruction: Culture and Mass Killing in the First World War* (Oxford University Press, 2007)

Kranjc, G., *To Walk with the Devil: Slovene Collaboration and Axis Occupation, 1941–1945* (University of Toronto Press, 2013)

Krivosheev, G., *Rossiya I SSSR v Voynach XX Veka: Poteri Vooruzhennyich Syl. Statystycheskoe Issledovanye* (Olma, Moscow, 2001)

Kukiel, M., *Dzieje Polski Porozbiorowe* (Świderski, London, 1961)

Kulski, J., *Stefan Starzyński w mojej pamięci* (Państwowe Wydawnictwo Naukowe, Warsaw, 1990)

Kulski, J., *The Color of Courage: A Boy at War: The World War II Diary of Julian Kulski* (Aquila Polonica Publishing, Los Angeles CA, 2014)

Kunert, A., *Generał Tadeusz Bór-Komorowski w Relacjach I Dokumentach* (Ofycina Wydawnicza RYTM, Warsaw, 2000)

Kunert, A. and Szyrmer, J., *Stefan Rowecki. Wspomnienia I Notatke Autobiograficzne 1906–1939* (Spółdzielnia Wydawnicza Czytelnik, Warsaw, 1988)

Kunźniar, R., *Poland's Foreign Policy After 1989* (Wydawnictwo Naukowe Scholar, Warsaw, 2009)

Kutsher, B. (trans. Marcus, G.), *Once There Was Warsaw* (Syracuse University Press, New York, 2024)

Laquer, W. and Baumel, J., *The Holocaust Encyclopaedia* (Yale University Press, New Haven CT, 2001)

Leslie, R., *The History of Poland Since 1863* (Cambridge University Press, 1983)

Lewandowska, S. and Martin, B. (eds), *Powstanie Warszawskie 1944: Praca Zbiorowa* (Wydawnictwo Polsko-Niemieckie, Warsaw, 1999)

Lichten, J., *Notes on the Assimilation and Acculturation of Jews in Poland 1863–1943* (Blackwell, Oxford, 1986)

Lifton, R., *Ärzte im Dritten Reich* (Ullstein, Berlin, 1998)

Likiernik, S., *By Devil's Luck: A Tale of Resistance in Wartime Warsaw* (Mainstream Publishing, Edinburgh, 2001)

Lochner, L., *What About Germany?* (Dodd, Mead & Co., New York, 1942)

Łojek, B., *Muzeum Katyńskie w Warszawie* (Polska Fundacja Katyńska, Warsaw, 2001)

Longerich, P., *Holocaust: The Nazi Persecution and Murder of the Jews* (Oxford University Press, 2010)

Lubetkin, C., *Zagłada i Powstanie, Żydowski Instytut Historyczny* (Książka i Wiedza, Warsaw, 1999)

Lubomirski, M., *Pamiętnik Księżnej Marii Zdzisławowej Lubomirskiej 1914–1918* (Wydawn. Poznańskie, Poznań, 1997)

Luck, H. von, *Panzer Commander* (Cassell, London, 2002)

Lukas, R., *Forgotten Holocaust: The Poles Under German Occupation 1939–1944* (Hippocrene Books, New York, 2012)

Machray, R., *Poland: 1914–1931* (Allen & Unwin, London, 1932)

MacLean, F., *The Cruel Hunters: SS-Sonderkommando Dirlewanger, Hitler's Most Notorious Anti-Partisan Unit* (Schiffer, Atglen PA, 1998)

Mallmann, K.-M., Böhler, J., and Matthäus, J., *Einsatzgruppen in Polen. Darstellung und Dokumentation* (WBG, Darmstadt, 2008)

Mark, B., *Dziennik Szmuela Wintera. Ważny dodatek do dokumentacji przedpowstaniowej* (Kwartalnik Historii Żydów 01/2019)

Melvin, M., *Manstein: Hitler's Greatest General* (Thomas Dunne, New York, 2011)

Mendelsohn, E., *The Jews of East Central Europe Between the World Wars* (Indiana University Press, Bloomington IN, 1984)

Michalka, W., *Deutsche Geschichte 1933–1945: Dokumente zur Innen- und Aussenpolitik* (Fischer Taschenbuch Verlag, Frankfurt am Main, 1994)

Mickiewicz, A., *Księgi narodu polskiego i pielgrzymstwa polskiego* (Księgarnia Luxemburgska, Paris, 1866)

Mikołajczyk, S., *The Rape of Poland: Pattern of Soviet Aggression* (Whittlesey House, New York, 1972)

Moczarski, K., Fitzpatrick, M., and Stroop, J., *Conversations with an Executioner* (Englewood Cliffs NJ, 1981)

Moczulski, L., *Wojna Prewencyjna: Czy Piłsudski Planowal Najazd na Niemcy?* (Bellona, Warsaw, 2017)

Moorhouse, R., *First to Fight: The Polish War 1939* (Vintage, London, 2020)

Musiał, B., *Sowjetische Partisanen in Weissrussland: Innenansichten aus dem Gebiet Baranoviči 1941–1944: Eine Dokumentation* (Oldenbourg, Munich, 2013)

Nałkowska, Z., *Dzienniki* (Czytelnik, Warsaw, 1976–96, 4 volumes)

Nash, D., *From the Realm of a Dying Sun. Volume I: IV. SS-Panzerkorps and the Battles for Warsaw, July–December 1944* (Casemate, Havertown PA, 2020)

Neitzel, S. and Welzer, H., *Soldiers: German POWs on Fighting, Killing, and Dying* (Random House, New York, 2012)

Nekrich, A., Ulam, A., and Freeze, G., *Pariahs, Partners, Predators: German-Soviet Relations, 1922–1941* (Columbia University Press, New York, 1997)

Neumann, J., *Die 4. Panzerdivision 1938–1943* (Verlag & Antiquariat für Zeitgeschichte, Bad Dürkheim, 1985)

Ney-Krwawicz, M., *Armia Krajowa: Siła Zbroina Polskiego Państwa Polskiego* (Wydawnictwa Szkolne I Pedagogiczne, Warsaw, 1993)

Noakes, J. and Pridham, G. (eds), *Nazism 1919–1945: Foreign Policy, War and Racial Extermination* (Exeter University Press, 1988, 4 volumes)

Nowak, J., *Courier from Warsaw* (Wayne State University Press, Detroit MI, 1982)

Official Documents Concerning Polish-German and Polish-Soviet Relations, 1933–1939: The Little White Book (Hutchinson, London, 1940)

Ordon, S. (trans. Anstruther, F.), *Fire over Warsaw* (Ksiażnica Polska, Glasgow, 1942)

Orska, I., *Silent is the Vistula: The Story of the Warsaw Uprising* (Longmans, Green and Co., Toronto, 1946)

Pachter, M., *Umierać też trzeba umieć* (Stowarzyszenie Centrum Badań nad Zagładą Żydów, Warsaw, 2015)

Paul, M., *A Tangled Web: Polish-Jewish Relations in Wartime Northeastern Poland and the Aftermath* (Perfina Press, Toronto, 2021, 2 volumes)

Paulsson, G., *Secret City: The Hidden Jews of Warsaw, 1940–1945* (Yale University Press, New Haven CT, 2002)

Person, K., *Assimilated Jews in the Warsaw Ghetto, 1940–1943* (Syracuse University Press, New York, 2014)

Person, K., *Warsaw Ghetto Police: The Jewish Order Service during the Nazi Occupation* (Cornell University Press, Ithaca NY, 2021)

Peszke, M., *The Polish Underground Army, the Western Allies, and the Failure of Strategic Unity in World War II* (McFarland, Jefferson NC, 2005)

Piłsudski, J., *Monitor Polski* (Drukarnia Państwowa w Warszawie, 1922)

Piłsudski, J., *The Memories of a Polish Revolutionary and Soldier* (AMS, New York, 1971)

Piotrkowski, S., *Dziennik Hansa Franka* (Wydawnictwo Prawnicze, Warsaw, 1957)

Piotrowski, T., *Poland's Holocaust: Ethnic Strife, Collaboration with Occupying Forces and Genocide in the Second Republic, 1918–1947* (McFarland, Jefferson NC, 1998)

Płoski, S., *Wspomnienia Więźniów Pawiaka* (Polska Akademia Nauka, Warsaw, 1964)

Pogonowski, F., *Podziemna Zbrokownia* (Wydawnictwo Ministerstwa Obrony Narodowej, Warsaw, 1975)

Polskie Siły Zbrojne w Drugiej Wojnie Swiatowej (Instytut Historyczny im. Gen. Sikorskiego, London, 1951, 3 volumes)

Polski Słownik Biograficzny (Polska Akademia Nauk I Polska Akademia Umiejętności, Kraków, 2001, 52 volumes)

Porter, B., *When Nationalism Began to Hate: Imagining Modern Politics in Nineteenth-Century Poland* (Oxford University Press, 2000)

Prazmowska, A., *Civil War in Poland 1942–1948* (Palgrave Macmillan, London, 2004)

Protassewicz, I. (trans. Zawadski, H.), *A Polish Woman's Experiences in World War II* (Bloomsbury, London, 2019)

Przygoński, A., *Powstanie Warszawskie w Sierpniu 1944* (Państwowe Wydawnictwo Nauowe, Warsaw, 1988)

Regulska, H., *Dziennik Z Oblężonej Warszawy* (PAX, Warsaw, 1978)

Richie, A., *Warsaw 1944: Hitler, Himmler, and the Crushing of a City* (William Collins, London, 2013)

Ringelblum, E., *Polish-Jewish Relations During the Second World War* (Northwestern University Press, Evanston IL, 1992)

Roberts, A., *Churchill: Walking with Destiny* (Allen Lane, London, 2018)

Robertson, J., *From Corsets to Communism: The Life and Times of Zofie Nałkowska* (Scotland Street Press, Edinburgh, 2019)

Ro'i Y., *Jews and Jewish Life in Russia and the Soviet Union* (Routledge, 1995)

Rosinski, J. and Hile, R., *The Warsaw Underground: A Memoir of Resistance, 1939–1945* (McFarland, Jefferson NC, 2014)

Rousseau, J.-J., *The Government of Poland* (Hackett, Indianapolis IN, 1985)

Rowecki, S., *Wspomnienia i notatki autobiograficzne (1918–1939)* (Czytelnik, Warsaw, 1988)

Rowińska, L., *That the Nightingale Return: Memoir of the Polish Resistance, the Warsaw Uprising and German P.O.W. Camps* (McFarland, Jefferson NC, 1999)

Rubinstein, W., *The Left, the Right, and the Jews* (Routledge, London 2017)

Sachslehner, J., *Zwei Millionen Ham'ma Erledigt: Odilo Globocnik – Hitlers Manager des Todes* (Styria Premium, Vienna, 2014)

Sakowska, R., Żbikowski, A., Tarnowska, M., Person, K., Epsztein, T., Rusiniak, M., Jarkowska-Natkaniec, A., Ferenc, M., and Laskowski, P., *Archiwum Ringelbluma: Konspiracyjne Archiwum Getta Warszawy* (Wydawnictwo Naukowe PWN, Warsaw, 1997, 6 volumes)

Salmonowicz, S., *Polskie Państwo Podziemne* (Wydawnictwa Szkolne i Pedagogiczne, Warsaw, 1994)

Sawicki, T., *Rozkaz: Zdławič Powstanie – Siły Zbrojne III Rzeszy w Walce z Powstaniem Warszawkim 1944* (Dom Wydawniczy Bellona, Warsaw, 2001)

Schäufler, H., *So Lebten und so Starben Sie: Das Buch vom Panzerregiment 35* (Kameradschaft ehemaliger Panzer-Regiment 35 e.V, Bamberg, 1983)

Schellenberg, W., *The Labyrinth: Memoirs of Walter Schellenberg, Hitler's Chief of Counterintelligence* (Da Capo, Boston MS, 1956)

Schelvis, J., *Sobibor: A History of a Nazi Death Camp* (Berg, Oxford, 2007)

Schenk, D., *Die Post von Danzig: Geschichte eines Deutschen Justizmords* (Rohwohlt, Hamburg, 1995)

Schenk, D., *Hitlers Mann in Danzig: Gauletier Forster und die NS-Verbrechen in Danzig-Westpreussen* (Dietz, Bonn, 2000)

Schoenfeld, J., *Jewish Life in Galicia under the Austro-Hungarian Empire and in Reborn Poland, 1898–1939* (Ktav, Hoboken NJ, 1985)

Schoenfeld, J. (ed.), *Holocaust Memoirs: Jews in the Lwów Ghetto, the Janowski Concentration Camp, and as Deportees in Siberia* (KTAV Publishing House, Hoboken NJ, 1985)

Sebag Montefiore, S., *Stalin: The Court of the Red Tsar* (Vintage, London, 2004)

Semenov, G., *Nastupayet Udarnaya* (Voyenizdat, Moscow, 1986)

Seton-Watson, H., *Eastern Europe Between the Wars, 1918–1941* (Cambridge University Press, 1946)

Shirer, W., *Berlin Diary: The Journal of a Foreign Correspondent 1934–1941* (Alfred A. Knopf, New York, 1941)

Shirer W., *The Rise and Fall of the Third Reich: A History of Nazi Germany* (Simon & Schuster, London, 1990)

Sloan, J. (ed.), *Notes from the Warsaw Ghetto: The Journal of Emmanuel Ringelblum* (Normanby Press, London, 2015)

Snyder, T., *Bloodlands: Europe Between Hitler and Stalin* (Vintage, London, 2011)

Sobieski, W. and Tymieniecki, K., *Dzieje Polski* (Wydawnictwo Antyk – Marcin Dybowski, Komorów, 2010, 3 volumes)

Stachiewicz, P., '*Parasol*'. *Dzieje Oddziału do Zadań Specialnych Kierownictwa Dywersii Komendy Głownej Armii Krajowej* (Instytut Wydawniczy Pax, Warsaw, 1984)

Stachura, P., *Poland, 1918–1945: An Interpretive and Documentary History of the Second Republic* (Routledge, Milton, 2004)

Stalin's Correspondence with Churchill, Attlee, Roosevelt and Truman, 1941–45 (Lawrence & Wishart, London, 1958)

Stańczyk, H., Smoliński, J., Panecki, T., Sikora, M., Żak, J., and Gotowiecki, P., *Polskie Siły Zbrojne na Zachodzie po II Wojnie Światowej: Klęska Zwycięzców* (Oficyna Wydawnicza Rytm, Warsaw, 2016)

Stawicki, T., *Rozkaz zdławić Powstanie: Niemcy i ich Sojusznicy w Walce z Powstaniem Warszawskim* (Bellona, Warsaw, 2010)

Stebelski, A., *The Fate of Polish Archives During World War II* (Państwowe Wydawn. Naukowe, Warsaw, 1964)

Storozynski, A., *The Peasant Prince: Tadeusz Koskiuszko and the Age of Revolution* (Tomas Dunne, New York, 2009)

Strzembosz, T., *Akcję Zbrojne Podziemnej Warszawy 1939–1944* (Państwowe Wydawnictwo Naukowe, Warsaw, 1983)

Suchcitz, A. and Maresch, E. (eds), *Armia Krajowa w Dokumentach, 1939–1945* (Instytut Pamięci Narodowej-Komisja Ścigania Zbrodni Przeciwko Narodowi Polskiemu, Warsaw, 2015, 2 volumes)

Szarota, T., *U progu Zagłady. Zajścia antyżydowskie i pogromy w okupowanej Europie* (Wydawnictwo Sic!, Warsaw, 2000)

Sziling, J. and Minczykowska, K. (eds), *Akcja Burza: Materiały z XXIV Sesji Naukowej w Toruniu w Dniu 18 Listopada 2014 Roku* (Fundacja General Elżbiety Zawackiej, Torún, 2015)

Szpilman, W., *The Pianist: The Extraordinary Story of One Man's Survival in Warsaw 1939–1945* (Picador, London, 2019)

Szuiecki, A. and Piotrowski, T., *The Polish Deportees of World War II: Recollections of Removal to the Soviet Union and Dispersal Throughout the World* (McFarland, Jefferson NC, 2004)

Tanikowski, A., Zieliński, K., and Silber, M., *Jew, Pole, Legionary: 1914–1920* (Museum of the History of Polish Jews, Warsaw, 2014)

Tazbir, S., *W obronie dzieci i młodzieży w Warszawie, 1939–1944* (Państwowy Instytut Wydawniczy, Warsaw, 1975)

Tebinka, J. and Zapalec, A., *Polska w Brytyjskiej Strategii Wspierania Ruchu Oporu. Historia Sekcji Kierownictwa Operacji Specjalnych (SOE),* (Neriton, Warsaw, 2021)

The Ringelblum Archive: Underground Archive of the Warsaw Ghetto (Żydowski Instytut Historyczny, Warsaw, 2017, 9 volumes)

Tooze, A., *The Wages of Destruction: The Making and Breaking of the Nazi Economy* (Penguin, Harmondsworth, 2006)

Trunk, I., *Judenrat: The Jewish Councils of Eastern Europe under Nazi Occupation* (University of Nebraska Press, Lincoln NE, 1996)

Ujazdowska, L. (ed.), *Zagłada Ochoty: Zbiór Relacji na Temat Zbrodni Hitlerowskiej Dokonanej na Ludności Ochoty w Czasie Powstania Warszawskiego* (Fronda, Warsaw, 2022)

Ulam, A., *Stalin: The Man and His Era* (Allen Lane, London, 1974)

Valcini, A., *Il Calvario di Varsavia, 1939–1945* (Garzanti, Milan, 1945)

Wagner, E., *Der Generalquartermeister. Briefe und Tagebuchaufzeichnungen des Generalquartermeisters des Heeres General der Artillerie Eduard Wagner* (Olzog, Munich, 1963)

Walicki, A., *Między filozofią, religią, i polityką* (Państwowy Instytut Wydawniczy, Warsaw, 1983)

Weinberg, G., *The Foreign Policy of Hitler's Germany: Starting World War II, 1937–39* (University of Chicago Press, 1980)

Weinberg, G., *Visions of Victory: The Hopes of Eight World War II Leaders* (Cambridge University Press, 2005)

Weissman, B., *The American Relief Administration in Russia, 1921–1923: A Case Study in the Interaction Between Opposing Political Systems* (PhD dissertation, Columbia University, 1968)

Wiernik, J., *A Year in Treblinka: An Inmate Who Escaped Tells the Day-to-Day Facts of One Year of his Torturous Experience* (American Representation of the General Jewish Workers' Union of Poland, New York, 1944)

Winchester, C. and Drury, I., *Hitler's War on Russia* (Bloomsbury, London, 2011)

Wojewoda, M. and Wojewoda, J., *Bitwa nad Bzura: Pierwsza Wśród Wielkich Bitew II Wojny Światowej* (Bellona, Warsaw, 2016)

Woodward, L., *British Foreign Policy in the Second World War* (HMSO, London, 1970, 5 volumes)

Wrochem, O. von, *Erich von Manstein: Vernichtungskrieg und Geschichtspolitik* (Brill Schöningh, Leiden, 2009)

Yahil, L., Friedman, I., and Galai, H., *The Holocaust: The Fate of European Jewry 1932–1945* (Oxford University Press, 1991)

Zaloga, S., *Poland 1939: The Birth of Blitzkrieg* (Osprey, Oxford, 2002)

Zamoyski, A., *Poland: A History* (HarperCollins Publishers, 2015)

Zaremba, Z., *Żeby chociaż świat wiedział* (Bellona, Warsaw, 2010)

Zawodny, J., *Nothing But Honour: The Story of the Warsaw Uprising, 1944* (Hoover Institution Press, Stanford CA, 1978)

Żerko, S. (ed.), *Polskie Dokumenty Dyplomatyczne, 1939* (Warsaw, 2005)

Zimmerer, J., *From Windhoek to Auschwitz? Reflections on the Relationship between Colonialism and National Socialism* (De Gruyter Oldenbourg, Berlin, 2023)

Zimmerman, J., *The Polish Underground and the Jews, 1939–1945* (Cambridge University Press, 2015)

Zych, G., *Oranienburg* (Ksiżka i Wiedza, Warsaw, 1962)

INDEX

Figures in bold refer to illustrations and tables.